THE ORGB SOLUTION

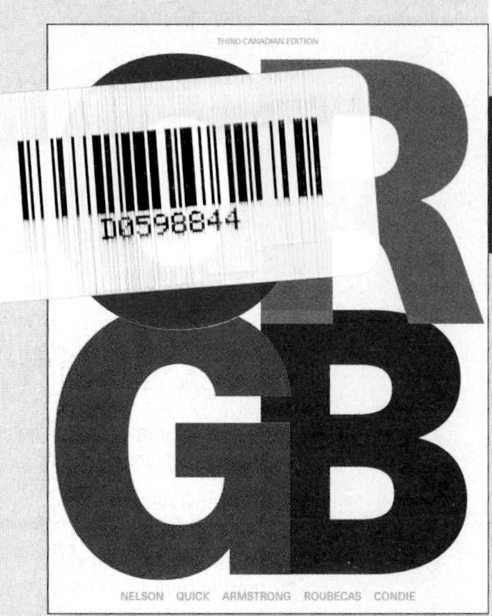

Print

ORGB 3CE delivers all the key terms and all the content for the **Organizational Behaviour** course through a visually engaging and easy-to-review print experience.

Digital

MindTap enables you to stay organized and study efficiently by providing a single location for all your course materials and study aids. Built-in apps leverage social media and the latest learning technology to help you succeed.

1. Open the Access Card included with this text.
2. Follow the steps on the card.
3. Study.

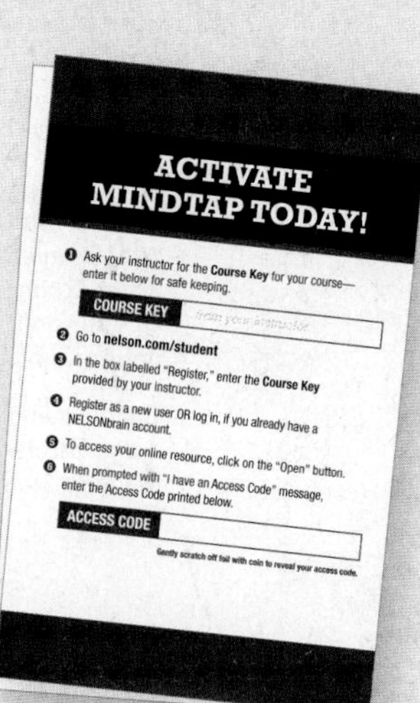

Student Resources

- Interactive eBook
- Flashcards
- Pre-Test Quizzes
- Post-Test Quizzes
- Chapter Videos
- Chapter Video Quiz
- Online Glossary
- Part-Ending Case Studies
- Matching Exercises
- Chapter Review Cards

Students: **nelson.com/student**

Instructor Resources

- Access to All Student Resources
- Instructor Companion Site
- PowerPoint® Slides
- Updated Test Bank
- LMS Integration
- Instructor Prep Cards
- Answers to Mini-case, Running case, and Part-ending case questions

Instructors: **nelson.com/instructor**

NELSON

ORGB, Third Canadian Edition

by Debra L. Nelson, James Campbell Quick, Ann Armstrong, Chris Roubecas, and Joan Condie

VP, Product Solutions, K–20:
Claudine O'Donnell

Director, Qualitative Disciplines:
Jackie Wood

Executive Marketing Manager:
Amanda Henry

Content Manager:
Suzanne Simpson Millar

Photo and Permissions Researcher:
Jessie Coffey

Senior Production Project Manager:
Jennifer Hare

Production Service:
MPS Limited

Copy Editor:
Karen Rolfe

Proofreader:
MPS Limited

Indexer:
MPS Limited

Design Director:
Ken Phipps

Post-secondary Design PM:
Pamela Johnston

Interior Design:
Cathryn Mayer

Cover Design:
Courtney Hellam

Compositor:
MPS Limited

Printed and bound in Canada
1 2 3 4 22 21 20 19

For more information contact Nelson Education Ltd., 1120 Birchmount Road, Toronto, Ontario, M1K 5G4. Or you can visit our Internet site at nelson.com

Library and Archives Canada Cataloguing in Publication Data

Title: ORGB / Nelson, Quick, Armstrong, Roubecas, Condie.
Other titles: Organizational behaviour
Names: Nelson, Debra L., 1956- author. | Quick, James C., author. | Armstrong, Ann, 1951- author. | Roubecas, Chris, author. | Condie, Joan, 1955- author.
Description: Third Canadian edition. | Written by Debra L. Nelson, James Campbell Quick, Ann Armstrong, Chris Roubecas, and Joan Condie. | Original Canadian edition by Debra L. Nelson ... et al. | Includes bibliographical references and index.
Identifiers: Canadiana 20189065222 | ISBN 9780176873387 (softcover)
Subjects: LCSH: Organizational behavior—Textbooks.
Classification: LCC HD58.7 .O76 2019 | DDC 302.3/5—dc23

ISBN-13: 978-0-17-687338-7
ISBN-10: 0-17-687338-4

ORGB[3]

BRIEF CONTENTS

CONTENTS

Part 1
INTRODUCTION

Hunter Bliss/Shutterstock.com

Part 2
INDIVIDUALS WITHIN ORGANIZATIONS

Cranach/Getty Images

Part 3
INTERPERSONAL PROCESSES AND BEHAVIOUR

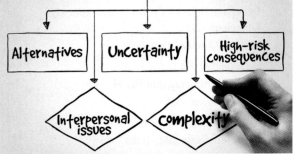

dizain/Shutterstock.com

14 Learning and Performance Management 254

Part 4 ORGANIZATIONAL PROCESSES AND STRUCTURES

kate_sept2004/E+/Getty Images

15 Jobs and the Design of Work 271

16 Organizational Design and Structure 291

17 Managing Change 313

18 Career Management 333

ABOUT THE AUTHORS

Ann Armstrong

Courtesy of James Kachan

Dr. Ann Armstrong received her Ph.D. from the Rotman School of Management. Her thesis examined, in a variety of organizations, several compensation systems innovations that help to reinforce team structures. Since then, her research has focused on the structures of and dynamics in social enterprises.

In addition to co-authoring two books with Nelson Education, Ann has co-authored two books on the social economy of Canada and the United States. She has written articles on a variety of subjects from greening curricula to measuring impact in the social economy.

Ann teaches at the undergraduate, graduate, and executive levels in Canada and abroad. She particularly enjoys teaching courses that have experiential activities and assignments. As well, Ann serves as the Academic Director of a program for Internationally Educated Professionals who have come recently to Canada and of a program that links graduate students with non-profit boards.

Ann's greatest claim to fame may be that she participated in a head shave for a United Way fundraiser. It was a successful fundraiser and an intriguing inadvertent social experiment!

Chris Roubecas

Courtesy of Chris Roubecas

Dr. Chris P. Roubecas got his start in business in 2000 with residential and commercial real estate development. He has been a professor in the School of Business at Southern Alberta Institute of Technology (SAIT) since 2005, and received his Ph.D. in organizational leadership in 2014, with a dissertation investigating the Organizational Behaviour concept of motivation crowding. Chris has taught numerous business courses offered in a variety of programs across SAIT, including Introduction to Business, Marketing, Management, Business Fundamentals, Human Resource Management, Recruitment & Selection, Training & Development, Small Business Management, Entrepreneurship, Tourism, Microeconomics, Macroeconomics, and his favourite, of course, Organizational Behaviour!

Across all of these programs, Chris has maintained excellent student evaluations, and has been awarded SAIT Instructor Excellence 10 consecutive times. He won the SAIT Student Association Teaching award twice, and has also been nominated three times for the SAIT-wide Ralph T. Scurfield Award of Excellence. Chris is a mentor in SAIT's training program for new faculty, and developed Lightboard v.2.0 as SAIT's 2019 Cisco E-Learning Chair. He is also currently developing the School of Business's first Study Aboard program in Organizational Behaviour where he will bring the world to SAIT and SAIT to the world.

Chris likes to spend his free time with his wife and their wonderful son, travelling to new places and learning new things.

ACKNOWLEDGMENTS

A special thank you to Joan Condie, Sheridan College, who has been a co-author of this text in previous editions and was integral in the considerable groundwork that went into this third edition.

We would like to thank the following faculty for providing feedback and recommendations that helped us develop this new edition:

Stan Arnold, Humber College

Anna Bortolon, Conestoga College

Debby Clevelend, British Columbia Institute of Technology

Charles Keim, MacEwan University

Mary Ann Lesperance, Niagara College

Roberta Swatzky, Okanagan College

And to those who helped with the creation of our supplement materials:

Rose Campbell, Southern Alberta Institute of Technology

Sonja Johnston, Southern Alberta Institute of Technology

Charissa Lee, Southern Alberta Institute of Technology

Michelle Poisson, Southern Alberta Institute of Technology

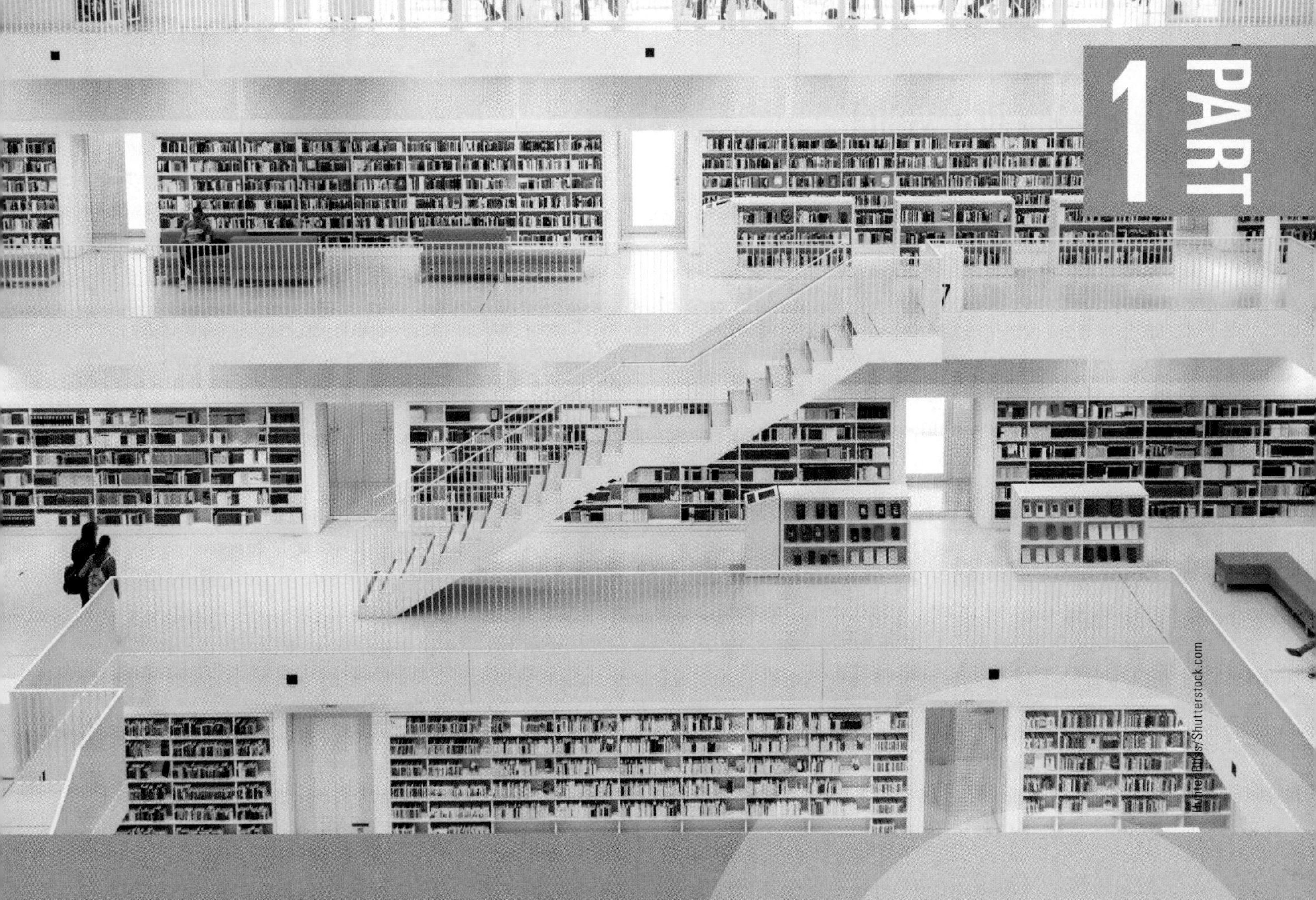

Hurtelectic/Shutterstock.com

Organizational Behaviour and Opportunities

1

LEARNING OUTCOMES

After reading this chapter, you should be able to do the following:

- 1-1 Define organizational behaviour.
- 1-2 Identify four action steps for responding positively in times of change.
- 1-3 Identify the important system components of an organization.
- 1-4 Describe the formal and informal elements of an organization.
- 1-5 Understand the diversity of organizations in the economy.
- 1-6 Evaluate the opportunities that change creates for organizational behaviour.
- 1-7 Demonstrate the value of objective knowledge and skill development in the study of organizational behaviour.
- 1-8 Explain the process of organizational design thinking.

See the end of this chapter for a list of available Study Tools, a "What about You?" Quiz, Mini Case, and the Shopify Running Case.

1-1 HUMAN BEHAVIOUR IN ORGANIZATIONS

> “Organizations have been described as clockworks, but they often seem like snake pits.[1]

Welcome to the field of organizational behaviour! Here you will learn about what happens in organizations at three levels of analysis—the individual, the team, and the organization. The more you understand about organizations, the more effective you will become as an organizational actor. Organizations have been studied for many years now and we have developed some robust theories and collected some useful empirical data. In this book, you will be exposed to many ideas and organizations that will enrich your understanding of the realities of the workplace. As you become familiar with the many aspects of organizational reality, you will be better prepared for your careers.

Human behaviour in organizations is complex and often difficult to understand. Organizations have been described as clockworks in which human behaviour is logical and rational, but they often seem like snake pits to those who work in them.[2] The clockwork metaphor reflects an orderly, idealized view of organizational behaviour devoid of conflict or dilemma because all the working parts (the people) are believed to mesh smoothly. The snake pit metaphor conveys the daily conflicts, distress, and struggle in organizations. Each metaphor reflects reality from a different perspective—the organization's versus the individual's point of view—and both reflect the complexity of human behaviour, the dark side of which is seen in cases of road rage and workplace violence. Still others have described organizations using a more nuanced approach. Bolman and Deal urge us to see organizations through four frames or metaphors—structural or machine, human resource or family, political or jungle, and symbolic or theatre. Managers, if they are to be effective, need to understand organizational situations through all four frames as doing so allows them to address the complexities of behaviours in organizations.[3]

opportunities Favourable times or chances for progress and advancement.

change The transformation or modification of an organization and/or its stakeholders.

challenge The call to competition, contest, or battle.

organizational behaviour The scientific study of individual behaviour, group dynamics, and structural choices in organizations.

This chapter introduces the field of organizational behaviour. The first section provides an overview of human behaviour in organizations, its interdisciplinary origins, and behaviour in times of change. The second section presents the organizational context within which behaviour occurs. The third section highlights the **opportunities** that exist in times of **change** and **challenge** for people at work.[4]

The fourth section addresses the ways people learn about organizational behaviour and explains how the text's pedagogical features relate to the various learning styles. The next section presents the plan for the book. It concludes with an account of design thinking.

Organizational behaviour is the study of individual behaviour, group processes, and structural dimensions of organizations. The study of organizational behaviour is primarily concerned with the psychosocial, interpersonal, and behavioural dynamics in organizations. Organizational variables that affect human behaviour at work are also relevant to the study of organizational behaviour. These organizational variables include jobs, the design of work, communication, performance appraisal, organizational design, and organizational structure. Many organizational behaviour theories use a contingency perspective. Any prescriptions depend on the characteristics of the particular situation, which must be analyzed carefully. There are therefore no universals in organizational behaviour: this is called the contingency perspective.

Understanding Human Behaviour

The vast majority of theories and models of human behaviour fall into two basic categories. One category has an internal perspective, and the other an external perspective. The internal perspective looks at individuals' minds to understand their behaviour. The internal perspective is psychodynamically oriented and its proponents understand human behaviour in terms of the thoughts, feelings, past experiences, and needs of the individual. The internal perspective explains people's actions and behaviour in terms of their history and personal value systems. The internal processes of thinking, feeling, perceiving, and judging lead people to act in specific ways. This perspective has given rise to a wide range of motivational and leadership theories. It implies that people are best understood from the inside and that people's behaviour is best interpreted alongside their thoughts and feelings.

The external perspective, on the other hand, focuses on factors outside the person to understand behaviour. People who subscribe to this view understand human behaviour in terms of the external events, consequences, and environmental forces to which a person is subject. From the external perspective, a person's history, feelings, thoughts, and personal value systems do not help interpret actions and behaviour. This perspective has given rise to an alternative set of motivational and leadership theories, which are covered in Chapters 5 and 12. The external perspective implies that examining the surrounding external events and environmental forces is the best way to understand behaviour.

The internal and external perspectives offer alternative explanations for human behaviour. For example, the internal perspective might say Aisha is an outstanding employee because she has a high need for achievement, whereas the external perspective might say it is because she is extremely well paid for her work. Some years ago, one influential thinker combined both perspectives with his argument that behaviour is a function of the interaction between the person and the environment.[5]

Interdisciplinary Influences

Organizational behaviour is a blended discipline that has grown out of contributions from numerous earlier fields of study. The sciences of psychology, sociology, engineering, anthropology, management, medicine, and economics have each contributed to our understanding of human behaviour in organizations. These interdisciplinary influences have evolved into the independent discipline of organizational behaviour.

Psychology, the science of human behaviour, developed during the closing decades of the 19th century. Psychology traces its own origins to philosophy and the science of physiology. One of the most prominent early psychologists, William James, held a degree in medicine. Since its origin, psychology has branched into a number of specialized fields, including clinical, experimental, organizational, industrial/organizational (often referred to as IO Psych), and social psychology. Social psychology, in particular, frequently overlaps with organizational behaviour; for instance, both investigate work motivation.[6] According to a survey of senior decision makers, most observed that personality was more important than an individual's skill set when it came to hiring.[7] Tests that used to understand personality include Myers-Briggs Temperament Index, the Big Five, and the DISC Behavior Inventory.

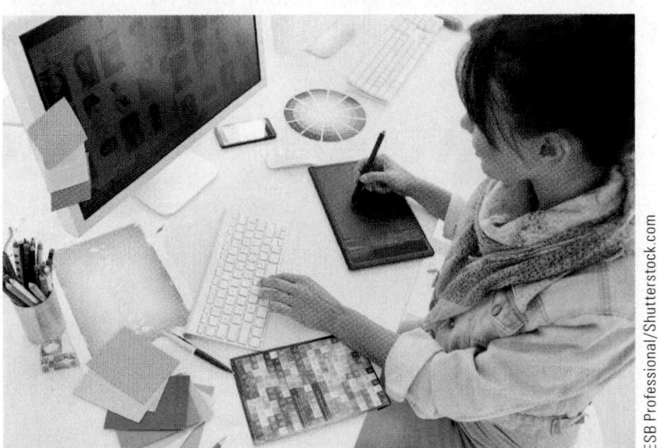
Effective work requires the fit between the person, the technology, and the organization.

ESB Professional/Shutterstock.com

The Canadarm is a key space innovation designed by several Canadian companies and used by NASA.

Stocktrek Images, Inc./Alamy Stock Photo

Sociology, the science of society, has contributed greatly to our knowledge of group and intergroup dynamics. Because sociology takes society rather than the individual as its point of departure, sociologists focus on the variety of roles within a society or culture, the norms and standards of behaviour in groups, and the consequences of compliant and deviant behaviour. One pre-eminent sociologist developed the idea of a bureaucracy as a design to professionalize organizations. While the term *bureaucracy* may have a negative association now, its original purpose was to create organizations that were administratively fair and free from nepotism.[8]

Engineering is the applied science of energy and matter. It enhances our understanding of the design of work. Frederick W. Taylor took basic engineering ideas and applied them to human behaviour at work, influencing the early study of organizational behaviour.[9] With his engineering background, Taylor placed special emphasis on human productivity and efficiency in work behaviour. His notions of performance standards and differential piece-rate systems still shape organizational goal-setting

psychology The science of human behaviour.

sociology The science of society.

engineering The applied science of energy and matter.

programs, such as those at Black & Decker, IBM, and Weyerhaeuser.[10]

Anthropology, the science of human learned behaviour, is especially important to our understanding of organizational culture. Cultural anthropology focuses on the origins of culture and the patterns of behaviour that develop with symbolic communication. Anthropological research has examined the effects of efficient cultures on organizational performance[11] and the ways pathological personalities may lead to dysfunctional organizational cultures.[12] Design firm IDEO, for example, hires anthropologists as well as other social scientists as they are able to gather and synthesize insights from interviews and observations. That way, IDEO's designs are more useful to their clients.[13] IDEO has designed an Apple watch camera band, the Levi's commuter trucker jacket, a creativity-developing app for children, to name a few.[14]

Management, originally called administrative science, is the study of overseeing activities and supervising people in organizations. It emphasizes the design, implementation, and management of various administrative and organizational systems. Management is the first discipline to take the modern corporation as the unit of analysis, a viewpoint that distinguishes its contribution to the study of organizational behaviour.

Medicine is the applied science of healing or treating diseases to enhance an individual's health and well-being. Medicine concerns itself with both physical and psychological health, as well as occupational mental health.[15] As modern care defeats acute diseases, medical attention has shifted to more chronic diseases, such as hypertension, and to occupational health and well-being.[16] These trends have contributed to the growth of organizational wellness programs, such as Johnson & Johnson's "Fit for Life" program.[17] Skyrocketing health care costs continue to contribute to increased organizational concern with wellness and health care in the workplace.[18]

Economics is the study of theories, principles, and models that seek to understand and explain how markets work. It attempts to explain how wealth is created and distributed. According to Adam Smith (1723–1790), often considered the founder of economics, "economics is the study of the nature and causes of nations' wealth or simply as the study of wealth."[19] There are two branches in economics: micro-economics, which looks at the individual unit and its decisions and macro-economics, which looks at systemic processes. More recently, behavioural economics (BE) has contributed to our understanding of organizational behaviour. Behavioural economists argue that we are not as rational as economists assume. Rather we tend "to act more like Homer Simpson than Mr. Spock" when we have to make complex decisions."[20] Organizations such as Canadian Tire and various banks are using BE ideas in designing ways to interact with their customers. In addition, behavioural economists have developed the idea of *nudges* as a useful tool to change behaviour in individuals. Nudges attempt to alter behaviour by using subtle suggestions, indirect incentives, and framing choices to help us make better decisions.

anthropology The science of the learned behaviour of human beings.

management The study of overseeing activities and supervising people in organizations.

medicine The applied science of healing or treatment of diseases to enhance an individual's health and well-being.

economics The study of theories, principles, and models that seek to understand and explain how markets work.

1-2 BEHAVIOUR IN TIMES OF CHANGE

Early research with individuals and organizations in the midst of environmental change found that people often experience change as a threat and respond by relying on well-learned and dominant forms of behaviour.[21] That is, in the midst of change, people often become rigid and reactive, rather than open and responsive. This behaviour works well in the face of gradual, incremental change. However, rigid and well-learned behaviour may be a counterproductive response to significant change. Outsourcing is a significant change in North American industry that has been forced by dramatic advances in the Internet and networking technology.[22] Big changes disrupt people's habitual behaviour and force them to learn new skills. One senior executive offers some sensible words of advice to see the opportunity in change.[23] He recommends adapting to change by seeing it as positive, and challenge as good rather than bad. His action steps for doing this are to (1) have a positive attitude,

Monkey Business Images/Shutterstock.com

Change requires a shared vision, innovative thinking, and a powerful change team.

(2) ask questions, (3) listen to the answers, and (4) be committed to success.

However, success is never guaranteed, and change often results in failure. If this happens, do not despair. Some of the world's greatest leaders, such as Nelson Mandela, experienced dramatic failures and successes. Their capacity to learn from the failures and to respond positively to new opportunities helped them overcome early setbacks. One venture capitalist with whom the authors have worked likes to ask those seeking to build a business to tell him about their greatest failure. He wants to hear how the executive responded to the failure and what they learned from the experience. Change carries both the risk of failure and the opportunity for success; our behaviour often determines the outcome. Success can come through enlightened opportunism, the accumulation of small wins, and the use of microprocesses, as has been found with middle managers engaged in institutional change.[24]

Some of the world's greatest leaders, such as Nelson Mandela, experienced dramatic failures and successes.

1-3 THE ORGANIZATIONAL CONTEXT

A complete understanding of organizational behaviour requires both an understanding of human behaviour and an understanding of the organizational context—that is, the specific setting—within which human behaviour is acted out.

Organizations as Open Systems

Just as two different perspectives offer complementary explanations for human behaviour, two views shape complementary explanations of organizations. Organizations are open systems of interacting components: people, tasks, technology, and structure. These internal components also interact with components in the organization's task environment. Open system organizations consist of people, technology, structure, and purpose, all interacting with elements in the organization's environment.

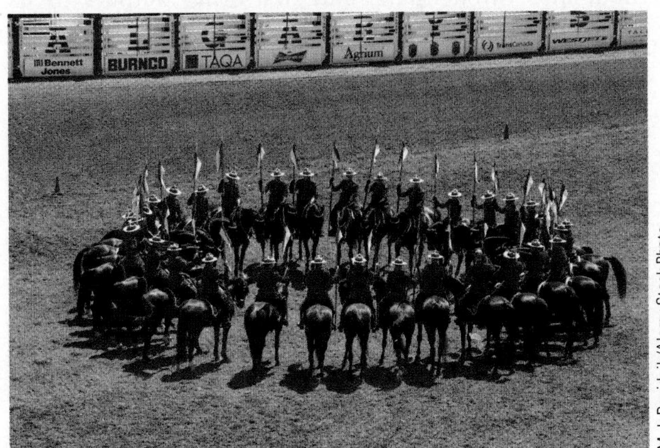

M.J. Daviduik/Alamy Stock Photo

The RCMP musical ride illustrates the delicate fit of many components.

What, exactly, then is an organization? Today, the corporation is the dominant organizational form for much of the Global North, but other organizational forms have dominated other societies. Religious organizations, such as the temple corporations of ancient Mesopotamia and the Catholic Church in 19th-century Quebec, can often dominate society.[25] So can military organizations, like the clans of the Scottish Highlands and the regional armies of the People's Republic of China.[26] All of these societies are woven together by family organizations, which themselves may vary from nuclear and extended families to small, collective communities.[27] The purpose and structure of the religious, military, and family organizational forms vary, but people within different organizations often behave alike. In fact, early discoveries about power and leadership in work organizations were remarkably similar to findings about power and leadership within families.[28]

Organizations may manufacture products, such as aircraft components or steel, or deliver services such as managing money or providing insurance protection. We must first understand the open system components of an organization and the components of its task environment in order to see how the organization functions. The four major internal components are structure, technology, people, and task. These four components, along with the organization's inputs, outputs, and key elements in the task environment, are depicted in Figure 1.1. The **structure** is the systems of communication, systems of authority, and the systems of workflow.

The technology is the wide range of tools, knowledge, processes, and/or techniques used to transform the inputs into outputs. The **people** are the human resources of the organization. The **task** of the organization is its mission, purpose, or goal for existing. In addition to these major internal components, the

structure The systems of communication, authority, and workflow.

people The human resources of the organization.

task An organization's mission, purpose, or goal for existing.

FIGURE 1.1 AN OPEN-SYSTEMS VIEW OF AN ORGANIZATION

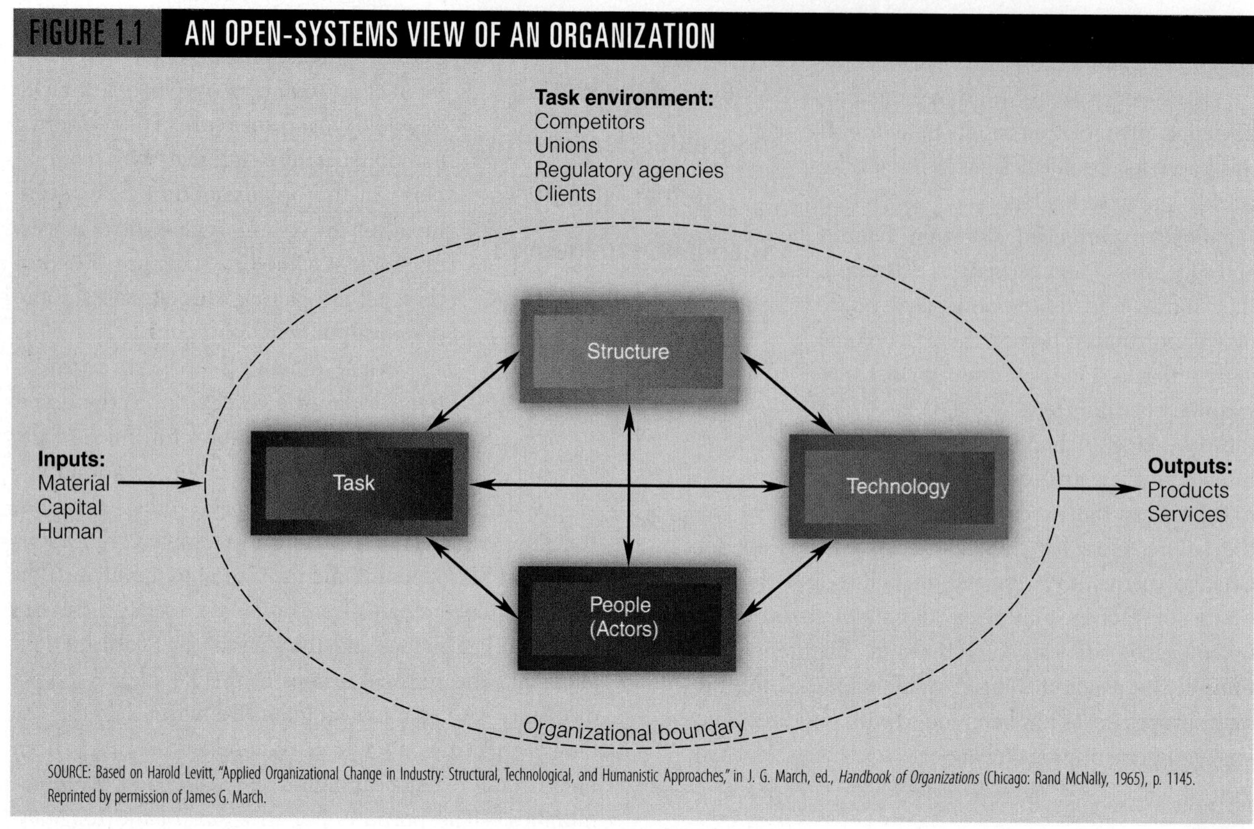

SOURCE: Based on Harold Levitt, "Applied Organizational Change in Industry: Structural, Technological, and Humanistic Approaches," in J. G. March, ed., *Handbook of Organizations* (Chicago: Rand McNally, 1965), p. 1145. Reprinted by permission of James G. March.

organization, as a system, also has an external task environment. The external task environment is composed of different constituents, such as suppliers, customers, and federal regulators. The task environment is that element of the environment related to the organization's degree of goal attainment; that is, the task environment is composed of those elements of the environment related to the organization's basic task.[29] For example, Tim Hortons is the chief competitor for Starbucks Canada and therefore a key element in Starbucks' task environment. Starbucks Canada must develop a business strategy and approach that considers the actions and activities of Tim Hortons. Similarly, Tim Hortons must do the same, especially as it has lost significant brand credibility in 2018.

The organization works by taking inputs, converting them into throughputs, and delivering outputs to its task environment. Inputs are the human, informational, material, and financial resources used by the organization. Throughputs are the materials and resources as they are transformed by the organization's technology component. Once the transformation is complete, they become outputs for customers, consumers, and clients.

The actions of suppliers, customers, regulators, and other elements of the task environment affect the organization and the behaviour of people at work. For example, businesses in the environmental field in Ontario are worried by the recent cancellation by Premier of Ontario of the GreenON rebate program. They are worried that households and businesses will not invest in their products and services.[30]

IN ACTION

McDonald's

North American corporations typically do things the North American way as they globalize and extend their reach into all parts of the world. The process of standardization is a uniquely American way of business since the advent of the Model T by Henry Ford. McDonald's has shown that it does not have to be that way. Instead of the Big Mac, the really successful Big Tasty was invented in Germany and launched in Sweden. France has the Croque McDo, which is ham and Swiss cheese on toast. The Netherlands has the McKroket—a deep-fried beef patty, and other countries have their own unique McDonald's specialties. McDonald's current global success is being achieved through accommodation, not through domination.

1-4 THE FORMAL AND INFORMAL ORGANIZATION

The open systems view of organization suggests that organizations are designed like clockwork with a neat, precise, interrelated functioning. The **formal organization** is the official, legitimate, and most visible part that enables people to think of organizations in logical and rational ways. **Scientific management**, developed by Frederick W. Taylor, is one of the best known models that suggests that organizations should operate like clockwork. The model argues that all work can be—and should be—broken down into the smallest possible tasks and processes. The snake-pit metaphor mentioned earlier originates from the study of the **informal organization**, which is unofficial and less visible. The **Hawthorne studies** were initiated in 1924 and were originally designed to study the relationship between illumination and productivity. While productivity increased, it was not caused by the illumination but by other factors. This unexpected finding triggered more research. Subsequent studies looked at the relationships between the changes in rest breaks and work hours and productivity. The analysis of the research concluded that the productivity must be attributable to "improved personal relations between workers and management"[31] and the workers' participation in the study itself. During the interview study, the third of the four Hawthorne studies, the researchers began to fully appreciate the informal elements of the Hawthorne Works as an organization.[32] (However, the generalizability of the Hawthorne effect—and the effect itself—has been challenged.) The formal and informal elements of the organization are depicted in Figure 1.2.

Since the formal and informal elements of an organization can sometimes conflict, we must understand both. Conflicts erupted in many organizations during the early years of the 20th century and were embodied in the union–management strife of that era. Sometimes formal–informal conflicts escalated into violence. For example, during the 1920s, supervisors at the Homestead Works of U.S. Steel were issued pistols "just in case" they felt it necessary to shoot unruly, dangerous steelworkers. Not all organizations are characterized by such potential formal–informal, management–labour conflict. During the same era, the progressive Eastman Kodak company helped with financial backing for employees' neighbourhood communities, such as Meadowbrook in Rochester, New York. Kodak's apparent concern for employees and attention to informal issues made unions unnecessary within the company.

The informal elements of the organization are often points

FIGURE 1.2 FORMAL AND INFORMAL ORGANIZATION

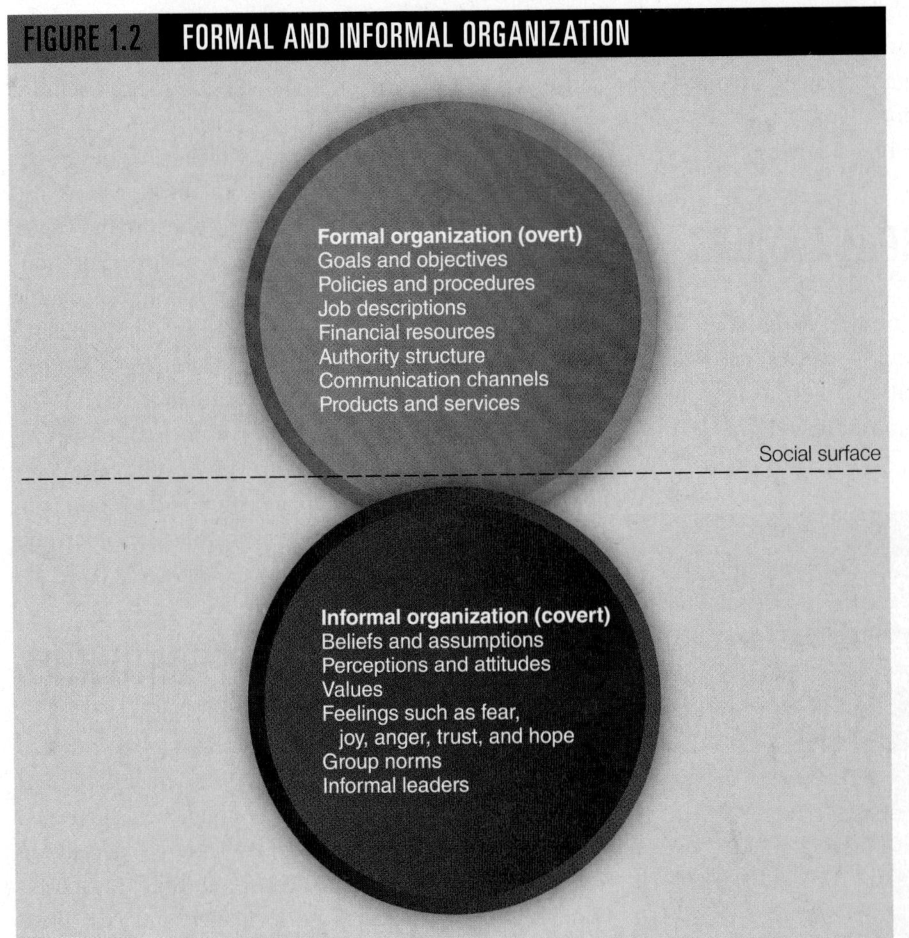

formal organization The official, legitimate, and most visible part of the system.

scientific management An atomistic view of management.

informal organization The unofficial and less visible part of the system.

Hawthorne studies Studies conducted during the 1920s and 1930s that discovered the existence of the informal organization.

IN ACTION

Marriott

Marriott is no Google, and it doesn't strive to be. Marriott employees *love* working at Marriott, and a large part of their affinity for the hotel chain can be attributed to its formal employee policies, from its hiring, flexible scheduling, and career development programs to its wide-ranging perks and benefits. These formal organizational elements have had a positive impact on worker attitudes and desire to remain with the company. Marriott employees consider each other as family rather than colleagues. By far, it is the company's recruitment and hiring practices that have the most positive effect on organizational outcomes. Marriott's EVP of HR believes that due to the company's practice of "hiring friendly and training technically," it has experienced lower turnover and increased numbers of employees who not only believe in serving their customers but delight in doing so.

SOURCE: L. Gallagher, "Why Employees Love Marriott," *Fortune*, 171 (March 15, 2015), 112–118 and Marriott International, Inc.

of diagnostic and intervention activities in organization development, though the formal elements must always be considered since they provide the context for the informal.[33] Informal elements are important because people's feelings, thoughts, and attitudes about their work affect their behaviour and performance. Individual behaviour plays out in the context of the formal and informal elements of the system, becoming organizational behaviour. Employees' moods, emotions, and dispositions all influence critical organizational outcomes, such as job performance, decision making, creativity, turnover, teamwork, negotiation, and leadership.[34]

1-5 DIVERSITY OF ORGANIZATIONS

Organizational behaviour always occurs in the context of a specific organizational setting. Most attempts at explaining or predicting organizational behaviour rely heavily on factors within the organization and give less weight to external environmental considerations.[35] Students can benefit from being sensitive to the industrial and sectoral context of organizations and from developing an appreciation for each organization as a whole.[36]

Large and small organizations operate in each sector of the economy. The private sectors play an important role in the economy. The manufacturing sector includes the production of basic materials, such as steel, and the production of finished products, such as automobiles and electronic equipment. The service sector includes transportation, financial services, insurance, and retail sales. The government sectors, which provide essential infrastructure, and nonprofit organizations are also important to our collective well-being because they meet needs that aren't addressed by other sectors. The nonprofit sector, for example, accounts for approximately 10 percent of Canada's gross domestic product (GDP).

Hundreds of small, medium, and large organizations contribute to Canada's economic health and human welfare. Throughout this book, we provide examples from a variety of organizations to help you develop a greater appreciation for your own organization and for others in the diverse world of business enterprises and nonprofit organizations.

Canada's 2016 GDP is worth US$1,529.76 billion or approximately 2.47 percent of the world economy. The foundation of the Canadian economy is foreign trade and the United States is by far the nation's largest trade partner. Foreign trade is responsible for about 45 percent of Canada's GDP. Canada is one of the few developed nations that is a net exporter of energy.

SOURCE: "Canada GDP," accessed from https://tradingeconomics.com/canada/gdp, May 4, 2018.

1-6 CHANGE CREATES OPPORTUNITIES

Change creates opportunities and risks. Global competition is a leading force driving change at work. Competition in the Canadian and world economies has increased significantly during the past few decades, especially in industries such as banking, finance, and air transportation. Competition creates performance and cost pressures, which have a ripple effect on people and their behaviour at work. While one risk for employees is the marginalization of part-time professionals, good management practice can ensure their integration.[37] Competition may lead to downsizing and restructuring, but it can provide the opportunity for revitalization.[38] Further, small companies don't necessarily lose in this competitive environment. For example, Squeeze Studio, a small 3D animation company in Quebec, competes globally. Product and service quality helps companies win in a competitive environment. Organizations as different as IBM, WestJet Airlines, and Arctic Co-operatives Limited Network all use problem-solving skills to achieve high-quality products and services.

Too much change leads to chaos; too little change leads to stagnation. Change in the coffee industry is a key stimulus for both Tim Hortons and Starbucks as they innovate and improve. Winning in a competitive industry can be a transient victory, however; staying ahead of the competition requires constant change.

Four Challenges for Managers Related to Change

Chapter 2 discusses four significant challenges for managers related to change in contemporary organizations: globalization, workforce diversity, ethics and character, and technological innovation. These four driving forces create and shape changes at work. Further, success in global competition requires organizations to respond to cultural, religious, and gender diversity and to personal integrity in the workforce, in addition to responding positively to the competition in the international marketplace. Workforce demographic change and diversity are critical challenges in themselves for the study and management of organizational behaviour.[39] The theories of motivation, leadership, and group behaviour based on research in a workforce of one composition may not be applicable in a workforce of a very different composition.[40] This may be especially problematic if cultural,

#HOT #TREND

Digital Health and One of Its Pioneers, Huda Idrees

Digital health is "the convergence of the digital and genomic revolutions with health, healthcare, living, and society." It's expected to reduce health care costs, create better health outcomes, and empower both patients and the health care providers. Digital health builds on already existing technologies such as smartphones and data analytics. In 2016, the global digital health market was estimated to be worth US$179.6 billion. Growth in the market is anticipated to rise at a compound annual growth rate of 13.4 percent between 2017 and 2025, reaching US$536.6 billion by the end of 2025.

Huda Idrees is one of Canada's "sheroes" who advocates for diversity and inclusion in STEM.

Huda Idrees is a pioneer in digital health. She founded her first startup when she was 12. Idrees has a well-established reputation in the global tech field as she has worked at Wattpad and Wealthsimple since graduating with a degree in engineering in 2013. She is now 27 and her new startup Dot Health is taking off. Dot Health aims to aggregate an individual's many health records in one place. That way, health records are in place online and easily accessible from a smartphone, tablet, or computer. Dot Health charges a monthly fee for the service. Idrees is motivated to solve a complex problem—the gap between health records and technology. As she notes, "it is a massive unfixed problem and nobody was looking at it because it doesn't have fast money in it. … This isn't a charity or a not-for-profit. But at the end of the day, we want this to have a positive impact. We're actually in it to do good for people."

SOURCES: "Definition of Digital Health," accessed from https://storyofdigitalhealth.com/definition, June 23, 2018; Quora "Is Digital Health the Future of Healthcare?" April 4, 2018, accessed from https://www.forbes.com/sites/quora/2018/04/04/is-digital-health-the-future-of-healthcare/#56284a022556, June 23, 2018; J. Leeder, "Toronto Startup Veteran Launches Digital Health-Records Platform," February 27, 2017, accessed from https://www.theglobeandmail.com/report-on-business/small-business/startups/toronto-startup-veteran-launches-digital-health-records-platform/article34124467, June 23, 2018.

gender, and/or religious differences lead to conflict between leaders and followers in organizations.

GLOBAL COMPETITION IN BUSINESS Managers and executives in North America face radical change in response to increased global competition, including an intense rivalry between the United States, Japan, and Europe in core industries.[41] Economic competition places pressure on all categories of employees to be productive and to add value to the firm. Corporate warfare and competition make employment uncertain for people in companies or industries that pursue cost-cutting strategies to achieve economic success. The global competition in the fragile automotive industry among the Japanese, North American, and European car companies embodies the intensity that other industries can expect in the future.

Some people feel that the future must be the focus in coming to grips with this international competition, whereas others believe we can deal with the future only by studying the past.[42] Global, economic, and organizational changes have dramatic effects on the study and management of organizational behaviour.

“Total quality isn't a panacea for all organizations and it doesn't guarantee unqualified success.”

CUSTOMER FOCUSED FOR HIGH QUALITY Global competition has challenged organizations to become more customer focused, to meet changing product and service demands, and to exceed customers' expectations of high quality. Quality has the potential to give organizations a competitive edge against international competition.

Quality became a rubric for products and services of high status. Total quality is defined in many ways.[43] Total quality management (TQM) is the total dedication to continuous improvement and to customers so that the customers' needs are met and their expectations exceeded. Quality is a customer-oriented philosophy of management with important implications for virtually all aspects of organizational behaviour. Quality cannot be optimized, because customer needs and expectations are always changing, but it is embedded in highly successful organizations. Part of what catapulted Toyota to the top of the auto industry is its attention to quality and detail throughout the organization. However, when Toyota decided to expand rapidly, it lost its quality focus. In 2010, the president of Toyota, Akio Toyoda, testified: “I would like to point out here that Toyota's priority has traditionally been the following: First, Safety; Second, Quality; and Third, Volume. These three priorities became confused and we were not able to stop, think, and make improvements as much as we were able to before, and our basic stance to listen to customers' voices to make better products has weakened somewhat.”[44]

Even though TQM consulting has experienced a boom-to-bust cycle, the main concepts underlying its initial rise in popularity are here to stay.

Quality improvement enhances the probability of organizational success in increasingly competitive industries. One study of 193 general medical hospitals examined seven TQM practices and found them positively related to the financial performance of the hospital.[45] Quality improvement is an enduring feature of an organization's culture and of the economic competition we face today. It leads to competitive advantage through customer responsiveness, results acceleration, and resource effectiveness.[46] The three key questions in evaluating quality-improvement ideas for people at work are as follows: (1) Does the idea improve customer response? (2) Does the idea accelerate results? (3) Does the idea increase the effectiveness of resources? A “yes” answer means the idea should be implemented to improve quality. Organizations as diverse as Diversicare Canada Management Services Co. Inc.; City of St. George, BC; ARSC Energy Services, Tri Ocean Engineering Ltd.; and Manulife Financial—Individual Wealth Management Operations have received the Canada Awards for Excellence in Quality from the National Quality Institute.[47]

Six Sigma is a philosophy for company-wide quality improvement developed by Motorola and popularized by General Electric. General Electric's plant in Bromont, Quebec, for example, is committed to achieving the highest Six Sigma standard. The Six Sigma program is characterized by its customer-driven approach, its emphasis on using quantitative data to make decisions, and its priority on saving money.[48] It has evolved into a high-performance system to execute business strategy. Part of its quality program is a 12-step problem-solving method specifically designed to lead a Six Sigma “Black Belt” to significant improvement within a defined process. Six Sigma tackles problems in four phases: (1) measure, (2) analyze, (3) improve, and (4) control. In addition, it forces executives to align the right objective and targets and quality-improvement teams to mobilize for action in order to accelerate and monitor sustained improvement. Six Sigma is set up so that it can be applied to a range of situations, from manufacturing

TABLE 1.1 CONTRASTING SIX SIGMA AND TOTAL QUALITY MANAGEMENT

Six Sigma	Total Quality Management
Executive ownership	Self-directed work teams
Business strategy execution system	Quality initiative
Truly cross-functional	Largely within a single function
Focused training with verifiable return on investment	No mass training in statistics and quality return on investment
Business results oriented	Quality oriented

SOURCE: M. Barney, "Motorola's Second Generation," *Six Sigma Forum Magazine* (May 2002): 13. Reprinted by permission of ASQ.

settings to service work environments. Table 1.1 contrasts Six Sigma and TQM. One study compared Six Sigma to two other methods for quality improvement (specifically, Taguchi's methods and the Shainin system) and found it to be the most complete strategy of the three, with a strong emphasis on exploiting statistical modelling techniques.[49]

BEHAVIOUR AND QUALITY AT WORK Whereas total quality may draw on reliability engineering or just-in-time management, total quality improvement can succeed only when employees have the skills and authority to respond to customer needs.[50] Total quality has important direct effects on the behaviour of employees at all levels in the organization, not just on employees working directly with customers. Chief executives can advance total quality by engaging in participative management, being willing to change anything, focusing quality efforts on customer service (not cost cutting), including quality as a criterion in reward systems, improving the flow of information about quality-improvement successes or failures, and being actively and personally involved in quality efforts. Developed by and for the manufacturing industry, Six Sigma is a quality and management trend with staying power. The fundamental goal of Six Sigma is to increase quality by reducing the variation between manufactured parts. To achieve Six Sigma, an organization must incur only 3.4 defective or nonstandard parts per million.[51] It's easy to see why organizations across a wide range of product and service industries are implementing Six Sigma techniques: the goal of stratospheric perfection is motivating and actually measurable.

Quality improvement is crucial to competitive success. The National Quality Institute, whose mission is "Helping Canada Live and Work Better," has an awards program to honour and to inspire a commitment to quality excellence. Organizations that do not respond to customer needs find their customers choosing alternative product and service suppliers who are willing to exceed customer expectations. *Quality* is one watchword for competitive success. Keep in mind, however, that total quality isn't a panacea for all organizations and it doesn't guarantee unqualified success.

MANAGING ORGANIZATIONAL BEHAVIOUR IN CHANGING TIMES Over and above the challenge of quality improvement to meet international competition, managing organizational behaviour during changing times is challenging for at least four reasons: (1) the increasing globalization of organizations' operating territory, (2) the increasing diversity of organizational workforces, (3) the continuing demand for higher levels of moral and ethical behaviour at work, and (4) continuing technological innovation with its companion need for skill enhancement.

Each of these four issues is explored in detail in Chapter 2 and highlighted throughout the text as they appear intertwined with contemporary organizational practices. For example, the issue of women in the workplace concerns workforce diversity and at the same time overlaps with the globalization issue. Gender roles are often defined differently in various cultures, and sexual harassment often plagues organizations in North America and elsewhere.

IN ACTION

Kicking Horse Coffee

The CEO of Kicking Horse, Elana Rosenfeld, has designed her company to reflect her values. She started the company in 1996, long before premium coffees became popular in the Canadian market. From the outset, Rosenfeld introduced whole bean, organic, fair trade coffee. To her, doing so was a "no-brainer." While Lavazza bought 80 percent of Kicking Horse, valued at $215 million in 2017, Rosenfeld is still the CEO and continues to be based in Invermere, BC. Rosenfeld goes on to note that Lavazza and Kicking Horse have philosophical similarities, although their brands are different.

SOURCE: S. Efron, "Kicking Horse Coffee CEO Elana Rosenfeld on Building a Business that Reflects her Personal Ethics," *The Globe and Mail*, April 15, 2018, accessed from https://www.theglobeandmail.com/business/careers/leadership/article-kicking-horse-coffee-ceo-elana-rosenfeld-on-building-a-business-that, May 4, 2018.

1-7 LEARNING ABOUT ORGANIZATIONAL BEHAVIOUR

Organizational behaviour is based on scientific knowledge, empirical findings, and applied practice. It involves the study of abstract ideas, such as valence and expectancy in motivation, as well as the study of concrete matters, such as observable behaviours and physical and emotional symptoms of distress at work. Therefore, learning about organizational behaviour includes at least three activities, as shown in Figure 1.3. First, the science of organizational behaviour requires the mastery of a certain body of **objective knowledge**. Objective knowledge results from research and scientific activities. Second, the practice of organizational behaviour requires **skill development** based on knowledge and an understanding of yourself in order to master the abilities essential to success. Both objective knowledge and skill development must be applied in real-world settings.

Learning is challenging and fun because we are all different. Within learning environments, student diversity is best addressed in the learning process when students have more options and can take greater responsibility as co-producers in the effort and fun of learning.[52] For those with learning exceptionalities, learning can be a special challenge. Teaching and learning styles should be aligned carefully and educators should be aware that teaching is no longer merely verbal and visual; it has now become virtual. If you are a visual learner, use charts, maps, PowerPoint slides, videos, the Internet, notes, or flash cards, and write things out for visual review. If you are an auditory learner, listen, take notes during lectures, and consider taping them so you can fill in gaps later; review your notes frequently; and recite key concepts out loud. If you are a tactile learner, trace words as you are saying them, write down facts several times, and make study sheets.

Objective Knowledge

Objective knowledge, in any field of study, is developed through basic and applied research. Research in organizational behaviour has continued since early research on scientific management. Acquiring objective knowledge requires the cognitive mastery of theories, conceptual models, and research findings. In this book, the objective knowledge in each chapter is reflected in the supporting notes. Mastering the concepts and ideas that come from these notes enables you to intelligently discuss topics such as motivation, performance, leadership,[53] and executive stress.[54]

objective knowledge Knowledge that results from research and scientific activities.

skill development The mastery of abilities essential to successful functioning in organizations.

We encourage instructors and students of organizational behaviour to think critically about the objective knowledge in organizational behaviour. Only by engaging in critical thinking can you question or challenge the results of specific research and responsibly consider how to apply research results in a particular work setting. Rote memorization does not prepare students to appreciate the complexity of specific theories or the intricacies of interrelated concepts, ideas, and topics. Good critical thinking, however, enables the student to identify inconsistencies and limitations in the current body of objective knowledge.

Critical thinking, based on knowledge and understanding of basic ideas, leads to inquisitive exploration and is a key to accepting the responsibility of co-producer in the learning process. A questioning, probing attitude is at the core of critical thinking. The student of organizational behaviour should evolve into a critical consumer of knowledge related to organizational behaviour—one who is able to intelligently question the latest research results and distinguish plausible, sound new approaches from fads that lack substance or adequate foundation. Ideally, the student of organizational behaviour develops into a scientific professional manager who is knowledgeable in the art and science of organizational behaviour.

FIGURE 1.3 LEARNING ABOUT ORGANIZATIONAL BEHAVIOUR

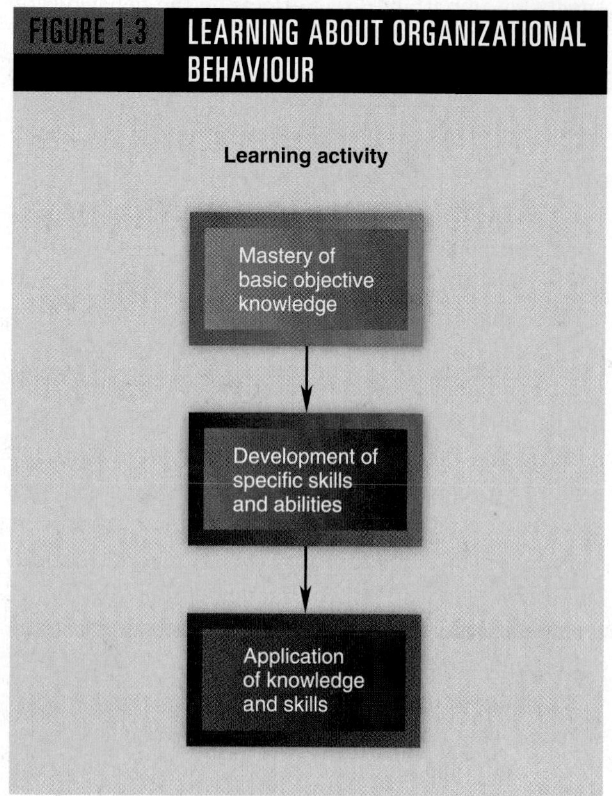

Skill Development

Learning about organizational behaviour requires doing as well as knowing. The development of skills and abilities requires that students be challenged by the instructor and by themselves. The Self-Assessment at the end of the chapter gives you a chance to learn about yourself, challenge yourself, and developmentally apply what you are learning.

Employment and Social Development Canada has identified nine "essential skills" for work, learning, and life. The nine were identified through research and are needed to be successful in most types of work and life. The nine are (1) reading, (2) document use, (3) numeracy, (4) writing, (5) oral communication, (6) working with others, (7) continuous learning, (8) thinking, and (9) computer use/digital skills. While the skills are used in different degrees and at different levels of complexity in different types of work, they are all needed.[55] All these skills are used in the study of organizational behaviour.

Developing skills is different from acquiring objective knowledge because it requires structured practice and feedback. A key function of experiential learning is engaging the student in individual or group activities that are systematically reviewed, leading to new skills and understandings. Objective knowledge acquisition and skill development are interrelated. The process for learning from structured or experiential activities is depicted in Figure 1.4. The student engages in an individual or group-structured activity and systematically reviews that activity, gaining new or modified knowledge and skills.

If skill development and structured learning occur in this way, there should be an inherently self-correcting element to learning because of the modification of the student's knowledge and skills over time.[56] To ensure that skill development does occur and that the learning is self-correcting as it occurs, three basic assumptions must be followed.

First, each student must accept responsibility for their own behaviour, actions, and learning. This is a key to the co-producer role in the learning process. A group cannot learn for its members. Each member must accept responsibility for what they do and learn. Denial of responsibility helps no one, least of all the learner.

Second, each student must actively participate in the individual or group-structured learning activity. Structured learning is not passive; it is active. In group activities, everyone suffers if just one person adopts a passive attitude. Therefore, everyone must actively participate.

Third, each student must be open to new information, new skills, new ideas, and experimentation. This does not mean that students need to be confessional. It does mean that students should have a nondefensive, open attitude so that they can learn and adjust to new ideas.

Application of Knowledge and Skills

Understanding organizational behaviour includes an appreciation and understanding of working realities, as well as of science and of yourself. One of the advantages of structured, experiential learning is that a person can explore new behaviours and skills in a comparatively safe environment. Losing your temper in a classroom activity and learning about the potentially adverse impact on other people will probably have dramatically different consequences from losing your temper with an important customer in a tense work situation. Learning spaces

FIGURE 1.4 LEARNING FROM STRUCTURED ACTIVITY

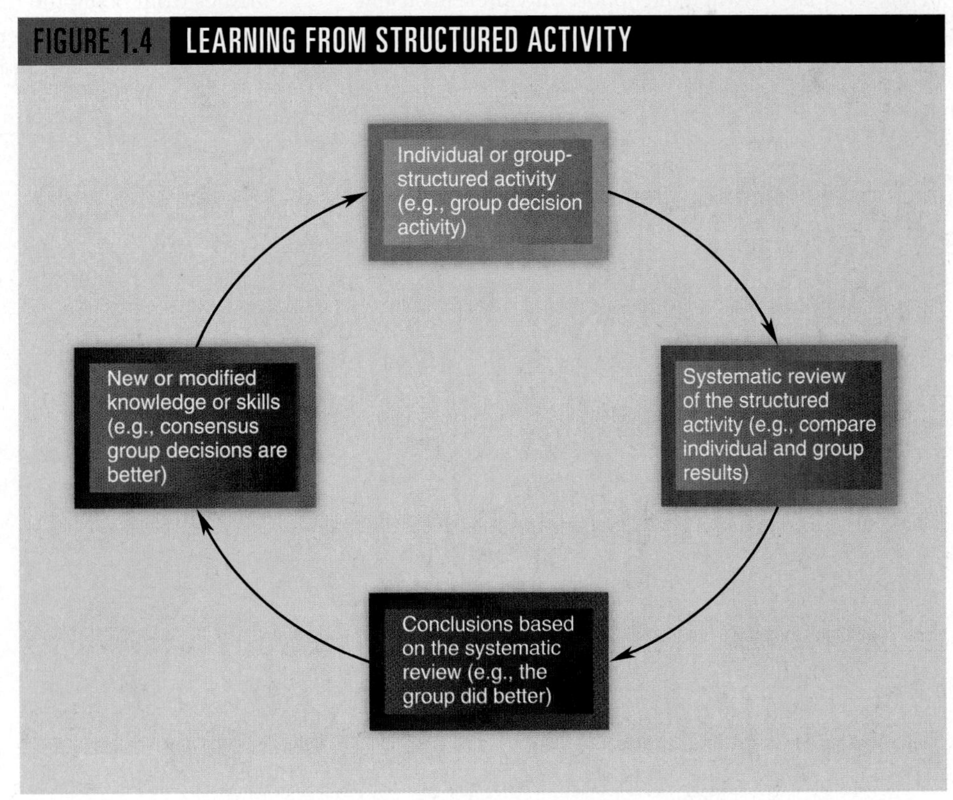

that offer the interface of student learning styles with institutional learning environments give learners safe spaces to engage their brains to form abstract hypotheses, to actively test these hypotheses through concrete experience, and to reflectively observe the outcomes in behaviour and experience.[57] The ultimate objective of skill application and experiential learning is that the student transfers the process employed in learning from structured activities in the classroom and learning spaces to learning from unstructured opportunities in the workplace. The Kolb Learning Style Model synthesizes the different ways that we use to learn. Kolb has found that we can learn through the processes of doing, feeling, thinking, and applying. While we each have our preferred learning process, we can learn the others. His view is that the more we can learn through all four processes, the stronger our learning.[58]

Although organizational behaviour is an applied discipline, students are not "trained" in organizational behaviour. Rather, they are "educated" in organizational behaviour and are co-producers in learning. The distinction between these two modes of learning is found in the degree of direct and immediate applicability of either knowledge or skills. As an activity, training more nearly ties direct objective knowledge or skill development to specific applications. By contrast, education enhances a person's residual pool of objective knowledge and skills that may then be selectively applied later—sometimes significantly later—when the opportunity presents itself. Hence, education is highly consistent with the concept of lifelong learning. Especially in a growing and engaging area of knowledge such as organizational behaviour, there is much to learn that can be applied immediately so that the student can be an effective organizational actor!

1-8 DESIGN THINKING

An exciting new idea is starting to shape managerial thinking and practice. It helps to bring together all the various elements of organizational behaviour. Design thinking is gaining traction among thoughtful organizational leaders. Roger Martin, a leading management guru, argues that "[in] a global economy, elegant design is becoming a competitive advantage. Trouble is, most business folks don't think like designers."[59] In his view, the design economy will replace the information economy. Managers will need to think like designers when they face a problem—they will accept the mystery of the problem, take on the abstract challenge, and design a solution rather than rely on past approaches and tools. Such managers will demonstrate "abductive" reasoning; that is, they will suggest something that could be and then explore it.[60] Apple is a fine example of an organization that understands design thinking in its work of creating "insanely great" products. Martin goes on to argue that businesspeople need to shift to becoming masters of heuristics from being the masters of algorithms.[61]

Such a shift is considerable and will require a new approach to managing people and organizations. Fusenet Inc., a Toronto-based firm that develops products and brands for the creation, storage, and delivery of digital media, allows its staff to spend a day a week to work on their own projects in a lab. It is an in-house business incubator. According to Fusenet's founder and CEO, Sanjay Singhal, "The lab gives them a safe environment in which they can tell us about [their project] and they'll know we won't steal the idea. Nothing changes other than we can invest in it and we know we won't lose the person a year down the road when it becomes commercial."[62]

Photo by Rawpixel on Unsplash

Diverse people working together can address global problems!

STUDY TOOLS 1

IN THE BOOK YOU CAN ...

☐ Rip out the **Chapter Review card** at the end of the book to review Key Concepts and Key Terms.

☐ Take a "What about You?" Quiz related to material in the chapter.

☐ Read additional cases in the Mini Case and Shopify Running Case sections.

ONLINE YOU CAN ...

NELSON.COM/STUDENT

☐ Take a "What about You?" Quiz related to material in the chapter.

☐ Test your understanding with a quick Multiple-Choice Pre-Test quiz.

☐ Read the eBook, which includes discussion points for questions posed in the Cases.

☐ Watch Videos related to chapter content.

☐ Use the available Flashcards and Matching Quizzes to test your understanding of key terms and concepts.

☐ See how much you've learned by taking a Post-Test.

WHAT ABOUT YOU?

Learning Style Inventory

This 24-item survey is not timed. Answer each question as honestly as you can, using one of the following words:

	Often	Sometimes	Seldom
1. Can remember more about a subject through the lecture method with information, explanations, and discussion.	☐	☐	☐
2. Prefer information to be written on the chalkboard, with the use of visual aids and assigned readings.	☐	☐	☐
3. Like to write things down or to take notes for visual review.	☐	☐	☐
4. Prefer to use posters, models, or actual practice and some activities in class.	☐	☐	☐
5. Require explanations of diagrams, graphs, or visual directions.	☐	☐	☐
6. Enjoy working with my hands or making things.	☐	☐	☐
7. Am skillful with and enjoy developing and making graphs and charts.	☐	☐	☐
8. Can tell if sounds match when presented with pairs of sounds.	☐	☐	☐
9. Remember best by writing things down several times.	☐	☐	☐
10. Can understand and follow directions on maps.	☐	☐	☐
11. Do better at academic subjects by listening to lectures and tapes.	☐	☐	☐
12. Play with coins or keys in pockets.	☐	☐	☐
13. Learn to spell better by repeating the word out loud than by writing the word on paper.	☐	☐	☐
14. Can better understand a news development by reading about it in the paper than by listening to the radio.	☐	☐	☐
15. Chew gum, smoke, or snack during studies.	☐	☐	☐
16. Feel the best way to remember is to picture it in your head.	☐	☐	☐
17. Learn spelling by "finger spelling" words.	☐	☐	☐

	Often	Sometimes	Seldom
18. Would rather listen to a good lecture or speech than read about the same material in a textbook.	☐	☐	☐
19. Am good at working and solving jigsaw puzzles and mazes.	☐	☐	☐
20. Grip objects in hands during learning period.	☐	☐	☐
21. Prefer listening to the news on the radio rather than reading about it in the newspaper.	☐	☐	☐
22. Obtain information on an interesting subject by reading relevant materials.	☐	☐	☐
23. Feel very comfortable touching others, hugging, shaking hands, etc.	☐	☐	☐
24. Follow oral directions better than written ones.	☐	☐	☐

Scoring Procedures

On the line next to each of your answers, write the corresponding point value. Score 5 points for each OFTEN, 3 points for each SOMETIMES, and 1 point for each SELDOM, then total your scores for the following groups of questions:

Visual Preference questions 2 + 3 + 7 + 10 + 14 + 16 + 19 + 22 = ______________

Auditory Preference questions 1 + 5 + 8 + 11 + 13 + 18 + 21 + 24 = ______________

Tactile Preference questions 4 + 6 + 9 + 12 + 15 + 17 + 20 + 23 = ______________

SOURCE: Adapted from J. N. Gardner and A. J. Jewler, *Your College Experience: Strategies for Success,* 3rd concise ed. (Belmont, CA: Wadsworth/ITP, 1998), pp. 62–63; E. Jensen, *Student Success Secrets,* 4th ed. (Hauppauge, N.Y.: Barron's, 1996), pp. 33–36.

MINI CASE

Brian Cowell

The afternoon was as gloomy as Brian's mood. It had not been a very productive day. All Brian could think about was the decision before him. He found the current situation interesting in that he had never before struggled with decisions. In the past, he had always been able to make quick and good decisions. His gut usually gave him the answer and he trusted his instincts. This time he felt nothing, and he was unsure how to proceed without that guiding force.

Brian Cowell was 52 years old and the CEO of Data Solutions, a company he had run for the last 20 years. Brian had been very successful at the helm of the company. Data Solutions had grown from a small data processing business to one of the largest employers in the area. Brian's good instincts had guided them through recent challenging times, and the company was in just the right place to meet the challenges ahead. Or was it? This was the question that plagued Brian.

Changes in technology were providing some interesting possibilities for the future. A part of Brian said that he needed to step up and help Data Solutions move into the global environment. He could lead Data Solutions into the global marketplace and continue the growth he had begun so many years ago. That was a big step and would take Brian down a very challenging road. The other option was to continue on the company's current path. Not a bad one: the company had been the most profitable in its history last year and everyone was very happy. Deep inside, Brian knew the answer. Move the company forward to the next logical step: globalization. But Brian was tired and really wanted to spend his last years at Data Solutions reaping the benefits of his hard work, not gearing up for the biggest challenge of his career. Didn't he deserve the right to enjoy his final years at Data Solutions?

Apply Your Understanding

1. Does Brian have an obligation to lead the company to globalization?
2. What is Brian's responsibility to himself and his family?
3. What would you do and why?

RUNNING CASE SHOPIFY

SHOPIFY: A CANADIAN SUCCESS

Shopify is one of Canada's start-up success stories. It was founded in 2006 in Ottawa by Tobias Lutke, Daniel Weinand, and Scott Lake. Shopify actually started in 2004 as an online outlet to sell snowboard equipment directly to other snowboarders. The co-founders soon realized that there were many other small businesses that did not have easy access to online platforms to sell their products. Shopify's mission is to support other e-commerce companies so that they can concentrate on making and selling their products. That way, the companies can spend more time working at the heart of their business rather than spending time on time-consuming administrative tasks. Shopify's key strategic differentiator is that it integrated all aspects of running a business from marketing, payments, checkout, and shipping on an integrated merchant dashboard. Shopify now allows its merchants to sell through other channels too, such as Facebook, Pinterest, and Amazon.

Shopify started off as a five-person company and has grown to 3,000 employees working in five offices across North America. In 2016, it had 600,000 active stores that generated $55 billion in sales. Shopify went public in 2015 in a successful IPO.

In 2015, Shopify was awarded the Employer of the Year in the 2014 Canadian Startup Awards. It has been recognized as one of Canada's most innovative companies. Shopify also recognizes its e-commerce partners through various awards such as best mobile commerce experience, best abandoned cart recovery experience, and best e-commerce course.

THE CANADIAN PRESS/Paul Chiasson

While Shopify remains one of the "darlings" of Canada's tech space, it has faced some controversies during its evolution from its modest beginning. In May 2017, Shopify stock fell rapidly as it faced criticism from an analyst that it was pushing "shady" business practices. It was accused of being an over-valued get-rich-quick scheme. A few months earlier, in February 2017, Shopify was forced to defend why it was hosting an e-commerce store for the alt-right media outlet Breitbart News. Shopify's CEO had received 10,000 messages in protest. However, the CEO claimed that to shut it down would be censorship and therefore he would not do so. He argued that "... products are a form of speech and that it's important to defend free speech, even if the company doesn't agree with some of the voices." (See the running case at the end of Chapters 4 and 10 for more details about the Breitbart incident.)

SOURCES: "About Us," accessed from https://www.shopify.ca/about, September 28, 2018; J. Koeftsier, Forget Ecommerce: Shopify Wants to Transform All Retail, Everywhere, Everywhen, Everyhow, December 8, 2013, accessed from https://venturebeat.com/2013/12/18/forget-ecommerce-shopify-wants-to-transform-all-retail-everywhere-everywhen-everyhow, September 28, 2018; S. M. Baldwin, "The Invisible Selling Machine," *Fortune*, March 15, 2017, accessed from http://fortune.com/2017/03/15/shopify-ecommerce-revolution, September 28, 2018; "Shopify Ecommerce Winner 2017," accessed from https://www.shopify.ca/commerceawards/winners September 28, 2018; CP, "Shares in Canada's Shopify Fall for 2nd Day After Claim It's a 'Get-Rich-Quick' Scheme," May 10, 2017, accessed from https://www.huffingtonpost.ca/2017/10/05/shares-in-canadas-shopify-fall-for-2nd-day-after-claim-its-a-get-rich-quick-scheme_a_23234064/?utm_hp_ref=ca-shopify, September 28, 2018; A. Posadzki, "Ottawa-based Shopify Defends Hosting Breitbart Store," *Huffington Post*, February 11, 2017, accessed from https://www.huffingtonpost.ca/2017/02/11/shopify-breitbart-store_n_14691414.html?utm_campaign=canada_dau, September 28, 2018.

Apply Your Understanding

1. What is innovative about Shopify's business model?
2. As Shopify gets larger, what challenges might it face?
3. Why would a vendor want to sell through Shopify?

2 Organizational Challenges for Today

LEARNING OUTCOMES

After reading this chapter, you should be able to do the following:

2-1 Describe the factors that affect organizations competing in the global economy.

2-2 Explain how cultural differences form the basis of work-related attitudes.

2-3 Describe the diverse groups that make up today's business environment.

2-4 Discuss the role of ethics, character, and personal integrity in the organization.

2-5 Explain five issues that pose ethical dilemmas for managers and employees.

2-6 Describe the effects of technological advances on today's workforce.

See the end of this chapter for a list of available Study Tools, a "What about You?" Quiz, Mini Case, and the Shopify Running Case.

Being a manager is not an easy job. Managers face many challenges, both internally and externally. Chapter 2 outlines several that today's managers and employees face. As Chapter 1 demonstrated, organizations are open systems and are therefore affected by changing system dynamics. Some of the pressing issues facing managers *today* are working in globalized and diverse organizations. As well, managers will likely confront decisions that require thoughtful analysis and nuanced ethical judgments. This chapter addresses these issues and provides some guidance for working effectively.

Many North American executives believe that organizations are encountering unprecedented global competition.[1] Globalization is being driven, on the one hand, by the spread of economic logic centred on freeing, opening, deregulating, and privatizing economies to attract investment and, on the other hand, by the technological digitization that is revolutionizing communication.[2] The challenges are manifest as both opportunities and threats.

> "Canada must play a leadership role in supporting an open global trading system at a time when protectionist forces threaten to reverse decades of progress.[3]"

What major challenges must Canadian managers overcome in order to remain competitive? According to the Canadian Council of Chief Executives, Canadian organizations face many significant challenges: (1) Canada remains an export-dependent economy that is highly dependent on the United States, its largest trading partner; (2) organizations in every sector face the challenge of a strong currency combined with a weak demand for products and services from our largest trading partner; and (3) Canada has low labour productivity growth. However, Canada weathered the 2008–2009 recession relatively unscathed.[4] In the first quarter of 2018, "the economy grew at an annualized pace of 1.3 per cent for the first three months of the year, slower than the annual pace of 1.7 per cent in the final three months of 2017."[5] The Business Council of Canada has expressed concern about the slow pace of Canada's growth and its continued low labour productivity growth. Among its recommendations is an ambitious trade strategy: "Canada must play a leadership role in supporting an open global trading system at a time when protectionist forces threaten to reverse decades of progress."[6]

2-1 COMPETING IN THE GLOBAL ECONOMY

Only a few years ago, business conducted across national borders was referred to as "international" activity. The word *international* implies that the individual's or the organization's nationality is held strongly in consciousness.[7] *Globalization,* by contrast, suggests that the world is free from national boundaries and is borderless.[8] North American workers now compete with workers in other countries. Organizations from other countries are locating subsidiaries in North America, such as the Canadian manufacturing locations of Honda, Toyota, 3M, and Black & Decker Manufacturing, to name a few.

Similarly, what were once called *multinational organizations* (organizations that did business in several countries) are now referred to as transnational organizations. In **transnational organizations**, the global viewpoint supersedes national issues.[9] Transnational organizations operate across long distances and employ a multicultural mix of workers. While there are few transnational organizations in Canada,[10] Magna International is well known and operates worldwide and locally with diverse populations of employees.

Social and Political Changes

Social and political upheavals have led organizations to change the way they conduct business and to encourage their members to think globally. For example, Toyota is learning to communicate with the 60-million-strong Generation Y, or millennials.[11]

Business ventures in China have become increasingly attractive to North American companies. One challenge managers have tackled is understanding the Chinese way of doing business. Chinese managers' business practices were shaped by the Communist Party, socialism, feudalistic values, and ***guanxi*** (building networks

transnational organization An organization in which the global viewpoint supersedes national issues.

guanxi The Chinese practice of building networks for social exchange.

for social exchange). Once *guanxi* is established, individuals can ask favours of each other with the expectation that the favour will be returned. For example, many Chinese use *guanxi,* or personal connections, to conduct business or obtain jobs. Use the Self-Assessment at the end of the chapter to think about yourself as a future global manager.

The concept of *guanxi* is not unique to China. There are similar concepts in many other countries, including Russia and Haiti. It is a broad term that can mean anything from strongly loyal relationships to ceremonial gift giving, sometimes seen as bribery. *Guanxi* is more common in societies with underdeveloped legal support for private businesses.[12] North Americans can learn to build their own *guanxi*; understand the Chinese chain of command and negotiate slow, general agreements in order to interact effectively with Chinese managers. Using the foreign government as the local franchisee may be effective in China. For example, KFC Corporation's operation in China is a joint venture between KFC (60 percent) and two Chinese government bodies (40 percent).[13]

In 1993, the European Union integrated 15 nations into a single market by removing trade barriers. At that time, the member nations of the European Union were Austria, Belgium, Denmark, Finland, France, Germany, Greece, Ireland, Italy, Luxembourg, the Netherlands, Portugal, Spain, Sweden, and the United Kingdom. By 2007, Bulgaria, Cyprus, the Czech Republic, Estonia, Hungary, Latvia, Lithuania, Malta, Poland, Slovakia, and Slovenia had also joined. Europe's integration provides many opportunities for North American organizations, with half a billion potential customers. Companies such as Ford Motor Company and IBM, which entered the market early with wholly owned subsidiaries, were able to capitalize on their much-anticipated head start.[14] Competition within the European Union will intensify, however, as will competition from Japan and the nations of the former Soviet Union.

Canada, the United States, and Mexico dramatically reduced trade barriers with the North American Free Trade Agreement (NAFTA), which took effect in 1994. Organizations found promising new markets for their products, and many companies located plants in Mexico to take advantage of low labour costs. The agreement immediately eliminated many of these tariffs and provided that the remaining tariffs be phased out over time. However, as of mid-2018, NAFTA has not been re-signed and the Trump administration has implemented many protectionist tariffs. As a result, Canada has retaliated in kind. The Trump administration has created trade barriers that are having significant employment impacts in both Canada and the United States.

Given these changes, managers must think globally and adopt a long-term view. Entering global markets requires long-term strategies and cultural fluency.

Cultural Differences

One key for any organization competing in the global marketplace is to understand diverse cultures. Whether managing culturally diverse individuals within a single location or managing individuals at remote locations around the globe, organizations must appreciate the differences between cultures. Edgar Schein suggests that to understand an organization's culture, or more broadly any culture, it is important to dig below the surface of visible artifacts and uncover the basic underlying assumptions at the core of the culture.[15]

Microcultural differences (i.e., differences within cultures) are key to our understanding of the global work

IN ACTION

Canada Goose

Canada Goose has started its international expansion by opening several flagship stores, in Tokyo, Boston, Chicago, and London. The London store is its largest and located on Regent Street, a prime retail location. Canada Goose plans a gradual international expansion, aiming for 15–20 new stores by 2020. "We have an opportunity to cherry pick the best locations and build world class, experiential stores in those areas," notes Canada Goose President and CEO Dani Reiss.

While Canada Goose enjoys high brand awareness in Canada, the 60-year-old firm is not well known yet in the United States. As well, Canada Goose has traditionally sold its products through retailers but is expanding its flagship stores and its e-commerce sites as part of its international expansion strategy.

SOURCE: J. Kell, "Canada Goose Is Practicing Patience with Its International Expansion," *Fortune*, May 11, accessed from http://fortune.com/2017/05/11/canada-goose-store-expansion/, June 29, 2018.

environment.[16] Differences in symbols are extremely important. The thumbs-up sign, for example, means approval in North America, whereas in Australia, it is an obscene gesture. Many European countries don't use manila file folders and, therefore do not recognize the icons used in Microsoft Office applications.[17]

Do cultural differences translate into differences in work-related attitudes?

Pioneering Dutch researcher Geert Hofstede investigated this question.[18] He and his colleagues surveyed 160,000 managers and employees of IBM working in 60 different countries[19] to study individuals from the same company in the same jobs, but living in different countries. Hofstede's studies showed that national culture explains more differences in work-related attitudes than do age, gender, profession, or position within the organization. Hofstede first found five dimensions of cultural differences that formed the basis for work-related attitudes. In his more recent research, he found a sixth dimension. Figure 2.1 highlights the six dimensions.

FIGURE 2.1 HOFSTEDE'S SIX DIMENSIONS OF CULTURAL DIFFERENCES

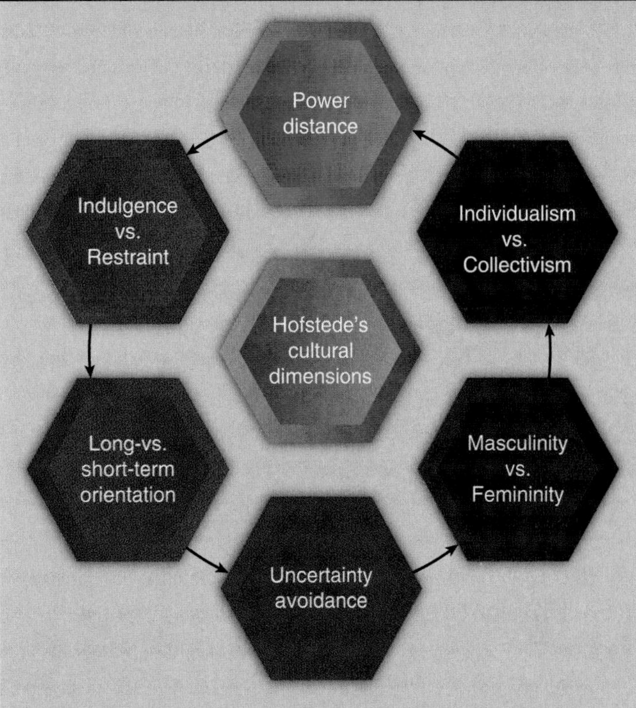

SOURCE: Hofstede's Cultural Dimensions, accessed from https://www.business-to-you.com/hofstedes-cultural-dimensions/, June 30, 2018.

Management careers have taken on a global dimension. Working in transnational organizations may give managers the opportunity to work in other countries. **Expatriate managers**, those who work in a country other than their home country, benefit greatly from knowledge of cultural differences.

International executives are executives whose jobs have international scope, whether in an expatriate assignment or in dealing with international issues. What kind of competencies should such executives have? There are several attributes that individuals should develop in order to prepare for an international career. Some of the key competencies are integrity, insightfulness, risk taking, courage to take a stand, and ability to bring out the best in people. Learning-oriented attributes of international executives include cultural adventurousness, flexibility, openness to criticism, desire to seek learning opportunities, and sensitivity to cultural differences.[20] Further, strong human capital generally has a positive effect on internationalization.[21]

> “Understanding cultural differences becomes especially important for organizations that are considering opening global offices.”

Because workplace customs vary widely, understanding cultural differences becomes especially important for organizations that are considering opening global offices. Carefully researching this information in advance helps organizations manage foreign operations. Consulate offices and companies operating within the foreign country provide excellent information about national customs and legal requirements. Table 2.1 presents a business guide to cultural differences in three countries: Japan, Mexico, and Saudi Arabia.

Another reality affecting global business practices is the cost of layoffs in other countries. Downsizing presents challenges worldwide. Dismissing a 45-year-old middle manager with 20 years of service and a $50,000 annual salary varies in cost from a low of $13,000 in Ireland to a high of $130,000 in Italy.[22] The wide variability in costs stems from the various legal protections that certain countries give workers. In Italy, laid-off employees must receive a “notice period” payment (one year's pay if they have nine years or more of service) plus a severance payment (based on pay and years of service). North American companies operating overseas often adopt the European tradition of training and retraining workers to avoid overstaffing and potential layoffs. Appreciating the customs and rules for doing business in another country is essential to global success.

expatriate manager A manager who works in a country other than their home country.

TABLE 2.1 BUSINESS GUIDE TO CULTURAL DIFFERENCES

Country	Appointments	Dress	Gifts	Negotiations
Japan	Punctuality is necessary when doing business here. It is considered rude to be late.	Conservative for men and women in large to medium companies, though pastel shirts are common. May be expected to remove shoes in temples and homes, as well as in some *ryokan* (inn) style restaurants. In that case, slip-on shoes should be worn.	Important part of Japanese business protocol. Gifts are typically exchanged among colleagues on July 15 and January 1 to commemorate mid-year and the year's end, respectively.	Business cards (*meishi*) are an important part of doing business in Japan and key for establishing credentials. One side of your card should be in English and the reverse in Japanese. It is an asset to include information such as membership in professional associations.
Mexico	Punctuality is not always as much of a priority in Mexican business culture. Nonetheless, Mexicans are accustomed to North Americans arriving on time, and most Mexicans in business, if not government, will try to return the favour.	Dark, conservative suits and ties are the norm for most men. Standard office attire for women includes dresses, skirted suits, or skirts and blouses. Femininity is strongly encouraged in women's dress. Women business travellers will want to bring hosiery and high heels.	Not usually a requirement in business dealings though presenting a small gift will generally be appreciated as a gesture of goodwill. If giving a gift, be aware that inquiring about what the receiver would like to receive can be offensive.	Mexicans avoid directly saying "no." A "no" is often disguised in responses such as "maybe" or "we'll see." You should also use this indirect approach in your dealings. Otherwise, your Mexican counterparts may perceive you as being rude and pushy.
Saudi Arabia	Customary to make appointments for times of day rather than precise hours. The importance Saudis attach to courtesy and hospitality can cause delays that prevent keeping to a strict schedule.	Only absolute requirement of dress code in the Kingdom is modesty. For men, this means covering everything from navel to knee. Females are required to cover everything except the face, hands, and feet in public; they can wear literally anything they want providing they cover it with an *abaya* (standard black cloak) and headscarf when they go out.	Should be given only to the most intimate of friends. For a Saudi to receive a present from a lesser acquaintance is so embarrassing that it is considered offensive.	Business cards are common but not essential. If used, the common practice is to have both English and Arabic printed, one on each side so that neither language is perceived as less important by being on the reverse of the same card.

SOURCE: Adapted from information obtained from business culture guides accessed online at http://www.executiveplanet.com.

2-2 CULTURAL DIFFERENCES AND WORK-RELATED ATTITUDES

individualism A cultural orientation in which people belong to loose social frameworks, and their primary concern is for themselves and their families.

collectivism A cultural orientation in which individuals belong to tightly knit social frameworks, and they depend strongly on large extended families or clans.

Hofstede's work has implications for work-related attitudes. However, it is worth noting that Hofstede's analysis is done by country. While this is valid for many countries, it does not hold in the countries where there are strong subcultures that are based on ethnicity of origin or geography. In Canada, for instance, there is a distinct French Canadian culture that has quite a different set of norms compared to English-speaking Canada. And in Italy, masculinity scores would differ between North and South.[23]

We'll now take a closer look at how Hofstede's six dimensions of cultural differences are manifest in a variety of countries. Figure 2.2 provides a graphical representation of the differences between Canada, the United States, and Mexico using Hofstede's dimensions.

Individualism/Collectivism

In cultures where **individualism** predominates, employees put loyalty to themselves first, and loyalty to their company and work group second. Cultures characterized by **collectivism** are tightly knit social frameworks in which individual members depend strongly on extended families or clans. Group decisions are valued and accepted.

FIGURE 2.2 COMPARISON OF HOFSTEDE'S SCORES BETWEEN CANADA, MEXICO, AND THE UNITED STATES

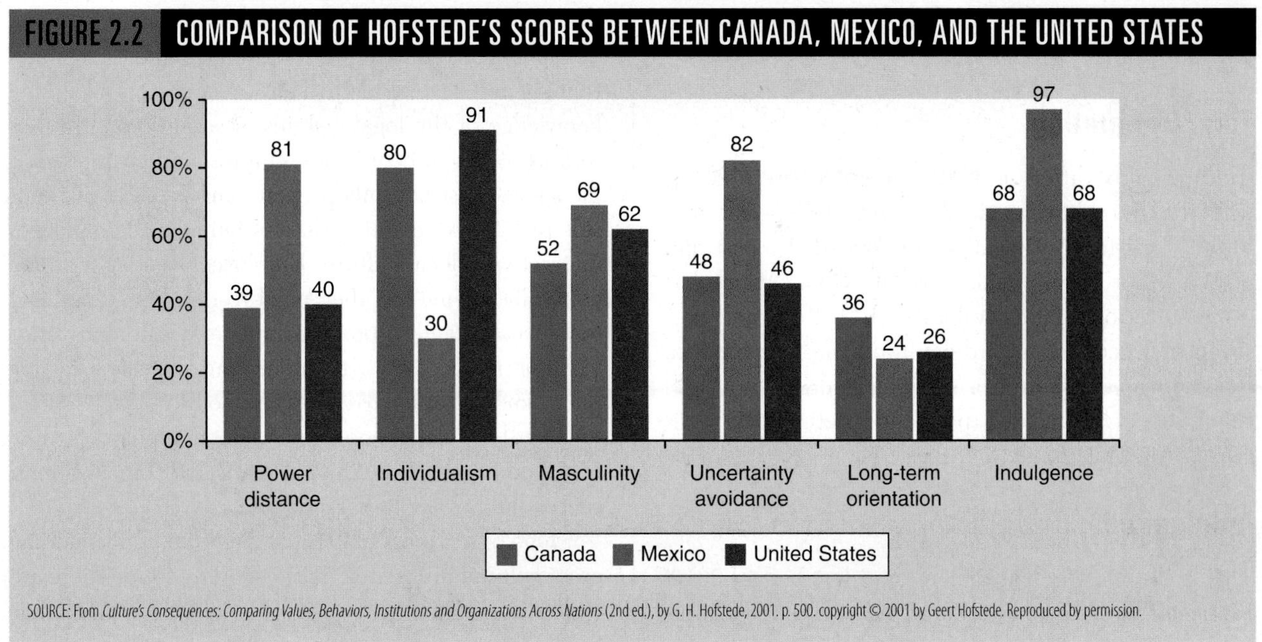

SOURCE: From *Culture's Consequences: Comparing Values, Behaviors, Institutions and Organizations Across Nations* (2nd ed.), by G. H. Hofstede, 2001. p. 500. copyright © 2001 by Geert Hofstede. Reproduced by permission.

The North American culture is individualistic in orientation. Individualistic managers, as found in Canada, Great Britain, and the Netherlands, emphasize and encourage individual achievement. In collectivist cultures, such as the Israeli kibbutzim and Japanese companies, people view group loyalty and unity as paramount. Collectivistic managers seek to fit harmoniously within the group. Managers also encourage these behaviours among their employees. The world's regions are patterned with varying degrees of cultural difference.

Because these dimensions vary widely, management practices should be adjusted to account for cultural differences. Managers in transnational organizations must learn as much as they can about other cultures in order to lead their culturally diverse organizations effectively.

Power Distance

Power distance relates to the acceptance of unequal distribution of power. In countries with a high **power distance**, bosses are afforded more power, titles are used, formality is the rule, and authority is seldom bypassed. Managers and employees see one another as fundamentally different kinds of people. India, Venezuela, and Mexico all demonstrate high power distance.

In societies with low power distance, people believe in minimizing inequality. People at various power levels are less threatened by, and more willing to trust, one another. Managers and employees judge each other equally. Managers are given power only if they have expertise. Employees frequently bypass the boss in order to get work done in countries with a low power distance, such as Denmark and Australia.

Uncertainty Avoidance

Cultures with high **uncertainty avoidance** are concerned with security and tend to avoid conflict. People need consensus and struggle constantly against the threat of life's inherent uncertainty. Cultures with low uncertainty avoidance tolerate ambiguity better. People are more willing to take risks and more comfortable with individual differences. Conflict is seen as constructive, and people accept dissenting viewpoints. Norwegians and Australians value job mobility because they have low uncertainty avoidance; Japan and Italy are characterized by high uncertainty avoidance, and not surprisingly, their cultures emphasize career stability.

Masculinity/Femininity

In cultures characterized by **masculinity**, assertiveness and materialism are valued. Men should be assertive, tough, and decisive, whereas women are expected to be nurturing, modest, and tender.[24] Money and possessions are important, and performance is what counts. Achievement is admired. Cultures characterized by **femininity** emphasize relationships and concern for others. Men and women are expected to assume both assertive and nurturing

power distance The degree to which a culture accepts unequal distribution of power.

uncertainty avoidance The degree to which a culture tolerates ambiguity and uncertainty.

masculinity The cultural orientation in which assertiveness and materialism are valued.

femininity The cultural orientation in which relationships and concern for others are valued.

roles. Quality of life is important, and people and the environment are emphasized.

Time Orientation

Cultures also differ in **time orientation**; that is, whether the culture's values are oriented toward the future (long-term orientation) or toward the past and present (short-term orientation).[25] In China, which has a long-term orientation, values such as thrift and persistence, which look toward the future, are emphasized. Russians generally have a short-term orientation and value respect for tradition (past) and meeting social obligations (present).

Indulgence

This is the most recent dimension, identified in 2010. Indulgent cultures tend to allow relatively free gratification of human desires related to enjoying life and having fun. Non-indulgent—or restrained—countries are more likely to believe that such gratification needs to be curbed and regulated by strict rules. Indulgent cultures value leisure time, freedom and personal control; restrained cultures do not.[26]

Developing Cross-cultural Sensitivity

In today's multicultural environment, it is imperative that organizations help their employees recognize and appreciate cultural differences. One way organizations do this is through cultural sensitivity training. Another way to develop sensitivity is by using cross-cultural task forces or teams. GE Medical Systems Group (GEMS) has 19,000 employees working worldwide. GEMS has developed a vehicle for bringing managers from each of its three regions (the Americas, Europe, and Asia) together to work on a variety of business projects. The Global Leadership Program forms several work groups made up of managers from various regions and has them work on important projects, such as worldwide employee integration, to increase employees' sense of belonging throughout the GEMS international organization.[27]

time orientation Whether a culture's values are oriented toward the future (long-term orientation) or toward the past and present (short-term orientation).

indulgence Indulgent cultures value leisure time, freedom, and personal control.

diversity All forms of individual differences, including culture, gender, age, ability, religion, personality, social status, and sexual orientation.

The globalization of business affects all parts of the organization, particularly human resource management. Human resource managers must adopt a global view of human resource planning, recruitment and selection, compensation, and training and development. They must possess a working knowledge of the legal systems in various countries, as well as of global economics, culture, and customs. HR managers must not only prepare employees to live outside their native country but also help global employees interact with local culture. Employees need to become culturally fluent, i.e., they need to develop "the ability to internalize and respond to a range of different worldviews or perspectives ... to understand a range of starting points and cultural currencies, and to be able to respond to [them] in related contexts."[28] Global human resource management is complex, but critical to organizations' success in the global marketplace.

One of the most influential guides to understanding cross-cultural differences is *The Culture Map*. There are eight dimensions that need to be measured to enhance communication across cultures. The eight are (1) Communicating: explicit vs. implicit, (2) Evaluating: direct negative feedback vs. indirect negative feedback, (3) Persuading: principles first vs. applications first, (4) Leading: egalitarian vs. hierarchical, (5) Deciding: consensual vs. top down, (6) Trusting: task vs. relationship, (7) Disagreeing: confrontational vs. avoid confrontation, and (8) Scheduling: structured vs. flexible.[29]

According to the culture mapping tool, Canada has the following characteristics: (1) its communication approach is explicit; (2) its evaluation approach is between giving direct and indirect negative feedback; (3) its persuading approach focuses on applications first; (4) its leading approach is quite egalitarian; (5) its deciding approach is between consensual and top-down; (6) its trust approach is task-focused; (7) its disagreeing style is between confrontational and avoiding confrontations; and (8) its approach to scheduling is structured, relying on linear-time.[30] Figure 2.3 shows Canada in comparison to Mexico and the United States, its NAFTA neighbours.

2-3 THE DIVERSE WORKFORCE

Canada is a very diverse country. In addition to our many different Indigenous peoples, and the Anglophone and Francophone communities, we have attracted people from the world over.

Cultural differences contribute a great deal to the diversity of the workforce, but there are other forms of diversity that are important as well. **Diversity** encompasses all forms of differences among individuals, including culture, gender, age, ability, religion, personality, social status, and sexual orientation. Diversity has garnered increasing attention in recent years, largely because of demographic changes in the working population. Many managers believe that dealing with diversity is a paramount concern for two reasons. First, managers need to motivate diverse work groups. Second, managers must communicate with employees who have different values and language skills.

Several demographic trends are affecting organizations. By the year 2020, the workforce will be more culturally diverse, more female, and older than ever. Recent legislation and new technologies have helped more individuals with disabilities enter the workforce. Therefore, learning to work together is an increasingly important skill, as is working with an open mind.[31]

FIGURE 2.3 CANADA'S CULTURE MAPPING, COMPARED TO MEXICO AND THE UNITED STATES

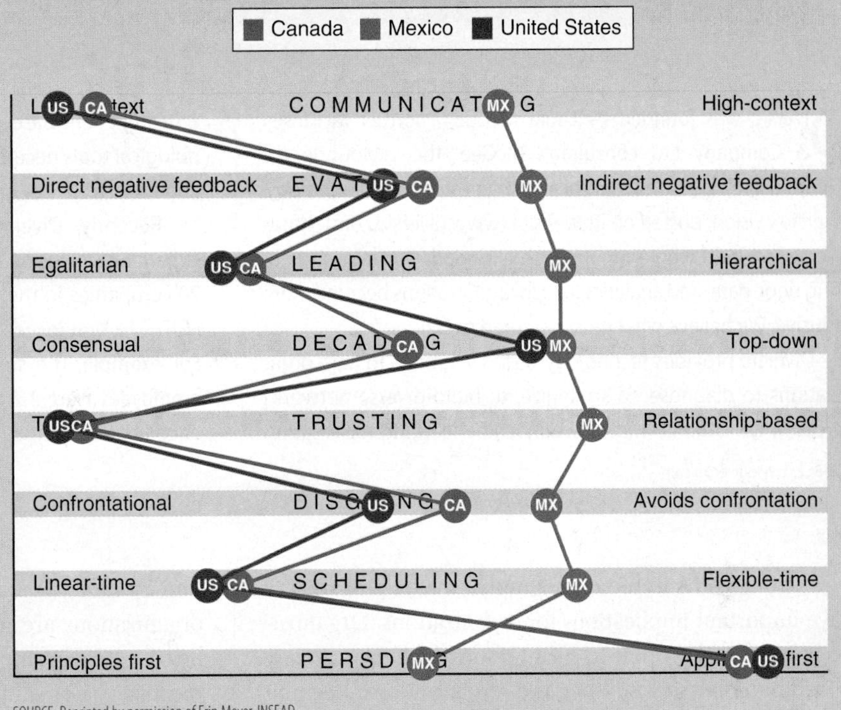

SOURCE: Reprinted by permission of Erin Meyer, INSEAD.

Calgary-based Agrium Inc. received an award in 2017 as one of Canada's best diversity employers. It provides mentoring, networking, and career development opportunities to women employees through formal women's leadership groups, mentoring dinners, and seminars on work–life balance and stress management. Based on the success of the women employees' leadership group, the company is launching a long-term, formal diversity and inclusiveness strategy with wider scope; the program is being led by the CEO and supported by an in-house diversity council.[32]

Cultural Diversity

The globalization of business is promoting cultural diversity in the workplace. In addition, changing domestic demographics affect organizations' cultural diversity.

The population who had an Aboriginal identity grew by 20.1% between 2006 and 2011 to reach 1.4 million in 2011, representing 4.3% of Canada's overall population. During the same period, the growth of the non-Aboriginal population was much smaller, at 5.2%.

Among the countries of the world with the largest foreign-born populations, Canada is currently ranked eighth, with about 7.5 million people. The size of the foreign-born population in Canada closely follows that of the United Arab Emirates, the United Kingdom and France. In 2011, close to 3 in 10 people in Ontario (28.5%) and British Columbia (27.6%) were foreign born. These two provinces had the highest proportions of foreign-born persons of all the provinces and territories. According to the reference scenario for the projections of the diversity of the Canadian population, South Asians and Chinese could continue to be the two largest visible minority groups in 2031, with populations of 3.6 million and 2.7 million, respectively.

SOURCE: Reproduced from Statistics Canada, Canadian Demographics at a Glance, Catalogue No. 91-003-XWE. Reproduced and distributed on an "as is" basis with the permission of Statistics Canada.

IN ACTION

Diversio and Laura McGee

Diversio was founded by Laura McGee, a former McKinsey & Company Ltd consultant. McGee, the co-founder of #GoSponsorHer, is a frequent speaker on diversity and technology. Diversio's vision, posted on its website (www.diversio.com), states "We see a world where no one feels excluded. Our mission is to bring rigor, data, and analytics to help organizations become more inclusive. We believe what gets measured gets done."

Diversio provides technology-based solutions to help organizations to diagnose, to strategize, to build diverse networks across organizations, and to use machine learning for creating a strong talent base. Diversio provides its clients with the technological tools necessary to build an organization that is diverse and inclusive.

Recently, Diversio examined how LGBTQ2+ employees experience inclusion at work. It surveyed 2,120 employees from 20 companies in the U.S., Canada, and the U.K. and found that LGBTQ2+ employees face significant barriers in the workplace. For example, the survey results demonstrated that LGBTQ2+ employees were 3.7 times more likely to say they have experienced harassment at work.

SOURCE: www.diversio.com

Strong shifts in the demographic makeup of society have important implications for organizations. Organizations need to be open to hiring individuals from many different countries so that the organizations become as diverse as the communities in which they operate. As Figure 2.4 shows, there has been considerable immigration to most of the provinces. However, Canada's organizations are not as diverse as they can and should be. A recent study of the labour market experience of racialized (i.e., subjected to racism) Ontarians found that racialized Ontarians are far more likely to live in poverty; to face barriers to Ontario's workplaces; and, even when they get a job, are more likely to earn less than the rest of Ontarians and controlling for age, immigration status, and education did not eliminate the gap.[33]

FIGURE 2.4 DISTRIBUTION OF RECENT IMMIGRANTS BY PROVINCE, 2011–2016

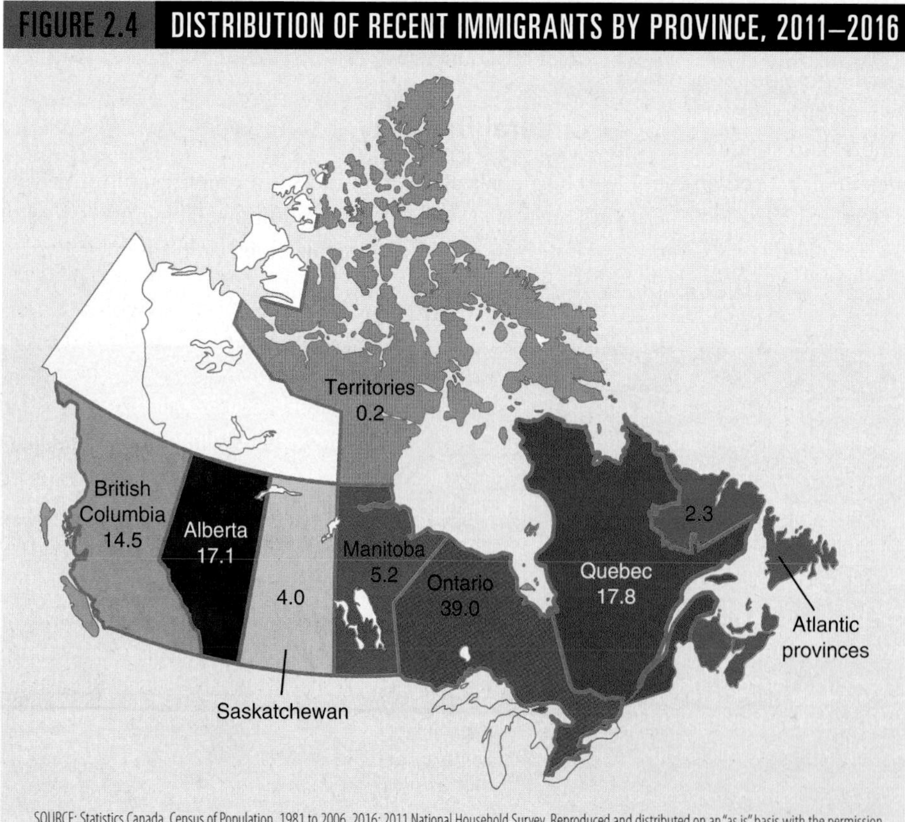

SOURCE: Statistics Canada, Census of Population, 1981 to 2006, 2016; 2011 National Household Survey. Reproduced and distributed on an "as is" basis with the permission of Statistics Canada.

It need not be this way. For example, Coca-Cola has made substantial progress on diversity by monitoring its human resource systems.[34] Similarly, RBC has made diversity central to its strategy. RBC, which has 52,500 employees, has set up cross-cultural training, mentorship programs, and employee resource groups. It works with nonprofit agencies to hire newcomers to Canada.[35] The globalization of business and changing demographic trends present organizations with a culturally diverse workforce, creating both challenge and risk.

The challenge is to harness the wealth of differences provided by cultural diversity. The risk is that prejudices and stereotypes may prevent managers and employees from having cooperative interactions to benefit the organization.

Gender Diversity

The workforce has feminized substantially. In 1976, 45.4 percent of women in Canada were in the workforce; by 2017, that had risen to 61.5 percent. Even so, Canada ranks eighth among 40 countries surveyed by the OECD on female participation.[36] However, according to a 2018 survey of Canadian organizations, "of the 540 Named Executive Officers, 489 are men and 51 are women. The number of women increased by three. In percentage terms, women now hold 9.44% of these important jobs compared to 9.02% a year ago and compared to only 4.62% in 2006."[37]

Nevertheless, women's share of authority and compensation is not increasing commensurately with their participation in the workforce. In addition to lower earnings, women face obstacles at work. The **glass ceiling** is a transparent barrier that keeps women from rising above a certain level in organizations. In Canada, it is still quite unusual to find women in positions above middle management.[38] The ultimate glass ceiling may well be the corporate boardroom and the professional partnership. In fact, "Osler Law's 2017 Diversity Disclosure Practices reported that women directors in TSX-listed companies have grown from 12 percent in 2015 to 14.5 percent in 2017."[39] Even if women do make it to the top, they may face the **glass cliff**, the phenomenon whereby senior women finding themselves disproportionately represented in untenable leadership positions that often resulted in failure.[40]

On a global basis, the leadership picture for women is improving somewhat. For example, the number of female political leaders has grown dramatically worldwide in recent decades. In the 1970s there were only five such leaders. In the 1990s, 21 female leaders came into power, and women around the world are leading major global companies. These global female business leaders do not come predominantly from North America or Europe. For example, Chanda Kochhar took over as managing director and CEO of ICICI Bank in 2009.[41] In addition, a large number of women have founded entrepreneurial businesses. For example, former chief of ICICI Venture Renuka Ramnath launched Multiples Alternate Asset Management in 2009.[42]

Removing obstacles to women's success continues to be a challenge for organizations. Organizations must develop policies that promote equity in pay and benefits, encourage benefit programs of special interest to women, and provide equal starting salaries for jobs of equal value. Organizations that shatter the glass ceiling share several practices. Upper managers demonstrate support for the advancement of women through mentoring programs. Leaders incorporate practices into their diversity management programs to ensure that women perceive the organization as attractive.[43] Women are represented on standing committees addressing key strategic business issues, and are targeted for participation in executive education programs. Systems are in place for identifying women with high potential for advancement.[44] Companies such as Motorola, Deloitte, and the Bank of Montreal offer excellent programs for advancing and developing women executives.[45]

Typically, women have adopted the caregiving role. Women are still largely responsible for home management, childcare, and often, elder care. Because of their multiple roles, women frequently experience conflicts between work and home. In response, organizations can offer incentives such as flexible work schedules, childcare, elder care, and work site health promotion programs to assist working women in managing the stress of their lives.[46]

Organizations must help their increasing numbers of female employees achieve their potential, or risk underutilizing the talents of more than half of the Canadian workforce.

LGBTQ2+ Diversity

According to StatsCan, the percentage of Canadians aged 18 to 59 who reported in 2014 that they consider themselves to be homosexual (gay or lesbian) is 1.7 percent of the population and 1.3 percent for who reported in 2014 that they consider themselves to be bisexual. Since same-sex marriages were legalized in 2005, the number of same-sex marriages between 2006 and 2011 increased 42.4 percent. As well, the number of children aged 24 and under living with female same-sex parents in 2011 was 7,700 and the number of children aged 24 and under living with male same-sex parents was 1,900.[47]

Members of the LGBTQ2+ community continue to face considerable discrimination in the workplace. "This disconnect between diversity and inclusion is experienced by women, aboriginal people and ethnic minorities, but

glass ceiling A transparent barrier that keeps women from rising above a certain level in organizations.

glass cliff Senior women finding themselves disproportionately represented in untenable leadership positions.

More and more organizations are recognizing the importance of creating cultures that include LGBTQ2+ employees.

it is especially marked for the LGBT (Lesbian, Gay, Bisexual, and Trans) community. … almost 30% of Canadian LGBT-identified respondents felt that they experienced discrimination in the workplace as opposed 2.9% of the general population."[48] More companies are trying to create organizational cultures that are actually inclusive. For example, Google offers Unconscious Bias at Work training to all Googlers by incorporating Busting Bias at Work training to every Googler's first day at Google. Similarly, on National Coming Out Day and in collaboration with all global RBC PRIDE initiatives, RBC ran a feature story in its intranet, profiling 13 international participants from the LGBT & Allies community sharing their stories, and a timeline of RBC's LGBT milestones.[49]

Coming out at work is still not easy. It is important therefore that organizations create a safe environment where employees are comfortable sharing their identity. Employee resource groups are one way to provide space for employees to be themselves. "By creating [such] resources and groups, organizations signal to individuals that the leaders and top management care about these issues and these rights."[50] IBM Canada has been a leader in creating spaces and resources for its LGBTQ2+ employees; for example, its domestic partner health care benefit program is in place for over 80% of employees worldwide.[51]

Age Diversity

The graying of the workforce is another source of workplace diversity. Aging baby boomers (those individuals born between 1946 and 1964) contribute to the rise of the median age and the number of middle-aged Canadians is rising dramatically. According to data from StatsCan, "the proportion of seniors within the population has been steadily growing since 1960. … According to all population projection scenarios, seniors are expected to comprise around 23% to 25% of the population by 2036, and around 24% to 28% in 2061." While the proportion of seniors is increasing, "similar to other countries, Canada's youth represent a smaller share of the population than in the past."[52]

This change in worker profile has profound implications for organizations. The job crunch among middle-aged workers will intensify as companies seek flatter organizations and eliminate middle management jobs. Older workers are often higher paid, and companies that employ large numbers of aging baby boomers may find these pay scales a handicap to competitiveness.[53] Conversely, a more experienced, stable, reliable, and healthier workforce can pay dividends to companies. The baby boomers are well trained and educated, and their knowledge is a definite asset to organizations.

The aging workforce is increasing intergenerational contact at work.[54] As organizations flatten, workers traditionally segregated by old corporate hierarchies find themselves working together. Four generations are cooperating: *the silent generation* (people born from 1930 through 1945), a small group; *the baby boomers*, whose substantial numbers give them a strong influence; *the baby bust generation, popularly known as Generation X* (those born from 1965 through 1976); and the subsequent generation, called *Generation Y*, *millennials*, or *the baby boomlet*.[55] The millennials bring new challenges to the workplace because of their early access to technology and their continuing connection to parents.[56]

The differences in attitudes and values among these four generations can be substantial, and managers struggle to integrate their workers into a cohesive group. Some leadership positions are held by members of the silent generation. Baby boomers regard the silent generation as complacent, strive for moral rights in the workplace, and take a more activist position regarding employee rights. The baby busters, newer to the workplace, are less patient, want more immediate gratification, and value family over work. They scorn the achievement orientation and materialism of the baby boomers. Younger workers may have false impressions of older workers, viewing them as resistant to change, unable to learn new work methods, less physically capable, and less creative than younger employees. Research indicates, however, that older employees are more satisfied with their jobs, more committed to the organization, and more internally motivated than their younger cohorts.[57] Research also indicates that direct experience with older workers reduces younger workers' negative beliefs.[58] Motivating aging workers and helping them maintain high levels of contribution to the organization is a key task for managers.

Ability Diversity

Employees with different abilities present yet another form of diversity. Individuals with disabilities are an underutilized human resource. According to StatsCan, one in seven Canadians aged 15 years or older reported a disability. In 2012, almost 14% of the Canadian population aged 15 years or older—3.8 million individuals—reported having a disability that limited their daily activities. In general, provinces in the east had a slightly higher prevalence of disability than did those in the west. Among the territories, the prevalence of disability was 14% in Yukon, 8% in the Northwest Territories, and 7% in Nunavut.[59]

While individuals with disabilities have entered the workforce in greater numbers, the progress is still slow. Some companies have recognized the value of employing workers with disabilities. McDonald's created McJOBS, a corporate plan to recruit, train, and retain individuals with disabilities that has hired more than 9,000 mentally and physically challenged individuals since 1981.[60]

Its participants include workers with visual, hearing, or orthopedic impairments; learning disabilities; and mental impairments. McJOBS holds sensitivity training sessions with managers and crew members before workers go onsite to help workers without disabilities understand what it means to be a worker with a disabling condition. Most McJOBS workers start part-time and advance according to their own abilities and the opportunities available.

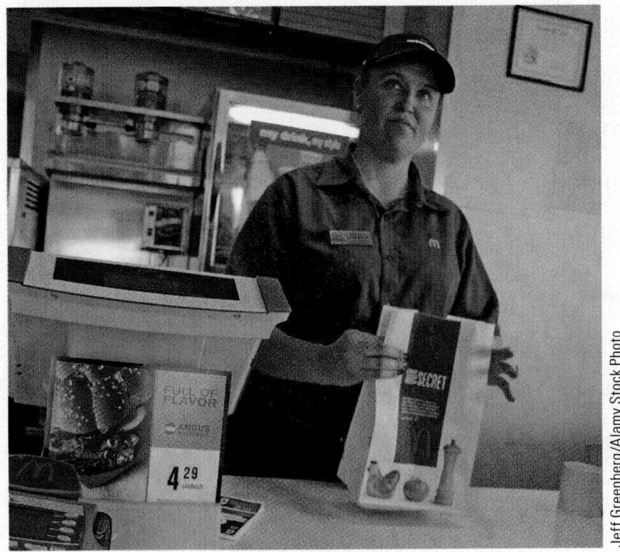

Jeff Greenberg/Alamy Stock Photo

A McDonald's employee who is integrated into its workforce.

Valuing Diversity

Diversity involves more than culture, gender, age, ability, and personality. It also encompasses religion, social status, and sexual orientation. These diversity types bring heterogeneity to the workforce.

Managers must combat prejudice and discrimination to manage diversity. Prejudice is an attitude, and discrimination describes behaviour; both diminish organizational productivity. Organizations benefit when they ensure that good workers are promoted and compensated fairly, but as the workforce becomes increasingly diverse, the potential for unfair treatment also increases as some individuals may discriminate more.

Diversity helps organizations in many ways. Some organizations recognize the potential benefits of aggressively working to increase the diversity of their workforces. Yum! Brands' Kentucky Fried Chicken (KFC) tries to attract and retain diverse group executives. A president of KFC's U.S. operations said, "We want to bring in the best people. If there are two equally qualified people, we'd clearly like to have diversity."[61]

In an effort to understand and appreciate diversity, Alcon Laboratories developed a diversity training class called Working Together. The course takes advantage of two key ideas. First, people work best when they are valued and when diversity is taken into account. Second, when people feel valued, they build relationships and work together as a team.[62] Even majority group managers may be more supportive of diversity training if they learn to appreciate their own ethnic identity. It is important to frame diversity training as part of a larger, more general, human resource development. One evaluation of diversity training found that participants preferred training that was described as focusing on human relations, rather than on diversity per se, and had a broad focus.[63] Further, women react more positively to diversity training than men.[64] Organizations should measure the effects of training so they can monitor its positive payoffs.

Managing diversity helps companies become more competitive. But managing diversity takes more than simply being a good organizational citizen or complying with employment equity.[65] Managing diversity requires a painful examination of employees' hidden assumptions. Biases and prejudices about people's differences must be uncovered through structured self-reflection and addressed so that differences can be celebrated and used to their full advantage.

TABLE 2.2 DIVERSITY'S BENEFITS AND PROBLEMS

Benefits	Problems
• Attracts and retains the best human talent	• Resistance to change
• Improves marketing efforts	• Lack of cohesiveness
• Promotes creativity and innovation	• Communication problems
• Results in better problem solving	• Interpersonal conflicts
• Enhances organizational flexibility	• Slowed decision making

Diversity's Benefits and Problems

Diversity enhances organizational performance. Table 2.2 summarizes the main benefits, as well as the problems, with diversity at work. Organizations reap five main benefits from diversity. First, diversity management helps firms attract and retain the best available human talent. The companies topping the "Best Places to Work" lists are usually excellent at managing diversity. Second, diversity aids marketing efforts. Just as workforces are diversifying, so are markets. A diverse workforce can improve a company's marketing plans by drawing on insights from various employees' cultural backgrounds. Third, diversity promotes creativity and innovation. The most innovative companies, such as Hewlett-Packard, deliberately build diverse teams to foster creativity. Fourth, diversity improves problem solving. Diverse groups bring more expertise and experience to bear on problems and decisions and they encourage higher levels of critical thinking. Fifth, diversity enhances organizational flexibility. Diversity makes an organization challenge old assumptions and become more adaptable. These five benefits add up to competitive advantage for companies with well-managed diversity.

We must also recognize diversity's potential problems. Five problems are particularly important: resistance to change, lack of cohesiveness, communication problems, conflicts, and decision making. People are attracted to, and more comfortable with, others like themselves. It stands to reason that workers may resist diversity efforts when they are forced to interact with others unlike themselves. Managers should be prepared for this resistance rather than naively assuming that everybody supports diversity. Another difficulty with diversity is the issue of cohesiveness, that invisible "glue" that holds a group together. Cohesive groups have higher morale and better communication, but diverse groups take longer to achieve cohesiveness, so they may also take longer to develop high morale.

Another obstacle to performance in diverse groups is communication. Culturally diverse groups may encounter special communication barriers. Misunderstandings can lower work group effectiveness by creating conflict and hampering decision making.[66] Now some organizations are looking beyond diversity to inclusion. The goal is to ensure that different individuals are actively engaged and are able to work together while being themselves. For example, Torys, a large law firm, has created a Women in Business Development Program, to boost women's profiles when women experience career interruptions.[67]

2-4 ETHICS, CHARACTER, AND PERSONAL INTEGRITY

Managers and employees frequently face ethical dilemmas and trade-offs. Some organizations display good character and have executives known for their personal integrity. Merck & Company, with some notable exceptions, manages ethical issues well and its emphasis on ethical behaviour has earned it recognition as one of the most admired companies in *Fortune*'s polls of CEOs.[68]

The toughest problems for managers to resolve include employee theft, environmental issues, comparable worth of employees, conflicts of interest, and sexual harassment.

Despite many organizations' careful handling of ethical issues, unethical conduct sometimes occurs. The toughest problems for managers to resolve include employee theft, environmental issues, comparable worth of employees, conflicts of interest, and sexual harassment.[69]

Ethical theories help us understand, evaluate, and classify moral arguments; make decisions; and then defend conclusions about what is right and wrong. Ethical theories can be classified as consequential, rule-based, or character.

Consequential Theories of Ethics

Consequential theories of ethics emphasize the consequences or results of behaviour. John Stuart Mill's utilitarianism, a well-known consequential theory, suggests the consequences of an action determine whether it is right or wrong.[70] "Good" is the ultimate moral value, and we should maximize good effects for the greatest number of people. But do good ethics make for good business?[71] Right actions do not always produce good consequences, and good consequences do not always follow right actions. And how do we determine the greatest good—in short-term or long-term consequences? Using the "greatest number" criterion implies that minorities (less than 50 percent) might be excluded in evaluating the morality of actions. An issue that matters to a minority but not to the majority might be ignored. These are some of the dilemmas raised by utilitarianism.

Organizations often subscribe to consequential ethics, partly due to the arguments of the Scottish political economist and moral philosopher Adam Smith.[72] He believed that the self-interest of human beings is religion's providence, not the government's. Smith set forth a doctrine of natural liberty, presenting the classical argument for open market competition and free trade. Within this framework, people should be allowed to pursue what is in their economic self-interest, and the natural efficiency of the marketplace would serve the well-being of society. However, virtue ethics offer an alternative rule-based theory.

Rule-based Theories of Ethics

Rule-based theories of ethics emphasize the character of the act itself, not its effects, in arriving at universal moral rights and wrongs.[73] Moral rights, the basis for legal rights, are associated with such theories. In a theological context, the Bible, the Talmud, and the Koran are rule-based guides to ethical behaviour. Immanuel Kant worked toward the ultimate moral principle in formulating his categorical imperative, a universal standard of behaviour.[74] Kant argued that individuals should be treated with respect and dignity and that they should not be used as a means to an end. He argued that we should put ourselves in the other person's position and ask if we would make the same decision if we were in that person's situation.

Character Theories of Ethics

Character theories of ethics emphasize the character of the individual and the intent of the actor, instead of the character of the act itself or its consequences. These theories emphasize virtues and are based on an Aristotelean approach to character. Robert Solomon is the best known advocate of the Aristotelean approach to business ethics.[75] He advocates a business ethics theory centred on the individual within the corporation, thus emphasizing both corporate roles and personal virtues. Aristotle shaped his vision around an individual's inner character and virtuousness, not the person's behaviour. Thus, the "good" person who acted out of virtuous and "right" intentions was one with integrity and ultimately good ethical standards. Solomon's six dimensions of virtue ethics are community, excellence, role identity, integrity, judgment (*phronesis*), and holism. The dimensions summarize the ideals defining good character. These include honesty, loyalty, sincerity, courage, reliability, trustworthiness, benevolence, sensitivity, helpfulness, cooperativeness, civility, decency, modesty, openness, gracefulness, and many others.

Cultural relativism contends that there are no universal ethical principles and that people should not impose their own ethical standards on others; local standards guide ethical behaviour. Cultural relativism encourages individuals to operate under the old adage "When in Rome, do as the Romans do." Unfortunately, people who adhere strictly to cultural relativism may avoid or ignore difficult ethical dilemmas by denying their own accountability.

ETHICAL DILEMMAS FACING THE ORGANIZATION TODAY

People need ethical theories to guide them through confusing, complex moral choices and ethical decisions. Contemporary organizations experience a wide variety of ethical and moral dilemmas. Here we address employee rights, sexual harassment, organizational justice, and whistle blowing. We conclude with a discussion of social responsibility and codes of ethics.

Employee Rights

Managing the rights of employees at work creates many ethical dilemmas in organizations. These dilemmas include privacy issues related to technology. Many believe that the monitoring of computer use, for example, to see what websites employees are visiting

consequential theory An ethical theory that emphasizes the consequences or results of behaviour.

rule-based theory An ethical theory that emphasizes the character of the act itself rather than its effects.

character theory An ethical theory that emphasizes the character, personal virtues, and integrity of the individual.

constitutes an invasion of privacy. Using employee data from computerized information systems presents many ethical concerns. Safeguarding the employee's right to privacy while preserving access to the data for those who need it forces managers to balance competing interests.

Drug testing, free speech, downsizing and layoffs, and due process are a few of the employee rights issues managers face. For example, the reality of HIV or AIDS in the workplace illustrates the difficulties managers face in balancing the interests of their employees and their organizations. Managers may face a conflict between the rights of HIV-infected workers and the rights of their coworkers who feel threatened. Employers are not required to make concessions to coworkers, but employers do have obligations to educate, reassure, and provide emotional support to coworkers.

Confidentiality may also present challenges. Some employees with HIV or AIDS fear stigmatization or reprisals and do not want to reveal their condition to their coworkers. Management should discuss the ramifications of trying to maintain confidentiality and should assure the affected employee that every effort will be made to prevent negative consequences for them in the workplace.[76]

Laws protect HIV-infected workers. How does a manager protect the dignity of the HIV-infected employee and preserve the morale and productivity of the work group when so much prejudice and ignorance still surround this disease? Many organizations believe the answer is education.[77] The Global Business Coalition on HIV/AIDS, Tuberculosis and Malaria comprises many organizations in different industries that bring health and opportunity to those afflicted with the three diseases. MTV Networks International, Bayer AG, Booz & Company, and MAC Cosmetics, to name only a few, are members of the Coalition.[78]

Sexual Harassment

Sexual harassment is unwelcome verbal or physical sexual attention that affects an employee's job conditions or creates a hostile working environment.[79] Sexual harassment is more likely to occur in male-dominated workplaces.[80] Managers can defend themselves by demonstrating that they took action to eliminate workplace harassment and that the complaining employee did not take advantage of company procedures to deal with harassment. Even the best sexual harassment policy, however, will not absolve a company when harassment leads to firing, demotions, or undesirable working assignments.[81] The Canadian Human Rights Commission recommends three critical steps to create a healthy workplace, free of harassment: (1) begin to change a culture of fear by discussing harassment, sharing information, and involving employees in the development of an anti-harassment policy; (2) illustrate what constitutes harassing behaviour and provide clear directions for filing complaints; and (3) monitor progress and engage in ongoing training.[82]

distributive justice The fairness of the outcomes that individuals receive in an organization.

There are three types of sexual harassment. *Gender harassment* includes crude comments or behaviours that convey hostility toward a particular gender. *Unwanted sexual attention* involves unwanted touching or repeated pressure for dates. *Sexual coercion* consists of implicit or explicit demands for sexual favours by threatening negative job-related consequences or promising job-related rewards.[83] Recent theory has focused attention on the aggressive behaviour of sexual harassers.[84]

Sexual harassment costs the typical Fortune 500 company $6.7 million per year in absenteeism, turnover, and lost productivity. Valeant Pharmaceuticals International paid out millions to settle several sexual harassment complaints against former CEO Milan Panic.[85] These sorts of costs do not take into account the negative publicity sexual harassment cases may attract. Sexual harassment victims are less satisfied with their work, supervisors, and coworkers and may psychologically withdraw at work. They may suffer poorer mental health, and even exhibit symptoms of post-traumatic stress disorder in conjunction with the harassment experience. Some victims report alcohol abuse, depression, headaches, and nausea.[86]

Several companies have created comprehensive sexual harassment programs. Atlantic Richfield (ARCO), owned by British Petroleum, now infamous for the world's largest oil spill and ecological disaster, and a player in the male-dominated energy industry, has a handbook on preventing sexual harassment that includes phone numbers of agencies where employees can file complaints. The openness seems to work. Lawsuits rarely happen at ARCO. When employees make sexual harassment complaints, the company investigates thoroughly. For example, ARCO fired the captain of an oil tanker for sexually harassing coworkers.

Organizational Justice

Organizational justice also generates moral and ethical dilemmas at work. **Distributive justice** concerns the fairness of outcomes individuals receive. For example, Japanese CEOs, in the past, have questioned the distributive justice of keeping North American CEOs' salaries so high while many companies were struggling and laying off workers.

Procedural justice concerns the fairness of the process by which outcomes are allocated. The ethical questions in procedural justice examine the process by which an organization distributes its resources. Has the organization used the correct procedures in allocating resources? Have the right considerations, such as competence and skill, been brought to bear in the decision process? And have the wrong considerations, such as race and gender, been excluded from the decision process? One study of work scheduling found voluntary turnover negatively related to advance notice and consistency, two dimensions of procedural justice.[87] Some research suggests cultural differences in the effects of distributive and procedural justice.[88]

Whistle Blowing

Whistle blowers are employees who inform authorities of wrongdoings by their companies or coworkers. Whistle blowers can be perceived as either heroes or "vile wretches" depending on their situations. Those seen as heroes generally report serious and high-magnitude ethical breaches widely perceived as abhorrent.[89] Others may see the whistle blower as a vile wretch if they feel the act of whistle blowing is more offensive than the situation reported.

Whistle blowing can be a powerful influence on corporate North America because committed organizational members sometimes engage in unethical behaviour in an intense desire to succeed. Organizations can manage whistle blowing by explaining the conditions that are appropriate for disclosing wrongdoing. Clearly delineating wrongful behaviour and the appropriate ways to respond are important organizational actions.

Social Responsibility

Corporate **social responsibility** is an organization's obligation to behave ethically in its social environment. Ethical conduct at the individual level can translate into social responsibility at the organizational level. Socially responsible actions are expected of organizations. Current concerns include protecting the environment, promoting worker safety, supporting social issues, and investing in the community, among others. Some organizations, such as IBM, loan executives to inner-city schools to teach science and math. Firms that are seen as socially responsible have a competitive advantage in attracting applicants.[90]

IN ACTION

Manitoba Hydro

In 2018, Manitoba Hydro was recognized as one of Canada's and Manitoba's Top 100 Employers. It was also recognized in 2018 as one of Canada's Best Diversity Employers. Among its commitments to diversity and inclusion are a pre-placement program for Indigenous candidates "to complete the academic prerequisites for entry into apprenticeship, while receiving on-the-job training and pay". In 2012, it established an employee resource group, the Indigenous Sharing Circle. As well, Manitoba Hydro, for a decade, has supported its DisAbility Access Program to help persons who have sustained severe brain injury reintegrate into the workforce; the program has since expanded to include individuals with intellectual disabilities.

Manitoba Hydro's approach to CSR focuses on sustainable development, grounded in "13 complementary guiding principles based on the principles and guidelines of sustainable development adopted by the Manitoba Round Table on Environment and Economy." The 13 principles are (1) stewardship of the economy and the environment; (2) shared responsibility; (3) integration of environmental and economic decisions; (4) economic enhancement; (5) efficient use of resources; (6) prevention and remedy; (7) conservation; (8) waste minimization; (9) access to adequate information; (10) public participation; (11) understanding and respect; (12) scientific and technological innovation; and (13) global responsibility.

SOURCES: Manitoba Hydro, Recognized as one of Canada's Best Diversity Employers, https://content.eluta.ca/top-employer-manitoba-hydro#diversity, accessed June 29, 2018; Sustainable Development Policy, https://www.hydro.mb.ca/environment/env_management/sdp.shtml#scientific, accessed June 29, 2018.

Codes of Ethics

Most mature professions guide their practitioners' actions and behaviour with codes of ethics. For example, the Hippocratic oath guides doctors. A profession's code of ethics becomes a standard against which members can measure themselves in the absence of internalized standards.

No universal code of ethics or oath exists for business as it does for medicine. However, Paul Harris and four business colleagues, who founded Rotary International in 1905, addressed

procedural justice The fairness of the process by which outcomes are allocated in an organization.

whistle blower An employee who informs authorities of the wrongdoings of their company or coworkers.

social responsibility The obligation of an organization to behave in ethical ways.

Purpose *and* Profit

Is it possible to achieve both purpose and profit? This is an issue that has generated much discussion recently. For example, BlackRock's CEO, Larry Fink, has criticized companies that focus on quarterly results at the expense of long-term thinking and doing. In his 2018 letter to CEOs, entitled *A Sense of Purpose,* he focuses on the need for businesses to create long-term value. Fink argues, "Without a sense of purpose, no company, either public or private, can achieve its full potential. It will ultimately lose the license to operate from key stakeholders." Fink has made it clear that if companies want BlackRock's support, they must contribute to society.

The "purpose *and* profit" approach represents a significant departure from the traditional short-term profit maximization approach that has governed much managerial action. It is seen as a response to many failures of capitalism that the economic meltdown of 2008 exposed. Julie Hanna, executive chair of Kiva, concludes "Great companies aren't great just because they make lots of money. They make lots of money precisely because they're great."

SOURCES: L. Fink, A Sense of Purpose, 2018 Letter to CEOs, https://www.blackrock.com/corporate/investor-relations/larry-fink-ceo-letter, accessed June 30 2018; J. Hanna, Startups don't need to choose between profit and purpose, May 11, 2016, http://www.wired.co.uk/article/julie-hannah-profit-purpose-startups, accessed June 30 2018; A.R. Sorkin, "BlackRock's Message: Contribute to Society, or Risk Losing Our Support," *New York Times*, January 15, 2018, https://www.nytimes.com/2018/01/15/business/dealbook/blackrock-laurence-fink-letter.html, accessed June 30, 2018.

FIGURE 2.5 THE FOUR-WAY TEST

The Four-Way Test
of what we think, say, or do

1. Is it the TRUTH?
2. Is it FAIR to all concerned?
3. Will it build GOODWILL and better friendships?
4. Will it be BENEFICIAL to all concerned?

SOURCE: Rotary International.

ethical and moral behaviour early. They developed the four-way test, shown in Figure 2.5, which is now used in more than 166 nations by 1.2 million Rotarians. The four-way test focuses the questioner on key ethical and moral questions. Beyond the individual and professional level, organizational culture is another excellent starting point for addressing ethics and morality. Sometimes codes articulate a corporation's ethics. Johnson & Johnson's credo helped hundreds of employees ethically address criminal tampering with Tylenol products. Students in business schools have developed graduation codes of ethics to guide them in their work.

technology The intellectual and mechanical processes used by an organization to transform inputs into products or services that meet organizational goals.

Individual codes of ethics, professional oaths, and organizational credos must all be anchored in a moral, ethical framework. We must continue using ethical theories to question and improve our individual current standards. Although a universal right and wrong may exist, it would be hard to agree upon a single code of ethics to which all individuals, professions, and organizations can subscribe.

TECHNOLOGICAL INNOVATION AND TODAY'S WORKFORCE

Another challenge that managers face is managing technological innovation. **Technology** can incorporate the intellectual and mechanical processes an organization uses to transform inputs into products or services that meet its goals. Managers must adapt to rapidly changing technology and ensure its optimum use in their organizations. Managers' inability to incorporate new technologies into their organizations limits economic growth in North America.[91] Although North America still leads the way in developing new technologies, it lags behind in using them productively in workplace settings.[92] Great organizations avoid technology fads and bandwagons, instead pioneer the application of carefully selected technologies.[93]

The Internet has radically changed organizations' communication and work performance. The Internet and electronic innovation have made surveillance of employees more widespread. However, companies need to balance the use of spyware, monitoring of employee e-mails and websites, and video monitoring systems with respect for employee rights to privacy. Managers with excellent interpersonal skills do more to ensure high productivity, commitment, and appropriate behaviour on the part of employees than intense employee performance monitoring systems. Organizations with clearly written policies spelling out their approach to monitoring employees walk the fine line between respecting employees' privacy and protecting the interests of the organization.

One fascinating technological change is the development of **expert systems**, computer-based applications that use a representation of human expertise in a specialized field of knowledge to solve problems. Expert systems can be used in many ways, including providing advice to non-experts, providing assistance to experts, replacing experts, and serving as a training and development tool in organizations.[94] They are used in medical decision making, diagnosis, and medical informatics.[95] Anheuser-Busch has used an expert system to assist managers in ensuring that personnel decisions comply with anti-discrimination laws.[96]

Japan leads the world in the use of **robotics** in organizations; while organizations in North America have fewer total robots than Japan, the gap is narrowing. As well, the growth in the use of robots is expected to come from the "BRICS countries," i.e., Brazil, Russia, India, China and South Africa.[97] Whereas Japanese workers are happy to let robots take over repetitive or dangerous work, North American employees and unions worry that they will be replaced by labour-saving robots.[98] However, the main reason for the reluctance of North American organizations to use robots is their slow payback. Robotics represents a big investment that does not pay off in the short term. Japanese managers are more willing to evaluate the effectiveness of robotics technology along a long-term horizon.

It is tempting to view technology from only the positive side; however, some realism is in order. Some firms that have been disappointed with costly technologies are electing to *de*-engineer: 42 percent of information technology projects are abandoned before completion, and half of all technology projects fail to meet managers' expectations. Pacific Gas and Electric (part of PG&E Corporation) spent tens of millions of dollars on a new IBM-based system. Then deregulation hit the utility industry, allowing customers to choose among utility companies. Keeping up with multiple suppliers and fast-changing prices was too much for the massive new system; it was scrapped in favour of a new project using the old first-generation computer system, which is still being updated and gradually replaced. Because some innovations fail to live up to expectations, managers have to handle both revolutionary and evolutionary approaches to technological transitions.[99]

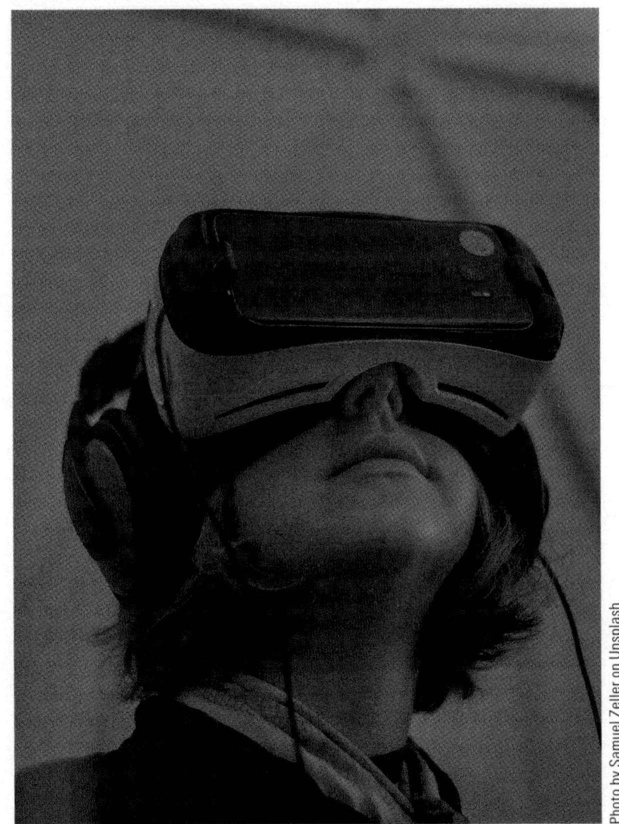

Photo by Samuel Zeller on Unsplash

Augmented reality technology is developing quickly.

Alternative Work Arrangements

Technological advances have prompted the advent of alternative work arrangements, the nontraditional work practices, settings, and locations that are now supplementing traditional workplaces. One alternative work arrangement is **telecommuting**, electronically transmitting work from a home computer to the office. IBM was one of the first companies to experiment with the notion of installing computer

expert system A computer-based application that uses a representation of human expertise in a specialized field of knowledge to solve problems.

robotics The use of robots in organizations.

telecommuting Electronically transmitting work from a home computer to the office.

terminals at employees' homes and having employees work at home. By telecommuting, employees gain flexibility, save the commute to work, and enjoy the comforts of being at home. Telecommuting also has disadvantages, however, including distractions and lack of opportunities to socialize with other workers. Despite these disadvantages, telecommuters still feel "plugged in" to the communication system at the office. Studies show that telecommuters often report higher satisfaction with office communication than do workers in traditional office environments.[100]

Telus Corp. sees telecommuting as part of its green strategy. Hundreds of Telus employees work from home offices and the results have included significant cost savings in office space, increased employee productivity, and savings of many tonnes in greenhouse gases.[101] Telecommuting lets companies access workers with key skills regardless of their locations. Alternative workplaces also give organizations an advantage in hiring and keeping talented employees, who find the flexibility of working at home very attractive.

Satellite offices comprise another alternative work arrangement. In such offices, large facilities are broken into a network of smaller workplaces located near employees' homes. Satellites are often located in comparatively inexpensive cities and suburban areas. They usually have simpler furnishings than the more centrally located offices. Satellites can save a company as much as 50 percent in real estate costs and can attract employees who do not want to work in a large urban area, thus broadening the pool of potential employees.[102]

These alternative work arrangements signal a trend toward *virtual offices,* in which people work anytime, anywhere, and with anyone. The concept suggests work occurring where people are, rather than people coming to work. Information technologies make connectivity, collaboration, and communication easy. Critical voicemails and messages can be delivered to and from the central office, a client's office, the airport, the car, or home. Wireless Internet access and online meeting software, such as zoom.com, allow employees to participate in meetings anywhere at any time.

Impact of Technology on Management

Technological innovation affects the very nature of the management job. Managers who once had to coax workers back to their desks from coffee breaks now find that they need to encourage workers mesmerized by new technology to take more frequent breaks.[103] Working with a computer can be stressful, both physically and psychologically. Long hours at computer terminals can cause eye, neck, and back strain, and headaches. In addition, workers accustomed to the fast response time of the computer come to expect the same from their coworkers and scold coworkers when they fail to match the computer's speed and accuracy. New technology, combined with globalization and intensified business pressures, has created extreme workers, pushing up the ranks of workaholics.[104] These extreme workers pay a price in relationships; other dimensions of a full, rich life; and increased stress.

Computerized monitoring provides managers with a wealth of information about employee performance, and it holds great potential for misuse. The telecommunications, airline, and mail-order merchandise industries make wide use of systems that secretly monitor employees' interactions with customers. Employers praise such systems for improving customer service. Workers, however, react to secret scrutiny with higher levels of depression, anxiety, and exhaustion. Bell Canada evaluated operators using a system that tabulated average working time with customers. Operators found the practice highly stressful, and they sabotaged the system by giving callers wrong directory assistance numbers rather than taking the time to look up the correct ones. Bell Canada now uses average working time scores for entire offices rather than for individuals.[105]

In a world of rapid technological innovation, managers must focus on helping workers manage the stress of their work. They must take advantage of the wealth of information available to motivate, coach, and counsel workers rather than to stringently control or police them.

New technologies and rapid innovation place a premium on a manager's technical skills. Managers must develop technical competence in order to gain workers' respect. Computer-integrated manufacturing systems, for example, require managers to use participative management styles, open communication, and greater technical expertise to be effective.[106]

Helping Employees Adjust to Technological Change

Most workers understand the benefits of modern technologies. Innovation has improved working conditions and increased the availability of skilled jobs. Technology is also bringing disadvantaged individuals into the workforce. Microchips have dramatically increased opportunities for workers with visual impairments. Information can be decoded into speech using a speech synthesizer, into braille using a hard-copy printer, or into enlarged print visible on a computer monitor.[107] Engineers at Carnegie Mellon University have developed PizzaBot, a robot that individuals with disabilities can operate using a voice-recognition system, to fill a pizza order from the crust to the toppings. Despite these and other benefits of new technology in the workplace, however, some employees may still resist change.

Technological innovations change employees' work environments, generating stress. Many workers react negatively to change that they feel threatens their work situation. Many of their fears centre around loss—of freedom, of control, of the things they like about their jobs.[108] Employees may fear diminished quality of work life and increased pressure. Further, employees may fear being replaced by technology or being displaced into jobs of lower skill levels.

Managers can take several actions to help employees adapt to changing technology. Encouraging workers' participation in early phases of decisions regarding technological changes is important. Individuals who participate in planning for the implementation of new technology learn about the potential changes in their jobs; therefore, they are less resistant to the change. Workers' input in early stages can smooth the transition into the new ways of performing work.

Managers should also keep in mind the effects that new technology has on the skill requirements of workers. Many employees support changes that increase the skill requirements of their jobs. Increased skill requirements often lead to increased job autonomy, responsibility, and (potentially) pay. Whenever possible, managers should select technology that increases workers' skill requirements.

Providing effective training is essential. Training helps employees perceive that they control the technology rather than being controlled by it. The training should be designed to match workers' needs, and it should increase the workers' sense of mastery of the new technology.

A related challenge is to encourage workers to invent new uses for existing technology. **Reinvention** is the term for creatively applying new technology.[109] Individuals who explore the boundaries of a new technology can personalize the technology and adapt it to their own job needs, and share this information with others in their work group.

Managers must lead organizations to adopt new technologies more humanely and effectively. Technological changes are essential for earnings growth and for expanded employment opportunities. The adoption of new technologies is a critical determinant of North American competitiveness in the global marketplace.

reinvention The creative application of new technology.

STUDY TOOLS 2

IN THE BOOK YOU CAN ...

- ☐ Rip out the **Chapter Review card** at the end of the book to review Key Concepts and Key Terms.
- ☐ Take a "What about You?" Quiz related to material in the chapter.
- ☐ Read additional cases in the Mini Case and Shopify Running Case sections.

ONLINE YOU CAN ...

NELSON.COM/STUDENT

- ☐ Take a "What about You?" Quiz related to material in the chapter.
- ☐ Test your understanding with a quick Multiple-Choice Pre-Test quiz.
- ☐ Read the eBook, which includes discussion points for questions posed in the Cases.
- ☐ Watch Videos related to chapter content.
- ☐ Use the available Flashcards and Matching Quizzes to test your understanding of key terms and concepts.
- ☐ See how much you've learned by taking a Post-Test.

WHAT ABOUT YOU?

Planning for a Global Career

Think of a country you would like to work in, do business in, or visit. Find out about its culture, using Hofstede's dimensions as guidelines. You can use a variety of sources to accomplish this, particularly your school library, government offices, faculty members, or others who have global experience. You will want to answer the following questions:

1. Is the culture individualistic or collectivist?
2. Is the power distance high or low?
3. Is uncertainty avoidance high or low?
4. Is the country masculine or feminine in its orientation?
5. Is the time orientation short term or long term?
6. Does the country have an indulgent orientation?
7. How did you arrive at your answers to the six questions?
8. How will these characteristics affect business practices in the country you chose to investigate/to visit?

MINI CASE

Jill Warner

Jill Warner, President of Ace Toys, sat looking at the monthly profit and loss statement. For the fifth month in a row, the company had lost money. Labour costs were killing them. Jill had done everything she could think of to reduce costs and still produce a quality product. She was beginning to face the fact that soon she would no longer be able to avoid the idea of outsourcing. It was a concept that Jill had done everything to avoid, but it was beginning to look inevitable.

Jill felt strongly about making a quality Canadian product using Canadian workers in a Canadian factory. But if things continued the way they were, she was going to have to do something. She owed it to her stockholders and board of directors to keep the company financially healthy. They had entrusted her with the future of the company, and she could not let them down. It was not her money or company to do with as she pleased. Her job was to make sure that Ace Toys flourished.

However, if she chose to outsource the production segment of the company, only management and the sales force would keep their jobs. How could she face the 500 people who would lose their jobs? How would the small community that depended on those 500 jobs survive? She also worried about the customers who had come to depend on Ace Toys to produce a safe product that they could give to their children with confidence. Would that quality suffer if she sent production halfway around the world? How could she ensure that the company she hired to produce the toys would live up to Ace's standards? Would the other company pay a fair wage and not employ children? The questions seemed endless, but Jill needed to decide how to save the company.

Apply Your Understanding

1. Is sending jobs out of the country unethical?
2. Using rule, virtue, rights, and justice theories, evaluate Jill's options.
3. What would you do and why?

RUNNING CASE SHOPIFY

DIVERSITY IN QUESTION

Shopify believes that effective organizational culture is created from blending great people, diversity and inclusion, and a clear set of articulated values. As part of its commitment to people, for example, it offers self-directed budgets for learning and also provides catering and house cleaning. Shopify recognizes the need for diversity as its merchant base is 50 percent women across 175 countries. Shopify was recognized in 2018 as a best place to work by Glassdoor and as a top Canadian company by G2 Crowd.

Even so, Shopify has been criticized for its lack of diversity in its board; it is overwhelmingly white and male. At its 2018 annual shareholders' meeting, one of Shopify's shareholders questioned the diversity of the board's composition. Meriel Bradford, a shareholder and a former vice-president of Teleglobe and senior bureaucrat at Global Affairs and other federal departments, commented, "diversity was important for any company aspiring to be global. . . .This board doesn't have it." In response, one of the board members said the board was looking for talent. Bradford then commented that "I suggest your search technique is poor."

Kevin Van Paassen/Bloomberg via Getty Images

Shopify's lack of diversity is emblematic of the tech industry in North America. There are several possible explanations. Computer science departments are still overwhelming male. As well, and most interestingly, a study from Stanford suggests that the actual recruiting processes may alienate women. The researchers observed 75 recruiting sessions for 60 companies and found, for example, that sexist jokes were told and presentation decks had only images of men. Male-dominated industries tend to use masculine language and therefore may alienate and exclude women. Further, women in STEM continue to make less money than men and individuals of racialized colour make less than their white peers. Even so, some in the tech sector consider the lack of diversity as a false issue. James Damore, a former Google engineer, wrote an anti-diversity memo that soon became viral. He commented that men and women were biologically different and were suited to different types of work; e.g., men were better engineers than women. The email caused a firestorm and Damore was fired from Google; Google's CEO, Sundar Pichai, said the memo violated its policies.

SOURCES: J. Bagnall, "Is Shopify's Board of Directors Too Male, Too White?" *Ottawa Citizen*, May 31, 2018, accessed from http://ottawacitizen.com/business/local-business/bagnall-is-shopifys-board-of-directors-too-male-too-white, September 28, 2018; "Life at Shopify," Shopify, accessed from https://www.shopify.com/careers/culture, July 3, 2018; B. Myers, "Women and Minorities, By the Numbers," *Wired*, March 27, 2018, accessed from https://www.wired.com/story/computer-science-graduates-diversity/, September 28, 2018; M. Ehrenkranz, "Let's be Very Clear about What Happened to James Damore," *Gizmodo*, January 17, 2018, accessed from https://gizmodo.com/lets-be-very-clear-about-what-happened-to-james-damore-1822160852, September 23, 2018.

Apply Your Understanding

1. Why are tech firms still not very diverse?
2. What can Shopify do to become more diverse?
3. What are the risks to Shopify if it does not become more diverse and inclusive?

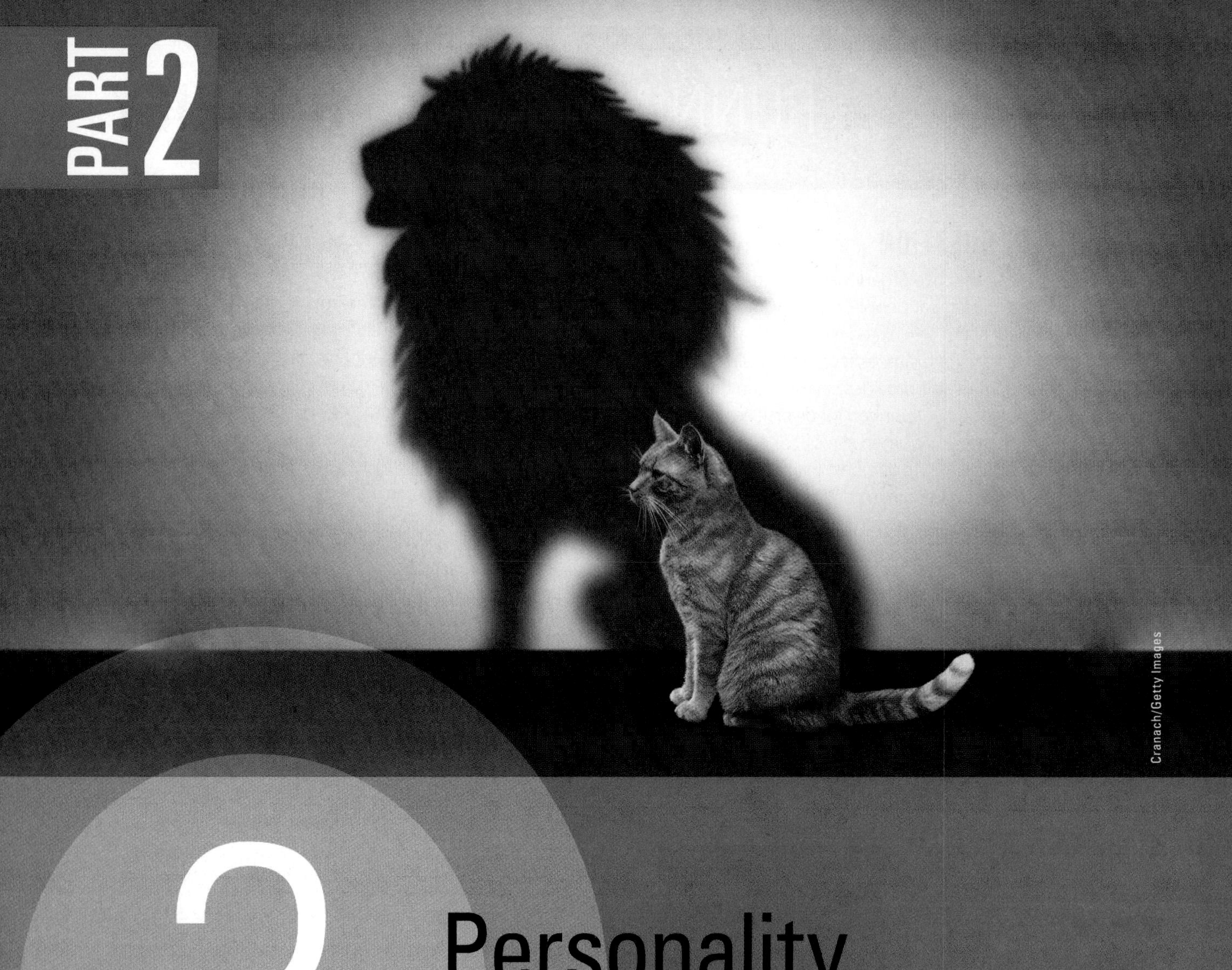

3 Personality and Perception

LEARNING OUTCOMES

After reading this chapter, you should be able to do the following:

3-1 Describe individual differences and their importance in understanding behaviour.

3-2 Explain how personality influences behaviour.

3-3 Discuss the practical assessment of personality in organizations.

3-4 Define *social perception* and explain the factors that affect it.

3-5 Identify how biases create barriers to social perception.

3-6 Describe how individuals manage others' impressions.

See the end of this chapter for a list of available Study Tools, a "What about You?" Quiz, Mini Case, and the Shopify Running Case.

Because personality is such a fundamental component of what makes each individual unique, the better one is able to understand and manage different personality traits, the better one is able to work with people in all organizational settings, from new introductions, to informal book clubs, to corporate work environments. But our understanding of personality is only as good as our social perception is accurate: Cognitive biases constantly undermine our perceptions.

> "Behaviour is the mirror in which everyone shows their image."
> —Johan Wolfgang von Goethe

3-1 INDIVIDUAL DIFFERENCES AND ORGANIZATIONAL BEHAVIOUR

The next two chapters of this text begin to explore the concept of **individual differences**, which describe how a person's skills and abilities, personality, perceptions, attitudes, emotions, and ethics combine to form the essence of who that person is at their most fundamental level. (Skills, abilities, personality, and perceptions will be discussed in this chapter, while attitudes, emotions, and ethics are discussed next, in Chapter 4.) It is our individual differences, and the seemingly infinite ways that these differences combine, that make directing and managing organizational behaviour challenging.

Individual differences are responsible for inconsistencies in motivation (Chapter 5); variable responses to stress (Chapter 6); challenges associated with decision making (Chapter 7); difficulties and misunderstandings in communication (Chapter 8); conflict within groups and teams and its resolution (Chapter 9 and 10); desire for power and influence (Chapter 11); discrepancies in styles of leadership and followership (Chapter 12); the creation, maintenance, and changing of culture (Chapter 13); disparities in learning styles and abilities (Chapter 14); perspectives on jobs and the design of work, as well as organizational structure (Chapters 15 and 16); and adaptability to change and careers (Chapters 17 and 18). In other words, recognizing, understanding, appreciating, and managing individual differences is the whole reason for studying organizational behaviour, because while no two people are exactly alike, no two people are completely different, either. The more one understands individual differences, the better they can work with and direct others. Figure 3.1 illustrates how some individual differences affect human behaviour.

The basis for understanding individual differences in a scientific and consistent way stems from early research in the field, which explained that behaviour is a function of the person and the environment.[1] This idea has been refined into what is now known as **interactional psychology**,[2] which has four basic propositions[3]:

1. Behaviour is a function of a continuous, multidirectional interaction between personality characteristics and situational characteristics.

FIGURE 3.1 VARIABLES INFLUENCING INDIVIDUAL BEHAVIOUR

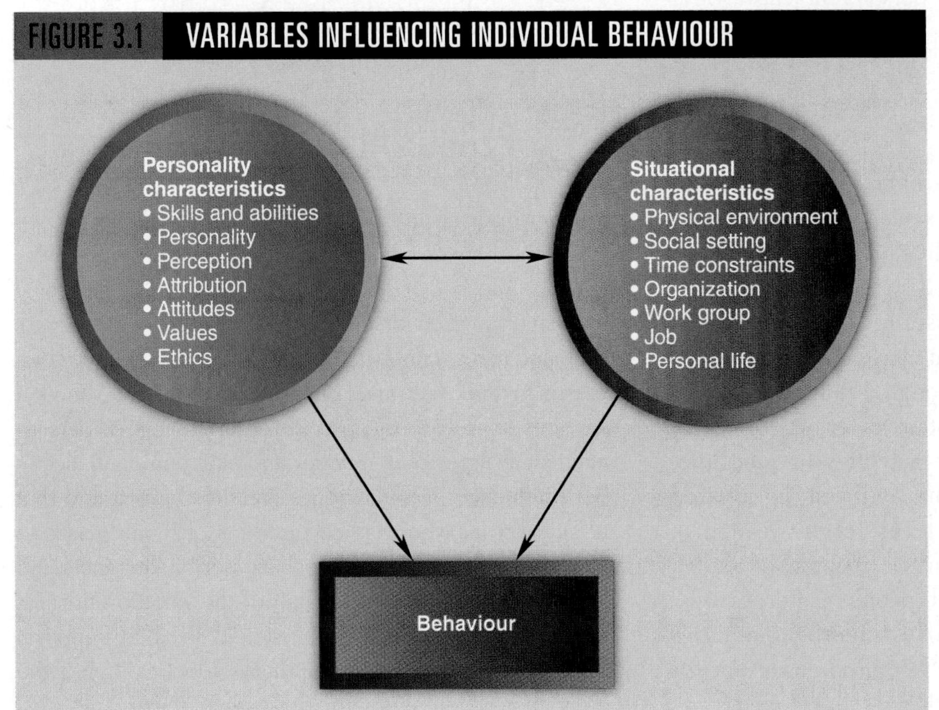

individual differences The way in which factors such as skills, abilities, personalities, perceptions, attitudes, values, and ethics differ from one individual to another.

interactional psychology The psychological approach that emphasizes that in order to understand human behaviour, we must know something about the person and about the situation.

Identical twins separated at birth share personality traits and preferences.

Personality characteristics include all factors that are internal to an individual, such as skills, attitudes, and perceptions. Situational characteristics include all factors that are external to an individual, such as physical location, social setting, and even variables like temperature and time of day.

2. The person is active in this process and is changed by situations and is also able to change situations.
3. People vary in many characteristics, including cognitive, affective, motivational, and ability factors.
4. Two interpretations of situations are important: the objective situation and the person's subjective view of the situation.

Skills and Abilities

Skills and abilities influence behavioural outcomes. **Abilities** describe natural capacities that allow an individual to perform a particular job or task successfully. **Skills** are talents that have been acquired through deliberate and sustained effort to carry out activities or job functions and can be related to ideas (cognitive skills), things (technical skills), and people (interpersonal skills). Underlying abilities are required in order for skills to be developed.

abilities Natural capacities that allow an individual to perform a particular task successfully.

skills Talents that have been acquired through deliberate and sustained effort.

***g* factor** A measure of an individual's general mental ability.

personality A relatively stable set of characteristics that influences an individual's behaviour.

The ***g* factor** is a measure of an individual's general mental *ability*, (i.e., natural capacity) and was conceptualized nearly 100 years ago when psychologists observed that children's performance across unrelated school subjects was positively correlated. (Children who performed well in one cognitive area often performed well in other cognitive areas.) IQ scores are commonly regarded as estimates of an individual's *g* factor. The existence of the *g* factor is well established and uncontroversial, and the most widely accepted theories of intelligence incorporate it. It is a significant predictor of individual differences in many social outcomes, particularly in education and employment,[4] and has also been been shown to be strongly correlated with work performance.[5]

3-2 PERSONALITY

Personality is an individual difference that lends consistency to a person's behaviour. **Personality** is the relatively stable set of characteristics that influences how consistent an individual is in their own behaviour across time and across contexts. Personality is the tendency of a person to think, feel, and behave in a certain way. Although researchers debate the precise determinants of personality, many agree that genetics and environmental factors both influence personality. Researchers have found that identical twins who were separated at birth and raised in very different environments share personality traits and preferences. Approximately half of the variation in traits like extraversion, impulsiveness, and flexibility appears to be genetically determined; that is, identical twins who grew up in different environments share these traits.[6]

Environment also serves as a personality determinant, shaping individual characteristics and behavioural responses through family, cultural, and educational influences, and other external stimuli. Though they are stable, personality traits are not fixed. They continue to develop and change to some degree through adulthood.[7]

Big Five Personality Trait Model

Personality theorists have argued that to understand individual behaviour, behavioural patterns must be broken down into a series of observable **traits**, which are distinguishing qualities or features belonging to a person. One popular personality classification is the Big Five Personality Trait model (also known as the Five Factor Model of personality). Based on many studies spanning nearly a century, personality researchers have found that nearly all personality traits can be mapped to one of the following five dimensions:[8] extraversion, agreeableness, conscientiousness, neuroticism, and openness to experience.[9] It is important to note that when we discuss each of these traits, we are really referencing the *dimensions* of that trait. One extreme of the extraversion dimension corresponds to individuals who are very extraverted, while the other extreme corresponds to very introverted individuals. Additionally, Big Five personality traits are "normally distributed," meaning that the majority of people score somewhere near average, and few individuals score at one extreme or another.

EXTRAVERSION–INTROVERSION The extraversion–introversion dimension is normally referred to simply as extraversion. This dimension describes how outgoing and energetic someone is, and how comfortable they are around people and in new social settings. People who are extreme extroverts enjoy being with other people, are talkative, full of energy, and often seen as attention seeking. Extroverts typically have little trouble with public speaking or performing in front of large audiences.

AGREEABLENESS–DISAGREEABLENESS The agreeableness–disagreeableness dimension is normally referred to as agreeableness. This dimension refers to how easygoing and friendly someone is. People who are extremely agreeable tend to get along with many different types of people in many different situations. They are compassionate, cooperative, and trusting of others, and are generally seen as well tempered.

CONSCIENTIOUSNESS–DISORGANIZED The conscientiousness–disorganized dimension is normally referred to as conscientiousness. This dimension denotes how organized and dependable someone is. People who are highly conscientious have high levels of self discipline, and are reliable, neat, punctual, and able to meet deadlines. Extreme conscientiousness can be perceived as inflexibility and obstinacy.

NEUROTICISM–EMOTIONAL STABILITY The neuroticism–emotional stability dimension is normally referred to as neuroticism. This dimension corresponds to how emotionally volatile someone is. People who are highly neurotic are emotionally reactive and prone to psychological stress. They tend to experience a greater degree of unpleasant emotions like anger, and anxiety, and often lack a degree of impulse control.

traits Distinguishing qualities or features of a person.

IN ACTION

Personality

Does your personality affect life outcomes? In a recent comprehensive review of research on the Big Five personality model, researchers found that the answer seems to be a resounding yes. Extraverts, for example, are happier, more satisfied with romantic relationships, and less likely to be depressed. Agreeable individuals are less likely to have heart disease, and more likely to have a positive leadership style. Conscientious people are healthier and enjoy greater occupational success, and they are less likely to engage in criminal or antisocial behaviours. Emotionally stable individuals experience greater job satisfaction, commitment, and occupational success. Those who are open to new experiences tend to choose occupations that involve creative and artistic skills, but they are also more likely to engage in substance abuse.

SOURCE: D. J. Ozer and V. Benet-Martínez, "Personality and the Prediction of Consequential Outcomes," *Annual Review of Psychology* 57 (2006): 401–421.

TABLE 3.1 THE "BIG FIVE" PERSONALITY TRAITS	
Extraversion	The person is gregarious, assertive, and sociable (as opposed to reserved, timid, and quiet).
Agreeableness	The person is cooperative, warm, and agreeable (rather than cold, disagreeable, and antagonistic).
Conscientiousness	The person is hardworking, organized, and dependable (as opposed to lazy, disorganized, and unreliable).
Neuroticism	The person is insecure, anxious, and depressed (as opposed to calm, self-confident, and cool).
Openness to experience	The person is creative, curious, and cultured (rather than practical with narrow interests).

SOURCES: P. T. Costa and R. R. McCrae, *The NEO-PI Personality Inventory* (Odessa, Fla.: Psychological Assessment Resources, 1992); J. F. Salgado, "The Five Factor Model of Personality and Job Performance in the European Community," *Journal of Applied Psychology* 82 (1997): 30–43.

OPENNESS TO EXPERIENCE–CAUTIOUS The openness to experience–cautious dimension is referred to as openness to experience. This dimension describes how much someone prefers variety and novelty. People who are highly open to experience are curious, creative, willing to try new things, and are open to new people, new ideas, and new ways of doing things.

In an organizational setting, we know that introverted and conscientious employees are less likely to be absent from work.[10] Individuals with high agreeableness tend to rate others more leniently on peer evaluations, while those with high conscientiousness tend to be tougher raters.[11] Extraverts tend to have higher salaries, receive more promotions, and be more satisfied with their careers.[12] Across many occupations, conscientious people are more motivated and are high performers.[13] When you examine specific occupations, however, different patterns of the Big Five factors are related to high performance. For customer service jobs, individuals high in emotional stability, agreeableness, and openness to experience perform best. Managers with emotional stability and extraversion are top performers.[14] Recent research results indicate that in work teams, the minimum level of agreeableness in a team and the mean levels of conscientiousness and openness to experience have a strong effect on overall team performance.[15] The Big Five framework has also shown itself to be a valid framework for studying personality in multinational studies.[16]

Everyone sees what you appear to be, few experience what you really are.

—Nicollò Machiavelli, The Prince

The trait approach has many critics. Some theorists argue that simply identifying traits is not enough, since personality is dynamic and never completely stable. Further, early trait theorists tended to ignore the influence of situations.[17] Also, the trait theory tends to ignore process—that is, how we get from a trait to a particular outcome.

The Dark Triad

Recent research has found that another set of trait dimensions collectively known as "the dark triad," which predict negative or antisocial behavioural outcomes that cannot fully be explained by the Big Five alone. As might be expected, people who are high in these traits tend toward socially dysfunctional behaviours, like aggressiveness, opportunism, and exploitativeness.[18] The dimensions of the dark triad are narcissism, psychopathy, and Machiavellianism.[19]

NARCISSISM (SELFLESSNESS) This dimension refers to how self-absorbed someone is. People who are high in narcissism spend an excessive amount of time thinking about themselves and have an inflated sense of pride and ego. Narcissistic individuals may post many selfies to their Instagram each day.

PSYCHOPATHY (EMPATHY) This dimension describes the degree to which someone cares about others. People who are high in psychopathy do not care about others' welfare, and experience little (or no) emotional response or remorse. Psychopathy is characterized by selfishness and antisocial behaviours.

MACHIAVELLIANISM (SCRUPULOUS) This dimension corresponds to the degree of morality that someone possesses. People who are high in Machiavellianism are manipulative and exploitative. High Machiavelli individuals are duplicitous, amoral, and focused solely on self-interest and personal gain.

HEXACO Personality Model

The HEXACO personality model incorporates the dark triad into the Big Five model to create a very robust model of personality traits.[20] Where the Big Five model describes personality across five dimensions, the HEXACO model describes personality across six dimensional traits:

H: Honesty/Humility–Dark Triad

E: Emotional Stability–Neuroticism

X: Extraversion–Introversion

A: Agreeableness–Disagreeableness

C: Conscientiousness–Disorganized

O: Openness to Experience–Closed-minded

You can see that the E, X, A, C and O traits are the same as those described by the Big Five model; Emotional stability; Extraversion; Agreeableness; Conscientiousness; and Openness to Experience. The Honesty/humility dimension is simply the other extreme of the Dark Triad personality characteristic described above.

The dimensions of personality are not the only important factors when considering something as complex as someone's personality.

OTHER IMPORTANT PERSONALITY TRAITS

While the Big Five personality traits provide a great deal of information, and the HEXACO personality model even more so, these five or six dimensions of personality are not the only important factors to consider when analyzing something as complex as someone's personality. There are many other aspects that may be considered, including core self-evaluation, self-monitoring, and affectivity.

Core Self-Evaluation (CSE)

Core self-evaluation (CSE) is a broad set of personality traits that refers to the positiveness of a person's self-concept.[21] It represents a subconscious, fundamental evaluation about a person's abilities. Those with high CSEs think positively of themselves, and have confidence in their own abilities. Core self-evaluation represents personality traits that are constant over time, and its four factors are locus of control, self-esteem, generalized self-efficacy, and neuroticism. Research suggests that people with high CSE are more popular,[22] make more money, have higher prestige jobs, and higher job satisfaction. Their more successful career paths are based partly on the fact that they are more likely to pursue further education and maintain better health.[23]

LOCUS OF CONTROL An individual's generalized belief about internal (self) versus external (situation or others) control is called **locus of control**. People who believe they control what happens to them have an *internal* locus of control, whereas people who believe that circumstances or other people control their fate have an *external* locus of control.[24] Internals (those with an internal locus of control) have higher job satisfaction, health, organizational commitment, job involvement, motivation, and career success. Their stress levels are lower, as are their levels of role ambiguity, role conflict, and work–family conflict.[25] It appears that internals' beliefs change their behaviour in such a way as to promote positive outcomes. The externals' perception of their passive role means they are less likely to deal directly with problems or initiate constructive actions.

Because internals believe they control what happens to them, they typically prefer to exercise control in their environment. Internals don't appreciate close supervision, and favor having input into decisions. Externals, in contrast, may appreciate a more structured task setting with greater supervision and assistance, and may not prefer to participate in decision making.

SELF-EFFICACY **General self-efficacy** is a person's overall view of themselves as being able to perform effectively in a wide variety of situations.[26] While *task-specific self-efficacy* describes a person's belief that they can perform a specific task ("I believe I can do this sales presentation today."), the CSE refers

core self-evaluation The positiveness of a person's self-concept; comprised of locus of control, self-esteem, self-efficacy, and neuroticism.

locus of control An individual's generalized belief about internal control (self-control) versus external control (control by the situation or by others).

general self-efficacy An individual's general belief that they are capable of meeting job demands in a wide variety of situations.

to general self-efficacy ("I believe I can perform well in just about any part of the job.").

People with high general self-efficacy have more confidence in their skills and innate abilities as well as other personal resources (e.g., energy, influence over others, etc.). People with low general self-efficacy often feel ineffective and may express doubts about performing a new task well. People who trust their own efficacy tend to attempt difficult tasks, to persist in overcoming obstacles, and to experience less anxiety when faced with adversity.[27] Because previous success is one of the most important determinants of self-efficacy, generalized self-efficacy tends to be self-fulfilling: An individual believes in their skills and abilities, attempts a new task, perseveres, achieves success, and then has a greater feeling of self-efficacy. Because they are confident in their capability to provide meaningful input, they value the opportunity to participate in decision making.[28] High self-efficacy has also been related to higher job satisfaction and performance.[29]

SELF-ESTEEM **Self-esteem** is an individual's general feeling of self-worth. Individuals with high self-esteem have positive feelings about themselves, perceive themselves to have strengths as well as weaknesses, and believe their strengths are more important than their weaknesses.[30] Individuals with low self-esteem view themselves negatively, and are more strongly affected by what other people think of them.[31] Self-esteem is also affected by situational factors. Success tends to raise self-esteem, while failure lowers it.

A person's self-esteem affects attitudes and behaviour in organizations. People with high self-esteem perform better and are more satisfied with their jobs,[32] and tend to seek out higher status jobs.[33] A team made up of individuals with high self-esteem is more likely to succeed than a team with low or average self-esteem.[34] Very high self-esteem, however, can have negative impacts: People with very high self-esteem may brag inappropriately when they find themselves in stressful situations.[35] Very high self-esteem may also lead to overconfidence and relationship conflicts.[36]

NEUROTICISM Neuroticism in the context of CSE is the same trait as described by the Big Five and the HEXACO models. It describes how emotionally volatile someone is. People who are highly neurotic are emotionally reactive, and prone to psychological stress. They tend to experience a greater degree of unpleasant emotions like anger, and anxiety, and are more susceptible to feelings of helplessness.[37] Locus of control, self-efficacy, self-esteem, and neuroticism together constitute the core self-evaluations. CSE is a strong predictor of both job satisfaction and job performance, next only to g factor.[38]

self-esteem An individual's general feeling of self-worth.

self-monitoring The extent to which people base their behaviour on cues from other people and situations.

#HOT TREND

High Self-Monitors

High self-monitors resemble good actors who are able to play different roles for different audiences. They have strong motives to succeed in social interactions, use humor in conversations, and speak first to break awkward silences. In addition, a recent study showed that high self-monitors are also likely to be social network brokers, connecting previously unacquainted people with each other. High self-monitors, when viewed by others as empathetic, can be effective at connecting people and building networks.

SOURCE: A. M. Kleinbaum, A. H. Jordan, and P. G. Audia, "An Altercentric Perspective on the Origins of Brokerage in Social Networks: How Perceived Empathy Moderates the Self-Monitoring Effect," *Organization Science*, published online February 13, 2015.

Self-Monitoring

Another important personality trait is **Self-monitoring**, which is the extent to which people base their behaviour on cues from other people and situations. Self-monitoring has a huge impact on behaviour in organizational and social settings.[39] Different situations often require different comportment, for instance behaviour that is acceptable at an office party (laughing, joking, drinking, and even dress codes) is often very different from what is acceptable in a meeting, even if the same group of people are involved. High self-monitors pay attention to what is appropriate in particular situations and to the behaviour of other people, and they modify their behaviour to reflect what is required by the current situation. High self-monitors present themselves in various ways in an attempt to impress others and receive positive feedback. Low self-monitors, in contrast, pay less attention to situational cues and act from internal states instead. As a result, low self-monitors' behaviour is consistent across different situations.

High self-monitors pay more attention to the subjective norms of behaviour in all contexts, and because high self-monitors base their behaviour on cues from others and from the situation, they demonstrate higher levels of self-awareness and assess their own behaviour more accurately than low-self-monitors.[40] According to research, high self-monitors are more motivated to attain high social status than low self-monitors, and they are more likely to be promoted as they accomplish tasks by meeting the expectations of others and because they seek out central positions in social networks.[41] They are also more likely to use self-promotion to make others aware of their skills and accomplishments. Managers who are high self-monitors are also good at reading their employees' needs and changing the way they interact with employees.[42]

However, the high self-monitor's behavioural variability may not be suited for every job, and the tendency to portray different behaviours in different situations may not fit every organization.[43] Because high self-monitors adapt their behaviours based on social cues, they are more susceptible to groupthink and other herd mentalities. The high self-monitoring person also runs the risk of being seen as hypocritical or two-faced by those who perceive the changes in behaviour as insincerity.[44]

Positive/Negative Affect

The final personality trait that we will discuss is positive/negative affect. Individuals who focus on the positive aspects of themselves, other people, and the world in general are said to have **positive affect**.[45] In contrast, those who accentuate the negative in themselves, others, and the world are said to possess **negative affect** (also called *negative affectivity*).[46] Positive affect has been linked to more life satisfaction and better performance across a variety of life and work domains.[47] Individuals with positive affect are more satisfied with their jobs,[48] are more likely to help others at work and engage in more organizational citizenship behaviours (OCBs),[49] and have have fewer absentee days.[50] Individual affect also influences the work group; positive individual affect produces positive team affect, which promotes cooperation and reduces conflict.[51] In this way, leader affectivity has the power to influence subordinate outcomes.

Situational Variables

Though knowledge of an individual's personality can provide some insights into a person's behaviour, knowledge of personality traits alone cannot predict behaviour in all instances. Recall that the interactional psychology model (Figure 3.1) requires knowledge of both person and situational characteristics to predict behaviour. Situational variables/characteristics include all moderators of behaviour that are external to the individual, such as physical location, social setting, time pressures, and expectations, among others.

Different situations affect different people in different ways. A given situation may seem to one individual as an opportunity, while another sees it as an insurmountable challenge. Some situations allow for a free expression of personality, while other situations provoke a narrower range of behaviour. This is known as *situational strength*. **Strong situations** overwhelm the effects of individual personalities because they exert clear pressure on all to act in a specific way. For example, behaviours in an elevator are typically very limited: When two strangers are in an elevator, they tend to stand as far away from one another as possible. They seldom make eye contact, and seldom speak to one another. When an elevator is full of strangers, the passengers typically stare straight ahead at the doors, or the floor buttons, and again, seldom make eye contact or speak to one another. This is an example of a strong situation where the established norms of behaviour tend to overwhelm individual personality.

Weak situations are open to many interpretations. They provide few cues to appropriate behaviour and no obvious rewards for any particular behaviour. Thus, individual personalities have a stronger influence in weak situations than in strong situations. Consider an encounter at the park, where two extraverted strangers who happen to meet may smile at one another, and may exchange a friendly greeting, perhaps even a brief conversation about neutral topics like the weather. Two introverts may pass one another without a glance, let alone speak to one another. The park is an example of a weak situation, where individual personality is more likely to be expressed.

Organizations have different combinations of strong and weak situations, and it follows that personality affects behaviour more in some situations than in others.[52]

PERSONALITY ASSESSMENT IN ORGANIZATIONS

An accurate understanding of employee personality can assist a manager in many ways. Combining compatible individuals in a team, matching jobs to individuals, choosing an appropriate management approach for each employee, and understanding what circumstances a person may find stressful or enticing are all factors that may be at least partially

positive affect An individual's tendency to accentuate the positive aspects of themselves, other people, and the world in general.

negative affect An individual's tendency to accentuate the negative aspects of themselves, other people, and the world in general.

strong situation A situation that overwhelms the effects of individual personalities by providing strong cues for appropriate behaviour.

understood through personality assessment. To apply personality theories in organizational settings, managers must first formally measure members' personalities. Projective tests, behavioural measures, and self-report questionnaires can all be used to measure personality.

Common Personality Assessment Tools

During **projective tests**, individuals are shown an ambiguous picture, abstract image, or photo and are asked to describe what they see or to tell a story about it. The rationale behind projective tests is that each individual responds to the stimulus in a way that reflects their unique personality. The Rorschach inkblot test is one of the most well-known projective tests used to assess personality.[53] Projective tests, however, have low reliability, which is to say that they do not provide stable and consistent results when repeated over time. The individual being assessed may look at the same picture and see different things at different times. In addition, the assessor might apply her or his own biases in interpreting the information about the individual's personality.

Behavioural measures of personality examine an individual's behaviour in a controlled situation. We might assess a person's sociability, for example, by counting the number of times they approach strangers at a party. The behaviour is then scored to produce an index of personality. There are, of course, potential problems with behavioural measures of personality, including the observer's ability to stay focused and the way the observer interprets the behaviour. Additionally, some people behave differently when they know they are being observed.

The most common method of assessing personality is the **self-report questionnaire**. An individual responds to a series of questions, usually in an agree/disagree or true/false format. One of the more widely recognized questionnaires is the Minnesota Multiphasic Personality Inventory (MMPI), a comprehensive test assessing a variety of traits that can help diagnose several neurotic or psychotic disorders. Another self-report questionnaire, the NEO Personality Inventory, measures the Big Five traits. Self-report questionnaires also suffer from limited reliability: It is difficult for an individual to assess their own personality objectively. People often answer questions in terms of how they want to be seen rather than as they really are.

projective tests A measure of personality that relies on an individual's interpretation of an ambiguous or abstract image.

behavioural measures A personality assessment that examines behaviour in a controlled environment.

self-report questionnaire A personality assessment tool that analyzes an individual's responses to a series of questions.

Myers-Briggs Type Indicator (MBTI)® instrument A self-report questionnaire personality assessment tool.

xpixel/Shutterstock.com

Each individual responds in a way that reflects their unique personality.

The Myers-Briggs Type Indicator® Instrument

The **Myers-Briggs Type Indicator®** (or **MBTI®**) is an instrument designed to formally evaluate people, and provide descriptive profiles of their personality types, which can provide insights about their individual differences. The MBTI instrument has been used in career counselling, team building, conflict management, and understanding management styles.[54]

The MBTI® is built on research done by Carl Jung who proposed that the population was made up of two basic types—Extraverted types and Introverted types.[55] He then identified how these two basic types differ in their styles when gathering information and making decisions. Jung suggested that human similarities and differences could be understood by describing preferences: We prefer and therefore choose one way of doing things over another, but we are not exclusively one way or another. Rather, we have a *preference* for Extraversion or Introversion, just as we have a preference for right-handedness or left-handedness. Jung's type theory argues that no preferences are better than others. Differences are to be understood, celebrated, and appreciated.

THE PREFERENCES Through a series of 100 self-reported questions, the MBTI identifies an individual's

TABLE 3.2 TYPE THEORY PREFERENCES AND DESCRIPTIONS

Extraversion (E)	Sensing (S)	Thinking (T)	Judging (J)
Outgoing	Practical	Analytical	Structured
Publicly expressive	Specific	Clarity	Time oriented
Interacting	Feet on the ground	Head	Decisive
Speaks, then thinks	Details	Justice	Makes lists/uses them
Gregarious	Concrete	Rules	Organized
Introversion (I)	**Intuition (N)**	**Feeling (F)**	**Perceiving (P)**
Quiet	General	Subjective	Flexible
Reserved	Abstract	Harmony	Open ended
Concentrating	Head in the clouds	Heart	Exploring
Thinks, then speaks	Possibilities	Mercy	Makes lists/loses them
Reflective	Theoretical	Circumstance	Spontaneous

preferences in four areas of personality. The combination of these preferences makes up an individual's psychological type. Table 3.2 shows these preferences.

The **Extraversion/Introversion** (E/I) scale represents how one prefers to direct and receive energy. The Extraverted type (E) is energized by interaction with other people and prefers to focus their energy and attention outward. The Introverted type (I) is energized by time alone and focuses energy inward on thoughts and introspection. Extraverted types typically have a wide social network, whereas Introverted types have a more narrow range of relationships. As articulated by Jung, this preference has nothing to do with social skills or with self-confidence. Many introverts have excellent social skills but prefer the internal world of ideas, thoughts, and concepts. Jung's theory holds that the Extraversion/Introversion preference reflects the most important distinction between individual personalities. Almost 52 percent of English-speaking Canadians report as extroverts; however, approximately 62.5 percent of French Canadians are extroverts.[56]

The **Sensing/Intuition** (S/N) dimension describes an individual's preference in information collection. The Sensing type (S) prefers "real" information that is gathered directly through the five senses. The Intuitive type (N) prefers information coming from associations and prefers to focus on possibilities rather than on what actually exists.[57] Sensing types prefer specific answers to questions and can be frustrated by vague instructions. They like tasks and projects that yield tangible results, and would rather use established skills than learn new ones. Intuitive types like solving new problems and quickly grow impatient with routine details. They enjoy learning new skills more than actually using them. They tend to think about several things at once and may appear absentminded. They like figuring out how things work just for the fun of it. Of English-speaking Canadians, approximately 54.5 percent report a preference for Sensing; however, approximately 62.4 percent of French Canadians prefer to use their five senses for information gathering.[58]

The **Thinking/Feeling** (T/F) preference describes the way we prefer to make decisions and come to conclusions. The Thinking type (T) prefers to analyze situations objectively, and makes decisions in a logical, impartial fashion, whereas the Feeling type (F) prefers to consider morals and motives, and makes decisions in a personal, value-oriented way. Thinking types tend to analyze decisions, while Feeling types empathize. Thinking types try to be impersonal, and tend to show less emotion and are less comfortable with emotional expression,

Extraversion (E) A preference for interaction with other people.

Introversion (I) A preference for spending time alone.

Sensing (S) A preference for gathering information through the five senses.

Intuition (N) A preference for gathering information through associations and focusing on what "could be" rather than what actually is.

Thinking (T) A preference for making decisions in a logical, objective fashion.

Feeling (F) A preference for making decisions in a personal, value-oriented way.

IN ACTION

Who Says Introverts Can't Be Leaders?

Do you have to be an extravert to be a leader? Some of the most influential leaders in business and politics would disagree—they're introverts!

Introverted leaders may succeed because of their natural capacity for introspection and thoughtful communication. They spend a lot of time listening and are more open to others' ideas, collaborating with others before making important decisions. Rather than interacting with a great number of people, introverts form genuine, deep ties to a smaller network of people they can rely on.

It's important to remember that introversion means getting energy from time alone. It has nothing to do with social skills; in fact, many of the leaders mentioned above have great social skills.

ZUMA Press, Inc/Alamy Stock Photo

Marissa Mayer, CEO of Yahoo

KATHY WILLENS/POOL/EPA/Newscom

Warren Buffett, famous investor and philanthropist, CEO of Berkshire Hathaway

Justin Sullivan/Getty Images

Larry Page, CEO and cofounder of Google

Featureflash/Shutterstock.com

President Barack Obama

JStone/Shutterstock.com

Hillary Clinton, former Secretary of State

Frederic Legrand-COMEO/Shutterstock.com

Mark Zuckerberg, cofounder of Facebook

© CENGAGE LEARNING / SOURCE: S. Cole, "7 Famous Leaders Who Prove Introverts Can Be Wildly Successful," *Fast Company*, http://www.fastcompany.com/3032028/the-future-of-work/7-famous-leaders-who-prove-introverts-can-be-wildly-successful, accessed June 18, 2014.

preferring to put things into a logical, rather than emotional, framework. Feeling types base their decisions on how the outcome will affect the people involved. They are more comfortable with emotion in the workplace, and they enjoy pleasing people and receiving frequent praise and encouragement.

Thinking/Feeling type preference is the only one to show a consistent difference between genders, with males somewhat more likely to show a Thinking preference and females a Feeling preference. Of English-speaking males, 73.3 percent have a preference for Thinking, while English-speaking females have a 56.4 percent preference for Feeling. (French Canadians share approximately the same distribution by gender.)[59]

Judging (J) A preference for closure and completion in making decisions.

Perceiving (P) A preference for exploring many alternatives and maintaining flexibility.

The **Judging/Perceiving** (J/P) dichotomy reflects a person's approach to the outer world. The Judging types (J) prefer closure. They prefer to lead planned, organized lives and like making decisions. Judging types love getting things accomplished and delight in checking off completed tasks on their calendars. On the other hand, Perceiving types (P) prefer flexible and spontaneous lives and like to keep options open. Perceiving types generally adopt a wait-and-see attitude, collecting new information instead of drawing conclusions. Perceiving types are curious and welcome new information. They may start many projects without finishing them. Of English-speaking Canadians, 55.9 percent report a preference for Judging, while 53.7 of French-speaking Canadians report a preference for Perceiving.[60]

THE SIXTEEN TYPES These preferences combine to form 16 distinct types. Keep in mind that there are no "good" or "bad" types; each type is simply a descriptor, and each has its own strengths and weaknesses that influence preferred behaviours. For example, the ESTJ type has preferences for Extraversion, Sensing, Thinking, and Judging. ESTJs have a preference for interacting with others (E); see the world as it is (S); make decisions objectively (T); and like structure, schedules, and order (J). Combining these qualities makes them ideal managers.[61] ESTJs are dependable, practical, and conscious of the chain of command, seeing work as a series of goals to be reached by following rules and regulations. They may have little tolerance for disorganization and have a high need for control.

USES AND MISUSES OF MBTI The Myers-Briggs Type Indicator® instrument (MBTI®) is one of the world's most popular self-report questionnaire assessment tools, used by more than 88 percent of Fortune 500 companies in 115 countries around the world. It is estimated that two million people are assessed worldwide each year.[62] The Vancouver Organizing Committee for the 2010 Olympic Winter Games used the MBTI for developing team effectiveness.[63] The test is widely used by organizations for staff development workshops, team building exercises, communication skills development, leadership training, conflict management, in new student orientation sessions at some reputable universities, and even in educational and vocational counselling. By giving people an increased understanding of their behaviour and preferences, MBTI can help people increase their productivity, build relationships, and make life choices that suit their personal needs.

Many supporters value type theory for its simplicity and accuracy, but the use of personality tests in personnel selection is controversial. Personality tests are poor predictors of employee performance, accounting for only about 15 percent of the variation in employee achievement.[64] This may be partially due to the fact that most personality tests are self-reported, but it also underscores the importance of situational variables on performance. While employee personalities are important considerations, employees are more significantly influenced by an organization's culture, the work group, and the specific tasks assigned.

OB researchers have also strongly criticized the idea that personality can be categorized into types. Recall from our earlier discussion that personality is normally distributed across trait dimensions, meaning that the majority of people score somewhere near average, and few individuals score at one extreme or another. Of the 25 MBTI questions designed to elicit E/I preference, one individual may respond to 13 questions as an extrovert, and 12 as an introvert. Another individual may respond to 22 questions as an extrovert and only 3 questions as an introvert. Both of these individuals would be categorized as extroverts, even though one is clearly more extroverted than the other. If the first person re-wrote the test, they may choose to answer just one question differently, and come away with 12 extrovert responses, and 13 introvert responses, and they would then be categorized as an introvert. Because people typically score near the average of a given trait dimension, many individuals find that if they re-take the MBTI test, they receive a different "type" classification.[65]

Information from the MBTI instrument can also be misused in organizational settings.[66] Through lack of understanding, or by subconscious attribution, supervisors may pigeonhole employees by their "type," restricting the opportunities extended to some employees ("They won't want to work on this new project because they are Sensing") or forcing them down a certain career trajectory that they may not want ("You need to go into sales because you're an Extrovert.") Other inappropriate uses include labelling coworkers, claiming results as a convenient excuse not to work with someone, and avoiding responsibility for one's shortcomings.

> The question is not what you look at, but what you see.
> —Henry David Thoreau

3-4 SOCIAL PERCEPTION

Perception is another psychological process that creates individual differences. Our perception is the vehicle through which we come to understand ourselves and our world. No two people see the world in the exact same way, because "there is no truth. There is only perception."[67] When it comes to interacting with other people, **social perception** is the process of interpreting information about another person (or a group) and

social perception The process of interpreting information about another person.

making inferences about them as individuals. In other words, it's how we "make sense" of other people.

People are naturally motivated to try to understand and predict the behaviour of those around them. We attempt this understanding through the four components of social perception: observation, attribution, integration, and confirmation.

Observation

Observation includes the raw data that can be collected in a situation and includes information about people, behaviours, and situations.[68] There are three components that commonly affect what we observe about others: characteristics of ourselves, as perceivers; characteristics of the target person; and characteristics of the situation in which the interaction takes place. Figure 3.2 models the observational component of social perception.

CHARACTERISTICS OF THE PERCEIVER Several characteristics of the perceiver can affect social perception. This is how two individuals who interact with a third party can come away from the interaction with completely different perceptions about that other individual. One such characteristic is the perceiver's *past experiences*. Our past experiences shape our expectations, and this can colour our expectations of others. If every experience an individual has with cats has led to them being scratched, they may have a negative view of all cats. This is a common basis for racism and sexism.

The perceiver's *values and attitudes* also affect social perception. If someone believes that pitbulls are vicious animals, ready to attack innocent bystanders without provocation, then they are likely to have a negative attitude toward anyone they see walking a dog that resembles a pitbull. This attitude will likely colour their perception of the individual. In a similar fashion, *mood* can have a strong influence on the way we perceive someone.[69] We think differently when we are happy than when we are sad, or frustrated, or embarrassed. When in a positive mood, we form more positive impressions of others. When in a negative mood, we tend to evaluate others unfavourably. Another factor that can affect social perception is the perceiver's *self-concept*. An individual with a positive self-concept tends to notice positive attributes in another person. In contrast, a negative self-concept can lead a perceiver to pick out negative traits in another person.

FIGURE 3.2 A MODEL FOR SOCIAL PERCEPTION

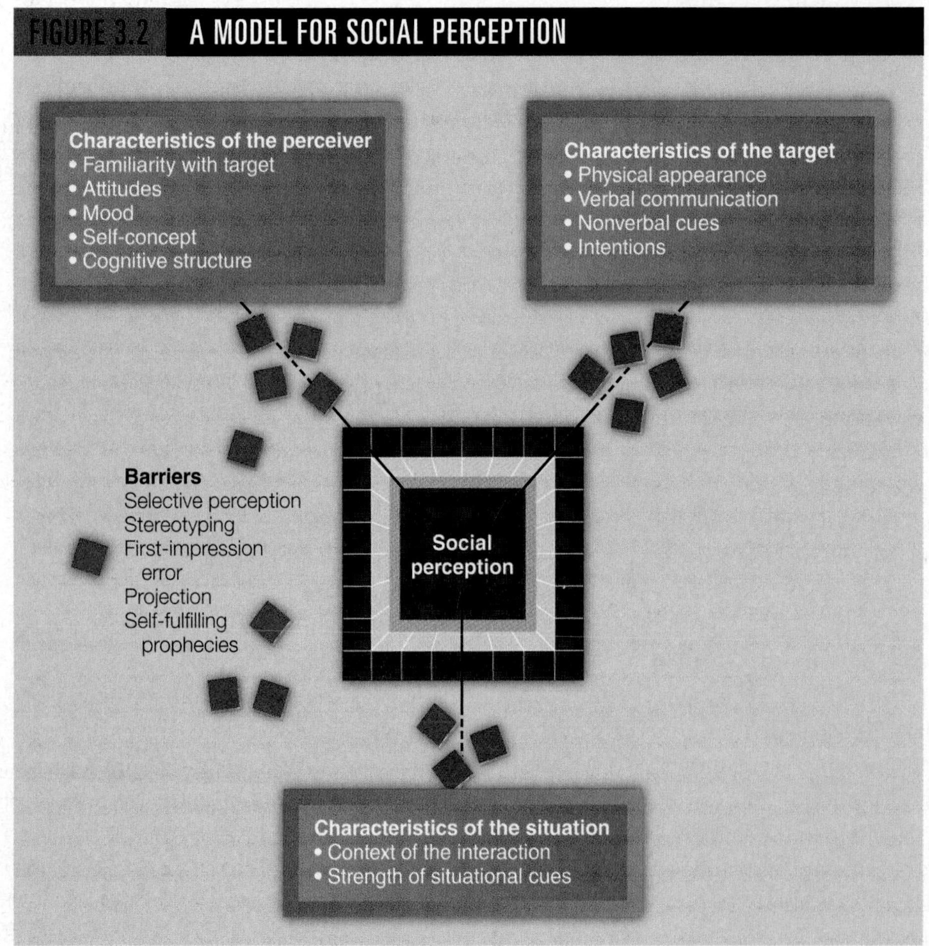

Finally, a *cognitive structure* is an individual's pattern of thinking. Cognitive structures affect social perception because they affect what we notice and remember about others. Some people tend to perceive physical traits, such as height, weight, and appearance, more readily ("I never forget a face"). Others focus on central traits, or personality dispositions.

CHARACTERISTICS OF THE TARGET As social beings, humans are very good at observing physical traits in others (even if it occurs subconsciously), and most people are able to accurately interpret emotions and attitudes from nonverbal behaviours such as body language, tone of voice, and facial

Jonathan Knowles/Stone/Getty Images

Several characteristics of the perceiver can affect social perception.

expressions. Characteristics of the target (the person being perceived) understandably influence social perception. *Physical appearance* plays a large role in our perception of others. The perceiver will notice physical features such as height, weight, estimated age, race, and gender. Physical attractiveness often colours our entire impression of another person. Interviewers rate attractive candidates more favourably and award them higher starting salaries.[70] Whether male or female, attractive people are judged more positively in terms of their occupational, academic, and interpersonal competence.[71]

Verbal communication affects our perception of a target: We listen to the topics they discuss, their voice tone, and their accent and make judgments based on this input. Similarly, *nonverbal communication* conveys a great deal of information about the target. Eye contact, facial expressions, body movements, and posture all are deciphered by the perceiver in an attempt to form an impression of the target.

The perceived *intentions* of the target also affect perception. If someone stops you on the street, your original perception may be that they are trying to sell you something, and your initial reaction may be negative; however, if that person says "you dropped your wallet" and gives it back to you, your perception of them is instantly changed.

Perceivers tend to notice characteristics that contrast with the norm, those that are intense, new, or unusual.[72] A loud person, one who dresses outlandishly, a very tall person, or a hyperactive child will be noticed because they stand out and draw attention to themselves. Novel individuals, like newcomers or minorities, also attract attention.

CHARACTERISTICS OF THE SITUATION The situation in which the interaction between the perceiver and the target takes place also influences perception. The physical context, as well as the *social context* of the interaction, is a major influence. Meeting a professor in their office for a scheduled appointment affects your impression of the subsequent interaction differently than a chance meeting in a local restaurant would.[73]

The *strength of situational cues* also affects social perception. As we discussed earlier in the chapter, some situations overwhelm the effects of individual personalities because they exert clear pressure on all to act in a specific way. In these situations, we assume that the individual's behaviour is explained by the situation, and not by the individual's disposition. This is the **discounting principle** in social perception.[74] For example, if you encountered an automobile salesperson who had a warm and personable manner, asked about your work and hobbies, and seemed genuinely interested in your taste in cars, you probably wouldn't assume that this behaviour reflects their true personality. You would reason that this person is trying to sell you a car, and they probably treat all customers in this manner.

Attribution

After observing someone, their behaviours, and situational contexts, individuals use the information collected to attempt to explain and understand others' behavior. This is known as *attribution.* Human beings are innately curious. We want to know *why* people behave the way they do. We also seek to understand and explain our own behaviour. **Attribution theory** explains how we pinpoint the causes of our own behaviour and that of other people.[75]

INTERNAL AND EXTERNAL ATTRIBUTIONS When seeking to assign the cause of behaviour, individuals may attribute the behaviour to internal characteristics (something within the individual's control) or an external (or situational) source (something outside the individual's control). If an individual performs well on an exam, they might say that it was because they are smart or because they studied hard; this internal attribution credits ability or effort. Alternatively, they might make an external attribution for their performance by saying the test was easy or that they had good luck.

discounting principle The assumption that an individual's behaviour is accounted for by situational factors, not personality.

attribution theory The process used by individuals to explain the causes of their own behaviour and that of others.

Attribution patterns differ among individuals,[76] and attribution theory has important implications for behaviour because the way individuals explain their own behaviour affects their motivation, while the way an individual explains someone else's behaviour affects their perception of that person. While some individuals attribute their failures to lack of effort (which motivates them to try harder next time), others attribute their failures to lack of ability, and they may develop feelings of incompetence (or even depression) as a result.[77] Women managers are less likely to attribute their success to their own ability. This may be because they are adhering to social norms that compel women to be modest or because they believe that success has more do to with hard work than ability.[78]

KELLEY'S COVARIATION MODEL (AN ATTRIBUTION THEORY) According to attribution theory, people make attributions (inferences) concerning others' behaviour and performance,[79] but these attributions are not always accurate. In organizations, attribution theory impacts not only our perception of others, but also our assessments of their performance and attitudes. Supervisors and employees who share perceptions and attitudes tend to evaluate each other highly.[80] Supervisors and employees who do not share perceptions and attitudes are more likely to blame each other for performance problems. Kelley's covariation model is the best-known attribution theory and was developed to assess whether an action should be attributed to an individual characteristic (internal attribution), or an environmental factor (external attribution). The term *covariation* simply means that a person has multiple observations and can see how behaviours are correlated with their causes.

Kelley proposed that individuals make attributions based on three kinds of "evidence"[81]: **Consensus** is the extent to which peers in the same situation behave the same way. For instance, in one peer has a glass of wine with lunch, but the other does not, the consensus is low. If both have wine, consensus is high. **Distinctiveness** is the degree to which the person behaves the same way in similar situations (or how novel is the behaviour?) For instance, if an individual has wine with lunch only when meeting with friends, the distinctiveness is high (it is a novel situation). If they have wine often, at lunch and dinner, the distinctiveness is low (it is a common occurrence). **Consistency** refers to the frequency of a particular behaviour over time. For instance, if an individual always orders wine when out for lunch with friends, the behaviour is consistent. If the wine at lunch was to celebrate an occasion, and is not a typical event, then consistency is low.

We form attributions based on whether these cues are low or high. Figure 3.3 shows how the combination of these cues fosters internal or external attributions. Suppose you have received several complaints from customers regarding one of your customer service representatives, John. You have not received complaints about your other service representatives (low consensus). Reviewing John's records, you find that he also received customer complaints during his previous job as a sales clerk (low distinctiveness). The complaints have been coming in steadily for three months (high consistency). In this case, you would most likely make an internal attribution and conclude that the complaints must stem from John's behaviour. The combination of low consensus, low distinctiveness, and high consistency suggests internal attributions.

Other combinations of these cues, however, produce external attributions. High consensus, high distinctiveness, and low consistency, for example, produce external

FIGURE 3.3 KELLEY'S ATTRIBUTION MODEL

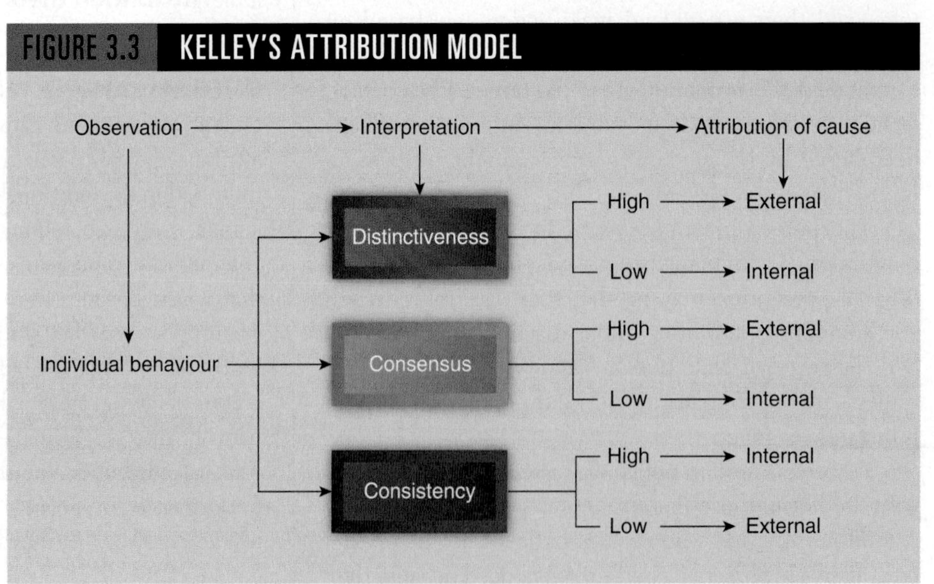

consensus An informational cue indicating the extent to which peers in the same situation behave in a similar fashion.

distinctiveness An informational cue indicating the degree to which an individual behaves the same way in other situations.

consistency An informational cue indicating the frequency of behaviour over time.

attributions. Suppose one of your employees, Maya is performing poorly on collecting overdue accounts. You find that the behaviour is widespread within your work team (high consensus) and that Maya is performing poorly only on this aspect of the job (high distinctiveness), and that most of the time she handles this aspect of the job well (low consistency). You will probably decide that something about the work situation caused the poor performance.

Stupidity and unconscious bias often work more damage than venality.

—Bertrand Russel

Integration and Confirmation

Integration is the process of forming impressions about others.[82] Once we have observed the person, their behaviours, and the situational context, and have attributed those behaviours to internal or external factors, we begin to form automatic impressions of that individual.[83] These impressions are often subconscious.[84] Once impressions are made, *confirmation* describes the ongoing efforts to integrate new information into the impression that we have already made.

3-5 BIAS AND BARRIERS TO SOCIAL PERCEPTION

Humans integrate their observations and attributions about others' behaviour very quickly. All of our opinions and beliefs about others are processed through what is called our **perceptual screen**, or our frame of reference, which is the psychological process that evaluates all input that we receive. On average, it takes people just 30 seconds to make an assessment about someone's personality and intelligence,[85] and significantly less time (only 1/10th of a second!) to make inferences about attractiveness, likeability, trustworthiness, and competence.[86] In order to process large amounts of information very (very!) quickly, our perceptual screens often use information-processing "rules of thumb," or mental shortcuts called **heuristics**. These heuristics often result in **cognitive biases**, which are mistakes in reasoning, evaluating, and remembering as a result of holding on to one's preferences and beliefs, sometimes even in light of contrary information. These biases create barriers, which prevent us from perceiving others accurately. People are often not aware of their bias, which is known as an **implicit bias**, and these biases influence our beliefs and opinions without our realizing.

Individuals like to believe that they are good judges of character, and that the decisions they make about the world are the result of objective and logical thinking, where all information is observed and properly evaluated. But researchers have catalogued and researched *hundreds* of cognitive biases that affect *all* aspects of our perception. Some of the more common cognitive biases in each component of social perception will be discussed, but remember, when making judgements about others, "there is no reality. There is only perception."

Biases in Observation

Selective perception is a cognitive bias where individuals have a tendency to prefer information that supports their viewpoints and often ignore or reject information that threatens those viewpoints. Information that is difficult or unpleasant to believe is automatically filtered and rejected. Proponents of homeopathic treatment for illness rely on anecdotal reports of treatment and reject scientific studies proving their ineffectiveness, often reacting angrily when others insist that homeopathy is chicanery.

Stereotypes are another bias that affect what we observe by affecting what we expect to observe. A **stereotype** is generalization about a group of people. Stereotypes reduce information about other people to a workable level, so that it can be compiled efficiently. Stereotypes become even stronger when they are shared with and validated by others.[87] Not all stereotypes are negative: Women are stereotypically seen as more warm and nurturing, Asians are often stereotyped as being better at math. Even when positive, however, inaccurate stereotypes can be harmful because they generate false impressions that may never be tested or changed.[88]

perceptual screen The psychological process that evaluates all input.

heuristic Mental shortcuts, or information-processing "rules of thumb" to reduce information to manageable levels.

cognitive bias Mistakes in reasoning, evaluating, and remembering as a result of holding on to one's preferences and beliefs.

implicit bias Biases that are subconscious or unrecognized.

selective perception The process of selecting information that supports one's viewpoints while discounting information that threatens those views.

stereotype A generalization about a group of people.

FIGURE 3.4 COGNITIVE BIAS CODEX

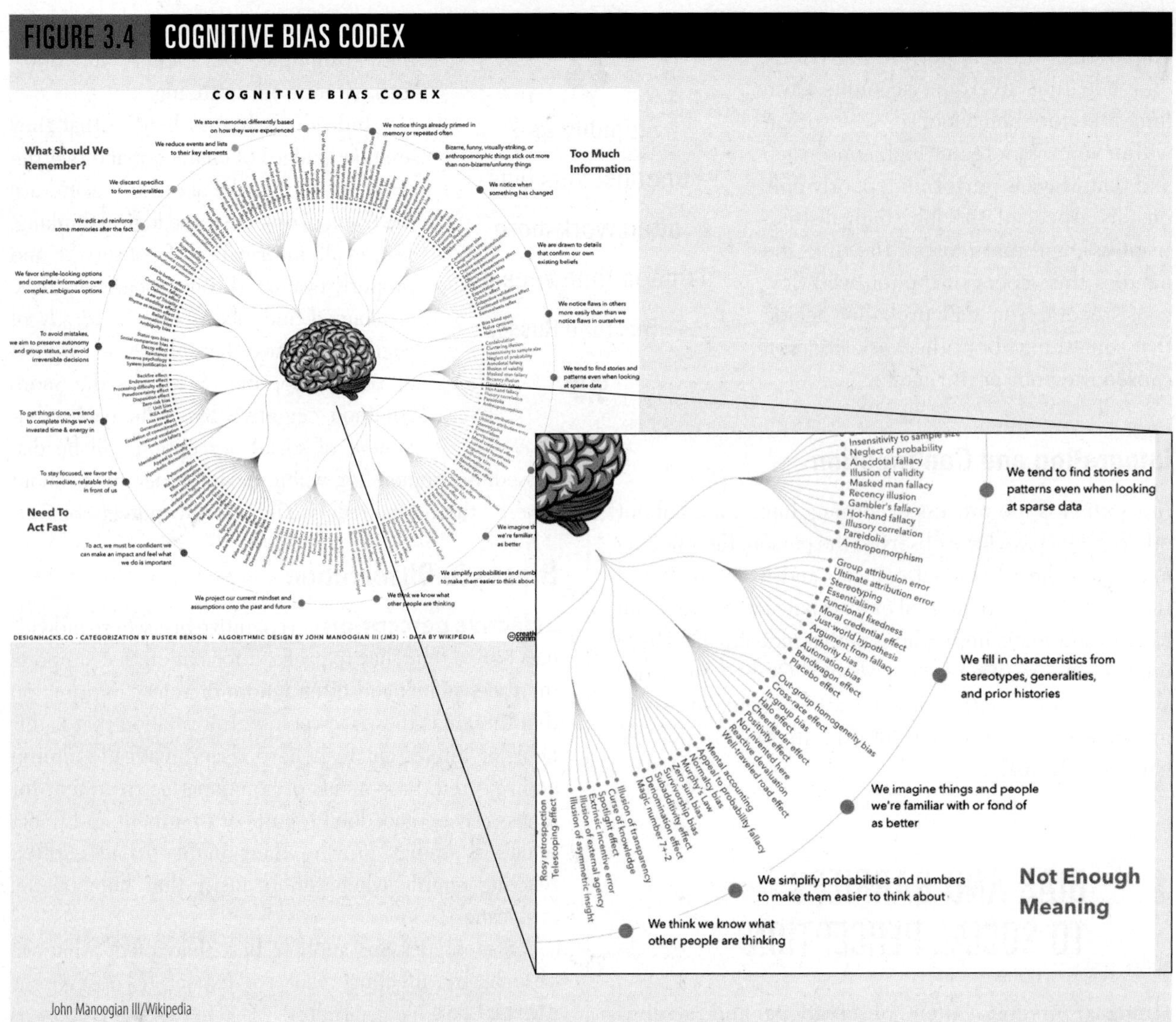

John Manoogian III/Wikipedia

IN ACTION

Is "Bossy" a Negative Stereotype for Women?

Strong, powerful women often get stereotyped as bossy, and it's seldom a compliment. Strong, assertive men, in contrast, are referred to as powerful or decisive. Sheryl Sandberg, COO of Facebook, teamed with former Secretary of State Condoleezza Rice and Girl Scouts' CEO Anna Maria Chavez to launch "Ban Bossy" (www.banbossy.com) to combat the stereotype by banning the word. The idea is that girls often don't want to lead because they don't want to be disliked and called bossy—meaning too aggressive, ambitious, and political and overstepping bounds. Many women joined the campaign, including Beyoncé, who said in her TV ad for the campaign, "I'm not bossy. I'm the boss."

The campaign has generated controversy, with some women arguing that rather than banning the "bossy" word, women should reclaim it by not worrying about being labelled as such, and by being confidently assertive.

All parties would probably agree that the stereotype exists. The key for both sexes lies in being assertive and strong while still being respectful. Neither sex fares well as leaders when seen as abrasive.

SOURCES: A. Fisher, "How Women Can Respond to That Other B-Word: Bossy," *Fortune*, http://fortune.com/2014/04/24/how-women-can-respond-to-that-other-b-word-bossy/, accessed April 20, 2014; J. Humphrey, "The End of Bitchy: Addressing Stereotypes of Women at Work," *Fast Company*, http://www.fastcompany.com/3041942/strong-female-lead/the-end-of-bitchy-addressing-stereotypes-of-women-at-work, accessed June 2, 2018.

Biases in Attribution

The attribution process is most commonly affected by two errors: the fundamental attribution error and the self-serving bias. People are more likely to attribute *others'* behaviours to dispositional (internal) causes while ignoring potential situational causes. This is known as the **fundamental attribution error**.[89] This means that we tend to blame people for their problems, even when the situation is the actual culprit, and we may credit people for their successes even when they did nothing to truly deserve it. For example, if you see someone fall on the stairs ahead of you, you are likely to assume that the person is clumsy or was not watching carefully (an internal attribution), whereas when the same thing happens to you, you may look for something on the stair that tripped you like a puddle or loose tread (an external attribution). Looking for external reasons for others' behaviours is complex and difficult because of limited information, so it is much faster and easier to assume internal causation.

However, when evaluating one's *own* behaviours, individuals tend to make internal attributions for their own successes and external attributions for their own failures.[90] This is known as **self-serving bias**. In other words, when we succeed, we take credit for it; when we fail, we blame the situation.

There are cultural differences in these two attribution errors. In fatalistic cultures, such as India's, people tend to believe that fate is responsible for much that happens. People in such cultures tend to emphasize external causes of behaviour.[91] In China, people are taught that hard work is the route to accomplishment. When faced with either a success or a failure, Chinese individuals first introspect about whether they tried hard enough or whether their attitude was correct. In analyzing a cause, they first look to their own effort.[92]

Projection, also known as the false-consensus effect, is the misperception of the commonness of our own beliefs, values, and behaviours that leads us to overestimate the number of others who share them. We assume that others are similar to us, and that our own values and beliefs are appropriate. People who are different are viewed as unusual and even deviant. Projection occurs most often when you surround yourself with others similar to you.[93]

Biases in Integration and Confirmation

First impressions are lasting impressions, so the saying goes. We tend to remember what we perceive first about a person, and sometimes we are quite reluctant to change our initial impressions.[94] **First-impression error** occurs when we observe a very brief bit of a person's behaviour in our first encounter and infer that this behaviour reflects what the person is really like. First-impression errors are especially common in interviews, given that individuals are specifically attempting to create a positive first impression. These impressions, however, may be the basis for long-term employment relationships. Something seemingly as unimportant as a handshake can leave a lasting impression. Despite all the relevant information that emerges in an interview following the initial handshake, the firmness of that handshake is significantly related to interview ratings.[95]

The **halo effect** occurs when one aspect of a person is viewed positively, resulting in all aspects of that person being assumed positive. Physical attractiveness produces a strong halo effect on perceived personality characteristics. Attractive individuals are often assumed to be successful, warm, kind, sensitive, poised, sociable, outgoing, and intelligent. Research shows that we treat attractive people better than unattractive people, giving them more attention, rewards, cooperation, and help,[96] and this is true of not only attractive strangers but also people with whom we are familiar. Is it a surprise that attractive people are healthier, more confident, and have better social skills?[97] The opposite effect is known as the horn effect (as in devil's horns); when an observer dislikes one aspect of an individual, they will tend to view all aspects of that individual more negatively.

The **recency effect** is the opposite of a first impression error in that it describes the tendency to weigh recent events more heavily than earlier events. Many employees take advantage of the recency effect by increasing their effort right before their annual appraisal, guessing, correctly, that the supervisor is more likely to be influenced by recent performance than errors made months ago.

Another perceptual bias is known as the **contrast effect**, which is the tendency to diminish or enhance the measure of one target through comparison with

fundamental attribution error The tendency to make attributions to internal causes when focusing on someone else's behaviour.

self-serving bias The tendency to attribute one's own successes to internal causes and one's failures to external causes.

projection Overestimating the number of people who share our own beliefs, values, and behaviours.

first-impression error The tendency to form lasting opinions about an individual based on initial perceptions.

halo effect When one aspect of a person is viewed positively, resulting in all aspects of that person being assumed positive.

recency effect The tendency to weigh recent events more than earlier events.

contrast effect The tendency to diminish or enhance the measure of one target through comparison with another recently observed target.

another recently observed target. This occurs because humans typically use comparisons to place things and people in context. Someone who is 6'1" standing beside someone who is 7'0" would be seen as short, but the same person, beside someone who is 5'4" would be seen as tall.

Self-fulfilling prophecies (also called the Pygmalion effect) are another way that our biases interfere with social perception. Sometimes our expectations affect the way we interact with others such that we get what we expect. Early studies of self-fulfilling prophecy were conducted in elementary school classrooms. Teachers were given bogus information that some of their pupils had high intellectual potential. These pupils were chosen randomly; there were really no differences among the students. Eight months later, the "gifted" pupils scored significantly higher on an IQ test. The teachers' expectations had elicited growth from these students, and the teachers had given them tougher assignments and more feedback on their performance.[98]

"Faking Good" Is Our Default Mode of Impression Management

Scientists have examined the brains of people engaged in either "faking good" (giving the best impression) or "faking bad" (giving an undesirable impression) using sophisticated brain imaging technology. Faking bad activates distinct regions of the brain and takes longer, whereas faking good happens more quickly and doesn't show as much patterned brain activity. This indicates that faking good may be so well practised that it's the default form of impression management.

SOURCE: T. F. D. Farrow, J. Burgess, I. D. Wilkinson, and M. D. Hunter, "Neural Correlates of Self-Deception and Impression Management," *Neuropsychologia* 67 (2015): 159–174.

IMPRESSION MANAGEMENT

Most people want to make favourable impressions on others. This is particularly true in organizations where individuals compete for jobs, favourable performance evaluations, and salary increases. The process by which individuals try to influence the impressions others have of them is called **impression management**.[99] Though impression management often has negative connotations, individuals engage in impression management in most social interactions. People use impression management to influence others based on how they want to be perceived: A person's *authentic persona* reflects the way they actually see themselves, and impression management in this style is used with true friends and family; the *ideal persona* is a reflection of how the individual wishes they were, and impression management in this style may be used on job interviews, and early in relationships in order to make a good impression; and the *tactical persona* is typically used to achieve a certain goal by manipulating others. Impression management by the tactical persona is more scheming, disingenuous, and more obviously seen as false. Impression management is sometimes referred to as self-presentation.

self-fulfilling prophecy
The situation in which our expectations about people affect our interaction with them in such a way that our expectations are fulfilled.

impression management
The process by which individuals try to control the impressions others have of them.

There are several methods of impression management, including self-disclosure, managing appearances, ingratiation, aligning actions, and altercasting. *Self-disclosure* involves conveying information about oneself and one's achievements to establish one's identity. People are typically happy to share certain details about themselves with others in order to establish themselves as being "worthy" of knowing. Details about one's work or other achievements are often conveyed to others, while details about accidents or mistakes are typically not conveyed.

Managing appearances involves controlling one's outward appearance by dressing a certain way, or behaving like others within the group in order to fit in. This is a style of impression management that virtually everyone engages in. Students keeping up with fashion trends are managing appearances, and business people who develop firm handshakes are also managing appearances.

Ingratiation is a method of impression management that is often seen as manipulative. Ingratiation means to make oneself more likeable to one's target, often by conforming to the expectations or opinions of that target. Saying that you love foreign films, when you really don't, because your target expressed an interest is ingratiating, as is using excessive praise or flattery. Ingratiation can also involve doing favours for someone, like bringing them coffee and donuts.

Aligning actions occurs when an individual attempts to present questionable behaviours in a more favourable light. Individuals who are attempting to align actions may laugh off an offensive comment as a joke, or may use excuses for why their behaviour is the way it is; for instance, missing a deadline would be blamed on an illness, rather than as a result of poor time management.

Finally, *altercasting* consists of imposing a different (alter) identity, and the corresponding set of expectations on to another. In altercasting, the impression manager casts the other person in a role, before making a request. Altercasting can be obvious "You're such a great writer, and you're always so helpful; would you mind editing my paper?" or it can be more subtle, such as when someone acts needy, other people tend to become more giving. Altercasting is an effective persuasion tool, but if not used effectively, altercasting can be seen as manipulative and deceptive.[100]

Research results indicate that job candidates who engage in impression management techniques perform better in interviews, are more likely to be hired, and are rated more favourably in performance appraisals than those who do not.[101] However, research also shows that there is no link between the use of those impression management techniques and actual performance on the job.[102]

STUDY TOOLS 3

IN THE BOOK YOU CAN ...

- ☐ Rip out the **Chapter Review card** at the end of the book to review Key Concepts and Key Terms.
- ☐ Take a What about You? Quiz related to material in the chapter.
- ☐ Read additional cases in the Mini Case and Shopify Running Case sections.

ONLINE YOU CAN ... NELSON.COM/STUDENT

- ☐ Take a What about You? Quiz related to material in the chapter.
- ☐ Test your understanding with a quick Multiple-Choice Pre-Test quiz.
- ☐ Read the eBook, which includes discussion points for questions posed in the Cases.
- ☐ Watch Videos related to chapter content.
- ☐ Use the available Flashcards and Matching Quizzes to test your understanding of key terms and concepts.
- ☐ See how much you've learned by taking a Post-Test.

WHAT ABOUT YOU?

Are You a High or Low Self-Monitor?

For the following items, circle T (true) if the statement is characteristic of your behaviour. Circle F (false) if the statement does not reflect your behaviour.

1. I find it hard to imitate the behaviour of other people. T F
2. At parties and social gatherings, I do not attempt to do or say things that others will like. T F
3. I can argue only for ideas that I already believe. T F
4. I can make impromptu speeches even on topics about which I have almost no information. T F
5. I guess I put on a show to impress or entertain others. T F
6. I would probably make a good actor. T F
7. In a group of people, I am rarely the centre of attention. T F
8. In different situations and with different people, I often act like very different persons. T F
9. I am not particularly good at making other people like me. T F
10. I am not always the person I appear to be. T F
11. I would not change my opinions (or the way I do things) in order to please others or win their favour. T F
12. I have considered being an entertainer. T F
13. I have never been good at games like charades or at improvisational acting. T F
14. I have trouble changing my behaviour to suit different people and different situations. T F
15. At a party, I let others keep the jokes and stories going. T F
16. I feel a bit awkward in company and do not show up quite as well as I should. T F
17. I can look anyone in the eye and tell a lie with a straight face (if it is for a good cause). T F

18. I may deceive people by being friendly when I really dislike them. T F

Scoring

To score this questionnaire, give yourself 1 point for each of the following items that you answered T (true): 4, 5, 6, 8, 10, 12, 17, and 18. Now give yourself 1 point for each of the following items that you answered F (false): 1, 2, 3, 7, 9, 11, 13, 14, 15, and 16. Add both subtotals to find your overall score. If you scored 11 or above, you are probably a *high self-monitor.* If you scored 10 or under, you are probably a *low self-monitor.*

SOURCE: From *Public Appearances, Private Realities: The Psychology of Self-Monitoring* by M. Snyder. Used with permission by M. Snyder.

MINI CASE

Race Problems in Canada

Most Canadians think that our country is more racially sensitive and inclusive than that of the Unites States. But some academics and journalists argue that Canada's race problem is far worse than that of the United States; it's just less visible.

Canada's Aboriginal populations include First Nations, Inuit, and Métis peoples, and account for almost 1.5 million Canadians, almost 50 percent of whom are under the age of 18. When comparing Aboriginal statistics in Canada to African-American statistics in the United States, a disturbing pattern becomes immediately apparent: In almost every category, Canada's Aboriginal populations suffer more adversity than the African American population in the United States. Unemployment rates are significantly higher; median income is lower; homicide rates are significantly higher; infant mortality rates are significantly higher; life expectancy is lower; high school dropout rates are significantly higher.

Despite comprising just over 4 percent of Canada's total population, more than 23 percent of the inmate populations in federal institutions are Aboriginal. The prime minister convened an inquiry into missing Aboriginal women to examine the systemic causes of all forms of violence against Indigenous women and girls because Aboriginal women in Canada are five times more likely to be murdered than non-Aboriginals. The National Inquiry into Missing and Murdered Indigenous Women and Girls explains, "We are exposing hard truths about the devastating impacts of colonization, racism and sexism—aspects of Canada that many Canadians are reluctant to accept."

But when Canadians are asked for their views on Aboriginal issues, many reply with derisive condemnations about governance problems on the reserves. They point to examples of Band administrators who blatantly defraud their own people, or they angrily reference tax exemptions and other financial aid programs that Aboriginal people are able to claim. Still others point to the perception of apathy among the Aboriginal people themselves, who appear unwilling to make the drastic changes needed to overhaul their whole system of governance.

Almost 50 percent of First Nations members live on remote reserves, nowhere near urban centres. In the Greater Toronto Area, not even 1 percent of the population comprises Aboriginal people, but the province of Manitoba reports 17 percent Aboriginal populations. In 2014, Winnipeg recorded the highest proportion of racist tweets of Canadian cities. In Manitoba and Saskatchewan, 1 in 3 residents believes that "racial stereotypes are accurate" and 52 percent of residents agree that Aboriginal economic problems are "mainly their fault" (only 36 percent of all Canadians feel this way.)

Robert Falcon-Ouellette is trying to change perceptions. Falcon-Ouellette is of Cree heritage, and is the director of the University of Manitoba's Aboriginal focus programs. He has his Ph.D. and two masters' degrees, and served in Canada's armed forces for 18 years. But when Falcon-Ouellette ran for mayor of Winnipeg in 2014, citizens wouldn't even shake his hand. He was told, "You Indians are the problem with the city. You're all lazy. You're drunks. The social problems we have in the city are all related to you." But Falcon-Ouellette persevered. In 2015 he was elected by a landslide to represent his Winnipeg riding in the Canadian House of Commons.

Apply Your Understanding

1. How could it be possible for most Canadians to believe that there is no race problem in Canada, even when confronted with the appalling statistics described in this case?
2. How can Robert Falcon-Ouellette use the integration and confirmation aspects of social perception to change people's views on Aboriginal people?
3. How can Robert Falcon-Ouellette use the techniques of impression management to his benefit?

RUNNING CASE SHOPIFY

BUILDING THE COMPANY

Tobias Lütke is an introvert. Though he manages an organization of more than 600,000 merchants, whose gross merchandise volume exceeded $55 billion in 2017, Lütke prefers to stay out of the spotlight. Though he owns a Tesla, he typically rides his bike to work, and he insists that employees call him Tobi. After meeting the successful entrepreneur, many describe him as unassuming and humble.

As a child growing up in Germany, Lütke was given a computer when he was just six years old. By the time he was 12, he was writing code and creating new games. He would even modify the computer's hardware, get new parts, and instal them himself. Lütke would do the minimum necessary to get through school in order to spend as much time as possible on the computer, and his parents grew so concerned with his obsession that they feared Lütke might have learning disabilities. After Grade 10, Lütke entered an apprenticeship program, but didn't appreciate that the company made him program in Java, a computer language that Lütke felt was too restrictive.

When Lütke decided that he wanted to sell snowboards, he couldn't find an e-commerce platform that met with his approval, so he set about designing one of his own. Even as he was selling snowboards, he realized that the platform he had built had the potential to help others who were trying to gain a foothold in the restrictive e-commerce market. Lütke likes to talk about how lucky he was when he began creating Shopify because, as a new CEO: "I think I was bad at everything. A hundred percent of everything."

But Lütke persevered, and as the company grew, he put the same amount of effort into finding his team as he did into developing his product. Although investors suggested he move to Silicon Valley, he remained in Ottawa, explaining that Canadians were the smartest people he'd met anywhere in the world. Lütke focused on developing a culture-driven organization to ensure that employees stayed happy and engaged, and one of Shopify's keys for maintaining that culture is that Lütke adamantly rejects the use of "personas" in the workplace, saying "I have serious, serious problems with personas [and] with unauthentic individuals."

Shopify employees acknowledge that Lütke is very difficult to work for. His expectations are very high, and his feedback is brutally honest and direct. Despite all this, Lütke is very good at reading people and getting the most out of them. He's even working on his feedback skills, if only because upsetting people makes things "less efficient."

SOURCE: Trevor Cole, Our CEO of the Year You Probably Haven't Heard of," *ROB*, November 27, 2014, accessed from https://www.theglobeandmail.com/report-on-business/rob-magazine/meet-our-ceo-of-the-year/article21734931, September 28, 2018.

Apply Your Understanding

1. Briefly assess Lütke's personality using the Big Five model.
2. How does Tobias Lütke rate on self-monitoring?
3. Would you say that Lütke has an internal or an external locus of control?

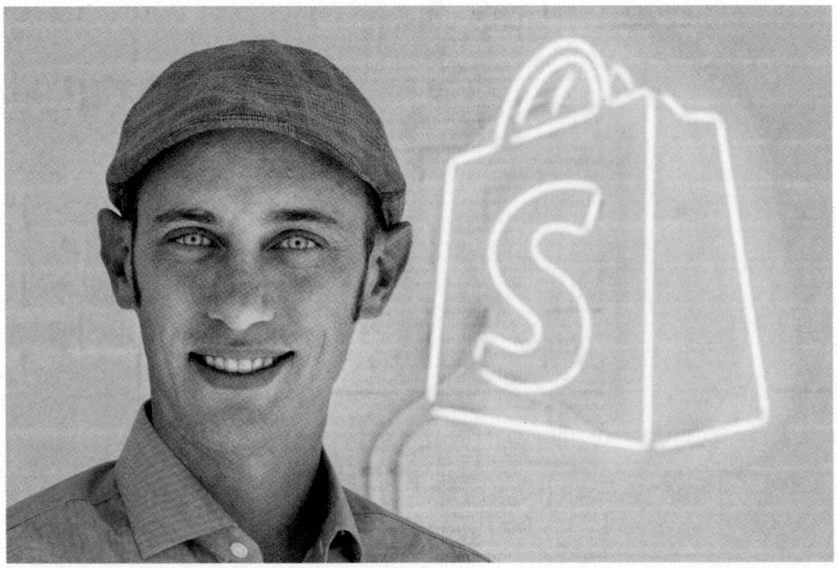

THE CANADIAN PRESS/Paul Chiasson

4 Emotions, Attitudes, and Ethics

LEARNING OUTCOMES

After reading this chapter, you should be able to do the following:

4-1 Discuss the definition and importance of emotions.

4-2 Explain the ABC model of an attitude.

4-3 Describe how attitudes are formed.

4-4 Identify the sources and consequences of work attitudes.

4-5 Describe how characteristics of the source, target, and message affect persuasion.

4-6 Describe the consequences of individual and organizational ethical behaviour.

4-7 Identify the factors that affect ethical behaviour.

See the end of this chapter for a list of available Study Tools, a "What about You?" Quiz, Mini Case, and the Shopify Running Case.

In continuing our examination of individual differences, this chapter examines the effects of emotion and attitudes on behaviour. How attitudes are formed, and how they are changed can have significant impacts on what people believe and what they do, and this is especially important when we consider how our attitudes impact ethical behaviours.

4-1 EMOTIONS

Emotions are instinctive mental states resulting from one's circumstances or mood. Emotions are states of feeling (as opposed to reasoning) typically directed at a specific object or person, and include feelings (fear, joy, anger), physiological changes (increased heart rate, dilated pupils), and the inclination to act.[1] Emotions are short-lived reactions to an event, can range from weak to intense, and they significantly affect thoughts and behaviours. Individuals differ in their capacity to experience both positive emotions (e.g., happiness, pride) and negative emotions (e.g., anger, fear, guilt).[2]

Your intellect may be confused, but your emotions will never lie to you.

—Robert Ebert

Emotions have the ability to affect memory, attention, and reasoning: Consider that experiences throughout one's lifetime are often remembered due to their associated emotional context, whether it be joy and pleasure, or sorrow and pain. Emotional stimuli can affect attention, and this is especially true for fear-based stimuli: It's not a coincidence that the person who is afraid of spiders is the one who notices the spider in a corner of the room.[3] Emotion also has a powerful influence over reason, and contributes to belief formation. Emotional instability is a root cause of human unhappiness, and is a common denominator in mental disorders.[4]

Emotions are unique psychological experiences in several different ways.[5] Some emotions are displayed in universally similar fashion regardless of age and cultural background. Humans tend to display happiness, surprise, fear, anger, contempt, disgust, and sadness using the same facial expressions.[6] Emotions are also seemingly stronger than our intentions, and they are often unable to be assuaged by reason. We can logically tell ourselves not to be sad or jealous when we don't get what we want, or not to be afraid of a little snake, but it seldom works because emotions often overpower rational thought. Finally, and perhaps most significantly, emotions tend to be less controlled than other psychological states, affecting virtually all aspects of cognition. When we are happy, everything we experience adds to our happiness, but when we are frustrated, all that we experience contributes to our frustration.

Traditional management theories held that emotions were "bad" for rational decision making. However, recent research has proven that emotions and cognitions are intertwined and that both are normal parts of human functioning and decision making. When organizational events are positive and goals are being met, people experience positive emotions and are inspired to perform more organizational citizenship behaviours.[7] Positive emotions improve cognitive functioning, physical and psychological health, and coping mechanisms.[8] People who experience positive emotions tend to do so repeatedly and to be more creative.[9] Overall, people who experience positive emotions are more successful across a variety of life domains and report higher life satisfaction. Negative emotions, on the other hand, lead to unhealthy coping behaviours and diminish cardiovascular function and physical health.[10] Negative emotions can get in the way of good decisions; for example, anger reactions can lead negotiators to reject offers that are in their best interests.[11]

Emotional Labour

Anyone who has worked in a customer service role of any kind knows that maintaining one's composure while dealing with rude or frustrating customers is challenging and stressful. The effort needed to manage your emotions in order to perform your job effectively is called **emotional labour**.[12] This effort can require intellectual, physical and emotional resources, as well as time. Emotional labour is a part of all human interactions and relationships, and the emotional labour involved in many jobs can be demanding. Police are expected to hide their anxiety in a dangerous situation; health professionals are expected to provide support to critically injured people when they themselves may be feeling sad or helpless in the situation.

The degree of an individual's emotional labour

emotions Mental states that typically include feelings, physiological changes, and the inclination to act.

emotional labour The need to manage emotions in order to perform one's job effectively.

(how much effort is needed to manage emotions) is directly related to **emotional dissonance**, which refers to the contradiction between the emotions that are experienced and the emotions that are expressed. Emotional dissonance is greater when the emotions displayed are significantly different from what is felt. People typically handle emotional labour by "acting a part." Individuals can use using surface acting, or deep acting. In *surface acting*, the individual is trying to mask their true feelings but have not changed their beliefs about the situation. As a result, they feel more stressed[13] and are more likely to appear insincere because their true feelings can leak out. In *deep acting*, individuals deal with the situation by attempting to change their thoughts about the situation to better match their true emotions with the required emotions. As a result, they feel less stress and are more effective in handling the situation. For example, some airlines have trained their service staff to handle difficult flyers by approaching them from the assumption that the customer's inappropriate behaviour is related to a fear of flying rather than an abusive personality.[14]

People vary in their ability to handle emotional labour and employers can do much to help them. First, if the demands of the job are made clear before hiring, candidates themselves can choose whether to pursue the opportunity, knowing that a high degree of emotional labour will be required. Upon hiring, employers can train employees in techniques both for managing their own emotions and for dealing with the emotions of others, for example, through role plays. By recognizing and understanding the inevitable stresses of dealing with emotional labour on an ongoing basis, employers can offer support and stress release throughregular breaks, timeout rooms to get away, appreciation for handling tough situations well, supportive coaching, and opportunities to socialize and share stories.

emotional dissonance
Conflict between what a person feels and what the person is expected to express.

emotional intelligence
The ability to understand and manage of emotions in oneself and others.

Emotional Intelligence

It has long been theorized that "people skills" (otherwise known as "soft" skills) can make a significant difference in how well someone is able to interact with others. This longstanding theory has been formally recognized by the research on emotional intelligence. **Emotional intelligence (EI)** refers to one's ability to recognize and label one's own feelings as well as those of others, and use that information to guide behaviour. EI encompasses four separate abilities: (1) perceiving emotions; (2) using emotions; (3) understanding emotions, and (4) managing emotions. Individuals who have high EI can also manage and adapt their emotions to their environments to better achieve their goals. Emotional intelligence is sometimes referred to as emotional quotient (EQ, as a play on intelligence quotient, or IQ), and has been shown to influence job performance above and beyond general mental ability and personality factors, particularly in jobs requiring high emotional labour.[15]

Emotional Display Rules

Part of emotional intelligence is awareness of others' emotions, but skill in recognizing others' emotions is complicated by the fact that those emotions are not

IN ACTION

Google's SIYLI

Google uses its Search Inside Yourself Leadership Institute (SIYLI) to train leaders in mindfulness practices and emotional intelligence skills. Based on studies of neuroscience, the program is focused on helping leaders become more resilient, more creative, and happier. SIYLI cofounder and chair Chade-Meng Tan is a Google engineer who believes work should be fun and enjoyable, and that it should create the conditions for world peace. Meng, also known as Google's Jolly Good Fellow, connected with emotional intelligence guru Daniel Goleman and mindfulness pioneer Jon Kabat Zinn to create the program, which was tested and refined at Google over a four-year period.

SIYLI is an intense two-day experience in which participants learn to train their attention, develop self-knowledge and self-mastery, and create useful mental habits. More than a thousand Google employees have been through SIYLI training, and there's a lengthy waitlist to get in. Now, SIYLI is offered worldwide. Maybe Meng's vision of creating world peace is not so far-fetched.

SOURCE: silyi.org

Brasil2/E+/Getty Images

EMOTIONAL CONTAGION

Emotion in group settings can be extended by **emotional contagion**, which is the process through which one person's emotions and related behaviours elicit similar emotions in others. The emotional contagion phenomenon has been observed in humans, other primates, and dogs.[18]

Emotions in organizations need to be managed because they can spread easily, depending on the level of task and social interdependence. Emotional contagion affects any job involving interpersonal interaction, and occurs primarily through nonverbal cues and the basic human tendency of mimicry. We tend to mimic each other's facial expressions, body language, speech patterns, vocal tones, and even emotions. Positive emotions that travel through a work group through emotional contagion produce cooperation and task performance.[19] The opposite also occurs when negative emotions destroy morale and performance.

always visible. Different groups of people have different expectations about what emotions are appropriate to express in specific situations; these are known as **emotional display rules**. Emotional recognition requires recognizing "hidden" emotions that are disguised by people conforming to their display rules.

> "Different groups of people have different expectations about what emotions are appropriate to express in specific situations"

Display rules vary widely with culture, and individualistic cultures are more expressive than collectivistic cultures overall.[16] A study comparing Canadian, American, and Japanese students[17] showed that Japanese display rules suppress displays of powerful negative emotion (anger, disgust, contempt) significantly more than North Americans and Japanese were less likely to endorse the display of positive emotions than were Canadians. The only difference between Canadians and Americans was that Canadians believed contempt should be expressed less than did the Americans.

If one were unfamiliar with the display rules, one might mistakenly accept the displayed emotion as the actual emotion. It would be easy for a Canadian unaware of Japanese display rules to assume that a Japanese colleague is not pleased because their reaction appears muted by Canadian expectations. It would also be easy to assume that the Japanese colleague accepts something that really is quite upsetting to them, because again, their display rules supress the visual cues associated with anger or contempt.

4-2 ATTITUDES

An **attitude** is a set of emotions, beliefs and behaviours that are expressed when we evaluate a person or an object with some degree of favour or disfavour.[20] Attitudes can form directly as a result of personal experience or observation and they can be developed through social norms. They can be explicit, meaning that one is consciously aware of them, and that they clearly and deliberately influence behaviours and beliefs, or they can be implicit, where

emotional display rules Expectations regarding what emotions are appropriate to express in specific situations.

emotional contagion A process through which one person's emotions and related behaviours elicit similar emotions in others.

attitude A set of emotions, beliefs and behaviours expressed when we evaluate a person or an object.

TABLE 4.1 THE ABC MODEL OF AN ATTITUDE

	Component	Measured By	Example
A	Affect	Physiological indicators Verbal statements about feelings	I don't like my boss.
B	Behavioural intentions	Observed behaviour Verbal statements about intentions	I want to transfer to another department.
C	Cognition	Attitude scales Verbal statements about beliefs	I believe my boss plays favourites at work.

SOURCE: Adapted from M. J. Rosenberg and C. I. Hovland, "Cognitive, Affective, and Behavioral Components of Attitude," in M. J. Rosenberg, C. I. Hovland, W. J. McGuire, R. P. Abelson, and J. H. Brehm, *Attitude Organization and Change* (New Haven, Conn.: Yale University Press, 1960). Copyright 1960 Yale University Press. Used with permission.

their impact is unconscious. We respond favourably or unfavourably toward many things: animals, coworkers, our own appearance, and politics, to name a few.

The ABC Model

Three components—**a**ffect, **b**ehavioural intentions, and **c**ognition—compose what we call the ABC model of an attitude.[21] An individual does not have an attitude until they respond to an person, object, situation, or issue, and this response can be affective, behavioural, or cognitive. The ABC model (see Table 4.1) shows we must consider all three components to understand an attitude.

Affect is the emotional component of an attitude. It refers to an individual's feeling about something or someone. Statements such as "I like this" or "I prefer that" reflect the affective component of an attitude. Affect is measured by physiological indicators, such as blood pressure, which show emotional changes by measuring physiological arousal.

The second component is the intention to behave in a certain way toward an object or person. Our attitudes toward management, for example, may be inferred from observing the way we treat a supervisor. We may be supportive, passive, or hostile, depending on our attitude. The behavioural component of an attitude is measured by observing behaviour or by asking a person about behaviour or intentions.

affect The emotional component of an attitude.

cognition The process of understanding through thought, experience, and the senses.

social learning The process of deriving attitudes from family, peer groups, and culture.

The third component of an attitude, **cognition** describes the process of understanding through thought, experience, and the senses. Cognition reflects a person's perceptions or beliefs. Cognitive elements are evaluative beliefs measured by attitude scales or by asking about thoughts. The statement "I believe Japanese workers are industrious" reflects the cognitive component of an attitude.

4-3 ATTITUDE FORMATION

Unlike personality, attitudes are learned, and our responses to people and issues are able to change and evolve over time. Two major influences on attitudes are direct experience and social learning.

Direct experience with something strongly influences attitudes toward it. How do you know that you like biology or dislike math? You have probably formed these attitudes from experience in studying the subjects. Research has shown that attitudes derived from direct experience are stronger, held more confidently, and more resistant to change than attitudes formed through indirect experience.[22] These attitudes are powerful because of their availability; they are easily accessed and active in our cognitive processes.[23]

In **social learning**, the family, peer groups, and culture act to shape an individual's attitudes indirectly.[24] Children adopt certain attitudes when their parents reinforce attitudes they approve of, and peer pressure moulds attitudes through acceptance of individuals who express popular attitudes and through sanctions, such as exclusion from the group, for individuals who espouse unpopular attitudes. Culture also plays a role in attitude development. Consider, for example, the contrast in the American and European attitudes toward vacation and leisure. The typical vacation in the United States is two weeks. In Europe, longer vacations are the norm, and in some countries, *holiday* means everyone taking a month off. The European attitude is that an investment in longer vacations is important to health and performance.

Substantial social learning occurs through modelling, in which individuals acquire attitudes by observing others. For example, research indicates that the example set by an ethical manager is more effective in altering employee attitudes than is formal ethical training.[25] Employers may rely on modelling in training approaches such as job shadowing. However, the effectiveness of learning from a model depends on attention, motivation, and practice.

IN ACTION

Learning from Observing

For an individual to learn from observing a model, four processes must take place:

1. The learner must focus attention on the model.
2. The learner must be motivated to learn from the model.
3. The learner must retain what was observed from the model. Retention is accomplished in two basic ways. In one, the learner "stamps in" what was observed by forming a verbal code for it. The other way is through symbolic rehearsal, by which the learner forms a mental image of themselves behaving like the model.
4. Behavioural reproduction must occur; that is, the learner must practise the behaviour.

Attitudes and Behaviour

The relationship between attitude and behaviour has been investigated by organizational behaviourists and social psychologists for quite some time. Researchers have found that ability to predict behaviour based on attitude depends on five things: attitude specificity, attitude relevance, timing of measurement, personality factors, and social constraints.[26]

ATTITUDE SPECIFICITY Individuals possess both general and specific attitudes, and general attitudes typically exert an influence over specific attitudes: "It's important to stay healthy" is a general attitude. "Sugar is bad, and people shouldn't eat processed foods" is a specific attitude. General attitudes typically have less predictive ability on specific behaviours. For instance, a person may be a health and fitness proponent (general attitude), yet may still take the elevator at work to go up two floors, and accept the cake offered by a colleague (two specific behaviours). These actions appear to weaken, or even contradict the link between attitudes and behaviours. These actions, however, are specific events, and are influenced by a variety of elements. An individual may choose to take an elevator up one floor because they don't want to get sweaty climbing the stairs and may accept the cake because it is a colleague's birthday and they do not want to offend. Given a choice of company benefits between a free gym membership or a parking space close to the building, this individual will probably choose the gym membership. In this instance, the general attitude is more predictive of behaviour because the behaviour is more general, and less dependent on specific conditions.[27] General attitudes are better able to predict general behaviours. The individual who has specific attitudes about sugar would not accept the cake offered by their colleague. In this instance, their specific attitude is able to predict their specific behaviour. It is unable to predict, however, whether this individual would choose the parking space or the gym membership.

RELEVANCE Another factor that affects the attitude–behaviour link is relevance.[28] Attitudes that address an issue in which we have some self-interest (either we stand to gain or lose from them) are more relevant for us, and our subsequent behaviour is consistent with our expressed attitude. Consider a proposal to raise income taxes for those earning $150,000 or more. A student earning nowhere near $150,000 will probably not find the issue of great personal relevance, and may not be motivated to vote on that particular issue. Individuals in that income bracket, however, will find it relevant, and their attitude toward the issue would be strongly predictive of whether they would vote for the tax increase.

TIMING The timing of the measurement also affects attitude–behaviour correspondence. The shorter the time between the attitude measurement and the observed behaviour, the stronger the relationship. For example, voter preference polls taken close to an election are more accurate than earlier polls.

PERSONALITY Personality factors also influence the attitude–behaviour link. One personality disposition that affects the consistency between attitudes and behaviour is self-monitoring. Recall from Chapter 3 that low self-monitors rely on their internal states when making decisions about behaviour, while high self-monitors are more responsive to situational cues. Low self-monitors therefore display greater correspondence between their attitudes and behaviours.[29] High self-monitors may display little correspondence between their attitudes and behaviour because they behave according to signals from others and from the environment.

SOCIAL CONSTRAINTS Finally, social constraints affect the relationship between attitudes and behaviour.[30] The social context provides information about acceptable attitudes and behaviours,[31] and new members of an organization often adopt new attitudes and behaviours after being exposed to the attitudes of their new peer group. A newcomer from Australia may casually use certain words that have a very negative connotation in Canada. The first time the Australian uses one of these terms it will likely be met with censure and condemnation. After seeing how group members respond to the term, it is unlikely that the Australian will use it again, even though it is commonly used in Australia and does not have such a negative meaning.

Attitude is a little thing that makes a big difference.

—Winston Churchill

Cognitive Dissonance

Individuals typically behave according to their attitudes. As rational beings, people prefer consistency (consonance) between their attitudes and behaviour. Anything that disrupts this consistency causes tension (dissonance), which motivates individuals to change either their attitudes or their behaviour to maintain consistency. The tension produced by a conflict between attitudes and behaviour is known as **cognitive dissonance**.[32] Cognitive dissonance can arise when individuals behave in a way that is contrary to their beliefs, when they attempt to hold two or more contradictory beliefs or values at the same time, or when they receive new information that is inconsistent with existing beliefs.

People respond to cognitive dissonance in one of four ways: They change their behaviour, they justify their behaviour, they change their attitudes, or they ignore or deny new information.[33] Returning to the example of going to the gym, from above: An individual may believe that exercise is required to maintain physical fitness and overall health; however, that individual may consistently fail to go to the gym. The difference between their beliefs (that exercise is necessary for physical health) and their behaviours (failing to get exercise) may cause them discomfort, due to cognitive dissonance. To resolve this dissonance, the individual may: Begin going to the gym (change the behaviour); they may insist they simply don't have time to go to the gym (justify their behaviour); they may decide that eating healthy is more important than exercise (change their attitudes); or they may argue that they are still healthy even if they don't use the gym, because smoking is what's really bad for health (ignore or deny.)

cognitive dissonance A state of tension that is produced through conflict between attitudes and behaviour.

Managers need to understand cognitive dissonance because employees often find themselves in situations in which their attitudes conflict with their behaviour. Employees who display sudden shifts in behaviour may be attempting to reduce dissonance. Some employees find the conflicts between strongly held attitudes and required work behaviour so uncomfortable that they leave the organization to escape the dissonance.

A manager can sometimes use dissonance deliberately to change an employee's attitude. This is done by involving the employee in a task that contradicts the underlying attitude. For example, a manager who wants an employee to take safety more seriously may ask the person to join the health and safety committee, emphasizing the importance of the role, how this employee is well suited to it, and allocating time for the commitment. It would be difficult for the employee to refuse. The employee would then be involved in audits of the workplace and meetings to discuss needed changes. This involvement contradicts an attitude that health and safety is a trivial concern, creating dissonance. But the involvement is public and cannot be retracted, leading the employee to resolve the dissonance by changing the attitude. Health and safety is now judged to be a more important concern, in line with the employee's observable behaviour.

4-4 WORK ATTITUDES

Attitudes at work are important because, directly or indirectly, they affect work behaviour. Employee work attitudes correlate with performance, absenteeism,

Thomas Soellner/Shutterstock.com

Attitudes correlate with performance, absenteeism, turnover, unionization, grievances, and even drug abuse.

Job satisfaction is not just related to on-the-job characteristics. Studies have found that workers with long commutes have higher levels of anxiety, are less productive at work, and report less satisfaction with their jobs than workers with shorter commutes. One study found that an additional 10 minutes of commute time in each direction (for a total of 20 additional minutes each day) has the same effect on job satisfaction as receiving a 19% pay cut. But researchers also routinely find that individuals select marginally higher paying jobs with significantly longer commutes. The researchers explain that these behaviours reflect individuals' inability to fully appreciate the psychological, emotional, and physical costs of increased travel times.

SOURCE: T. Loudenback, "Adding 20 minutes to your commute makes you as miserable as getting a 10 percent pay cut," *Inc.*, https://www.inc.com/business-insider/study-reveals-commute-time-impacts-job-satisfaction.html, accessed June 4, 2018.

turnover, unionization, grievances, and even drug abuse.[34] Studies have shown employee attitudes to be predictive of financial performance measures such as market share,[35] and to be related to customer satisfaction. Chief among the things that negatively affect employees' work attitudes are demanding jobs over which they have little control.[36] A positive climate, on the other hand, can generate positive attitudes and good performance.[37] A field experiment demonstrated that hotel customers developed a more positive attitude toward the hotel when offered helpful, concerned service by employees. Customers responded to employee warmth by increasing loyalty and a willingness to pay more for the service.[38] Because of the power of attitudes, it is important to know how employees feel about their work, and what influences lie behind those attitudes so action can be taken to guide attitudes in a constructive way where possible.

Job Satisfaction

Job satisfaction is a pleasurable or positive emotional state resulting from the appraisal of one's job or job experiences.[39] It has been treated both as a general attitude and as satisfaction with specific dimensions of the job such as pay, the work itself, promotion opportunities, supervision, and coworkers.[40] An individual may hold different attitudes toward various aspects of a job. For example, an employee may like their job responsibilities but be dissatisfied with the opportunities for promotion.

Many organizations formally survey job satisfaction in their employees. The two most extensively validated measures of job satisfaction are *the Job Descriptive Index (JDI)* and the *Minnesota Satisfaction Questionnaire (MSQ)*. The Job Descriptive Index measures the specific facets of satisfaction by asking employees to respond "yes," "no," or "cannot decide" to a series of statements describing their jobs. The Minnesota Satisfaction Questionnaire asks employees to respond to statements about their jobs using a five-point scale that ranges from very dissatisfied to very satisfied. Figure 4.1 presents sample items from each measure.

These tools have been of value to practitioners because they examine how employees react to specific aspects of the job and circumstances, which provides more information than global measures of job satisfaction (which simply ask "Overall, how satisfied are you with your job?"). Global measures of job satisfaction are highly correlated with measures like the JDI and MSQ, and a lot easier, cheaper, and quicker to administer. However, if job satisfaction is not high, the global measure does not allow exploration of the underlying issues.

Studies have shown the importance of good relations with management and interesting work,[41] coworker support,[42] good pay, and security.[43] Factors important for job satisfaction will vary with the individual. For example, more educated workers are more likely to emphasize the intrinsic job content (interesting job, meets your abilities, opportunity to use initiative, useful for society) and less educated workers are more likely to endorse extrinsic factors such as pay, good hours, and generous holidays.[44] Personality research shows that those with high core self-evaluation will tend to be more satisfied with their work, no matter what they are doing, than people with low core self-evaluation.[45] Employees with negative affectivity (who tend toward being distressed, pessimistic, and generally dissatisfied) will tend to be less satisfied with any job they have than those with positive affectivity.[46] One study showed that affective

job satisfaction A pleasurable or positive emotional state resulting from the appraisal of one's job or job experiences.

FIGURE 4.1 SAMPLE ITEMS FROM SATISFACTION QUESTIONNAIRES

Job Descriptive Index

Think of the work you do at present. How well does each of the following words or phrases describe your work? In the blank beside each word given below, write

__Y__ for "Yes" if it describes your work
__N__ for "No" if it does NOT describe it
__?__ if you cannot decide

WORK ON YOUR PRESENT JOB:

______ Routine
______ Satisfying
______ Good

Think of the majority of the people you work with now or the people you meet in connection with your work. How well does each of the following words or phrases describe these people? In the blank beside each word, write

__Y__ for "Yes" if it describes the people you work with
__N__ for "No" if it does NOT describe them
__?__ if you cannot decide

CO-WORKERS (PEOPLE):

______ Boring
______ Responsible
______ Intelligent

Minnesota Satisfaction Questionnaire

1 = Very dissatisfied
2 = Dissatisfied
3 = I can't decide whether I am satisfied or not
4 = Satisfied
5 = Very satisfied

On my present job, this is how I feel about:

______ The chance to work alone on the job (independence)
______ My chances for advancement on this job (advancement)
______ The chance to tell people what to do (authority)
______ The praise I get for a good job (recognition)
______ My pay and the amount of work I do (compensation)

SOURCES: (Top) The Job Descriptive Index adapted from Bowling Green State University. The complete forms, scoring key, instructions, and norms can be obtained from Dr. Patricia C. Smith, Department of Psychology, Bowling Green State University, Bowling Green, OH 43403. (Bottom) Minnesota Satisfaction Questionnaire from D.J. Adapted from Weiss, R.V. Davis, G.W. England, and L.H. Lofquist, Manual for the Minnesota Satisfaction Questionnaire (University of Minnesota Vocational Psychology Research, 1967).

disposition measured when the participants were 15 to 18 years of age correlated significantly with their job satisfaction measured 40 years later.[47]

Orla/ Shutterstock.com

Employee satisfaction predicts organizational performance.

Managers and employees believe that happy or "satisfied" employees are more productive at work. The satisfaction–performance link is, in fact, more complex than that. There is a correlation between the two,[48] and individuals who are satisfied do tend to be better performers, but job satisfaction explains only a modest amount of the variation in performance. Many factors influence an individual's performance, and there are many exceptions to the satisfaction–performance link, where satisfied workers do not perform well and dissatisfied workers work effectively.

Even in those cases where satisfaction and performance are closely linked, it is unclear whether satisfaction leads to performance, or strong performance leads to personal satisfaction, or another variable mediates both, or if all are true. We do know that job satisfaction is a better predictor of performance in complex professional jobs. Rewards also appear to act as a link between satisfaction and performance, influencing both: Employees who receive valued rewards are more satisfied, and employees who receive rewards that are contingent on performance (the higher the performance, the larger the reward) tend to perform better.

Although job satisfaction does not predict individual performance reliably, researchers have found a strong link between job satisfaction and organizational performance. Companies with satisfied workers have better performance than companies with dissatisfied workers.[49] This may be due to the more intangible elements of performance, like organizational citizenship behaviour, that contribute to organizational effectiveness but aren't necessarily captured by measuring individual job performance.

Dissatisfied workers, on the other hand, are more likely to skip work and quit their jobs, driving up the cost of turnover. Dissatisfied workers also report more psychological and medical problems than do satisfied employees.[50]

Organizational Citizenship versus Workplace Deviance

Job satisfaction encourages **organizational citizenship behaviour**—behaviour that is above and beyond the call of duty. Satisfied employees are more likely to help their coworkers, make positive comments about the company, and refrain from complaining when things at work go poorly.[51] Going beyond the call of duty is especially important to organizations using teams, where extra help from each other can get things accomplished more effectively and efficiently.

Satisfied workers are more likely to want to give something back to the organization because they want to reciprocate their positive experiences.[52] Employees may feel that citizenship behaviours are not recognized by the organization because they occur outside the confines of normal job responsibilities. Organizational citizenship behaviours (OCBs) do, however, influence performance evaluations. Employees who help others, suggest innovations, and develop their skills receive higher performance ratings[53] and are recognized through reward allocations.

Individuals who identify strongly with the organization are more likely to perform OCBs.[54] High self-monitors, who base their behaviour on cues from the situation, are also more likely to perform these behaviours.[55] One study found that individual workers were more likely to offer OCBs when doing so was the norm among other team members. The impact of one worker's OCBs can spread throughout an entire department.[56] Worker satisfaction does not simply impact team interactions; OCBs influence "bottom-line" effectiveness in the organization, and have been shown to relate to productivity, efficiency, reduced costs, customer satisfaction, and unit-level turnover.[57]

Given the value of OCBs, organizations have a vested interest in inspiring and motivating employees to engage in these behaviours. At the outset, managers can focus on selecting employees likely to engage in OCBs, using structured interviews designed to assess this propensity,[58] and looking for evidence of conscientiousness. Managers can also take steps to ensure work decisions are fair and are perceived to be fair; consider using a transformational leadership style where possible (discussed in Chapter 12); and address issues that detract from employee attitudes such as job satisfaction and commitment.[59]

In contrast to organizational citizenship behaviours, workplace deviance behaviour (WDB) occurs when employees are dissatisfied with their jobs and have negative attitudes. **Workplace deviance behaviour** consists of counterproductive behaviour that violates organizational norms and harms others or the organization.[60] Examples of such behaviour include gossiping about coworkers, sabotaging others' projects, and theft from the company or colleagues.

Negative events such as downsizing and technological insecurities are generally considered responsible for spikes in workplace deviance. Layoffs may inspire anger and hostility toward the organization, causing employees to develop negative attitudes and to feel the desire to retaliate. Even when an employee keeps their job but believes the procedure used to determine the layoff is unfair, they may still take revenge against the manager.[61] Perceived unfairness at work is a major cause of deviance, sabotage, and retaliation. Positive attitudes decrease deviance.

Organizational Commitment and Job Satisfaction

The strength of an individual's identification with an organization is known as **organizational commitment**. There are three kinds of organizational commitment: affective, continuance, and normative. **Affective commitment** is an employee's intention to remain in an organization because of a strong desire to do so. Affective commitment encompasses loyalty and a deep concern for the organization's welfare. Affective commitment consists of three factors: a belief in the goals and values of the organization, a willingness to put forth effort on behalf of the organization, and a desire to remain a member of the organization.[62]

Continuance commitment is an employee's tendency to remain in an organization because the person cannot afford to leave.[63] Sometimes, employees believe that if they leave, they will lose a great deal of their investments

organizational citizenship behaviour Behaviour that is above and beyond the call of duty.

workplace deviance behaviour Counterproductive behaviour that violates organizational norms and harms others or the organization.

organizational commitment The strength of an individual's identification with an organization.

affective commitment The type of organizational commitment that is based on an individual's desire to remain in an organization.

continuance commitment The type of organizational commitment that is based on the fact that an individual cannot afford to leave.

in time, effort, and benefits. **Normative commitment** is a perceived obligation to remain with the organization. Individuals who experience normative commitment stay with the organization because they feel that they should.[64]

All three types of commitment are related to lower turnover, but research shows that employees with affective commitment show higher attendance; better performance; higher OCB; and, on a personal level, less stress and less work–family conflict.[65] Normative commitment is also associated with these desirable outcomes, but not as strongly, while continuance commitment is not associated with any desirable outcomes other than lower turnover.

Managers can increase affective commitment by communicating their appreciation of employees' contributions, and their concern for employees' well-being.[66] Affective commitment also increases when the organization and employees share the same values, and when the organization emphasizes values such as moral integrity, fairness, creativity, and openness.[67] Negative experiences at work, such as perceived age discrimination, diminish affective commitment.[68]

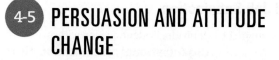

4-5 PERSUASION AND ATTITUDE CHANGE

The days of command-and-control management, when supervisors simply told employees what to do and employees complied, are over. Modern managers must instead aim to change attitudes, and thus need to understand, and be skilled in the art of persuasion.[69] Through persuasion, one individual (the source) tries to change the attitude of another person (the target) in regard to a certain issue (the message).[70] Persuasion is little more than a sales pitch; where the source attempts to "sell" a new attitude (the message) to the target. Characteristics of the source, target, and message all combine to affect how successful the attempt at persuasion will be.

Source Characteristics That Affect Persuasion

Three major characteristics of the source (the individual who is trying to change another's attitude) that affect persuasion are expertise, trustworthiness, and attractiveness.[71] The perception of the source's expertise is a judgment made by the target. The target will see the source as an expert if they have relevant information, like credentials and experience. A source that is perceived as an expert is particularly persuasive, because that expertise increases the credibility of the message. This is why advertisements often use doctors or professionals to deliver their message. A source's level of expertise also contributes to their level of trustworthiness. A trustworthy source is more likely to be persuasive. The use of actors and athletes to advertise products relies on people's implicit assumptions that the people they admire are trustworthy, and thus, that their message is more dependable.

normative commitment
The type of organizational commitment that is based on an individual's perceived obligation to remain with an organization.

Attractive sources, particularly attractive female sources, induce significantly greater levels of persuasion in targets.[72] This increased persuasiveness may be the result of the halo effect (where one positive trait causes other traits to be viewed more positively), or may be the result of social conditioning such that attractive people are often more outgoing (see Chapter 3 for a discussion on social perception) and better communicators. Many individuals feel that they are unable to affect their level of attractiveness, but this has been shown to be untrue. There is much that can be done to increase one's perceived attractiveness: taking care with one's self-presentation is a necessary first step (see impression management of the ideal persona in Chapter 3), and research has also demonstrated that the perceived attractiveness of a team member can go down significantly if that person proves to be lazy and uncooperative, or up significantly when the person is hard working and well liked.[73] Respect, familiarity, and the perception that one is contributing to shared goals all enhance how physical attractiveness is judged.

Target Characteristics That Affect Persuasion

Individuals differ widely in their susceptibility to persuasion, and attention, intelligence, self-esteem, mood, and age all affect how persuasive a message is likely to be. Attention is a key component of affecting persuasion because if the target is not paying attention to the message, they are unlikely to be persuaded by it.[74] This is yet another reason that marketing companies use actors, musicians, athletes and other famous figures in their advertising. Individuals are more willing to pay attention to famous people that they admire.

In general, targets who are less intelligent are more easily persuaded, and individuals with moderate self-esteem are more likely to change their attitudes than individuals with lower or higher self-esteem.[75] Individuals who hold very extreme attitudes are more resistant to persuasion, while people who are in a good mood are easier to persuade.[76] Finally, young adults ages 18–25 are more persuadable than older adults.[77]

Message Characteristics That Affect Persuasion

The source and the target are understandably important in estimating how persuasive an argument is likely to be, but the features of the message itself are paramount. Some messages are simply more persuasive than others; for instance, "let's do this and then go get a drink" is likely to be more persuasive than any version of "I'm going to need you to come in on the weekend." All things being equal, however, subtly presented messages have been shown to be more persuasive than obvious ones.[78] Undisguised deliberate attempts at changing attitudes may actually entrench attitudes, driving them further in the original direction, and decreasing the likelihood of adopting change. This is most likely to occur when the target of the persuasive communication feels that their freedom of choice is being threatened.[79] Less-threatening approaches are less likely to elicit negative reactions, and are thus more likely to be successful.

Persuasion is often more effectual than force.

—Aesop

A message with more arguments (i.e., more reasons "why") will be more likely to influence attitude change,[80] and, when the target is not motivated to change, presenting both sides of an issue can increase persuasivity by refuting the "other" side, which makes it harder for the targets to hang on to their previous attitudes. Showing support for one side of the issue while acknowledging that another side exists can help decrease the directness of the message, reducing the perceived threat to freedom of choice. Finally, the emotional tone of the message is also important. Messages framed using an emotional appeal (such as jealousy, fear, indignation, and humour) are also more persuasive[81]; again, consider their use in advertising campaigns.

Cognitive Routes to Persuasion

The *elaboration likelihood model* of persuasion suggests that people can change their attitudes as a result of persuasion through two possible avenues: the *central route* and the *peripheral route*.[82] The routes are differentiated by the amount of elaboration, or scrutiny, the target is motivated to give the message. The elaboration likelihood model is presented in Figure 4.2.

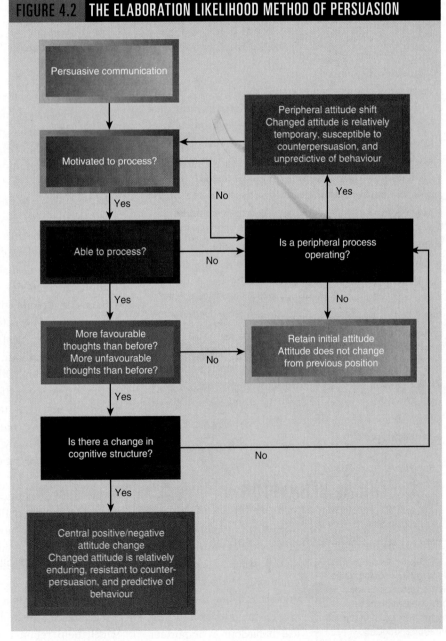

FIGURE 4.2 THE ELABORATION LIKELIHOOD METHOD OF PERSUASION

Persuasive communication

Motivated to process?

Yes

No

Able to process?

Yes

No

More favourable thoughts than before? More unfavourable thoughts than before?

Yes

No

Is there a change in cognitive structure?

Yes

No

Central positive/negative attitude change
Changed attitude is relatively enduring, resistant to counter-persuasion, and predictive of behaviour

Is a peripheral process operating?

Yes

No

Peripheral attitude shift
Changed attitude is relatively temporary, susceptible to counterpersuasion, and unpredictive of behaviour

Retain initial attitude
Attitude does not change from previous position

The *central route* of persuasion is used when targets are motivated to pay attention, and have the ability to think critically about the message being received. Targets processing information centrally are likely to give thoughtful consideration to the information presented to them, and persuasion involves direct cognitive processing of the message's content. The listener may nod their head at strong arguments and shake their head at weak ones.[83] Using the central route, logical and convincing arguments are able to elicit lasting change in attitudes.[84]

FIGURE 4.3 MOST REPORTED ETHICAL LAPSES IN 2017, BY ISSUE

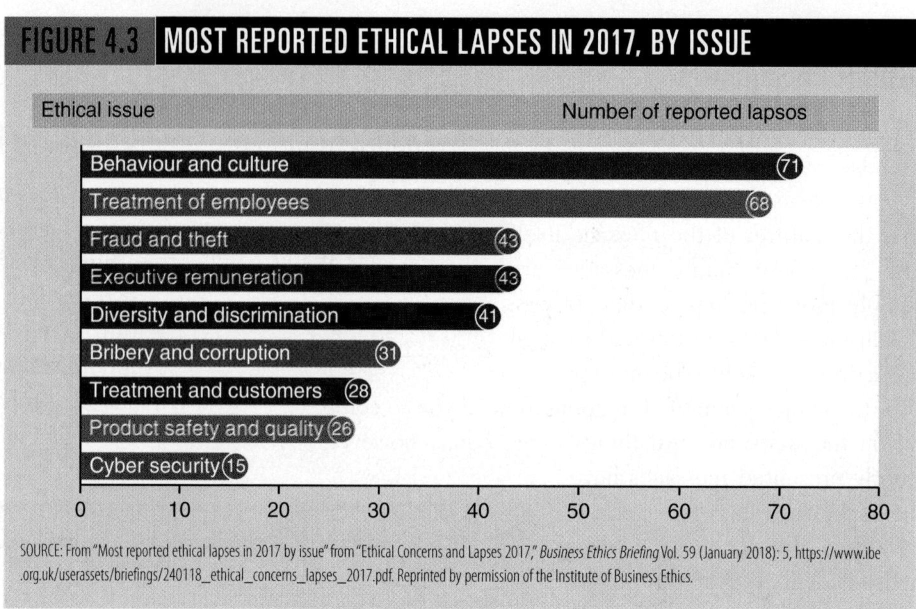

SOURCE: From "Most reported ethical lapses in 2017 by issue" from "Ethical Concerns and Lapses 2017," *Business Ethics Briefing* Vol. 59 (January 2018): 5, https://www.ibe.org.uk/userassets/briefings/240118_ethical_concerns_lapses_2017.pdf. Reprinted by permission of the Institute of Business Ethics.

In the *peripheral route* to persuasion, the individual is not motivated to pay attention to the logical quality of the message, or is unable to process the message content. Targets processing information peripherally do not examine information thoroughly, and instead persuasion is influenced heuristically by characteristics of the source; for example, their expertise, trustworthiness, and attractiveness. Alternatively, the individual may be persuaded by statistics, the number of arguments presented, or the method of presentation—all of which are nonsubstantial aspects of the message.[85] Using the peripheral route, targets may change their attitude temporarily, but because the attitude change is superficial, it is likely to be changed with the next message received.

The elaboration likelihood model shows that the target's level of involvement with the issue is important. That involvement also determines which route to persuasion will be more effective. In some cases, attitude change comes about through both the central and the peripheral routes.[86]

4-6 ETHICAL BEHAVIOUR

Ethics is the study of moral values and moral behaviour. **Ethical behaviour** is acting in ways consistent with one's personal values and the commonly held values of the organization and society.[87]

ethical behaviour Acting in ways consistent with one's personal values and the commonly held values of the organization and society.

Paying attention to ethical behaviour is important in many ways, and for many reasons, for an organization. Most individuals do not want to be associated with organizations that have unethical reputations, and having such a reputation, whether for a community basketball team or an international business, leads to fewer members, fewer partnerships, and fewer customers, all of which combine to create fewer opportunities for organizational growth. See Figure 4.3 for a list of common ethical lapses that affect organizations.

When new members do not want to join the organization, the potential talent pool is severely restricted, leading to stagnancy within the ranks, and potentially decreasing membership as older members leave the organization. Alternatively, unethical individuals may be attracted to organizations with reputations for allowing malfeasant behaviour, thus increasing the organization's amoral reputation. Other organizations may also choose to limit their association with those perceived as unethical so as not to be tainted themselves, which leads to fewer strategic partnerships, which in turn leads to less development. Finally, consumers shy away from products and services if a company has an unethical reputation. Of course, illegal actions also lead to liability and financial risk. Unethical behaviour can also impact organizational members through increased stress, lower job satisfaction, and turnover.[88]

On the positive side, organizations with ethical reputations create goodwill in the communities in which they operate, building customer loyalty and creating relationships with suppliers and even competitors. Ethical behaviour can create more positive work environments, which help retain and develop good employees, and

IN ACTION

B Corps

B Corps (Certified Benefit Corporations) are companies that use the power of business as a force for good. To be designated a B Corp, a company must meet tough standards in environmental performance, social responsibility, accountability, and transparency. Today, there are more than two thousand certified B Corps in more than fifty countries representing one hundred and thirty different industries. B Corps aim not only to be the best in the world but also to be the best *for* the world. For example, when compared to other sustainable businesses, B Corps are more likely to donate at least 10 percent of their profits to charity, use on-site renewable energy, and use suppliers from low-income communities. B Corps you may recognize include Ben & Jerry's, Patagonia, miEnergy, Libro Credit Union, and HiMama, among others.

SOURCE: bcorporation.net

attract more applicants,[89] creating a larger hiring pool, which allows respected firms to choose higher quality applicants. Doing the right thing can have a positive effect on an organization's performance.[90]

Even if an organization has a reputation for acting ethically, unethical behaviour by employees can affect individuals and work teams, and, if allowed to go unchecked, an individual's behaviour can eventually impact the organization. Organizations thus depend on individuals to act ethically. The early 2000s saw a spate of ethical scandals lead to organizational crises, and from that point on, organizations have modified their ethics codes from generally communicated ideals to specific, measured edicts.

Individuals face complex ethical issues at work. A review of articles in one week of *The Wall Street Journal* revealed over 60 articles dealing with ethical issues in business.[91] As Table 4.2 suggests, few of these issues are clear-cut. They depend on the specifics of the situation, and their interpretation depends on the characteristics of the individuals examining them. Consider lying, for instance. Many people tell "white lies." Is this acceptable? The perception of what constitutes ethical versus unethical behaviour in organizations varies among people.

Corporate Social Responsibility

If one considers ethical behaviour to be "values in action," one of the ways in which many Canadian organizations are demonstrating those values is through their corporate social responsibility (CSR). Tim Hortons Children's Foundation sends over 19,000 children to camp each year, and Home Depot's volunteer program,

TABLE 4.2 ETHICAL ISSUES FROM REVIEWED ARTICLES IN ONE WEEK IN *THE WALL STREET JOURNAL*

1. Stealing	Taking things that don't belong to you
2. Lying	Saying things you know aren't true
3. Fraud and deceit	Creating or perpetuating false impressions
4. Conflict of interest and influence buying	Bribes, payoffs, and kickbacks
5. Hiding versus divulging information	Concealing information that another party has a right to know or failing to protect personal or proprietary information
6. Cheating	Taking unfair advantage of a situation
7. Personal decadence	Aiming below excellence in terms of work performance (e.g., careless or sloppy work)
8. Interpersonal abuse	Behaviours that are abusive of others (e.g., sexism, racism, emotional abuse)
9. Organizational abuse	Organizational practices that abuse members (e.g., inequitable compensation, misuses of power)
10. Rule violations	Breaking organizational rules
11. Accessory to unethical acts	Knowing about unethical behaviour and failing to report it
12. Ethical dilemmas	Choosing between two equally desirable or undesirable options

SOURCE: Kluwer Academic Publishers, by J. O. Cherrington and D. J. Cherrington, "A Menu of Moral Issues: One Week in the Life of The Wall Street Journal," *Journal of Business Ethics* 11 (1992): 255–265. Reprinted with kind permission of Springer Science and Business Media. © Cengage Learning.

CPimages.ca PHOTO/The Home Depot Canada

Home Depot Employees Work with Habitat for Humanity

Team Depot, has seen thousands of employees build homes with Habitat for Humanity and build or improve community playgrounds through its partnership with KaBOOM! Eighteen percent of Canadian organizations encourage employees to do volunteer work during work hours and pay for that time.[92] CSR initiatives like these can be instrumental in team building, in enhancing corporate pride and identity, and in reinforcing an ethical climate within the organization.

4-7 FACTORS THAT AFFECT ETHICAL BEHAVIOUR

Two sets of factors—individual characteristics and organizational factors—influence ethical behaviour.[93] See Figure 4.4. In this section, we will examine individual influences on ethical behaviour. Organizational influences on ethical behaviour will be discussed throughout the remainder of the text.

values Enduring beliefs that a specific behaviour or end state of existence is preferable.

Ethical decision making requires three qualities of individuals that are influenced by personality factors such as value systems, locus of control, Machiavellianism, and cognitive moral development. The three qualities required for ethical decision making are:[94]

1. The competence to identify ethical issues and evaluate the consequences of alternative courses of action
2. The self-confidence to seek out different opinions about the issue and decide what is right in terms of a particular situation
3. Toughmindedness—the willingness to make decisions when all that needs to be known cannot be known and when the ethical issue has no established, unambiguous solution.

> "There is no such thing as business ethics. There is only one kind—you have to adhere to the highest standards."
>
> —Marvin Bower

Values

Different values generate different ethical behaviours. Though values vary widely among individuals, we use them to evaluate our own behaviour and that of others. **Values** are enduring beliefs that a specific behaviour or end state of existence is personally or socially preferable.[95] Values represent a person's judgments about what is good versus what is bad. As a general belief about what is right and what is wrong, values are deeply held and quite stable, forming the basis for ethical behaviour.

Parents and other respected role models influence value development by providing guidance about what is right and wrong. As individuals grow and mature, their values may change as the individual develops a sense of self. Cultures, societies, and organizations all shape one's values.

Age and Culture in Values

Although relatively fixed, values can and do change over time. Values also shift between generations. Baby boomers' values contrast with both Generation X and millennial values to a large extent: baby boomers tend to be more driven, and have a work-oriented value

FIGURE 4.4 INDIVIDUAL/ORGANIZATIONAL MODEL OF ETHICAL BEHAVIOUR

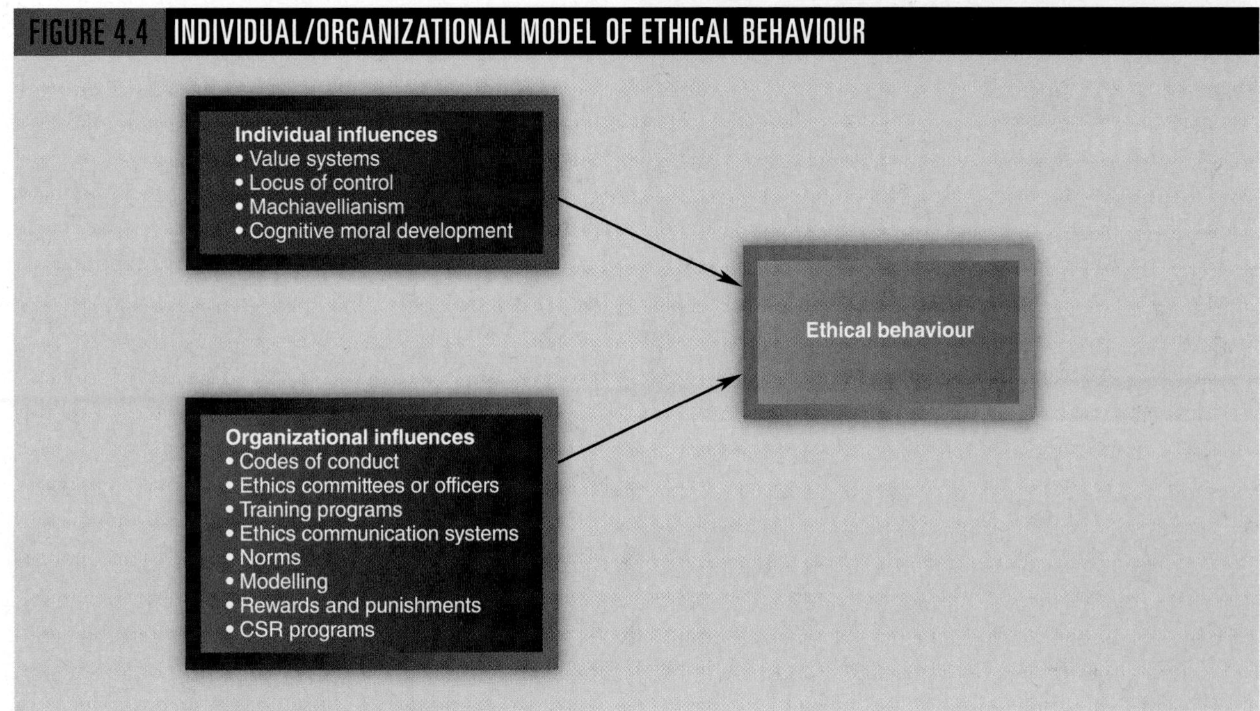

system that emphasizes achievement values. Millennials typically value self-reliance, individualism, and balance between family and work life.[96] See Table 4.3 for a brief comparison.

Organizations facing the challenges of an increasingly diverse workforce and a global marketplace must also recognize cultures' influence on values. Doing business in a global marketplace often means encountering a clash of values among different cultures. Consider loyalty, for example. In Japan, loyalty means "compassionate overtime." Even when you have no work yourself, you should stay late to provide moral support for your peers who are working late.[97] In contrast, Koreans value loyalty to the person for whom you work.[98] In Canada, family and other personal loyalties are held above loyalty to the organization or supervisor.

TABLE 4.3 DIFFERENCES BETWEEN GENERATIONS

	Baby Boomers	Generation X	Millennials
Birth Years	1946–64	1965–80	1981–2000
	Assume diversity	Accept diversity	Celebrate diversity
	Pragmatic/idealist	Pragmatic/practical	Optimistic/realist
	Self-expansive	Self-involved	Self-inventive
	Reject rules	Desire rules	Rewrites rules
	Were laissez-faire kids	Were latch-key kids	Were nurtured kids
	Freedom to seek and achieve	No link between hard work and success	High expectations
	Future is now	Future is closing	Future is open
	Categorization	Labels	Personalization and Customization

When faced with ethical dilemmas, individuals who voice their decision using a foreign language rather than their native tongue will likely make decisions that are less ethical. Communicating in a learned language allows individuals to psychologically distance themselves from issues and make less emotional, utilitarian decisions.

SOURCE: A. Lukis, "Moral Decisions May Depend on Language; People Make More Pragmatic Decisions in Languages Other Than Their Native Tongue," *Wall Street Journal* (May 12, 2014).

Cultures also differ in the individual contributions they value at work. Collectivist cultures such as China and Mexico value a person's contributions to relationships in the work team. In contrast, individualist cultures (Canada, the Netherlands) value a person's contribution to task accomplishment. Both collectivist and individualist cultures value rewards based on individual performance.[99] Iran's collectivist managers demonstrate little tolerance for ambiguity, high need for structure, and willingness to sacrifice for the good of society—all values they derive from Islam, which promotes belonging, harmony, humility, and simplicity.[100]

Values also affect individuals' views of what constitutes authority. French managers value authority as a right of office and rank. Their behaviour reflects this value, as they tend to exercise power based on their position in the organization. In contrast, managers from the Netherlands value group inputs to decisions and expect employees to challenge and discuss their decisions.[101] It is human nature to judge the value systems of others, but tolerating diverse values can help us understand other cultures. Value systems of other nations are not necessarily right or wrong—they are merely different.

WORK VALUES Work values also influence individual perceptions of right and wrong on the job.[102] While most individuals value fairness, honesty, achievement, and concern for others, the relative weight they assign to each value will influence their decisions and their behaviours. For example, if someone values achievement above honesty, they may be more inclined to stretch the truth, or use a colleague's resources without permission in the process of achieving their goals. If an individual values honesty above all else, they may be more likely to show less concern for others' feelings by not observing social niceties and politeness when assessing another's performance. Sharing values with work colleagues means less stress and easier relationships. Employees who share their supervisors' values are more satisfied with their jobs and more committed to the organization.[103]

Values also have a profound effect on job choice. Most organizations say they value diversity, but fail to live up to those values in their recruiting and promoting programs. Minority candidates will judge the sincerity of diversity claims and this judgment will affect their interest in working for the company.[104] If they discover that the recruiting sales job on diversity was misleading, they are likely to leave.[105]

Locus of Control

Another individual influence on ethical behaviour is locus of control. Recall from Chapter 3 that individuals with an internal locus of control believe that they control events in their lives and that they are responsible for their own experiences. Those with an external locus of control believe that outside forces such as fate, chance, or other people control what happens to them.[106] Internals are more likely to take personal responsibility for the consequences of their ethical or unethical behaviour, while externals are more apt to believe that external forces caused their ethical or unethical behaviour. Research has shown that internals make more ethical decisions than do externals.[107] Internals also are more resistant to social pressure and are less willing to hurt another person, even if ordered to do so by an authority figure.[108]

Machiavellianism

Machiavellianism also influences ethical behaviour. Recall from Chapter 3 that Machiavellianism is a personality characteristic indicating your willingness to do whatever it takes to get your own way.[109] An individual who ranks highly in Machiavellianism (known as a high-Mach) operates from the notion that it is better to be feared than loved. High-Machs tend to be deceitful, have a cynical view of human nature, and care little for conventional notions of right and wrong.[110] They are skilled manipulators, relying on their persuasive abilities. Low-Machs, in contrast, value loyalty and relationships. They are less willing to manipulate others for personal gain and are concerned with others' opinions.

High-Machs believe that the desired ends justify any means; therefore, they are willing to manipulate

TABLE 4.4 KOHLBERG'S LEVELS OF MORAL DEVELOPMENT

Level I: Premoral **Ethical behaviour based on self-interest**	
Stage 1	Obey rules to avoid punishment
Stage 2	Follow rules if in own best interest, if rewards follow
Level II: Conventional **Ethical behaviour based on others' expectations**	
Stage 3	Live up to expectations of others close to you
Stage 4	Live up to expectations of society
Level III: Principled **Ethical behaviour based on universal values**	
Stage 5	Act on principles of justice and rights
Stage 6	Act on own self-selected principles

others in order to achieve a goal.[111] They are emotionally detached from other people and focus on the objective aspects of situations. And high-Machs are more likely to engage in ethically questionable behaviour.[112] Employees can counter Machiavellian individuals by focusing on teamwork instead of on one-on-one relationships, where high-Machs have the upper hand. Making interpersonal agreements public reduces their susceptibility to Machiavellian manipulation.

Cognitive Moral Development

An individual's level of **cognitive moral development** also affects ethical behaviour. Psychologist Lawrence Kohlberg proposed that as individuals mature, they move through a series of six stages of moral development.[113] (See Table 4.4). With each successive stage, they become less dependent on other people's opinions of right and wrong and less self-centred (focusing less on their own interests). At higher levels of moral development, individuals are concerned with broad principles of justice and with their self-chosen ethical principles. Kohlberg's model focuses on the decision-making process and on how individuals justify ethical decisions. His cognitive developmental theory explains how people decide what is right and wrong and how the decision-making process changes through interaction with peers and the environment.

In the premoral first stage typical of children, the focus is on doing what's best for yourself. Think of the child who tells a lie to avoid punishment. At level II, typical of most adults and therefore suitably labelled "conventional," people focus on the expectations of others. At the final, principled level, what is "right" is determined by universal values. The person sees beyond laws, rules, and the expectations of others.

Since it was proposed, more than 30 years ago, Kohlberg's model of cognitive moral development has been supported by a great deal of research. Individuals at higher stages of development are less likely to cheat,[114] more likely to engage in whistleblowing,[115] and more likely to make ethical business decisions.[116]

Individual differences in values, locus of control, Machiavellianism, and cognitive moral development all influence ethical behaviour in organizations. Organizations might use this knowledge to promote ethical behaviour by hiring and promoting individuals who share the organization's values or hiring and promoting only internals, low-Machs, and individuals at higher stages of cognitive moral development. This strategy obviously presents practical and legal problems. As values, locus of control, and cognitive moral development are fairly stable in adults, an organization is unlikely to change them through training. The best way to use the knowledge of individual differences may be to recognize that they help explain why ethical behaviour differs among individuals and to focus managerial efforts on creating a work situation supporting ethical behaviour.

Most workers are susceptible to external influences and look to their organization for guidance. Managers can offer such guidance by encouraging ethical behaviour through codes of conduct, ethics committees, training programs, ethics communication systems, norms, modelling, rewards and punishments, and CSR programs. We discuss some of these areas further in Chapter 17.

cognitive moral development The process of moving through stages of maturity in terms of making ethical decisions.

STUDY TOOLS 4

IN THE BOOK YOU CAN ...

- ☐ Rip out the **Chapter Review card** at the end of the book to review Key Concepts and Key Terms.
- ☐ Take a "What about You?" Quiz related to material in the chapter.
- ☐ Read additional cases in the Mini Case and Shopify Running Case sections.

ONLINE YOU CAN ...

NELSON.COM/STUDENT

- ☐ Take a "What about You?" Quiz related to material in the chapter.
- ☐ Test your understanding with a quick Multiple-Choice Pre-Test quiz.
- ☐ Read the eBook, which includes discussion points for questions posed in the Cases.
- ☐ Watch Videos related to chapter content.
- ☐ Use the available Flashcards and Matching Quizzes to test your understanding of key terms and concepts.
- ☐ See how much you've learned by taking a Post-Test.

WHAT ABOUT YOU?

Assess Your Job Satisfaction

Think of the job you have now or a job you've had in the past. Indicate how satisfied you are with each aspect of your job below, using the following scale:

1 = Extremely dissatisfied 2 = Dissatisfied 3 = Slightly dissatisfied 4 = Neutral 5 = Slightly satisfied 6 = Satisfied 7 = Extremely satisfied

1. The amount of job security I have.
2. The amount of pay and fringe benefits I receive.
3. The amount of personal growth and development I get in doing my job.
4. The people I talk to and work with on my job.
5. The degree of respect and fair treatment I receive from my boss.
6. The feeling of worthwhile accomplishment I get from doing my job.
7. The chance to get to know other people while on the job.
8. The amount of support and guidance I receive from my supervisor.
9. The degree to which I am fairly paid for what I contribute to this organization.
10. The amount of independent thought and action I can exercise in my job.
11. How secure things look for me in the future in this organization.
12. The chance to help other people while at work.
13. The amount of challenge in my job.
14. The overall quality of the supervision I receive on my work.

Now, compute your scores for the facets of job satisfaction.

Pay satisfaction:

Q2 + Q9 = ___ Divided by 2: ___

Security satisfaction:

Q1 + Q11 = ___ Divided by 2: ___

Social satisfaction:

Q4 + Q7 + Q12 = ___ Divided by 3: ___

Supervisory satisfaction:

Q5 + Q8 + Q14 = ___ Divided by 3: ___

Growth satisfaction:

Q3 + Q6 + Q10 + Q13 = ___ Divided by 4: ___

Scores on the facets range from 1 to 7. (Scores lower than 4 suggest there is room for change.)

This questionnaire is an abbreviated version of the Job Diagnostic Survey, a widely used tool for assessing individuals' attitudes about their jobs. Compare your scores on each facet to the following norms for a large sample of managers.

Pay satisfaction: 4.6 Security satisfaction: 5.2 Social satisfaction: 5.6 Supervisory satisfaction: 5.2 Growth satisfaction: 5.3

How do your scores compare? Are there actions you can take to improve your job satisfaction?

SOURCE: J. RICHARD HACKMAN & GREG R. OLDHAM, *WORK REDESIGN*, 1st Edition, © 1980. Reprinted by permission of Pearson Education, Inc., Upper Saddle River, N.J.

MINI CASE

Doing All That Is Necessary? SNC Lavalin

The World Bank has a published blacklist of corrupt and fraudulent companies. These companies have been banned from receiving project funding due to fraud, corruption, collusion, or coercion. Stephen Zimmerman, director of operations of the World Bank's Integrity Division, says "We're not a global policeman but what we can do is facilitate the global conversation against corruption [...] the World Bank is unique in that it's the only office in the world that looks at corruption cases globally; law enforcement tends to be national by its nature."

More than 600 companies have been barred from doing business with the World Bank, and of those, 117 are Canadian; the most of any country in the world. The United States has the second most companies with 46, while Indonesia is third with 43 companies barred. Of the 117 Canadian companies barred from doing business with the World Bank, 115 represent SNC-Lavalin and its subsidiaries. SNC-Lavalin is the largest engineering firm in Canada, based in Montreal, with offices in over 50 countries and operations in over 160 countries. SNC employs more than 50,000 people in a variety of industries, including infrastructure and construction, mining and metallurgy, oil and gas, environment and water, and clean energy. The company also advertises that it can provide clients with financing, asset management, engineering, construction, procurement, and operations management.

In 2010, allegations of bribery were levelled against company executives, and the company began a series of internal ethics initiatives. Executives from the firm even met with Quebec's premier to reassure political leaders that the company had taken the necessary steps to improve its corporate governance. In 2012, however, SNC's CEO was arrested on fraud charges, and in 2013, four company executives resigned from the organization for various undisclosed reasons.

Also in 2013, ethical violations began to come to light when one company vice president was jailed in Switzerland for suspicion of corruption, fraud, and money laundering in North Africa. Another executive, Stephane Roy, was on trial for fraud, bribery, and contravening a United Nations act. Roy alleges that he was acting on orders by his superiors, and that he had been framed and scapegoated by higher-level executives who called him a rogue employee. Roy told reporters that SNC-Lavalin created "a corporate culture where it was common practice to do all that was necessary, including the payment of 'commissions' and other benefits to obtain contracts, including in Libya."

A preliminary hearing on federal corruption and fraud charges against the company is scheduled to begin in September 2018, involving wrongdoing related to contracts that SNC had in Libya between 2001 and 2011, when $47.7 million was paid to public officials in Libya to influence government decisions. The company acknowledged that there were incidents of corporate malfeasance in the North African country, but says that it has undergone a complete overhaul of its ethics and compliance procedures since then, and that all executives who were with the company at that time have been removed from the organization.

SOURCE: J. RICHARD HACKMAN & GREG R. OLDHAM, WORK REDESIGN, 1st Edition, © 2018. Reprinted by permission of Pearson Education, Inc., New York, New York.

Apply Your Understanding

1. How might examples of executive corruption at SNC influence attitude formation in company employees?
2. How might cognitive dissonance play a role in unethical behaviour?
3. What factors influenced Stephane Roy's (un) ethical behaviour?

SHOPIFY RUNNING CASE

IN SUPPORT OF FREE SPEECH

When activists targeted Shopify for hosting Breitbart's online merchandise store, the hashtag #DeleteShopify, was circulated an attempt to persuade Shopify to drop Breitbart as a merchant. In spite of significant bad press, and pressure from other merchants as well as Shopify employees, Tobias Lütke held firm to his values, and refused to remove Breitbart from their merchants list. In 2017, Lütke penned an open letter called "In Support of Free Speech" explaining his justification. In that letter, Lütke explained that the reasons Shopify would continue to host Breitbart's e-commerce site were "nuanced," and "require[d] thought." He explained that he himself is a liberal immigrant, who runs a liberal company, and is against exclusion of any kind, but he went on to argue that he did not feel that he was in a position to assert his moral position onto another, no matter how controversial or distasteful he may have found them.

Lütke explained that for as long as Shopify has existed there have been demands from some groups to remove products that they disagree with, and Breitbart was no different. He rationalized that, living in a democracy, it was up to individuals as consumers to cast their vote on retailers by choosing which products to purchase —that purchase decisions would express a community's moral evaluation of a company and the company would either succeed or fail due to market forces, rather than censorship. Lütke also argued that products are a form of speech and the principle of free speech should protect both the producers and consumers of products, even when the product/message was controversial.

A portion of that letter reads, "If we start blocking out voices, we would fall short of our goals as a company to make commerce better for everyone. Instead, we would have a biased and diminished platform."

Apply Your Understanding

1. Describe the emotional labour likely experienced by Tobias Lütke.
2. Using the *Elaboration Likelihood Model*, explain how Tobias Lütke's open letter could have been received by his audience.
3. Describe how Tobias Lütke's values affected his decision to continue to host Breitbart merchandise.

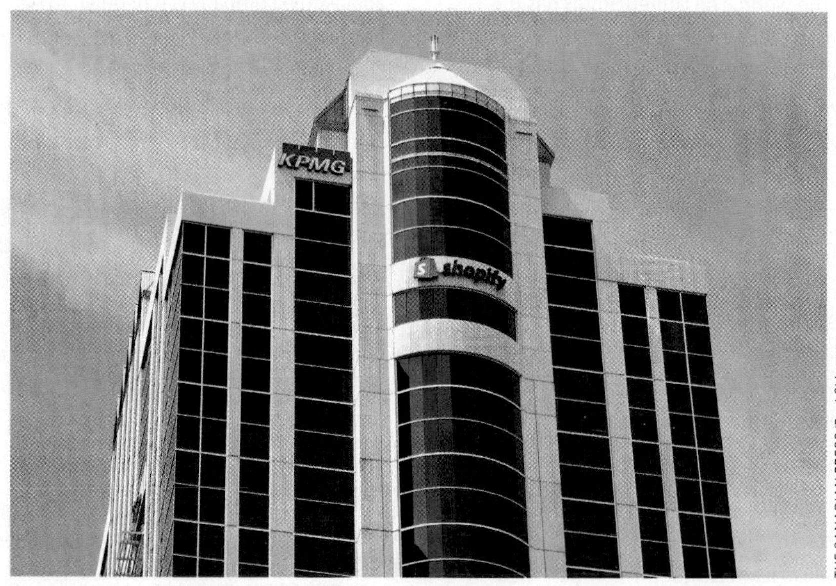

THE CANADIAN PRESS/Paul Chiasson

5 Motivation

LEARNING OUTCOMES

After reading this chapter, you should be able to do the following:

- 5-1 Define *motivation* and explain the difference between needs theories and process theories of motivation.
- 5-2 Explain how Maslow's need hierarchy is related to Theory X and Theory Y and ERG theory.
- 5-3 Discuss the needs for achievement, power, and affiliation.
- 5-4 Describe the role of inequity in motivation.
- 5-5 Describe the expectancy theory of motivation.
- 5-6 Explain how goal setting can motivate performance.
- 5-7 Describe the cultural differences in motivation.

See the end of this chapter for a list of available Study Tools, a "What about You?" Quiz, Mini Case, and the Shopify Running Case.

Motivation is one of the most critical components of an organization's success. There is clear evidence that people who are motivated try harder, and achieve more than individuals who are not motivated, but how can organizations influence an individual's level of motivation? Why are some people motivated by rewards, but others are motivated by praise? Can motivation be directed and sustained? There are few topics more thoroughly researched, or more hotly debated, in the field of organizational behaviour than motivation.

5-1 MOTIVATION

Motivation is the process of arousing and sustaining goal-directed behaviour, and it describes the forces that influence the direction, intensity, and persistence of a person's efforts. Every organization, from community sports teams to multinational conglomerates, wants to get the highest level of effort and the best possible performance from their members, and motivational levels play a significant role in typical performance.[1] From a productivity perspective, no component of organizational behaviour has a more significant impact on the organization than motivation.[2] Motivated employees are more likely to have higher levels of organizational engagement and commitment, and are more efficient and effective than unmotivated employees, which can increase productivity, and lower costs for the organization. Motivated employees are also more likely to collaborate and problem solve, leading to improved outcomes, positive relationships, and improved organizational culture. Because of its importance, there are few topics more thoroughly researched, or more hotly debated, in the field than motivation.

Motivation theories first attempt to predict and explain behaviour, and then use that understanding to implement organizational systems to enhance and encourage desired behaviours. A comprehensive approach to understanding motivation, behaviour, and performance must consider three elements of the work situation—the individual, the task, and the environment—and how these elements interact.[3] Motivation theories are broadly classified into two different categories: needs theories and process theories.

Needs theories of motivation give primary consideration to variables *within* the individual that lead to motivation and behaviour. The underlying premise is that people are motivated by unfulfilled needs and will engage in certain behaviours in an attempt to meet those needs. Needs theories focus on the psychological requirements of performance and motivation. **Needs** are insufficiencies that provoke some type of behavioural response, and they can be psychological (mental) or physiological (physical). Needs theories of motivation are content theories, and they focus on *what* motivates someone. **Process theories** of motivation describe individual motivation as being controlled by external environmental forces, and focus on *how* motivation works, and what factors direct and sustain it. Process theories typically rely on data to improve performance metrics.

> "Understanding motivation is one of the most important things we can do in our lives, because it has such a bearing on why we do the things we do and whether we enjoy them or not.
> —Clayton Christensen"

Motivation theories have passed through seven distinct stages in the last century, oscillating between process theories, which rely on normative data to improve performance metrics, and needs theories, which focus on the psychological requirements of performance and motivation.[4] As motivation theories are developed and continue to be refined, there has been a shift away from overarching broad conceptual theories of human motivation in general towards more strictly defined theories that focus on specific components of individual motivation

motivation The forces that influence the direction, intensity, and persistence of effort.

needs theories Theories of motivation based on the premise that people are motivated by unfulfilled needs.

needs physiological or psychological insufficiencies that provoke some type of behavioural response.

process theories Theories of motivation that emphasize the nature of the interaction between the individual and their environment.

Internal Motivators and External Incentives

Internal needs, or motivators, are intangible factors that arise from within an individual. They come from a person's desire to do something for its own sake, and the behaviour itself is its own reward. Internal motivators include enjoyment or excitement, the challenge of accomplishment, pride, and even fear. For instance, some people run marathons because they enjoy running; they may enjoy the physical challenge of pushing their bodies, the overall level of fitness that they are able to maintain, the feeling of success at having accomplished a difficult task, or any of a number of different reasons. Other people do crossword or Sudoku puzzles, again, because they enjoy the mental stimulation and the challenge of completion. On the other hand, some people may dress or speak a certain way out of fear of being judged by their peers, some parents are overly protective of their children out of fear that something bad might happen, while other people refuse to fly in commercial airplanes out of fear of crashing. In all cases, the behaviour stems from some internal belief or desire held by the individual.

External incentives, or extrinsic motivators, are tangible rewards or punishments that come from outside a person and are awarded, (or withheld) by somebody else. External motivators include things such as awards, pay and bonuses, and also penalties, fines, and punishments. For instance, some students study in order to achieve high marks; other students work to achieve high marks in order to avoid being reprimanded by their parents. In both cases, the behaviour stems from the desire to get something, or to avoid something unpleasant. Most economic assumptions about human motivation emphasize financial incentives and assume that people are motivated by self-interest for economic gain to provide the necessities and conveniences of life.[5]

MOTIVATION THEORIES TIMELINE: SCIENTIFIC MANAGEMENT AND THE HAWTHORNE STUDIES

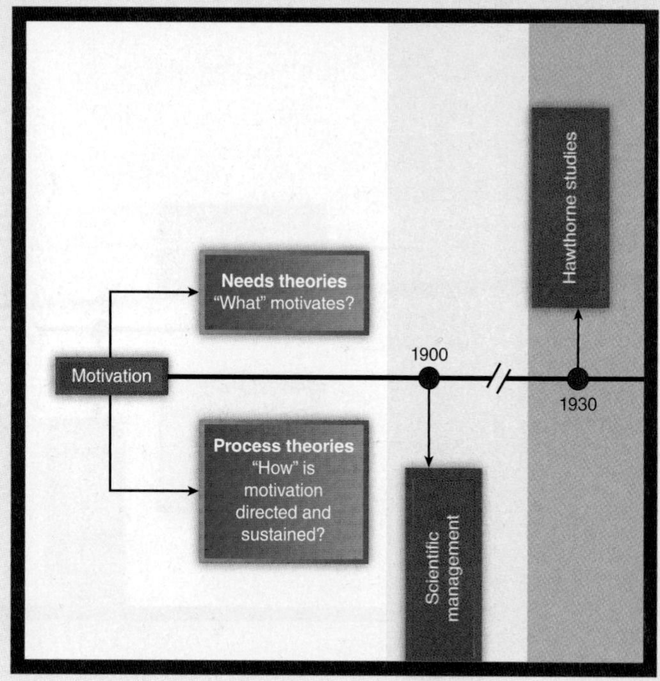

Scientific Management—A Process Theory

In the early 1900s, with the dawn of the Industrial Revolution, the first formal theory of motivation was introduced by Frederick Taylor.[6] Scientific management was designed to motivate individual productivity by rewarding increased performance with increased compensation, but little concern was paid to working

IN ACTION

Intrinsic Factors and External Incentives Work Together

Which affects employee performance more, intrinsic rewards or external incentives? According to a recent study, it depends. Researchers reviewed four decades of research and nine previous meta-analyses to answer that question along with other questions about the relative impact of intrinsic versus extrinsic motivation on performance outcomes. They found that both are instrumental. However, the most *important* method depended on the performance context. Intrinsic motivation was a better predictor of performance when quality was desired. For those tasks that require a great deal of personal investment, require judgment, or are complex, intrinsic motivation mattered most. On the other hand, external incentives were a better predictor of performance for quantity, when tasks were straightforward, noncomplex, and repetitive. Motivation tactics do not work in isolation. Managers should consider the desired performance to determine whether to rely on intrinsic rewards or external incentives to motivate employee behavior.

SOURCE: C. P. Cerasoli, J. M. Nicklin, and M. T. Ford, "Intrinsic Motivation and Extrinsic Incentives Jointly Predict Performance: A 40-Year Meta-Analysis," *Psychological Bulletin* 140 (2014): 980–1008.

MOTIVATION THEORIES TIMELINE: MASLOW'S NEED HIERARCHY, THEORY X AND THEORY Y, AND ERG THEORY

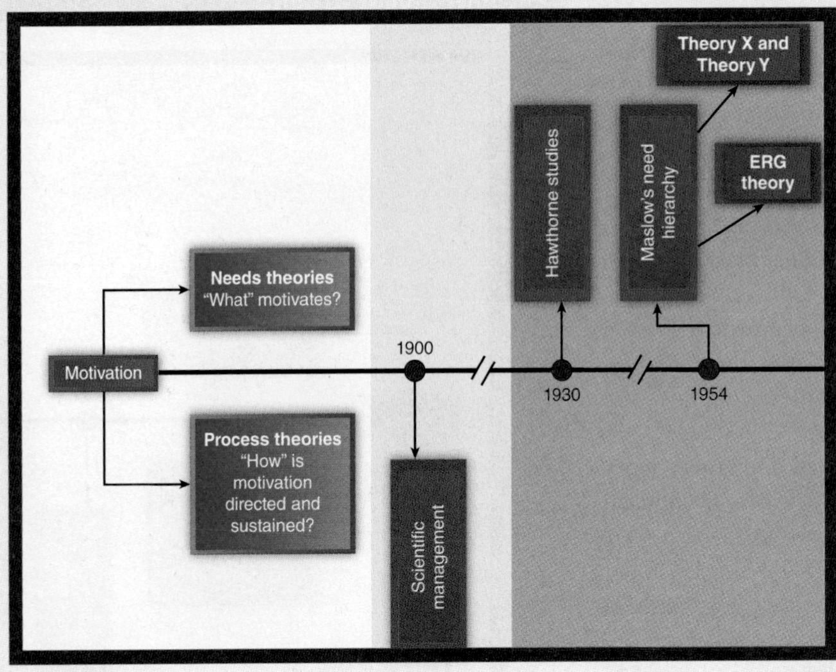

conditions or employment standards, and absolutely no concern was paid to employee morale. Under the scientific management strategy, factory conditions were poor, and workers were commonly exploited.[7] The Industrial Revolution changed how labour was performed, by changing the lengths to which organizations would go to achieve results. Workers were pushed until they began pushing back, and as individuals began to collectively identify with the labour movement, scientific management began to falter. Workers began resisting the scientific management strategy, and as early as 1911, laws were passed that banned the use of stop-watches on production floors. Despite its many shortcomings, most specifically in the treatment of human beings as machines, Taylor's view of motivation profoundly influenced all subsequent process-based motivational paradigms.

The Hawthorne Studies—A Needs Theory

The Great Depression (1930s) changed the social and political landscape in a fundamental way. The working class began to focus on social and labour welfare, and this time frame saw governments enact legislation to protect labourers (social security, employment insurance, and labour standards). The Hawthorne studies[8] (discussed in Chapter 1) are one of the most widely recognized management research projects ever conducted on human relations[9] and one of the few studies to claim that compensation is not the most important motivator of employee behaviour. The Hawthorne studies found that peer influence and social expectations have at least as much influence over productivity as compensation and incentives. The Hawthorne studies and other research conducted during the 1930s suggest that motivating employees can best be attained by resolving morale problems and improving social relations at work. Though this work has been largely discredited, it set the foundation for needs-based theories of motivation.

5-2 MASLOW'S NEED HIERARCHY—A NEEDS THEORY

After World War II, the United States experienced its most significant period of economic growth and expansion. This period of unparalleled economic development saw increases in productivity without any corresponding change in an organization's motivational technique, and needs theories which focused on employee empowerment and human relations remained the dominant motivational paradigm. Maslow's hierarchy of needs was introduced in 1943, and became a dominant theory of motivation in the late 1950s, as another tool for explaining human needs.

Maslow created a visual pyramid to represent the relative importance of five basic needs he believed to be true for all humans.[10] According to Maslow, our physiological

Sergey Nivens/Shutterstock.com

An unsatisfied need is a motivating need.

needs are of prime importance and we will do anything to ensure we have the means for survival (food, water, air). Safety and security needs are a close second, followed by love or social needs, and then esteem needs (the need to feel important or recognized). Self-actualization at the tip of the pyramid represents the need to discover oneself and realize one's potential. Maslow claimed that an unsatisfied need is a motivating need, and when more than one need is unsatisfied, the one closer to the base of the pyramid takes precedence because unsatisfied lower needs make it more difficult to fulfill higher needs.

The distinguishing feature of Maslow's need hierarchy is the *progression hypothesis*, which suggests that we are able to progress up the pyramid as the lower-level needs are met. There is a widely held mistaken view that lower-level needs must be fully satisfied before progressing. In truth, Maslow stated that everyone has unsatisfied needs at every level (after all, hunger is recurring, and everyone feels that their safety needs are unmet sometimes) but the more that lower needs are met, the more attention and resources can be directed at achieving higher needs.[11] A single action can also meet more than one need; for example, a meal fulfills physiological needs (hunger), but may also fill social needs (family gatherings often involve meals), and esteem needs (the chef may take pride in having cooked a gourmet meal that everyone enjoys).

Though Maslow's hierarchy has been challenged by researchers,[12] and has not found much empirical support in predicting individual needs, it laid the groundwork for the idea that everyone has different categories of needs, and that even within an individual, needs are constantly progressing and changing. The work was something of a revelation for organizations to consider that for the majority of employees, whose basic needs are met, keeping them motivated means offering opportunities to meet social, esteem, and self-actualization needs. Table 5.1 presents some examples of how employers can meet needs at various levels of the hierarchy.

> What a man can be, he must be. This need we call self-actualization.
> —Abraham Maslow

TABLE 5.1 WAYS IN WHICH EMPLOYERS CAN ADDRESS NEEDS IDENTIFIED BY MASLOW

Physiological Needs	Meals Access to cafeteria, vending machines, drinking fountains Working conditions: temperature, cleanliness, space, noise, lighting, ventilation Rest periods
Safety and Security Needs	
Economic	Wages and salaries Benefits (medical, retirement, etc.)
Psychological	Job descriptions Thorough training Managerial availability Avoid abrupt changes Clear communication
Physical	Prevent hazards Training in safety practices
Love/Social Needs	Opportunities to work in teams Social interaction Social activities
Esteem Needs	Opportunities for responsibility Recognition Participation in decisions Challenging goals
Self-actualization Needs	Opportunities for creative and challenging tasks/jobs Autonomy to pursue own interests Training

Theory X and Theory Y—A Needs Theory

Two other theories of motivation were built upon the framework of Maslow's model: Theory X and Theory Y, and

BLOOMimage/Getty Images

edhar yuralaits/Alamy Stock Photo

'X and Y": A mnemonic device to remember Theory X vs. Theory Y.

ERG theory. Theory X and Theory Y was created using Maslow's need hierarchy to explain motivation from a manager's perspective. The theory groups the physiological and safety needs presented in Maslow's model as "lower-order needs," and the social, esteem, and self-actualization needs as "upper-order needs."

According to Theory X and Theory Y, managers categorize employees into one of two categories depending on the factors that the manager believes motivates behaviour. **Theory X** management believes that employees are motivated by lower-order needs; that they are inherently lazy, that they will avoid responsibility where possible, that they dislike their work, and that they are working only for a sustainable income. Theory X managers believe that workers need to be closely supervised, and that control systems of rewards and punishments are required in order to properly motivate behaviours. Theory X managers emphasize production and output. **Theory Y** supervisors, on the other hand, believe that employees are self-directed and are internally motivated by higher-order needs, which are fulfilled through work. Theory Y supervisors prefer a participative style of management, and emphasize employee commitment to the organization and its goals. These assumptions are listed in Table 5.2 and have been mapped onto Maslow's hierarchy, from which they derive, in Figure 5.1.[13]

Theory X and Theory Y are not opposite ends of the same spectrum, but represent two different spectra. In order to achieve the highest level of employee output, a combination of both theories should be used (see Chapter 12 for a discussion of leadership contingency theory).[14] Like Maslow's, this theory proposes that self-actualization is the highest level of achievement for individuals, and Theory Y assumptions are the inspiration for employee participation programs which encourage employee involvement to support high-performance achievements.[15]

Theory X Management assumption that workers are lazy and dislike responsibility.

Theory Y Management assumption that workers like work and will seek responsibility.

ERG Theory—A Needs Theory

ERG theory recognized Maslow's contribution to understanding motivation, but believed that the needs hierarchy failed to accurately identify and categorize human needs.[16] Instead, ERG theory condenses Maslow's five needs into only three categories: **E**xistence, **R**elatedness, and **G**rowth (or ERG).[17] (Maslow's physiological and physical safety needs comprise the existence category; Maslow's interpersonal safety, love, and interpersonal esteem needs comprise ERG's relatedness need category; and Maslow's self-actualization and self-esteem needs represent ERG's growth category.)

ERG theory added a *regression* hypothesis to Maslow's original progression hypothesis, which suggests

FIGURE 5.1 MASLOW'S NEEDS AND THEORY X AND THEORY Y

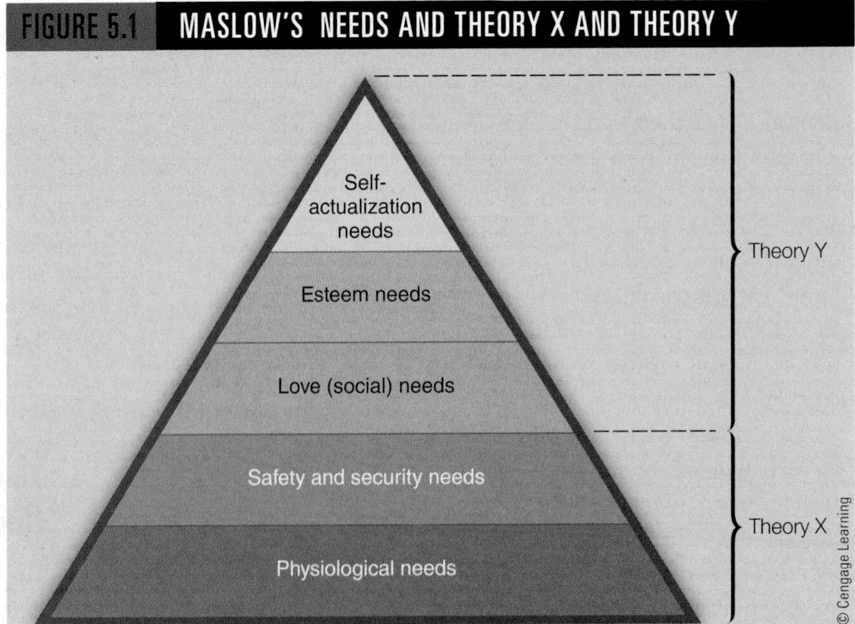

© Cengage Learning

TABLE 5.2 ASSUMPTIONS ABOUT PEOPLE

Theory X	Theory Y
• People are by nature indolent. That is, they work as little as possible. • People lack ambition, dislike responsibility, and prefer to be led. • People are inherently self-centred and indifferent to organizational needs. • People are by nature resistant to change. • People are gullible and not very bright, the ready dupes of the charlatan and the demagogue.	• People are not by nature passive or resistant to organizational needs. They have become so as a result of experience in organizations. • The motivation, the potential for development, the capacity for assuming responsibility, and the readiness to direct behaviour toward organizational goals are all present in people. Management does not put them there. It is a responsibility of management to make it possible for people to recognize and develop these human characteristics for themselves. • The essential task of management is to arrange conditions and methods of operation so that people can achieve their own goals best by directing their own efforts toward organizational objectives.

SOURCE: From "The Human Side of Enterprise" by Douglas M. McGregor; reprinted from *Management Review*, November 1957.

that when people are frustrated by their inability to meet needs at the next higher level in the hierarchy, they regress to lower-level needs and intensify their desire to gratify these needs. This regression hypothesis proposes that an already-satisfied need can continue to motivate when a higher need cannot be achieved.

For example, if a person is continually denied in their attempts to satisfy their growth needs, relatedness needs can become key motivators. An employee may desire growth opportunities that simply are not available at their current place of employment. The employee may not choose to quit and seek another job, but may instead refocus on social opportunities available at work through friendships and social contact.

ERG theory also allows the order of needs to differ between individuals (in other words, needs do not have to progress from E to R to G,) which allows it to explain behaviours that Maslow's hierarchy struggles with, like the "starving artist," whose physical needs are not well met, but whose growth needs are fulfilled. The artist, failing to fulfill their higher order need of physical comfort, may regress and continue to fulfill their lower order need of growth by continuing to focus on their art.

5-3 McCLELLAND'S NEED THEORY—A NEEDS THEORY

McClelland's need theory of motivation focuses on personality, and identifies three learned or acquired needs.[18] These are the needs for *achievement, power*, and *affiliation*. McClelland stated that all people have these three types of motivation in varying degrees, regardless of culture, gender, age, or race, and that life experiences led to different needs being dominant in different people.

Need theory posits that each individual's needs for achievement, power, and affiliation are subconscious,

Motivation

Psychologists and other behavioural researchers have recognized that motivation is not as simple as rewarding desired behaviour and punishing undesired behaviour. Research consistently finds that rewards offered to encourage a given behaviour can instead reduce the very behaviour intended to be encouraged. For instance, when Britain began rewarding people for donating blood, researchers found that blood donations became higher among individuals who were not offered compensation. Similarly, fines and punishments sometimes fail to reduce undesired behaviours, but instead appear to encourage them. Daycares that implemented fines for parents who were late picking up their children found that even more parents arrived late after the policy was implemented.

This effect has been given many names including the over-justification hypothesis, the corruption effect, the hidden cost of reward, cognitive evaluation theory, and motivation crowding.

SOURCE: B. Frey, and R. Jegen, "Motivation Crowding Theory," *Journal of Economic Surveys* 15(5) (2001): 589–623.

MOTIVATION THEORIES TIMELINE: MCCLELLAND'S NEED THEORY

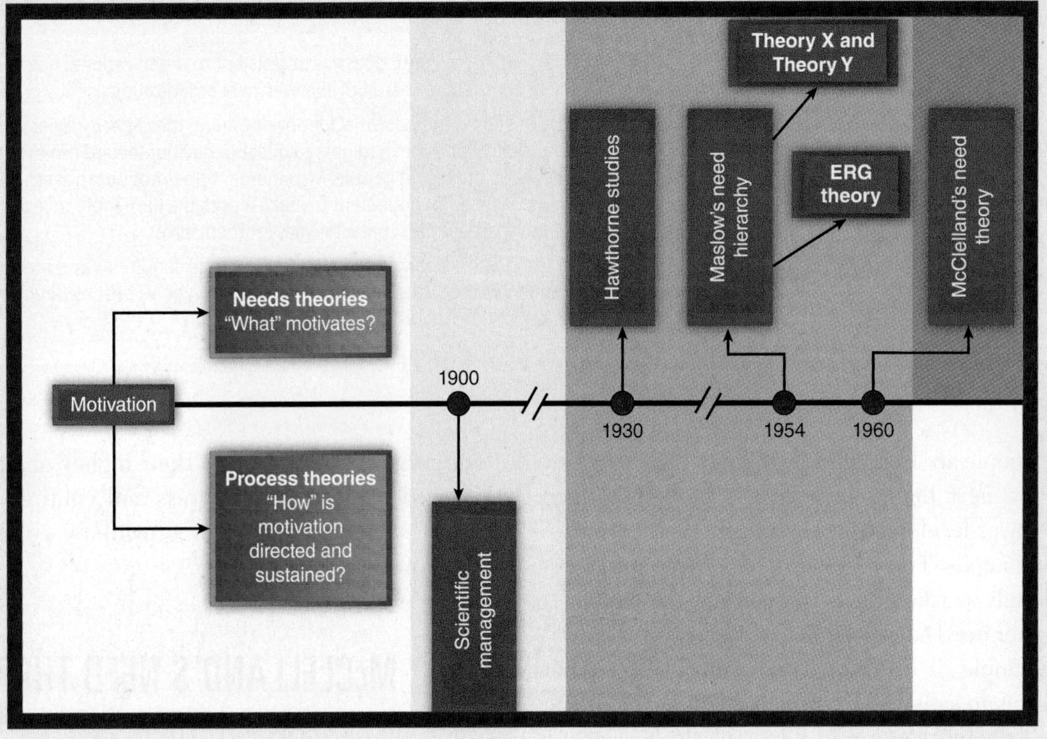

and that an individual could not simply describe their needs if asked. A projective test (called the Thematic Apperception Test[19]) is used wherein individuals are shown a standard set of pictures, and are asked to create stories about them. Those stories are then analyzed for their motivational themes. McClelland believed that people's own needs were subconscious or below their own awareness, but that those needs are **manifest** or easily perceived by others. A manager who knows their staff well can reasonably determine who would like power, who cherishes affiliation opportunities, and who particularly values achievement.

Where victims see adversity, extreme achievers see opportunity.

—Robin Sharma

manifest needs Learned or acquired needs that are subconscious but easily perceived by others.

need for achievement (nAch) Individuals motivated by a manifest need for competition, challenging goals, persistence, and overcoming difficulties.

Need for Achievement (nAch)

The **need for achievement** (often abbreviated as nAch) describes individuals who are motivated by competition, challenging goals, persistence, and overcoming difficulties.[20] McClelland found that people with a high need for achievement perform better than those with lower nAch levels. High need for achievement individuals typically share three characteristics: First, they set goals that are moderately difficult, yet achievable. Second, they like to receive feedback on their progress toward these goals. Third, they do not like having external events or other people interfere with their progress toward the goals.

High achievers often hope and plan for success. They may be quite content to work alone or with other people—whichever is more appropriate to their task. High achievers like being very good at what they do, and they develop expertise and competence in their chosen endeavours. The need for achievement generalizes well across countries with adults who are employed full-time, but researchers have found international differences in the tendency for achievement.[21] Achievement tendencies are highest in individualistic cultures and lowest in collectivistic societies.[22]

Need for Power (nPow)

The **need for power** (often abbreviated as nPow) includes the desire to influence others, the urge to change people or events, and the wish to make a difference. The need for power is interpersonal because it involves influence over other people. McClelland distinguishes between socialized power, which is used for the benefit of many, and personalized power, which is used for individual gain. The former is a constructive force, whereas the latter may be a very disruptive, destructive force. According to McClelland's research, the best managers have a high need for socialized power, as opposed to personalized power.[23] They are concerned for others; have an interest in organizational goals; and want to be useful to the larger group, organization, and society.

Need for Affiliation (nAff)

The **need for affiliation** (often abbreviated nAff) describes an urge to establish and maintain warm, close relationships with others.[24] People with a high need for affiliation enjoy being part of groups, and have a desire to feel loved and accepted. Individuals with high nAff prefer collaboration over competition, and are motivated to express their emotions to others and expect others to do the same in return. They find conflicts disturbing and are strongly motivated to work through any such barriers to closeness.

A need that is not addressed directly by McClelland's need theory, but that has emerged in research, is the need for autonomy. This is the desire for independence and freedom from constraints. People with a high need for autonomy prefer to work alone and to control the pace of their work, and dislike bureaucratic rules, regulations, and procedures. The need for autonomy is common in many cultures: A study comparing employee need patterns in eight foreign subsidiaries of a multinational company (Belgium, Spain, Germany, Italy, Venezuela, Mexico, Columbia, and Japan) found that the need to control the environment was strong in all.[25]

Art Babych/Shutterstock.com

High nPow individuals are motivated by a need to influence others, and change people or events.

Research has shown that motivation is not always characterized by self-interest: Given the chance for respectful contact with the beneficiaries of their work, some workers show substantial increases in effort and performance. In a longitudinal field experiment with fundraising callers, one group was given ten minutes of direct contact with a student whose scholarship had been funded partly through their fundraising efforts. The control groups had either indirect contact (a letter from a beneficiary) or no exposure. One month later, the direct contact group showed significantly greater persistence (142 percent more phone time) and job performance (171 percent more money raised) than the control groups. Having direct contact with beneficiaries makes the work more meaningful and purposeful. It makes the worker feel better about doing it.

Is this self-interest or altruism? In the end, that does not matter because both the individual and the organization gain.

SOURCES: A. M. Grant, "Relational Job Design and the Motivation to Make a Prosocial Difference," *Academy of Management Review* 32(2007): 393–417; A. M. Grant, E. M. Campbell, G. Chen, K. Cottone, D. Lapedis, and K. Lee, "Impact and the Art of Motivation Maintenance: The Effects of Contact with Beneficiaries on Persistence Behavior," *Organizational Behavior and Human Decision Processes* 103 (2007) 53–67.

Figure 5.2 shows the parallel structures of Maslow's, Theory X and Theory Y, ERG, and McClelland's theories of motivation.

It is important to note that McClelland's need theory believes that the needs which drive motivation are fixed within the individual and cannot be changed by external forces. Managers must use their knowledge of employees' needs to provide opportunities for them to meet their specific needs, but they cannot change the needs themselves. For example, a manager may want to promote a staff member; however, if the employee has a high need for affiliation but a moderate need for achievement and a low need for power, the employee will resist this opportunity. Getting promoted would mean being pulled away from friends or being put in charge of them, which would be even worse. While the manager may believe that being promoted is a chance

need for power (nPow) Individuals motivated by a manifest need to make an impact, influence others, change people or events, and make a difference.

need for affiliation (nAff) Individuals motivated by a manifest need to establish and maintain warm, close relationships with other people.

FIGURE 5.2 NEED THEORIES OF MOTIVATION

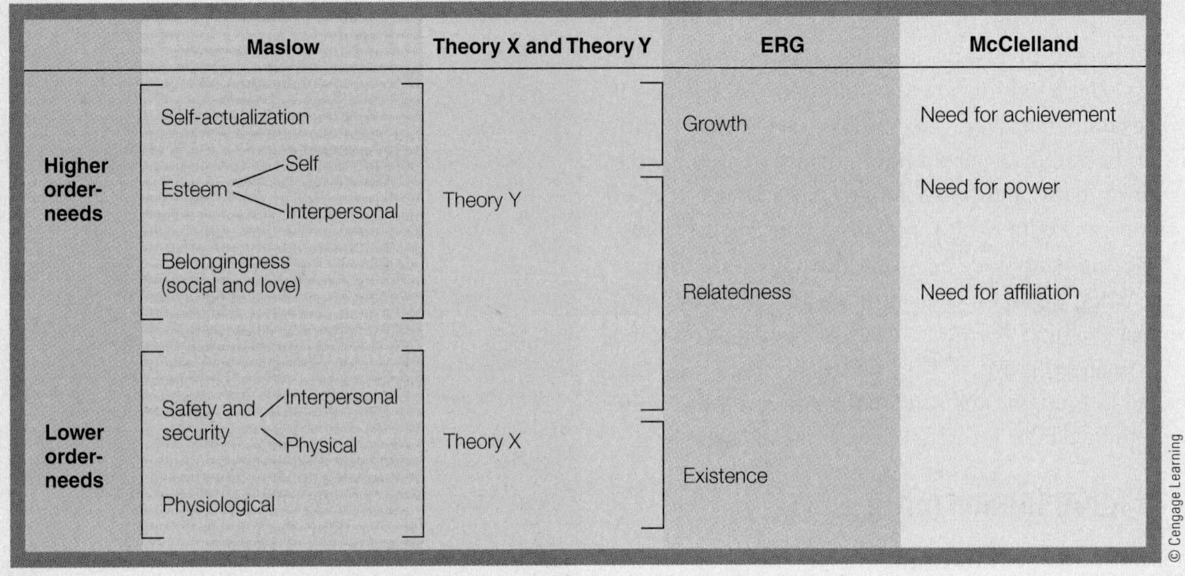

for recognition, to make more money, and pursue more interesting work, they cannot project their own needs, or motivators, on to others.

Maslow
Theory X and Theory Y
ERG
McClelland
Higher order-needs
Self-actualization
Esteem
Self
Interpersonal
Belongingness (social and love)
Theory Y
Growth
Relatedness
Need for achievement
Need for power
Need for affiliation
Lower order-needs
Safety and security
Interpersonal
Physical
Physiological
Theory X
Existence
© Cengage Learning

5-4 EQUITY THEORY—A PROCESS THEORY

Equity theory states that motivation is a function of perceived fairness (equity) in the social exchange and that inequity (unfairness) is an important motivator. The theory proposes that all employees perceive that they contribute *inputs* to an organization (such as time, experience, creativity, etc.) and receive *outcomes* from the organization in return (in the form of pay, awards, benefits, recognition, etc.). Employees then create a subjective ratio measuring their outcomes against their *perceived* contributions. Employees also create ratios for others within the organization, comparing others' *perceived* outcomes against their *perceived* inputs. Employees then weigh their outcome/input ratio against that of the comparison other. The comparison is seen as fair if the ratios are approximately the same. Both parties do not have to contribute in equal amounts, or receive equal outcomes, so long as the ratio of outcomes/inputs is similar. Therefore, it is acceptable to receive greater outcomes if one's inputs were also greater; it is also acceptable to receive less if one's input was commensurately smaller. In equity theory, it is the ratio of outcome to input that matters. If the ratios of outcomes to inputs are not matched, however, there is **inequity**. Inequity creates tension, which motivates a person to take action to resolve the inequity.[26]

inequity When a person perceives that they are receiving less than they are giving, or is giving less than they are receiving in comparison with another.

Equity theory has several important considerations in an organizational setting. The first, which has been mentioned (but is worth repeating) is that it is the *ratio* of outcomes to inputs that is important, not the absolute measure of either factor. Some parents with young children or some people with certain illnesses will happily accept less pay in return for increased flexibility. The next, and arguably the most important, consideration in equity theory is that it is the *perceived* outcomes and inputs that are being measured and compared, and as Chapter 3 made clear, people's perceptions can be vastly different. Nontangible and invisible inputs, such as emotional investment, and nontangible outcomes, such as job satisfaction, may well enter into a person's equity equation, drastically changing the resulting ratio.

Pay inequity, where women are traditionally paid less (outcome) for the same work (input), has been a thorny issue for women in some organizations. This inequity has led to the notion of "equal pay for work of equal value" when determining pay for female- versus male-dominated jobs (in some Canadian jurisdictions).[27] As organizations grow internationally, they may have

MOTIVATION THEORIES TIMELINE: EQUITY THEORY

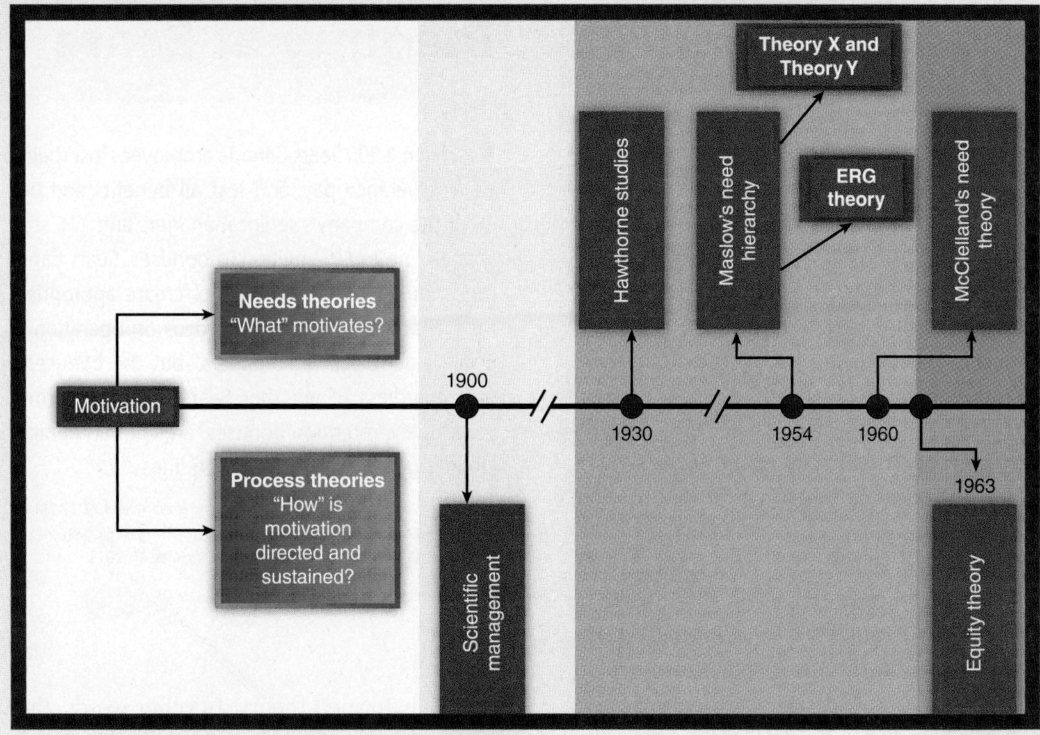

trouble determining pay and benefit equity/inequity across national borders as cost of living and other local market factors affect the ratio of outcomes to inputs for employees in different locations.

Figure 5.3 shows one equity situation and two inequity situations, one negative and one positive. A negative inequity (b) occurs when the individual perceives that they are receiving less for the same level of input (or are putting in more effort for the same level of outcome); for instance, non-smokers often resent their peers who smoke, because smokers take three or four 15-minute breaks each workday but are paid the same amount as the non-smokers, who put in an extra hour of effort each day. A positive inequity (c) occurs when the individual perceives that they are receiving more than the comparison other for the same level of input (or are putting in less inputs for the same level of outcome), for instance, a male colleague who is paid a higher salary than a female in the same role.

The Resolution of Inequity

Once a person establishes the existence of a perceived inequity, they might use a number of strategies to restore equity. Equity theory highlights seven basic strategies for restoring equity: (1) alter one's outcomes, (2) alter one's inputs, (3) alter the comparison other's outcomes, (4) alter the comparison other's inputs, (5) change who is used as a comparison other, (6) rationalize the inequity, and (7) leave the organizational situation.

An employee who receives a bonus that is smaller than what the comparison other received, or who feels

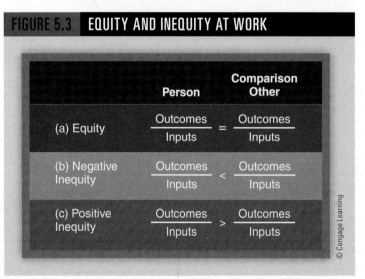

FIGURE 5.3 EQUITY AND INEQUITY AT WORK

	Person		Comparison Other
(a) Equity	Outcomes / Inputs	=	Outcomes / Inputs
(b) Negative Inequity	Outcomes / Inputs	<	Outcomes / Inputs
(c) Positive Inequity	Outcomes / Inputs	>	Outcomes / Inputs

that they worked harder than their colleagues will perceive a negative inequity. That employee could (1) try to convince their supervisor to increase the bonus or recognize their work in another way; (2) decide to work less moving forward to bring their efforts in line with the bonus; (3) try to get the colleague's bonus cut; (4) insist that the colleague take on a bigger part of the workload; (5) realize that they are lucky to get such a bonus in the first place, because their brother works longer hours at his job, earns less, and got no bonus at all; (6) re-assess their own contributions, and determine that they were not giving enough credit to the colleague; or (7) quit.

The selection of a strategy and the tactics used to reduce inequity is a sensitive issue with possible long-term consequences. In this example, a strategy aimed at reducing the comparison other's outcomes (by trying to get the colleague's bonus cut) may have the desired short-term effect of restoring equity but will reduce morale and productivity in the long term, and will likely lead to retaliation and increased conflict. Equity theory only proposes that these are the mechanisms by which an individual will redress perceived inequities. It does not include a hierarchy predicting which inequity reduction strategy a person will or should choose, but it is nevertheless a reminder of the importance of fairness. Workers who perceive compensation decisions as equitable based on performance report greater job satisfaction and organizational commitment.[28]

Evidence shows strong support for equity theory's contention that undercompensated workers react with negative attitudes[29] and lowered performance.[30] However, research does not appear to support the contention that employees who feel overcompensated will be motivated to restore equity by, for example, increasing their own inputs or decreasing their outcomes. People seem to be able to rationalize inequity in their own favour quite easily.

IN ACTION

Inequity at Sears

When 2,900 Sears Canada employees lost their jobs without severance pay, and lost all benefits and pension plans, 43 of the company's senior managers and 116 store managers received up to $9.2 million in bonuses. Sears Canada says that the bonuses were designed to "create appropriate incentives for management to stay and focus on operation and to maximize value for all stakeholders," but the bonuses will be paid out regardless of whether Sears meets performance targets. Bankruptcy "retention bonuses" are common practice, but they create significant perceived inequities.

SOURCE: K. Dangerfield, "Sears Managers, Executives Get $9.2M in Bonuses While Thousands Laid Off," July 14, 2017, accessed from https://globalnews.ca/news/3598469/sears-canada-lay-offs-management-bonuses, May 20, 2018.

equity sensitive An individual who prefers an equity ratio equal to that of their comparison other.

benevolent An individual who is comfortable with an equity ratio less than that of their comparison other.

entitled An individual who is comfortable with an equity ratio greater than that of their comparison other.

New Perspectives on Equity Theory: Equity Sensitivity

Equity theory has been revisited in light of new theories and research. One important theoretical revision proposes three types of individuals based on preferences for equity.[31] **Equity sensitives** prefer equity based on the originally formed theory. In other words, they want the ratio between their outcomes to inputs to be equivalent to that of their comparison others, and feel distressed when under-rewarded, and guilt when over-rewarded. **Benevolents** are comfortable with an equity ratio less than that of their comparison other,[32] and may be thought of as givers. Benevolents show less distress in inequitable situations and are more likely to engage in OCBs in a team environment.[33] **Entitleds** are comfortable with an equity ratio greater than that of their comparison other,[34] and may be thought of as takers.

The equity sensitivity construct may also serve to explain how individuals differ in their perceptions of

Entitleds place a higher emphasis on external tangible organizational rewards.

inputs and outcomes. For a task that is particularly challenging, benevolents are more likely to perceive the satisfaction of accomplishing the challenge as an outcome thus not requiring any additional reward, while entitleds are more likely to perceive the higher level of work involved as an input, and expect to be compensated accordingly. Additionally, benevolents seem to put more emphasis on intrinsic outcomes at work whereas entitleds place a higher emphasis on external tangible organizational outcomes such as pay.[35] Interestingly, there may be cultural differences in equity sensitivity. One study found that Chinese employees had more of a benevolent orientation, whereas British and French employees were more entitlement oriented.[36]

Equity theory has also been supplemented by research on other issues of organizational justice. Where equity theory focuses on distributive justice (fairness in who gets what), it appears that people are also sensitive to **procedural justice** (fairness in how things are done) and **interactional justice** (fairness in how they are treated). People who feel fairly treated are more likely to engage in OCBs, giving back to the people and organization that have been good to them. People who feel unfairly treated are not only less likely to help others but also more likely to engage in theft,[37] sabotage,[38] and retaliation.[39]

The general conclusion from equity theory is fairly straightforward: Treating employees fairly is critical to motivation. The application of equity theory, however, is significantly more challenging, particularly when considering the advice of needs-based motivational theories to customize rewards based on the individual's particular motivating factors. Organizations find themselves in a position of trying to reward people differently (based on needs) while trying to ensure that the differences are fair (as per equity theory). Giving employees a choice of rewards and allowing them to choose which benefits are most valuable to them can help guard against perceived inequities,[40] and making the reward processes as transparent as possible can help to preserve equity as well as procedural and interactional justice.

5-5 EXPECTANCY THEORY— A PROCESS THEORY

While equity theory focuses on a social exchange, expectancy theory of motivation focuses on personal perceptions of the performance process. This cognitive process theory is founded on two notions: First, that people *expect* certain outcomes of behaviour and performance, which may be thought of as rewards or consequences of behaviour, and, second, that people believe there is a relationship between the effort they put forth, the performance they achieve, and the outcomes they receive.

Expectancy theory attempts to explain why individuals choose one behavioural option over another, and proposes that an individual will choose a certain behaviour because of their expectations about what the results of that behaviour will be.[41] The motivation for the behaviour is determined by the desirability of the outcome. Expectancy theory has been used in a wide variety of contexts, including test-taking motivation among students.[42]

The key elements of expectancy theory are expectancy, instrumentality, and the valence of an outcome.[43] **Expectancy** is the belief that effort leads to performance ("If I try harder, I can do better"). Expectancy is usually based on past experience, self-efficacy, and the perceived difficulty of the goal.[44] **Instrumentality** is the belief that performance is related to outcomes ("If I perform better, I will get more pay"). Instrumentality depends on a person's level of trust in the one measuring performance and allocating rewards. **Valence** is the value or importance an individual places on a particular outcome, and can be affected by individual values, needs, goals, and preferences. Valence can be positive or negative, depending on whether the person wants the outcome or not. Expectancy and instrumentality are attitudes, and valence is a value assessment.

Expectancy, instrumentality, and valence all influence a person's motivation. Expectancy and instrumentality concern a person's beliefs about how effort, performance, and rewards are related. While one person might believe that an increase in effort has a direct, positive effect on performance, another might have very different beliefs about the effort–performance link. The perceived relationship between effort and performance varies from person to person and from activity to activity. In a similar fashion, people's beliefs about the performance–reward link vary. From a motivation perspective, it is the person's *belief* about the relationships between these constructs that is important, not the actual nature of the relationship.

procedural justice The fairness of the process by which outcomes are allocated in an organization.

interactional justice Fairness in how people are treated.

expectancy The belief that effort leads to performance.

instrumentality The belief that performance is related to outcomes.

valence The value or importance one places on a particular reward.

MOTIVATION THEORIES TIMELINE: EQUITY THEORY

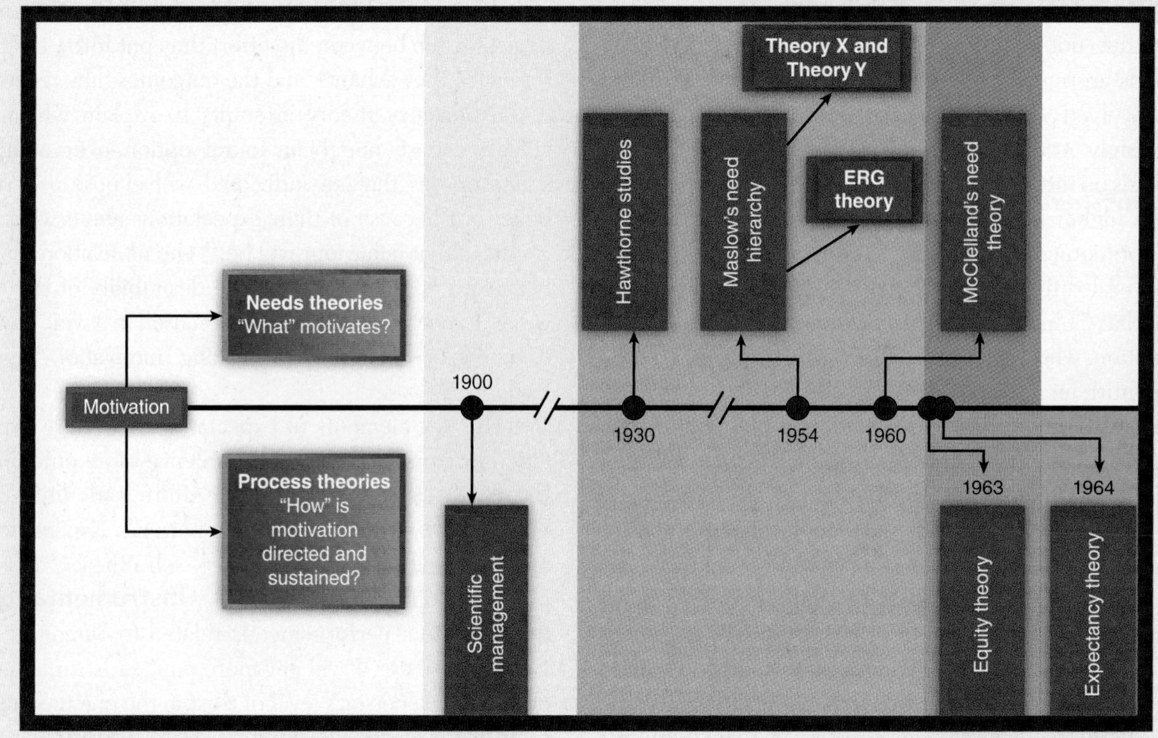

The motivation that a person experiences can be describes as follows:

Motivation = Expectancy × Instrumentality × Valence

When deciding among behavioural options, an individual will select the option with the highest resulting level of motivation. Figure 5.4 models the expectancy theory notions of effort, performance, and rewards.

Expectancy theory explains that it is important for employees to see a strong link between their efforts and results, to see that differential results lead to different outcomes, and for those outcomes to be relevant to employees. Valence and expectancy are particularly important in establishing priorities for people pursuing multiple goals.[45] Managers can take steps to enhance these links. To enhance *expectancy*, managers can match

FIGURE 5.4 AN EXPECTANCY MODEL FOR MOTIVATION

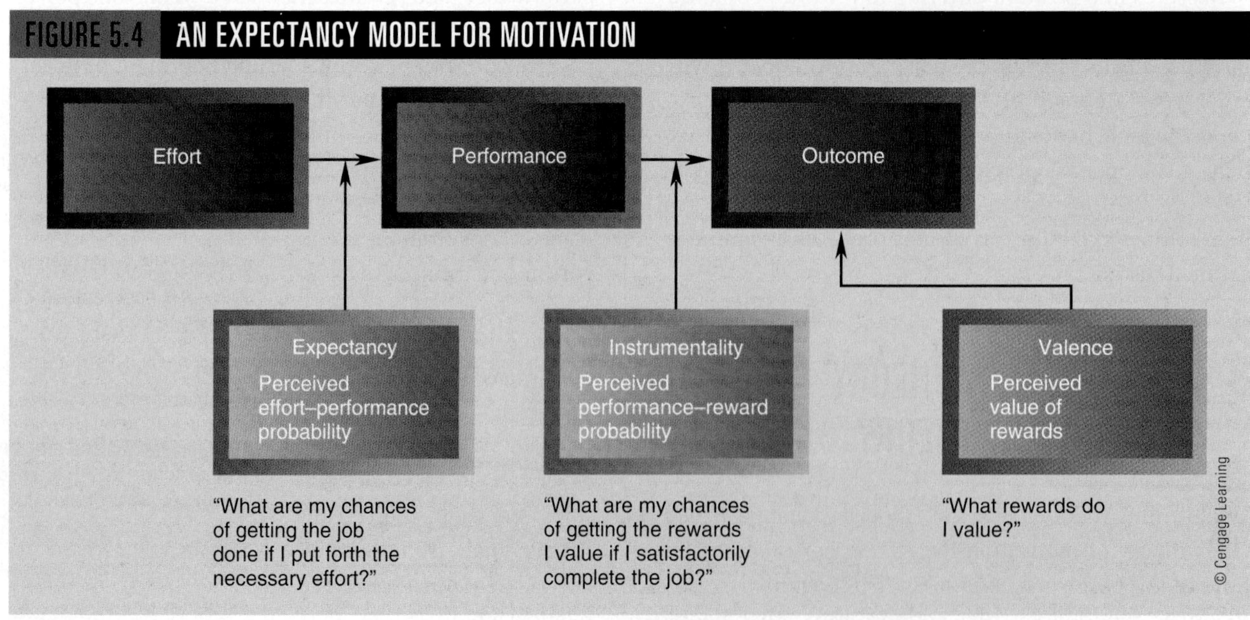

people to jobs and tasks and provide training, resources, and support so employees believe they can be successful. *Instrumentality* is enhanced when a manager observes and responds to varying performance levels. Managers can respond to strong, moderate, and weak performances differently. Managers should be sensitive to the *valence* of various rewards to individuals and do whatever is possible to attach valued rewards to strong performance.[46] This means the manager must be willing to treat people differently, e.g., rewarding one with time off and another with a bonus, keeping in mind the need to be seen as fair at the same time.

Motivational Problems

Expectancy theory attributes motivational problems to three basic causes:

1. Disbelief in a relationship between effort and performance. If the motivational problem stems from low expectancy (i.e., the person does not believe that effort will improve performance), the solution is to show how an increase in effort or an alteration in the kind of effort put forth can be converted into improved performance. Training programs can help increase self-efficacy which, in turn, will help strengthen expectancy.
2. Lack of trust in the relationship between performance and rewards. Organizations must strive to ensure that compensation systems tie rewards to performance in order to reduce uncertainty in instrumentality. The person can be shown how an increase in performance or a somewhat altered form of performance will be converted into rewards, by demonstrating that others who have achieved the outcome have gained the rewards.
3. Lack of desire for the rewards offered. A reward that is not valued is no reward at all. If the motivational problem is related to the value placed on certain rewards, there are two possible solutions: to alter the value placed on the rewards or to alter the rewards themselves.

Research results on expectancy theory have been mixed.[47] The theory predicts job satisfaction accurately, but its complexity makes it difficult to test the full model, and the measures of instrumentality, valence, and expectancy have only weak validity.[48] In addition, measuring the expectancy constructs is time consuming, and the values for each construct change over time for an individual. Finally, the theory assumes the individual is totally rational and acts as a minicomputer, calculating probabilities and values, ignoring emotional responses. In reality, the theory may be more complex than people as they typically function.

Motivation and Moral Maturity

Expectancy theory predicts that people will work to maximize their personal outcomes, and so the theory cannot explain altruistic behaviour for the benefit of others. Therefore, it may be necessary to consider an individual's **moral maturity** in order to understand altruistic, fair, and equitable behaviour. Moral maturity is the measure of a person's cognitive moral development, which was discussed in Chapter 4. Morally mature people act and behave based on universal ethical principles, whereas morally immature people act and behave based on egocentric motivations.[49]

5-6 GOAL-SETTING THEORY—A NEEDS THEORY

> "You can motivate by fear, and you can motivate by reward. But both those methods are only temporary. The only lasting thing is self-motivation.
> —Homer Rice"

The social climate in the 1980s became short-term oriented, and goal-setting theories became popular again, signalling the return to a focus on clear objectives and tangible, numerical outcomes. **Goal setting** is the process of establishing desired results that guide and direct behaviour and is one of the most robust theories of motivation, with research strongly supporting its basic principles. According to this theory, people with specific, challenging goals will outperform those with general, "do your best goals" or no goals at all. The higher the goal, the better the performance; that is, people work harder to reach difficult goals, as long as they are committed to the goal and have the skills to achieve it.[50] Goal-setting theory states that five goal-setting principles can improve success: clarity, challenge, commitment, feedback, and task complexity.

moral maturity The measure of a person's cognitive moral development.

goal setting The process of establishing desired results that guide and direct behaviour.

MOTIVATION THEORIES TIMELINE: GOAL-SETTING THEORY

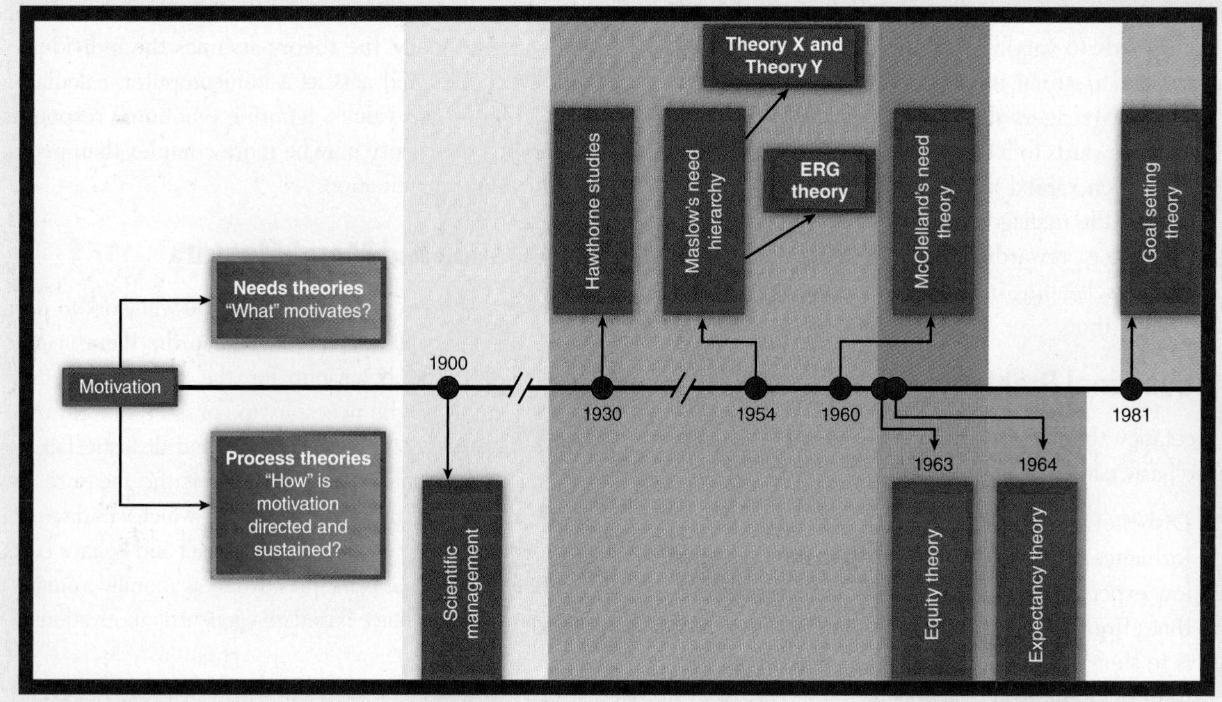

Clarity

Goals can be effective motivators only when they are specific. The SMART acronym is often used to create effective goals by ensuring that goals are:

Specific—Goals must be clear and precise in order to focus one's efforts.

Measurable—Goals must be measurable in order to be able to track progress and know when success has been achieved.

Achievable—Goals should stretch one's abilities, but must be realistic and attainable in order to be motivational.

Specific, challenging goals guide and direct behaviour.

Relevant—Goals must be worthwhile and valuable, or else they are not worth achieving.

Time-bound—Goals must have a deadline or target date.

Challenge

People are motivated by challenging goals, but it is important not to set impossible goals. Challenge can arise from the complexity of the task itself, from the balance between pressure and performance, from timelines and deadlines for performance and even from competition from peers who are also attempting to accomplish their own goals. Research has found that the highest level of effort occurs when tasks are moderately difficult—not very easy, and not very hard.[51]

Commitment

Goal commitment is the key component of motivation in goal-setting theory. An individual who is not truly committed to a goal will lack the motivation to achieve it. An individual's level of commitment can be influenced by three factors:[52]

1. The importance of the expected outcomes of goal attainment. If the goal is an absolute priority for an individual, they are more likely to be committed to its attainment.

2. If an individual believes very strongly that they are able to achieve their goal, more likely to be committed to its attainment. Managers can take steps to raise the self-efficacy of their subordinates by ensuring appropriate training, providing role models with whom the employee can identify, and expressing confidence in the employee. Interestingly, the mere fact of assigning a difficult goal in itself tends to raise self-efficacy because it is a sign that the manager believes in the employee[53]; and
3. If an individual has made promises or commitments to others about a certain goal, they are more likely to be committed to its attainment.

Being committed to a specific and ambitious goal that one has the ability to attain can affect outcomes in several ways:[54] Goals narrow one's attention by directing efforts toward goal-achievement-related activities and away from non-goal-oriented activities; ambitious goals serve to increase effort, with high goals leading to greater effort than easily achievable ones. Goals also affect persistence, making individuals more willing to work through temporary setbacks, and willing to spend more time working toward the goal. Finally, goals can create new habits and new cognitive processes, which can cause someone to develop or change their behaviours over the long term.

Employee commitment to goals can be increased in a variety of ways: having subordinates participate in setting the goals so they feel ownership; getting the employee to make a public commitment to the goal[55]; having the leader provide an inspiring vision and behaving supportively[56]; providing a clear rationale when assigning goals; and offering incentives. A large and difficult goal can be broken down into smaller, more immediate, and achievable goals. Providing ongoing feedback on progress is important in all cases.

Feedback

In addition to selecting the right goals, and being committed to them, feedback is an important component of performance. Accurate and timely feedback allows one to gauge how well they are progressing toward their goal. It allows them to assess whether their current strategies are working effectively, or if they should re-evaluate their goals or behaviours. Feedback also allows managers to clarify expectations. Feedback may come from supervisors, or external parties, or may be a self-check.

Task Complexity

Research shows that people work harder to reach difficult goals, as long as they are committed to the goal and have the skills to achieve it.[57] Task complexity refers to how difficult a specific task is, as it pertains to the likelihood of successful achievement. Simply put, simple goals are more likely to be achieved than complex goals. And even when an individual commits to challenging, complex goals, it can be easy to become overwhelmed once the real work starts. When individuals attempt complex tasks, they are ineffective at discovering suitable task strategies and may easily become demotivated if they have no prior training or experience, if there is high pressure to perform well, and if there is a significant time constraint.[58] In order to achieve complex tasks, they should be broken down into smaller, more manageable parts, where each part has its own specific goals.

5-7 CULTURAL DIFFERENCES IN MOTIVATION

Most motivation theories in use today have been developed by North Americans for use on North American workers.[59] These theories and practices propose that rewards should differ for different people, depending on their performance.[60] When researchers examine the universality of these theories, they find cultural differences in the way people are motivated, especially in collectivistic cultures and those with low power distance, where the rule of equality (all should be treated the same) or the rule of need (people should be treated according to their needs) may prevail.

North European countries, for example, have a greater level of collectivism (compared to North Americans). In the Netherlands, 19 percent of the workforce uses pay-for-performance reward systems, and this drops to only 4 percent of the German workforce.[61] Swedes, who have low power distance, express a preference for allocation rules that favour equality, followed by needs, and only then merit, whereas Americans favour the merit rule above all others and view the needs rule negatively.[62] In India, the order of preference was need, equality, and then merit.[63] Attempts to implement individual-based incentive plans that use individual performance appraisal as the criterion are often rejected in collectivistic, low power distance cultures.[64]

Even the goal-setting model of motivation is subject to cultural influences. Although North Americans respond well both to participative and assigned goals (as long as they accept the reasonableness of those goals), a study comparing Israel and the United States showed

IN ACTION

Money for Gold

Despite cultural differences in motivation, many countries attempt to motivate their Olympic athletes in the same way—by offering cash awards. Countries as varied as Taiwan, China, Russia, South Korea, Indonesia, Brazil, Canada, and the United States all reward medals with money.

SOURCE: C. Leung, "Which Country Rewards Athletes Best for Olympic Success?" *CNN*, (August 2016) accessed from https://edition.cnn.com/2016/08/19/sport/olympic-rewards-by-country/index.html, May 25, 2018.

that the performance of Israelis was significantly lower when goals were assigned to them than when they participated in setting the goals, but equal to the Americans when goals were participatively set. The Israelis are a more collectivistic and lower power distance culture and reacted much more negatively to goal assignment than the more individualistic, higher power distance Americans.[65]

STUDY TOOLS 5

IN THE BOOK YOU CAN ...

- ☐ Rip out the **Chapter Review card** at the end of the book to review Key Concepts and Key Terms.
- ☐ Take a "What about You?" Quiz related to material in the chapter.
- ☐ Read additional cases in the Mini Case and Shopify Running Case sections.

ONLINE YOU CAN ...

NELSON.COM/STUDENT

- ☐ Take a "What about You?" Quiz related to material in the chapter.
- ☐ Test your understanding with a quick Multiple-Choice Pre-Test quiz.
- ☐ Read the eBook, which includes discussion points for questions posed in the Cases.
- ☐ Watch Videos related to chapter content.
- ☐ Use the available Flashcards and Matching Quizzes to test your understanding of key terms and concepts.
- ☐ See how much you've learned by taking a Post-Test.

WHAT ABOUT YOU?

What's Important to Employees?

There are many possible job rewards that employees may receive. Listed below are 10 possible job reward factors. Rank these factors three times. First, rank them as you think the average employee would rank them. Second, rank them as you think the average employee's supervisor would rank them for the employee. Finally, rank them according to what you consider important. Your instructor has normative data for 1,000 employees and their supervisors that will help you interpret your results and place the results in the context of Maslow's need hierarchy.

Employee	Supervisor	You	
____	____	____	**1.** job security
____	____	____	**2.** full appreciation of work done
____	____	____	**3.** promotion and growth in the organization
____	____	____	**4.** good wages
____	____	____	**5.** interesting work

____ ____ ____ 6. good working conditions

____ ____ ____ 7. tactful discipline

____ ____ ____ 8. sympathetic help with personal problems

____ ____ ____ 9. personal loyalty to employees

____ ____ ____ 10. a feeling of being in on things

SOURCE: "Crossed Wires on Employee Motivation," *Training and Development* 49 (1995): 59–60. American Society for Training and Development. Reproduced with permission of AMERICAN SOCIETY FOR TRAINING AND DEVELOPMENT (VA) in the format Textbook via Copyright Clearance Center.

Apply Your Understanding

1. What does expectancy theory suggest about the stagnant levels of engagement and motivation in Canadian organizations?
2. Using concepts from McClelland's need theory, categorize the seven components of employee engagement.
3. Using Theory X and Theory Y, which management style would lead to higher levels of engagement/motivation?

MINI CASE

Engage!

Whether employee engagement leads to motivation, or motivation leads to employee engagement remains unclear. What researchers know for certain, is that employees who report high levels of engagement demonstrate higher levels of Organizational Citizenship Behaviours (OCB), higher performance levels, have better working relationships, and lead to more satisfied customers than their less-engaged counterparts. Actively disengaged employees, on the other hand, lower department and organizational productivity, are often unwilling to do work beyond their job description, and are more likely to be involved in interpersonal conflict and dysfunctional work relationships. Surprisingly, research shows that disengaged employees do not simply leave the organization by quitting or through repeated absences – they remain and do lasting damage to relationships and productivity.

Canadian organizations' employee engagement scores (as measured by The Conference Board of Canada,) have been stagnant since 2010, and in some cases are declining. The report indicates that employee engagement scores dropped during 2008, most likely due to the recession, but despite improved economic conditions, reported levels of engagement have failed to rebound. Though higher than global averages, the majority of Canadians interviewed reported that engagement is a problem within their organization, and most believed that it was very important that their companies address employee engagement issues.

In a report released in 2016, The Conference Board of Canada describes seven factors that can influence an employee's reported level of engagement. In order of importance, these factors include: 1) confidence in senior leadership; 2) relationship with manager; 3) interesting and challenging work; 4) professional and personal growth; 5) acknowledgement and recognition, 6) relationships with co-workers, and; 7) autonomy.

The report found that the most engaged employees were those who occupied management positions, those who were new to the organization, those working for small businesses, and those working in the not-for profit sector. The least engaged employees were employees who had been with the organization for a long time, technical and skilled trades, and federal government employees.

SOURCE: http://www.psychometrics.com/wp-content/uploads/2015/04/engagement_study.pdf

Apply Your Understanding

1. What does Expectancy theory suggest about the stagnant levels of engagement and motivation in Canadian organizations?
2. Using concepts from McClelland's Need Theory, categorize the seven components of employee engagement.
3. Using Theory X and Theory Y, which management style would lead to higher levels of engagement/motivation?

SHOPIFY RUNNING CASE

EMPLOYEE MOTIVATION WITH SPINIFY

Motivating employees is one of the most important requirements for success. It's also one of the most difficult aspects of management. In an effort to help their merchants be as successful as possible, Shopify offers a tie-in feature called "Spinify," which is a sales tracker built right in to the Shopify platform. Spinify allows merchants to track customized performance metrics in real time, and display the resulting data in a fun and personalized way to help engage employees and help motivate performance.

Spinify allows merchants to set custom performance targets for employees, which can be anything the merchant wants; from phone calls made, to units produced, to sales, to files opened or closed, to customer reviews. Any aspect of production that can be measured can be set as a performance target within Spinify. The program then creates leaderboards (a scoreboard, showing the names, and current scores of the leading competitors) to acknowledge and celebrate employees who move up the ranking based on those pre-set targets. Spinify also awards milestones, and can allow members to earn points and badges as they progress through milestones. Spinify progress data is always available in real time so employees always know where they stand with respect to the competition.

Spinify has a whole suite of tools designed to provide information about employee skills and weaknesses such as a performance grid that measures employee performance across two different attributes, and score cards to show employee achievements in activities, outcomes, and points and badges earned. These tools allow a customized managerial approach to coaching and motivating, and Shopify merchants who use Spinify report increases in performance metrics for individual and team targets.

Apply Your Understanding

1. What need(s) from Maslow's hierarchy are addressed using Spinify?
2. How can Spinify reduce perceived inequity?
3. How does Spinify conform to goal-setting theory?

Paul McKinnon/Shutterstock.com

Mikadun/Shutterstock.com

Stress and Well-Being at Work

6

LEARNING OUTCOMES

After reading this chapter, you should be able to do the following:

6-1 Define *stress*, *stressor*, and *distress*.

6-2 Compare four approaches to stress.

6-3 Explain the psychophysiology of the stress response.

6-4 Identify work and nonwork causes of stress.

6-5 Explain the JDCS and ERI models that link stress to negative consequences.

6-6 Describe the consequences of stress.

6-7 Discuss individual factors that influence a person's response to stress and strain.

6-8 Identify the stages of preventive stress management.

See the end of this chapter for a list of available Study Tools, a "What about You?" Quiz, Mini Case, and the Shopify Running Case.

Stress is an important topic in organizational behaviour. It affects everyone and every organization on a regular basis. It influences each person's quality of life and a wide variety of behaviours significant to an organization's success including productivity, turnover, employee satisfaction, and absenteeism. It is important to understand stress so that you can learn to manage your stress and that of others. A 2017 survey found that 25 percent of Canadians have left their jobs because of (negative) stress and another 17 percent are considering doing so.[1]

6-1 WHAT IS STRESS?

Stress has many interpretations: even stress experts do not agree on its definition. Stress carries a negative connotation for some people, as though it were to be avoided. This is unfortunate because stress is a great asset in managing legitimate emergencies and achieving peak performance. We define *stress*, or the stress response, as the unconscious preparation to fight or flee that a person experiences when faced with any demand.[2] A **stressor**, or demand, is the person or event that triggers the stress response. **Distress** or **strain** refers to the adverse psychological, physical, behavioural, and organizational consequences that *may* occur as a result of stressful events.

Stress—A Worldwide Issue

Stress is a common work phenomenon and a costly one. Fifty-eight percent of Canadians report feeling overworked.[3] In 2001 one in four Canadian workers worked over 50 hours a week.[4] In 2014, 4 percent of Canadians worked very long hours; however, this is less than the OECD Better Life Index's average of 9 percent.[5] Stress-related absences cost Canadian employers billions of dollars each year.[6] Stress affects all sectors, as shown in Canadian research focused on workers as varied as sawmill workers,[7] hospital staff,[8] and financial services workers.[9]

Increasing levels of work stress seem to be a global concern. European studies show that stress is the second most common work-related health problem (affecting 28 percent of workers and second only to backache).[10] The majority of European employees report working at high speeds or under tight deadlines more than 50 percent of the time and this percentage has increased significantly since the 90s.[11] In Australia, compensation claims due to work stress increased 62 percent from 1996 to 2003.[12] Stress has become an increasing concern in Chinese[13] and South African[14] workplaces. In 2004, the European Union level social partners (participating countries) signed a voluntary agreement on workplace stress, recognizing the importance of the problem and creating a framework to combat stress at work. This agreement was a catalyst for awareness and action in a broad spectrum of countries, each of which took its own approach.[15] The United Kingdom's Health and Safety Executive created an extensive management education system called the Management Standards approach, creating and distributing training materials to enhance the awareness of stress issues and the understanding of suitable organizational actions for preventing and dealing with stress.[16] It has created a stress code that requires employers to protect their employees from stress or risk legal action.[17] Some of those standards are illustrated later in the chapter.

An important advancement in understanding stress is the increasing realization that individual interventions are not sufficient, and stress is something that can and should be tackled by organizations. For example, the World Health Organization (WHO) has said that "Most of the causes of work stress concern the way work is designed and the way in which organizations are managed."[18]

> "Stress is a common work phenomenon and a costly one."

stress The unconscious preparation to fight or flee that a person experiences when faced with any demand.

stressor The person or event that triggers the stress response.

distress The adverse psychological, physical, behavioural, and organizational consequences that may arise as a result of stressful events.

strain Distress.

6-2 FOUR APPROACHES TO STRESS

One of the pioneers of stress research was Canadian Hans Selye, who is noted as one of the most prolific scientists of all time.[19] It was Selye who popularized the now common understanding that chronic stress increases vulnerability to health problems. According to Selye, stress is the nonspecific response of the body to demands put on it,[20] whether those are pleasant demands (such as preparing for a birth) or unpleasant ones (such as awaiting a critical performance review). Later researchers defined stress differently than Selye, however, so we will review four different approaches to defining stress: the homeostatic/medical, cognitive appraisal, person–environment fit, and psychoanalytic approaches.

IN ACTION

Jack.org

The charity Jack.org was started in 2010 by the parents of Jack Windeler who died by suicide at age 18 in his first year at Queen's University. His parents wanted to make sure that resources would be available to help students and to prevent such tragedies. Jack.org's vision is "a Canada where all young people understand how to take care of their own mental health and look out for each other. A Canada without shame, and where all those who need support get the help they deserve. With thousands of young leaders across every province and territory in Canada, we're only just getting started." In 2018, the Canadian government made a $50,000 donation to Jack.org in honour of the birth of Prince Louis of England.

Universities and colleges are coming together to address students' stress. (See the Self-Assessment at the end of the chapter to examine your stressors.) In a 2016 survey, 15 percent of Ontario postsecondary students reported they'd been treated for depression or diagnosed with it in the previous year. For anxiety, the figure was 18 percent. This is an increase from 2013, when 10 percent of students reported depression and 12 percent reported anxiety. In response, half of Canadian universities have created drop-in opportunities for students to relax with therapy dogs. Other responses include video counselling and 24-hour crisis lines.

SOURCES: "Jack.org 101," accessed from https://jack.org/About/Jack-org-101 and "About," accessed from https://jack.org/About/Our-History, July 20, 2018. Reprinted by permission of Jack.org; Wendy Glauser, "Postsecondary Campuses Responding to Record Anxiety and Depression Levels," CMAJ (189) December 4, 2017: E1501-2, accessed from http://www.cmaj.ca/content/cmaj/189/48/E1501.full.pdf, July 20, 2018.

The Homeostatic/Medical Approach

Walter Cannon was the first to describe the "emergency response" as an animal's response to threat. This is the basis of our current concept of the fight-or-flight response. According to Cannon, stress results when an external, environmental demand upsets the person's natural steady-state balance.[21] He referred to this steady-state balance, or equilibrium, as **homeostasis**. Cannon believed the body was designed with natural defence mechanisms to keep it in homeostasis. He was especially interested in the role of the sympathetic nervous system in activating a person under stressful conditions.[22]

The Cognitive Appraisal Approach

Richard Lazarus was more concerned with the psychology of stress, emphasizing instead the psychological and cognitive aspects of the response.[23] Like Cannon, Lazarus saw stress as a result of a person–environment interaction, yet he emphasized the person's cognitive appraisal in classifying persons or events as stressful or not. Individuals differ in their appraisal of events and people. Perception and cognitive appraisal are important processes in determining what is stressful. For example, people who are higher in neuroticism (or lower in emotional stability, as described in Chapter 3, when discussing the Big Five personality characteristics), seem to have a propensity to perceive threat. Given the same situation, those who make a threat appraisal and those who make a challenge appraisal react with different physiological patterns to the stressor and experience different emotions.[24] In addition to cognitive appraisal, Lazarus introduced the concepts of problem-focused and emotion-focused coping. Problem-focused coping emphasizes managing the stressor, and emotion-focused coping emphasizes managing individual response.

The Person–Environment Fit Approach

Robert Kahn was concerned with the social psychology of stress, so his approach emphasized how confusing and conflicting expectations of a person in a social role create stress for the person.[25] He extended the approach to examine a person's fit in the environment. A good person–environment fit occurs when a person's skills and abilities match a clearly defined, consistent set of role expectations. Stress occurs when the role expectations are confusing and/or conflict with a person's skills and abilities. After a period of such stress, the person can expect to experience strain, for example, depression.

The Psychoanalytic Approach

Harry Levinson defined stress based on Freudian psychoanalytic theory.[26] Levinson believed that two elements

homeostasis A steady state of bodily functioning and equilibrium.

of the personality interact to cause stress. The first element is the **ego-ideal**—the embodiment of a person's perfect self. The second element is the **self-image**—how the person really sees him- or herself, both positively and negatively. Although not sharply defined, the ego-ideal encompasses admirable attributes of parental personalities, desired and/or imaginable qualities, and the absence of any negative or distasteful qualities. Stress results from the discrepancy between the idealized self (ego-ideal) and the real self-image; the greater the discrepancy, the more stress a person experiences. More generally, psychoanalytic theory helps us understand the role of unconscious personality factors as causes of stress within a person.

> "Prolonged stress is dangerous. For example, research now shows that stress plays a role in triggering or worsening depression and cardiovascular disease and in speeding the progression of HIV/AIDS."

6-3 THE STRESS RESPONSE

Whether activated by an ego-ideal/self-image discrepancy, a poorly defined social role, cognitive appraisal suggesting threat, or a lack of balance, the resulting stress response is characterized by a predictable sequence of mind and body events as first observed by Selye. The stress response begins with the release of chemical messengers, primarily adrenaline, into the bloodstream. These messengers activate the sympathetic nervous system and the endocrine (hormone) system. These two systems work together and trigger mind–body changes to prepare the person for fight or flight.

In preparing to fight—or flee—the body (1) redirects blood to the brain and large-muscle groups; (2) increases alertness through improved vision, hearing, and other sensory processes; (3) releases glucose (blood sugar) and fatty acids into the bloodstream to sustain the body during the stressful event; and (4) suppresses the immune system as well as restorative and emergent processes (such as digestion).

As the body responds, the person shifts from a neutral posture to an offensive posture. The stress response can be very functional in preparing a person to handle legitimate emergencies through peak performance. It is neither inherently bad nor necessarily destructive.

ego-ideal The embodiment of a person's perfect self.

self-image How a person sees him- or herself, both positively and negatively.

However, prolonged stress is dangerous. For example, research now shows that stress plays a role in triggering or worsening depression and cardiovascular disease and in speeding the progression of HIV/AIDS.[27]

6-4 SOURCES OF WORK STRESS

Work stress is caused both by factors in the work environment and by nonwork (external) pressures that "spill over" into the workplace. An example of an external pressure is when a working mother or father is called at work to come pick up a sick child from daycare. Therefore, the two major categories of sources of work stress are the work demands and nonwork demands shown in Table 6.1.

Work Demands

Work demands become stressful when there is a mismatch with the skills and resources of the workers, whether this is time, equipment, or knowledge.

TABLE 6.1 WORK AND NONWORK DEMANDS

Work Demands	
Task Demands	**Role Demands**
Change Lack of control Career progress New technologies Time pressure	Role conflict: • Interrole • Intrarole • Person-role Role ambiguity
Interpersonal Demands	**Physical Demands**
Emotional toxins Sexual harassment Poor leadership	Extreme environments Strenuous activities Hazardous substances Global travel
Nonwork Demands	
Home Demands	**Personal Demands**
Family expectations Child-rearing/daycare arrangements Parental care	Workaholism Civic and volunteer work Traumatic events

TASK DEMANDS We have already seen that an intensification of work seems to have occurred for many, whether this is in workload, responsibilities, or time pressures. Globalization is creating dramatic changes at work, causing on-the-job pressure and stress.[28] Change leads to uncertainty in a person's daily tasks and activities, and may be caused by job insecurity related to difficult economic times.

Technological innovation creates change and uncertainty for many employees, requiring additional training, education, and skill development. Additionally, new technologies create both career stress and "technostress" for people at work who wonder if "smart" machines will replace them.[29] Although they enhance the organization's productive capacity, new technologies may be viewed as the enemy by employees who must ultimately learn to use them. This creates a real dilemma for management.

Intended to make work easier and more convenient, information technology may have a paradoxical effect and incur stress rather than relieve it, especially if it blurs the line between work and private life; for example, leading people to think they need to respond to those late-evening e-mails from work.

Lack of control is a second major task-related source of stress, especially in work environments that are difficult and psychologically demanding. The lack of control may be caused by the inability to (1) influence the timing of tasks and activities, (2) select tools or methods for accomplishing the work, (3) make decisions that influence work outcomes, and (4) exercise direct action to affect the work outcomes.

Concerns over career progress and time pressures (or work overload) are two additional task demands triggering stress for the person at work. Career stress has occurred in many organizations as the middle-manager ranks have been thinned due to mergers, acquisitions, and downsizing during the past two decades.[30] Leaner organizations, unfortunately, mean overload for the employees who remain. Fewer people doing the same amount (or more) of work creates time pressure, a leading cause of stress often associated with work overload. It may also result from poor time management skills.

Not all task demands are negative. Challenge stressors that promote personal growth and achievement are positively related to job satisfaction and organizational commitment.[31]

© iStockphoto.com/Lauri Wiberg

Firefighters have to overcome the anatomical response that pushes them to flee and make running into the burning building a conditioned response.

ROLE DEMANDS The social–psychological demands of the work environment may be every bit as stressful as task demands at work. People encounter two major categories of role stress at work: role conflict and role ambiguity.[32] Role conflict results from inconsistent or incompatible expectations communicated to a person. The conflict may be an interrole, intrarole, or person–role conflict.

Interrole conflict is caused by conflicting expectations related to two separate roles, such as employee and parent. For example, the employee with a major sales presentation on Monday and a sick child at home Sunday night is likely to experience interrole conflict. Work–family conflicts like these can lead individuals to withdrawal behaviours.[33]

Intrarole conflict is caused by conflicting expectations related to a single role, such as employee. For example, the manager who presses employees for both very fast work *and* high-quality work may be viewed at some point as creating a conflict for employees.

Ethics violations are likely to cause person–role conflicts. Employees expected to behave in ways that violate personal values, beliefs, or principles experience conflict. Person–role conflicts and ethics violations create a sense of divided loyalty for an employee.

The second major cause of role stress is role ambiguity. Role ambiguity is the confusion a person experiences related to the expectations of others. Role ambiguity may be caused by not understanding what is expected, not knowing how to do it, or not knowing the result of failure to do it. For example, a new magazine employee asked to copyedit a manuscript for the next issue may experience confusion because of lack of familiarity with copyediting procedures and conventions for the specific magazine.

The case *Zorn-Smith vs the Bank of Montreal* exemplifies the stress caused by task and role demands, the impact on the employee, and the trouble it can lead to

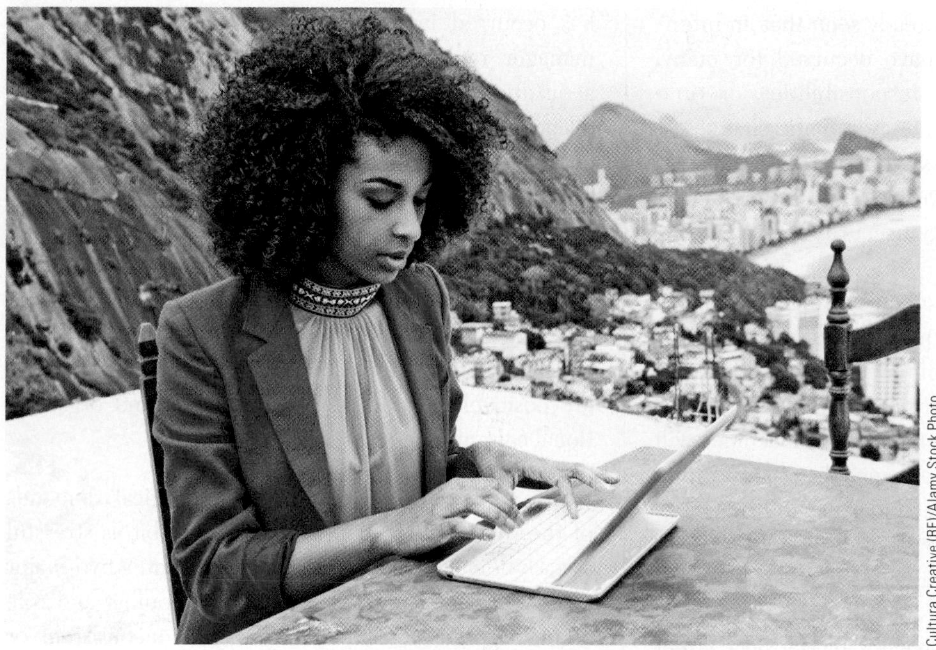
Cultura Creative (RF)/Alamy Stock Photo

Role conflict and spillover can cause significant stress.

for the employer. It is a sad story of a hard-working, committed long-term employee who ended up depressed and jobless. Zorn-Smith was originally pressured to take a promotion although she was not provided with the necessary training, then required to perform at a high level and supervise others despite the lack of training. Asking for a demotion due to the stress, she then had to cover for her replacement, who went on leave.[34] Zorn-Smith took sick leave and then was terminated when she refused to do part-time work. The court hearing the case ordered BMO to pay wrongful dismissal damages as well as damages for creating the work environment that led to her stress, stating, "This callous disregard for the health of an employee was flagrant and outrageous. That Susanne Zorn-Smith would suffer a further burnout was predictable—the only question was when it would come ... I find that the Bank's conduct was the primary cause of Susanne Zorn-Smith's adjustment disorder with depressed and anxious mood."[35]

INTERPERSONAL DEMANDS Emotional toxins, such as sexual harassment and poor leadership in the organization, are interpersonal demands for people at work. Emotional toxins are often generated at work by abrasive personalities.[36] These emotional toxins can spread through a work environment and cause a range of disturbances. Even emotional dissonance can be a cause of work stress.[37] Organizations are increasingly less tolerant of sexual harassment, a gender-related interpersonal demand that creates a stressful working environment both for the person being harassed and for others. The vast majority of sexual harassment is directed at women in the workplace and is a chronic yet preventable workplace problem.[38] Poor leadership in organizations or excessive, demanding management styles or leadership styles mismatched to employees are leading causes of work stress for employees. Employees who feel secure with strong, directive leadership may be anxious with an open management style. Those comfortable with participative leaders may feel restrained by a directive style. Trust is an important characteristic of the leader–follower interpersonal relationship, so a threat to a worker's reputation with their supervisor may be especially stressful.[39] Functional diversity in project groups also causes difficulty in the establishment of trusting relationships, thus increasing job stress, which leads to lower cohesiveness within the group.[40]

While workers in construction and manufacturing jobs can easily identify on-site risks to their health and safety, office employees often consider their work spaces safe havens. However, many offices cause stress and other health problems in a number of unexpected ways. The close quarters of office buildings expose employees

FAST FACT

The WHO's Special Programme on Health and Environment has identified noise and occupational health and air quality as major health concerns across all nations. According to the WHO, one of the most disturbing aspects of noise is chronic exposure. The chronic din of construction sites, airports, and even leaf blowers triggers the stress response with all of its associated "fight-or-flight" hormones. Urban, occupational, and everyday noise is often under the radar, yet it has a constant wear and tear effect on a person's mind and body. While the chronic exposure to noise is unlikely to be lethal, it does lead to fatigue, irritability, and poor concentration along with sleep disturbance.

SOURCE: R. Weiss, "Health," *The Washington Post* (5 June 2007): F-1.

to influenza and other contagious diseases. Poor or abusive management causes psychological stress and can increase the risk of cardiovascular disorders. Working 55 or more hours a week exposes workers to the risk of diminished capacity in memory and mental tasks. Working 41 or fewer hours a week is considered healthy. Computerized work places the entire muscular-skeletal system under stress. Inadequately designed chairs and poor posture put stress on the lower vertebrae, while repetitive actions such as typing can damage the upper arms and hands. Finally, inactive office work often results in a sedentary lifestyle, causing weight gain, fatigue, and depression.[41]

Canadian law is increasingly recognizing the link between interpersonal treatment at work and stress. Nancy Sulz was awarded nearly $1 million in damages when her mental health was damaged by her RCMP superiors' treatment of her.[42] Workers exposed to harassment and bullying are now protected by provincial anti-harassment legislation in Quebec (2002), Saskatchewan (2007), and Ontario (2010).

PHYSICAL DEMANDS Extreme environments, strenuous activities, hazardous substances, and global travel create physical demands for people at work. One cross-cultural study that examined the effects of national culture and ambient temperature on role stress concluded that ambient temperature does affect human well-being, leading to the term *sweat shop* for inhumane working conditions.[43] The unique physical demands of work are often occupation-specific, such as the risk of gravitationally induced loss of consciousness for military pilots flying high-performance fighters[44] or jet lag and loss of sleep for globe-trotting CEOs. Despite the fact that there are many positive aspects to business travel, the associated demands are increasingly recognized as sources of stress.[45] Some organizations are now relying more on technology for meeting to reduce travel costs, environmental costs, and stress.

Office work has its physical hazards as well. Noisy, crowded offices, such as those of some stock brokerages, can prove stressful as well as harmful. Working with a computer can also be stressful, especially if the ergonomic fit between the person and machine is not correct. Eyestrain, neck stiffness, and arm and wrist problems may result. Office designs that use partitions rather than full walls may create stress, by offering little privacy for the occupant and little protection from interruptions. Open plan offices, while in vogue, have been found to increase the cognitive load on workers through high density or low privacy, both of which increase distraction. As a result, employees collaborate less and suffer strain more. In an intriguing recent study, researchers found that open plan offices subtly promoted sexism.[46] They note "many women became hyper-aware of being constantly watched and their appearance constantly evaluated; multiple women told them that 'there isn't anywhere that you don't feel watched.' Of the men interviewed, there was no evidence they felt similarly or changed their actions as a result of the lack of privacy."[47] Both these studies highlight how office space design can have a notable impact on an individual's stress at work.

Nonwork Demands

Nonwork demands also create stress for people, which may carry over into the work environment, or vice versa.[48] Nonwork demands may broadly be identified as home demands from an individual's personal life environment and personal demands that are self-imposed.

HOME DEMANDS The wide range of home and family arrangements in contemporary Canadian society has created great diversity in the home demand arena. Traditional families may experience demands that create role conflicts or overloads that are difficult to manage. For example, the loss of good daycare for children may be especially stressful for dual-career and single-parent families.[49] The tension between work and family may lead to a real struggle to achieve balance in life. As a result of the maturing of the Canadian population, an increasing number of people face the added demand of parental care. Even when a person works to achieve an integrative social identity, integrating many social roles into a "whole" identity for a more stress-free balance in work and nonwork identities, the process of integration is not an easy one.[50]

PERSONAL DEMANDS Self-imposed, personal demands are the second major category of nonwork demands identified in Table 6.1. Although self-imposed and personal, these demands contribute to work stress on the job. **Workaholism** may be the most notable of these demands that causes stress for people at work and has been identified as a form of addiction.[51] Some of the early warning signs of workaholism include over-commitment to work, inability to enjoy vacations and respites from work, preoccupation with work problems when away from the workplace, and constantly taking work home on the weekend. Another type of personal

workaholism An imbalanced preoccupation with work at the expense of home and personal life satisfaction.

demand comes from civic activities, volunteer work, and nonwork organizational commitments, such as in religious and public service organizations. These demands become more or less stressful depending on their compatibility with the person's work and family life and their capacity to provide alternative satisfactions for the person.

6-5 TWO MODELS LINKING STRESS SOURCES TO NEGATIVE CONSEQUENCES

The many sources of stress described above have been pulled together by two comprehensive models: the job demand-control-support model and the effort–reward imbalance model.

Job Demand-Control-Support Model

Karasek's **job demand-control-support model (JDCS)** asserts that high demands (work or nonwork), low control, and low support all contribute to strain, and strain can be modified or prevented by altering these factors. In its original form, the model focused only on the stress related to job demands and level of control a worker has over the job. If a worker has a heavy workload, the work is complex, and there are deadlines to meet, that job is high in demands. If the worker has a lot of decision latitude—able to decide how, when, and what to do—Karasek believed that control would make the high demands more bearable. Job strain is created when the high demands are intensified by low control, having to meet expectations but unable to control the situation.[52] Research supports this claim, showing that high demands combined with low control increase the risk of physical and mental health conditions. Chronic job strain is a predictor for initial[53] and recurrent[54] heart attacks.[55] A study of BC sawmill workers showed that high psychological demands were associated with a higher risk of neurotic disorders.[56] Data from a Canadian mental health survey showed that those who reported high demand and low control in the workplace were more likely to have had depression or anxiety disorders.[57] A longitudinal study of Finnish dentists found that job demands predicted burnout and depression.[58]

job demand-control-support model (JDCS) This stress model asserts that high demands, low control, and low support all contribute to strain.

effort–reward imbalance model (ERI) This stress model attributes strain to a combination of high effort and low reward.

The importance of the control aspect of the model is clear in the finding that voluntary overtime is not seen as stressful (even when there is no reward), whereas mandated overtime is associated with fatigue and low satisfaction.[59] A study with the leaders of several hundred addiction treatment centres found that the emotional exhaustion associated with the high demands in their job was decreased if their centres engaged in long-term planning, which gave a greater sense of control.[60] Firefighters all face stressful critical events on a regular basis. The likelihood of their turning to alcohol as a stress release turns out to be strongly associated with the resources provided to their particular unit. Those units with good resources (e.g., quality and availability of apparatus, tools, support services, and information) have a significantly lower level of drinking, likely because the greater resources give the firefighters a greater sense of control.[61]

The support dimension of the Karasek model was added later when it became clear that low support at work can magnify the strain in a high demand/low control job but also that low support on its own can be very stressful. A study of 14,000 Belgian men over three years showed that those with low social support at work experienced a higher risk of coronary heart disease.[62] Nurses given support from their coworkers and supervisors experience less fatigue and higher intrinsic motivation when job demands increase.[63] Research with Canadian prison employees showed that if people feel supported by coworkers, they were less likely to suffer psychological stress when exposed to injustice.[64]

Effort–Reward Imbalance Model

Siegrist's model attributes job strain to a combination of high effort and low reward.[65] Like the inequity model of motivation discussed in Chapter 5, the **effort–reward imbalance model (ERI)** is a reciprocity model that says people look for a balance between what they put out and what they receive in return. In the ERI model, if a person expends high effort and receives little reward in return, strain is created and adverse health conditions may follow. The ERI model explains that the effort may arise from external sources (time pressure, workload, interruptions, responsibilities) but may also be generated internally (by a worker's need to surpass him- or herself, need for approval, and satisfaction from tackling challenging situations). Low rewards can arise from low wages, being treated with a lack of respect or esteem

FIGURE 6.1 THE COSTS OF AN UNHEALTHY WORKPLACE

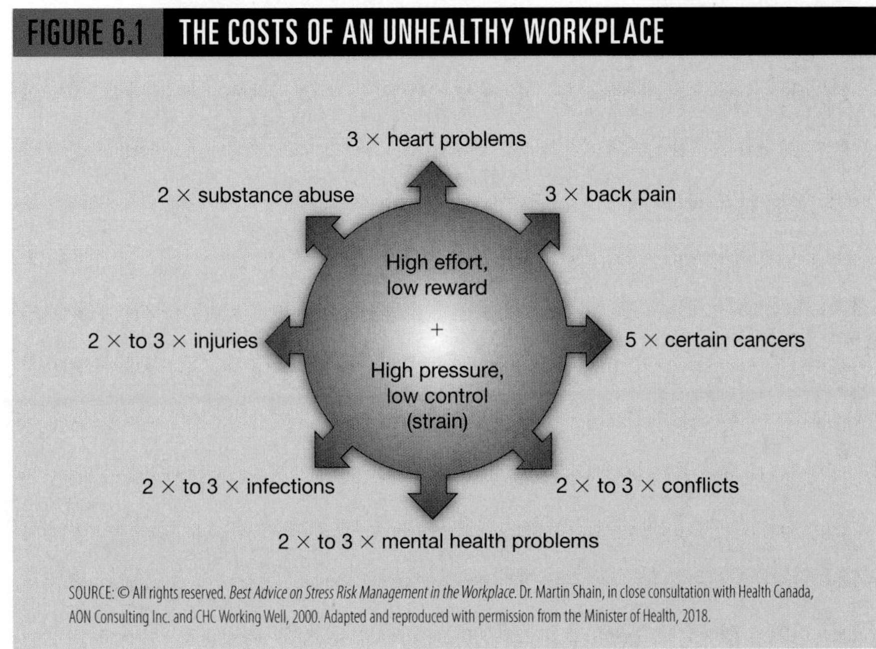

 Best Advice on Stress Risk Management in the Workplace. Dr. Martin Shain, in close consultation with Health Canada, AON Consulting Inc. and CHC Working Well, 2000. Adapted and reproduced with permission from the Minister of Health, 2018.

for the work, job insecurity, and lack of career opportunities. Reducing or preventing strain can be achieved if the organization modifies the efforts required and improves the rewards offered, thereby righting the balance.

The ERI model helps explain the high stress level in many service jobs because of the high effort involved and the fact that many interactions are not rewarding. The self-control involved in service jobs requires significant effort that is often not matched by appreciation from customers. This imbalance can be associated with emotional exhaustion and anxiety.[66]

The ERI model has strong research support, demonstrating that a high effort–reward imbalance is associated with higher risk for depression, anxiety, and psychotropic drug consumption[67]; cardiovascular disease[68]; and neck and back injuries.[69]

The ERI and JDCS models are not mutually exclusive and, in fact, can complement each other. A Canadian study showed that the two models together were a better predictor of self-reported health status in a group of BC workers than either model alone.[70] An interesting addition to the recent research literature is the evidence that perceived unfairness can be a significant contributor to experienced stress.[71] Injustice could be interpreted as a lack of control, a lack of support, or a lack of reward so it fits into either model.

Figure 6.1 is a summary from Health Canada of the link between negative effects from constant exposure to high demands and low control, or high effort and low rewards in the workplace.[72]

6-6 THE POSITIVE CONSEQUENCES OF STRESS

So far our discussion has focused on the link between stress and negative consequences, e.g., medical, performance, and behavioural problems. Stress may be positive, however, creating a healthy, thriving work environment.

Some managers and executives thrive under pressure because they practise what world-class athletes already know.[73] that bringing mind, body, and spirit to peak condition requires recovering energy, which is as important as expending energy. Hence, world-class athletes and managers get high marks on any "stress test" because they use stress-induced energy in positive, healthy, and productive ways. The consequences of healthy, normal stress (called *eustress,* for "euphoria stress") include a number of performance and health benefits to be balanced against the more commonly known costs of individual and organizational distress.[74] An organization striving for high-quality products and services needs a healthy workforce to support the effort. Eustress is a characteristic of healthy people; distress is not.

> An organization striving for high-quality products and services needs a healthy workforce to support the effort. Eustress is a characteristic of healthy people; distress is not.

Positive stress can bring performance and health benefits. The Yerkes-Dodson law, shown in Figure 6.2, indicates that stress leads to improved performance up to an optimum point.[75]

FIGURE 6.2 YERKES-DODSON LAW

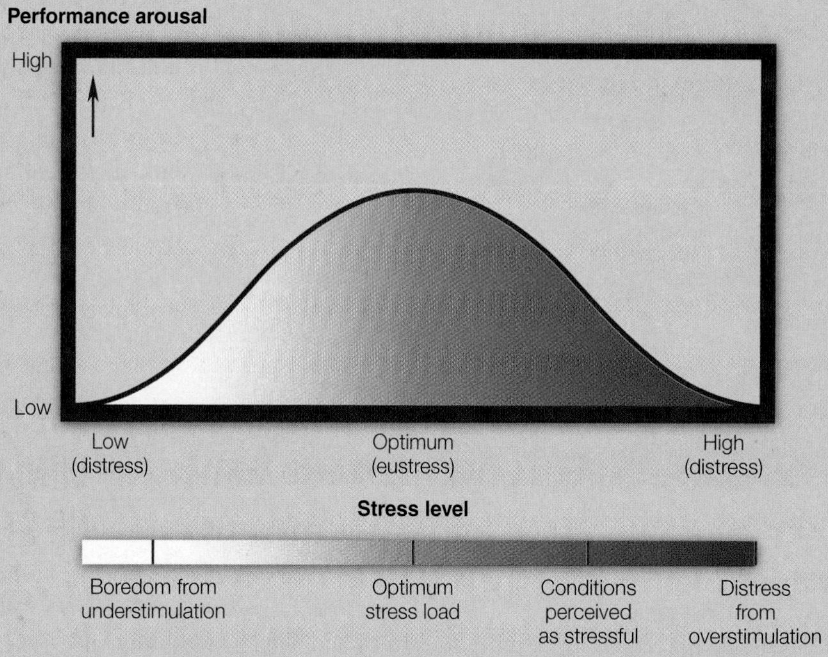

Performance arousal

High

Low

Low (distress) | Optimum (eustress) | High (distress)

Stress level

Boredom from understimulation | Optimum stress load | Conditions perceived as stressful | Distress from overstimulation

Beyond the optimum point, further stress and arousal have a detrimental effect on performance. Therefore, healthy amounts of eustress are desirable to improve performance by arousing a person to action. It is in the mid-range of the curve that the greatest performance benefits from stress are achieved. You can likely recall instances where you have produced some of your best work or come up with a great idea when "under the gun." Adrenaline can be a great motivator. The stress response does provide momentary strength and physical force for brief periods of exertion, thus providing a basis for peak performance in athletic competition or other events.

6-7 INDIVIDUAL DIFFERENCES IN THE STRESS–STRAIN RELATIONSHIP

Individual differences play a central role in the stress–strain relationship. The weak organ hypothesis in medicine, also known as the Achilles' heel phenomenon, suggests that a person breaks down at their weakest point. Individual differences, such as negative affectivity and Type A behaviour pattern, enhance vulnerability to strain under stressful conditions. Other individual differences, such as personality hardiness, self-esteem, self-efficacy, and self-reliance, reduce vulnerability to strain under stressful conditions.

Self-Esteem, Self-Efficacy, and Negative Affectivity

Several personality characteristics discussed in Chapter 3 are linked to stress vulnerability. Self-esteem (feelings of personal worth) and self-efficacy (belief in personal capability to meet demands) seem to buffer people from stress whereas negative affectivity seems to make stress more likely.

Those with high self-esteem react differently to stressors and are ultimately less harmed[76] than those with low self-esteem because they appraise the situation differently and use more effective coping strategies. For example, in a study that experimentally induced rejection from an online "date," those with low self-esteem showed greater cortisol reactivity (a physiological measure), appraised themselves more negatively, made more self-blaming attributions, and were more likely to derogate the rejecter.[77]

The fact that self-efficacy is associated with lower levels of stress is not surprising since it suggests a greater sense of personal control. Research in China showed that primary and secondary school teachers with high self-efficacy were less stressed and were more likely to use active coping and positive thinking strategies whereas those with low self-efficacy were more likely to use emotion-focused coping.[78] When those with high self-efficacy are given greater job control, it reduces their stress level, whereas greater job control can actually be stressful for those with low self-efficacy.[79]

People with negative affectivity (tendency to accentuate the negative aspects of the world around them) seem to be sensitized to experience threat and respond strongly to it. Physiological measures show that those with high negative affectivity show greater muscle tension during stress and are slower to recover normal muscle tension and skin temperature after the stress is over than those low on negative affectivity.[80] Those with high negative affectivity are also more likely to react to stress with counterproductive work behaviours (harming the organization or its members) because they get angry more easily and tend to be impulsive.[81] Not surprisingly, the other personality characteristic that predicts counterproductive work behaviours in response to stress is low conscientiousness.[82]

Type A Behaviour Pattern

Type A behaviour pattern is also labelled *coronary-prone behaviour*.[83] **Type A behaviour pattern** is a combination of personality and behavioural characteristics, including competitiveness, time urgency, social status insecurity aggression, hostility, and a quest for achievements. The main indicators of Type A behavioural pattern are (1) a sense of time urgency (a kind of "hurry sickness"); (2) the quest for numbers (success is measured by the number of achievements); (3) status insecurity (feeling unsure of yourself deep down inside); and (4) aggression and hostility expressed in response to frustration and conflict. There are two primary hypotheses concerning the lethal part of the Type A behaviour pattern. One hypothesis suggests that the problem is time urgency, whereas the other hypothesis suggests that it is hostility and aggression. The weight of evidence suggests that hostility and aggression, not time urgency, are the lethal agents.[84]

The alternative to the Type A behaviour pattern is the Type B behaviour pattern. People with Type B personalities are relatively free of the Type A behaviours and characteristics. Type B people are less coronary prone, but if they do have a heart attack, they do not appear to recover as well as those with Type A personalities. Organizations can also be characterized as Type A or Type B.[85] Type A individuals in Type B organizations and Type B individuals in Type A organizations experience stress related to a misfit between their personality type and the predominant type of the organization.

Type A behaviour can be modified. The first step is recognizing that an individual is prone to the Type A pattern and, possibly, spending time with Type B individuals. Type B people often recognize Type A

Type A behaviour pattern A complex of personality and behavioural characteristics, including competitiveness, time urgency, social status insecurity, aggression, hostility, and a quest for achievements.

IN ACTION

Goldman Sachs Is a Great Place to Work for Type A Employees

Individuals with Type A personalities are known for their quest for numbers and hurried lifestyles. Conventional wisdom suggests that the last thing Type A employees need is a Type A workplace. However, Goldman Sachs employees defy conventional wisdom. Walk into Goldman's lower Manhattan offices, and you might see groups of employees participating in meditation sessions, being implored to "let go of the day's stresses." These meditation sessions are part of Goldman's "resiliency week," which is designed to help its employees focus on stress management, happiness, and work–life balance in the midst of routinely long workweeks and gruelling work hours. Goldman Sachs employees, like those of other large investment firms, command high salaries, some averaging $380,000 per year. But ask employees why Goldman Sachs is No. 45 on *Fortune's* 100 Best Companies to Work, and they may tell you it's the inclusive culture, the ability to balance work with family, and the emphasis on managing stress. The pay's not bad, either.

SOURCE: C. Matthews. "Why People Love Working at Goldman Sachs: It's Not Just the Money," *Time* (January 16, 2014); A. Vandermey. "Yes, Goldman Sachs Really Is a Great Place to Work," *Fortune* (February 3, 2014): 97–104.

personality hardiness A personality resistant to distress and characterized by commitment, control, and challenge.

resilience Rather than being knocked down by failure, resilient individuals are able to bounce back.

transformational coping A way of managing stressful events by changing them into less subjectively stressful events.

self-reliance A healthy, secure, *interdependent* pattern of behaviour related to how people form and maintain supportive attachments with others.

behaviour and can help Type A individuals judge situations realistically. Type A individuals can also learn to pace themselves, manage their time well, and try not to do multiple things at once. Focusing only on the task at hand and its completion, rather than worrying about other tasks, can help Type A individuals cope more effectively.

Personality Hardiness

People who have personality hardiness resist strain reactions when subjected to stressful events more effectively than do people who are not hardy.[86] The components of **personality hardiness** are commitment, control, and challenge. Commitment is an engagement with your environment that leads to the experience of activities as interesting and enjoyable. Control is an ability to influence the process and outcomes of events that leads to the experience of activities as personal choices. Challenge is the viewing of change as a stimulus to personal development, which leads to the experience of activities with openness. Hardiness is akin to **resilience**. Resilience is described as "that ineffable quality that allows some people to be knocked down by life and come back stronger than ever."[87]

The hardy personality appears to use these three components actively to engage in transformational coping when faced with stressful events.[88] **Transformational coping** is the act of actively changing an event into something less subjectively stressful by viewing it in a broader life perspective, by altering the course and outcome of the event through action, and/or by achieving greater understanding of the process. The alternative to transformational coping is regressive coping, characterized by a passive avoidance of events and decreased interaction with the environment. Regressive coping may lead to short-term stress reduction at the cost of long-term healthy life adjustment.

HARDY	NOT HARDY
Commitment	Alienation
Control	Powerlessness
Challenge	Threat

Self-Reliance

There is increasing evidence that social relationships have an important impact on health and life expectancy.[89] **Self-reliance** is a personality attribute related to how people form and maintain supportive attachments with others. Self-reliance was originally based in attachment theory, a theory about normal human development.[90] The theory identifies three distinct patterns of attachment, and research suggests that these patterns extend into behavioural strategies during adulthood, in professional as well as personal relationships.[91] Self-reliance results in a secure pattern of attachment and interdependent behaviour. Interpersonal attachment is emotional and psychological connectedness to another person. The two insecure patterns of attachment are counterdependence and overdependence.

Self-reliance is a healthy, secure, *interdependent* pattern of behaviour. It may appear paradoxical because a person appears independent while maintaining a host of supportive attachments.[92] Self-reliant people respond to stressful, threatening situations by reaching out to others appropriately. Self-reliance is a flexible, responsive strategy of forming and maintaining multiple, diverse relationships. Self-reliant people are confident, enthusiastic, and persistent in facing challenges.

IN ACTION

Delta Hotels

Delta Hotels has been on the *Maclean's* list of 50 Best Employers since the start of the rankings. Delta focuses more on employee engagement than employee satisfaction and believes that its focus contributes to employee well-being and productivity. Delta Hotels has focused on mental health as its main focal point for improving the all-important engagement metric. It hosted a Mental Health Week to highlight the high numbers of mental health and mental illness issues in the workplace to help address the stigma still surrounding mental health. It also shared ways for employers to encourage their employees to give voice to their mental health challenges. Under Bill Pallett's leadership, Delta Hotels created its Valuing Healthy Minds program, a mental health and wellness initiative. The initiative received Excellence Canada's Award for Excellence—Healthy Workplace® Award and the Order of Excellence Award.

SOURCES: How Delta Hotels Prioritizes Mental Health, March 30, 2017, https://risepeople.com/blog/10-companies-with-amazing-workplace-wellness-programs/, accessed July 20, 2018; About, W.J. Pallett & Associates, http://www.wjpassociates.ca/index.php/about, accessed July 20, 2018.

Counterdependence is an unhealthy, insecure pattern of behaviour that leads to separation in relationships with other people. When faced with stressful and threatening situations, counterdependent people withdraw. Counterdependence may be characterized as a rigid, dismissing denial of the need for other people in difficult and stressful times. Counterdependent people exhibit a fearless, aggressive, and actively powerful response to challenges.

Overdependence is also an unhealthy, insecure pattern of behaviour. Overdependent people respond to stressful and threatening situations by clinging to other people in any way possible. Overdependence may be characterized as a desperate, preoccupied attempt to achieve a sense of security through relationships. Overdependent people exhibit an active but disorganized and anxious response to challenges. Overdependence prevents a person from being able to organize and maintain healthy relationships and thus creates much distress. It is interesting to note that both counterdependence and overdependence are exhibited by some military personnel who are experiencing adjustment difficulties during the first 30 days of basic training.[93] In particular, basic military trainees who have the most difficulty have overdependence problems and find it difficult to function on their own during the rigours of training.

6-8 PREVENTIVE STRESS MANAGEMENT

Stress is an inevitable feature of work and personal life. **Preventive stress management** is an organizational approach about people and organizations taking joint responsibility for promoting health and preventing distress and strain. Preventive stress management is rooted in the public health notions of prevention, which were first used in preventive medicine. The three stages of prevention are primary, secondary, and tertiary prevention. A framework for understanding preventive stress management is presented in Table 6.2.

Primary prevention is intended to reduce, modify, or

TABLE 6.2 A FRAMEWORK FOR PREVENTIVE STRESS MANAGEMENT

Focus	Level	Aim
Organizational stressors	Primary prevention: stressor directed	**Prevent the stress:** Reduce work demands Increase control Flexibility Appropriate selection and training Fairness Provide support Management development Clear structure and practices Clear expectations Strong communication Healthy change processes Culture
Stress responses	Secondary prevention: response directed	**Influence the reaction to stressful events:** Encourage challenge appraisal rather than threat appraisal Give employees more control Give employees support
Distress	Tertiary prevention: symptom directed	**Help employees deal with stress symptoms:** Debriefing/defusing sessions EAP Time off Adjust work demands Work with employee to plan changes that will reduce stress

SOURCE: J. D. Quick, R. S. Horn, and J. C. Quick, "Health Consequences of Stress," *Journal of Organizational Behavior Management* 8(2) figure 1 (Fall 1986): 21. Reprinted by permission of the publisher (Taylor & Francis Group, http://www.informaworld.com).

counterdependence An unhealthy, insecure pattern of behaviour that leads to separation in relationships with other people.

overdependence An unhealthy, insecure pattern of behaviour that leads to preoccupied attempts to achieve security through relationships.

preventive stress management An organizational approach that holds that people and organizations should take joint responsibility for promoting health and preventing distress and strain.

primary prevention The stage in preventive stress management designed to reduce, modify, or eliminate the demand or stressor causing stress.

eliminate the demand or stressor causing stress. The idea behind primary prevention is to eliminate or alleviate the source of a problem. True organizational stress prevention is largely primary in nature because it changes and shapes the demands the organization places on people at work. **Secondary prevention** is intended to alter or modify the individual's or the organization's response to a demand or stressor. People must learn to manage the inevitable, inalterable work stressors and demands to avert distress and strain while promoting health and well-being. **Tertiary prevention** is intended to heal individual or organizational symptoms of distress and strain. The symptoms may range from early warning signs (such as headaches or absenteeism) to more severe forms of distress (such as hypertension, work stoppages, and strikes). We discuss the stages of prevention in the context of organizational prevention and individual prevention.

Organizational Stress Prevention

PRIMARY PREVENTION As seen in the research emerging from the JDCS model, a natural starting point for preventing stress is to remove or reduce high job demands, give workers more control over their circumstances, and offer support. Physical demands can be reduced through better ergonomics, job rotation, and better planning that distributes work over time and employees. Task demands can be modified through improved work systems, increased staffing levels, and having more realistic expectations. Organizations can enhance employee control by inviting their participation in organizational decisions that affect them, and by giving workers more flexibility in how they do their job, when, and where (e.g., permitting flexible work schedules and telecommuting). If workers have been well matched to their position through appropriate selection, training, and promotion, they will have a stronger sense of self-efficacy. A focus on fairness in all organizational processes and decisions will also enhance employees' sense of control and predictability. Support comes in two forms: socioemotional and instrumental. Socioemotional support makes the person feel accepted, trusted, and appreciated, and comes from positive social interactions with management and coworkers, responsibilities entrusted, and recognition offered. Instrumental support lies in a worker knowing they will get assistance when it is needed. These all point to the critical role of management. Research[94] on stress in thousands of Canadians leads researchers to suggest more support from managers will come from giving them the skills for people management (e.g., training in project planning and giving feedback), the tools to manage people (e.g., appropriate policies, training on implementing alternative work arrangements), the time they need to manage people, and the incentives to focus on the people part of their job (e.g., measurement and accountability, 360-feedback, and rewards recognizing good people skills).

secondary prevention The stage in preventive stress management designed to alter or modify the response to a demand or stressor.

tertiary prevention The stage in preventive stress management designed to heal symptoms of distress and strain.

A great deal of stress can be prevented by having clear structure, policies, and practices, and clearly communicating expectations. If workers know exactly what they are expected to do, why, and how; what they are accountable for achieving; what the rules are; what to do when things do not go as expected; and what resources they have, it helps tremendously by reducing role ambiguity and role conflict and giving them a sense of security. Job descriptions, regular team meetings, manager availability, and the use of goal setting have all been shown to be important contributors to clear expectations.

When organizational change is underway, demands seem to inevitably increase, but research in Norway[95] and the United States[96] shows that a healthy change process (see Chapter 17) can greatly reduce the stress. Good practice includes communicating what the change involves, why it is happening, and exactly where the employee fits in; providing ongoing support (accepting resistance as natural); and enhancing control through active participation by employees.

Organizational culture can also play a role in preventing or creating stress. In some companies, the culture encourages long hours and putting work over family. People feel guilty if they leave work on time or if they say no to a request that means overload. Promotions are limited to those who put in significant unpaid overtime.[97] Ironically, in many organizations where the workers deal with stressful critical incidents on a regular basis (e.g., ambulance workers, police) and one would expect support, the culture stigmatizes vulnerability so workers are reluctant to admit they need help.[98] A culture that values employees and work–life balance is more likely to make reasonable demands in the first place, offer support and employee control, and be proactive in dealing with the stresses that inevitably occur.

Table 6.3 shows a selection of the Management Standards created by the UK's Health and Safety Executive as part of its stress management educational program.[99] Its recommendations fit closely with the suggestions for primary prevention just discussed.

TABLE 6.3 SELECTED MANAGEMENT COMPETENCIES FOR PREVENTING AND REDUCING STRESS AT WORK FROM UNITED KINGDOM HEALTH AND SAFETY EXECUTIVE'S MANAGEMENT STANDARDS, 2007

Management Standard	Competency	Examples of Positive Manager Behaviour	Examples of Negative Manager Behaviour
Demands	Managing workload and resources	• Bringing in additional resources to handle workload • Awareness of team members' abilities • Monitoring team workload • Refusing to take on additional work when team is under pressure	• Delegating work unequally to team members • Creating unrealistic deadlines • Showing lack of awareness of how much pressure team is under • Asking for tasks without checking workload first
Control	Participative approach	• Providing opportunities to express opinions • Regular team meetings • Knowing when to consult employees and when to make decisions	• Not listening when employee asks for help • Presenting a final solution • Making decisions without consultations
Support	Accessible/visible	• Communicating that employees can talk to them any time • Having an open-door policy • Making time to talk to employees at their desks or work stations	• Being constantly at meetings away from office • Saying "don't bother me now" • Not attending lunches or social events
Support	Individual consideration	• Provides regular one-on-ones • Flexible when employee needs time off • Provides information on additional sources of support • Regularly asks "how are you?"	• Assuming everyone is OK • Badgering employees to tell them what is wrong • Not giving enough notice of shift changes • No consideration of work–life balance

SOURCE: *Management Competencies for Preventing and Reducing Stress at Work: Identifying and Developing the Management Behaviours Necessary to Implement the HSE Management Standard*, by Joanna Yarker, Rachel Lewis, Emma Donaldson-Feilder, Paul Flaxman; Health and Safety Executive, 2007; http://www.hse.gov.uk/research/rrpdf/rr553.pdf. Contains public sector information published by the Health and Safety Executive and licensed under the Open Government Licence v1.0.

SECONDARY PREVENTION One of the ways in which organizations can help employees deal with stress is to influence their interpretation of the stressful events so they perceive the event in a positive way (recall Lazarus's cognitive appraisal approach to stress). Positive appraisals are linked to more effective active coping strategies whereas negative appraisals are associated with less effective escapist strategies.[100] Stressors seen as a challenge tend to increase performance. They are motivating, associated with positive emotions, and seen as under the employee's control.[101] When stressors are seen as a hindrance, they tend to decrease performance and are associated with negative emotions. For example, if an employer knows the organization must undergo a change and must communicate that to his or her staff, the way in which he or she presents the change will shape their reaction. If employees see it as an opportunity that, although demanding, is within their ability to handle, they will be less stressed than if they see it as a threat. An intriguing study demonstrated the importance of a task's description. Glynn[102] gave experimental subjects the same puzzle to do but introduced the task differently. Those in the work condition were told they were production managers performing the activity and those in the play condition were told they were starship captains playing a game. This small manipulation affected information processing and behaviours in the activity itself, with "play" subjects focusing more on performance quality and "work" subjects focusing on quantity.

When employees face stressful events, the employer may also be in a position to assist them by giving them greater control through which they can tackle the challenge[103] and giving them support, both emotionally and in practical, instrumental ways. A team from Laval University worked with several Quebec health units to mitigate the high levels of stress in their workplaces. A range of staff participated in identifying constraints, proposing interventions, disseminating information, and monitoring the implementation of the changes. Comparison to control units before and after the intervention showed that in the units with the participatory intervention, there was a lowering of psychological demands and burnout rates, sleep problems were lessened, and there were fewer issues with quality of work.[104]

TERTIARY PREVENTION The first step in dealing with the symptoms of stress is detecting their existence. Employees may be visibly upset, irritable, or aggressive but frequently the signs are more subtle and the employer needs to be alert for changes in absenteeism, performance level, accidents, mistakes, and client complaints.[105] If work conditions are such that the employer or manager suspects stress may be an issue, it is important to ask the employee how they are doing, asking if there are any problems.

When critical incidents happen, some organizations are formally set up to offer debriefing and defusing sessions in which employees can talk through the stressful incident with knowledgeable and supportive people.[106] More commonly, though, employees must cope on their own with stressful events. A sensitive manager can help by steering the employee to support through the organization's Employee Assistance Program (EAP) or through referral to other supportive services. Time off may help ease the stress reaction. The manager can also work collaboratively with the employee to adjust demands underlying the stress.

Individual Prevention

Clinical research shows that individuals may use a number of self-directed interventions to help prevent distress and enhance positive well-being.[107]

POSITIVE THINKING The power of positive thinking is found as an optimistic, nonnegative thinking style used by people to explain the good and bad events in their lives to themselves.[108] A positive, optimistic explanatory style is a habit of thinking learned over time, though some people are predisposed to positive thinking. Pessimism is an alternative explanatory style leading to depression, physical health problems, and low levels of achievement. In contrast, positive thinking and optimism enhance physical health and achievement and avert susceptibility to depression. Positive thinking does not mean ignoring real stress and challenge, though.

Optimistic people avoid distress by viewing the bad events and difficult times in their lives as temporary, limited, and caused by an external event. Optimistic people face difficult times and adversity with hope, and take more credit for the good events in their lives, which they see as more pervasive and generalized. Learned optimism begins with identifying pessimistic thoughts and then distracting oneself from these thoughts or disputing them with evidence and alternative thoughts. Learned optimism is nonnegative thinking.

TIME MANAGEMENT Time pressure is one of the major sources of stress for people both at work and in school. The leading symptoms of poor time management include constant rushing, missed deadlines, work overload and the sense of being overwhelmed, insufficient rest time, and indecision. Effective time managers are "macro" time managers who use a GP3 method of time management.[109] The GP3 method includes (1) *setting* goals that are challenging yet attainable; (2) *prioritizing* these goals in terms of their relative importance; (3) *planning* for goal attainment through specific tasks, activities, scheduling, and even delegation; and (4) *praising* yourself for specific achievements along the way. Setting concrete goals and prioritizing these goals are the most important first steps in time management skills, ensuring that the most important work and study activities receive enough time and attention. This system of time management enables a person to track his or her success over time and goes a long way toward reducing unnecessary stress and confusion.

LEISURE TIME ACTIVITIES Unremitting striving characterizes many people with a high need for achievement. Leisure time activities provide employees an opportunity for rest and recovery from strenuous activities either at home or at work. When asked what they do with their leisure time, many individuals say that they clean the house or mow the lawn. These activities are fine, as long as the individual gets the stress-reducing benefit of pleasure from them. Some say our work ethic is a cultural barrier to pleasure. We work longer hours, and two-income families are the norm. Leisure is increasingly a luxury among working people. The key to the effective use of leisure time is enjoyment. Leisure time can be used for spontaneity, joy, and connection with others in our lives. Although vacations can be a relief from job burnout, they may suffer fade-out effects.[110] Hence, leisure time and vacations must be periodic, recurring activities.

PHYSICAL EXERCISE Different types of physical exercise are important stress prevention activities for individuals. Aerobic exercise improves a person's responsiveness to stressful activities. Research has found that aerobically fit people (1) have lower levels of adrenaline in their blood at rest; (2) have a slower, stronger heart functioning; and (3) recover from stressful events more quickly.[111]

Flexibility training is an important type of exercise because of the muscular contractions associated with the

© iStockphoto.com/ranplett

There is compelling evidence that exercise reduces stress.

stress response. One component of the stress response is the contraction of the flexor muscles, which prepares a person to fight or flee. Flexibility training enables a person to stretch and relax these muscles to prevent the accumulation of unnecessary muscular tension.[112] Flexibility exercises help maintain joint mobility, increase strength, and play an important role in the prevention of injury.

RELAXATION TRAINING Herbert Benson was one of the first people to identify the relaxation response as the natural counter-response to the stress response.[113] In studying Western and Eastern peoples, Benson found that Judeo-Christian people have elicited this response through their time-honoured tradition of prayer, whereas Eastern people have elicited it through meditation. The relaxation response does not require a theological or religious component. If you have a practice of regular prayer or meditation, you may already elicit the relaxation response regularly.

DIET Diet may play an indirect role in stress and stress management. High sugar content in the diet can stimulate the stress response, and foods high in cholesterol can adversely affect blood chemistry. Good dietary practices contribute to a person's overall health, making the person less vulnerable to distress.

#HOT TREND

Say No to the Borderless Workday

Technology is blurring the borders of the workday, inviting people to take their work with them whenever and wherever they are. Does this make us more productive? Research now shows that a clear separation between work and nonwork time is important to well-being and to performance at work. Studies with German and Swiss employees showed that those thinking about or actively working on "work" in the evening were more fatigued the next day at work, and more likely to be tense and distressed. Those who engaged in relaxing activities were more at ease the next day. Those who engaged in mastery activities (e.g., playing a sport or music) felt stronger and more active at work the next day. Interestingly, the need for psychological detachment is especially strong for those employees who are intensely involved in their jobs. What is the role of the employer in ensuring this separation? The CEO of Cisco Systems told all employees to take vacation from December 23 to January 4 and not to send text messages or e-mails to colleagues during that time. It is interesting that he needed to encourage people to take true holiday time and that he recognized the importance of doing it.

SOURCES: S. Sonnentag, C. Binnewies, and E. J. Mojza, "Did You Have a Nice Evening?" A Day-level Study on Recovery Experiences, Sleep, and Affect," *Journal of Applied Psychology* 93 (2008): 674–684; S. Sonnentag, E. J. Mojza, C. Binnewies, and A. Scholl, "Being Engaged at Work and Detached at Home: A Week-level Study of Work Engagement, Psychological Detachment and Affect," *Work & Stress* 22 (2008): 257–276; W. Immen, "Surviving the January Grind," *The Globe and Mail* (January 9, 2010): B15.

Yulia Sverdlova/Shutterstock.com

A healthy diet, like exercise, can reduce stress.

OPENING UP Everyone experiences a traumatic, stressful, or painful event in life at one time or another. One of the most therapeutic, curative responses to such an event is to confide in another person.[114] Discussing difficult experiences with another person is not always easy, yet health benefits, immune system improvement, and healing accrue through self-disclosure. In one study comparing those who wrote once a week about traumatic events with those who wrote about nontraumatic events, significant health benefits and reduced absenteeism were found in the first group.[115] Confession need not be through a personal relationship with friends. It may occur through a private diary. The process of opening up and confessing appears to counter the detrimental effects of stress.

PROFESSIONAL HELP Confession and opening up may occur through professional helping relationships. People who need healing have psychological counselling, career counselling, physical therapy, medical treatment, surgical intervention, and other therapeutic techniques available. Employee assistance programs may be very helpful in referring employees to the appropriate caregivers. Even combat soldiers who experience battle stress reactions severe enough to take them out of action can heal and be ready for subsequent combat duty.[116] The early detection of distress and strain reactions, coupled with prompt professional treatment, can be instrumental in averting permanent physical and psychological damage.

Whereas organizational stress prevention programs are aimed at eliminating health risks at work, comprehensive health promotion programs are aimed at establishing a "strong and resistant host" by teaching individual prevention and lifestyle change.[117] Physical fitness and exercise programs characterize corporate health promotion programs in the United States and Canada.[118] A health and wellness survey of accredited medical schools in the United States, Canada, and Puerto Rico found that these programs place significant emphasis on physical well-being and minor emphasis on spiritual well-being.[119] A new approach to comprehensive health promotion places emphasis on the organization and organizational wellness.[120] Still, social and cognitive processes are key considerations in the successful implementation of stress prevention programs.[121] Johnson & Johnson has developed a comprehensive health promotion program with a wide array of educational modules for individuals and groups. Each of these educational modules addresses a specific topic, such as Type A behaviour, stress, diet, and risk assessment (through regular health evaluations for participants). Upon implementation of this health promotion program, Johnson & Johnson found that the health status of employees improved, even if they didn't participate in the program.

STUDY TOOLS 6

IN THE BOOK YOU CAN ...

- ☐ Rip out the **Chapter Review** card at the end of the book to review Key Concepts and Key Terms.
- ☐ Take a "What about You?" Quiz related to material in the chapter.
- ☐ Read additional cases in the Mini Case and Shopify Running Case sections.

ONLINE YOU CAN ...

NELSON.COM/STUDENT

- ☐ Take a "What about You?" Quiz related to material in the chapter.
- ☐ Test your understanding with a quick Multiple-Choice Pre-Test quiz.
- ☐ Read the eBook, which includes discussion points for questions posed in the Cases.
- ☐ Watch Videos related to chapter content.
- ☐ Use the available Flashcards and Matching Quizzes to test your understanding of key terms and concepts.
- ☐ See how much you've learned by taking a Post-Test.

WHAT ABOUT YOU?

Are You Self-Reliant?

Each of the following questions relates to how you form relationships with people at work, at home, and in other areas of your life. Read each statement carefully and rate each on a scale from 0 (strongly disagree) to 5 (strongly agree) to describe your degree of disagreement or agreement with the statement.

Answer all 16 questions.

____ 1. I feel secure in my ability to meet life's challenges.

____ 2. It is difficult to make a decision without consulting others.

____ 3. I can perform high-quality work with little support from others.

____ 4. Friends are a waste of time because in the end they will desert you.

____ 5. On some tasks I can work effectively without other people.

____ 6. It is difficult for me to delegate works to others.

____ 7. Life would be much easier if I didn't have to deal with other people.

____ 8. I put myself at risk if I ever let anyone know I need them.

____ 9. Difficult situations can be overcome.

____ 10. I'm more comfortable being a follower than a leader.

____ 11. I am successful at what I do.

____ 12. There is no one who can understand things in my life.

____ 13. People will always reject you when they find out what you are really like.

____ 14. The actions that I take are usually right.

____ 15. I don't like it when people try to find out too much about me.

____ 16. Needing someone is a sign of weakness.

Scoring:

Follow the instructions to determine your score for each subscale of the Self-Reliance Inventory.

Counterdependence

Step 1: Total your responses to Questions 4, 7, 8, 12, 13, 15 and 16 ___

The score range for counterdependence is 0 to 35. Scores above 22 suggest counterdependence.

Self-Reliance

Step 2: Total your responses to Questions 1, 3, 5, 9, 11 and 14 ___

The score range for self-reliance is 0 to 30. Scores above 17 suggest self-reliance.

Overdependence

Step 3: Total your responses to Questions 2, 6 and 10 ___

The score range for overdependence is 0 to 15. Scores above 9 suggest overdependence.

A set of scores less than 13 in Step 1, greater than 17 in Step 2, and less than 7 in Step 3 indicate self-reliance.

SOURCE: J. R. W. Joplin, D. L., Nelson, J. C. Quick, and J. D. Quick, *The Self-Reliance Inventory* (Arlington, TX: The University of Texas at Arlington).

MINI CASE

69 Days of Stress

On August 5, 2010, 33 miners started their regular shift at a gold and copper mine under the Atacama Desert in northern Chile. It was a dangerous job but they had learned to cope with the constant awareness that something could go very wrong. And then it did. A mine collapse buried them 700 metres underground. For 17 days no one knew they were alive. They had two days of emergency food. The humidity was at 80 percent and the temperature was over 36 degrees Celsius. One miner had diabetes, another hypertension; two had a lung disease called silicosis. Some developed dental infections, others fungal infections and body sores from the conditions. They were finally rescued 69 days after the mine disaster. How did they cope? Why did they not give up?

Initial Reaction

When the collapse first occurred, it took hours for the dust to settle. Then the shift foreman, Luis Urzua, took a crew of three to explore the site. "I saw the collapsed rock. Many thought it would be two days. But when I saw it, I knew otherwise." Important decisions were made at this point, ones which saved their lives. Critically, Urzua rationed the emergency food so they ate two spoonfuls of tuna every other day, making it last over two weeks. And they ate together, with no one taking a mouthful until everyone had their share. They used a bulldozer to carve into a natural water deposit for drinking but otherwise limited use of vehicles to protect air quality. Urzua drew detailed topographical maps of the area that included more than 2 km of tunnels, caves, and a 35 m^2 refuge. He planned how to use the space—a work area, a sleep area, and a sanitary facility. The men were organized into shifts and a disciplined routine was set in place. They reinforced the roof, monitored gas levels, and patrolled the area to check for structural integrity.

Contact Made

When a rescue drill made contact on August 22 and the miners could start communicating with the outside world, they became active participants in their rescue. For example, they needed to design and create drainage and holding pools to shunt water into canals away from their living quarters in case one of the rescue alternatives was implemented, which would lead to a great deal of water entering their refuge. The disciplined structuring of their days continued. They were divided into three groups, Grupo Refugio, Grupo Rampa, and Grupo 105—named after the "shelter," the "ramp," and "Level 105" (sections of the mine where they slept). Lights shone from 7:30 am until 10 pm, mimicking daylight. Urzua wrote each of the men an official job description. All had purpose and meaning in their days. There was daily contact with a doctor, a psychologist, and a miner updating technical aspects of the rescue operation. Supplies came down to the miners. They had phone and video links for communication with relatives. One watched a video of his child being born.

When off duty, they slept, played games, told stories and jokes, exercised, and sent messages to their families. An Elvis fan led regular sing-alongs. Realizing that their ordeal might lead to opportunity, they asked rescuers to send down a book on public speaking so they could talk effectively to the media when they emerged. Long before their rescue was assured, a psychologist with NASA who went to Chile to share NASA's experience with human isolation in extreme environments said, "I fully believe they will do it. The miners are quite hearty, quite resilient ... They have shown every sign that they can organize themselves; that they are masters of their own fate."

One feature of their success was their solidarity, their "leave no man behind" culture. They argued over who would be the last man rescued, all wanting to be at the end of the line, not the beginning. They made a pact that all would share in telling their story for the inevitable film. When they emerged from the mine after 69 days trapped underground, they hired an accountant to track their earnings from public appearances and equitably distribute it among the 33. Did Urzua and the others ever doubt their future? "There were times when I flinched a little, but then I found the strength to talk to the other miners and explain to them what was going on." "We had strength, we had spirit, we wanted to fight, we wanted to fight for our families, and that was the greatest thing."

SOURCES: W. Longbottom, "Last Man Standing: The Foreman Who Refused to Give up and Remained 2,000ft down Until All His men Were Safe," *Daily Mail UK*, October 14, 2010, accessed http://www.dailymail.co.uk/news/article-1320371/CHILEAN-MINERS-RESCUE-Luis-Urzua-foreman-refused-up.html, September 6, 2018; J. Franklin, "Luis Urzua: The Foreman Keeping Hope Alive for Chile's Trapped Miners," *The Observer*, September 5, 2010, accessed http://www.guardian.co.uk/world/2010/sep/05/luis-urzua-chile-trapped-miners, September 6, 2018; M.A Roldan (AFP), "Chile's Luis Urzua: Last Miner out After 70-Hour Day Shift," *Vancouver Sun*, October 14, 2010, accessed http://www.vancouversun.com/news/Chile+Luis+Urzua+Last+miner+after+shift/3671846/story.html, accessed October 18, 2010; BBC News Latin America and Caribbean, "Jubilation as Chile Mine Rescue Ends," October 14, 2010, accessed (http://www.bbc.co.uk/news/world-latin-america-11539182, September 6, 2018.

Apply Your Understanding

1. Identify the work demands that are causing stress for the miners.
2. Explain how Urzua appears to be using transformational coping.
3. Describe what stress management steps were likely important in helping the miners deal with their situation.

SHOPIFY RUNNING CASE

AVOIDING TALENT DRAIN

Tech companies are known for providing benefits that appeal particularly to millennials. One of the reasons for providing attractive benefits is to recruit and to retain talent. Canadian tech companies compete with Silicon Valley for technical talent. Companies such as Google and Facebook are well known for having imaginative benefits such as free gourmet healthy food to onsite massages to 24/7 gyms. Such perks are designed to increase job satisfaction and to reduce stress.

Shopify is well aware of the talent drain. To keep Canadian talent in Canada, Shopify offers access to valuable perks such as four hours of housecleaning a month, a baby bonus, and a monthly allowance until a child turns five. These are in addition to the more common benefits of snacks, gym memberships, and lunches. At Shopify, the benefits include providing support to help employees start their own businesses as well as a free store on its e-commerce platform. There is increased coverage for mental health and wellness through flexible time and vacation policies. Shopify now offers full-time employees $5,000 to spend on house-cleaning, health–care/fitness-related expenses, starting a business, or retirement plan contributions. According to Jen McInnis, talent success lead at Shopify, the aim is to "encourage employees to be their holistic self at work." One employee notes on Glassdoor.ca that Shopify has "benefits that truly help to improve your quality of life. Another values the "healthcare package, cheap gym membership, [and] allocations for personal development and physical wellness." As well, all employees can get stock options.

Shopify offers many benefits that support stress reduction at work and, by allowing employees to select their particular benefits, it provides a high level of autonomy to its employees.

SOURCES: "Shopify Benefits," Glassdoor, accessed from https://www.glassdoor.ca/Benefits/Shopify-Canada-Benefits-EI_IE675933.0,7_IL.8,14_IN3_IP4.htm, July 21, 2018; Evan Hamilton, "How Canadian Tech Companies Are Upping the Benefits Ante, *Benefits Canada*," November 15, 2016, accessed from https://www.benefitscanada.com/benefits/other/how-canadian-tech-companies-are-upping-the-benefits-ante-89902, September 28, 2018.

Apply Your Understanding

1. What tactics does Shopify use to retain its talent?
2. How can benefits packages be useful for addressing stress?
3. How does work autonomy reduce stress? How might autonomy increase stress?

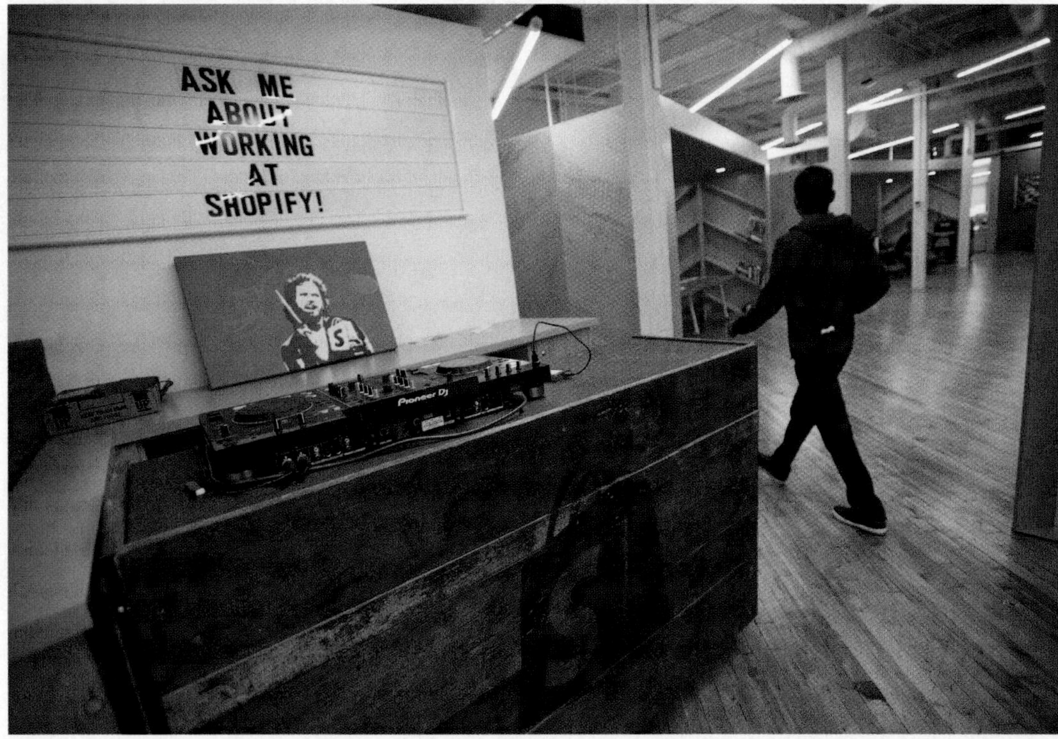

Kevin Van Paassen/Bloomberg via Getty Images

7 Decision Making by Individuals and Groups

LEARNING OUTCOMES

After reading this chapter, you should be able to do the following:

- 7-1 Identify the steps in the decision-making process.
- 7-2 Describe various models of decision making.
- 7-3 Discuss the individual influences that affect decision making.
- 7-4 Explain how groups make decisions.
- 7-5 Describe the role culture plays in decision making.
- 7-6 Explain how organizations can improve the quality of decisions through participation.

See the end of this chapter for a list of available Study Tools, a "What about You?" Quiz, Mini Case, and the Shopify Running Case.

Decisions, decisions, decisions! Every day, employees and managers face decisions, large and small, as we all do. This chapter will provide you some guidance on how to be a better decision maker. We know, from research, that we are flawed decision makers. We are subject to bias, even if we think we are not, and our biases shape our assumptions and decisions. The more you know about how decisions are actually made—as opposed to how they should be—the more effective you will be.

7-1 THE DECISION-MAKING PROCESS

Decision making is a critical activity in organizations. Managers can face decisions ranging from very simple, routine matters for which the manager has an established decision rule (**programmed decisions**) to new and complex decisions that require creative solutions (**nonprogrammed decisions**).[1] Scheduling lunch hours for a work group is a programmed decision. The manager performs the decision activity on a daily basis, using an established procedure with the same clear goal in mind. In contrast, decisions such as buying out another company are nonprogrammed. The decision to acquire a company is a unique, unstructured situation and requires considerable judgment. Regardless of the type of decision made, it is helpful to understand as much as possible about how individuals and groups make decisions.

Decision making, in its *idealized* form, is a process involving a series of steps. The first step is recognizing the problem; that is, the manager realizes that a decision must be made. Identifying the actual problem is important; otherwise, the manager may be reacting to symptoms rather than dealing with the root cause of the problem. Next, a manager must identify the objective of the decision. In other words, the manager must determine what is to be accomplished by the decision.

The third step in the decision-making process is gathering information relevant to the problem. The manager must accumulate sufficient information about why the problem occurred. This involves conducting a thorough diagnosis of the situation and going on a fact-finding mission.

The fourth step is listing and evaluating alternative courses of action. During this step, a thorough "what-if" analysis should also be conducted to determine the various factors that could influence the outcome. It is important to generate a wide range of options and creative solutions in order to be able to move on to the next step.

Next, the manager selects the alternative that best meets the decision objective. If the problem has been diagnosed correctly and sufficient alternatives have been identified, this step is much easier.

Finally, the solution is implemented. The situation must then be monitored to see whether the decision met its objective. Consistent monitoring and periodic feedback are essential parts of the follow-up process.

Decision making can be stressful. Managers must make decisions with significant risk and uncertainty, and often with limited information. They must trust and rely on others in their decision-making process, but they are ultimately responsible for the final decision. Sometimes decisions are painful and involve exiting businesses, firing people, and admitting wrong. Cirque du Soleil, for example, has a history of making effective—and recently, painful—decisions.

“ Decision making can be stressful. Managers must make decisions with significant risk and uncertainty, and often with limited information.

7-2 MODELS AND LIMITS OF DECISION MAKING

The success of any organization depends on managers' abilities to make **effective decisions**. An effective decision is timely, is acceptable to the individuals affected by it, and meets the desired objective.[2] This section describes five models of decision making: the rational model, the bounded rationality model, the Vroom-Yetton-Jago model, the Z model, and the garbage can model. The section will conclude with a discussion of the limits of decision-making techniques.

Rational Model

Rationality refers to a logical, step-by-step approach to decision making, with a thorough analysis of alternatives and their consequences. The rational model of decision making

programmed decision A simple, routine matter for which a manager has an established decision rule.

nonprogrammed decision A new, complex decision that requires a creative solution.

effective decision A timely decision that meets a desired objective and is acceptable to those individuals affected by it.

rationality A logical, step-by-step approach to decision making, with a thorough analysis of alternatives and their consequences.

IN ACTION

Cirque du Soleil

Cirque du Soleil has successfully used a **blue ocean approach** by entering into a new market, creating a true innovation and, as a result, transforming our understanding of a circus. A blue ocean approach argues "companies are better off searching for ways to gain 'uncontested market space' over competing with similar companies."

It made decisions about four key competitive issues: (1) Which of the factors that the industry takes for granted should be eliminated? (2) Which factors should be reduced well below the industry's standard? (3) Which factors should be raised well above the industry's standard? and (4) Which factors should be created that the industry has never offered? The blue ocean approach enabled Cirque du Soleil to create a new domain where it could set its own direction. It has enjoyed extraordinary success and has been seen by millions of people around the world. It has become one of Canada's best known cultural exports since it was created by a group of street performers in 1984.

Guy Laliberté, the founder, and Daniel Lamarre, the CEO, work together in making the critical decisions about the direction of Cirque du Soleil. According to Lamarre, Laliberté has never overturned one of his decisions as "... the communication is so fluid between us, I will never put myself in that position. I've been good in reading him." In 2015, Cirque du Soleil made a strategic decision of considerable import. It was acquired by TPG Capital and two other investors. At the time, Lamarre told the investors "You can come into my office ten times a day if you so desire, I'll give you all the financial information you need, all the operation information you need. But you shouldn't go into the creative department because that's the core of the company, and I don't want them to be disturbed by any changes we are making."

Photo by Robert Marquardt/Getty Images

SOURCES: C. Edwards, "Blue Ocean Strategy: Creating Your Own Market," *Business News Daily*, July 13, 2018, accessed from https://www.businessnewsdaily.com/5647-blue-ocean-strategy.html, September 7, 2018; "What Is Blue Ocean Strategy?" *The Wall Street Journal* 2009, accessed from http://guides.wsj.com/management/strategy/what-is-blue-ocean-strategy, September 7, 2018; G. Pitts, "Daniel Lamarre: Cirque du Soleil," *The Globe and Mail*, August 27, 2007, http://www.theglobeandmail.com/report-on-business/article778263.ece; and M. Lev-Ram, "How to Manage a Bunch of Clowns: Q&A with the CEO of Cirque du Soleil," *Fortune*, February 24 2017, accessed from http://fortune.com/2017/02/24/cirque-du-soleil-ceo, September 7, 2018.

comes from classic economic theory and contends that the decision maker is completely rational in his or her approach. The rational model assumes the following: (1) The outcome will be completely rational; (2) The decision maker has a consistent system of preferences, which is used to choose the best alternative; (3) The decision maker is aware of all the possible alternatives; and (4) The decision maker can calculate the probability of success for each alternative.[3] These assumptions are based on economic models that are now considered unrealistic. In the rational model, the decision maker strives to optimize, that is, to select the best possible alternative.

blue ocean approach
Companies are better off to entering new spaces rather than competing with existing companies in the market.

Given the assumptions of the rational model, it is unrealistic. There are time constraints and limits to human knowledge and information-processing capabilities. In addition, a manager's preferences and needs change often. The rational model is thus an ideal that managers strive for in making decisions. It captures the way a decision should be made but does *not* reflect the reality of managerial decision making.[4]

Bounded Rationality Model

Recognizing the deficiencies of the rational model, Herbert Simon suggested that there are limits on how rational a decision maker can actually be. His decision theory, the bounded rationality model, earned a Nobel Prize in 1978.

Simon's model, also referred to as the "administrative man" theory, rests on the idea that there are constraints that force a decision maker to be less than completely rational. The bounded rationality model has four assumptions:

1. Managers select the first alternative that is satisfactory.
2. Managers recognize that their conception of the world is simple.
3. Managers are comfortable making decisions without determining all the alternatives.
4. Managers make decisions by rules of thumb or heuristics.

Bounded rationality assumes that managers **satisfice**; that is, they select the first alternative that is "good enough," because the costs of optimizing in terms of time and effort are too great.[5] Further, the theory assumes that managers develop shortcuts, called heuristics, to make decisions in order to save mental activity. Heuristics are rules of thumb that allow managers to make decisions based on what has worked in past experiences.

Does the bounded rationality model more realistically portray the managerial decision process? Research indicates that it does.[6] One of the reasons managers face limits to their rationality is that they must make decisions under risk and time pressure. The situation they find themselves in is highly uncertain, and the probability of success is not known.

Vroom-Yetton-Jago Normative Decision Model

Vroom, Yetton, and Jago developed and refined the normative decision model, which helps leaders and managers determine the appropriate level of employee participation in decision making. The model recognizes the benefits of authoritative, democratic, and consultive styles of leader behaviour.[7] Five forms of decision making are described in the model:

- *Decide*. The manager makes the decision alone and either announces it or "sells" it to the group.
- *Consult individually*. The manager presents the problem to the group members individually, gets their input, and then makes the decision.
- *Consult group*. The manager presents the problem to the group members in a meeting, gets their inputs, and then makes the decision.
- *Facilitate*. The manager presents the problem to the group in a meeting and acts as a facilitator, defining the problem and the boundaries that surround the decision. The manager's ideas are not given more weight than any other group members' ideas. The objective is to get concurrence.
- *Delegate*. The manager permits the group to make the decision within the prescribed limits, providing needed resources and encouragement.[8]

The key to the normative decision model is that a manager should use the decision method most appropriate for a given decision situation. The manager arrives at the proper method by working through the model. Factors such as decision significance, commitment, and leader expertise are the situational factors in the normative decision model. Although the model offers very explicit predictions as well as prescriptions for leaders, its utility is limited to the leader decision-making tasks.

Z Model

Isabel Briggs Myers, co-creator of the MBTI, described in Chapter 3, also developed the Z problem-solving model, which capitalizes on the strengths of the four separate preferences (sensing, intuiting, thinking, and feeling). By using the Z problem-solving model, managers can use both their preferences and non-preferences to make decisions more effectively. According to this model, good problem solving has four steps:

1. *Examine the facts and details.* Use sensing to gather information about the problem.
2. *Generate alternatives.* Use intuiting to develop possibilities.
3. *Analyze the alternatives objectively.* Use thinking to logically determine the effects of each alternative.
4. *Weigh the impact.* Use feeling to determine how the people involved will be affected.

Using the Z model can help an individual develop his or her nonpreferences. Another way to use the Z model is to rely on others to perform the nonpreferred activities. For example, an individual who is an NF (Intuitive–Feeling) might want to turn to a trusted NT (Intuitive–Thinking) for help in analyzing alternatives objectively.

Garbage Can Model

The **garbage can model** of decision making emerged as a critique of Simon's model. The garbage can model asserts that decision

bounded rationality A theory that suggests that there are limits to how rational a decision maker can actually be.

satisfice To select the first alternative that is "good enough" because the costs in time and effort are too great to optimize.

garbage can model Decision making is a process of organizational anarchy.

making is fundamentally a process characterized by organizational anarchy.[9] Organizations function like garbage cans into which go problems, solutions, participants with different preferences, and choice opportunities. As Figure 7.1 illustrates, they can come together in different ways in different organizational subunits. The garbage can model can help us understand why sometimes solutions drive problems, and why individuals with power can control the outcomes of decisions. It gives us further insight into the nonrational processes in decision making. The theory has been used notably in the study of public-sector budget decision making.[10]

The model also has been used to understand UN peacekeeping. "The UN is particularly amenable to models focusing on agenda setting and decision making in organized anarchies or settings characterized by uncertain preferences, unclear organizational processes, and fluid participation in decision making, since these features accurately describe the UN."[11]

escalation of commitment The tendency to continue to support a failing course of action.

Escalation of Commitment

Each decision-making model carries its own limits. This is, however, one limitation that they all share: the decision maker's unwillingness to abandon a bad decision. Continuing to support a failing course of action is known as **escalation of commitment**.[12] In situations characterized by escalation of commitment, individuals who make decisions that turn out to be poor choices tend to hold fast to those choices, even when substantial costs are incurred.[13]An example of escalation is the price wars that often occur between airlines. The airlines reduce their prices in response to competitors until at a certain stage, the airlines are in a "no-win" situation. They continue to compete despite the heavy losses they are incurring. The desire to win is a motivation to continue to escalate, and each airline continues to reduce prices (lose money) based on the belief that the other airline will pull out of the price war. Another example of escalation of commitment is NASA's enormous International Space Station. Originally estimated to cost $8 billion, the Space Station

FIGURE 7.1 GARBAGE CAN MODEL OF DECISION MAKING

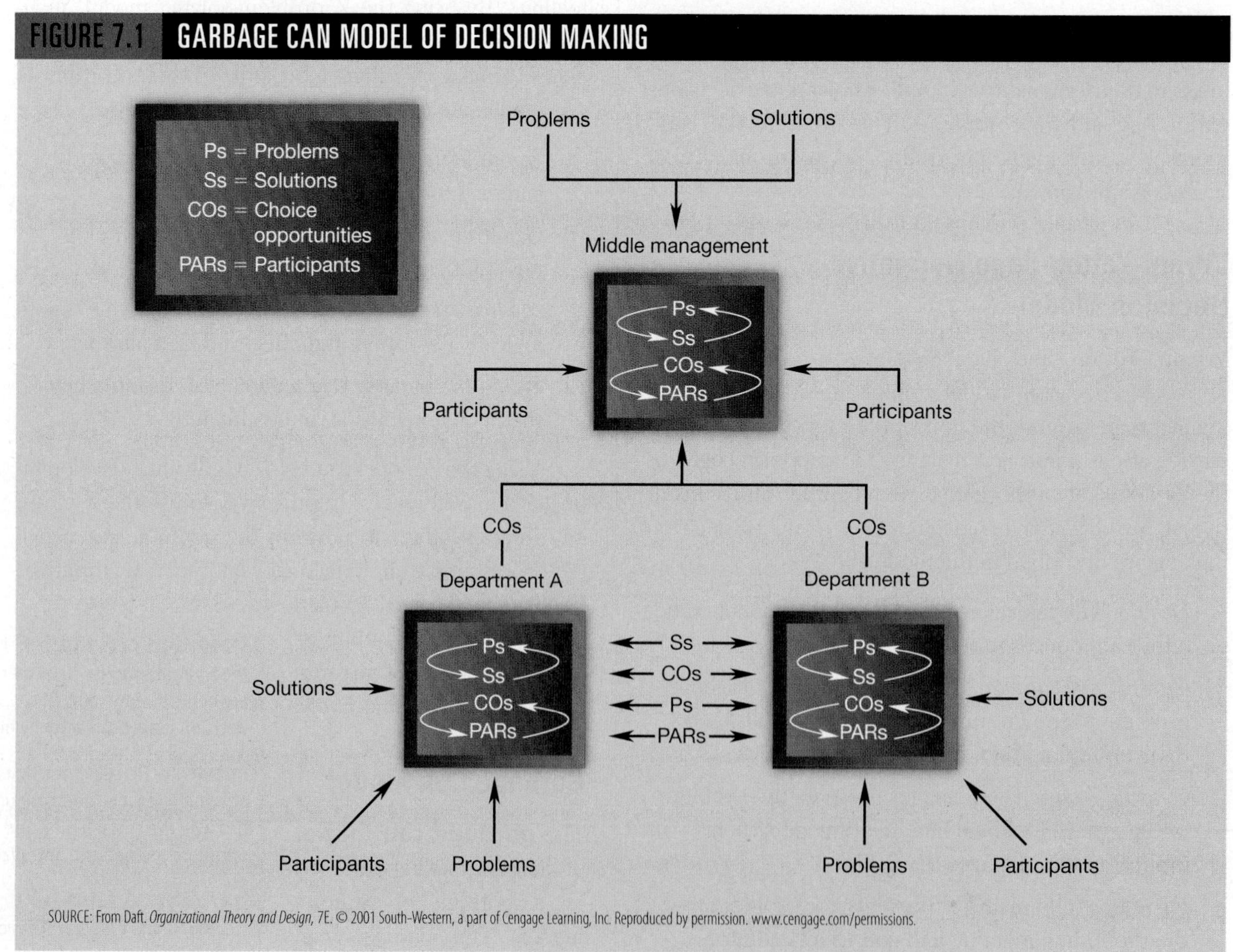

SOURCE: From Daft. *Organizational Theory and Design*, 7E. © 2001 South-Western, a part of Cengage Learning, Inc. Reproduced by permission. www.cengage.com/permissions.

has been redesigned five times and was completed in 2011. Some pundits speculate that the total bill may reach $100 billion for what physicist Robert Park describes as "the biggest technological blunder in history."[14] In 2015, its costs were a staggering $US150 billion![15]

Why does escalation of commitment occur? One explanation is offered by cognitive dissonance theory, as we discussed in Chapter 4. This theory assumes that humans dislike inconsistency and that when inconsistency exists among their attitudes or between their attitudes and behaviour, they strive to reduce the dissonance.[16]

Other reasons people may hang on to a losing course of action are optimism and control. Some people are overly optimistic and overestimate the likelihood that positive things will happen to them. Other people operate under an illusion of control—that they have special skills to control the future that other people don't have.[17] The closer a project is to completion, the more likely escalation is to occur.[18]

Hanging on to a poor decision can be costly to organizations. While most American airlines originally placed orders for the prestigious Mach 2 *Concorde* airliner during the 1960s, their orders for the plane were eventually cancelled, leaving only British Airways and Air France as customers. While these two firms doggedly held on to their marginally profitable *Concorde* operations for almost three decades, a crash in 2000 led to closer scrutiny of the aging fleet, which was eventually retired in 2003. Industry insiders estimate that every customer who took the *Concorde* rather than a 747 cost British Airways more than $1,200 in profits.[19]

Organizations can deal with escalation of commitment in several ways. One is to split the responsibility for project decisions, by allowing different individuals to make decisions at different project stages. Organizations have also tried to eliminate escalation of commitment by closely monitoring decision makers.[20] Another suggestion is to provide individuals with a graceful exit from poor decisions so that their self-images are not threatened. One way of accomplishing this is to reward people who admit to poor decisions before escalating their commitment to them, or having groups make an initial investment decision. Participants in group decision making may experience a diffusion of responsibility for the failed decision rather than feeling personally responsible; thus, they can pull out of a bad decision without threatening their image.[21]

Individuals are imperfect decision makers! There are many cognitive limits on their ability to make effective decisions. Here are a few examples. (1) *Halo (and horn) effect:* A tendency to conclude that a person who does X well will do Y and Z well too. Similarly, you will conclude that a person who does X poorly will do Y and Z poorly too. We therefore overestimate the importance of some characteristics and devalue others. (2) *Recency effect:* Individuals value information that they have received the most recently. (3) *Confirmation bias:* We look for information that confirms our own views. and (4) *Central tendency:* We tend toward leniency (or the middle point in evaluations) as we want to avoid extremes in our assessments.

> "Individuals are imperfect decision makers!"

Daniel Kahneman, winner of the Nobel Prize in Economics, first uncovered some key limitations to individuals' cognitive abilities. In his seminal 1974 article, coauthored with Amos Tversky, he found that individuals rely on heuristics when they are faced with judgments under uncertainty. While the heuristics can be helpful, they can lead to errors. Kahneman and Tversky found, for example, that individuals tend to disregard sample size and tend not to make sufficient adjustments to their starting point as they stay anchored there. As a result of relying on heuristics, people develop cognitive biases that affect their ability to make good decisions.[22]

More recently, researchers have uncovered how our decisions are shaped by our blind spots or **unconscious or implicit bias**. Such biases "... are unconscious feelings we have towards other people—unconscious feelings that play a strong part in influencing our judgement of certain people and groups, away from being balanced or even-handed, in many different areas of life."[23] It is important to note that we all have such biases: "Implicit biases are a natural process by which we take information, and we judge people on the basis of generalizations [and stereotypes] regarding that information. We all do it."[24] Such biases have several characteristics: (1) We generally tend to hold implicit biases that favour our own ingroup, though research has shown that we can still hold implicit biases against our ingroup; (2) Implicit biases are malleable. Our brains are incredibly complex, and our implicit associations can be gradually unlearned through debiasing techniques; (3) The implicit associations we hold do not necessarily align with our declared beliefs or even reflect stances we would explicitly endorse; and (4) Implicit and explicit biases

unconscious or implicit bias Our unconscious, subtle feelings toward others that influence our judgments about them.

are related but distinct mental constructs. They are not mutually exclusive and may even reinforce each other.[25]

A recent study found that preschool teachers focused more on the behaviour of black boys and considered their behaviour as challenging even though all the children, black and white girls and boys, displayed similar and non-challenging behaviours. Black children account for roughly 19 percent of all preschoolers, but nearly half of preschoolers who get suspended.[26] In a workplace context, such biases can have a serious impact on the fairness of performance appraisals in organizations, for example. Table 7.1 describes 20 of our cognitive biases.

We have seen that there are many limits to how rational a manager can be in making decisions. Most managerial decisions involve considerable uncertainty and risk, and individuals react differently to risk situations.

TABLE 7.1 20 COGNITIVE BIASES THAT SCREW UP YOUR DECISIONS

Anchoring Bias	**Availability Heuristic**	**Bandwagon Effect**	**Blind-Spot Bias**	**Choice-Supportive Bias**
People are over-reliant on the first piece of information they hear. In a salary negotiation, whoever makes the first offer establishes a range of reasonable possibilities in each person's mind.	People overestimate the important of information that is available to them. A person might argue that smoking is not unhealthy because they know someone who lived to 100 years and smoked three packs a day.	The probability of one person adopting a belief increases based on the number of people who hold that belief. This is a powerful form of groupthink and is reason why meetings are often unproductive.	Failing to recognize your own cognitive biases is a bias in itself. People notice cognitive and motivational biases much more in others than in themselves.	When you choose something, you tend to feel positive about it, even if that choice has flaws. Like how you think your dog is awesome—even if it bites people every once in a while.
Clustering Illusion	**Confirmation Bias**	**Conservatism Bias**	**Information Bias**	**Ostrich Effect**
This is the tendency to see patterns in random events. It is key to various gambling fallacies, like the idea that red is more or less likely to turn up on a roulette table after a string of reds.	We tend to listen only to information that confirms our preconceptions—one of the many reasons it's so hard to have an intelligent conversation about climate change.	Where people favour prior evidence over new evidence or information that has emerged. People were slow to accept that the Earth was round because they maintained their earlier understanding that the planet was flat.	The tendency to seek information when it does not affect action. More information is not always better. With less information people can often make more accurate predictions.	The decision to ignore dangerous or negative information by "burying" one's head in the sand, like an ostrich. Research suggests that investors check the value of their holdings significantly less often during bad markets.
Outcome Bias	**Overconfidence**	**Placebo Effect**	**Pro-Innovation Bias**	**Recency**
Judging a decision based on the outcome, rather than how exactly the decision was made in the moment. Just because you won a lot in Vegas doesn't mean gambling your money was a smart decision.	Some of us are too confident about our abilities, and this causes us to take greater risks in our daily lives. Experts are more prone to this bias than laypeople, since they are more convinced they are right.	When simply believing that something will have a certain effect on you causes it to have that effect. In medicine, people given "fake" pills can experience the same physiological effects as people given the real thing.	When a proponent of an innovation tends to overvalue its usefulness and undervalue its limitations. Sound familiar, Silicon Valley?	The tendency to weigh the latest information more heavily than older data. Investors often think the market will always look the way it looks today and make unwise decisions.
Salience	**Selective Perception**	**Stereotyping**	**Survivorship Bias**	**Zero-Risk Bias**
Our tendency to focus on the most easily recognizable features of a person or concept. When you think about dying, you might worry about being mauled by a lion, as opposed to what is more likely, like dying in a car accident.	Allowing our expectations to influence how we perceive the world. An experiment involving a football game between students from two universities showed that one team saw the opposing team commit more infractions.	Expecting a group or person to have certain qualities without having real information about the person. It allows us to quickly identify strangers as friends or enemies, but people tend to overuse and abuse it.	An error that comes from focusing only on surviving examples, causing us to misjudge a situation. For instance, we might think that being an entrepreneur is easy because we haven't heard of all those who have failed.	Sociologists have found that we love certainty—even if it's counterproductive. Eliminating risk entirely means there is no chance of harm being caused.

SOURCE: From S. Lee and S. Lebowitz, "20 Cognitive Biases That Screw Up Your Decisions," *Business Insider*, August 26 2015, http://www.businessinsider.com/cognitive-biases-that-affect-decisions-2015-8, accessed July 30, 2018.

7-3 INDIVIDUAL INFLUENCES ON DECISION MAKING

No decision is made in a vacuum. In many ways, decisions reflect the people who make them, so it is appropriate to examine the individual influences on decision making: comfort with risk, **cognitive style**, personality, intuition, and creativity.

Risk and the Manager

Many decisions involve some element of risk. For managers, hiring decisions, promotions, delegation, acquisitions and mergers, overseas expansions, new product development, and other decisions make risk a part of the job.

Individuals differ in terms of their willingness to take risks. Some people experience **risk aversion**. They choose options that entail fewer risks, preferring familiarity and certainty. Other individuals are risk takers; that is, they accept greater potential for loss in decisions, tolerate greater uncertainty, and in general are more likely to make risky decisions. Risk takers are also more likely to take the lead in group discussions.[27]

Some earlier research indicated that women are more averse to risk taking than men and that older, more experienced managers are more risk averse than younger managers. However, more recently, the view that women are more risk averse has been challenged.[28] There is also some evidence that successful managers take more risks than unsuccessful managers.[29] However, the tendency to take risks or avoid them is only part of behaviour toward risk. Risk taking is influenced by not only an individual's tendency but also organizational factors. In commercial banks, loan decisions that require the assessment of risk are made every day.

Many decisions involve some element of risk and ambiguity.

Upper-level managers face a tough task in managing risk-taking behaviour. By discouraging lower-level managers from taking risks, they may stifle creativity and innovation. If upper-level managers are going to encourage risk taking, however, they must allow employees to fail without fear of punishment. One way to accomplish this is to consider failure "enlightened trial and error."[30] The key is establishing a consistent attitude toward risk within the organization.

When individuals take risks, losses may occur. Suppose an oil producer thinks there is an opportunity to uncover oil by reentering an old drilling site. She gathers a group of investors and shows them the logs, and they chip in to finance the venture. The reentry is drilled to a certain depth, and nothing is found. Convinced they did not drill deep enough, the producer goes back to the investors and requests additional financial backing to continue drilling. The investors consent, and she drills deeper, only to find nothing. She approaches the investors, and after lengthy discussion, they agree to provide more money to drill deeper. Why do decision makers sometimes throw good money after bad?

Cognitive Styles

Cognitive styles refer to how we typically think, remember, and address problems. They influence our attitudes, values, and social interaction. Further, cognitive styles are seen as bipolar variables as they indicate a tendency that is relatively fixed. Abilities, on the other hand, are unipolar so that having more of an ability is generally considered to be better.[31] Researchers have identified various cognitive styles and have developed instruments to measure them. Field dependence/independence has been studied extensively. Field dependent individuals are most affected by their environment. They tend to get the whole idea whereas the field independent individuals conduct an analytical procedure and are more likely to break a model into different sections and details and tend to depend on their inner knowledge.[32]

Studies have shown that a manager's cognitive style can have an impact on what sorts of strategies they prefer. "In practice, understanding the differences which are connected with the views of strategies is important when members of the top management team are replaced

cognitive style An individual's preference for gathering information and evaluating alternatives.

risk aversion The tendency to choose options that entail fewer risks and less uncertainty.

IN ACTION

Bombardier Inc.

The events of September 11, 2001, had a significant impact on Bombardier and other plane manufacturers. That same year, Bombardier expanded considerably through acquisitions in its rail and recreational groups. According to Pierre Beaudoin, CEO since 2008, "... [as a result,] a lot of the rocks came to the surface in terms of Bombardier's capabilities and structure." He notes that "... in 2001, we had an organization that was very proud of being number one ... But when we talked to our customers, they were saying we weren't very good."

Beaudoin and his leadership team soon realized that the company's managers, while acknowledging that there were problems, insisted that the problems were not in their departments. They surveyed their employees and the employees observed that the company focused too much on hardware. Based on the survey results and on observing the managers, Beaudoin realized that Bombardier would need to move beyond particular fixes and needed to get to the core of the company. As Beaudoin put it, "[We] needed employees to understand we were flying people, not planes." Beaudoin then made the decision to focus on culture to transform Bombardier.

Beaudoin identified three priorities—creating a rewarding and safe workplace, providing excellent customer service, and reducing waste—and then asked Bombardier's top leaders how they would realize the priorities. One of the many challenges that Beaudoin faced was employees wondering why he had decided to focus on "soft" issues such as creating a rewarding workplace. However, Beaudoin also emphasized that "hard" goals needed to be met, e.g., a $500 million performance improvement gain.

SOURCES: B.Simpson, "'Flying People, not Planes': The CEO of Bombardier on Building a World-Class Culture," *McKinsey Quarterly*, March 2011, accessed from https://www.mckinsey.com/business-functions/organization/our-insights/and-8220flying-people-not-planes-and-8221-the-ceo-of-bombardier-on-building-a-world-class-culture, September 7, 2018.

by new ones."[33] Managers tend to select successors like themselves, rather than selecting individuals with different cognitive styles and personalities.

intuition A fast, positive force in decision making that is utilized at a level below consciousness and involves learned patterns of information.

Personality, Attitudes, and Values

In addition to all of the individual differences variables (discussed in Chapters 3 and 4), personality characteristics, attitudes, and values, managers must use both their logic and their creativity to make effective decisions. Most of us are more comfortable using either logic or creativity, and we show that preference in everyday decision making.

Our brains have two lateral halves. The right side is the centre for creative functions, while the left side is the centre for logic, detail, and planning. There are advantages to both kinds of thinking, so the ideal situation is to be "brain-lateralized" or to be able to use either logic or creativity or both, depending on the situation. There are ways to develop the side of the brain you are not accustomed to using. To develop your right side, or creative side, you can ask "what-if" questions, engage in play, and follow your intuition. To develop the left side, you can set goals for completing tasks and work to attain these goals. For managers, it is important to see the big picture, craft a vision, and plan strategically—all of which require right-brain skills. It is equally important to be able to understand day-to-day operations and flow chart work processes, which are left-brain skills. Brain hemispheric dominance is related to students' postsecondary education choices. Left-brained students gravitate toward business, engineering, and sciences, whereas right-brained students are attracted to education, nursing, communication, and literature.[34]

Intuition

There is evidence that managers use their **intuition** to make decisions.[35] Henry Mintzberg, in his work on managerial roles, found that in many cases managers do not appear to use a systematic, step-by-step approach to decision making. Rather, Mintzberg argued, managers make judgments based on "hunches."[36] Daniel Isenberg studied the way senior managers make decisions and found that intuition was used extensively, especially as a mechanism to evaluate decisions made more rationally.[37] A study of the way managers at Bank of America made decisions about the future direction of the company following the deregulation of the banking industry found they used intuition as an antidote to "analysis paralysis," or the tendency to analyze decisions rather than develop innovative solutions.[38] Similarly, a series of studies conducted with the U.S. Navy, U.S. Army, and firefighters, found that decision makers normally relied on intuition in unfamiliar, challenging situations. These decisions were superior to those made after careful evaluation of information and potential alternatives.[39]

Just what is intuition? In Jungian theory, intuiting (N) is one preference used to gather data. This is only one way that the concept of intuition has been applied to managerial decision making, and it is perhaps the most widely researched form of the concept of intuition. There are, however, many definitions of *intuition* in the managerial literature. Chester Barnard, one of the early influential management researchers, argued that intuition's main attributes were speed and the inability of the decision maker to determine how the decision was made.[40] Other researchers have contended that intuition occurs at an unconscious level and that this is why the decision maker cannot verbalize how the decision was made.[41]

Intuition has been variously described as follows:

1. The ability to know or recognize quickly and readily the possibilities of a situation.[42]
2. Smooth automatic performance of learned behaviour sequences.[43]
3. Simple analyses frozen into habit and into the capacity for rapid response through recognition.[44]

These definitions share some common assumptions. First, there seems to be a notion that intuition is fast. Second, intuition is used at a level below consciousness. Third, there seems to be agreement that intuition involves learned patterns of information. Fourth, intuition appears to be a positive force in decision making.

The use of intuition may lead to more ethical decisions. Intuition allows an individual to take on another's role with ease, and role taking is a fundamental part of developing moral reasoning. You will recall from Chapter 4 the role of cognitive moral development in ethical decision making. One study found a strong link between cognitive moral development and intuition. The development of new perspectives through intuition leads to higher moral growth, and thus to more ethical decisions.[45]

One question that arises is whether managers can be taught to use their intuition. After giving intuition tests to more than 10,000 executives, Agor has concluded that in most cases, higher management positions are held by individuals with higher levels of intuition. Just as the brain needs both hemispheres to work, Agor cautions that organizations need both analytical and intuitive minds to function at their peak. Agor suggests relaxation techniques, using images to guide the mind, and taking creative pauses before making a decision.[46] In his autobiography, Lee Iacocca, once CEO of Chrysler, spends pages extolling intuition: "To a certain extent, I've always operated by gut feeling."[47] A review of the research on intuition suggests that although intuition itself cannot be taught, managers can be trained to rely more fully on the promptings of their intuition.[48]

“

Although intuition itself cannot be taught, managers can be trained to rely more fully on the promptings of their intuition.

Intuition, with many definitions, is an elusive concept. Some researchers view "rational" methods as preferable to intuition, yet satisfaction with a rational decision is usually determined by how the decision feels intuitively.[49] Intuition appears to have a positive effect on managerial decision making, but it is not without controversy. Some writers argue that intuition has its place and that instincts should be trusted, but not as a substitute for reason. With new technologies, managers can analyze a lot more information in a lot less time, making the rational method less time consuming than it once was.[50]

Creativity

In some ways, creativity is as elusive a concept as intuition. (We know it when we encounter it and feel its absence.) Even though creativity is also highly individual, it is also collective. Personal creativity plays a role in the decisions made in organizations every day. **Creativity** is a process influenced by individual and organizational factors that results in the production of novel and useful ideas, products, or both.[51]

The four stages of the creative process are preparation, incubation, illumination, and verification.[52] Preparation means seeking out new experiences and opportunities to learn, because creativity grows from a base of knowledge. Incubation is a process of reflective thought and is often conducted subconsciously. During incubation, the individual engages in other pursuits while the mind considers the problem and works on it. Illumination occurs when the individual senses an insight for solving the problem. Finally, verification is conducted to determine if the solution or idea is valid. Verification is accomplished by thinking through the implications of the decision, presenting the idea to another person, or trying out the decision. Momentary quieting of the brain through relaxation can increase "coherence" or the ability of different parts of the brain to work together.[53] Both individual and organizational influences affect the creative process.

creativity A process influenced by individual and organizational factors that results in the production of novel and useful ideas, products, or both.

INDIVIDUAL INFLUENCES Several individual variables are related to creativity. One group of factors involves the cognitive processes that creative individuals tend to use. One cognitive process is divergent thinking, meaning the individual's ability to generate several potential solutions to a problem.[54] In addition, associational abilities and the use of imagery are associated with creativity.[55] Unconscious processes such as dreams are also essential cognitive processes related to creative thinking.[56]

Personality factors have also been related to creativity in studies of individuals from several different occupations. These characteristics include intellectual and artistic values, breadth of interests, high energy, concern with achievement, independence of judgment, intuition, self-confidence, and a creative self-image.[57] Tolerance of ambiguity, intrinsic motivation, risk taking, and a desire for recognition are also associated with creativity.[58]

There is also evidence that people who are in a good mood are more creative.[59] Positive affect is related to creativity in work teams because being in a positive mood allows team members to explore new ways of thinking.[60] Positive emotions enhance creativity by broadening your cognitive patterns and resources. These positive emotions initiate thoughts and actions that are novel and unscripted.[61] Moreover, it is a cyclical process: thinking positively makes us more creative, and being more creative makes us think positively.[62]

Conversely, it has been found that people in negative moods perform better at tasks involving considerable cognitive demands. When an individual experiences negative moods or emotions, it is a signal to the individual that all is not well, and leads to more attention and vigilance in cognitive activity. Try the Self-Assessment now!

ORGANIZATIONAL INFLUENCES The organizational environment in which people work can either support creativity or impede creative efforts. Creativity killers include focusing on how work will be evaluated, being closely monitored while you are working, and competing with other people in win–lose situations. In contrast, creativity facilitators include feelings of autonomy, being part of a team with diverse skills, and having creative supervisors and coworkers.[63] High-quality, supportive relationships with supervisors are related to creativity.[64] High-quality social networks that are cohesive can have a positive impact on creative decision making. Such social networks encourage creative decision making by facilitating shared sensemaking of relevant information and consensus building.[65] Flexible organizational structures and participative decision making have also been associated with creativity.

IN ACTION

Adobe's Kickbox Stimulates Creative Ideas

Adobe, the digital marketing and media company, developed an approach to creativity called Kickbox, and it was so successful within Adobe that it is now open sourced. The instructions are free, so any company can create its own kickbox. It is a red cardboard box that includes a pen, sticky notes, a timer, a small notebook for bad ideas, a spiral notebook, a sea salt and caramel chocolate bar, and a $10 Starbucks gift card. Also included is a $1,000 prepaid card that employees can spend without having to justify their expense to management.

Inside the box is a five-step model to develop a creative idea: inception, ideate, improve, investigate, and infiltrate. Each step has detailed instructions on how to complete the step. It's a highly systematic process, and more than 1,000 employees at Adobe have used a Kickbox. Of these, 23 have received major investments from Adobe to move their ideas ahead.

Adobe's VP of Creativity, Mark Randall, came up with the Kickbox idea. He surveyed employees to see what kept them from pursuing creative ideas. The number-one response was "convincing management." Kickbox eliminates that barrier and unboxes creativity and innovation.

SOURCES: D. Burkus, "Inside Adobe's Innovation Kit," *Harvard Business Review*, accessed from https://hbr.org/2015/02/inside-adobes-innovation-kit,; M. Wilson, "Adobe's Kickbox: The Kit to Launch Your Next Big Idea," *Fast Company*, February 9, 2015, accessed from http://www.fastcodesign.com/3042128/adobes-kickbox-the-kit-to-launch-your-next-big-idea, September 7, 2018.

An organization can also present impediments to creativity. These barriers include internal political problems, harsh criticism of new ideas, destructive internal competition, and avoidance of risk.[66] The physical environment can also hamper creativity. Companies such as Oticon, a Danish hearing-aid manufacturer, and Ethicon Endo-Surgery, a division of Johnson & Johnson, use open-plan offices that eliminate office walls and cubicles as they believe that employees will interact more frequently. When people mix, ideas mix as well.[67] Organizations can, therefore, enhance individuals' creative decision making by providing a supportive environment, participative decision making, and a flexible structure.

INDIVIDUAL/ORGANIZATION FIT Research has indicated that creative performance is highest when there is a match, or fit, between the individual and organizational influences on creativity. When individuals who desire to be creative are matched with an organization that values creative ideas, the result is more creative performance.[68]

A common mistaken assumption about creativity is that either you have it or you do not. Research refutes this myth and has shown that individuals can be trained to be more creative.[69] The Disney Institute features a wide range of programs offered to organizations, and one of its best-sellers is creativity training. Part of creativity training involves learning to open up mental locks that keep us from generating creative alternatives to a decision or problem. Studies of the role of organizational rewards in encouraging creativity have mixed results. Some studies have shown that monetary incentives improve creative performance, whereas others have found that material rewards do not influence innovative activity. Still other studies have indicated that explicitly contracting to obtain a reward led to lower levels of creativity when compared with contracting for no reward, being presented with just the task, or being presented with the task and receiving the reward later.[70]

The following are some mental locks that diminish creativity:

- Searching for the "right" answer
- Trying to be logical
- Following the rules
- Avoiding ambiguity
- Striving for practicality
- Being afraid to look foolish
- Avoiding problems outside our own expertise
- Fearing failure
- Believing we are not really creative
- Not making play a part of work[71]

Note that many of these mental locks stem from values within organizations. Organizations can facilitate creative decision making in many ways. Rewarding creativity, allowing employees to fail, making work more fun, and providing creativity training are a few suggestions. Organizations can encourage creativity by exposing employees to new ideas through job rotation, for example, which moves employees through different jobs and gives them exposure to different information, projects, and teams, either within or outside the company. Finally, managers can encourage employees to surround themselves with stimuli that they have found to enhance their creative processes. These may be music, artwork, books, or anything else that encourages creative thinking.[72]

We have seen that both individual and organizational factors can produce creativity. Creativity also means finding problems as well as fixing them. Recently, four different types of creativity have been proposed, based on the source of the trigger (internal or external) and the source of the problem (presented versus discovered). Responsive creativity means responding to a problem that is presented to you by others because it is part of your job. Expected creativity is discovering problems because you are expected to by the organization. Contributory creativity is responding to problems presented to you because you want to be creative. Proactive creativity is discovering problems because you want to be creative.[73]

3M consistently ranks among the top ten in *Fortune*'s annual list of most admired corporations. It earned this reputation through innovation: more than one-quarter of 3M's sales are from products less than four years old. Post-It Notes, for example, were created by a worker who wanted little adhesive papers to mark hymns for church service. He thought of another worker who had perfected a light adhesive, and the two spent their "free time" developing Post-It Notes. 3M has continued its tradition of innovation with Post-It Flags, Pop-Up Tape Strips, and Nexcare Ease-Off Bandages.[74]

Leaders can play key roles in modelling creative behaviour. Sir Richard Branson, founder and chairman of U.K.–based Virgin Group, believes that if you do not use your employees' creative potential, you are doomed to failure. At Virgin Group, the culture encourages risk taking and rewards innovation. Rules and regulations are not its thing, nor is analyzing ideas to death. Branson says that an employee can have an idea in the morning and implement it in the afternoon.[75]

THE GROUP DECISION-MAKING PROCESS

Managers use groups to make decisions for several reasons. One is **synergy**, which occurs when group members stimulate new solutions to problems through the process of mutual influence and encouragement within the group. Another reason for using a group is to gain commitment to a decision. Groups also bring more knowledge and experience to the problem-solving situation.

synergy A positive force that occurs in groups when group members stimulate new solutions to problems through the process of mutual influence and encouragement within the group.

Group decisions can sometimes be predicted by comparing the views of the initial group members with the final group decision. These simple relationships are known as **social decision schemes**. One social decision scheme is the majority-wins rule, in which the group supports whatever position is taken by the majority of its members. Another scheme, the truth-wins rule, predicts that the correct decision will emerge as an increasing number of members realize its appropriateness. The two-thirds-majority rule means that the decision favoured by two-thirds or more of the members is supported. Finally, the first-shift rule states that members support a decision represented by the first shift in opinion shown by a member.

Research indicates that these social decision schemes can predict a group decision as much as 80 percent of the time.[76] Current research is aimed at discovering which rules are used in particular types of tasks. For example, studies indicate that the majority-wins rule is used most often in judgment tasks (that is, when the decision is a matter of preference or opinion), whereas the truth-wins rule predicts decisions best when the task is an intellective one (that is, when the decision has a correct answer).[77]

Advantages and Disadvantages of Group Decision Making

Group decision making has advantages and disadvantages. The advantages include (1) more knowledge and information through the pooling of group member resources; (2) increased acceptance of and commitment to the decision because the members had a voice in it; and (3) greater understanding of the decision because members were involved in the various stages of the decision process. The disadvantages of group decision making include (1) pressure within the group to conform and fit in; (2) domination of the group by one forceful member or a dominant clique, who may ramrod the decision; and (3) the amount of time required, because a group makes decisions more slowly than an individual.[78]

In light of these advantages and disadvantages, should an individual or a group make a decision? Substantial empirical research indicates that effectively making that determination depends on the type of task involved. For judgment tasks requiring an estimate or a prediction, groups are usually superior to individuals because of the breadth of experience that multiple individuals bring to the problem.[79] On tasks that have a correct solution, other studies have indicated that the most competent individual outperforms the group.[80] However, this finding has been called into question. Much of the previous research on groups was conducted in the laboratory, where group members interacted only for short periods of time. Researchers wanted to know how a longer group experience would affect decisions. Their study showed that groups who worked together for longer periods of time outperformed the most competent member 70 percent of the time. As groups gained experience, the best members became less important to the group's success.[81] This study demonstrated that experience in the group is an important variable to consider when evaluating the individual versus group decision-making question.

social decision schemes Simple rules used to determine final group decisions.

groupthink A deterioration of mental efficiency, reality testing, and moral judgment resulting from pressures within the group.

Given the emphasis on teams in the workplace, many managers believe that groups produce better decisions than individuals, yet the evidence is mixed. More research needs to be conducted in organizational settings to help answer this question.

Limits of Group Decision Making

Two potential liabilities are found in group decision making: groupthink and group polarization. These problems are discussed next.

GROUPTHINK One liability of a cohesive group is its tendency to develop **groupthink**, a dysfunctional process. Irving Janis, the originator of the groupthink concept, describes groupthink as "a deterioration of mental efficiency, reality testing, and moral judgment" resulting from pressures within the group.[82]

Certain conditions favour the development of groupthink. One of the conditions is high cohesiveness. Cohesive groups tend to favour solidarity because members identify strongly with the group.[83] High-ranking teams that make decisions without outside help are especially prone to groupthink because they are likely to have shared mental models; that is, they are more likely to think alike.[84] Homogeneous groups (ones with little to no diversity among members) are more likely to suffer from groupthink.[85] Two other conditions that encourage groupthink are having to make a highly consequential decision and time constraints.[86] A highly consequential decision is one that will have a great impact on the group members and on outside parties. When group members feel that they have a limited time in which to make a decision, they may rush through the process. These antecedents cause members to prefer concurrence in decisions and to fail to evaluate one another's suggestions critically. A group suffering from groupthink shows recognizable symptoms.

An incident cited as a prime example of groupthink is the 1986 *Challenger* disaster, in which the shuttle exploded and killed all seven crew members. A presidential commission concluded that flawed decision making was the primary cause of the accident. In 2003, the shuttle *Columbia* exploded over Texas upon reentering the earth's atmosphere, killing all seven crew members. Within days of the *Columbia* disaster, questions began to surface about the decision-making process that led flight engineers to assume that damage caused to the shuttle upon takeoff was minor and to continue the mission. The subsequent investigation of the disaster led observers to note that NASA's decision-making process appeared just as flawed in 2003 as it was in 1986, exhibiting all the classic symptoms of groupthink. The final accident report blamed the NASA culture that downplayed risk and suppressed dissent for the decision.[87]

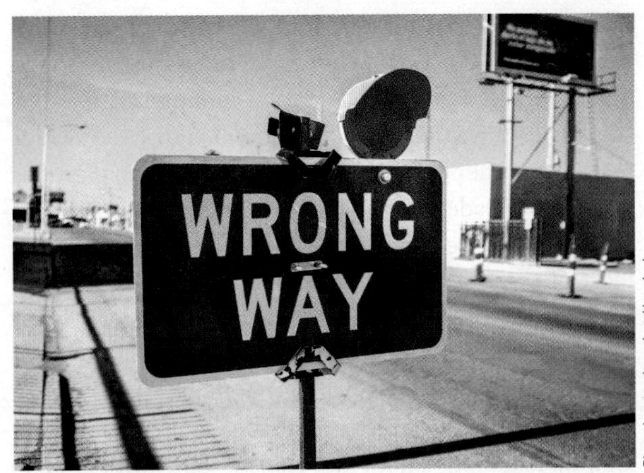

Photo by neonbrand on Unsplash

Poor decision-making can lead to catastrophic consequences.

Consequences of groupthink include an incomplete survey of alternatives, failure to evaluate the risks of the preferred course of action, biased information processing, and a failure to work out contingency plans. Evident in the *Challenger* situation, the overall result of groupthink is defective decision making. The group considered only two alternatives: launch or no launch. Group members failed to consider the risks of their decision to launch the shuttle, and they did not develop any contingency plans.

Table 7.2 presents the symptoms of groupthink and Janis's guidelines for avoiding groupthink. Many of these suggestions centre around ensuring that decisions are evaluated completely, with opportunities for discussion from all group members. This strategy encourages members to evaluate one another's ideas critically. Groups that are educated about the value of diversity tend to perform better at decision-making tasks. On the other hand, groups that are homogenous and are not educated about the value of diversity do not accrue such benefits in decision making.[88]

Janis has used the groupthink framework to conduct historical analyses of several political and military fiascoes. One review of the decision situation in the *Challenger* incident

TABLE 7.2 SYMPTOMS OF GROUPTHINK AND HOW TO PREVENT IT

Symptoms of Groupthink

- *Illusions of invulnerability.* Group members feel that they are above criticism. This symptom leads to excessive optimism and risk taking.
- *Illusions of group morality.* Group members feel they are moral in their actions and therefore above reproach. This symptom leads the group to ignore the ethical implications of their decisions.
- *Illusions of unanimity.* Group members believe there is unanimous agreement on the decisions. Silence is misconstrued as consent.
- *Rationalization.* Group members concoct explanations for their decisions to make them appear rational and correct. The results are that other alternatives are not considered, and there is an unwillingness to reconsider the group's assumptions.
- *Stereotyping the enemy.* Competitors are stereotyped as evil or stupid. This leads the group to underestimate its opposition.
- *Self-censorship.* Members do not express their doubts or concerns about the course of action. This prevents critical analysis of the decisions.
- *Peer pressure.* Any members who express doubts or concerns are pressured by other group members who question their loyalty.
- *Mindguards.* Some members take it upon themselves to protect the group from negative feedback. Group members are thus shielded from information that might lead them to question their actions.

Guidelines for Preventing Groupthink

- Ask each group member to assume the role of the critical evaluator who actively voices objections or doubts.
- Have the leader avoid stating his or her position on the issue prior to the group decision.
- Create several groups that work on the decision simultaneously.
- Bring in outside experts to evaluate the group process.
- Appoint a devil's advocate to question the group's course of action consistently.
- Evaluate the competition carefully, posing as many different motivations and intentions as possible.
- Once consensus is reached, encourage the group to rethink its position by reexamining the alternatives.

SOURCE: From Janis. *Groupthink*, 2E. © 1982 Wadsworth, a part of Cengage Learning, Inc. Reproduced by permission. www.cengage.com/permissions.

proposed that two variables, time and leadership style, are important to include.[89] When a decision must be made quickly, there is more potential for groupthink. Leadership style can either promote groupthink (if the leader makes his or her opinion known up front) or avoid groupthink (if the leader encourages open and frank discussion).

There are few empirical studies of groupthink, and most of these involved students in a laboratory setting. More applied research may be seen in the future, however, as a questionnaire has been developed to measure the constructs associated with groupthink.[90] Janis's work on groupthink has led to several interdisciplinary efforts at understanding policy decisions.[91] The work underscores the need to examine multiple explanations for failed decisions. Teams that experience cognitive (task-based) conflict are found to make better decisions than teams that experience affective (emotion-based) conflict. As such, one prescription for managers has been to encourage cognitive conflict while minimizing affective conflict. However, these two forms of conflict can also occur together and more research is needed on how one can be encouraged while minimizing the other.[92]

GROUP POLARIZATION Another group phenomenon was discovered by a graduate student. His study showed that groups and individuals within the group made riskier decisions and accepted greater levels of risk following a group discussion of the issue. Subsequent studies uncovered another shift—toward caution. Thus, group discussion produced shifts both toward more risky positions and toward more cautious positions.[93] Further research revealed that individual group members' attitudes became more extreme simply following group discussion. Individuals who were initially against an issue became more radically opposed, and individuals who were in favour of the issue became more strongly supportive following discussion. These shifts came to be known as **group polarization**.[94]

group polarization The tendency for group discussion to produce shifts toward more extreme attitudes among members.

The tendency toward polarization has important implications for group decision making. Groups whose initial views lean a certain way can be expected to adopt more extreme views following interaction.

Several ideas have been proposed to explain why group polarization occurs. One explanation is the social comparison approach. Prior to group discussion, individuals believe they hold better views than the other members. During group discussion, they see that their views are not so far from average, so they shift to more extreme positions.[95] A second explanation is the persuasive arguments view. It contends that group discussion reinforces the initial views of the members, so they take a more extreme position.[96] Both explanations are supported by research. It may be that both processes, along with others, cause the group to develop more polarized attitudes.

Group polarization leads groups to adopt extreme attitudes. In some cases, this can be disastrous. For instance, if individuals are leaning toward a dangerous decision, they are likely to support it more strongly following discussion. Both groupthink and group polarization are potential liabilities of group decision making, but several techniques can be used to help prevent or control these two liabilities.

Techniques for Group Decision Making

Once a manager has determined that a group decision approach should be used, he or she can determine the technique that is best suited to the decision situation.

Photo by Brendan Church on Unsplash

Group polarization leads groups to adopt extreme and inflexible ideas.

Seven techniques will be briefly summarized: brainstorming, nominal group technique, devil's advocacy, dialectical inquiry, quality circles and quality teams, and self-managed teams.

BRAINSTORMING Brainstorming is a good technique for generating alternatives. The idea behind **brainstorming** is to generate as many ideas as possible, suspending evaluation until all of the ideas have been suggested. Participants are encouraged to build upon the suggestions of others, and imagination is emphasized. One company that benefits from brainstorming is Toyota. Despite its success with the baby-boomer generation, Toyota's executives realized that they were failing to connect with younger buyers, who viewed the firm as stodgy. In response, Toyota assembled a group of younger employees to brainstorm new products for this market. The result was the Toyota Echo, as well as Scion, an entirely new line of boxy crossover vehicles aimed at the younger set.[97] Similarly, Cirque du Soleil has a group, the Trend Group, composed of young people, to gather ideas from all over the world.[98]

Evidence suggests, however, that group brainstorming is less effective than a comparable number of individuals working alone. In groups, participants engage in discussions that can make them lose their focus.[99]

NOMINAL GROUP TECHNIQUE A structured approach to decision making that focuses on generating alternatives and choosing one is called **nominal group technique (NGT)**. NGT involves the following discrete steps: (1) Individuals silently list their ideas; (2) Ideas are written on a chart one at a time until all ideas are listed; (3) Discussion is permitted but only to clarify the ideas. No criticism is allowed; and (4) A written vote is taken. NGT is a good technique to use in a situation where group members fear criticism from others.[100]

DEVIL'S ADVOCACY In the **devil's advocacy** decision method, a group or individual is given the role of critic. This devil's advocate has the task of coming up with the potential problems of a proposed decision. This helps organizations avoid costly mistakes in decision making by identifying potential pitfalls in advance.[101] A devil's advocate who challenges the CEO and top management team can help sustain the vitality and performance of the upper echelon.

DIALECTICAL INQUIRY **Dialectical inquiry** is essentially a debate between two opposing sets of recommendations. Although it sets up a conflict, it is a constructive approach because it brings out the benefits and limitations of both sets of ideas.[102] When using this technique, it is important to guard against a win–lose attitude and to concentrate on reaching the most effective solution for all concerned. Research has shown that the way a decision is framed (that is, win–win versus win–lose) is very important. A decision's outcome could be viewed as a gain or a loss, depending on the way the decision is framed.[103]

QUALITY CIRCLES AND QUALITY TEAMS **Quality circles** are small groups that voluntarily meet to provide input for solving quality or production problems. Quality circles also extend participative decision making into teams. Managers often listen to recommendations from quality circles and implement the suggestions. Involvement in the decision-making process is the primary reward.

Quality circles are not empowered to implement their own recommendations. They operate in parallel fashion to the organization's structure, and they rely on voluntary participation.[104] In Japan, quality circles have been integrated into the organization instead of added on. This may be one reason for Japan's success with this technique. In contrast, the North American experience is not as positive. It has been estimated that 60 to 75 percent of the quality circles have failed. Reasons for the failures have included lack of top management support and lack of problem-solving skills among quality circle members.[105]

Quality teams, in contrast, are included in total quality management and other quality improvement efforts as part of a change in the organization's structure. Quality teams are generated from the top down and are empowered to act on their own recommendations. Although quality circles emphasize the generation of ideas, quality teams make data-based decisions about improving product and service quality. Various

brainstorming A technique for generating as many ideas as possible on a given subject, while suspending evaluation until all the ideas have been suggested.

nominal group technique (NGT) A structured approach to group decision making that focuses on generating alternatives and choosing one.

devil's advocacy A technique for preventing groupthink in which a group or individual is given the role of critic during decision making.

dialectical inquiry A debate between two opposing sets of recommendations.

quality circle A small group of employees who work voluntarily on company time, typically one hour per week, to address work-related problems such as quality control, cost reduction, production planning and techniques, and even product design.

quality team A team that is part of an organization's structure and is empowered to act on its decisions regarding product and service quality.

decision-making techniques are employed in quality teams. Brainstorming, flow charts, and cause-and-effect diagrams help pinpoint problems that affect quality.

Quality circles and quality teams are methods for using groups in the decision-making process. Self-managed teams take the concept of participation one step further.

SELF-MANAGED TEAMS Another group decision-making method is the use of self-managed teams. The decision-making activities of self-managed teams are more broadly focused than those of quality circles and quality teams. Self-managed teams make many of the decisions that were once reserved for managers, such as work scheduling, job assignments, and staffing.

Factors in Selecting the Appropriate Technique

Before choosing a group decision-making technique, the manager should carefully evaluate the group members and the decision situation. Only then can the best method for accomplishing the objectives of the group decision-making process be selected. If the goal is generating a large number of alternatives, for example, brainstorming would be a good choice. If group members are reluctant to contribute ideas, the nominal group technique would be appropriate. To guard against groupthink, devil's advocacy or dialectical inquiry would be effective. Decisions that concern quality or production would benefit from the advice of quality circles or the empowered decisions of quality teams. Moreover, recent research results suggest that if individuals within a team are made accountable for the process of decision making (rather than the end decision itself), then such teams are more likely to gather diverse information, share information, and eventually make better decisions.[106] Finally, a manager who wants to provide total empowerment to a group should consider self-managed teams.

Special Decision-making Groups

Even though in organizations many types of groups make collective decisions, quality-oriented groups and self-managed teams have higher levels of involvement and authority in group decision making.

Many organizations have claimed success with self-managed teams. GE has used self-managed teams in its aerospace division with some considerable success.[107] Research evidence shows that self-managed teams can lead to higher productivity, lower turnover among employees, and flatter organization structure.[108]

#HOT #TREND

Electronic Brainstorming

Electronic brainstorming overcomes two common problems that can produce group brainstorming failure: production blocking and evaluation apprehension. Production blocking occurs when you forget what *you* wanted to contribute because you were concentrating on listening to *others* in the session. In electronic brainstorming, ideas are recorded electronically, so participants can focus on the ideas they want to share free from interruption. Electronic brainstorming also overcomes evaluation apprehension, which occurs when individuals fear that others might respond negatively to their ideas. In electronic brainstorming, input is anonymous, so evaluation apprehension is reduced. Studies indicate that anonymous electronic brainstorming groups outperform face-to-face brainstorming groups in the number of ideas generated.

SOURCES: B. A. Nijstad, W. Stroebe, and H. F. M. Lodewijkx, "Production Blocking and Idea Generation: Does Blocking Interfere with Cognitive Processes?" *Journal of Experimental Social Psychology* 39 (2003): 531–549; W. H. Cooper, R. B. Gallupe, S. Pollard, and J. Cadsby, "Some Liberating Effects of Anonymous Electronic Brainstorming," *Small Group Research* 29 (1998): 147–178.

Self-managed teams, like any cohesive group, can fall victim to groupthink. The key to stimulating innovation and better problem solving in these groups is welcoming dissent among members. Dissent breaks down complacency and sets in motion a process that results in better decisions. Team members must know that dissent is permissible so that they won't fear embarrassment or ridicule.[109]

A 2013 study from the Wharton School found that 15 minutes of mindfulness meditation can help decision makers make "smarter choices." Mindfulness helped individuals to consider information available in the present moment and therefore helped them make better decisions. The results suggested "that increased mindfulness reduces the tendency to allow unrecoverable prior costs to influence current decisions."

SOURCES: C. Bergland, "The Neuroscience of Making a Decision," Psychology Today Canada, May 6, 2015, https://www.psychologytoday.com/ca/blog/the-athletes-way/201505/the-neuroscience-making-decision, accessed July 28 2018; A.C. Hafenbrack, Z. Kinias, and S.G. Barsade, "Debiasing the Mind Through Meditation: Mindfulness and the Sunk-Cost Bias," *Psychological Science* 25, 2: 369–376.

7-5 DIVERSITY AND CULTURE IN DECISION MAKING

Styles of decision making vary greatly among cultures. Many of the dimensions proposed by Hofstede that were presented in Chapter 2 affect decision making. Uncertainty avoidance, for example, can affect the way people view decisions. In Canada, a culture with low uncertainty avoidance, decisions are seen as opportunities for change. In contrast, cultures such as those of Indonesia and Malaysia attempt to accept situations as they are rather than to change them.[110] Power distance also affects decision making. In more hierarchical cultures, such as India, top-level managers make decisions. In countries with low power distance, lower-level employees make many decisions. The Swedish culture exemplifies this type.

The individualist/collectivist dimension has implications for decision making. Japan, with its collectivist emphasis, favours group decisions. Canada has a more difficult time with group decisions because it is an individualistic culture. Time orientation affects the frame of reference of the decision. In China, with its long-term view, decisions are made with the future in mind. In Canada, many decisions are made considering the short term.

The masculine/feminine dimension can be compared to the Jungian thinking/feeling preferences for decision making. Masculine cultures, as in many Latin American countries, value quick, assertive decisions. Feminine cultures, as in many Scandinavian countries, value decisions that reflect concern for others.

Research examining the effects of cultural diversity on decision making has found that when individuals in a group are racially dissimilar, they engage in more open information sharing, encourage dissenting perspectives, and arrive at better decisions than racially similar groups.[111] Other kinds of diversity such as functional background have been studied as well. Top management teams that have members who come from a variety of functional backgrounds (for example, marketing, accounting, information systems) engage in greater debate in decision making than top management teams in which the members come from similar backgrounds. This diversity results in better financial performance for the firm.[112] Research also indicates that strategic decision making in firms can vary widely by culture. For example, one such source of variation stems from the differential emphasis placed on environmental scanning in different cultures. Furthermore, strategic decision making might appear rational but is also informed by firm level and national characteristics.[113]

7-6 PARTICIPATION IN DECISION MAKING

Effective management of people can improve an organization's economic performance. Firms that capitalize on this fact share several common practices. Chief among them is participation of employees in decision making.[114] Many do this through highly empowered self-managed teams. Even in situations where formal teams are not feasible, decision authority can be handed down to frontline employees who have the knowledge and skills to make a difference. At many hotels, for example, guest services personnel are empowered to do whatever is necessary to make guests happy—without consulting their superiors.

The Effects of Participation

Participative decision making occurs when individuals who are affected by decisions influence the making of those decisions. Participation buffers employees from the negative experiences of organizational politics.[115] Participation in decisions such as how technology is developed has been found to affect employees' attitudes toward the technology and how they use it.[116] In addition, participative management has been found to increase employee creativity, job satisfaction, and productivity.[117]

As the economy becomes increasingly based on knowledge work and as new technologies make it easier for decentralized decision makers to connect, participative decision making will undoubtedly increase.[118] Needing to adopt a single messaging system to meet the requirements of more than 20,000 users, one municipal organization faced a huge challenge in getting all the users to provide input into the decision. Technology helped craft a system that balanced the needs of all the groups involved, and IT planners developed a 28-page spreadsheet to pull together the needs and desires of all 60 departments into a focused decision matrix. Within two years, 90 percent of the users had agreed on and moved to a single system, reducing costs and complexity.[119]

Foundations for Participation and Empowerment

Organizational and individual foundations underlie empowerment that enhances task motivation and performance. The organizational

participative decision making Decision making in which individuals who are affected by decisions influence the making of those decisions.

foundations for empowerment include a participative, supportive organizational culture and a team-oriented work design. A supportive work environment is essential because of the uncertainty that empowerment can cause within the organization. Empowerment requires that lower-level organizational members be able to make decisions and take action on those decisions. As operational employees become empowered to make decisions, real fear, anxiety, or even terror can be created among middle managers in the organization.[120] Senior leadership must create an organizational culture that is supportive and reassuring for these middle managers as the power dynamics of the system change.

A second organizational foundation for empowerment concerns the design of work. The old factory system relied on work specialization and narrow tasks with the intent of achieving routinized efficiency.[121] This approach to the design of work had some economic advantages, but it also had some distressing disadvantages leading to monotony and fatigue. This approach to the design of work is inconsistent with participation because the individual feels absolved of much responsibility for a whole piece of work. Team-oriented work designs are a key organizational foundation because they lead to broader tasks and a greater sense of responsibility. For example, Volvo builds cars using a team-oriented work design in which each person does many different tasks and each person has direct responsibility for the finished product.[122] These work designs create a context for effective participation as long as the empowered individuals meet necessary individual prerequisites.

The three individual prerequisites for participation and empowerment are (1) the capability to become psychologically involved in participative activities, (2) the motivation to act autonomously, and (3) the capacity to see the relevance of participation for personal well-being.[123] First, people must be psychologically equipped to become involved in participative activities if they are to be empowered and become effective team members. Not all people are so predisposed. For example, Germany has an authoritarian tradition that runs counter to participation and empowerment at the individual and group levels. General Motors encountered significant difficulties implementing quality circles in its German plants because workers expected to be directed by supervisors, not to engage in participative problem solving. The German initiatives to establish supervisory/worker boards in corporations are intended to change this authoritarian tradition.

A second individual prerequisite is the motivation to act autonomously. People with dependent personalities are predisposed to be told what to do and to rely on external motivation rather than internal, intrinsic motivation.[124] These dependent people are not effective contributors to decision making.

Courtesy of Volvo Car Corporation.

Volvo Cars designed a car by women for women.

Finally, if participative decision making is to work, people must be able to see how it provides a personal benefit to them. The personal payoff for the individual need not be short term. It may be a long-term benefit that results in people receiving greater rewards through enhanced organizational profitability.

What Level of Participation?

Participative decision making is complex, and managers must understand that employees can be involved in some, or all, of the stages of the decision-making process. For example, employees could be variously involved in identifying problems, generating alternatives, selecting solutions, planning implementations, or evaluating results. Research shows that greater involvement in all five of these stages has a cumulative effect. Employees who are involved in all five processes have higher satisfaction and performance levels. And, all decision processes are not created equal. If employees can't be provided with full participation in all stages, the highest payoffs seem to come with involvement in generating alternatives, planning implementations, and evaluating results.[125] Styles of participation in decision making may need to change as the company grows or as its culture changes.

STUDY TOOLS 7

IN THE BOOK YOU CAN ...

- ☐ Rip out the **Chapter Review card** at the end of the book to review Key Concepts and Key Terms.
- ☐ Take a "What about You?" Quiz related to material in the chapter.
- ☐ Read additional cases in the Mini Case and Shopify Running Case sections.

ONLINE YOU CAN ... NELSON.COM/STUDENT

- ☐ Take a "What about You?" Quiz related to material in the chapter.
- ☐ Test your understanding with a quick Multiple-Choice Pre-Test quiz.
- ☐ Read the eBook, which includes discussion points for questions posed in the Cases.
- ☐ Watch Videos related to chapter content.
- ☐ Use the available Flashcards and Matching Quizzes to test your understanding of key terms and concepts.
- ☐ See how much you've learned by taking a Post-Test.

WHAT ABOUT YOU?

Who Owns the Fish?

This exercise is attributed to Albert Einstein!

There are five houses in a row and in five different colours. In each house lives a person from a different country. Each person drinks a certain drink, plays a certain game, and keeps a certain pet. No two people drink the same drink, play the same game, or keep the same pet.

The Brit on lives in a red house.

The Swede keeps dogs.

The Dane drinks tea.

The green house is on the left of the white house.

The green house owner drinks coffee.

The person who plays tennis rears birds.

The owner of the yellow house plays chess.

The man living in the house right in the centre drinks milk.

The Norwegian lives in the first house.

The man who plays poker lives next to the man who keeps cats.

The man who keeps horses lives next to the one who plays chess.

The man who plays billiards drinks beer.

The German plays golf.

The Norwegian lives next to the blue house.

The man who plays poker has a neighbour who drinks water.

Question

1. Who owns the fish?

MINI CASE

And the Grammy Goes To ...

Imagine that you are the president of the music industry's biggest, most prestigious, and only peer-recognized award, the Grammy. For several years, you've received criticism that the number of Grammy awards dilutes the awards' impact. How do you respond? If you're Grammy president and CEO Neil Portnow, the decision is rather straightforward—consolidate some award categories and eliminate others altogether. Portnow should have expected dissatisfaction from some artists about the decision, especially from those whose category would be eliminated. But what Portnow could not have anticipated was that the decision to restructure the awards would lead to threats of legal action, allegations of racism, and calls to boycott the telecast. The Grammy awards have undergone many changes over the years, from the expansion of award categories to changes in the nomination and voting process, most of the changes that are in response to a changing music industry. What began with 28 award categories in 1959 had increased 289 percent to 109 in 2010, leading to criticism that the increased number of categories not only confused consumers but also reduced the perceived value of winning a Grammy. The 2011 review of the Grammy award structure was its first-ever comprehensive evaluation.

Some of the most highly publicized changes included the elimination of gender-specific subcategories in the R&B, pop and country fields; the elimination of the Zydeco and Cajun category and its consolidation into a "regional roots music" category with Hawaiian and Native American music; and the reduction of awards in the R&B category, from eight to four. Critics of the changes insisted that the Academy's restructuring of the awards unfairly targeted ethnic music. Latin jazz musician Bobby Sanabria called the decision "the most blatant example of racism in the history of any arts organization and a slap in the face to cultural and musical diversity." Sanabria attributes his own mainstream success to having been nominated for a Grammy in 2001 and again in 2008. He and other Latin jazz artists claimed that the Academy's decision to restructure the awards would negatively affect their ability to make a living.

Apply Your Understanding

1. Is Sanabria justified in his claim that consolidating "ethnic" category awards will reduce the Grammy's musical and cultural diversity? Explain.
2. To what extent should the Academy of Recording Arts and Sciences have considered representation of the different genres in its restructuring decision?
3. Was the decision to consolidate actually straightforward? Why/why not?

SOURCES: J.C. McKinley, Jr., "Academy Defends Cutting Grammy categories," *The New York Times* (July 17, 2011); N.M. Moody, "Coalition Announces Boycott of CBS over Grammys," *Associated Press* (June 30, 2011); B. Sisario, "Grammys Cutting More than 30 categories," *The New York Times* (April 6, 2011).

SHOPIFY RUNNING CASE

BRICKS, MORTAR, AND GREEN

Shopify is about to become the online platform for the sale of legal marijuana in British Columbia. BC plans to house its supply of marijuana in a warehouse in Richmond, BC, and to use Shopify as its distribution channel. Shopify was selected because "because of its proven record of on-time service, user-friendly design and approach to anticipating consumer needs." While Shopify approached all the provinces and territories to provide distribution services, only its BC and Ontario bids were successful. In the case of BC, Shopify will create two separate websites to fulfill online orders: one for consumers, and another that will allow private retail stores to verify the age of purchasers on the BC Cannabis Stores' retail website. Couriers will be required to also verify the age of buyers at delivery.

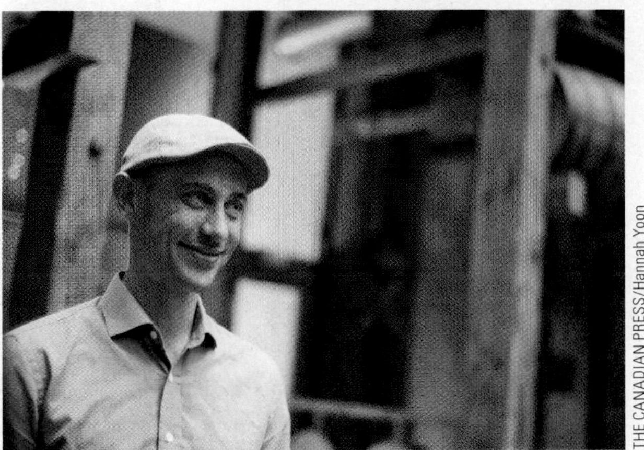

THE CANADIAN PRESS/Hannah Yoon

In July 2018 Shopify announced that it will have its first bricks-and-mortar location. Shopify will create a permanent space for its merchants in Los Angeles. Its space is in ROW DTLA, a creative and commercial area located in a historic area and a major hub for the distribution of produce across the region. Shopify chose the location as many of its merchants work in the Los Angeles region. Shopify plans to provide various services such as in-person support, events, and workshops. Shopify hopes that its downtown LA location will help its merchants grow and will attract more diverse merchants in the future.

SOURCES: M. Hager, "B.C. Announces Richmond Warehouse, Shopify Platform for Online Pot Sales," *The Globe and Mail*, June 22, 2018, accessed from https://www.theglobeandmail.com/canada/british-columbia/article-bc-announces-richmond-warehouse-shopify-platform-for-online-pot, September 28, 2018; "ROWDTLA," accessed from https://rowdtla.com/history, July 28, 2018; Shopify Team, "Shopify's First Permanent Home for Helping Merchants in Person Is Coming to LA," July 25, 2018, accessed from https://www.shopify.com/press/news/shopifys-first-permanent-home-for-helping-merchants-in-person-is-coming-to-la, September 28, 2018.

Apply Your Understanding

1. Should Shopify support the marijuana industry? Why or why not?
2. What are the advantages and disadvantages of Shopify having a physical space for its merchants?
3. Should Shopify expand its physical presence? If so, what sort of decision process should it use to consider the possibility?

Vasin Lee/Shutterstock.com

8 Communication

LEARNING OUTCOMES

After reading this chapter, you should be able to do the following:

8-1 Describe the interpersonal communication process.

8-2 Explain common communication barriers and gateways through them.

8-3 Distinguish between defensive and nondefensive communication.

8-4 Explain the impact of nonverbal communication.

8-5 Identify how social media and communication technologies affect communication.

8-6 Describe four communication skills of effective managers.

See the end of this chapter for a list of available Study Tools, a "What about You?" Quiz, Mini Case, and the Shopify Running Case.

Communication is the most important component of interacting with others. It is how we begin, maintain, and end relationships. What we say and how we say it are important, but ultimately, what is *understood* is all that matters. Communication is a process that is ongoing and dynamic, and enlarging your repertoire of communication skills so you can employ strategies that are most effective under various circumstances can help ensure that what is meant is understood, which in turn helps us improve our effectiveness both personally and professionally.

Communication—the human connection—is the key to personal and career success

—Paul J. Meyer

8-1 INTERPERSONAL COMMUNICATION

Communication evokes a shared or common meaning in another person. It is how we bridge the gap from individual processes to interpersonal processes. In order for communication to be considered effective, information must be not only transferred, but also understood. The value and importance of effective communication is difficult to overestimate, because in personal and professional settings, "if you can't communicate then it doesn't matter what you know."[1] **Interpersonal communication** occurs between two or more people in an organization, and is important in building and sustaining human relationships at work.

An Interpersonal Communication Model

The interpersonal communication model in Figure 8.1 illustrates the key elements of interpersonal communication. The **communicator** is the person originating the message; this person has a message to share. The communicator **encodes** their information and ideas into a message by describing them using words, pictures, symbols, gestures, and/or tone of voice. The **message** contains two components that the communicator intends to evoke in the receiver: The thought or *conceptual component* of the message is its content, and is contained in the words, ideas, symbols, and concepts chosen to relay the message. The feeling or *emotional component* of the message is its affect, and is contained in the demeanour, intensity, force, and the gestures of the communicator. The emotional component of the message adds the overtones of joy, anger, fear, or pain to the conceptual component. This addition often enriches and helps to clarify the message. The communicator then **transmits** their encoded message using any number of transmission methods based on the content, urgency, and intended recipient of their message.

The **receiver** is the person the message is being sent to; this is who the communicator wants to evoke a shared or common meaning with. The receiver **decodes** the message, hopefully into something very similar to what the communicator originally intended, but this is not always the case. **Feedback** may or may not occur during specific instances of communication. Feedback occurs when the receiver provides the communicator with a response to the message. That response can be a vague acknowledgement of receipt of the original communication, or it may be a more specific response, such as agreement, or a request for more information. When feedback occurs, communication is said to be two-way.

Perceptual screens are the subconscious filters through which we interpret our world. Perceptual screens are built upon individual attributes and traits, and are affected by age, gender, values, beliefs, past experiences, cultural influences, and individual needs. The communicator's and the receiver's respective perceptual screens will influence the quality, accuracy, and clarity of all messages sent between them. The more closely the receiver's and the communicator's perceptual screens align (in other words, the more attributes and traits the sender and receiver have in common), typically the clearer and less distorted communication between them will be. If there are significant differences between the sender's and the receiver's perceptual screens, (for instance, age, gender, language, and culture) there will be more static, noise, and distortion in the message, and the meaning evoked through the communication may not be accurately interpreted, or commonly shared.

communication The evoking of a shared or common meaning in another person.

interpersonal communication Communication between two or more people in an organization.

communicator The person originating a message.

encode To convert information into a form that may be transmitted.

message The thoughts and feelings that the communicator is attempting to elicit in the receiver.

transmit The way that an encoded message is conveyed to another.

receiver The person receiving a message.

decode To interpret a message that has been received.

feedback Information fed back that completes two-way communication.

FIGURE 8.1 A BASIC INTERPERSONAL COMMUNICATION MODEL

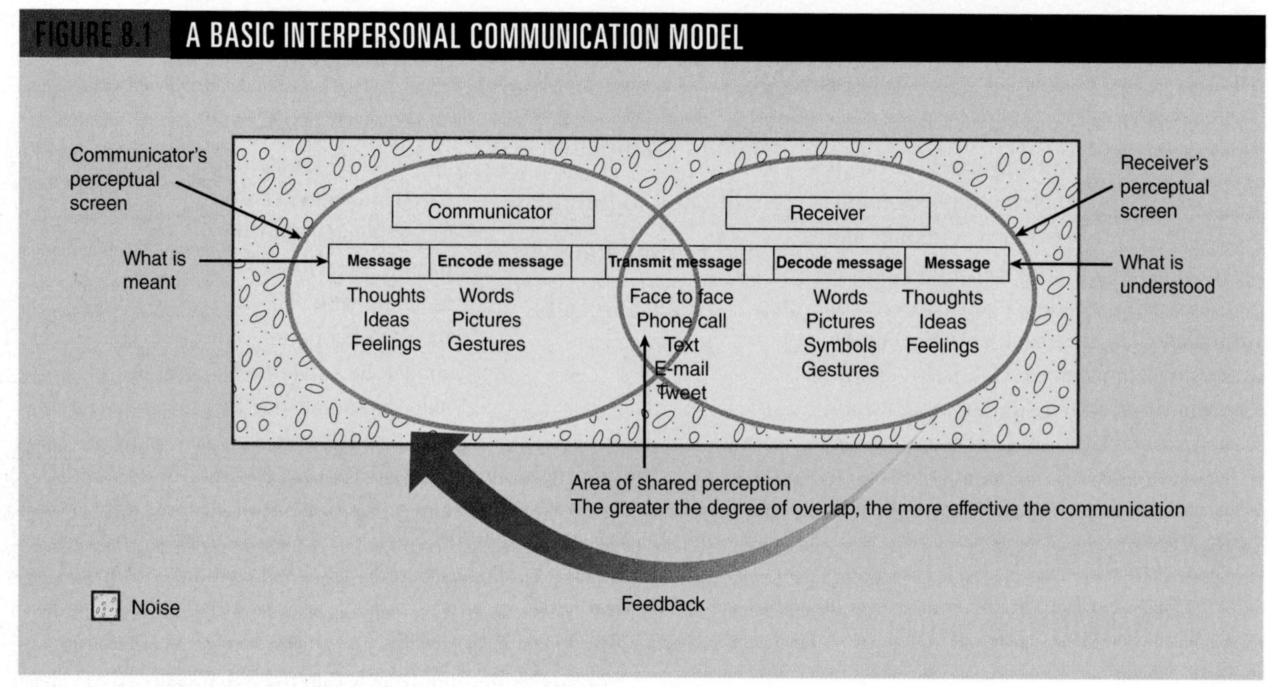

The **language** of the message describes more than just words and their pronunciation. Language also encompasses industry-specific jargon or acronyms, culturally specific idiom, regional colloquialisms, and all the methods of combining how words are used and understood by a community of people.

Data are the uninterpreted, unanalyzed elements of a message—the characters or symbols that are transmitted using a *medium* such as a telephone or face-to-face discussion. **Information** is data with meaning to a person who has interpreted or analyzed them. To put it more simply, information is what a person takes out of the data that has been transmitted to him or her. Since messages are conveyed through a medium, they differ in **richness** according to the ability of the medium to transmit meaning to the receiver.[2] Table 8.1 compares different media in terms of information richness. Some mediums, such as face-to-face communication, are considered very rich because they can convey a huge amount of information to the receiver: In addition to the words used by the communicator, data is transmitted in the form of body language, tone of voice, volume, etc., which enhances the meaning of the message. Other mediums, such as texts, are much more limited in the data which they can transmit, and they are said to have low levels of richness. This lack of richness severely limits the information that can be decoded because words (and emojis) are limited in their ability to convey complex and layered meaning.

Most people believe that they are good communicators yet breakdowns in communication occur

language The words, their pronunciation, and the methods of combining them used and understood by a group of people.

data Uninterpreted and unanalyzed facts.

information Data that have been interpreted, analyzed, and have meaning to a user.

richness The ability of a medium or channel to elicit or evoke meaning in the receiver.

TABLE 8.1 COMMUNICATION MEDIA: INFORMATION RICHNESS

Medium	Information Richness
Face-to-face discussion	Highest
Telephone	High
E-mail	Moderate
Blog	Moderate
Individualized letter	Moderate
Personalized note or memo	Moderate
Texting or tweeting	Moderate to low
Formal written report	Low
Flyer or bulletin	Low
Formal numeric report	Lowest

SOURCE: Adapted from E. A. Gerloff, "Information Richness: A New Approach to Managerial Behavior and Organizational Design," by R. L. Daft and R. H. Lengel in *Research in Organizational Behavior* 6 (1984): 191–233. Reprinted by permission of JAI Press Inc.

This Is Your Brain on Human Contact

According to Harvard Medical School assistant clinical professor and NeuroBusiness Group CEO Dr. Srini Pillay, our brains respond differently when we interact with individuals face-to-face than virtually. The human brain contains "mirror neurons" that help the brain mirror other's behavior, resulting in feelings of familiarity that the brain doesn't register when communicating by telephone or e-mail. During face-to-face interactions, the brain tucks away information about who we are and what we feel so that it is easily accessible during future interactions.

SOURCE: S. Dembling, "This is Your Brain on Human Contact," *Entrepreneur* 42 (2014): 28.

very frequently in organizational and social settings. Breakdowns even occur between people who have a long history of communicating together. It has been observed that "most people do not listen with the intent to understand; they listen with the intent to reply. They're either speaking or preparing to speak. They're filtering everything through their own paradigms."[3] Communication breakdowns and misunderstandings can be alleviated by using reflective listening techniques, which help ensure that communication feedback is incorporated into all instances of communication.

Reflective Listening

Effective message decoding is essential to effective communication. Message decoding entails more than just receiving the message: it requires receiving the message and understanding what was *meant* to be conveyed. The only way to confirm understanding of what was meant versus what was understood is to use feedback to confirm our understanding with the message sender. This process of confirming understanding is known as **reflective listening**. It is the skill of carefully listening to another person and repeating back to the speaker the heard message to correct any inaccuracies or misunderstandings. Though we use the word *listening* here, reflective listening is not just for verbal communication. Reflecting back all types of messages helps the receiver confirm, clarify, and sharpen the communicator's intended meaning, and can help reduce perceptual distortions, and overcome interpersonal barriers that lead to communication failures. Especially useful in problem solving, reflective listening can be learned in a short time with positive effects on behaviours and emotions in organizational situations.[4]

ONE-WAY VERSUS TWO-WAY COMMUNICATION

Reflective listening encourages two-way communication. **Two-way communication** is an interactive form of communication in which there is an exchange of thoughts, feelings, or both and through which shared meaning often occurs. Problem solving and decision making are often examples of two-way communication. **One-way communication** occurs when a person sends a message to another person and no feedback, questions, or interaction follow. Giving instructions or giving directions are examples of one-way communication. One-way communication occurs whenever a person sends a one-directional message to a receiver with no reflective listening or feedback in the communication.

One-way communication is often less accurate than two-way communication and is typically only used to convey simple, factual information (think of advertisements and other public service announcements). When time and accuracy are both important to the successful completion of a task, such as in combat or emergency situations, extensive training enhances the understanding of one-way communication without the need for overdrawn two-way communication.[5] Firefighters and military combat personnel train extensively to minimize the need for full communication loops during emergencies. These highly trained professionals rely on fast, abbreviated communication and feedback as a shorthand for more complex information exchanges ("stat," "roger that," "10-4"). However, this communication works only within the range of situations for which the professionals are specifically trained because the meanings behind those short-forms have already been discussed in detail.

reflective listening A skill intended to help the receiver and communicator clearly and fully understand the message sent.

two-way communication A form of communication in which the communicator and receiver interact.

one-way communication Communication in which a person sends a message to another person and no feedback, questions, or interaction follows.

8-2 BARRIERS AND GATEWAYS TO COMMUNICATION

No matter how carefully a communicator encodes and transmits their message, or how diligently a receiver decodes the message using their reflective listening skills, there are certain elements in all social situations that impede the ease and the success of communication. **Barriers to communication** are factors that block or significantly distort successful communication. **Gateways to communication** are tools, habits, and techniques that can help to clarify messages and reduce communication static, providing clear pathways for shared meaning in order to better evoke a common understanding. Awareness and recognition of communication barriers are always the first steps in opening the gateways, and active listening, seeking and providing feedback, choosing appropriate language, and selecting communication mediums carefully are all easy ways to reduce temporary or simple barriers. About 20 percent of communication problems can be prevented or resolved simply by implementing communication policy guidelines.[6]

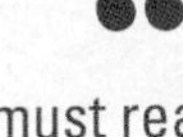

We must realize that we are all different in the way we perceive the world and use this understanding as a guide to our communication with others.

—Tony Robbins

Barriers to communication in the workplace may be obvious, temporary, and easily resolved. Obvious barriers include physical separation and status differences. Not so obvious are barriers to communication that involve what a receiver is willing or able to decode at any given time, and many factors influence how we perceive information. Finally—but no less important—are the barriers caused by different communication styles, cultural diversity, and language. These barriers may be deeply rooted and systemic and are more difficult to overcome.

Perceptual Filters

As mentioned at the beginning of the chapter, what is communicated to others, and what is understood from others, is greatly affected by our perceptual screens. Perceptual screens are created by fundamental characteristics, such as personality, experience, and culture, but also by variable characteristics such as motivation, and emotion. It has been repeatedly established that individuals prefer to communicate with others who share their beliefs, and are more likely to accept information from people with whom they share an opinion,[7] even when that information can be proven false. People are significantly affected by subconscious biases and stereotypes, (See Chapter 3 for a more complete discussion about attribution errors,) and these biases affect who we choose to communicate with, and what information we process.

Individuals also have a limited capacity for absorbing, sorting, and using information, and anything received beyond that capacity is known as **information overload**. Information overload is common when information is new, but it can also

barriers to communication Aspects of the communication content and context that can impair effective communication in a workplace.

gateways to communication Pathways through barriers to communication and antidotes to communication problems.

information overload When information provided exceeds our limited capacity for absorbing, sorting, and using it.

retrorocket/Shutterstock.com

Barriers to communication block and distort successful communication.

occur due to volume of information presented at one time. When information overload occurs, the surplus is ignored, forgotten, or confused.

Finally, emotion and mood play a significant role in our willingness and ability to communicate. In general, people are more willing to commit to feedback loops and active listening practices when they are in a positive mood, and more likely to be dismissive or make snap judgments when experiencing negative moods. Someone feeling stressed or anxious will interpret an emotionally ambiguous message differently than someone feeling confident. The stronger the emotion (positive or negative) the larger the impact on effective communication as objective exchange gives way to emotional overtures.

Masculine vs. Feminine Communication Differences

Communication barriers can be attributed, in part, to differences in conversational styles.[8] As mentioned above, when people with different perceptual screens converse, what the receiver decodes and understands may not be what the communicator intended. (Though discussions of gender are outside the purview of this text, we will broadly classify personalities and communication styles as either masculine or feminine.) Masculine and feminine personalities, for a variety of reasons, often have markedly different perceptual screens, which results in different communication preferences. For example, feminine personalities are typically considered more sensitive and empathetic. They are more likely to engage in and receive communication, and are also more likely to reciprocate communication. For feminine personalities, communication is often about the process and is used as a bonding mechanism to build and strengthen interpersonal relationships. Feminine personalities are typically better at reading body language and understanding nonverbal cues, and they are more likely to display empathy. They are also more likely to process ideas or "think" aloud. To masculine personalities, these traits can be interpreted as lacking substance, being overly emotional, and appearing weak. Masculine personalities, on the other hand, tend to use communication as an impersonal tool to achieve a specific objective. Masculine personalities tend to be more blunt and focused, and are more likely to be confrontational, which can come across as aggressive or insensitive.

Nonverbal signals are also interpreted differently, depending on communication style: nodding, to feminine personalities can be a signal of agreement, but may also be used to signal empathy, encouragement, and attention, whereas masculine communicators typically use nods to indicate agreement and nothing more. Feminine personalities typically prefer eye contact and make more facial and physical reactions when communicating, while their masculine counterparts remain more emotionally distant and stoic during a conversation. Masculine communicators typically use only three tones when communicating, while feminine communicators use, on average, five tones when speaking. This can cause masculine personalities to be seen as bored or uninterested to their more vocal feminine counterparts.[9]

An important gateway through the gender barrier to communication is developing an awareness of how other people communicate by recognizing differences in tone, gesture, and purpose of communication. These differences can enrich organizational communication and empower professional relationships.[10] A second gateway is to actively seek clarification of the person's meaning rather than freely interpreting meaning from your own frame of reference. There is a time and place for both masculine and feminine communication styles and the most effective communicators are masters at balancing power and empathy signals, so that they come across as both confident and caring. Understand your own "default" communication style, and learn how to adapt to different communication styles so that you can use masculine and feminine communication styles appropriately given the situation.

IN ACTION

Who Speaks More?

It has often been said that women speak more than men do—that they use significantly more words per day, and start significantly more conversations than their male counterparts, but this myth is not borne out in the research. A meta-analysis of more than 30 years of research on language and communication differences between men and women shows that men and women communicate in very similar ways—in fact, the degree of overlap between male and female speaking abilities is 99.75%! While men are found to interrupt more, and women are more likely to disclose personal information, use more accurate spelling, and smile more, even these differences are relatively minor. Differences *among* gender groups have been found to be significantly larger than differences *between* gender groups.

SOURCE: D. Cameron, *The Myth of Mars and Venus*. Oxford University Press. https://www.theguardian.com/world/2007/oct/01/gender.books, accessed April 1, 2018.

Cultural Diversity

Culture is a filter that affects all communication, both verbal and nonverbal. It shapes all aspects of communication, yet cultural values and patterns of behaviour can be very confusing barriers to communication because most cultural differences are invisible and silent. **Culture** is the accumulated pattern of values, beliefs, and behaviours shared by a group of people with a common history (See Chapter 13 for a discussion about culture.) However, there is no way of recognizing someone's culture without getting to know them; there is no way of knowing when you first meet someone how they feel about things such as the importance of gender roles, or religion, yet these are important components of one's perceptual screen, and have critical implications for communication. Even cultures that seem very similar on the surface and speak the same language use different meanings for different symbols. In England, to "bomb" an exam means to perform very well, while in Canada, "bombing a test" is understood to mean performing poorly.

FIGURE 8.2 ELEMENTS OF CULTURE

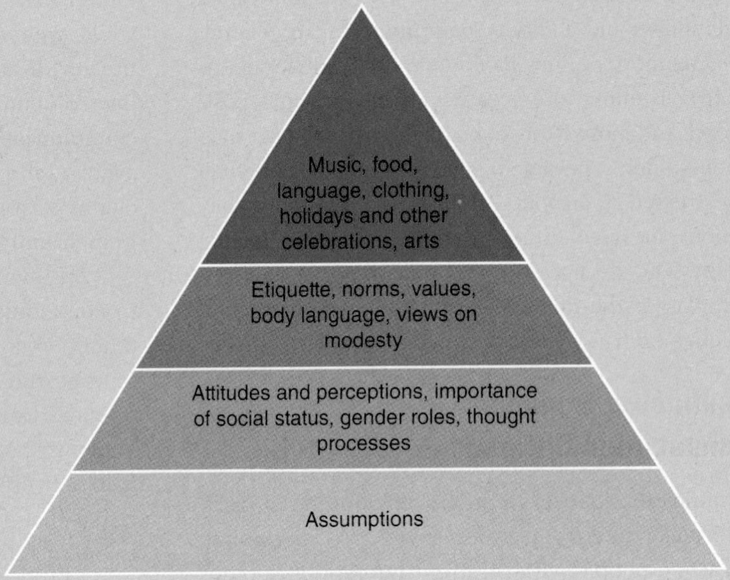

There are significant differences in work-related values as measured between countries and these differences often create invisible, systemic barriers to communication (see Figure 8.2). Canadians are different, for instance, than people from Germany, the United Kingdom, Japan, Saudi Arabia, and other nations,[11] and these cultural differences impact motivation, leadership, and teamwork in work organizations.[12] For example, German culture typically places greater value on authority and more importance in hierarchical differences than Canadian culture does. It is therefore more difficult for German workers to engage in direct, open communication with their supervisors than it is for Canadian workers.[13]

There are countless examples of clashes between communication styles across cultures, and these clashes are very often the basis of persistent stereotypes. For example, in Canada and the United States, speech is a very highly valued communication device. Good leaders are good orators, and we typically use direct and personal styles of verbal communication. We are judged and we judge others based on how well they communicate their thoughts and ideas using words. Criticisms and negative feedback, while phrased "nicely" are still vocalized. In other cultures, like those of Japan and Korea, a more indirect and impersonal style of communication is used, where silence is a tool to signify disagreement and respect without having to articulate the underlying message. This fundamental difference in cultural communication has led to the Asian stereotype that North Americans are aggressive and arrogant and, thus, insensitive and unapproachable. And conversely, the North American stereotype of the Korean and Japanese is that they are mild and subservient, unable to be appropriately strong and assertive.

Individuals typically use their own culture as the basis for judging *all* aspects of another culture.[14] This is known as **ethnocentricity**. Ethnocentrism is a universal phenomenon, and it while it serves to maintain and protect culture by fostering group commitment, it also clouds our perceptions of others and is a barrier to intercultural communication. Rather than seeing the person with whom we wish to communicate, we rely on stereotypes and see others as members of their cultural group rather than as individuals. (We see others as "Middle Eastern" or "a woman" or "a millennial" rather than as "Fatima" or "Sefa"). Truly, people of differing cultures communicate from separate worlds, and the degree of difference between cultures corresponds

culture The pattern of values, beliefs, and behaviours shared by a group.

ethnocentricity The habit of judging other cultures by the standards of our own.

to the distance separating these worlds. Our habit of judging others' communication by our own standards, combined with the filter of culture though which all communication passes implies that during intercultural communication, very frequently the message sent is not the message that is received.

The most important gateway through the communication barrier of cultural diversity is to increase cultural awareness and sensitivity. Remembering that intercultural communication is a process and practising reflective listening can enable us to learn new ways of communicating, which can grow our communication repertoire and help reduce our ethnocentricities and use of stereotypes. Organizations can also provide formal training for expatriate employees as part of their training for overseas or international assignments.

FIGURE 8.3 CANADIAN JARGON

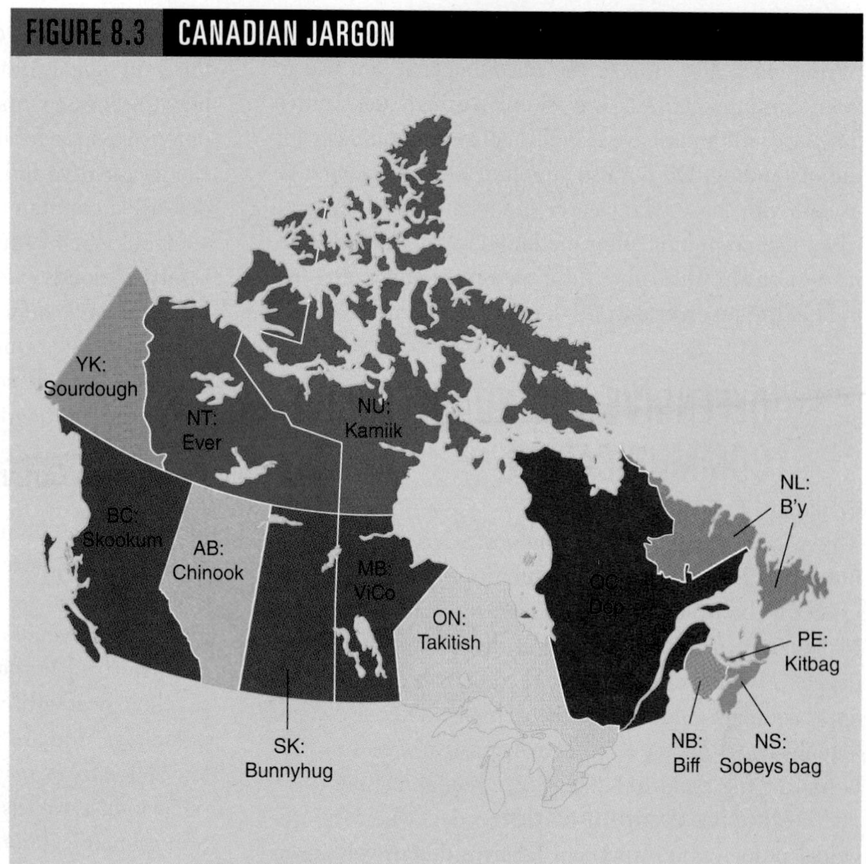

Language

As mentioned earlier in the chapter, the language of a message describes how words are used *and understood* by a community of people. When two people speak different languages, there are obvious barriers to communication, but even subtle differences within the same language can create noise and distort a message, resulting in communication confusion. The word *lift* means an elevator in Great Britain and a ride in Canada. Similarly, the words *jumper, trainers,* and *boot* have different meanings to the British than they do to Canadians. If you're having a verbal conversation, differences in accent and pronunciation can cue a perceptive listener that some words need to be decoded differently. However, if all communication is in writing, the lack of richness in that medium means that those necessary nonverbal signals will be missing from the message, and temporary misunderstandings may result. Another common miscommunication occurs when Canadians and Americans talk about the weather—"it's 30 degrees today!" means something very different to someone living in Calgary (who measures temperature in Celsius, where 30 degrees is a warm day), than it does to someone living in Miami (who uses the Fahrenheit scale, where 30 degrees is below freezing).

In a different vein, language barriers are created across disciplines and professional boundaries by technical terminology or industry **jargon**. Jargon is just a type of slang, where expressions have a specific meaning within a specific (usually organizational) context. Acronyms may be very useful to those on the inside of a profession or discipline as a means of shorthand communication, and technical terms can convey precise meaning between professionals; however, acronyms, technical terms and jargon often confuse people unfamiliar with their meaning and derail any attempt at clear communication. Consider a conversation between two people from the marketing and accounting departments within the same firm; their perceptual screens are quite different, and so their message encoding (through word choice) may also be very different. When someone from marketing says that he needs "buy-in" from their team, someone from accounting who is unfamiliar with that jargon might logically think they need their team members to pay some sort of monetary admission. In the same vein, "his performance is under par" is typically meant to imply that the performance is lacking; however, being below par is good in the game of golf and a golfer unfamiliar with business slang may interpret being called "under par" as a compliment. See Figure 8.3 for examples of regional jargon across Canada.

jargon Refers to words or expressions used by a group that have special or unique meanings.

Gateways through language-based barriers include paying close attention to the encoding that you use in your communications. Use simple, direct, declarative language until you have established a common basis for understanding. Do not use jargon or technical language except with those who clearly understand it. When possible, use communication mediums with elevated richness to ensure that more information is being conveyed to help the receiver decode the message accurately.

8-3 DEFENSIVE AND NONDEFENSIVE COMMUNICATION

The way in which we communicate has a significant impact on how our communications are received. If you expect to be ridiculed or criticized, you are more likely to present yourself and your ideas defensively than if you expect a warm, supportive, and friendly reception. But approaching a communication exchange defensively can actually cause people to react in a negative way, thus perpetuating the cycle and damaging communication.

Defensive communication occurs when an individual perceives a threat and behaves defensively in an effort to protect themselves. The threat doesn't have to be physical; criticism and rejection of a person or of their ideas can threaten their sense of self and cause them to behave defensively. Defensive communication is an attempt to avoid the process of communication,[15] and can include aggressive and hostile communications designed to win or dominate the exchange, as well as passive, withdrawing communication used to avoid or abbreviate the exchange as much as possible. Defensive communication in organizations leads to a wide range of problems, including injured feelings, communication breakdowns, alienation in working relationships, destructive and retaliatory behaviours, nonproductive efforts, and problem-solving failures. When such problems arise in organizations, it is common for employees to blame others for what is not working.[16] Such responses tend to lend heat, not light, to the communication process.

defensive communication Communication that can be aggressive, attacking, and angry, or passive and withdrawing.

nondefensive communication Communication that is assertive, direct, and powerful.

subordinate defensiveness Characterized by meek, submissive, and passive behaviour.

dominant defensiveness Characterized by aggressive and offensive behaviour.

passive-aggressive behaviour Defensive behaviour that begins as subordinate defensiveness, but ends as dominant defensiveness.

Nondefensive communication occurs when the individual is more focused on their message than on how the message may be (negatively) interpreted. Nondefensive does not mean meek or weak. Communication can be assertive and direct without being defensive. Nondefensive communication provides a basis for asserting yourself when attacked, without being defensive. An assertive, nondefensive style maintains or restores order, balance, and effectiveness in working relationships. While defensive communication in organizations creates barriers between people, nondefensive communication helps open up relationships.[17]

Defensive Communication at Work

Defensive communication often elicits defensive communication in response. The two basic patterns of defensive communication are subordinate defensiveness and dominant defensiveness. **Subordinate defensiveness** is characterized by passive or submissive behaviour. The psychological attitude of the subordinately defensive person is, "You are right, and I am wrong." People with low self-esteem may be prone to this form of defensive behaviour, as well as people at lower organizational levels. Subordinately defensive people do not adequately assert their thoughts and feelings, so their input is likely to be lost even if it is critical to organizational performance.[18] By contrast, **dominant defensiveness** is characterized by active, aggressive, domineering behaviour, which is offensive in nature. The psychological attitude of the dominantly defensive person is "I am right, and you are wrong." People who are egotistical or overcompensating for low self-esteem may exhibit this pattern of behaviour, as well as people who are taking advantage of higher-level positions within the organization. Dominant defensiveness, when left unchecked, can result in harassment. **Passive-aggressive behaviour** is behaviour that appears passive but, in fact, masks underlying aggression and hostility, and is a form of defensiveness that begins as subordinate defensiveness and may end up as dominant defensiveness.

Defensive Tactics

Defensive tactics describe how defensive communication is acted out. Unfortunately, defensive tactics are common in many organizations. Until defensiveness and defensive tactics are recognized and identified for what they are, it is difficult either to change them or to respond to them in nondefensive ways. In many cases, such tactics raise difficult ethical dilemmas for victims and supervisors. At what point does simple defensiveness become unethical behaviour?

Defensive tactics raise difficult ethical dilemmas for victims and supervisors.

Power plays are tactics used to manipulate by overtly using power to dominate and control or otherwise gain the upper hand in the relationship. Power plays can involve intentionally ignoring or misunderstanding others, undermining them, or even displaying overt aggression through bullying and insulting.

Labelling is often used to portray another person as abnormal or deficient in some regard. Psychological labels are often used out of context for this purpose, such as calling a person "paranoid," or "insane" or even "sick." A form of labelling can also be used to raise doubts about a person's abilities, values, orientation, or other aspects of his or her life.

Misleading is the selective presentation of information designed to leave a false or inaccurate impression. It refers to intentionally failing to provide or giving inaccurate or incomplete information in order to deceive someone or reframe the narrative. Defensive individuals may blame other people for their mistakes and wrongdoing. Scapegoating is a common method of shifting responsibility for an error onto the wrong person.

Finally, **hostile jokes** are a passive-aggressive defensive tactic and should not be confused with good humour, which is both therapeutic and nondefensive. Antagonistic and overtly mean sentiments can be delivered in a way that can be defended as "just joking"; however, the message contained within a hostile joke is intended to abuse, insult, and criticize the target. Jokes made at the expense of others are destructive to self-esteem and workplace communication.

Nondefensive Communication

Nondefensive communication is a constructive, healthy alternative to defensive communication in working relationships, and can help encourage feedback to ensure accurate communication.[19] A person who communicates nondefensively may be characterized as centred, assertive, controlled, informative, realistic, and honest. Nondefensive communication is powerful because it allows a communicator to exhibit self-control and self-possession without rejecting the receiver. Nondefensive communication should be self-affirming without being self-aggrandizing.

Converting defensive patterns of communication to nondefensive ones can be very difficult as our patterns of communication can become engrained in our perceptual screens. However, efforts to improve nondefensive communication skills are well worth pursuing as nondefensive communication enhances relationship building. Relationship-building behaviours and communication help reduce adverse responses, such as blame and anger following negative events.[20] The subordinately defensive person can learn to be more assertive by reporting what is intended and inviting confirmation, rather than asking for permission to do something. Another way is to stop using self-deprecating words, and convert messages into self-assertive, declarative statements. Conversely, the person prone to being dominantly defensive needs to be less aggressive, and needs to become more sensitive to feedback from others about their behaviour.

8-4 NONVERBAL COMMUNICATION

Most of the meaning in a verbal message (an estimated 65 to 90 percent) is conveyed through nonverbal communication.[21] **Nonverbal communication** includes all the elements of communication that do not use words or involve language. This can include (but is not limited to) gestures, facial expressions, eye contact, tone or volume of voice, touch, posture, clothing and other body adornments, body positioning, and the use of space.[22] The interpretation of nonverbal communication is specific to the context of the interaction, and relies on the communicator, the receiver, and the environment. Nonverbal communication is culturally bound and is influenced by both psychological and physiological processes.[23]

power play Manipulating others through direct use of power.

labelling Using labels out of context to affect how another is perceived.

misleading Deliberately providing inaccurate information in order to manipulate.

hostile jokes Passive-aggressive tactic used to mask aggression.

nonverbal communication All elements of communication that do not involve words.

#HOT TREND Disfluencies

Disfluencies in speech refer to all the natural breaks and pauses we take when we're talking. "Um" or "uh" are organic features of speech that occur as the speaker links thoughts together before speaking them. Disfluencies have been found to provide useful nonverbal indications to the listener to focus on what's coming: Because the speaker has specifically stopped to gather their thoughts, what follows disfluency is typically contextually significant. People have been found to remember the content of what they hear better when an average number disfluencies are included in a passage (approximately 2 disfluencies out of every 100 words spoken). Designers of synthesized voice systems have even begun experimenting with adding disfluencies into artificial speech.

SOURCE: J. Sedivy, "Your Speech Is Packed with Misunderstood, Unconscious Messages," *Nautilus* (Mar 20, 2018), https://nautil.us/blog/-your-speech-is-packed-with-misunderstood-unconscious-messages, accessed March 31, 2018.

When nonverbal signals align with verbal ones, they can help relay and reinforce a message by enhancing the message's tone and emphasis. However, nonverbal cues can detract from a message, or be used to convey the exact opposite meaning of just the words used. Tone of voice alone is usually enough to convey sarcasm in a conversation. Consider the words "oh really." When "oh really" is used along with raised eyebrows, direct eye contact, a partial smile, a raised inflection, and open arms it means that the person is interested in your story and wants to hear more. Compare this with "oh really" when paired with only one raised eyebrow, rolled eyes, a downward vocal inflection, and crossed arms, which is more likely to convey that the person does not believe you or is uninterested in your story. When there is a mismatch between the verbal and the nonverbal message, receivers believe the nonverbal cues.[24]

> "What you do speaks so loud I cannot hear what you say.
>
> —Ralph Waldo Emerson"

The three most important categories of nonverbal communication are kinesics, paralanguage, and proxemics.

kinesics The study of gestures, facial expressions, head movement, eye contact, and posture.

Kinesics

Kinesics is the study of gestures, facial expressions, head movements, eye contact, and posture.[25] Kinesics is culturally bound and interpreting kinesic signals requires consideration of the cultural conditions.

FabrikaSimf/Shutterstock.com

Nonverbal communication does not involve words.

Gestures can be used in three distinct ways[26]: they can be unconscious signals of our internal state conveying anxiety or nervousness, like clicking a pen or twirling hair when giving a presentation; They can have culturally agreed-upon meanings, either good or bad, like the thumbs-up sign or a raised middle finger; or they can be used to illustrate and enhance the verbal message that they accompany; for instance, the thumb and forefinger held very close together indicated that something is very small.

Facial expression and *eye contact* are both rich sources of nonverbal information. The face and eyes are the main point of focus during conversations and can easily and sometimes subconsciously convey our innermost thoughts. Dynamic facial actions and expressions are key clues of truthfulness, especially in deception situations.[27] Facial expressions conveying happiness, sadness, fear, anger, and disgust, are almost universally identifiable across cultures,[28] and can help set the tone for a given discussion. Facial expressions are also used to assess a speaker's credibility, competence, and level of engagement.

As mentioned earlier, eye contact can enhance reflective listening and, along with smiling, is one good way of displaying positive emotion.[29] However, norms regarding eye contact must be understood within the cultural context, as too much eye contact can be considered intimidating or threatening. A direct gaze indicates honesty and directness in North America, but this may not be true in other cultures. For example, television journalist Barbara Walters was uncomfortable interviewing Muammar al-Qaddafi in Libya because he did not look directly at her. However, in Libya, it is an offence for a man to look directly at a woman.[30] In Asian cultures it is considered respectful to bow the head in deference to a superior rather than make eye contact.

Head movements and *posture* are also used to convey a wide variety of nonverbal information. Consider the headshake used to convey the work "no" or the head tilt used by someone listening carefully to instructions, both of which convey different meanings and levels of attention without words.

Haptics is communication through touch. Touch can be welcoming, comforting, persuasive, or threatening depending on how it is received. A firm handshake or a pat on the shoulder conveys very different information than holding hands, or patting someone on the head.

FIGURE 8.4 ZONES OF TERRITORIAL SPACE IN NORTH AMERICAN CULTURE

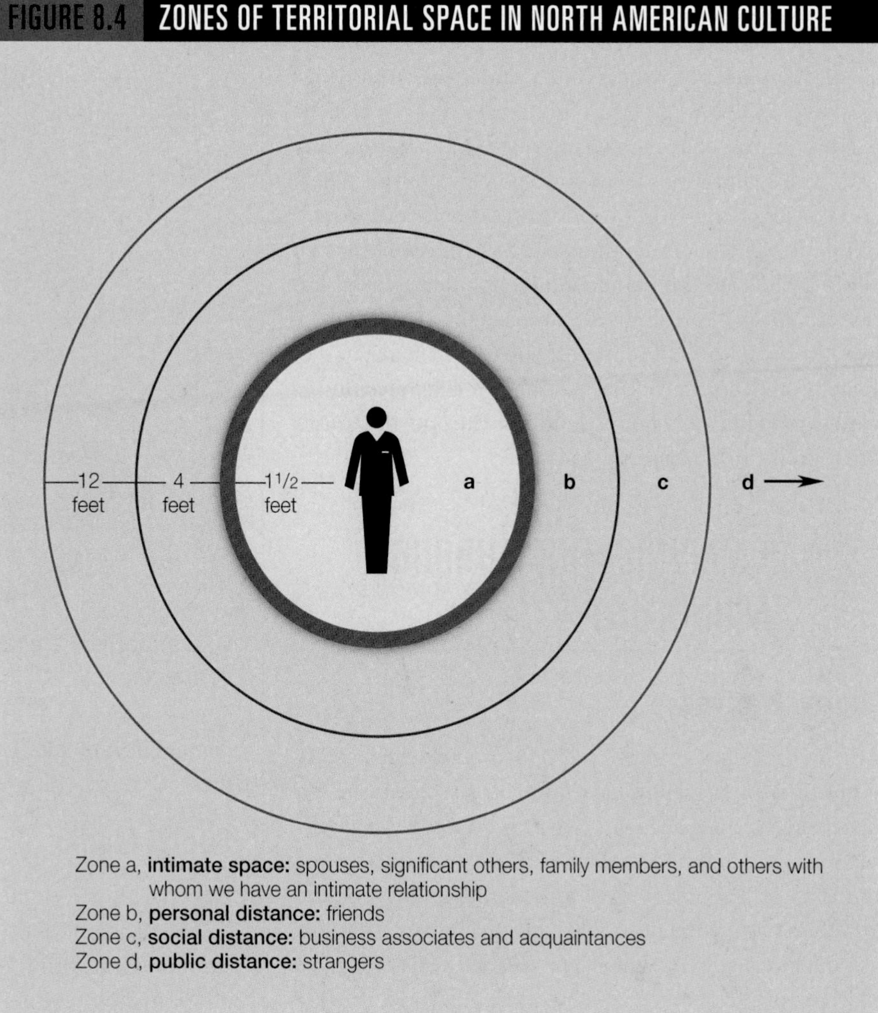

Zone a, **intimate space:** spouses, significant others, family members, and others with whom we have an intimate relationship
Zone b, **personal distance:** friends
Zone c, **social distance:** business associates and acquaintances
Zone d, **public distance:** strangers

Paralanguage

Paralanguage consists of variations in speech, such as pitch, volume, tempo, tone, duration, laughing, and crying.[31] Paralanguage helps communicate the intensity of a message and regulate conversational flow. Even babies recognize that sentences that end with a higher pitch are generally recognized as a question, while falling emphasis is often used to frame a farewell. We often make assumptions about the sender of a message by deciphering paralanguage cues: someone who speaks slightly faster than average may be seen as credible and intelligent, so long as they speak clearly and articulate well, while someone who speaks much too quickly is difficult to understand. Conversely, someone who speaks slightly slower than average may be seen as charming, while someone who speaks much too slowly is seen as doddering and boring. A high-pitched, breathy voice may be interpreted as dumb or vacuous, while rapid, loud speech may be taken as a sign of nervousness or anger.

Proxemics

The study of an individual's perception and use of space, including territorial space, is called **proxemics**.[32] *Territorial space* refers to bands of space extending outward from the body. These bands constitute comfort zones, and like kinesics, proxemics is culturally conditional. Figure 8.4 presents four zones of territorial space based on North American culture. Our relationships shape our use of territorial space and we hold hands with, or put an arm around, significant others to pull them into our intimate space. Territorial space varies greatly around the world. Both the sizes of comfort zones and their acceptable modes of interaction are culturally defined, and people often become uncomfortable when operating in territorial spaces different from those in which they are familiar.

paralanguage nonverbal variations in speech, such as pitch, volume, tempo, and tone.

proxemics The study of an individual's use of space in communication.

North Americans typically prefer a larger territorial space than Middle Easterners, but a smaller territorial space than people from Nordic countries. Americans working in the Middle East tend to back away to achieve a comfortable conversation distance when interacting with Arabs, and Arabs sometimes perceive this distance, and consequently North Americans, as cold and aloof.[33] Similarly, Americans communicating with Swedes often come away from the interaction feeling that Swedes are distant and standoffish. Personal space tends to be larger in cultures with cool climates, such as Canada, Great Britain, and northern Europe, and smaller in cultures with warm climates, such as southern Europe, the Caribbean, India, or South America.[34]

rnl/Shutterstock.com

Digital natives are accustomed to being digitally connected.

8-5 COMMUNICATING THROUGH TECHNOLOGY

Digital Natives

Much of the chapter thus far has focused on verbal communication and face-to-face interactions; however, our increasing reliance on technology is undoubtedly changing the way we communicate. There is a great divide between the level of technology used in generations born before 1980 and those born after 2000 who are known commonly as "millennials." Millennials are **digital natives**, most having grown up in the digitally connected world, who are fluent in the use of smartphones, tablets, the Internet, and everything that being digitally connected represents. Research has shown that digital technology has changed the way that millennials think, process and access information, and view institutions and relationships.[35] Younger people can have vastly different rituals, routines, and expectations with regard to communication, which can create situations where people feel alienated, disrespected, or just plain left out of the loop if they fail to adopt these same communication processes. Digital natives have different values, beliefs and behaviours than previous generations. Recall that this is the very definition of cultural differences. Millennials are misunderstood by older generations so frequently because they literally have a different culture than non-digital natives, and ethnocentric approaches to communication often lead to misunderstandings between these different cultures.

> "People have become so accustomed to texting that they're actually startled when the phone rings."
>
> —Ellen DeGeneres

digital native Someone who has grown up in a digitally connected world

Social Media

Digital natives recognize that the Internet is a tool of mass communication, and have no compunctions using it to communicate with friends from around the world, many of whom they have never met, and will never meet. Social media describes any computer-mediated technology that creates and maintains virtual communities and networks, allowing members to create and share information with whomever they choose, whenever they choose, and download, discuss, and modify content that is posted by others. Social media allows people to be connected to real or online communities. Facebook has more than 2 billion registered users, YouTube more than 1.5 billion users, WhatsApp 1.2 billion, WeChat more than 900 million, and Instagram more than 700 million.[36] This constant connection to vast social networks has had a significant impact on what people choose to share about themselves.

One thing that must be made clear to all users of communication technology is that when information is shared on social medial, that information is no longer private. *All* aspects of digital communication are permanent, and *all* social media content is public. A message

FIGURE 8.5 INTERNET COMMUNITIES' POPULARITY ON GOOGLE TRENDS (2004–2018)

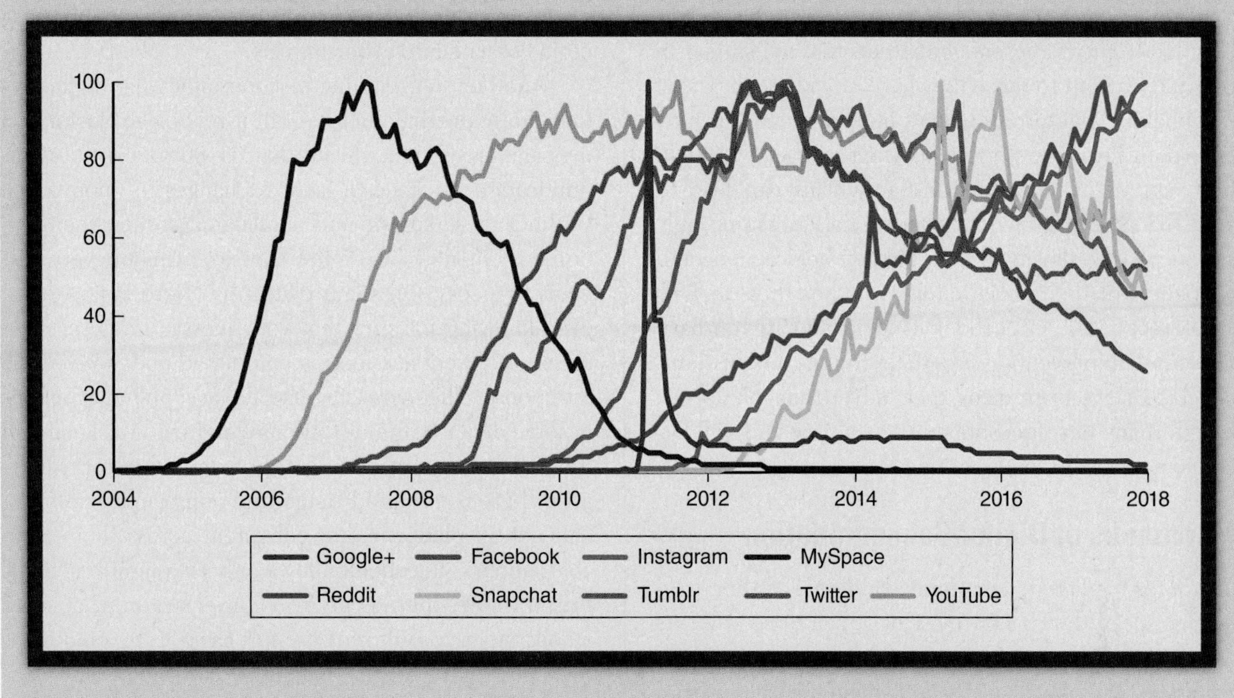

sent via computer or phone is processed through a server, where a record is kept. It is then sent to the receiver, who can also choose to keep the message and use it however they want. Social media data may be collected without the user's knowledge or consent by law enforcement or by companies engaged in data mining. Employers consistently check a potential employee's social media accounts (Facebook, LinkedIn) and make hiring determinations based on the information that users have posted.[37]

The way in which the Internet connects global and local communities through bottom-up and decentralized interactions represents a complete break with previous mass communication models from the past like print and television, which were top-down, centralized, linear, and mostly one-directional. This fundamental shift in how information is presented and communicated has had significant impacts on political discourse and cultural exchange. According to polling by Ipsos many millennials spend upward of 7 hours per day accessing the Internet.[38] This time is spent in a variety of ways: using social media, e-mailing, texting, playing games, shopping, and pursuing many other interests and hobbies. Younger individuals are more likely than previous generations to obtain their local and global news from digital sources, rather than local print or television media. It has been reported that 88 percent of millennials get news from Facebook occasionally, while 57 percent report using Facebook at least once per day to access news stories. Millennials also use other social media platforms to access news, including 83 percent who use YouTube, 50 percent who use Instagram, and significant proportions who use other social media platforms such as Pinterest (36 percent), Twitter (33 percent), Reddit (23 percent) and Tumblr (21 percent).[39] See Figure 8.5.

IN ACTION

Who's on What Social Media

New Pew Research Center survey results show that Facebook and YouTube are by far the most significant social media sites accessed by older Americans with 68% of U.S. adults (ages 25–64) using Facebook. Those between the ages of 18 and 24 have embraced a variety of platforms including YouTube, Snapchat, Twitter and Instagram, and 73% of respondents say they use more than one social media platforms to connect and communicate with their various social circles. Adults 65 and older represent only 37% of social media sites users.

SOURCE: Pew Research Center. *Social Media Use in 2018*. http://assets.pewresearch.org/wp-content/uploads/sites/14/2018/03/01105133/PI_2018.03.01_Social-Media_FINAL.pdf, accessed March 31, 2018.

This raises questions about who is "feeding" them their news as social media and news aggregators personalize content through machine-learning models, designed to provide users news items that are similar in tone and content to those they have already read. Using Facebook or Twitter also allows individuals to instantly share their favourite stories with their contacts, who can then "agree" or "disagree" instantly. This can lead to an **echo chamber** wherein individuals consume only content that conforms to their already-held beliefs, and the beliefs of their social circle, whether those beliefs are correct or not.[40] Facebook, Google, and Twitter have committed to preventing sites that promote and disseminate fake news from using their advertising platforms; though many have questioned their ability and willingness to actually do so.

Drawbacks of Digital Communication

Computer-mediated communication has other significant social drawbacks, most of which arise from its impersonal and often anonymous nature. Instant messaging, texting, e-mail, and tweets shield the sender from personal interaction. It is possible, and even easy, to make a negative or inappropriate comment yet avoid the social sanctions or reprisals that would follow in face-to-face communications. Comments on media platforms, news stories, and YouTube videos can be submitted anonymously (or by pseudonym), which eliminates personal accountability in communication, allowing people to say things online that they would never say in person.[41] Interpersonal skills such as tact and graciousness diminish online, and people tend to be more blunt when using electronic media. People who participate in discussions quietly and politely when face-to-face may become impolite, more intimate, and uninhibited when they communicate using a keyboard.[42] It has been argued that Twitter enables and encourages interactions that are simple, impulsive, and uncivil.[43]

Studies show that using computer-mediated technologies results in an increase in **trolling**, where a person posts deliberately provocative comments (often racist, sexist, homophobic, and/or ablest) with the aim of upsetting someone and **flaming**, which is making rude or obscene outbursts by computer, usually in anger, in response to something seen or read.[44] These patterns of aggressive and hostile communication are forms of dominant defensiveness, and because there is frequently no regulation or control over what is posted online, trolling and flaming often escalate into cyberbullying.

echo chamber When individuals consume digital content that conforms to their already-held opinions.

trolling Posting deliberately provocative material with the aim of eliciting a negative response.

flaming Making excessively rude or provocative comments through digital communication.

Another shortcoming of communicating digitally is that the nonverbal cues we often rely on to decipher a message are absent. Recall that 65–90 percent of communication in face-to-face exchanges is nonverbal. Without these kinesic and paralanguage cues, the emotional element of a digital message can be very difficult to assess. On some platforms, there is no way of even knowing for sure that your message was received unless the feedback loop is completed and you receive a response. The increasing use and acceptance of emojis in some digital communications can provide a signal into the emotional perspective of the communicator[45]; however, there is a limited range of emojis to choose from, and not all platforms are consistent across their available emojis—Facebook allows only six emoji reactions. Furthermore, there is no firm consensus on what some emojis mean to different users.[46] Even using emoticons that have agreed-upon meanings conveys a only one-dimensional "emotion"—there is no nuance or strength parameter to let someone know how strongly you "feel" that emoji, so oftentimes, multiple emojis are used together; however, this can increase confusion as to what is meant. While emojis can help signal emotional context, they are considered informal and casual, and are not acceptable in certain digital communications, such as e-mails and memos that are sent within a corporate environment. In e-mail and other written digital communications, the communicator must be careful to encode the message clearly.

What does a unicorn mean?

IN ACTION

Avoid E-mail Overload

The ever-present nature of e-mail has the potential to lead to e-mail overload. Here are five ways to prevent that from happening. First, don't try to solve problems using e-mail. Huddling the right people into a brief 7–15 minute meeting at the same time each week is more productive than spending 90 minutes e-mailing back and forth. Keep your e-mail subject lines specific to prevent others from wasting precious time searching inboxes for messages. Next, insist that e-mails are "Twitter-tight," not exceeding specified maximum number of words or characters. Fourth, avoid e-mails with multiple parts. Opt instead to one topic per e-mail. Finally, close e-mails quickly. Try putting a simple yes-or-no response in the subject line followed by "EOM" meaning "end of message." That way, recipients will not have to open the e-mail.

SOURCE: V. Harnish. "Five Ways to Liberate Your Team From Email Overload," *Fortune* 169 (2014): 52.

Benefits of Digital Communication

Digital communication is not all bad, however. It can change group interaction in positive ways by equalizing participation and input among group members. Barriers to communication that prevent some people from participating in face-to-face discussions can be eliminated, allowing people with social anxiety to share their thoughts from a safe environment, or individuals with language or cultural barriers to prepare statements in advance, providing them with the necessary time to carefully phrase their responses, which can reduce intercultural communication barriers. Studies of groups that make decisions via computer interaction have shown that the computer-mediated groups took longer to reach consensus than face-to-face groups. In addition, they were more uninhibited, less cooperative, and there was less influence from any one dominant person, which can result in less groupthink and hive mind behaviours.[47] Groups that communicate by computer seem to experience a breakdown of social norms and organizational barriers, and this is not always a bad thing.

Digital Communication at Work

Information communication technology (ICT) describes all of the ways that information can be sent digitally. ICT provides instant exchange of information in minutes or seconds across geographic boundaries and time zones. Not only is information available more quickly, but also the sheer volume of information that can be obtained on virtually any topic is staggering. An individual can easily become overwhelmed by information and must learn to be selective about the information accessed.

While ICT has increased productivity, normal considerations of time and distance have become irrelevant. E-mail, instant messaging, texting, and many other digital communication methods are **asynchronous**, meaning that the communicator and the receiver do not have to be coordinated in time, yet, many people fall into the habit of being constantly available, making it difficult to disengage from the pressures and demands of others. Many people find it difficult to disconnect themselves from their jobs because their phone is always with them, and they feel like they must be in constant contact, responding to e-mails and texts immediately, rather than waiting for business hours.

In addition, the use of new technologies encourages polyphasic, or multitasking activity (that is, doing more than one thing at a time). Managers can simultaneously make phone calls, send computer messages, and work on memos. Polyphasic activity has its advantages in terms of getting more done—but only up to a point. Paying attention to more than one task at a time splits a person's attention and reduces effectiveness at individual tasks. Constantly focusing on multiple tasks can become a habit, making it psychologically difficult for a person to let go of work.

Finally, technology may make people less patient with face-to-face communication. The speed advantage of the electronic media may translate into an expectation of greater speed in all forms of communication. However, individuals may miss the social interaction with others and may find their social needs unmet. Communicating by computer

information communication technology (ICT) Technologies, such as e-mail, voice mail, teleconferencing, and wireless access, which are used for interpersonal communication.

asynchronous Not coordinated in time.

means an absence of small talk; people tend to get to the point right away.

8-6 COMMUNICATION SKILLS FOR EFFECTIVE MANAGERS

Interpersonal communication is a critical foundation for effective performance in organizations for all employees, but especially for managers who are often required to coordinate and orchestrate work projects across organizational divisions, communicate goals and motivate performance among all employees, facilitate and resolve both personal and professional conflicts, and manage the day-to-day aspects of productivity and profitability. Language and power are intertwined in the communication that occurs between managers and their employees[48] and communication is the foundation of employee engagement and performance.[49] Studies have found that managers with the most effective work units consistently engaged in routine communication with their employees, whether it's face-to-face, via phone, or using digital technology, the important thing is that communication is reliable, frequent, and on-going. Studies have also found that managers with the highest promotion rates consistently engaged in networking activities with their superiors.[50]

An analysis of the research on communication between managers and their employees identified four communication skills that distinguish good managers from bad ones.[51] These skills include expressiveness, empathy and sensitivity, persuasiveness, and having an informative managing style. While it is possible to be an effective manager without possessing all these skills, and while some situations or organizations might favour some skills over others, interactive relationships are at the core of organization-based communication, and so possessing all four skills can make a manager more effective in communicating to employees.[52]

Expressiveness

Effective managers express their thoughts, ideas, and feelings openly and don't hesitate to voice their opinions (in a positive and constructive way) when needed. They tend toward extroversion, and they let the people they work with know where they stand on an issue, what they believe is required in a given situation, how they feel about what's going on, and why they feel the way they do. This communication allows employees to act with confidence, knowing how their opinions will be received, and understanding what work needs to be done for any given project and why things are happening the way they are. Supervisors who are not talkative or who tend toward introversion may at times leave their employees wondering what is expected of them, unsure about what their supervisors are thinking or feeling about certain issues, and at a loss as to what needs to be done.

Empathy and Sensitivity

In addition to being expressive speakers, good managers are willing, empathic listeners who use their reflective listening skills. Recall from earlier in the chapter that messages have two components; thoughts and feelings. Empathic listeners are able to recognize and decode the emotional components of the messages they receive. Good managers are approachable and willing to listen to suggestions and complaints, and are also better able to offer constructive criticisms.[53]

Better managers are also sensitive to the feelings, self-image, and psychological defences of their employees. Being able to recognize and understand the nuances of emotional reactions in others, and regulate one's own emotional response is known as emotional intelligence (EI) and is directly correlated to empathy and sensitivity and the ability to decode feelings from messages that are transmitted.

Persuasiveness

All supervisors and managers must exercise power and influence in organizations if they want to ensure performance and motivate employees to achieve organizational goals. Managers can be only as effective as their ability to induce compliance or influence their followers. Thus, effective managers are persuasive leaders who are able to align the goals of the employee with the goals of the organization, and then guide and motivate employees to consistently achieve those goals. The methods required to motivate employees can vary greatly depending on the employee, the project, and the circumstance, and good managers are able to use their communication skills to evoke a shared vision and achieve buy-in from employees.

Informative Managing Style

Finally, good managers keep their employees well informed, while appropriately and selectively disseminating information. The ability to coordinate the efforts of a group requires good communication and organization. Managers are responsible for the communication of goals, procedures, and expectations of the production process to the employees who ultimately carry out the work. Having an informative management style requires knowing what employees need to be successful, and ensuring that they have the right information at the right time. Failing to effectively filter information may lead to either information overload or a lack of sufficient information for task accomplishment. Good managers are transparent, and communicate openly and honestly about their expectations and feelings, which leads to increased trust and engagement from employees.[54]

STUDY TOOLS 8

IN THE BOOK YOU CAN ...

- ☐ Rip out the **Chapter Review card** at the end of the book to review Key Concepts and Key Terms.
- ☐ Take a "What about You?" Quiz related to material in the chapter.
- ☐ Read additional cases in the Mini Case and Shopify Running Case sections.

ONLINE YOU CAN ... (NELSON.COM/STUDENT)

- ☐ Take a "What about You?" Quiz related to material in the chapter.
- ☐ Test your understanding with a quick Multiple-Choice Pre-Test quiz.
- ☐ Read the eBook, which includes discussion points for questions posed in the Cases.
- ☐ Watch Videos related to chapter content.
- ☐ Use the available Flashcards and Matching Quizzes to test your understanding of key terms and concepts.
- ☐ See how much you've learned by taking a Post-Test.

WHAT ABOUT YOU?

Are You an Active Listener?

Reflective listening is a skill that you can practise and learn. Here are ten tips to help you become a better listener.

1. Stop talking. You cannot listen if your mouth is moving.
2. Put the speaker at ease. Break the ice to help the speaker relax. Smile!
3. Show the speaker you want to listen. Put away your work. Do not look at your watch. Maintain good eye contact.
4. Remove distractions. Close your door. Do not answer the telephone.
5. Empathize with the speaker. Put yourself in the speaker's shoes.
6. Be patient. Not everyone delivers messages at the same pace.
7. Hold your temper. Do not fly off the handle.
8. Go easy on criticism. Criticizing the speaker can stifle communication.
9. Ask questions. Paraphrase and clarify the speaker's message.
10. Stop talking. By this stage, you are probably very tempted to start talking, but do not. Be sure the speaker has finished.

Think of the last time you had a difficult communication with someone at work or school. Evaluate yourself in that situation against each of the ten items. Which one(s) do you need to improve on the most?

SOURCE: Republished with permission of IEEE, from "Steps to Better Listening" by C. Hamilton and B. H. Kleiner, *Engineering Management Review*, Vol. 15, No. 13, Copyright © 1987 IEEE; permission conveyed through Copyright Clearance Center, Inc.

MINI CASE

Smartphones: Promoting Communication Connectedness or Disconnectedness?

Many of us feel naked without our smartphones. They keep us continually connected to work, friends and family, teams, and social media groups. Most people keep their phones right in their pocket so that the phone is readily available to check the time, check the weather, check social media, check transit schedules, take photos and videos, and on, and on, and on. Smartphones entertain, fill gaps in our day, and demand our attention with an endless string of notifications. Smartphones offer a convenient alternative to face-to-face conversations, and at times they interrupt the conversations we do have.

Interestingly, with all that smartphones can do to facilitate communications, they have also undermined verbal communication and promoted incivility in the communications process. "Friends hardly call each other. People resist protocols that call for verbal communication. . . . People don't like using their phones to make calls or listen to voice mails." Texting seems to be the preferred mode, especially for younger people, when communicating with others.

People use their phones as a shield to protect them from having to have difficult, embarrassing, or emotional conversations: People use Facebook to notify friends and family about engagements, births, and even deaths and funerals. People end relationships via text, or use Twitter to vent complaints against companies and service providers.

College students in a recent survey indicated that they send and receive more than 100 messages every day, and check for messages more than 16 times an hour. They admit to texting while on a date, while in the shower, and even in the middle of religious services and funerals. Ninety percent of respondents admit to texting while eating, and 80 percent said they text while using the washroom, and neither of these locations was considered an inappropriate texting setting. Texting during a face-to-face conversation with someone, during a movie, and during class were all deemed inappropriate texting settings, but students admitted to frequently sending texts during these times. "People calling, texting and responding to e-mails at inappropriate times and places have become an issue in both a professional and business context." *The Wall Street Journal* reports.

SOURCES: J. De Avila, "The Unused Cellphone App: 'Calling,'" *The Wall Street Journal* (Eastern edition), February 24, 2010: D1; S. Hill. "Are Smartphones Killing the Art of Face-to-Face Conversation? We Ask the Experts," https://www.digitaltrends.com/mobile/are-smartphones-really-killing-the-art-of-conversation/; A. Mozes, "College Students Admit Texting in the Most Inappropriate Places" *CBS News*, https://www.cbsnews.com/news/college-students-admit-texting-in-the-most-inappropriate-places/; B. Pachter, "Mind Your Business Manners: Etiquette Suggestions for Success," *CPA Practice Management Forum* 6(5) (May 2010): 16 (3 pages).

Apply Your Understanding

1. Can the basic interpersonal communication model be used as an aid in understanding the impact of smartphone usage? If so, how?
2. How have smartphones transformed the way in which college and university students communicate?
3. Do you think that as people become more connected technologically they become less connected interpersonally? Why or why not?

RUNNING CASE SHOPIFY

SHOPIFY INTRODUCES TIMELINE

In early 2016, Shopify introduced a new communication feature, called Timeline, which is free for all Shopify merchants and available on all Shopify plans. Timeline is an internal communication tool designed to provide administrative users and staff members with an intuitive, social media-style framework to link the production aspects of their business quickly and efficiently to the sales aspects, whether those are people or products. Timeline allows authorized users to view detailed histories of products or customers, and write notes and comments for orders, customers, and transfers directly in Shopify. These notes and comments are then "attached" to the order or customer, and are available for all staff members to see and respond to, in real time, while the comments remain hidden from customers and other users. Timeline notes can include simple text notes, QR codes, and even files, and allow for emojis and profile photos.

Using tools that users will be familiar with from other social media platforms, such as the @mention feature, combined with push notifications and link and embed features, Shopify merchants and employees can use Timeline as a central communication method focused on single orders or customers, rather than having to coordinate through more traditional methods such as email or paper purchase orders. Even single-merchant businesses can use Timeline to post reminders to themselves about customers or order requirements, eliminating, or at least reducing, the need for external lists and Post-It notes.

Apply Your Understanding

1. What barriers to communication does Timeline resolve? What barriers to communication might Timeline cause?
2. What is the significance of adding emoji capabilities to Timeline?
3. What is the significance of ensuring that customers cannot see the information described in Timeline?

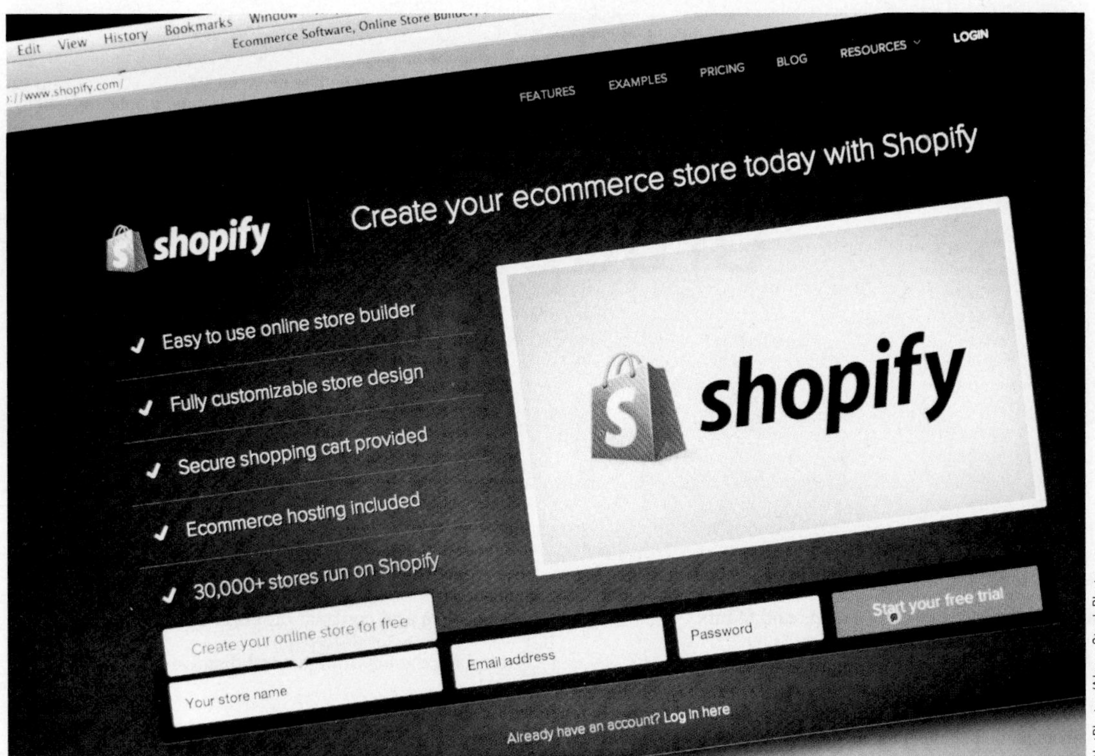

NetPhotos/Alamy Stock Photo

LWA/Photographer's Choice/Getty Images

9 Groups and Teams

LEARNING OUTCOMES

After reading this chapter, you should be able to do the following:

9-1 Define and distinguish between groups and teams.

9-2 Describe how groups form and develop.

9-3 Identify the factors that influence group behaviour and group effectiveness.

9-4 Compare and contrast different types of teams.

9-5 Explain the advantages and disadvantages of teams.

See the end of this chapter for a list of available Study Tools, a "What about You?" Quiz, Mini Case, and the Shopify Running Case.

Two heads are better than one, and more heads are better than two. Usually. There is no denying the importance of teams in modern organizations: When they work well, teams make better decisions and make fewer mistakes than individuals working alone. But just because people work together doesn't make them a team, not all teams work well together, and not all projects require a team effort.

9-1 GROUPS AND TEAMS

A **group** is formed whenever people interact with common interests and objectives. Groups can be just two people, or they can be whole societies; they can be formal with specified meetings and goals, or casual and informal with no set task or function apart from social interaction. The salient feature of a group is that people within the group call themselves "we," and distinguish themselves from those not in the group. Group members tend to maintain individual autonomy, individual accountability, and individual work products. A **team** is a type of group, with more in common than just interests and objectives. A team (1) is composed of people with complementary skills, (2) exists to accomplish a goal, (3) with members who work interdependently, (4) who hold each other mutually accountable for their performance.[1] Teams also normally operate as a unit within a larger organization that imposes resources, structure, leadership, climate, and culture onto the team, all of which influence the team's performance. Work teams typically emphasize shared leadership, mutual accountability, and collective work products.

Talent wins games, but teamwork and intelligence win championships.

—Michael Jordan

While all teams are groups, not all groups are teams. Where groups tend to have one leader, teams tend to share leadership: One person may be the team's task master who sets the agenda, initiates much of the work activity, and ensures that the team meets its deadlines. Another team member may take a leadership role in maintaining effective interpersonal relationships in the group. Shared leadership is very feasible in teams.

9-2 GROUP FORMATION AND DEVELOPMENT

Group Formation

Formal and informal groups develop in organizations for different reasons. Formal groups are sometimes called *official* or *assigned* groups, and informal groups may be called *unofficial* or *emergent* groups. Formal groups, such as project task forces, boards of directors, and temporary committees, gather to perform various tasks that are typically assigned by the organization. Formal groups typically have established goals, and metrics for measuring their success. Informal groups more commonly evolve in response to social needs that may not be met by formal groups. For example, organizational members' inclusion and affirmation needs might be satisfied through informal athletic or specialized interest groups.

Diversity

Diversity is an important consideration in the formation of groups, and a group's function often determines its level of diversity. Informal social groups typically have a more homogenous makeup because they are voluntarily formed around a specific activity or need, and attract members who are similar in that one regard. Homogeneous groups with little diversity typically have high levels of conformity, and have been shown to promote favourable interpersonal interaction, yield high levels of cohesiveness, increase member attachment and satisfaction, and reduce member uncertainty. In a workplace setting, formal teams are often created by the organization, and are brought together to analyze and solve complex organizational problems. Work teams typically benefit from greater levels of diversity. Ethnic, gender, and cultural diversity can enhance group performance by providing new perspectives, and a variety of skills and abilities from which the group can draw. Diverse work teams have been shown to make better decisions, develop and deliver better products and services, and create more engaged and committed employees.[2] However, while diversity typically delivers better organizational outcomes, it also creates more intergroup conflict and less group cohesion.

TEAM PARTICIPANT ROLES Individual diversity refers to differences in personality that are not necessarily explained by cultural, gender, or ethnic differences. Different personalities commonly found within a group include the

group Two or more people with common interests, objectives, and continuing interaction.

team A group of people with complementary skills who are committed to common goals, and hold themselves mutually accountable for their performance.

contributor, the collaborator, the communicator, and the challenger.[3] The *contributor* is data driven, supplies necessary information, and adheres to high performance standards. The *collaborator* sees the big picture and is able to keep a constant focus on the mission and urge other members to join efforts for mission accomplishment. The *communicator* listens well, facilitates the group's process, and humanizes the collective effort. The *challenger* is the devil's advocate who questions everything from the group's mission, purpose, and methods to its ethics. Members may exhibit one or more of these four basic styles over the team's life cycle. In addition, an effective group must have an integrator[4] who is able to link the group's output to the external environment. This is known as **boundary spanning**.

Achieving Diverse Work Teams Goes beyond Checking Boxes

Three additional forms of diversity should be considered when assembling productive and long-lasting work teams. Cognitive diversity will enhance creativity. Age/experience diversity will ensure the right balance between what's been done before and what is possible. Proximity diversity, the mix of virtual and traditional interactions, is an important predictor of success. The best managers use legally mandated criteria only as a starting point to achieving a much larger, more effective way of achieving true workplace diversity.

SOURCE: K. Rich, "Diversity's Central Paradox," *Forbes* 195 (2015): 34.

Models of Group Development

All groups, whether they are formal or informal, go through stages of development, some more successfully than others. Groups emerging successfully become a mature and productive unit. Mature groups are able to work through the complexities of interpersonal relationships and their associated conflicts, and establish group responsibilities and individual member roles, to achieve at high levels.

boundary spanning
Linking a group's output to the external environment.

TUCKMAN'S FIVE-STAGE MODEL The five-stage model of group development proposes that team behaviour progresses through five stages: forming, storming, norming, performing, and adjourning.[5] These stages are

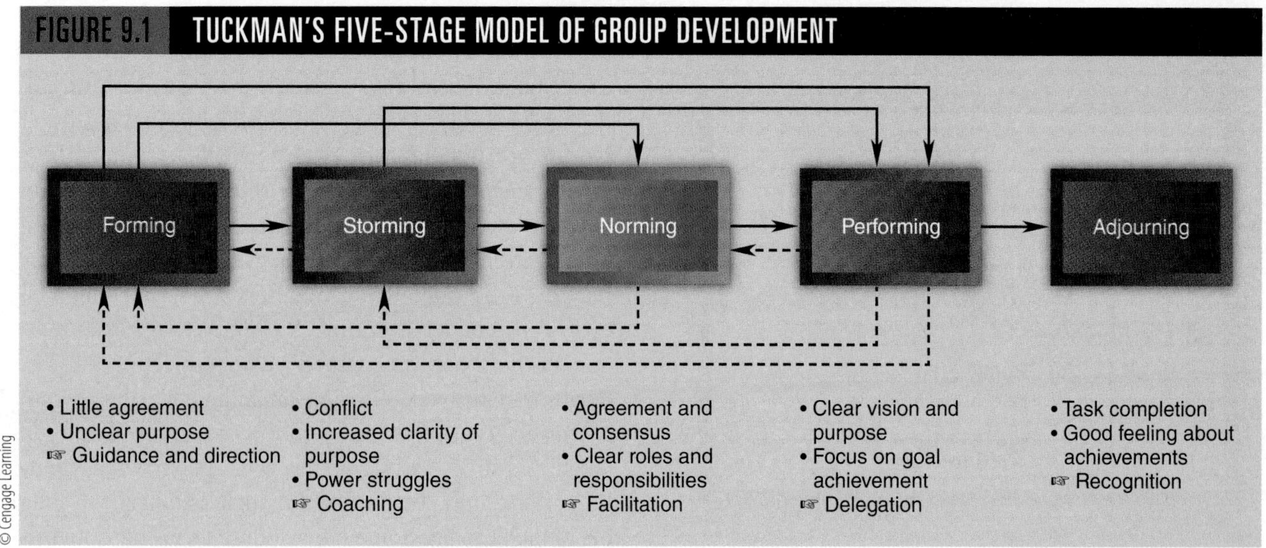

shown in Figure 9.1. It is important to note this process is not necessarily sequential: There are feedback loops at every different stage and there is no guarantee that all teams will progress through all five levels. Many teams experience relational conflicts at different times and in different contexts, and some teams may get "stuck" in one stage or may cycle between two stages, never moving on to the performing stage. Other groups may not progress linearly from one step to another in a predetermined sequence. However, the five-stage model provides insights into the process requirements of group formation.

The first step in group development is called the *forming* stage, where team members are unclear about individual roles and responsibilities and tend to be polite while they determine what is expected of them. Members are discovering the team's purpose, objectives, and external relationships and are testing those boundaries.

Team members compete for position in the *storming* stage. As the name suggests, there is considerable conflict as the norms of behaviour begin to be established, and power struggles, cliques, and factions within the group begin to form. Clarity of purpose increases, but uncertainties still exist at this stage.

Agreement and consensus are characteristic of team members in the *norming* stage. It is in this stage that roles and responsibilities become clear and accepted, with major decisions being made by group agreement. The focus turns from interpersonal relations to decision-making activities related to the group's task accomplishment.

Coming together is a beginning, staying together is progress, and working together is success.

—Henry Ford

As a team moves into the *performing* stage, it becomes more strategically aware and clear about its mission and purpose. In this stage of development, the group has successfully worked through the necessary interpersonal, task, and authority issues.

Members at this stage do not need to be instructed but may ask for assistance from the leader with personal or interpersonal development. Some groups stop at this stage, and the team remains permanently together, performing.

The final stage of group development is the *adjourning* stage. If/when the group's purpose is completed, the group disbands and everyone on the team can move on.

Punctuated Equilibrium Model

The punctuated equilibrium model of group development focuses on the timing of group achievements and status changes. As mentioned, though teams often go through different stages of group development, with each stage representing a different group dynamic, these stages do not happen linearly. The punctuated equilibrium model recognizes that groups typically alternate between periods of inertia with little visible progress toward goal achievement *punctuated* by bursts of energy as work groups develop. It is in these periods of energy where the majority of a group's work is accomplished.[6]

One interesting finding of research done on the punctuated equilibrium model is that groups, regardless of their project, take virtually the same trajectory through the stages of development toward completion.

FIGURE 9.2 PUNCTUATED EQUILIBRIUM

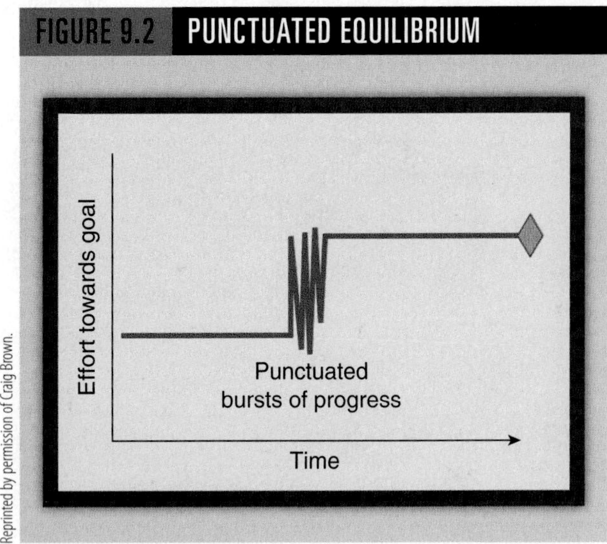

Reprinted by permission of Craig Brown.

This trajectory is illustrated in Figure 9.2. Phase 1 of the project lasts until approximately half of the allotted time has passed, no matter how much time was originally allotted. At the midpoint, the group undergoes a transition where the groups patterns of behaviour change dramatically, and the group spends the last half of the allotted time (no matter how long that is) working toward the group's goals. Studies have shown that whether groups are working on a project that is scheduled to take one hour, or one year, the transition consistently occurs at halfway between the first meeting and the deadline.[7]

The punctuated equilibrium model is not incompatible with the five-stage model.[8] Combining the two suggests that groups begin by combining the forming and norming stages, then go through a period of low performing, followed by storming, then a period of high performing, and finally adjourning.

9-3 GROUP BEHAVIOUR AND EFFECTIVENESS

Factors That Influence Group Behaviour

How groups form, and how successfully they move into the performing phase of group development, been a subject of interest in social psychology for a long time, and many different aspects of group behaviour have been studied. Two factors that significantly affect how well groups work together are norms of behaviour and group cohesion.

norms of behaviour The understood standards of behaviour within a group.

group cohesion How effectively a group ensures adherence to norms of behaviour.

NORMS OF BEHAVIOUR The standards that a group uses to evaluate the behaviour of its members are known as its behavioural norms. **Norms of behaviour** are the understood standards of behaviour within a group.[9] Norms are benchmarks against which team members are evaluated and judged by other members. Team norms may be implicit or explicit; they may be written or unwritten, expressly stated, or silently expected, they may even be unconsciously determined, and they can evolve and change over time. So long as individual members of the group understand what is expected of them, norms can be very effective in influencing behaviour. Norms may specify what members of a group should do (such as a dress code), or they may specify what members of a group should not do (such as taking too long on a lunch break). Some behavioural norms become formalized rules, such as an attendance policy or an ethical code, while other norms remain informal, such as dress codes and norms about after-hours socializing.

Behavioural norms (both formal and informal) do not just manage social behaviour, but also evolve around performance and productivity.[10] A group's productivity norms may or may not be consistent with the organization's productivity standards. A high-performance team sets productivity standards above organizational expectations, average teams set productivity standards consistent with organizational expectations, and noncompliant or counterproductive teams may set productivity standards below organizational expectations with the intent of damaging the organization or creating change. Performance norms are among the most important group norms from the organization's perspective. Even when group members work in isolation on creative projects, they display conformity to group norms.[11] Group norms of cooperative behaviour within a team can lead to members working for mutual benefit, which in turn facilitates team performance.[12] Finally, norms that create awareness of emotions and help regulate emotions are critical to groups' effectiveness.[13]

Group Cohesion

The "interpersonal glue" that makes the members of a group stick together is known as cohesion. **Group cohesion** enables a group to exercise effective control over its members in relation to its behavioural norms. Groups that have higher levels of group cohesion are able to exert influence over members to ensure that norms of behaviour are maintained, which can enhance job satisfaction and improve organizational productivity.[14] Increased job complexity and task autonomy have been shown to lead to increased

#HOT TREND "Six Thinking Hats" for Building Consensus among Team Members

How do you build consensus among more than 200 scientists at eight different corporate labs, two government labs, and five university campuses with varying levels of expertise? IBM Fellow and chief scientist Dharmendra Modha used a process called six thinking hats whereby team members used colours (six, in fact) to characterize their arguments and focus their thinking: white for facts, yellow for optimism, red for feelings, green for alternatives, black for caution, and blue for process. Modha credits the process with encouraging a greater diversity of ideas from team members.

SOURCE: A.T. Lii, J. Allsever, J. Hempel, and D. Roberts, "The New Teamwork," *Fortune* 169 (2014): 78–82.

group cohesiveness and better performance.[15] Also, member satisfaction, commitment, and communication are greater in more cohesive groups. Threats to a group's cohesion include goal conflict, unpleasant experiences, and domination of a subgroup. Groups with low levels of cohesion have greater difficulty exercising control and enforcing their standards of behaviour; hence, they are more vulnerable to such threats.

Group cohesion evolves gradually over time as group norms are established and entrenched, and group members who do not conform choose to leave the group. Smaller groups are more cohesive than larger groups, and homogenous groups typically have higher levels of cohesion because group members share the same values and perceptual screens. Prestige, social status, and other external pressures tend to enhance cohesion, while internal competition usually reduces cooperative interpersonal activity, thus decreasing cohesion within a team.[16]

The ratio of We's to I's is the best indicator of the development of a team.

—Louis B. Ergen

Factors That Influence Group Effectiveness

Group (and team) effectiveness requires attention to group structure, group process, and task and maintenance behaviours.[17]

GROUP STRUCTURE Group (and team) structure describes what the group has set out to achieve, and what tools they have at their disposal to achieve those goals. It describes the *who*, the *what*, the *where*, the *when*, and the *why* of the group. A team's goals and objectives specify what must be achieved, while the operating guidelines set the organizational boundaries and decision-making limits within which the team must function. The group also needs to know what measures are being used to assess its performance. Finally, group structure requires a clearly specified set of roles for all group members. These role specifications should include information about expectations of (and limits on) required role behaviours, such as decision making and task performance.

GROUP PROCESS Group (and team) process is the second dimension of group effectiveness, and it describes *how* the group is going to achieve. Group process issues describe the behavioural components of group effectiveness and encompasses whether groups get along or not. Group process describes how groups manage cooperative and competitive behaviours. Both sets of behaviours are necessary for group task accomplishment, and they should be viewed as complementary. **Cooperative behaviours** typically describe interpersonal teamwork skills and include communication skills, trust, personal integrity, positive interdependence, and mutual support. On the other hand, **competitive behaviours** typically describe achievement skills, and include the ability to enjoy competition, play fair, and be a good winner or loser. Competitive rewards have been found to enhance the speed of performance, while cooperative rewards appear to enhance the accuracy of performance.[18]

cooperative behaviours
Interpersonal teamwork skills.

competitive behaviours
Achievement skills.

"AS TEAM-BUILDING EXERCISES GO I'VE SEEN WORSE."

CartoonStock.com

IN ACTION

Google's Project Aristotle

In 2012, Google began a project known as Project Aristotle, in an effort to discover how to create the perfect team. Google had long believed adages like "introverts work best together" and "teams are more effective when members are friends," but the People Operations department (consisting of researchers, statisticians, psychologists, sociologists, and engineers) spent millions analyzing data from more than 180 teams spread throughout the company, over the course of three years, in an effort to determine whether those bits of conventional wisdom were actually true.

Google examined how employees eat together (and found that the most productive employees typically varied their dining companions, but not always). They examined which traits the best managers have (which, unsurprisingly, turned out to be good communication and avoiding micro-management, again, this wasn't always the case). In fact, despite all the metrics measured, Google found no patterns of behaviour that could predict whether a team would be a success or a failure. What Google did find was that teams that allowed members to speak in equal proportion, and that were able to assess how members felt based on nonverbal cues, were significantly more successful than other teams. These group skills contribute to psychological safety, and Google concluded that more than anything else, psychological safety is critical to making a team work.

SOURCE: C. Duhigg, "What Google Learned from Its Quest to Build the Perfect Team," *The New York Times Magazine*, February 25, 2016, accessed from https://www.nytimes.com/2016/02/28/magazine/what-google-learned-from-its-quest-to-build-the-perfect-team.html, April 10, 2018.

TASK AND MAINTENANCE FUNCTIONS An effective group or team carries out task functions to perform its work successfully and maintenance functions to ensure member satisfaction and a sense of team spirit.[19] Table 9.1 presents nine task and nine maintenance functions in teams or groups.

Task functions are those activities directly related to the effective completion of the team's work. For example, the task of initiating activity involves suggesting ideas, defining problems, and proposing approaches and/or solutions to problems, while the task of seeking information involves asking for ideas, suggestions, information, or facts. Accomplishing task functions leads to the success of the group, and effective teams have members who fulfill various task functions as they are required. Different task functions vary in importance throughout the life cycle of a group.

Maintenance functions are those activities essential to the effective, satisfying interpersonal relationships within a group or team. Task functions often cause tension in teams and groups working together, and maintenance functions are necessary to drain off negative or destructive feelings. Humour and joking behaviour have been found to be common maintenance functions that serve to enhance social relationships in groups.[20] Maintenance functions enhance togetherness, cooperation, and teamwork, enabling members to achieve psychological intimacy while furthering the success of the team.

TABLE 9.1 TASK AND MAINTENANCE FUNCTIONS IN TEAMS OR GROUPS

Task Functions	Maintenance Functions
Initiating activities	Supporting others
Seeking information	Following others' leads
Giving information	Gatekeeping communication
Elaborating concepts	Setting standards
Coordinating activities	Expressing member feelings
Summarizing ideas	Testing group decisions
Testing ideas	Consensus testing
Evaluating effectiveness	Harmonizing conflict
Diagnosing problems	Reducing tension

9-4 TYPES OF TEAMS

Teams can take on any number of logistical styles depending on what their objectives and resources are: Some teams are like baseball teams where members have set responsibilities or "positions"; others are like football teams working through coordinated action, and still other teams work like doubles tennis teams, where members have primary yet flexible responsibilities. Each type of team may have a useful role in an organization, and sometimes a team is not what's best: at the right time and in the right context, the individual expert should not be overlooked.[21] Individual members with particular skills or abilities must be allowed to shine.

Recall from earlier that teams differ from groups in that teams have workflow interdependence, and require mutual accountability. Teams rely on collaboration and the sharing of information and abilities to make decisions that will best achieve group goals, and **teamwork** requires that team members put aside individual interests in favour of unity. When different people have different knowledge, talents, and abilities, and tasks require integrated and collaborative efforts to accomplish, teams must bring together members with different specialties and knowledge, and teamwork is often the only solution. Teams with experience working together can produce valuable innovations, and individual contributions within teams are valuable as well.[22]

Because teams can take almost any form they wish, it can be difficult to classify

task function An activity directly related to the effective completion of a team's work.

maintenance function An activity essential to effective, satisfying interpersonal relationships within a team or group.

teamwork Joint action by a team of people in which individual interests are subordinated to team unity.

Teams can take almost any form they wish.

and distinguish teams; however, in the broadest sense, teams can be classified based on their "type" within the organizational context. These types include (1) production, (2) service, (3) management, (4) project, (5) action and performing, and (6) advisory. These different types of teams can be further analyzed using three broad categories: **team permanence**, which describes how long the team plans to stay together; **skill differentiation**, which describes how varied the team members' skills are from one another; and **authority differentiation**, which describes how much decision-making ability is distributed among team members.[23] See Table 9.2 for an example of how different types of teams can be classified.

team permanence How long the team plans to stay together.

skill differentiation How varied the team members' skills are from one another.

authority differentiation How much autonomy and decision-making responsibility is distributed among team members.

There is no one style of team that works best in every situation; each team is dependent on its members and its objectives, and what's best for achieving one goal may not be best for the next goal, even with the same team members. Three other important styles of teams that have emerged in the organizational environment are cross-functional teams, self-managed teams, and virtual teams. Any team type can be cross-functional

TABLE 9.2 TYPES OF TEAMS

Team Type	Example	Description	Permanence	Skill Differentiation	Authority Differentiation
Production	Accounting team	Core employees who produce a tangible product.	High. The team will continue to exist, even if new members are added or other members leave.	Low. Members typically have similar skills.	High. Only one or two members (typically managers) will have decision-making authority.
Service	Customer Service	Core employees who engage with customers.	High. The team will continue to exist, even if new members are added or other members leave.	Low. Members typically have similar skills.	High. Only one or two members (typically managers) will have decision-making authority.
Management	Senior managers, Executives	Responsible for setting business objectives and directing and coordinating employees.	Medium. The team will continue to exist if new members are added or other members leave; however, it may look and act differently, depending on the organization's goals.	Low. Members typically have similar skills (though a broad range of skills).	Low. Management teams typically have authority to make decisions within their department.
Project	Development teams	Teams that come together to complete an entire project and then disband.	Low. The team will exist only until their goal is achieved, and then will disband.	Medium–High. Development teams draw members with the needed skill sets. Depending on the project, these skills can be highly varied.	Medium–Low. Project teams are typically given the authority required to complete the project. All members of the team will be able to make decisions as required.
Action/Performing	Crisis management teams	Teams of interdependent experts who come together for one performance event.	Low. The team will exist only until the emergency is called off, and will then disband.	Medium. The team is usually made up of a variety of skill sets, however they are all related in some way.	Low. Typically, action teams are given the authority required to resolve the crisis situation, and all members of the team will be able to make decisions.
Advisory	Review panels	These teams provide recommendations to decision makers.	Varies. Some advisory councils review one product or service element, while others are permanent organizational fixtures.	Medium. Team members must be able to advise regarding many aspects of the project.	High. Advisory teams make recommendations, but typically have no ultimate authority to implement their recommendations.

TABLE 9.2 TYPES OF TEAMS (*Continued*)

***Special Classifications of Teams**					
Cross-functional		Teams made up of people with different areas of expertise and experience.	Varies with team type	High. The purpose of a cross-functional team is to bring together people with a wide range of skills.	Varies. Depending on the goals of the virtual team, members may or may not all have the ability to make independent decisions.
Self-managed		Teams that have complete autonomy over goal setting, scheduling, and procedures.	Varies with team type	High. Self-directed work teams operate with little to no organizational supervision, so group members must have all necessary skills.	Low. Self-directed work teams have control over inputs, and outputs with little organizational oversight
Virtual		These teams operate without regard to space or time, often collaborating across organizational and geographic boundaries.	Varies with team type	High. The organization can access expertise from around the world. This typically results in high skills differentiation.	Varies. Depending on the goals of the virtual team, members may or may not all have the ability to make independent decisions.
Non-Organizational Teams					
Community	Typically social groups	These teams have less-defined goals and objectives and are typically social clubs (e.g., community soccer teams).	High. These teams typically exist independent of their members, and will go on as new members join and old members leave.	Low. Members typically come together to enjoy social aspects of an event, and have similar skills.	Low. There are typically not formal goals associated with community teams; however, each member is able to make whatever independent decisions they wish.

or self-managed, and any team can be virtual, though because these teams require greater resources and have greater responsibilities, they are typically reserved for management, project, action, and advisory teams.

Cross-Functional Teams

A **cross-functional team** is any group of people who have different areas of expertise and experience working together to achieve a common goal. Cross-functional teams in business often include members from marketing, finance, engineering, human resources and other organizational departments.[24] Cross-functional teams may even include people from outside of the organization, such as suppliers, clients, or consultants.

Self-Managed Teams

Self-managed teams, also called *self-directed teams* or *autonomous work groups*, are cross-functional groups that are organized based on a specific project or goal, and the team sees the project through its entire life cycle, from conception to implementation. These teams are common in manufacturing, and service industries where new products and services are being developed, created, tested, and implemented. The thing that sets self-managed teams apart from other styles is that they are empowered to make *all* decisions regarding the project within the team, and have very low levels of managerial oversight. Managers may provide leadership and influence to self-managed teams,[25] but the team has the autonomy to plan, organize, and implement work practices as the team decides. Self-managed teams require a very high level of autonomy and empowerment at the organizational level, as well as the individual level.

cross-functional team
People with different expertise and experience working toward a common goal.

self-managed teams
Teams with the autonomy to plan, organize, and implement work practices without managerial oversight.

Virtual Teams

Virtual teams do not meet face to face, and instead rely on digital tools of communication to plan and execute their tasks. Virtual team members may be located anywhere geographically or status-wise in an organization, and are common in knowledge-based industries, as well as international or global organizations. Virtual teams typically employ a very diverse group of individuals both in terms of employee skill sets and ethnic and cultural backgrounds. This diversity requires that virtual team members have strong communication skills in order to be successful.

virtual teams Teams that do not meet face to face, and instead rely on digital tools of communication to plan and execute their tasks.

> "Great things in business are never done by one person. They're done by a team of people."
>
> —Steve Jobs

Whether a traditional group, a self-managed work team, or a virtual team, groups and teams continue to play a vital role in organizational behaviour and performance at work.

9-5 ADVANTAGES AND DISADVANTAGES OF TEAMS

Individual limitations can often be overcome, and problems can be resolved through teamwork and collaboration. Teams can be very good at performing work that is more complicated and/or more voluminous than one person can handle, and in the past several decades,

IN ACTION

Getting Virtual Teams Right

With increased technology, most professionals can perform their jobs from anywhere in the world. Despite the benefits of virtual teams, however, 66% of IT projects outsourced to virtual teams failed to satisfy their client's requirements. Research finds that most people consider virtual communication less productive than face-to-face interaction, nearly half feeling confused and overwhelmed by the technology. It's not all bad news. A more recent study found that well-managed virtual teams can actually outperform traditional ones and have the potential for productivity gains upwards of 43%. High-performing virtual teams share the following characteristics:

- Team members are suited to work in virtual teams, possessing good communication skills, high emotional intelligence, and the ability to work independently. Team size is manageable, with no more than ten people, and roles are clearly defined.
- Teams are led by individuals who foster trust among team members, encouraging dialogue, and clarifying goals and deadlines.
- Though dispersed geographically, virtual teams come together and meet face-to-face at several critical times during the relationship—at kickoff, during onboarding, and to celebrate milestones.

Rawpixel/Shutterstock.com

- Teams have the right technology that integrates a variety of communications media as appropriate for different types of collaboration. This includes conference calling, direct calling and text messaging, and discussion forums.

SOURCE: K. Ferrazzi, "Managing Yourself," *Harvard Business Review* 92 (2014): 120–123.

organizations have made work teams a part of their organizational structure to keep up with dynamic and highly competitive markets.[26] When teams work well they can make better decisions, develop and deliver better products and services, and create more engaged and committed employees. Teams, however, do not always work well. The use of teams can result in increased costs, increased personal and organizational conflict, worse decisions, and decreased employee satisfaction.

Advantages of Teams

Teams benefit an organization by bringing multiple points of view and opinions to bear on a problem, which allows for broader and deeper explorations of potential solutions and can present a wider variety of decision alternatives than may have been achieved by an individual reviewing the same problem. More simply put: having more people consider a problem often leads to more resolution ideas in a shorter time. Group decisions are generally more accurate than personal ones. Teams also provide a variety of skill sets and knowledge bases and can draw on members' varied expertise to implement potential solutions, arriving at the most efficient and effective resolution. When teams are organized and integrated, they can share information and coordinate tasks faster and more accurately than individuals, and can accomplish more work more quickly and effectively. When a group is able to produce more than expected from each individual member, it is called a **process gain**,[27] and process gains are the goal of every team. These synergies allow teams to achieve specific performance goals more quickly and effectively than people working alone. In competitive industries, creative and complex problem solving and effective and efficient solutions can be the key to a long-term operational advantage.

Cohesive teams also encourage employee engagement and satisfaction. Belonging to a team can provide meaning and emotional fulfillment for employees and can define a part of those individuals' **social identity**, which is their sense of who they are based on how they fit within a group. Teams can also lead to greater individual motivation and productivity because as team members feel accountable to the group, achieving group goals can provide personal satisfaction.

Social Benefits to Individuals

Being on a productive team has obvious benefits for the organization, but the individual members of a team derive personal, social benefits from the collective experience of teamwork as well. These individual benefits can be described as psychological intimacy and achieving integrated involvement.[28]

Psychological intimacy is emotional and psychological closeness to other team or group members. It is the feeling of friendship and results in feelings of affection and warmth, unconditional positive regard, opportunity for emotional expression, openness, security, and emotional support. Failure to achieve psychological intimacy may result in feelings of emotional isolation and loneliness. This may be especially problematic for executives who often report experiencing loneliness at the top of the organizational hierarchy with no one to confide in. Psychological intimacy is important for emotional health and well-being; however, it does not necessarily have to be achieved at work.

Integrated involvement is closeness achieved through tasks and activities. It is a feeling of productivity and competence, and results in enjoyment of work, self-confidence, engagement, social identity, being valued for one's skills and abilities, opportunity for power and influence, conditional positive regard, and support for one's beliefs and values. Failure to achieve integrated involvement may result in social isolation.

Disadvantages of Teams

When they work, teams can increase productivity, solve problems more quickly, and implement solutions more effectively. However, teams are not always as effective as individuals. There are significant costs associated with forming and maintaining teams, most of which have to do with the social costs of maintaining a group. These costs include time and efforts directed at defining and enforcing group roles, resolving differences, establishing norms, etc. These costs can quickly overrun any productivity increases the team may have experienced, and result in **process losses**, which occur when groups perform worse than expected of individual members.[29]

Process losses commonly occur for the simple reason that it can be difficult to work with other people. **Coordination losses** occur because coordinating the efforts of a group can be challenging, especially when one person's inputs depend on another's outputs. Time

process gain When a group is able to produce more than expected from its members.

social identity A person's sense of who they are based on group membership.

psychological intimacy Emotional and psychological closeness to other team or group members.

integrated involvement Closeness achieved through tasks and activities.

process losses When groups perform worse than expected based on the individual members.

coordination losses Process losses that occur due to challenges associated with coordinating the efforts of a group.

wasted waiting on other people is a common concern in team settings, and these process losses can increase a group's project completion time over that of an individual. The challenges associated with coordinating a group increase as the group grows.

Some process losses are not just a function of coordination losses, but motivation losses. When group members are not committed or do not feel accountable to the team, the group setting may actually encourage them to withhold their efforts. **Social loafing** occurs when one or more group members exert less effort than they would if they were working alone. Loafers rely on the efforts of other group members and fail to contribute their own time, effort, thoughts, or other resources.[30] Social loafing (sometimes known as free riding) is more likely to occur when individual efforts are hard to observe, which occurs more commonly in larger teams. Team members who possess high levels of conscientiousness and agreeableness tend to compensate for social loafers so that team performance is not reduced,[31] but this can increase dissatisfaction and increase group conflict.

Social loafing decreases as team commitment increases because members' individual interests are subordinated to team unity. Social loafing can also be reduced when the individual contributions to the group product can be assessed, and this is more easily accomplished in smaller teams. Having valid member self-evaluation systems is another way to combat free-riding behaviours.

Group conformity is another process loss associated with poorly functioning teams. One of the critical process gains made by teams is their ability to access various perspectives and areas of expertise. Group decisions are better than individual decisions only when the thoughts and ideas of all group members are being considered. Groupthink, and polarization, as discussed in Chapter 7, can occur when team members feel compelled to conform to the prevailing mindset of the group and fail to express contradictory opinions or dissenting information.

Group conformity is taken to its extreme in instances of **loss of individuality**, which is a social process in which individual group members lose self-awareness and its accompanying sense of accountability, inhibition, and responsibility for individual behaviour.[32] People may engage in morally reprehensible acts and even violent behaviour as members of a group or organization when their individuality is lost. Loss of individuality was a contributing factor in one of the most shameful incidents in Canada's recent military history—the torture of a Somali teenager by Canadian peacekeepers.[33] Loss of individuality is not always negative or destructive, however. The loosening of normal ego control mechanisms in the individual may lead to prosocial behaviour and heroic acts in dangerous situations.[34]

social loafing When one or more group members exert less effort than they would if they were working alone.

loss of individuality A social process in which individual group members lose self-awareness and its accompanying sense of accountability, inhibition, and responsibility for individual behaviour.

IN ACTION

When Teams Don't Work

Teams are not the answer to every organizational problem. In fact, research consistently reveals that teams do worse—not better—than the sum of individuals' contributions. Groups can suffer from so many different process losses in coordination, collaboration, and motivation that they are significantly more likely to underperform. There are many reasons teams don't work, but the most common reasons include:

- *Lack of clarity about the team's purpose:* Clarity on the objectives is a must for the team to perform and yet it is often lacking. Unless the team knows exactly what is expected of it, they will struggle to coordinate their efforts
- *Lack of authority or leadership:* Self-managed work teams get a lot of good press, but not every team is able to manage their own project without oversight. Leadership and authority are important for directing the team efforts, and maintaining order among team members.
- *Challenges of coordination:* Everyone has a unique perceptual screen that influences their thoughts and actions. Expecting everyone to be in agreement just because they belong to the same team is unrealistic.
- *Lack of supportive context:* Teamwork is about collaborative efforts. Achievement requires team members to subordinate personal preferences to team unity. Too often, teamwork becomes lost in fostering interactions or resolving interpersonal conflicts.
- *Collective effort vs. individualism:* Collective effort can sometimes suffocate creativity and prevent people from voicing opinions and ideas when problems are being analyzed.

SOURCE: S. Bhasin, "5 Reasons Why Teams Don't Work," July 1, 2016, from https://www.peoplematters.in/article/watercooler/5-reasons-why-teams-dont-work-13598, accessed April 11, 2018.

STUDY TOOLS 9

IN THE BOOK YOU CAN ...

- ☐ Rip out the **Chapter Review card** at the end of the book to review Key Concepts and Key Terms.
- ☐ Take a "What about You?" Quiz related to material in the chapter.
- ☐ Read additional cases in the Mini Case and Shopify Running Case sections.

ONLINE YOU CAN ...

NELSON.COM/STUDENT

- ☐ Take a "What about You?" Quiz related to material in the chapter.
- ☐ Test your understanding with a quick Multiple-Choice Pre-Test quiz.
- ☐ Read the eBook, which includes discussion points for questions posed in the Cases.
- ☐ Watch Videos related to chapter content.
- ☐ Use the available Flashcards and Matching Quizzes to test your understanding of key terms and concepts.
- ☐ See how much you've learned by taking a Post-Test.

WHAT ABOUT YOU?

How Cohesive Is Your Group?

Think about a group of which you are a member. Answer each of the following questions in relation to this group by circling the number next to the alternative that best reflects your feelings.

1. Do you feel that you are really a part of your group?

   5—Really a part of the group.

   4—Included in most ways.

   3—Included in some ways, but not in others.

   2—Do not feel I really belong.

   1—Do not work with any one group of people.

2. If you had a chance to do the same activities in another group, for the same pay if it is a work group, how would you feel about moving?

   1—Would want very much to move.

   2—Would rather move than stay where I am.

   3—Would make no difference to me.

   4—Would rather stay where I am than move.

   5—Would want very much to stay where I am.

3. How does your group compare with other groups with which you are familiar on each of the following points?

   - The way people get along together.

     5—Better than most.

     3—About the same as most.

     1—Not as good as most.

   - The way people stick together.

     5—Better than most.

     3—About the same as most.

     1—Not as good as most.

   - The way people help one another on the job.

     5—Better than most.

     3—About the same as most.

     1—Not as good as most.

Add up your circled responses. If you have a number of 20 or above, you view your group as highly cohesive. If you have a number between 10 and 19, you view your group's cohesion as average. If you have a number of 7 or less, you view your group as very low in cohesion.

SOURCE: From S. E. Seashore, *Group Cohesiveness in the Industrial Work Group* (University of Michigan, 1954). Reprinted by permission.

MINI CASE

F1 Pit Crews Are the Epitome of Teamwork

There are few teams as cohesive and coordinated as Formula One (F1) race pit crews. F1 race cars make between one and four scheduled pit stops during each race, primarily for the purpose of changing tires, adjusting the front wing, cleaning the rear wing, cleaning the visor, and clearing radiators.

Pit crews are typically made up of 20 mechanics:

- 4 "Gun men," one at each corner, responsible for using the pneumatic wrench to unlock the lug nut from each tire, and then relock the lug nut on the new tire.
- 8 Tire carriers, two at each corner of the car. One is responsible for removing the old tire, and the other is responsible for attaching the new tire.
- 2 Stabilizers, at each side of the car, responsible for holding the car steady while it is lifted.
- 2 "Jack men," positioned in front and rear, responsible for jacking the car off the ground. The front jack man is the most dangerous position in the pit crew as it requires standing directly in front of the vehicle as it enters the pit. The rear jack man is the only member of the pit crew *not* in position when the car arrives, and has to quickly move into position and coordinate with the front jack man to lift the car smoothly.
- 1–2 Front wing men, responsible for minor repairs and adjustments.
- 1 Fire extinguisher.
- 1 Starter who stands ready to restart the car should the driver stall the engine.

Consider all that a pit crew does: The driver must stop directly on the marks, or else all members of the pit crew have to adjust their position, which costs valuable time. The rear jack man has to get in position to lift the car. The car is hoisted, the gun men have to position the pneumatic wrench onto the lug nut correctly, and the tire carriers have to coordinate removal and replacement of heavy tires at awkward angles smoothly. Then the gun men have to re-secure the lug nut, and the jacks have to come away smoothly while the driver is putting car in gear so that the wheels start spinning the second they touch down. All of this happens in less than three seconds. Less than two seconds, on a good day.

Pit crews practise for hours to perfect their technique, but speed is not the focus of their efforts. Rather, consistency and coordination are the key to fast pit stops. All four corners of the car have to act in concert—if all four tires don't come off at the same time, the car can start rocking and tilting, which makes it harder for the new tires to go on, and costs fractions of seconds.

When a pit stop is perfect, you can hear it. There are only two noises: the sound of four wheel guns firing at the exact same time, twice—the first time to take the tires off, and the second to re-secure the new tires. 1.9 seconds apart.

SOURCE: https://www.formula1.com/en/latest/features/2017/1/f1-quest-perfect-pit-stop.html

Apply Your Understanding

1. If pit crews only "work" together for three seconds, can they really be considered a team?
2. Are task or maintenance functions more important for a typical pit crew? Explain.
3. Pit crews are not traditional work teams. Based on the types of teams described in the text, how would you classify a pit crew?

RUNNING CASE SHOPIFY

PROVIDING THE NARRATIVE FOR CUSTOMERS

One of Shopify's goals is to ensure that their clients have the best tools available for their websites so that merchants can present their goods and make sales as efficiently as possible. Shopify has identified web performance, which refers to how quickly web pages are downloaded and displayed to the user, as one of the most important considerations for increasing sales. Research indicates that a mobile page that loads 1 second faster can help to increase sales by up to 27 percent, and so Shopify aims to have customer web pages load in as few seconds as possible This goal of increasing processing/loading speed, however, conflicts with the layout used by traditional merchant pages, which are uniquely customized by the seller to showcase their products in a predominantly visual format using videos, interactive images, sounds, and high-resolution photos. Images and videos, however, are notoriously time consuming to load in a web browser, so often, the more visually appealing a webpage is, the slower it is to load.

Kevin Van Paassen/Bloomberg via Getty Images

To help reduce performance bottlenecks without losing the interactive abilities that merchants require to attract customers, the Shopify themes team created Narrative, a Shopify theme specifically designed for "storytelling". Shopify brought together their design team and their web developers to collaborate on creating a product that would allow merchants to tell the story of their product, but allow that story to load quickly, even on mobile browsers. Narrative's lead designer acknowledged that while the point of Narrative was to allow merchants to tell their story in a visual way, performance, compatibility and web page load times could not be sacrificed.

To create Narrative, Shopify design and development teams established a performance budget and collected performance data to discover the bottlenecks that were impacting client pages. The Narrative team was able to decrease initial page render time by 50 percent and decrease total page weight by 85 percent, allowing merchants the freedom to display their products in a visually rich format without sacrificing loading time or sales.

Apply Your Understanding

1. Why would Shopify have used a team to design Narrative, rather than assigning the project to a single developer? Was this the right decision?
2. What makes the Narrative people a team rather than a group?
3. Briefly discuss the diversity that might have been required by the Narrative team.
4. What type of team was most likely used by Shopify to create Narrative?

10 Conflict and Negotiation

LEARNING OUTCOMES

After reading this chapter, you should be able to do the following:

- 10-1 Describe the nature of conflicts in organizations.
- 10-2 Explain the sources of conflict in organizations.
- 10-3 Discuss different approaches to conflict.
- 10-4 Describe conflict management techniques.
- 10-5 Explain the process of negotiation.
- 10-6 Describe third-party conflict interventions.

See the end of this chapter for a list of available Study Tools, a "What about You?" Quiz, Mini Case, and the Shopify Running Case

Conflict is an emotionally taxing part of social interaction. In organizations, conflict is inevitable as people work together with different goals and different perspectives and personalities, and while conflict does not *have* to be destructive, it often is. When it comes to managing organizational conflict, negotiation is often the best—but not the only—option.

> Conflict is inevitable but combat is optional.
> —Max Lucado

Increasing organizational competition, globalization, organizational diversity, and the use of teams can magnify differences among people and highlight incompatibilities in personality, values, attitudes, perceptions, languages, cultures, and national backgrounds.[2] Workplace conflict can be more prevalent than conflict in a social setting, and more stressful, because individuals who work together do not have the option of simply ignoring differences of opinion and moving on to other topics; most projects depend on selecting one course of action, whether everyone approves or not. Also, individuals who work together must interact on a consistent basis and cannot avoid one another the way social contacts can, which can allow, and even encourage, small frustrations to escalate into major disputes. Conflict is also more likely in an organizational setting because parties have different goals, agendas, and motivations, and individuals attempting to further their own aims may be at odds with others doing the same thing.

10-1 THE NATURE OF CONFLICTS IN ORGANIZATIONS

Conflict occurs when incompatible goals, attitudes, emotions, or behaviours lead to disagreement or opposition between two or more parties.[1] Conflict can arise due to differences of opinion or misunderstandings where emotional commitment remains low and tensions are easily diffused, or conflict can escalate to physical confrontation, where emotions run high, and results are destructive.

conflict When incompatible goals, attitudes, emotions, or behaviours lead to disagreement or opposition between two or more parties.

A study of conflict in Canadian Workplaces found that 99% of HR professionals deal with conflict! These HR professionals say:

- 86% of workplace conflict is warring egos and personality clashes
- 73% of workplace conflict involves poor leadership
- 67% of workplace conflict involves lack of honesty
- 64% of workplace conflict involves stress
- 76% have seen conflict result in personal insults and attacks.
- 81% have seen someone leave the organization because of conflict.

YET:

- 77% say that conflict has led to a better understanding of others
- 51% say that conflict has led to better solutions
- 40% say that conflict has led to higher team performance
- 31% say that conflict has led to increased motivation
- 21% say that conflict has led to major innovations

Clearly conflict has some benefits, but at what cost?

SOURCE: "Warring Egos, Toxic Individuals, Feeble Leadership: A Study of Conflict in the Canadian Workplace," 2009, accessed from http://www.psychometrics.com/wp-content/uploads/2015/04/conflictstudy_09.pdf

TABLE 10.1 CONSEQUENCES OF CONFLICT	
Positive Consequences	**Negative Consequences**
• Leads to new ideas	• Diverts energy from work
• Stimulates creativity	• Threatens psychological safety
• Motivates change	• Wastes resources
• Promotes organizational vitality	• Creates a negative climate
• Helps individuals and groups establish identities	• Breaks down group cohesion
• Serves as a safety valve to indicate problems	• Can increase hostility and aggressive behaviours

Functional versus Dysfunctional Conflict

Though conflict is inevitable, it need not be destructive. While some types of conflict are more productive than others, and some are more easily resolved, it is not the source of conflict that damages productivity and trust; it is how conflict is handled that either strengthens or damages relationships. Table 10.1 shows the consequences of conflict can be positive or negative.

Functional conflict is conflict that improves performance (eventually), and is a constructive disagreement between two or more people. Functional conflict is a healthy way for people to express different opinions, and can produce new ideas, stimulate creativity and innovation,[3] improve the quality of decision making, and encourage growth among individuals.[4] Functional conflict can improve working relationships because once the parties have worked through their disagreement, they have a better understanding of one another moving forward, they have built a level of trust with one another, and they have improved their personal communication model, reducing the likelihood of future conflicts.[5] Constructive conflict can even release tension, and by solving problems through teamwork, overall morale can be improved.[6] Functional conflict is a necessary and desirable component of having a diverse team; recall that passing through a stage of conflict (*storming*) is considered a necessary step of group formation (see Chapter 9), and teams that do not experience any conflict might be suffering from group think, or subordinate defensive communication (see Chapter 8), where members are not voicing their opinions for fear of reprisal. It has been said that in a business setting if two people agree on everything, one of them can be eliminated.

functional conflict Conflict that improves performance.

dysfunctional conflict An unhealthy, destructive disagreement between two or more people.

Dysfunctional conflict is conflict that hinders performance, and is an unhealthy, destructive disagreement between two or more people. Dysfunctional conflict takes the focus away from the work to be done and places the focus on the conflict itself and the parties involved. Dysfunctional conflicts can destroy team cohesion, and damage social relationships. Disagreements that involve personalized anger and resentment directed at specific individuals rather than specific ideas are dysfunctional.[7] When parties are involved in a dysfunctional conflict, they tend to entrench their position, which serves to escalate the intensity of the disagreement and compound their areas of incompatibility. As tensions escalate, dysfunctional conflict becomes about who is "right," and "winning" becomes the goal, rather than finding a mutually satisfactory resolution. Dysfunctional conflict that is allowed to persist can lead to stress, reduced job satisfaction, and higher turnover.[8]

Phases of Conflict

Conflict is volatile and dynamic, but it typically moves in only one direction; what may begin as a minor functional conflict, which could have been easily resolved, can easily, and quickly, escalate into dysfunctional conflict from which no satisfactory resolution can be made.

There are four distinct phases for every major conflict situation: (1) The prelude or latent conflict, where conflict hasn't arisen yet, but the potential for conflict exists; (2) the trigger event, where the conflict becomes apparent; (3) the conflict stage, where opposing views are expressed and may become entrenched; and finally, (4) (ideally) resolution and dispute settlement.[9] The duration and intensity of each phase depend on the individuals involved in the conflict situation: Strong personalities conflicting over major differences in personal values will have a short phase 1, an explosive phase 2, a drawn-out phase 3, and may never reach phase 4. On the other hand, meek personalities in conflict over a misunderstanding will have a long phase 1, a relatively mild phase 2, a short phase 3, and move quickly on to phase 4.

FIGURE 10.1 PHASES OF CONFLICTS

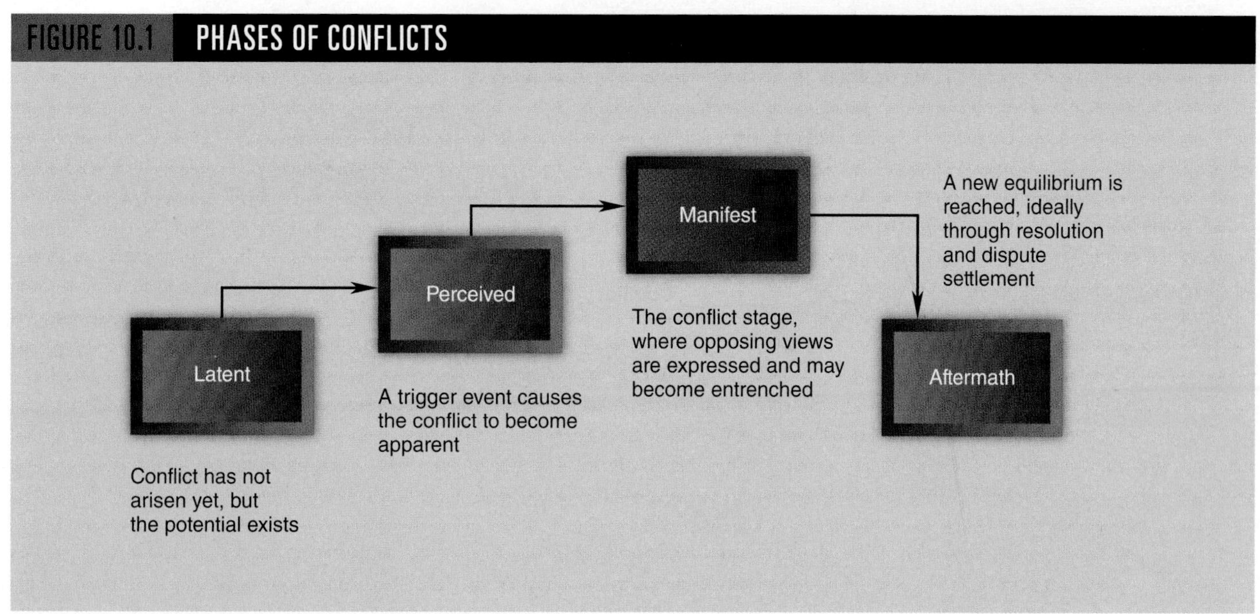
Manifest
A new equilibrium is reached, ideally through resolution and dispute settlement
Perceived
The conflict stage, where opposing views are expressed and may become entrenched
Latent
A trigger event causes the conflict to become apparent
Aftermath
Conflict has not arisen yet, but the potential exists

10-2 SOURCES OF CONFLICT IN ORGANIZATIONS

There are three sources of conflict in an organization[10]: (1) **task conflict** arises from differences in perspectives about work details and goals, (2) **process conflict** describes disagreements about how work will be accomplished, and (3) **relationship conflict** arises due to difficulties in interpersonal interactions.[11] These sources are sometimes referred to as **cognitive conflict**, which groups task and process conflict together, and **affective conflict**, which refers to relationship conflict.

Figure 10.2 summarizes the sources of conflict within each category.

Task Conflict

Task conflict most commonly involves goal differences between parties, and typically occurs between "equals" within an organization, whose knowledge base and opinions are equally valid. (For instance, task conflict does not typically occur between a manager and subordinate, because the manager is assumed to have the authority to set goals.) Task conflict can occur between two individuals on the same team if the team's purpose has not been clearly defined, or between two different groups in the organization who may have competing goals (e.g., sales vs. engineering). Task conflict is typically functional, and tends to positively impact team performance because it forces team members to reach common understanding and agreement of the issue at hand. Task conflict promotes the evaluation of others' ideas, and is usually easily resolved through communication or brief manager intervention.

Process Conflict

Process conflict occurs when parties have differing ideas about how organizational goals are to be accomplished or through disagreements about resources or responsibilities. Common sources of process conflict include:

- *Task interdependence*: when one person's (or group's) inputs depend on another person's (or group's) outputs, delays may cause frustration and conflict, especially if the final group bears the brunt of any penalties for lateness.
- *Common resources*: any time a resource must be shared there is the potential for conflict. Common resources may include machinery, people, funding, work space, materials, etc.
- *Responsibility*: who is responsible for what portion of a project is a common source of frustration. Who has to do what work, who pays, who benefits, who receives credit, or blame, and who is responsible for maintenance are all areas where conflict occurs.

task conflict Arises dues to different perspectives about work details and goals.

process conflict Arises due to disagreements about how tasks will be accomplished.

relationship conflict Arises due to challenges in interpersonal interactions.

cognitive conflict Conflict that is task or process oriented.

affective conflict Conflict that is emotional in origin.

FIGURE 10.2 CAUSES OF CONFLICT IN ORGANIZATIONS

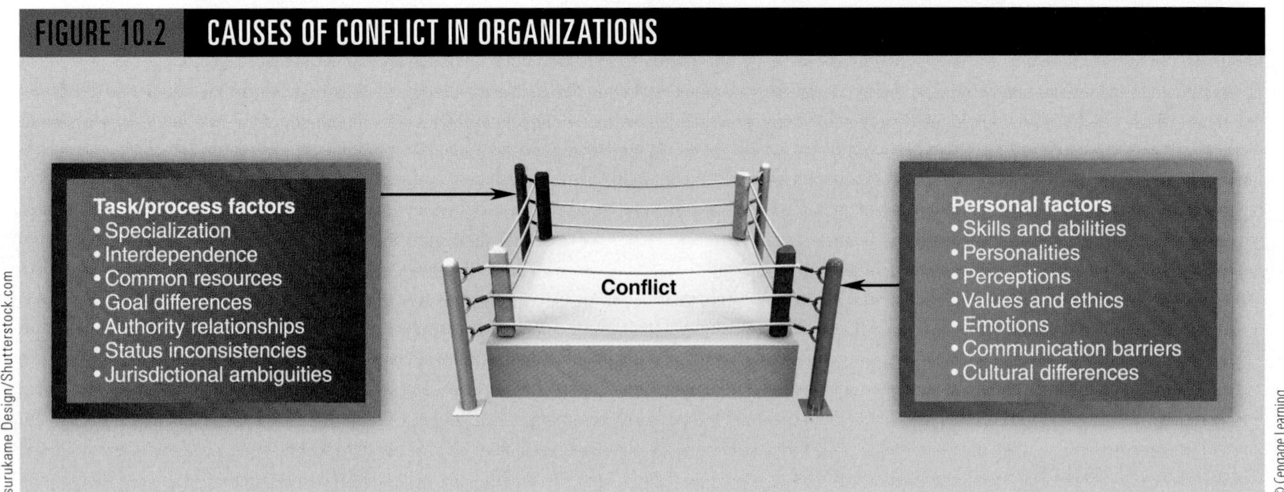

Tsurukame Design/Shutterstock.com

© Cengage Learning

Process conflict can occur between individuals or teams at any level of the organization (even executive management teams may disagree about who owns what resources, or whose project should have priority). Process conflict can be functional or dysfunctional (or, more commonly, begins as functional but escalates into dysfunctional conflict). When functional, process conflict can serve to clarify participants' roles in a project, solidify resource allocation, and can encourage critical assessment of potential avenues for work efforts. Process conflicts, however, frequently deteriorate into power struggles and politicking behaviours, distracting parties from work issues, causing them to spend more time arguing.

> Where all think alike, no one thinks very much.
>
> —Walter Lippmann

Relationship Conflict

Relationship conflict involves personal issues as opposed to work issues, and occurs when personalities clash. Relationship conflict can occur between individuals of teams at any level of the organization due to skills differences, personalities, values and ethics, communication barriers, and cultural differences. Relationship conflict is usually dysfunctional, and commonly escalates into hostility among group members, which has negative impacts on performance and feelings of trust and psychological safety.

In an organizational setting, task, process, and relationship conflicts are often tied together. Disagreements over task and process issues can lead to personal attacks that result in relationship conflicts. Likewise, relationship conflicts lead to increased task and process disagreements when individuals allow personal feelings to interrupt team productivity.

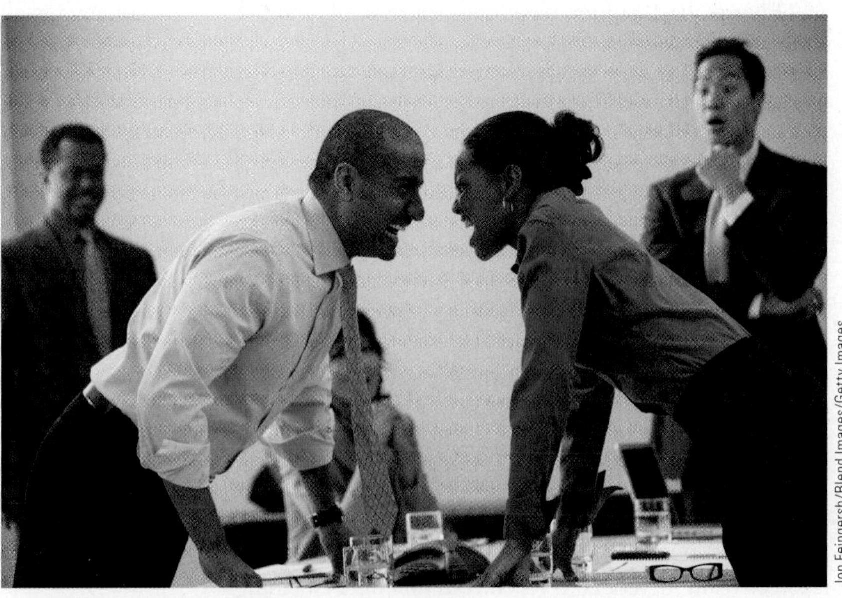

Jon Feingersh/Blend Images/Getty Images

Ensure that the conversation is productive.

IN ACTION

Relationship Conflict

Relationship conflicts can be dysfunctional and damaging to friendships and work progress, but they are also sometimes unavoidable. When confronted by a relationship conflict, try to:

1. *Pause*. Don't say the first thing that pops into your head, and don't fire off an angry e-mail. Take a minute (or 10) to step away from the conflict and think about your reaction. If you're angry, think about why you're feeling that way. Are you insulted? Embarrassed? Frustrated? Actively decide how to proceed. In most situations it is acceptable to say "Let's address this issue at another time."
2. *Address the issue privately*. It is tempting to vent your frustrations to a friend, or gain support by explaining your side, but personal conflicts should remain personal. If a conflict arises in a public forum, simply state that the issue will be addressed privately.
3. *Determine the most appropriate way to deal with the issue*. When possible, in-person conversations are better at resolving conflict because body language can be interpreted, and emotions can be more easily expressed. Some people prefer to have difficult conversations via e-mail because they have the time to think about and edit their thoughts.
4. *Allow the conversation*. Don't just begin by re-telling your version of events. Acknowledge that there is a situation; describe all sides, as clearly and accurately as you can, not just your own, and give everyone involved the opportunity to say what they need to say, without allowing the conflict to escalate. Use "I" statements to address emotions. Avoid being defensive, avoid interrupting, and avoid resorting to insults or personal criticisms. This can be very difficult.
5. *Use active listening techniques*. Be engaged in the conversation. Give feedback as you listen. Restate issues to clarify understanding.
6. *Ensure that the conversation is productive*. Recognize that for some conflicts, there is no resolution possible. If participants cannot rationally discuss the issue, or aren't moving forward toward a resolution, enlist help.

10-3 APPROACHES TO CONFLICT

Conflict is unavoidable in organizational settings. Many conflicts cannot be fully resolved, and oftentimes, one party and potentially all parties involved will not be completely satisfied with the outcome. Thus, when considering how to deal with conflict and minimize its negative consequences, it is better to approach the topic from a "management" perspective, rather than "resolution" perspective.

Framing the Conflict

The best conflict management strategy must first consider how the conflict appears to those engaged in it. A **zero-sum** situation describes any time a gain for one side is offset by a corresponding loss for the other side. Zero-sum situations are also known as win–lose situations because whatever is won by one side is lost by the other side. In a zero-sum conflict, both parties will be heavily invested in winning, and will be less likely to consider or accept mutually beneficial solutions or compromises. Dividing up a fixed budget is a zero-sum situation; whatever one side gains comes at the expense of the other side. Zero-sum situations lead to competitive strategies of conflict management and often entail dishonest communication, mistrust, and a rigid uncompromising position from both parties.[12] Zero-sum situations cause individuals and groups to focus on **assertiveness**, which means they are focused on maximizing outcomes for themselves.

Win–win situations, on the other hand, can be resolved with both sides improving their position. Win–win conflicts can allow both parties to arrive at a settlement that meets their needs and so both sides will be more willing to compromise. Deciding how to proceed through production shortages can be an example of a win–win situation. Win–win situations lead to cooperative strategies of conflict management and include honest communication, trust, openness to risk and vulnerability, and the notion that the whole may be greater than the sum of

zero-sum (win–lose) When gains on one side are offset by losses on the other side.

assertiveness Focused on achieving personal outcomes.

win–win When both sides can improve their position.

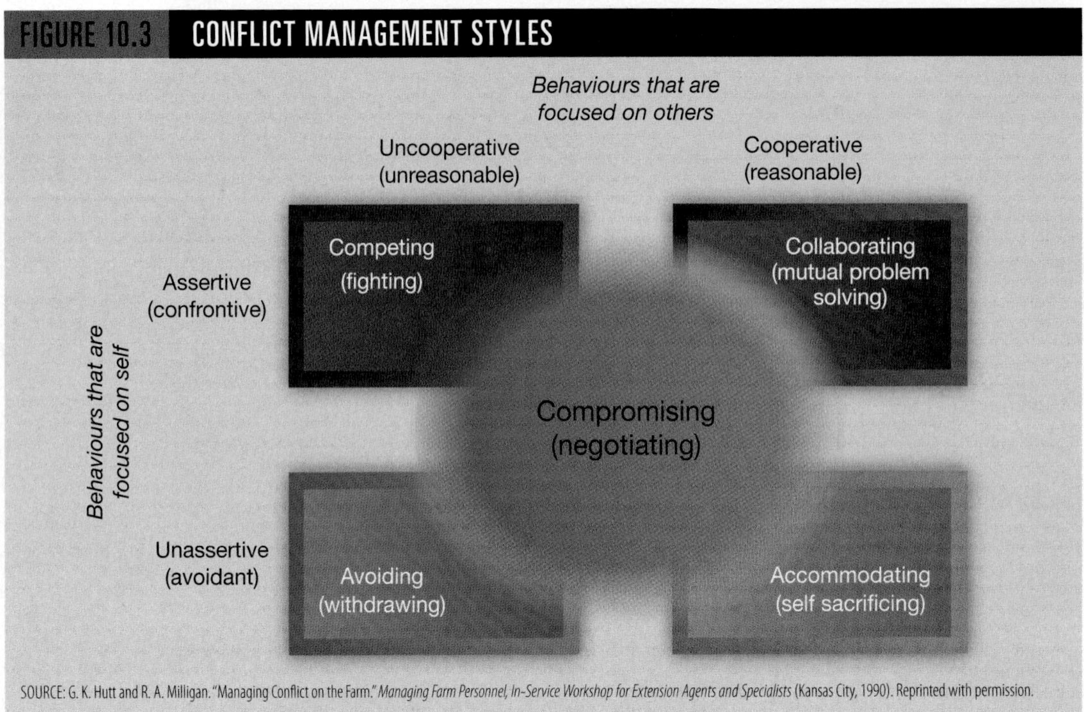

FIGURE 10.3 CONFLICT MANAGEMENT STYLES

SOURCE: G. K. Hutt and R. A. Milligan. "Managing Conflict on the Farm." *Managing Farm Personnel, In-Service Workshop for Extension Agents and Specialists* (Kansas City, 1990). Reprinted with permission.

the parts. Win–win situations can allow individuals and groups to focus on **cooperativeness**, which means they can focus on (or at least consider) satisfying other's concerns.

Conflict Management Styles

The degree of assertiveness (the extent to which you want your goals met) and cooperativeness (the extent to which you want to see the other party's concerns met)[13] act together to determine the conflict management style that is used in a given situation. People and teams may use different approaches to conflict depending on their personalities, the conflict issue itself, and their social relationship.

Figure 10.3 graphs the five conflict management styles derived between degrees of assertiveness and cooperativeness. Table 10.2 lists appropriate situations for using each conflict management style.

cooperativeness Focus on satisfying others' concerns.

avoiding A deliberate decision to take no action on a conflict or to stay out of a conflict situation.

accommodating (yielding) When one party gives in to the demands of the other party.

AVOIDING Avoiding a conflict is low on both the assertiveness and the cooperativeness scales. **Avoiding** is a deliberate decision to take no action on a conflict or to stay out of a conflict situation. For some relationship conflict-causing topics such as political or religious ideology, that have no bearing on work function, avoiding discussions of these topics indefinitely may be an appropriate strategy[14] as this avoidance prevents the conflict trigger from occurring (recall from earlier the phases of conflict). Once conflict has already been triggered, however, avoiding is seldom the best long-term conflict management style. When parties are already angry and need time to cool down, it may be wise to use avoidance in the very short term; however, avoidance can lead to increased frustration, which can escalate the conflict over time. Research shows that overuse of this style results in negative evaluations from others in the workplace.[15]

ACCOMMODATING Accommodating is a conflict management style that is low on the assertiveness scale, but high on the cooperativeness scale. **Accommodating**, also known as *yielding*, occurs when one party capitulates to the demands of the other party. Accommodating is a win–lose approach that may be an appropriate conflict management style when one side has significantly less information than the other, when one side is wrong, when there is a significant power differential that cannot be circumvented, when letting the other party have their way will grant similar treatment (repayment) later, or when the relationship is more important than the outcome. Overreliance on accommodating has long-term consequences: Those who constantly defer to others may find that others lose respect for them and may become frustrated and

TABLE 10.2 USES OF FIVE STYLES OF CONFLICT MANAGEMENT

Conflict-handling Style	Appropriate Situation
Forcing (Competing)	**1.** When quick, decisive action is vital (e.g., emergencies). **2.** On important issues where unpopular actions need implementing (e.g., cost cutting, enforcing unpopular rules, discipline). **3.** On issues vital to company welfare when you know you are right. **4.** Against people who take advantage of noncompetitive behaviour.
Collaborating	**1.** To find an integrative solution when both sets of concerns are too important to be compromised. **2.** When your objective is to learn. **3.** To merge insights from people with different perspectives. **4.** To gain commitment by incorporating concerns into a consensus. **5.** To work through feelings that have interfered with a relationship.
Compromising	**1.** When goals are important but not worth the effort or potential disruption of more assertive modes. **2.** When opponents with equal power are committed to mutually exclusive goals. **3.** To achieve temporary settlements to complex issues. **4.** To arrive at expedient solutions under time pressure. **5.** As a backup when collaboration or competition is unsuccessful.
Avoiding	**1.** When an issue is trivial or more important issues are pressing. **2.** When you perceive no chance of satisfying your concerns. **3.** When potential disruption outweighs the benefits of resolution. **4.** To let people cool down and regain perspective. **5.** When gathering information supersedes immediate decision. **6.** When others can resolve the conflict more effectively. **7.** When issues seem tangential or symptomatic of other issues.
Accommodating (Yielding)	**1.** When you find you are wrong—to allow a better position to be heard, to learn, and to show your reasonableness. **2.** When issues are more important to others than to yourself—to satisfy others and maintain cooperation. **3.** To build social credits for later issues. **4.** To minimize loss when you are outmatched and losing. **5.** When harmony and stability are especially important. **6.** To allow employees to develop by learning from mistakes.

SOURCE: K. W. Thomas, "Toward Multi-Dimensional Values in Teaching: The Example of Conflict Behaviors," *Academy of Management Review* 2 (1977): 309–325. Reproduced by permission of the publisher via Copyright Clearance Center, Inc. © Cengage Learning.

resentful when their own needs are never met, and they may lose self-esteem.[16]

FORCING Forcing is a conflict style that is very assertive and uncooperative (i.e., high on the assertiveness scale, but low on the cooperativeness scale). **Forcing** (or *competing*) in a conflict situation occurs when someone intends to satisfy their own interests and is willing to do so at the other party's expense. Forcing strategies occur in zero-sum situations where one side must lose. In an emergency, or in situations where you *know* you are right, it may be appropriate to use a forcing style, but relying on forcing strategies is dangerous: those who do so may become reluctant to admit when they are wrong and may find themselves surrounded by people who are afraid to disagree with them. Forcing also leads to increased relationship conflicts and all its attendant problems.[17]

COMPROMISING The compromising style is intermediate on both the assertiveness and the cooperativeness scales. In a **compromise** (or *negotiation*) each party gives up something to reach a solution to the conflict. Compromises are often

forcing When someone intends to satisfy their own interests at the other party's expense.

compromising When each party gives up something to reach a solution to the conflict.

#HOT TREND

Twitter is one of the most popular social media platforms, and many people view its anonymous structure as a platform for open and unrestricted conversations about contentious issues. Research shows, however, that Twitter is an echo chamber, where participants receive information selectively, and choose to associate with like-minded individuals. When Twitter users do choose communicate with people outside their bubble, they tend to focus on controversial topics, and use words that are more negative (*kill* and *hate*) than when they talk with those inside their bubble (when they use words like *thank* and *great*). Research shows that more than 70% of all tweets and replies between people with different ideologies were "disagreement" tweets, while about 8% of tweets between members of differing ideological groups were personal attacks. The echo chamber effect makes people more willing to attack or challenge people with conflicting views on Twitter, which serves only to escalate conflict, and reinforce the echo chamber.

SOURCE: Z. Liu and I. Weber, "Is Twitter a Public Sphere for Online Conflicts? A Cross-Ideological and Cross-Hierarchical Look. *Social Informatics: 6th International Conference* (2014): 11–13.

made between equals in the final hours of negotiations, when time is of the essence. Compromise may be an effective backup style when efforts toward collaboration are not successful[18]; however, compromise means partially surrendering your position for the sake of coming to terms, thus compromises are *not* optimal solutions because both parties leave the conflict unsatisfied. When people know that they will compromising, they often inflate their original demands in order to have more to "give" in order to receive comparable concessions, which undermines honest communication and can increase frustrations when the first offer is seen as unreasonable. Solutions reached through compromise may be only temporary, and often compromises do nothing to improve relationships between the parties in the conflict.

> "Whenever you're in conflict with someone, there is one factor that can make the difference between damaging your relationship and deepening it. That factor is attitude."
> —William James

COLLABORATING **Collaborating** is a win–win style that is high on both the assertiveness and the cooperativeness scales. Collaborating involves an open and thorough discussion of the conflict to arrive at a solution that is satisfactory to both parties. Finding collaborative solutions is time consuming and challenging, so while collaboration may be the best approach in theory, it cannot always be achieved in practice. Situations where collaboration may be effective include times when both parties need to be committed to a final solution or when a combination of different perspectives can be formed into a solution. Collaborating requires open, trusting behaviour and sharing information for the benefit of both parties. Long term, it leads to improved relationships and effective performance.[19]

collaborating Arriving at mutually beneficial outcomes.

Research on the five styles of conflict management indicates that although most managers favour a certain style, they have the capacity to change styles as the situation demands.[20] A study of project managers found that managers who used a combination of competing and avoiding styles were seen as ineffective by the engineers who worked on their project teams.[21] In another study of conflicts between R&D project managers and technical staff, competing and avoiding styles resulted in more frequent conflict and lower performance, whereas the collaborating style resulted in less frequent conflict and better performance.[22]

10-4 CONFLICT MANAGEMENT TECHNIQUES

How individuals approach conflict is an important determinant in how they engage others, and what their pattern of conflict will be; however, some conflicts can be managed with relatively straightforward techniques to reduce or remove the conflict conditions. These techniques include appealing to superordinate goals, expanding resources, changing personnel, changing structure, improving communication, and negotiating.

Superordinate Goals

An organizational goal that is more important to both parties than their individual or group conflicts is a **superordinate goal**.[23] Superordinate goals cannot be achieved by one individual or group alone. The achievement of these goals requires cooperation by both parties and reminding parties of a larger issue on which they both agree helps them realize their similarities rather than their differences, which can encourage cooperation.

Expanding Resources

This conflict resolution technique is so simple that it may be overlooked: If the conflict's source is common or scarce resources, providing more resources may be a solution. Organizations with tight budgets may not have the luxury of obtaining additional resources, but the costs of additional resources must be weighed against the costs of conflict within the organization.

Changing Personnel

In some cases, long-running severe conflict may be traced to a specific individual. For example, managers with lower levels of emotional intelligence (EI) have been demonstrated to have more negative work attitudes, to exhibit less altruistic behaviour, and to produce more negative work outcomes. A chronically disgruntled manager who exhibits low EI may not only frustrate his or her employees but also impede the department's performance. In such cases, transferring or firing an individual may be the best solution (but only after due process, of course).[24]

Changing Structure

Another way to resolve a conflict is to change the structure of the organization to facilitate cooperation. One way of accomplishing this is to create an integrator role within the organization. An *integrator* acts as a go-between, or a liaison between groups with very different interests, helping to mediate interactions, and promoting coordination between groups that have difficulty communicating.[25] In severe conflicts, the integrator should be a neutral third party.[26] Using cross-functional teams is another way of changing the organization's structure to manage conflict. Though cross-functional teams have their own conflict challenges, they can help overcome communication barriers and goal differences between functional departments within an organization. When putting together cross-functional teams, organizations should emphasize superordinate goals and educate individual members in other functional areas so that everyone in the team can have a shared language.[27]

Improving Communication

Another simple, yet often overlooked method to reduce conflict between individuals or groups is to improve the communication between them. Many instances of task and process conflict can be resolved, or even prevented by improving communication between parties (beware though—the potential for relationship conflict increases with increased interactions). Improving communication means giving people the chance to come together from a social perspective to find common ground and build trust, and while this can be accomplished using an integrator, it can also be accomplished by giving people the opportunity to interact in a stress-free environment without organizational edicts or deadlines. Improving communication also means improving organizational communication policies. It requires clarifying roles, permissions, and expectations for all organizational members to reduce uncertainty and reduce task and process conflicts. Finally, improving communication means reducing unchecked gossip. While gossip and the grapevine have valid roles within the organization, they are often the source of relationship conflict.

Negotiating

Negotiating is such a key conflict management strategy that it has its own section, below (See Learning Objective 10-5.)

INEFFECTIVE CONFLICT MANAGEMENT TECHNIQUES

Being involved in a conflict situation is emotionally and socially taxing. Whether a party to the actual conflict, or an independent observer, conflict is awkward and uncomfortable. People often react poorly and ineffectively to conflict situations, allowing or encouraging the situation to escalate. As each player's "stake" in the argument is amplified, the chances of a peaceful resolution decrease, and the possibility that the relationship will be damaged before a resolution is found increases. Behaviours that can result in escalating conflict include avoidance, hostile verbal and nonverbal displays, retribution and retaliation, character assassination, and coalition building.[28]

Avoidance is doing nothing in hopes that the conflict will disappear. Generally, this is not a good technique, because most

superordinate goal An organizational goal that is more important to both parties in a conflict than their individual or group goals.

Cheryl Ann Quigley/Shutterstock.com

Hostility escalates conflict by eliminating the possibility of rational discussion.

conflicts do not go away, and the individuals involved in the conflict react with frustration. Avoiding an argument while tempers are high is a good idea, but do not avoid the conflict situation altogether or it will continue to build. The opposite of avoiding a conflict is to react with **hostility** by being unnecessarily antagonistic or aggressive. Conflict situations often cause embarrassment or shame, which can result in anger and anger is often conveyed through verbal and nonverbal communication displays. Hostility escalates conflict by eliminating the possibility of rational discussion.

Retribution and retaliation occur when an individual feels justified in taking some course of action, because the other party did it too. Commonly known as "payback," retribution commonly happens when one party criticizes the other and the other party responds in kind, but it can also happen if one party misses a deadline, and the other party delays his or her outcome as well, or if one party uses too much of a resource, so the other party consumes more than his or her fair share in retaliation. When parties retaliate, conflict escalates quickly and the ability and willingness to resolve the conflict will decrease commensurately. While it is tempting to return insults and attempt to level the playing field when we perceive injustices, retribution and retaliation have no positive impacts on conflict.

Character assassination is an attempt to label or discredit an opponent to cause them to lose face in front of others. Character assassination is what moves task and process conflicts into relationship conflicts through name calling and accusations (which are often reciprocated), and both parties can end up losing credibility and respect in the eyes of those who witness the conflict. Though it can be challenging, keep the discussion focused on the conflict issue and not on the other person.

Coalition building occurs when the individuals involved in the dispute attempt to convince others of the merits of their own position, while simultaneously criticizing their opponent's position. Coalitions attempt to shift the balance of power in a conflict and create an "us versus them" mentality. Coalitions polarize environments and can spark conflicts among individuals who have nothing to do with the original situation.

hostility Reacting with antagonism and/or aggression.

retribution When an individual feels justified in taking some course of action, because the other party did it too.

character assassination An attempt to label or discredit an opponent.

coalition building Attempting to shift the balance of power by convincing others of the merits of the position.

IN ACTION

Don't Fight Other People's Fights

There are few instances where inviting uninvolved third parties into a conflict can bring about a resolution. This is especially true when the conflict is being voiced through Twitter. When U.S. Vice President Mike Pence was booed by audience members, and called out by the cast at a performance of the Broadway musical *Hamilton*, Donald Trump tweeted his "defence" of his VP, and demanded an apology. Some of Trump's followers also tweeted their displeasure over the slight, demanding apologies on behalf of Mike Pence, and vowing to boycott the show. The problem? They tagged Hamilton Theater Inc., a small theater run in Hamilton, Ontario, Canada, rather than Hamilton, the Broadway musical production.

SOURCE: D. Shum, "Donald Trump supporters mistakenly tweet Hamilton, Ont. theatre in Mike Pence spat," *Global News*, https://globalnews.ca/news/3078921/donald-trump-supporters-pick-on-wrong-hamilton-theatre-in-mike-pence-spat/, November 21, 2016, accessed May 7, 2018.

10-5 NEGOTIATION AS A CONFLICT MANAGEMENT TECHNIQUE

Negotiation is the fundamental form of conflict resolution. In its most simple form, **negotiation** involves two parties working toward agreement from different starting positions. Negotiation *should* be a joint process of finding a mutually acceptable solution to a conflict, and negotiation can be done in a cooperative environment, known as **integrative negotiation**, or in a competitive way which is known as **distributive negotiating**.[29]

Integrative negotiation (sometimes referred to as principled negotiation) is an approach to negotiating focused on interests and issues, where there is a reasonable expectation of arriving at a mutually beneficial agreement. Integrative negotiation is about "creating value" and approaches conflict using a collaborative (win–win) style (see Learning Objective 10-3), where the parties' goals are not seen as mutually exclusive. For integrative negotiation to be successful, the parties must have a common goal, faith in their problem-solving abilities, a belief in the validity of the other party's position, motivation to work together, mutual trust, and clear communication.[30] Integrative negotiation is characterized by (1) separating the person from the problem, (2) focusing on interests rather than on positions, (3) generating several different options before coming to an agreement, and (4) ensuring that the agreement is supported by objective criteria.[31]

> The most difficult thing in any negotiation, almost, is making sure that you strip it of the emotion and deal with the facts.
>
> —Howard Baker

Distributive negotiating occurs when both parties approach the conflict from a competitive perspective, believing the outcome to be zero-sum (see Learning Objective 10-3). Distributive negotiating is about "claiming value" and is adversarial, occurring when parties are interdependent and goals are incompatible, resources are limited, or parties are focused on "winning" rather than finding common ground.[32] A negotiator who wants to maximize the value of a single deal and is not worried about maintaining a good relationship with the other party may elect to follow a distributive negotiation strategy.

Cultural Differences in Negotiation

Cultural differences in negotiation must be considered before beginning any cross-cultural negotiation process. The collectivism–individualism dimension (discussed in Chapter 2) has a significant impact on negotiation styles. North Americans (and others from individualistic cultures) negotiate from a position of self-interest and are often significantly more assertive and less cooperative; while Japanese (and other collectivist cultures) focus on the good of the group, and tend toward less assertive and more cooperative bargaining styles.[33]

Gender stereotypes also affect the negotiating process. There appears to be no evidence that men are better negotiators than women or vice versa;

simonmcconico/E+/Getty Images

Negotiation should be a *joint* process of finding a *mutually acceptable* solution.

negotiation Two parties working toward agreement from different starting positions.

integrative negotiation A cooperative negotiation approach focused on the issues seeking a mutually beneficial solution.

distributive negotiating A competitive negotiation approach where each party seeks to maximize its own outcome.

however, women are frequently discriminated against in offers made during negotiations.[34] Feminine personalities may be seen as accommodating, conciliatory, and emotional (which are considered negatives in negotiations) while masculine personalities may be seen as assertive, powerful, and convincing (which are considered positive in negotiations).

Before Negotiating

Negotiations do not ensure that all parties will achieve their best potential outcome from any given conflict. Every negotiator or participant in a negotiation should be aware of, and try to improve, their "**BATNA**," which is the **B**est **A**lternative **t**o a **N**egotiated **A**greement, so as to avoid negotiating an outcome that is worse than he or she would have gotten some other way.[35] If a proposed negotiated agreement is better than the "best alternative," participants know that they should accept the terms, solidify the agreement, and close the deal. If a proposed agreement is not as good as the BATNA, however, participants should either go back to the negotiating table, or leave the negotiation to pursue other options.

The party with the best BATNA will have the strongest negotiating position, and will be less inclined to make concessions during negotiations so it is in all parties' best interests to make their BATNA as strong as possible prior to negotiations, and to publicize the strength of their BATNA. This strategy, however, often leads parties to believe that they have options outside negotiations that they do not really have. They overestimate their alternatives and believe that they would prevail should the conflict continue to escalate (for instance, to a strike or a lawsuit) and walk away from negotiations, receiving less that they would have had they remained in negotiation.[36]

BATNA **B**est **A**lternative **t**o a **N**egotiated **A**greement.

ZOPA **Z**one **o**f **P**otential **A**greement between parties. Overlap between negotiation limits.

negative bargaining zone When there is no overlap between negotiating parties' minimum limits. No negotiation agreement is possible.

mediator Helps conflicting parties negotiate a non-binding agreement.

The Zone of Potential Agreement (ZOPA)

In addition to knowing their BATNA, parties in a negotiation must decide, before negotiation start, what their limit is. In other words, what is the minimum that they will voluntarily accept, beyond which they will abandon the negotiation. As long as there is some overlap in what both parties will accept as a resolution from a conflict situation, however small, there is potential to form an agreement. This is known as the **Z**one **o**f **P**otential **A**greement **(ZOPA)** or the bargaining range. If there is no overlap between what both parties will accept, this is known as a **negative bargaining zone**, and there can be no negotiated agreement.[37]

FIGURE 10.4 ZONE OF POTENTIAL AGREEMENT (ZOPA)

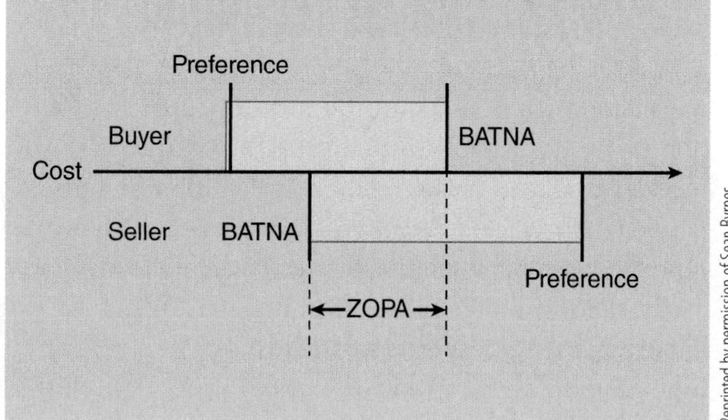

Reprinted by permission of Sean Byrnes

10-6 BEYOND NEGOTIATING

In situations where the parties are unable to negotiate, or even communicate effectively, when conflict has become too heated and positions are entrenched, it is unlikely that the participants will be able to effectively resolve the issue without external assistance. Outside facilitators can help manage hostilities, build trust, open communication, create and implement solutions, and gain commitment to the solutions from participants. Facilitators to conflict (known as intermediaries) do not attempt to prevent or eliminate conflict; instead, they attempt to find positive resolutions to conflict situations by (re-) establishing communication, ensuring that both sides are respectful, reducing tensions, and hopefully finding common ground. Conflict facilitators can be arbitrators, or mediators, and they can be distinguished by their level of control over the conflict process and their level of control over the implementation of a resolution.[38] Table 10.3 highlights the main differences between various ways to address conflict.

A **mediator** helps the conflicting parties negotiate an agreement. The resolutions that arise through mediation are non-binding, which means that parties have the option to accept or reject them. Mediators help focus discussions on problem solving and negotiating an agreement to the dispute, and the goal of mediation is help conflicting parties to come to a resolution on their own. Mediation is effective at allowing parties to fully

TABLE 10.3 NEGOTIATION, MEDIATION, ARBITRATION, AND LITIGATION—HOW THEY WORK

	How It Happens	Who Is Involved	How Does the Process Work	Outcome
Negotiation	By agreement/ contract	Two or more parties communicate with each other and make decisions	The parties determine the process	Contract is final and binding
Mediation	By agreement/contract Court-ordered	A neutral third party acts as communicator and facilitator to help parties make their own decisions to resolve the dispute	A neutral third party leads the parties through stages in private, caucus, and together. **1.** Opening statements **2.** Defining the issues **3.** Developing understanding of issues **4.** Developing solution	Written or oral agreement which morally or legally binds the parties
Arbitration	By agreement/ contract By legislation Court-ordered	A neutral third party acts as decision-maker	By e-mail, fax and conference calls, the arbitrator leads the parties through stages: **1.** Parties structure proceedings and schedule **2.** Submission of claims, preliminary matters, defence, answers, evidence, argument **3.** In-person hearing if requested **4.** Cross-examination **5.** Summation (unless parties agree to a less formal process)	The arbitrator's award is final and binding on the parties and enforceable by the courts
Litigation	Either party may initiate	Judge acts as decision-maker	Judge takes the parties through stages: **1.** Opening statements **2.** Argument/evidence **3.** Examination in chief **4.** Cross-examination **5.** Summation	A decision by the judge which is final and binding on the parties subject to the right of appeal

SOURCE: ADR Institute of Ontario (ADRIO), http://www.adrontario.ca/services/ProfessionalReferrals.cfm.

IN ACTION

Negotiation Mistakes

Avoid these mistakes—otherwise you will negotiate ineffectively!

1. Viewing negotiation as a fixed pie.
2. Over-valuing your assets.
3. Going on a power trip.
4. Not knowing what you really want.
5. Binding yourself too tightly into a particular outcome.

SOURCE: Program on Negotiation, Harvard School of Law (n.d.). Five Common Business Negotiation Mistakes, http://www.pon.harvard.edu/free-reports.

catalogue their grievances, and allows both sides to fully understand the other's position.

An **arbitrator** is a trusted outsider to the conflict situation who agrees to act as a judge. The arbitrator examines all aspects of the conflict, and then makes a resolution determination that the parties have promised to accept. Parties enter arbitration voluntarily and the resolutions that arise through arbitration are binding and typically cannot be appealed, which means that participants have no choice but to accept them. The outcomes of arbitration typically force one or both sides to do something that they probably wouldn't have on their own.

When negotiation, mediation, and arbitration fail, the final recourse for conflict is litigation.

arbitrator A trusted outsider to the conflict situation who renders a binding decision.

STUDY TOOLS 10

IN THE BOOK YOU CAN ...

- ☐ Rip out the **Chapter Review card** at the end of the book to review Key Concepts and Key Terms.
- ☐ Take a "What about You?" Quiz related to material in the chapter.
- ☐ Read additional cases in the Mini Case and Shopify Running Case sections.

ONLINE YOU CAN ...

NELSON.COM/STUDENT

- ☐ Take a "What about You?" Quiz related to material in the chapter.
- ☐ Test your understanding with a quick Multiple-Choice Pre-Test quiz.
- ☐ Read the eBook, which includes discussion points for questions posed in the Cases.
- ☐ Watch Videos related to chapter content.
- ☐ Use the available Flashcards and Matching Quizzes to test your understanding of key terms and concepts.
- ☐ See how much you've learned by taking a Post-Test.

WHAT ABOUT YOU?

What Is Your Conflict-handling Style?

Instructions:

For each of the 15 items, indicate how often you rely on that tactic by selecting the appropriate number.

Rarely 1_______2_______3_______4_______5 **Always**

1. I argue my case with my coworkers to show the merits of my position.
2. I negotiate with my coworkers so that a compromise can be reached.
3. I try to satisfy the expectations of my coworkers.
4. I try to investigate an issue with my coworkers to find a solution acceptable to us.
5. I am firm in pursuing my side of the issue.
6. I attempt to avoid being "put on the spot" and try to keep my conflict with my coworkers to myself.
7. I hold on to my solution to a problem.
8. I use "give and take" so that a compromise can be made.
9. I exchange accurate information with my coworkers to solve a problem together.
10. I avoid open discussion of my differences with my coworkers.
11. I accommodate the wishes of my coworkers.
12. I try to bring all our concerns out in the open so that the issues can be resolved in the best possible way.
13. I propose a middle ground for breaking deadlocks.
14. I go along with the suggestions of my coworkers.
15. I try to keep my disagreements with my coworkers to myself in order to avoid hard feelings.

Scoring Key:

Collaborating	Accommodating	Competing	Avoiding	Compromising
Item Score	Item Score	Item Score	Item Score	Item Score
4.____	3.____	1.____	6.____	2.____
9.____	11.____	5.____	10.____	8.____
12.____	14.____	7.____	15.____	13.____
Total = ____	**Total** = ____	**Total** = ____	**Total** = ____	**Total** = ____

Your primary conflict-handling style is: _____

(The category with the highest total.)

Your backup conflict-handling style is: _____

(The category with the second highest total.)

SOURCE: Reprinted with permission of Academy of Management, PO Box 3020, Briarcliff Manor, N.Y. 10510-8020. A Measure of Styles of Handling Interpersonal Conflict (Adaptation), M. A. Rahim, *Academy of Management Journal*, June 1983. Reproduced by permission of the publisher via Copyright Clearance Center, Inc.

MINI CASE

Conflict Escalation between Neighbours

Since 1953, the Kinder Morgan Trans Mountain Pipeline has transported crude and refined oil from Alberta to the west coast of British Columbia, which gets approximately 90 percent of its gasoline from that pipeline. In 2013, Kinder Morgan applied to build a second, larger pipeline, running parallel to the first, at an estimated cost of $7.4 billion. Alberta sees the pipeline as critical to its economic future, but in early 2016, British Columbia's NDP government said that it did not support the pipeline, partly due to environmental risks associated with oil spills. In late 2016, the federal government approved the Kinder Morgan expansion project, and assured Canadians that the approval was "subject to 157 binding conditions that will address potential Indigenous, socioeconomic and environmental impacts, including project engineering, safety and emergency preparedness."

In January 2018, British Columbia announced that oil imports from Alberta should be restricted until a study could be completed on the environmental impact of a potential spill. Alberta's premier (a member of the NDP) called the announcement a "stall tactic" and retaliated by blocking imports of wine from British Columbia. These sanctions were lifted two weeks later. Both governments have appealed to the federal government for assistance, and both governments have filed lawsuits in federal court. The federal government has referred the provinces to dispute mediation while those lawsuits progress.

In April 2018, Kinder Morgan suspended "non-essential" pipeline activities because British Columbia's continued opposition was putting shareholder resources at risk. Alberta responded by proposing to restrict the amount of crude oil, natural gas, and refined fuel being sent to British Columbia, essentially cutting off that province's gas supply, and Mayor of Calgary Naheed Nenshi criticized the British Columbia premier, saying, "It's very clear that Mr. Horgan, who I think is one of the worst politicians that we have seen in Canada in decades, appeals to populism in a way that is not based on fact." What started as a legitimate conflict between competing interests has become a bitter dispute between Alberta and British Columbia, between Canada's NDP leaders, and between provincial and federal governments.

In late May 2018, the federal government bought the Trans Mountain pipeline from Kinder Morgan for $4.5 billion. The government has stated that it does not plan to be a long-term owner of the pipeline, and is in negotiations with investors, including Indigenous communities, pension funds, and the Alberta government to sell the pipeline once it has been completed.

SOURCE: "The Kinder Morgan Pipeline Debate, Explained," *Maclean's*, accessed from http://www.macleans.ca/politics/the-kinder-morgan-pipeline-debate-explained, October 5, 2018; "Ottawa Buying Kinder Morgan's Trans Mountain Pipeline, Terminal for $4.5 Billion," *Maclean's*, May 28, 2018, accessed from https://www.macleans.ca/politics/ottawa/kinder-morgan-pipeline-bill-morneau-to-announce-if-ottawa-is-buying-trans-mountain-live-video, October 5, 2018.

Apply Your Understanding

1. Describe the organizational sources of conflict described in this case.
2. Is this conflict zero-sum? Can it be framed as a win–win?
3. Describe several ineffective conflict management techniques that have been used in this instance.

SHOPIFY RUNNING CASE

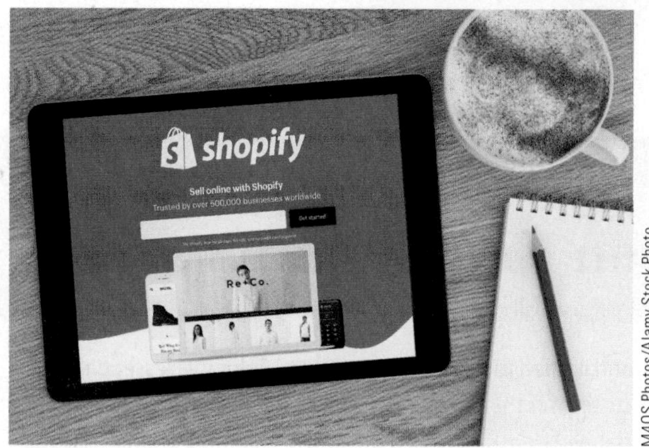

M4OS Photos/Alamy Stock Photo

#DELETESHOPIFY

In 2017, Shopify was targeted by activists who objected to one of Shopify's merchants; the ultra-right wing "news" outlet Breitbart, which has been described as a platform for incendiary alt-right views that are openly opposed to many aspects of equality, including feminism, multiculturalism, gender nonconformity, and homosexuality.

Protesters directly targeted hundreds of businesses who advertised through Breitbart media, and almost 1,000 organizations publicly pledged to stop their advertising campaigns and sever ties with the news outlet. Then the protesters turned their attentions to third-party agencies. Though Shopify doesn't even sell directly to consumers, the company provides back-end support (by connecting vendors to their suppliers) for 400,000 online stores, including Breitbart. The #DeleteShopify campaign was an attempt to curtail Breitbart by eliminating its other revenue streams, namely merchandise sales, which were being hosted by Shopify. Protesters urged people to #DeleteShopify, arguing that the products being sold through the Shopify store not only were offensive but also were helping Breitbart to fund its expansion efforts. Protesters also claimed that Breitbart's products violated Shopify's terms of service, which allows Shopify to remove content it deems "offensive, threatening, libelous, defamatory, pornographic, obscene, or otherwise objectionable."

More than 204,000 people signed a petition urging Shopify to remove Breitbart as a client. Almost 16,000 of those signatures were other Shopify merchants who threatened to take their business elsewhere. Shopify employees also wanted Shopify to end their relationship with the controversial store. Internal emails and chats were written, and employees even wrote a letter to the CEO urging him to reconsider Shopify's stance on the issue. Due to this pressure, Shopify hosted a town hall meeting with all employees to discuss the issue. When the issue wasn't resolved to their satisfaction, several employees quit.

Tobias Lütke explained to employees and to the public that Shopify was not in the business of censoring its merchants, and that it would continue host Breitbart merchandise on the site. Protesters angrily responded that Shopify was helping to fund hate speech. More than 10,000 emails, tweets, and messages were sent to Shopify's CEO, and thousands of Facebook messages and comments were posted on the organization's Facebook page urging the company to reconsider, but Lütke has held firm, and, as of September 2018, Breitbart is still using Shopify to sell merchandise.

Apply Your Understanding

1. Describe the various types of conflict that occurred in this scenario.
2. Describe how this scenario went through each step in the phases of conflict.
3. What style of conflict did Tobias Lütke use to approach the issue?

11 Power and Political Behaviour

LEARNING OUTCOMES

After reading this chapter, you should be able to do the following:

11-1 Describe the concept of power.

11-2 Identify sources and bases of power in organizations.

11-3 Describe how people increase their power and abuse their power.

11-4 Explain how to ensure that power is used ethically.

11-5 Describe political behaviour and influence tactics.

11-6 Identify ways to manage political behaviour in organizations.

See the end of this chapter for a list of available Study Tools, a "What about You?" Quiz, Mini Case, and the Shopify Running Case.

Power describes how things get done in organizations. From setting goals to allocating resources, and from creating teams to awarding credit, virtually all decisions made within the organizations are affected by people asserting their influence. All organizations have varying degrees of political behaviour. Those who have more power get more resources and get better results, so it is important to understand how some people acquire power and use it effectively, while others do not.

11-1 WHAT IS POWER

Power is having the ability to direct or influence the behaviour of other people, or the course of events. Power doesn't have to be exercised in order to exist; it is simply the *ability* (or potential) to act or produce an effect that constitutes power. Power is an important resource for anyone working in an organizational setting, because power often corresponds to control: control of people, control of projects, and control of resources. More powerful people are better able to satisfy their wants and needs, while individuals who have little power are more dependent on other people to achieve their goals.[1] Power has two component parts: the first is dependence, and the second is context.

With great power there must also come ... great responsibility!

—Stan Lee

Dependence describes the degree that someone must rely on someone else to achieve their goals. To the extent that person A depends on person B, person B has power over person A.[2] Dependence may be real or *perceived*, but it is only the perception of dependence that influences power. If an individual can convince others that they control access to a given resource, whether it is true or not, they have established their power over others in that regard. Likewise, if individual A refuses to acknowledge that person B has control over an asset, and sets about achieving their goals some other way, then person B has no power over person A.

The second component of power is that it exists only in **context** of the circumstances that form the relationship or the event in which power is being exercised. This is to say that power does not reside in people, but in relationships between people and situations. When the situation changes, the power dynamic changes as well. This contextual component sets power apart from dominance, which is the tendency for a person to be assertive and forceful in all situations (though dominance can be a predictor of power).[3]

Influence is the process of directing the behaviour of another person, or affecting the outcome of an event. Influence is the action of exerting power, and **authority** is having the right to influence another person.[4] It is important to understand the subtle differences among these terms. Managers may have authority over people, but no power: they may have the right, by virtue of their position, to tell someone what to do, but they may not have the skill or ability to influence other people to achieve the desired behaviour.

When someone exerts power over another, the person being directed can comply, commit, or resist. *Compliance* describes an obedient response in accordance with the request where behaviours and expressed attitudes conform, but underlying thoughts do not change. Compliance implies that behaviours may persist only while they are being monitored. *Commitment* describes genuine agreement, and an internalized acceptance of the request, such that it becomes the new standard of behaviour. Commitment behaviours will persist even without monitoring. Finally, *resistance* describes the situation where the person is opposed to the request and actively tries to deny it by refusing or avoiding it.

power The ability to direct or influence the behaviour of other people or the course of events.

dependence The degree to which someone relies on another to achieve their goals.

context The circumstances that form the setting for an event or an idea.

influence The process of directing behaviour, or affecting the outcome of an event.

authority Having the right to influence another person.

11-2 SOURCES AND BASES OF POWER IN ORGANIZATIONS

There are two sources of power in organizational settings; power can either come from the organization or from the individual. Positional sources of power are those that are derived from the power holder's formal role within the organization, while personal sources of power reside within the person and are not awarded by the organization. Within these two sources of power are six power bases, which describe the way that power is exercised: legitimate, reward, coercive, informational, referent, and expert.

Positional Bases of Power

There are four positional bases of power that can be given to an individual by an organization. They are legitimate, reward, coercive, and informational power.[5]

Legitimate power is typically based on hierarchical position and mutual agreement. Organizational members have agreed that people in certain roles have the authority to request certain behaviours from others. The most common example of legitimate power is a manager who has the authority to tell employees what work is to be done. Legitimate power gives the power holder the authority to request behaviours within a certain range, and employees recognize that the manager has been given that power as a function of his or her position within the hierarchy of the organization. Managers cannot ask employees to perform behaviours that are outside of the agreed-upon range (for instance, working in unsafe conditions) because employees also have legitimate power granted to them by rights legislation and the law. Legitimate power typically results in compliance or commitment to requests that are within the acceptable range, and refusal for requests outside of that range. Though it is the most common base of power used in organizations, legitimate power has not been linked to organizational effectiveness or to employee satisfaction.[6]

Reward power is power based on the power holder's ability to control and allocate rewards that are desired. These rewards can be financial or nonfinancial. Managers control rewards like salary increases, bonuses, recognition, preferred shifts, and promotions. Reward power can be used to motivate better performance, but only as long as the employee sees a clear link between performance and rewards. Reward power typically results in compliance behaviours where once the reward is achieved, or is no longer being offered, the desired behaviour stops.

Coercive power is based on the fear of negative consequences associated with disobeying or not complying. Coercive power comes from power holder's ability to punish or cause the target to have an unpleasant experience, and it forces people to act in a way that they wouldn't without duress. Managers blatantly use coercive power when they threaten to dismiss or demote employees, or assign them tasks that are embarrassing, but they can also use coercive power more subtly by criticizing work efforts, or excluding others from the social group. Individuals at any level can use coercion, for instance, by threatening to reveal secrets about another unless they get what they want.

IN ACTION

Information Is Power: Cambridge Analytica

In 2014, Cambridge Analytica, a British consulting firm, began collecting personally identifiable information through an in-app personality survey available on Facebook that several hundred thousand users agreed to complete. The company collected psychographic data from people who agreed to take the survey, as well as all of the people in their social network. In total, personal information was collected on an estimated 87 million Facebook users. In March 2018, a company whistle blower unearthed the depths of information collected, and explained that the data was allegedly used to predict and influence voter opinions on behalf of those who hired them, including American and British politicians.

SOURCE: E. Graham-Harrison, and C. Cadwalladr, "Revealed: 50 Million Facebook Profiles Harvested for Cambridge Analytica in Major Data Breach," *The Guardian*, March 17, 2018. https://www.theguardian.com/news/2018/mar/17/cambridge-analytica-facebook-influence-us-election, accessed May 1, 2018.

Coercive power results in only compliance behaviours, because once the threat of punishment is removed, the desired behaviour stops.[7]

Informational power is the ability to collect, control, and disseminate information that other people need or want. In the age of information technology, the ability to collect and distribute information can award a great deal of power and influence (consider the power wielded globally by Cambridge Analytica).[8] Unlike all other sources of power, informational power is transitory and short term; once the information is shared, the power is gone, but in the short run, information is power.

Personal Bases of Power

Referent power is an elusive power that is based on interpersonal attraction. Someone is said to have referent power over others

legitimate power Power based on position and mutual agreement.

reward power Power based on the ability to control and allocate rewards that a target wants.

coercive power Power based on the ability to punish or cause an unpleasant experience for a target.

informational power The ability to collect and disseminate useful information.

referent power An elusive power that is based on interpersonal attraction.

FIGURE 11.1 POWER DIAGRAM

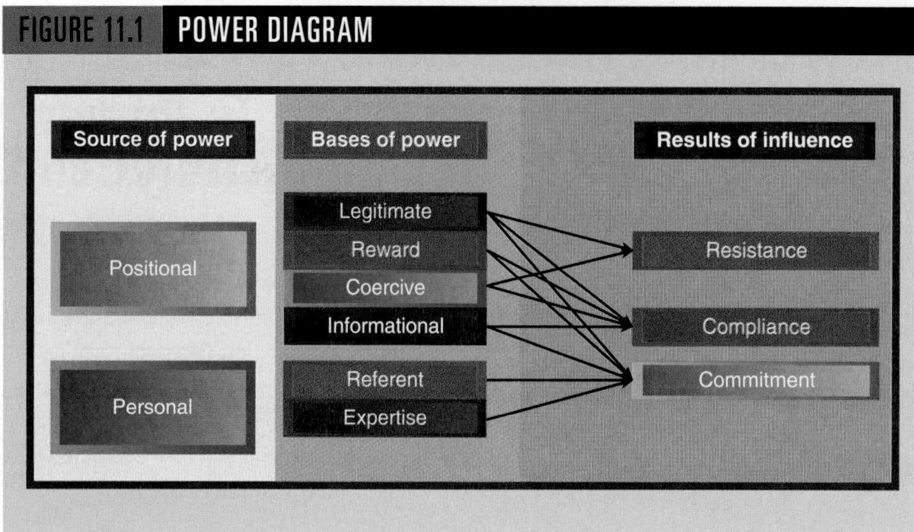

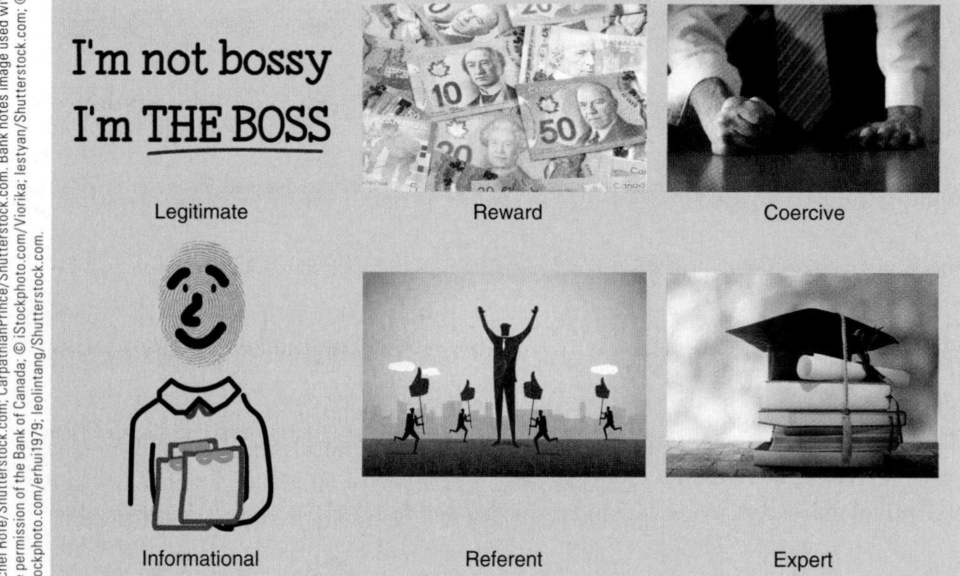

Rachel Rofe/Shutterstock.com; CarpathianPrince/Shutterstock.com. Bank notes image used with the permission of the Bank of Canada; © iStockphoto.com/Viorika; Iestyan/Shutterstock.com; © iStockphoto.com/erhui1979; leolintang/Shutterstock.com.

through reputation, and the greater the expertise, the greater the power. Expert power has been called the power of the future,[9] and it is how essential skills, abilities, and knowledge are passed on within the organization as employees commit to what they observe and learn from those they perceive as experts. Of the six bases of power, it has the strongest correlation to performance and satisfaction. See Figure 11.1 for a graphical representation of the interaction between bases of power and results of influence.

Groups and teams within an organization can derive power, and thus influence, from the same power bases as individuals. One of the common sources of intergroup power is control of critical resources.[10] When one group controls an important resource that another group requires or desires, such as money,

when the target identifies with the power holder in some way. There is no status component to referent power and people who do not have status within an organization may still have the capacity to influence others. Charismatic individuals have high levels of referent power. Referent power often leads to commitment behaviours as others attempt to secure favour with the power holder, but can also lead to compliance.

expert power The power that exists when one has specialized knowledge or skills.

strategic contingencies Activities that other groups depend on in order to complete their tasks.

Expert power is the power that exists when one has specialized knowledge, abilities, or skills that are in demand. Expertise can be demonstrated by credentials or

the first group holds power, and can influence the actions of the less powerful group. Groups seen as powerful tend to be given more resources from top management, making them more powerful.[11] Groups have power to the extent that they control **strategic contingencies**,[12] which are the activities that other groups depend on in order to complete their tasks.[13] The greater the degree of dependence, the greater the power.

Research suggests that there is no best base of power to use in all situations and that the most appropriate and effective power base depends on specific circumstances. The effectiveness of the six bases of power poses something of a challenge to those who wish to use power in organizational settings: The least effective power bases—legitimate, reward, and coercive (the ones that are simply inherited by the manager when they accept the supervisory position)—are the power bases most likely to be used by managers.[14] The most effective power bases—referent and expert—must be developed and strengthened through education, training, and interpersonal relationship skills. An important consideration in any power relationship is the context in which that power is used. Because power often implies dependent relationships, the abuse of power is a concern for any organization.

> "The key to successful leadership today is influence, not authority.
> —Ken Blanchard"

11-3 USING AND ABUSING POWER IN ORGANIZATIONS

Influence Maps

While organizational charts can show who has authority, they do not reveal much about who has power within the ranks, so it can be worthwhile for an organization to create an influence map to help visualize the distribution of power within its membership.[15] Influence maps help to clarify relationships between individuals and groups, and can identify strengths and highlight internal weaknesses within the official hierarchy. In one study, 3,000 managers were surveyed to see if there was a fit between their hierarchical level and their power. The study revealed that many managers were quite powerless and that their departments were suffering a power vacuum.[16] On an influence map, individuals and groups are listed on a page and their overall level of power is represented by the size of their location on the map. Relationships between parties are represented by arrows running between them, and the amount of influence is represented by the heaviness of the lines between them. See Figure 11.2 for an example of an influence map.

Increasing Power

Recall from above that power depends on two factors: dependence and context. Increasing the level of dependence and setting or changing context can increase or decrease the amount of power that someone might have in a given situation. There are several factors that can affect dependence and situational context to give a person (or a group) more leverage.[17] The first is *substitutability*. If someone (or some group) controls a resource that has no close substitutes or alternatives, then he or she has a greater degree of power over everyone who wants that resource. (Whoever holds the password to the wifi holds the power.) The desired resource could be physical goods, intangible services, or intellectual expertise. Conversely, if there are many alternatives to that resource, or many other sources of the same resource, then there is very little power in controlling some small portion of it.

FIGURE 11.2 INFLUENCE MAP

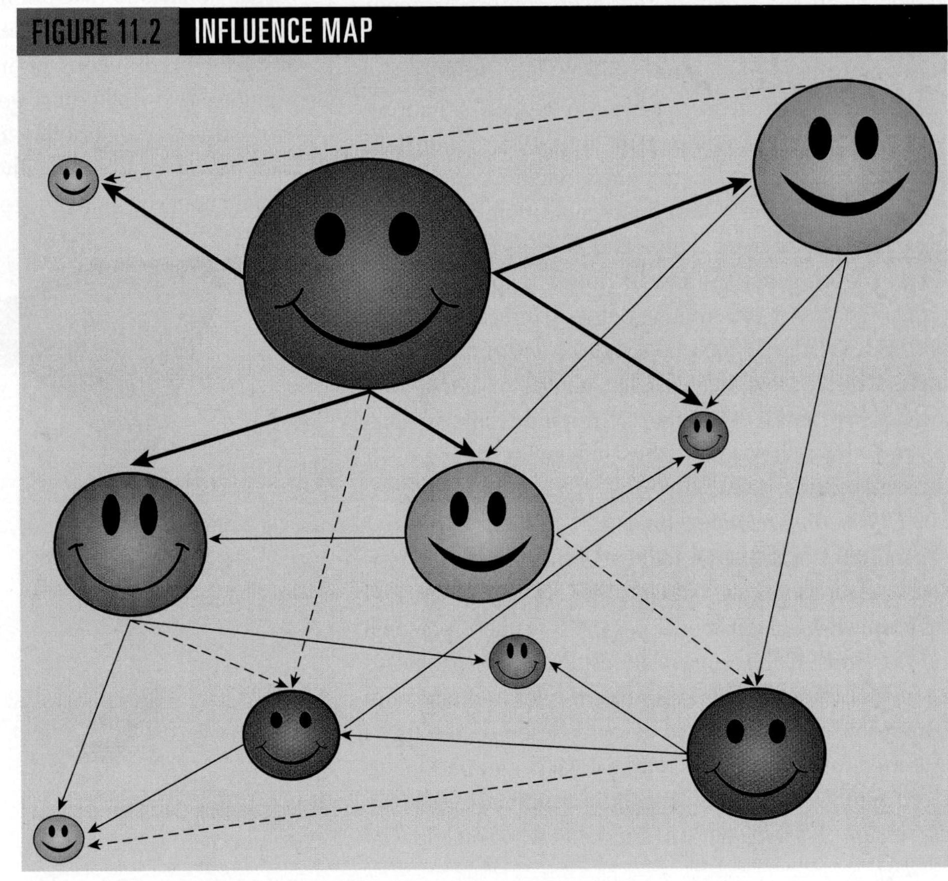

The second factor that can influence the level of power an individual (or a group) possesses is his or her *centrality*. Centrality can refer to both the number of dependants, and the degree of dependence an individual has. In other words, how many people depend on that someone, and to what degree are they dependent? Someone who oversees 100 other people who require input or assistance for their day-to-day tasks has a high degree of centrality, and is likely important to achieving organizational objectives. This person will have a greater level of power due to their number of dependants. Similarly, an individual responsible for making final decisions on important issues has a great deal of centrality due to the high level of dependence that others have on them, and this high level of dependence correlates to high levels of power. Conversely, if an employee was absent from work for one or two days, and no one was adversely affected, he or she would be said to have a low degree of centrality, and thus very little power.

> "Power is always dangerous. Power attracts the worst and corrupts the best.
> —Edward Abbey"

Visibility is another factor that can enhance the potential for influence that an individual might exercise. Visibility refers to how familiar one is, and how well known he or she is within the given context. In many organizations, there is a "go-to" person for common tasks, and that person, due to his or her visibility and familiarity, has increased power in certain situations. Visibility can refer to the person himself, or to her skills and qualifications. No matter one's qualifications, if they are unknown by the rest of the organization, one cannot draw any power from them. This is especially true for exercising personal sources of power (expert and referent). Specialists often hang degrees and certifications on their walls and stock bookshelves with intimidating texts, while others may display photos or newspaper articles in prominent locations to remind others of what, and/or whom they know, thus enhancing their power through increased visibility.

Cultivating relationships is a way that people can expand their sphere of influence by developing personal relationships with their superiors and peers, and then drawing organizational power from those personal relationships. Cultivating relationships allows people to borrow or trade on the power that resides in others, and may result in personal favours or undeserved resources that are awarded due to the relationship, and not due to merit. Cultivating relationships is best summarized by the expression "It's not what you know, but who you know."

Coalitions are another way of increasing power by joining together with others in an alliance in order to achieve a goal. Coalitions allow people to pool their power, allowing members to increase their centrality and their visibility. Trade unions are an example of coalitions giving people, who would otherwise have little influence, a great deal of power.

Finally, an individual's level of *authority* is a key component of how much influence he or she is a able to bring to bear on a given situation. Authority in this context refers to the level of discretion that an individual has to make and enforce his or her decisions. If an individual is able to make the final decision, and have it be binding, then he or she has a greater degree of power than someone who must ask permission before making a decision, or whose decision may be overturned.

ABUSING POWER IN ORGANIZATIONS Harassment in organizational settings is usually an attempt by one person to exert power over another person. The Canadian Human Rights Commission describes harassment as a form of discrimination, and a behaviour that persists over time, and "involves any unwanted physical or verbal behaviour that offends or humiliates."[18] Harassment occurs when someone makes unwelcome remarks or jokes, or threatens or intimidates because of race, religion, sex (including gender identity and gender expression), age, disability, or any other grounds of discrimination, or intentionally makes unwelcome physical contact with you including touching, patting, or pinching.

George Rudy/Shutterstock.com

Harassment is an attempt by one person to exert power over another.

IN ACTION

Understanding Coercive Power

Every student of organizational behaviour should know about the Milgram experiments and the Stanford Prison Study. Though the experiments were conducted in the 1960s and 70s, and have been widely criticized, they have significant implications for how people respond to, and abuse, power and both continue to be analyzed almost 60 years later.

The Milgram Experiments

The Milgram experiments investigated how obedient individuals could be to authority figures. Participants in the experiment were ordered to apply increasingly powerful electric shocks to "learners" when the learner made an error. (The "learner" was actually one of the researchers pretending to be a volunteer, and the electrical shocks were not real, but participants did not know this.) When participants resisted increasing the power of the shock, they were told, "Please continue; the experiment requires you to continue; it is absolutely essential you continue; you have no other choice but to continue." Two-thirds of the participants continued to administer increasingly powerful "shocks," up to the highest possible level of 450 volts, which, had they been real, would have been fatal.

The Stanford Prison Study

The Stanford Prison Experiment investigated the effects of *perceived* power by selecting 24 healthy, psychologically stable college-aged men and randomly assigning them to one of two roles: prisoner or guard. The simulation was supposed to last two weeks, but was stopped after only six days because the behaviour of the participants acting in the role of guards had grown abusive and psychologically damaging. The "prisoners" were forced to use plastic buckets as toilets, and sleep on a concrete floor with no mattress. Some were forced to go without clothing, and one prisoner was even locked in "solitary confinement"—a dark closet. Even though the "prisoners" knew that they could leave the experiment at any time, none chose to do so and most of the guards were upset when the experiment was halted. More than 50 people were observing the experiment, but only one questioned its morality.

SOURCE: M. Konnikova, "The Real Lesson of the Stanford Prison Experiment," *The New Yorker*, June 12, 2015, accessed from https://www.newyorker.com/science/maria-konnikova/the-real-lesson-of-the-stanford-prison-experiment, April 23, 2018.

Bullying

Workplace bullying, much like schoolyard bullying, is the persistent mistreatment of a person and can take the form of verbal abuse; conduct or behaviours that are threatening, intimidating, or embarrassing; sabotage that prevents work from getting done; or some combination of the three.[19] Expressing differences of opinion, offering feedback or guidance about work-related behaviour, and reasonable disciplinary action do not constitute bullying. Bullying is a form of coercive power designed to push the one being bullied into a powerless and defenceless position, and bullying behaviour can contribute to creating toxic workplaces.[20]

According to a survey conducted by Public Service Alliance of Canada, 45 percent of respondents have experienced bullying at their workplace. One-third of respondents said that being bullied caused them health problems, and more than a quarter of them claimed that the only way to stop the bullying was to quit their job.[21] Other research finds that the majority of bullies (70 percent) are men, while the majority of targets (60 percent) are women and minorities. Sixty percent of bullying is done by those in a managerial or supervisory role.[22] The top 10 bullying tactics in the workplace have been identified as: (1) blame for errors, (2) unreasonable job demands, (3) criticism of ability, (4) inconsistent compliance with rules, (5) threatening job loss, (6) insults and put-downs, (7) discounting or denial of successes, (8) exclusion, (9) yelling and screaming, and (10) stealing credit.[23] See Table 11.1 for steps to take if you feel that you are being bullied in an organizational setting.

TABLE 11.1 WHAT TO DO ABOUT HARASSMENT IN ORGANIZATIONS

Make it clear to the perpetrator that a line has been crossed. Many times, harassment begins subtly, maybe even jokingly, but then crosses the line. As soon as you feel that the line has been crossed, say something, and say something every time the behaviour reoccurs.
If the unwanted behaviour continues, tell a person in authority about the situation. (Either a manager or a supervisor, or a union representative or member of the employee association.) Tell the authority figure every time the behaviour reoccurs.
Document all alleged incidents, including when and where they occurred, the nature of the behaviour, the names of any witnesses, and any other relevant information. Document every time the behaviour reoccurs.
If the behaviour persists, or corrective action is not taken, a complaint may be made with the appropriate Human Rights Commission. Typically, a complaint must be made within one year of the alleged incident.

SOURCE: Alberta Human Rights Commission, October 2017, from https://www.albertahumanrights.ab.ca/publications/bulletins_sheets_booklets/sheets/hr_and_employment/Pages/sexual_harassment.aspx, accessed April 25, 2018.

#MeToo: 195 Countries, 6.5 Million Tweets

The "Me Too" movement was founded long before it became a hashtag, but in the wake of several prominent sexual harassment and assault scandals in the entertainment industry, the #MeToo social media movement was conceptualized to illustrate how many women have faced sexual harassment and sexual assault. Celebrities quickly promoted the hashtag, many tweeting their stories, and encouraging others to do the same. Google Trends show that #MeToo has been searched from 195 countries across the world. More than 12 million Facebook users have added the hashtag to a post, and more than 6.5 million tweets have been shared.

SOURCE: S. Chou, "Millions Say #MeToo. But Not Everyone is Heard Equally," January 23, 2018, from https://www.pri.org/stories/2018-01-23/millions-say-metoo-not-everyone-heard-equally, accessed April 30, 2018.

Sexual Harassment

Sexual harassment is harassment where the underlying context is sexual in nature. While both women and men engage in sexual harassment, men are more likely to be the transgressors, and women and transgender people are far more likely to be targeted. Forty-three percent of women, and 12 percent of men, have reported being sexually harassed in their workplace,[24] while young women have been found to experience particularly severe forms of harassment online.[25] In some cases, sexual harassment can be difficult to interpret or categorize because sexual harassment often starts subtly as a mutually acceptable friendly exchange, but then crosses the line into unwanted overtures or expectations. Perpetrators of sexual harassment may also believe that they are being complimentary with their gestures or comments, and do not recognize that they are harassing their targets.

In most provinces, employers are responsible for maintaining a work environment that is free from sexual harassment for all employees and customers. See Table 11.1 for steps to take if you feel that you are being harassed in an organizational setting.

11-4 USING POWER ETHICALLY

To the degree that power is a skill, practising can improve performance and results. Developing the skills required by each base of power, and using those forms of power, *without* overshooting into harassing behaviours, can provide individuals with increased influence, which can continue to grow with continued practice. Research shows that power has a significant and transformative impact on an individual's psychological state: Those who believe that they are powerful behave more assertively, tend to enjoy a higher self-esteem, and behave in more effective ways that actually serve to increase their power.[26] But increasing power can have negative consequences as well: corruption, selfishness, and decreased empathy are all behaviours associated with increased power.[27] Using power appropriately means using it ethically. Coercive power, for example, requires careful administration if it is to be used in an ethical manner without becoming abusive. Table 11.2 shows some guidelines for the ethical use of all six bases of power.

Determining whether a power-related behaviour is ethical or not can be difficult because the interpretation of behaviour is often dependent on perception—the person exercising power may believe that he or she is justified in the behaviour, while the person being acted upon may feel that he or she is being bullied. An objective way to determine whether the use of power is ethical in a given situation is to answer the following three questions:[28]

1. *Does the behaviour produce a good outcome for people both inside and outside the organization?* If the power-related behaviour serves only the individual's self-interest and fails to help the organization reach its goals, it should be considered unethical. A salesperson might be tempted to discount a product in order to make a sale, but doing so does not benefit the organization.
2. *Does the behaviour respect the rights of all parties?* Free speech, privacy, security, and due process (among others) are individual rights that are guaranteed to everyone by the Canadian Charter of Rights and Freedoms. These rights must be respected at all times and power-related behaviours that violate these rights are unethical.
3. *Does the behaviour treat all parties equitably and fairly?* Power-related behaviour that treats one party arbitrarily, or benefits one party at the expense of another, is unethical.

To be considered completely ethical, power-related behaviour must meet all three criteria. If the behaviour fails to meet the criteria, then alternative actions should be considered. Unfortunately, most power-related

TABLE 11.2 GUIDELINES FOR THE ETHICAL USE OF POWER

Form of Power	Guidelines for Ethical Use
Reward power	Verify compliance. Make feasible, reasonable requests. Make only ethical requests. Offer rewards desired by subordinates. Offer only credible rewards.
Coercive power	Inform subordinates of rules and penalties. Warn before punishing. Administer punishment consistently and uniformly. Understand the situation before acting. Maintain credibility. Fit punishment to the infraction. Punish in private.
Legitimate power	Be cordial and polite. Be confident. Be clear and follow up to verify understanding. Make sure request is appropriate. Explain reasons for request. Follow proper channels. Exercise power consistently. Enforce compliance. Be sensitive to subordinates' concerns.
Referent power	Treat subordinates fairly. Defend subordinates' interests. Be sensitive to subordinates' needs and feelings. Select subordinates similar to yourself. Engage in role modelling.
Expert power	Maintain credibility. Act confidently and decisively. Keep informed. Recognize employee concerns. Avoid threatening subordinates' self-esteem.
Informational power	Relay information completely and accurately. Refrain from framing the information to introduce "spin." Relay information in a timely manner. Relay updates as they become available.

SOURCE: G. Yukl, 1981. *Leadership in Organizations,* 7e. New Jersey: Pearson Education, Inc.

behaviours are not easy to analyze. Conflicts often exist among the criteria; for example, a given behaviour may maximize the greatest good for the greatest number of people but may not treat all parties equitably. While these criteria may not provide easy or certain answers, they can be used on a case-by-case basis to sort through the complex ethical issues surrounding the use of power.

11-5 POLITICAL BEHAVIOUR IN ORGANIZATIONS

Though the term is often used derogatorily, **organizational politics** is not necessarily negative; it is simply the use of power and influence in organizations. Leaders and managers routinely use their influence to organize and direct activities in order to meet organizational goals. Without some form(s) of power, a leader could not be a leader because he or she would hold no sway over followers.

Power and influence, however, are often exercised outside formal organizational roles, with aims other than achieving organizational goals and directing workflow. In most organizational settings, people have competing interests and they often act to achieve their own goals, capitalize on their own advantages, and maximize their own returns. In order to accomplish this, people use various tactics and strategies to acquire power and expand their power bases in order to affect decision making. Some of these tactics and strategies are sanctioned (acceptable to the organization); others are not. **Political behaviour** describes actions that (1) attempt to influence others in the organization, (2) are not part of one's formal role within the organization, (3) are not officially sanctioned by an organization, and (4) are aimed at protecting the self-interests of individuals (or groups).[29] What separates political behaviour from organizational politics is the self-serving nature of the behaviour; political behaviour is undertaken for personal gain, and its objective is to displace or manipulate the legitimate power that may be exercised in an organizational setting.[30] Due to the very likely possibility of resistance, people who engage in political behaviour often attempt to conceal or disguise their influence attempts, or attempt to camouflage their true intent behind organizationally approved reasons. This misdirection makes political behaviour secretive and underhanded.

Politics is a controversial topic. Some people take a favourable view of

organizational politics The use of power and influence in organizations.

political behaviour Actions not officially sanctioned by an organization that are taken to influence others in order to meet personal goals.

Devrimb/Getty Images

Political behaviour involves influencing others to achieve personal goals.

political behaviour while others see it as detrimental to the organization. Some workers, who perceive their workplace as highly political, actually find the use of political tactics more satisfying and report greater job satisfaction when they engage in political behaviour, while others find office politics distasteful and stressful.[31] Whether they enjoy engaging in it or not, most people are very good at recognizing political behaviour at all levels of the organization.[32]

> In our age there is no such thing as 'keeping out of politics.' All issues are political issues.
>
> —George Orwell

Dimensions of Political Behaviour

Political behaviour exists across three dimensions: internal vs. external, vertical vs. lateral, and legitimate vs. illegitimate,[33] and each organization is unique in the degree and direction of its political behaviour. Recall that power is contextual, and does not remain static over time. Typically, when individuals engage in political behaviours, other individuals respond with other political behaviours and power dynamics shift and vary over time.

The first dimension describes whether resources are being pursued internal to the organization, or with the assistance of "outsiders." When behaviour is confined to the organization, such as coalition forming, or exchanging favours or reprisals, it is said to be internal. Whistle blowing and leaking information to the press or investors involve outsiders and are examples of external forms of political behaviour.

The vertical–lateral dimension describes the direction of the political behaviours within the organization. Vertical political behaviours describe attempts to exercise power upward or downward through the organizational hierarchy. Upward political behaviours include bypassing the chain of command with complaints or appeals, or using gifts or flattery with supervisors in an attempt to gain favour. Downward influence attempts include exchanging favours with subordinates. Lateral political behaviours encompass all behaviours that move across the organizational hierarchy, including alliances, and coalition forming with peers.

Finally, the legitimate–illegitimate dimension describes the degree to which the behaviours are accepted by organizational norms or violate the accepted rules for conduct within the organization. While some organizations are naturally more politically inclined than others, sabotage, and illegal behaviours are examples of behaviour that are considered illegitimate in all organizations.

Organizational conditions often encourage political activity. Unclear goals, significant changes within the organization, lack of transparency, autocratic decision making, ambiguous lines of authority, scarce resources, and the degree of uncertainty can all have significant impacts on political behaviours.[34] Organizational climates tend to become more political at higher levels and less political at lower levels, and certain functional areas within organizations tend toward more political activities, such as marketing and sales.[35] Even activities that are supposed to be objective are affected by politics: A study of 60 executives who had extensive experience in employee evaluation indicated that political considerations were nearly always part of the performance appraisal process.[36]

The effects of political behaviour in organizations can be quite negative; when employees view the organization's political climate as extreme, they experience more anxiety, tension, fatigue, and burnout. They are also more dissatisfied with their jobs and are more likely to leave.[37] But not all political behaviour is destructive. When self-interest aligns with organizational goals, political behaviour is perceived positively by employees. Political behaviour is also viewed positively when it is seen as the only means by which to accomplish something.

Influence Tactics

Recall that influence is the process of directing the behaviour of another person, or affecting the outcome of an event. **Influence tactics** are the ways that power is translated into specific actions. There are 11 basic types of influence tactics listed and described in Table 11.3.[38] The influence tactics described here are listed from most pressure to least pressure, and politically savvy individuals recognize that different tactics should be used for different purposes, and for different people. Influence attempts with subordinates, for example, usually involve assigning tasks or changing behaviour. With peers, the objective is often to request help, and with superiors influence attempts are often made to request approval, or gain resources and support.

influence tactics The ways that power is translated into specific actions.

TABLE 11.3 INFLUENCE TACTICS USED IN ORGANIZATIONS

Tactics	Description	Examples
Pressure	Demands or threats used to convince others to comply with a request or to support a proposal.	"If you don't do this, you're fired." "You have until 5:00 to change your mind, or I'm going without you."
Assertiveness	Repeated requests, firm timelines, and expressing anger toward those who fail to meet expectations.	"I've already asked you twice." "Get it done by tomorrow night."
Legitimating	Using legitimate power.	"As the manager, I am telling you to do this." "The rules say that you have to do it this way."
Coalition	Using the support of others as an argument to persuade compliance.	"All the other supervisors agree with me." "I'll ask you in front of the group."
Exchange	Explicit or implicit promise of rewards or tangible benefits for compliance. (Or a reminder of favour that is owed.)	"I'll take you to lunch if you'll support me." "You owe me for last time."
Upward appeals	Seeking approval from those higher in the chain of command before making the request.	"My boss supports this idea." "Your manager already agreed."
Ingratiation	Attempting to become more likeable or be viewed more favourably.	"Only you can do this job right." Using flattery and compliments.
Rational persuasion	Logical arguments and factual evidence used to persuade.	"This will save us $150,000 in overhead." "It makes sense to hire John; he has the most experience."
Personal appeals	Relying on personal relationships or requesting special favors.	"Can you do me a favour?" Asking for workplace favours outside of work.
Inspirational appeals	Making an emotional request or proposal that arouses enthusiasm by appealing to values and ideals.	"Being environmentally conscious is the *right* thing." "Just *imagine* if we did this."
Consultation	Seeking participation and input into decision making or planning.	"What do you think we can do here?""How would you do this?"

SOURCE: G. Yukl and C. M. Falbe, "Influence Tactics and Objectives in Upward, Downward, and Lateral Influence Attempts," *Journal of Applied Psychology* 75 (1990): 132–140; A. Hall and L. Barrett. "Influence: The Essence of Leadership." University of Nebraska – Lincoln Extension, March 2007, http://extensionpublications.unl.edu/assets/pdf/g1695.pdf.

Pressure tactics refer to using demands and threats to force others to comply. Pressure tactics often rely on repeated interactions until the target agrees to change behaviour. Pressure tactics can be effective in emergency situations or when a person is not acting in his or her best interests and must be forced to change course; for instance, to get assistance with substance abuse problems.

Assertiveness tactics include repeated requests and firm reminders to influence behaviour. Those relying on assertiveness tactics routinely display their displeasure when tasks are not completed, in order to encourage compliance. Assertiveness tactics are closely related to pressure tactics, but occur within legitimate organizational channels.

Legitimating tactics occur when the request is made through legitimate channels and is based on the authority conferred by the organization or by one's position. Legitimating tactics rely on rules and regulations to encourage behaviour. Legitimating tactics can often be seen as heavy handed and coercive if not used appropriately.

Coalition tactics describes a group working together towards a common goal of influencing others. Coalitions take advantage of peer pressure to make demands, encourage behaviour, and attain goals. Unions and trade groups often use coalition tactics to achieve their goals.

Exchange tactics refer to reciprocal give-and-take scenarios where one party does another a favour, and then a favour is owed in return. It is human nature to repay obligations, and exchange tactics often rely on this sense of indebtedness to achieve compliance.

Upward appeals tactics are behaviours that go outside the normal chain of command in order to obtain commitment from those higher in the organization prior to asking for the favour. Upward appeals rely on the authority of the higher-up to achieve the goals.

Ingratiation tactics describe various forms of making others feel good either before or during the influence attempt. Ingratiation typically relies on flattery and compliments, and can be very effective at manipulating behaviour. Ingratiation can be genuine and honest, but failed attempts can be seen as irritating and offensive.

Rational persuasion tactics involve using factual data and logical arguments to convince others to act a certain way. Rational persuasion is the most commonly applied influence tactic, and can work on upward, downward, or lateral attempts at influence. Rational persuasion works best if the information presented is clear, relevant, and timely.

Personal appeals tactics refer to helping another person due to interpersonal relationships. People are more likely to agree to something when asked by someone familiar and liked.

Inspirational appeals tactics attempt to gain support for a request by appealing to emotions and values. Inspirational appeals can be valuable for achieving buy-in for organizational vision and for communicating the need for change.

Consultation tactics involve asking others for their input or assistance in influencing another group, and can be very effective for cross-functional projects, or in organizations that value democratic decision making. See Figure 11.3 for a visual representation of the bases of power that are typically used with each influence tactic, and the typical result.

FIGURE 11.3 SOURCES AND BASES OF POWER, PLUS INFLUENCE TACTICS

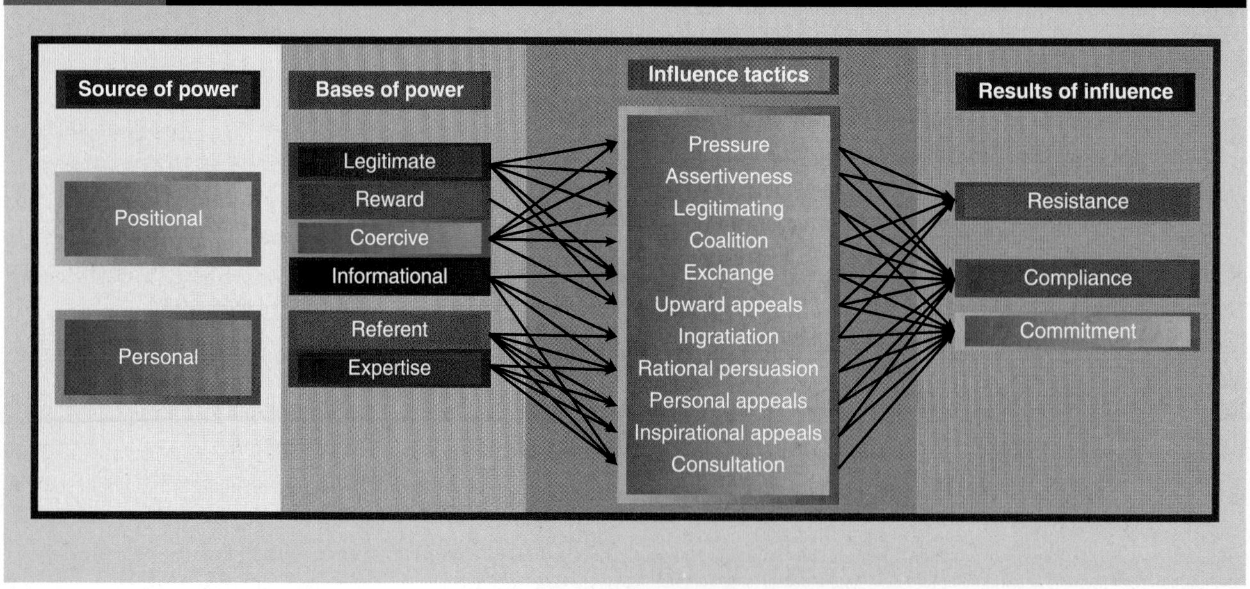

Political Skill

Political skill is the ability to accomplish things through interpersonal relationships outside the formally prescribed organizational mechanisms. More simply put, it is having the ability to leverage power and use influence to achieve desired outcomes. It is a distinct interpersonal attribute that is important for managerial success.[39] Research suggests that that political skill has a positive effect on team performance, trust for the leader, and support for the leader.[40] But political skill is not just for managers: Individuals who have the ability to accurately understand others and use this knowledge to influence others effectively are more likely to achieve personal goals and increase their resources in personal and organizational settings.

Political skill is made up of four components: social awareness, interpersonal influence, networking ability, and sincerity.[41] *Social awareness* refers to the accurate perception and evaluation of social situations. Socially astute individuals understand the behaviour and motives of others, are better able to anticipate and respond to these behaviours, and are able to manage social situations in ways that present them in the most favourable light. *Interpersonal influence* describes an individual's ability to influence and engage others. Individuals with high levels of interpersonal influence are able to put others at ease, establish rapport, and communicate with others in positive and supportive ways. *Networking ability* is an individual's skill at building relationships with others. People who are good at networking develop and retain extensive professional and social networks, and are effective at building successful alliances and coalitions. Finally, *sincerity* refers to an individual's ability to be authentic and genuine with others. Individuals who are sincere inspire more confidence and trust, making them more successful at influencing other people.[42]

#HOT #TREND

How Much Klout Do You Have?

How much influence do you have on social media? Klout is a mobile app that uses social media analytics to rank its users according to their online social influence, using many social media platforms, but specifically Facebook, Twitter, LinkedIn, and Instagram. Klout measures more than 12 billion user signals every day, such as number of followers, retweets, and unique mentions from various social media sites, and compiles data on each user. Users are given a numerical score between 1 and 100, with higher scores corresponding to higher levels of influence. Klout also measures "true reach," which is the size of a user's engaged audience; "amplification," which measures how likely one's messages will be mentioned or retweeted; and "network impact," which measures how influential a person's network is.

SOURCE: A. Rao, N. Spasojevic, Z. Li, and T. Dsouza. "Klout Score: Measuring Influence across Multiple Social Networks," presented at Big Data, 2015.

11-6 MANAGING POLITICAL BEHAVIOUR

Politics is an undeniable and unavoidable component of organizational behavior. Competition for resources combined with motivated self-interest invariably leads to political manoeuvring in virtually all group settings, and thus politics and political behaviours cannot be eliminated from any organizational setting. Managing political behaviour at work *is* important, though, because the perception of dysfunctional political behaviour can lead to dissatisfaction[43]: When employees perceive that there are dominant interest groups or cliques at work, or when they believe that the organization's reward practices are influenced by who you know rather than how well you perform, they are less satisfied.[44] Managers can take a proactive stance and manage the political behaviour that inevitably occurs[45] through open communication, clear expectations about performance and rewards, participative decision-making practices, work group cooperation, effective management of scarce resources, and a supportive organizational climate.

Open communication is the key to managing political behaviour. Lack of communication leads to low trust, role ambiguity, and uncertainty, and these factors tend to increase political behaviours. One way to open communication with respect to political behaviours is to clarify the sanctioned and nonsanctioned political behaviours in the organization. Communication can also serve to clarify expectations regarding performance through the use of clear, quantifiable goals and through the establishment of a clear connection between goal accomplishment and rewards.[46]

Participative management can also help manage political behaviour. Often, people engage in political behaviour when they feel excluded from decision-making processes in the organization. By including others in decision making,

political skill The ability to get things done through favourable interpersonal relationships outside formally prescribed organizational mechanisms.

behind-the-scenes manoeuvring can be significantly curtailed. Encouraging cooperation is another strategy for managing political behaviour whereby managers can instill a unity of purpose among work teams, rewarding cooperative behaviour and implementing activities that emphasize the integration of team efforts toward common goals.[47]

When individuals feel that reward systems are zero-sum, or that resources are limited, they may be motivated to engage in political behaviours in order to secure their resources or position within the organization. Managing resources appropriately can reduce these unwanted political behaviours. Clarifying the resource allocation process and making sure that the connection between performance and rewards is explicit can help discourage dysfunctional political behaviour.

Creating a supportive organizational climate is another way to manage political behaviour effectively. A supportive climate allows employees to discuss controversial issues promptly and openly, and this prevents the issue from festering and potentially causing friction among employees.[48] A successful leader must recognize internal powerbrokers who have influence over their peers, and cultivate strong relationships with those individuals in order to manage them and prevent them from working in opposition.

Sharing Power: Empowerment

Another positive strategy for managing political behaviour is **empowerment**—sharing power within an organization by giving employees the authority or power to make their own decisions with respect to their work role or task. As modern organizations have grown flatter and have eliminated layers of management, the concept of empowerment has become more important.[49] Empowerment describes the movement away from hierarchical authority structures toward self-determination and autonomy, giving individuals (and teams) the ability and responsibility to act on their own authority, and at their own discretion. Empowerment distributes control over resources to the employees actually performing the work, allowing them to make the decisions that best use their skills and abilities to improve service or performance.

An individual must have or believe four things in order to feel empowered: meaning, competence, self-determination, and impact.[50] *Meaning* describes sense of purpose or personal connection to the work. People who are empowered believe that their work is important. If individuals don't care about their work, they cannot feel empowered. *Competence* is an individual's belief that he or she has the skills and ability to do the job well. Without a sense of competence, people feel inadequate and abandoned, not empowered. *Self-determination* is the feeling of having control over the way work is accomplished. Employees who do not feel that they are controlling work flow, or who feel that they are just following orders, cannot feel empowered. Finally, *impact* is an individual's belief that his or her contributions matter to the organization, and he or she can influence the system or the process in which he or she works. Without a sense of contributing, individuals feel like they don't matter and cannot feel empowered.[51]

empowerment Giving employees the authority or power to make their own decisions.

Empowerment is easy to advocate but difficult to put into practice. Because the workforce is so diverse, managers should recognize that some employees are more ready for empowerment than others, and some positions are more readily empowered than others. Fortunately, empowerment is not a one-size approach. Empowerment can and should be customized. The manager must diagnose situations and determine the degree of empowerment to extend to employees. "[Power] in empowered organizations is not 'shared power,' where all decisions are made by consensus. It is not about throwing out procedures and letting everyone do their

IN ACTION

Gucci: Fine Fashion, Finer Management

Robert Polet, CEO of the Gucci Group, strongly believes in empowering his design teams, so each of Gucci's brands operates autonomously to a large extent. Each team is captained by a creative director who oversees the creative process of design, while a CEO for each team oversees the packaging and advertising part of the business. Polet has articulated a clear vision for Gucci and translated it into clearly defined roles and responsibilities for key organizational players whom he has empowered to carry out the responsibilities effectively. Most importantly, Polet has been adept at emphasizing the importance of the Gucci brand over people associated with it so that employees never lose sight of organizational goals. Polet's principles have worked. Since his arrival at Gucci, income is up 44 percent and some of the company's unprofitable brands are making a turnaround.

SOURCE: J. L. Yang, "Managing Top Talent at Gucci Group," *Fortune*, July 17, 2007, from http://archive.fortune.com/magazines/fortune/fortune_archive/2007/07/23/100135662/index.htm?postversion=2007071809, April 25, 2018.

own thing."[52] Rather, "[organizational] empowerment is about ensuring that people can influence decisions commensurate with their positions and interests in the organization."[53]

Managers must first have and then express confidence in employees and set high performance expectations. Positive expectations can go a long way toward enabling good performance. Managers must also create opportunities for employees to actively participate in decision making. This means participation in both voice and choice. Employees should not just be asked to contribute their opinions about any issue; they should also have a vote in the decision that is made.

Next, managers should examine and, where possible, remove bureaucratic constraints that stifle autonomy. Often, organizations have antiquated rules and policies that prevent employees from managing themselves. These restrictions often include unnecessary signature requirements, where the manager has to sign off on certain contracts or resources, or limitations on physical access to resources where managers control access to resources such as supply closets. Finally, managers should set inspirational and meaningful goals, and then step back, to allow empowered employees to achieve them.

Managing Up

One of the least discussed aspects of power and politics is the relationship between an individual and his or her boss. This is a crucial relationship because one's boss is the most important link to the rest of the organization.[54] Virtually everyone has a boss, yet few people consider practising their influence tactics and actively managing their power bases in this context. The employee–boss relationship is one of mutual dependence; an individual depends on the boss to give performance feedback, provide resources, and supply critical information. The boss depends on the individual for performance, information, and support. As a mutual relationship, individuals should take an active role in managing up. Using the skills and techniques discussed in this chapter and applying them to one's supervisor can help increase one's power in the organization.

Table 11.4 shows the basic considerations for managing a relationship with the boss. The first step is to try to increase awareness about what motivates the boss's behaviours and expectations. It is naïve to expect the boss to be perfect. Everyone has strengths, weaknesses, and blind spots. Attempt to discover directly or through observation what the boss's preferred work style is; some people prefer appointments, while others prefer an open-door policy. Once the factors that motivate the boss have been determined, they can be managed more accurately and effectively.

TABLE 11.4 MANAGING YOUR RELATIONSHIP WITH YOUR BOSS

Understand What Motivates Behaviours and Expectations
Their goals and objectives.
The pressures they face.
Their strengths, weaknesses, and blind spots.
Their preferred work and communication style.
Assess Yourself and Your Needs, Including
Your own strengths and weaknesses.
Your preferred work and communication style.
Your predisposition toward dependence on authority figures.
Develop and Maintain a Relationship That
Fits both your needs and styles.
Is characterized by mutual expectations.
Keeps your boss informed.
Is based on dependability and honesty.
Selectively uses your boss's time and resources.

SOURCE: Reprinted by permission of Harvard Business Review. From "Managing Your Boss," by J. J. Gabarro and J. P. Kotter, (May–June 1993): 155.

The second step in managing this important relationship is for the individual to assess him- or herself and his or her own needs much in the same way. Taking the time to assess one's strengths, and weaknesses, determining one's work and communication style, and assessing how one relates to authority figures can help employees to establish rapport and begin to communicate in positive and effective ways.

Once an employee has a basic awareness of the boss's expectations and preferences, and has done a self-analysis to determine his or her own needs and expectations, the next step is to work to develop an effective relationship that accommodates both parties' needs and work and communication styles. Clarifying goals and developing a plan for work objectives can be done explicitly or implicitly and can have positive impacts on rapport and communication.[55] The employee–boss relationship must be based on dependability and honesty. This means giving and receiving positive and negative feedback objectively. Finally, employees need to remember that the boss is on the same team. The golden rule is to make the boss look good because workers expect the boss to do the same for them.

STUDY TOOLS 11

IN THE BOOK YOU CAN ...

- ☐ Rip out the **Chapter Review card** at the end of the book to review Key Concepts and Key Terms.
- ☐ Take a "What about You?" Quiz related to material in the chapter.
- ☐ Read additional cases in the Mini Case and Shopify Running Case sections.

ONLINE YOU CAN ...

NELSON.COM/STUDENT

- ☐ Take a "What about You?" Quiz related to material in the chapter.
- ☐ Test your understanding with a quick Multiple-Choice Pre-Test quiz.
- ☐ Read the eBook, which includes discussion points for questions posed in the Cases.
- ☐ Watch Videos related to chapter content.
- ☐ Use the available Flashcards and Matching Quizzes to test your understanding of key terms and concepts.
- ☐ See how much you've learned by taking a Post-Test.

WHAT ABOUT YOU?

How Politically Skilled Are You?

Using the following 7-point scale, please place the number on the blank before each item that best describes how much you agree with each statement about yourself.

1 = strongly disagree

2 = disagree

3 = slightly disagree

4 = neutral

5 = slightly agree

6 = agree

7 = strongly agree

____ **1.** I spend a lot of time and effort at work networking with others.

____ **2.** I am able to make most people feel comfortable and at ease around me.

____ **3.** I am able to communicate easily and effectively with others.

____ **4.** It is easy for me to develop good rapport with most people.

____ **5.** I understand people very well.

____ **6.** I am good at building relationships with influential people at work.

____ **7.** I am particularly good at sensing the motivations and hidden agendas of others.

____ **8.** When communicating with others, I try to be genuine in what I say and do.

____ **9.** I have developed a large network of colleagues and associates at work whom I can call on for support when I really need to get things done.

____ **10.** At work, I know a lot of important people and am well connected.

____ **11.** I spend a lot of time at work developing connections with others.

____ **12.** I am good at getting people to like me.

____ **13.** It is important that people believe I am sincere in what I say and do.

____ **14.** I try to show a genuine interest in other people.

____ **15.** I am good at using my connections and network to make things happen at work.

____ **16.** I have good intuition or savvy about how to present myself to others.

____ **17.** I always seem to instinctively know the right things to say or do to influence others.

____ **18.** I pay close attention to people's facial expressions.

A higher score indicates better political skill than a lower score.

SOURCE: G. Ferris, S. L. Davidson, and P. L. Perrewe, *Political Skill at Work: Impact on Work Effectiveness* (Davies-Black Publishing: Boston, MA. 2005). © Cengage Learning

MINI CASE

Sexual Harassment in Parliament

Sexual harassment is an unfortunately common occurrence in organizational settings, and our nation's leaders are not exempt. Members of Canada's Parliament have come forward to share their stories of sexual misconduct. In a survey conducted in December 2017, 58 percent of female respondents said that they had personally been the target of various forms of sexual harassment. One MP, who chose to remain anonymous, explained that while she has never personally experienced sexual harassment on Parliament Hill, she has heard her male colleagues make inappropriate comments and jokes about other women, even after she explained that the jokes and comments were offensive and unwelcome. This suggests that perhaps the anonymous MP doesn't properly understand the definition of sexual harassment, rather than that she has not personally experienced it.

NDP leader Jagmeet Singh has a zero-tolerance policy for sexual harassment behaviours within his party. Singh has publicly declared that his first response to any accusation of sexual harassment is to "believe survivors," which is parlance for accepting the allegations at face value, and assume from the outset that the incident occurred as described. When MP Erin Weir was accused of harassment, it was no surprise that the NDP leader took the allegations very seriously. But this particular story of sexual harassment is atypical.

The initial allegations of misconduct were indirectly levelled at Weir by another MP, Christine Moore: When Weir was seeking the position of caucus chair, Moore sent an email objecting to Weir's promotion saying "as a woman, I would not feel comfortable to meet with you alone." This email, with its vague and indirect accusation of impropriety, caused Singh to begin an investigation into Weir's behaviours.

The independent investigator hired by Singh found that "Mr. Weir failed to read non-verbal cues in social settings. And that his behaviour resulted in significant negative impact to the complainants." However, even Singh acknowledges that when Weir was told explicitly that his advances were unwelcome, he stopped. After meeting with Weir to discuss the issue, Singh expelled Weir from caucus because he felt that Weir was not sufficiently remorseful nor willing to accept full responsibility for the offences.

Finally, Christine Moore, the woman who originally levelled the complaint against Weir has, herself, been accused of improper sexual conduct and using her position of power to pursue a relationship with a veteran of the war in Afghanistan. It is alleged that Moore used her political position to secure a meeting with the veteran, offered him drinks, and insisted even after he refused, and then followed him back to his hotel, where she spent the night. Moore allegedly sent explicit text messages, followed him when he went on vacation, and showed up at his house before the veteran made it clear that her advances were unwelcome. In spite of the evidence against her, Christine Moore was cleared of sexual misconduct and was permitted to remain in caucus.

SOURCES: J. Smith, "MPs share stories of sexual misconduct on and off Parliament Hill," CBC News, January 2, 2018, http://www.cbc.ca/news/politics/survey-female-mps-harassment-1.4469920, accessed May 8, 2018; N. Macdonald, "Jagmeet Singh says he always believes survivors. Well, here's another one," *CBC News*, May 8, 2018, http://www.cbc.ca/news/opinion/jagmeet-singh-says-he-always-believes-survivors-well-here-s-another-one-1.4652795, accessed May 8, 2018.

Apply Your Understanding

1. What *power bases* can Jagmeet Singh use to help reduce sexual harassment on Parliament Hill?
2. Which influence tactics can victims of sexual harassment and bullying, and their allies, use to help change the behaviour of those who would abuse their power?
3. How are Moore's behaviours indicative of sexual harassment?

SHOPIFY RUNNING CASE

POLITICAL BEHAVIOUR

When protesters urged people to #DeleteShopify, arguing that products being sold through Shopify were helping Breitbart to spread hate speech and intolerance, employees at Shopify agreed. Employees made personal and professional requests to CEO Tobias Lütke to remove Breitbart, and prevent the offensive client from being able to use the vendor platform to sell ultra right wing wares.

Internal emails and open letters were written, Slack chats and meetings were held, and employees signed and delivered a petition to the CEO urging him to reconsider Shopify's stance on the issue. Employees claimed that Breitbart violated Shopify's vision statement and culture and was against everything the company stood for. Due to this pressure, Shopify hosted a town hall meeting with all employees to discuss the issue. Tobias Lütke explained that, personally, he does not like Breitbart, or their message, and has publicly announced that he would be "delighted" if Breitbart switched to another service provider. However, Lütke went on to explain that Shopify was not in the business of censoring its merchants, and that the company would remain neutral in the debate, while continuing to host Breitbart merchandise on the site. Lütke went on to say that he would respect those who felt they had to leave if they disagreed.

Kevin Van Paassen/Bloomberg via Getty Images

Many employees, particularly women, Muslims, and LGBTs, left the meeting feeling ignored and dismissed. Several employees quit the organization in protest, among them developer Tessa Thornton, who went public with her objections, tweeting that she couldn't stand the cognitive dissonance any longer.

Apply Your Understanding

1. Describe the dimensions of political behaviour exhibited in this case.
2. Describe the bases of power used by Shopify CEO Tobias Lütke.
3. Briefly discuss the influence tactics that employees attempted to use to change Shopify's position on hosting Breitbart merchandise.

Michael Shake/Shutterstock.com

12 Leadership

LEARNING OUTCOMES

After reading this chapter, you should be able to do the following:

12-1 Discuss the differences between leadership and management.

12-2 Explain the role of trait theory in describing leaders.

12-3 Describe behavioural research in the development of leadership theories.

12-4 Describe and compare three contingency theories of leadership.

12-5 Consider a transactional theory of leadership.

12-6 Discuss inspirational leadership styles.

12-7 Discuss how issues of emotional intelligence, trust, ethics, and gender affect leadership.

12-8 Define *followership* and identify different types of followers.

12-9 Synthesize historical leadership research into key guidelines for leaders.

See the end of this chapter for a list of available Study Tools, a "What about You?" Quiz, Mini Case, and the Shopify Running Case.

While the leader and the manager may both know what needs to be accomplished, it is the leader who knows how to accomplish it, and who sets about mobilizing others toward that target. A manager can move pieces on the chess board, but a leader can get the pieces to move themselves, especially over the long run. There are many theories of leadership, and while none is a universal theory of how to lead, an effective leader can learn from each of them and adapt their style to the situation, to the task, and to the followers.

12-1 LEADERSHIP VERSUS MANAGEMENT

There are few topics in Organizational Behaviour more complex, more researched, and yet less understood than leadership. It can generally be agreed that a leader's primary role is to achieve organizational objectives using organizational resources.[1] By this measure, we can assess whether someone *is* an effective leader (they either achieve results, or they do not), but there are few concrete theories as to how and why some people are able to lead while others are not. Why do some individuals inspire others to put forth their best efforts, while others inspire little but contempt? In traditional business discussions, the terms *leadership* and *management* are often used interchangeably. In discussions of organizational behaviour, however, they represent very distinct but complimentary systems of action.[2]

“Management is doing things right; leadership is doing the right things.

—Peter F. Drucker

Leadership in organizations is the process of motivating, influencing, and enabling others to contribute toward the achievement of organizational goals. Leadership involves (1) setting [or changing] the direction for the organization; (2) aligning people with that direction through communication; and (3) motivating people to action, partly through empowerment and partly through basic need gratification. Effective leaders not only control the future of the organization but also act as enablers of change in organizations. They disturb existing patterns of behaviours, promote novel ideas, and help organizational members make sense of the change process.[3] **Management** consists of controlling resources to accomplish tasks through (1) planning and budgeting, (2) organizing and staffing, and (3) controlling and problem solving.

leadership The process of motivating, influencing, and enabling others toward achievement of organizational goals.

management The process of controlling resources to accomplish tasks.

Leadership and management deliver different outcomes; management produces stability, predictability, order, and efficiency, to help the organization achieve short-term results. Leadership, on the other hand, produces change. Leadership sets long-term goals, and challenges the status quo, which moves organizations into the future. Healthy organizations need both effective leadership and good management. For much of the 20th century, good management was enough to achieve organizational success, but the changes brought by the 21st century mean that organizations can no longer rely solely on traditional management and hope to maintain their success.

Leadership Theories

A brief word about leadership theories: There are many of them! Learning Outcomes 12-2 through 12-6 attempt to break up the vast field of leadership theories into (hopefully) digestible categories. The leadership theories presented here are classified by type, but students should recognize that this is a small sampling of the many theories that exist, and that the timelines are only approximate. Finally, these theories are not mutually exclusive; as is the case with much behavioural research, new theories are built on the theories that have come before, so even though some theories have been discounted, they still deserve a brief discussion because they are the foundation of future work in the field.

Refer to the In Review card at the end of this book for a figure that encompasses all of the leadership theories presented here.

12-2 TRAIT THEORIES

The first studies of leadership began as early as the mid-1800s and began with the underlying belief that the elements that made someone a good leader were intrinsic–that good leaders were simply born with certain

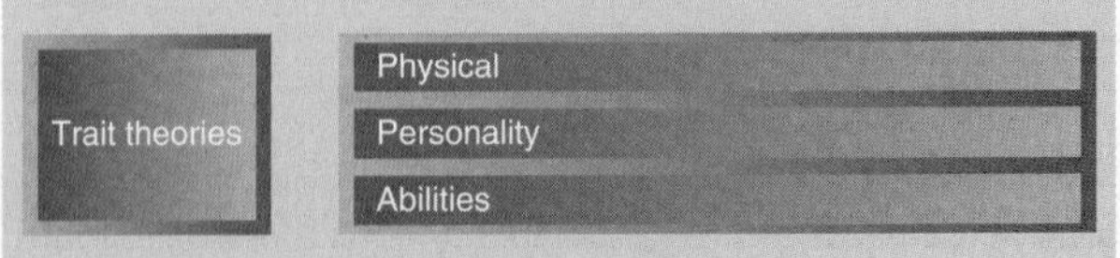

Rich Lindie/Shutterstock.com

A trait is a distinguishing quality or characteristic.

traits that made them seek out, and excel in leadership roles. A **trait** is a distinguishing quality or characteristic of a person. Trait theories attempted to identify and measure those distinguishing qualities and characteristics by focusing on physical attributes, personality characteristics, and abilities that distinguished leaders from other members of a group.[4]

Physical attributes including height, weight, physique, energy, health, appearance, and even age have been examined, and very few valid generalizations have emerged from this line of inquiry. Therefore, there is insufficient evidence to conclude that leaders can be distinguished from followers on the basis of physical attributes. Leader personality characteristics have been examined in great detail. These characteristics include (but are not limited to) originality, adaptability, introversion–extroversion, dominance, self-confidence, integrity, conviction, mood optimism, and emotional control. With regard to leader abilities, research has been conducted focusing on abilities such as social skills, intelligence, scholarship, speech fluency, cooperativeness, and insight.

Trait theory research has found some evidence that leaders may be more energetic, self-confident, emotionally stable, intelligent, cooperative, and sensitive to others than the average group member,[5] though this research is by

trait A distinguishing quality or characteristic of a person.

Narcissistic CEOs, Big Signatures

Does a large signature mean the CEO is a narcissist? A recent study indicates that it may. Researchers compared the signatures of 605 CEOs of U.S. companies from annual reports and proxy filings and analyzed the size of the signatures using a custom software program to find that larger signatures were more common among narcissists. CEOs with the largest signatures were also found to overinvest in research and development, have lower sales growth, and lower returns on investments. Despite lower financial performance, CEOs with large signatures enjoyed higher compensation than their peers, but shorter tenures.

The researchers describe narcissism as egotism, conceit, and disregard for others. Narcissistic leaders hold high opinions of themselves, belittle others, and ignore useful data and alternate opinions presented by subordinates. And narcissism is on the rise, making it more likely that you may encounter narcissists in the workplace. The best strategy may be to try to avoid working for one.

SOURCE: C. Ham, N. Seybert, and S. Wang, "Narcissism Is a Bad Sign: CEO Signature Size, Investment, and Performance," UNC Kenan-Flagler Research Paper No. 2013-1, June 4, 2014, http://ssrn.com/abstract=2144419; P. Korkki, "Bosses Who Love Them-selves," New York Times, March 8, 2015, http://www.nytimes.com/2015/03/08/business/the-perils-of-narcissists-in-the-workplace.html?_r=0, accessed May 20, 2018.

no means definitive. In short, research on trait theories has found no solid conclusions. Though there are some traits that appear to differentiate leaders from others, these traits are not universal: All leaders do not share the same set of traits, and there are plenty of people who have these traits but who are not leaders.

12-3 BEHAVIOURAL THEORIES

Behavioural theories emerged as a response to the deficiencies of the trait theories. Rather than searching for the characteristics that made a leader, behavioural theories attempt to identify the actions that leaders used to achieve results. According to the behavioural approach, people can learn to become leaders, and can improve their leadership skills by improving or changing their behaviours.

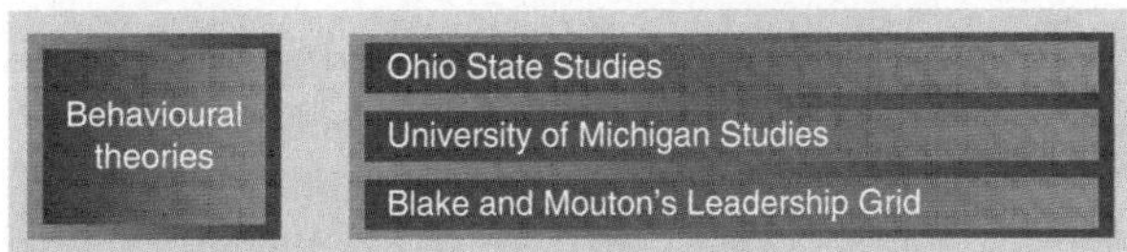

Foundations of Behavioural Research

There are two important studies that form the foundation for modern leadership theories: the Ohio State studies and the Michigan studies.

OHIO STATE STUDIES In the 1940s, the leadership research program at Ohio State University designed the Leaders Behavior Description Questionnaire (LBDQ), which attempted to identify common leadership behaviours. The questionnaire was administered to individuals ranging in backgrounds from college students to college administrators, and working in various settings from private companies to the military. After analyzing the results of the survey, researchers determined that there were two groups of behaviours that are strongly correlated: initiating structure and consideration.[6]

initiating structure Task-oriented leader behaviour aimed at defining and organizing work relationships and roles, as well as establishing clear patterns of organization and communication.

consideration Leader behaviour aimed at nurturing friendly, warm working relationships, as well as encouraging mutual trust and interpersonal respect within the work unit.

Leadership Grid® A graphical representation of a leader's concern for production *and* concern for people.

Initiating structure is leader behaviour aimed at defining, implementing, and improving organizational structure. Initiating structure is *task-oriented* behaviour focused on organizing work roles and goals, as well as establishing operating procedures and clear patterns of communication. **Consideration** is leader behaviour aimed at nurturing friendly, warm working relationships as well as encouraging mutual trust and interpersonal respect within the unit. These two leader behaviours are independent of each other. That is, a leader may be high on both, low on both, or high on one while low on the other.[7]

THE MICHIGAN STUDIES In the 1950s, studies conducted at the University of Michigan attempted to determine which leadership styles led to greater productivity and increased job satisfaction for workers. The research identified two broad leadership styles: production-oriented and employee-oriented.[8] (These findings are very similar to the Ohio State Studies findings of initiating structure and consideration behaviours.) The Michigan leadership studies also established the importance of participative leadership. A production-oriented leader created a work environment where the focus was on getting things done using close supervision or many written and unwritten rules and regulations to control behaviour. In comparison, employee-oriented leadership styles created a work environment that focused on relationships; the leader exhibited less direct supervision and established fewer rules and regulations for behaviour. The general conclusion of the studies was that less direct control allows employees to be more productive and engaged.

The Ohio State studies and the University of Michigan studies identified two critical characteristics of effective leaders: task-oriented behaviours and people-oriented behaviours.

The Leadership Grid®

The discovery that task orientation and people orientation represented two independent dimensions led to the development of Robert Blake and Jane Mouton's **Leadership Grid®** (sometimes called the management grid); a graphical representation of how a leader rates in both task and people orientations.[9] The horizontal axis of the grid is labelled *Concern for Results* (task-oriented), and the vertical axis is labelled *Concern for People* (people-oriented). Each dimension ranges from low (1) to high (9) and yields coordinates written in the form of (x,y), where the x value corresponds to the level of concern for production, and the y value corresponds to the level of concern for people. Blake and Mouton identified five distinct leadership styles

FIGURE 12.1 THE LEADERSHIP GRID®

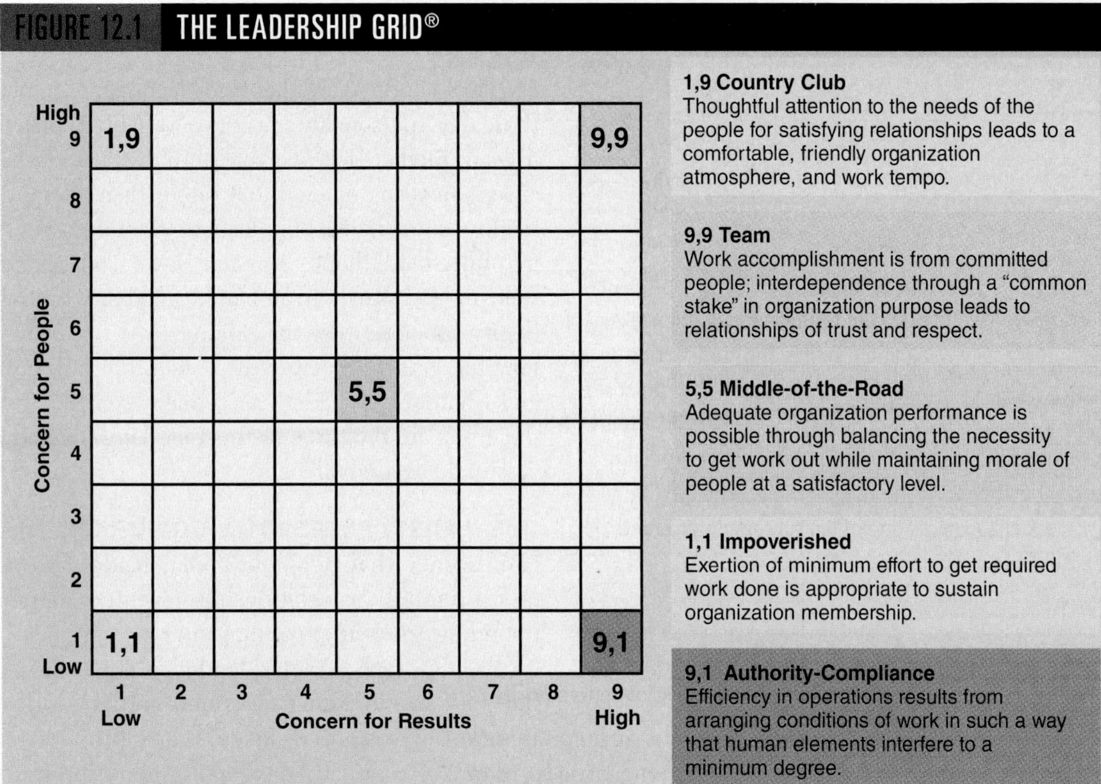

High
9
8
7
6
5
4
3
2
1
Low
Concern for People
1,9
9,9
5,5
1,1
9,1
1 2 3 4 5 6 7 8 9
Low
Concern for Results
High
1,9 Country Club
Thoughtful attention to the needs of the people for satisfying relationships leads to a comfortable, friendly organization atmosphere, and work tempo.
9,9 Team
Work accomplishment is from committed people; interdependence through a "common stake" in organization purpose leads to relationships of trust and respect.
5,5 Middle-of-the-Road
Adequate organization performance is possible through balancing the necessity to get work out while maintaining morale of people at a satisfactory level.
1,1 Impoverished
Exertion of minimum effort to get required work done is appropriate to sustain organization membership.
9,1 Authority-Compliance
Efficiency in operations results from arranging conditions of work in such a way that human elements interfere to a minimum degree.

SOURCE: © Cengage Learning / Bottom: "The Leadership Grid(r)" figure, *Paternalism Figure and Opportunism from Leadership Dilemmas Grid Solutions*, by Robert R. Blake and Anne Adams McCanse (Formerly the *Managerial Grid* by Robert R. Blake and Jane S. Mouton). Houston: Gulf Publishing Company (Grid Figure: p. 29; Paternalism Figure: p. 30, Opportunism Figure: p. 31). Copyright 1991 by Blake and Mouton, and Scientific Methods, Inc. Reproduced by permission of the owners.

corresponding to regions of the Leadership Grid®, as shown in Figure 12.1.

Impoverished (1,1) has low concern for both production and people, and is often referred to as a laissez-faire leader. This leader avoids taking sides, and stays out of conflicts; the impoverished manager does just enough to get by.

Authority-compliance (9,1) has a high concern for production, and a low concern for people, and is also known as the dictatorial leader. This leader desires tight control in order to get tasks done efficiently and considers creativity and human relations unnecessary. Authority-compliance managers may become so focused on achieving that they resort to tactics such as bullying. This form of abuse is quite common, with one in six North American workers reporting that they have been bullied by a manager.[10]

Middle-of-the-road (5,5) has balanced, medium concern for both production and people and is a compromising style where the leader attempts to balance a concern for both people and production without a commitment to either, resulting in average performance and average satisfaction.

Country club (1,9) has a low concern for production, and a high concern for people. A "country club" leader attempts to avoid conflict, and seeks to be well liked. This leader's goal is to keep people happy through good interpersonal relations, which are more important than the task.

Team (9,9) has high concern for both people and production. This leader works to motivate employees to reach their highest levels of accomplishment, and this style of leadership has been identified by Blake and Mouton as the most effective.

Behavioural theories of leadership have provided some useful insights into the dimensions of leadership; namely, that all organizations require both production and people leadership. These two functions of leadership are regarded as universal as they apply across organizations, industries, and cultures, but how they are performed and to what degree leaders focus on people versus production varies according to the situation.[11]

Like trait theories, there is no one specific behaviour or leadership style that can be applied to all situations to ensure successful outcomes.

impoverished (1,1) A leader who exerts just enough effort to get by.

authority-compliance (9,1) A leader who emphasizes efficient production.

middle-of-the-road (5,5) A leader who compromises, meeting neither production nor employee needs fully.

country club (1,9) A leader who creates a happy, comfortable work environment.

team (9,9) A leader who builds a highly productive team of committed people.

IN ACTION

How Mark Zuckerberg Hires

Facebook CEO Mark Zuckerberg thinks that hiring top talent is important. He has a rule for hiring individuals that takes the way we traditionally think about hiring and turns it upside down. Most managers may think, "Do I want this person working for me?" Instead, Zuckerberg says, "I would only hire someone to work directly for me if I would work for that person." His hiring decisions have been pretty good so far. He cites Sheryl Sandberg, Facebook's COO, as one of his successful hires and a person he would enjoy reporting to.

SOURCE: J. Bercovici, "Mark Zuckerberg Shares His Secret to Recruiting the Best Employees," *Inc.*, March 4, 2015, http://www.inc.com/jeff-bercovici/mark-zuckerberg-hiring-rule.html, accessed May 20, 2018.

12-4 CONTINGENCY THEORIES

Contingency theories were developed to investigate the criticisms levelled at trait and behavioural theories of leadership that some traits and some behaviours are more effective in certain situations and less effective in others. According to contingency theories, no leadership style is best in all situations. Instead, these theories propose that leadership outcomes may be more successful if leader traits and behaviours are considered in relation to situational contingencies. Success depends upon a number of variables, including the leader's preferred style, the capabilities and behaviours of the followers, and aspects of the situation. We examine three such theories, including Fiedler's contingency theory, path–goal theory, and situational leadership theory.

least-preferred coworker (LPC) The person with whom the leader works the least well.

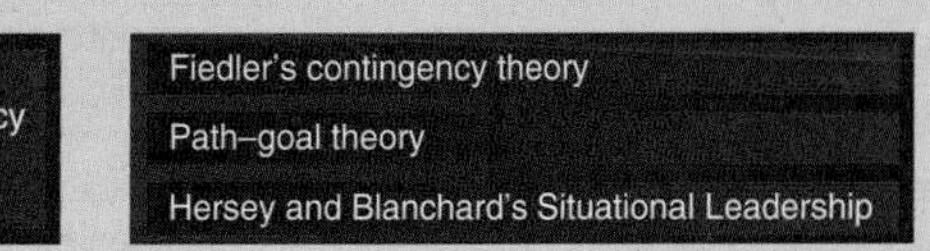

"Leadership is the art of getting someone else to do something you want done because he wants to do it.
—Dwight D. Eisenhower"

Fiedler's Contingency Theory

Fiedler's contingency theory of leadership emphasizes the leader's personality as a critical variable in their ability to lead. Fiedler believed that an individual's leadership style is unchanging, and that rather than attempting to modify one's behaviour, leaders should instead seek to understand their particular style, and match that style to the situation at hand.[12] Fiedler's contingency theory proposes that in addition to the leader's style, how the group perceives the leader, the task involved, and whether the leader can actually exert control over the group are the three factors that determine how successful the leader will be.

THE LEAST PREFERRED COWORKER Fiedler's contingency theory assumes that leaders are either task oriented or relationship oriented, depending upon how the leaders obtain their primary need gratification.[13] (Task-oriented leaders are primarily gratified by accomplishing tasks and getting work done. Relationship-oriented leaders are primarily gratified by developing good interpersonal relationships.) Fiedler assesses leadership orientation (which is assumed to be fixed, and either people-oriented or task-oriented) using the Least Preferred Coworker (LPC) scale.[14] The LPC scale is a projective technique that asks the leader to think about the people they work with, and then describe the person with whom they work the least well (their **least preferred coworker (LPC)**, in other words). On a scale of 1 to 8, the leader is asked to describe this least preferred coworker using 16 opposing measures of personality. For instance:

Pleasant	8 • 7 • 6 • 5 • 4 • 3 • 2 • 1	Unpleasant
Unfriendly	1 • 2 • 3 • 4 • 5 • 6 • 7 • 8	Friendly
Rejecting	1 • 2 • 3 • 4 • 5 • 6 • 7 • 8	Accepting
Tense	1 • 2 • 3 • 4 • 5 • 6 • 7 • 8	Relaxed
Supportive	8 • 7 • 6 • 5 • 4 • 3 • 2 • 1	Hostile
Open	8 • 7 • 6 • 5 • 4 • 3 • 2 • 1	Guarded
Insincere	1 • 2 • 3 • 4 • 5 • 6 • 7 • 8	Sincere

Scores are calculated based on the numerical value that leaders ascribed to each component of their LPC. Notice that positive terms have a higher value than negative terms. Leaders who describe their least preferred coworker in positive terms will have a higher numerical value, and are thus classified as high LPC, or relationship-oriented, leaders. Those who describe their least preferred coworker in negative terms will have a low numerical value, and are classified as low LPC, or task-oriented leaders.[15]

The LPC scale is not about the least preferred coworker at all, but is designed to measure the leadership style of the person who is taking the test and is quite controversial in organizational behavioural research.[16] The LPC score has been critiqued conceptually and methodologically because it is a projective technique with low measurement reliability.

SITUATIONAL FAVOURABLENESS Situational favourableness describes the leader's ability to exert control over the group. Leaders with situational control are able to ensure that their demands are carried out, while leaders without situational control cannot exert their authority over the rest of the group. Situational control is critical for leadership effectiveness, and is broken down into three components: task structure, position power, and leader–member relations.[17] Based on these three dimensions, the situation is either favourable or unfavourable for the leader.

Task structure describes how well group tasks are clearly defined, and refers to the number and clarity of rules, regulations, and procedures for getting the work done. **Position power** refers to the leader's legitimate authority to evaluate and reward performance, punish errors, and demote group members. Finally, **leader–member relations** describes the degree of trust, respect, and confidence that exists between the leader and the subordinates.

A favourable leadership situation is one with a structured task for the work group, strong position power for the leader, and good leader–member relations. In contrast, an unfavourable leadership situation is one with an unstructured task, weak position power for the leader, and moderately poor leader–member relations. Between these two extremes, the leadership situation has varying degrees of moderate favourableness for the leader.

	Favourable Situation	Unfavourable Situation
Task Structure	Structured	Unstructured
Position Power	Strong	Weak
Leader–Member Relations	Good	Poor

LEADERSHIP EFFECTIVENESS Contingency theory suggests that both low and high LPC leaders can be effective if placed in the right situation.[18] Specifically, low LPC (task-oriented) leaders are most effective in either very favourable or very unfavourable leadership situations. In contrast, high LPC (relationship-oriented) leaders are most effective in situations of intermediate favourableness. Research has shown that relationship-oriented leaders can perform well in leading new product development teams by encouraging team learning and innovativeness, which helps products get to market faster. In short, the right team leader can help get creative new products out the door faster, while a mismatch between the leader and the situation can have the opposite effect.[19]

What happens when a low LPC leader is in a moderately favourable situation or when a high LPC leader is in a highly favourable or highly unfavourable situation? According to the theory, leadership style is fixed, so Fiedler recommends that the leader's situation be changed to fit the leader's style.[20] A moderately favourable situation would be reengineered to be more favourable and therefore more suitable for the low LPC leader. A highly favourable or highly unfavourable situation would be changed to one that is moderately favourable and more suitable for the high LPC leader.

Path–Goal Theory

Martin Evans and Robert House developed the path–goal theory of leader effectiveness based on the expectancy theory of motivation (see Chapter 5 for a discussion of expectancy theory).[21] This theory posits that the basic role of the leader is to clear the subordinate's path to the goal and that, through enabling others, the leader forms a connection between subordinate goals and the organization's goals. Path–goal theory proposes that a leader's role is to provide what is missing in the situational circumstance by examining the nature of the task, the operating environment, and subordinate skills and abilities to determine which of the following four leader behaviours are best suited to improving subordinate performance and satisfaction. The four leader behaviours are directive, supportive, achievement-oriented, and participative.[22]

task structure The degree of clarity, or ambiguity, in the work activities assigned to the group.

position power The authority associated with the leader's formal position in the organization.

leader–member relations The quality of interpersonal relationships among a leader and the group members.

The *directive* style is used when the leader must give specific guidance about work tasks, schedule work, and let followers know what is expected. Directive leadership achieves positive results when the task is ambiguous but can have a negative impact on subordinates when the task is clear or routine. The *supportive* style is used when the leader needs to express concern for followers' well-being and social status. Supportive leadership increases the satisfaction for employees who work on tasks that are stressful, unpleasant, or frustrating. The *participative* style is used when the leader must engage in joint decision-making activities with followers. Participative leadership allows subordinates to be involved in decision making, which promotes satisfaction. The *achievement-oriented* style is used when the leader must set challenging goals for followers and show strong confidence in those followers. Achievement-oriented leadership encourages high performance by setting challenging goals, which can improve confidence. The key concepts in the theory are shown in Figure 12.2.

In selecting the appropriate leader behaviour style, the leader must consider:

SITUATIONAL FACTORS

- Ability level describes the employee's skills and aptitudes as they relate to performing tasks and achieving goals.
- Authoritarianism, which is the degree to which employees prefer to be told what to do, and how to do a job.
- Locus of control is the extent to which employees believe they have control over goal achievement (internal locus of control) or that goal achievement is controlled by outside forces (external locus of control).

ENVIRONMENTAL FACTORS

- Task structure describes the repetitiveness of the job.
- Work group describes the relationships between followers.
- Formal authority describes the extent of the leader's position power.

Consider two cases: first, where the followers are inexperienced and working on an ambiguous, unstructured task. The leader in this situation might best use a directive style. Next, consider followers who are highly trained professionals, and the task is a difficult, yet achievable one. The leader in this situation might best use an achievement-oriented style. The path–goal theory assumes that leaders adapt their behaviour and style to fit the characteristics of the followers and the environment in which they work.

Actual tests of the path–goal theory and its propositions have yielded conflicting results.[23] Path–goal theory has intuitive appeal and reinforces the idea that the appropriate leadership style depends on both the work situation and the followers; however, it is an autocratic theory that assumes that group members do not know what is best for them, and that they require the leader to show the way. The whole theory is based on the leader's interpretation of the situation, and if the leader is flawed, or if the leader is removed from the equation for some reason, path–goal theory suggests that the whole system could fail.

FIGURE 12.2 THE PATH–GOAL THEORY OF LEADERSHIP

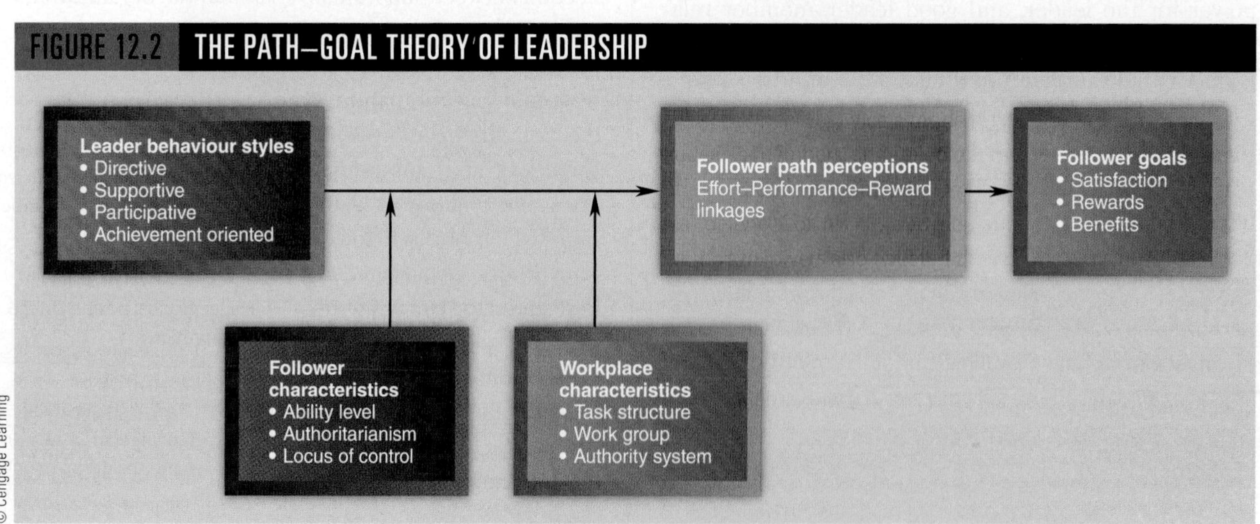

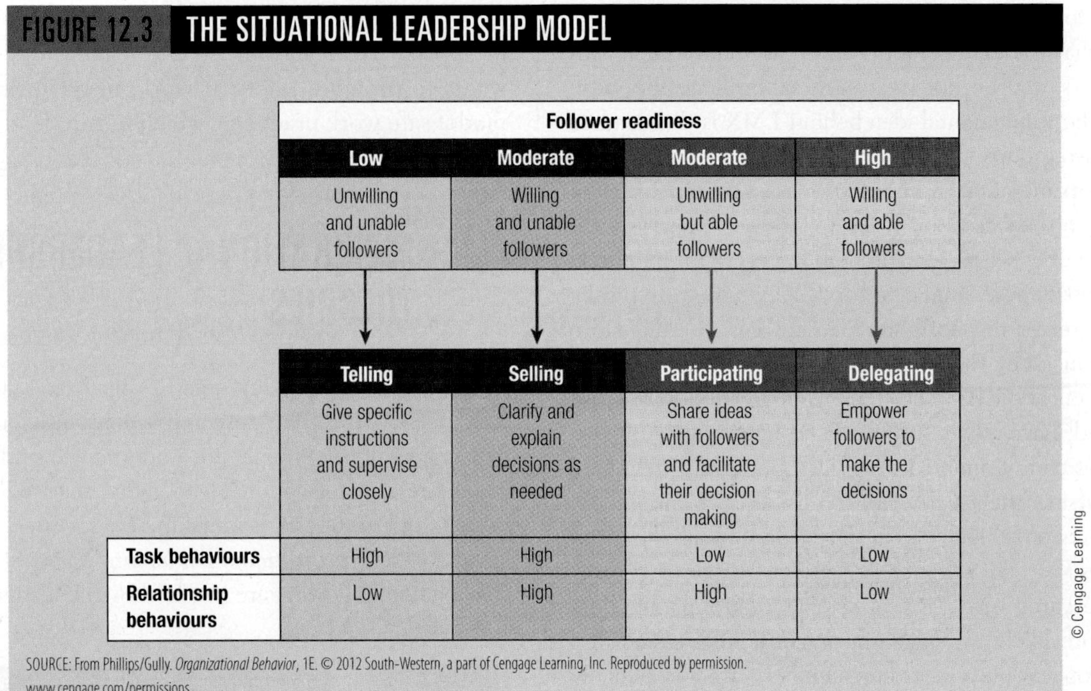

Follower readiness
Low
Moderate
Moderate
High
Unwilling and unable followers
Willing and unable followers
Unwilling but able followers
Willing and able followers
Telling
Selling
Participating
Delegating
Give specific instructions and supervise closely
Clarify and explain decisions as needed
Share ideas with followers and facilitate their decision making
Empower followers to make the decisions
Task behaviours
High
High
Low
Low
Relationship behaviours
Low
High
High
Low
© Cengage Learning

FIGURE 12.3 THE SITUATIONAL LEADERSHIP MODEL

SOURCE: From Phillips/Gully. *Organizational Behavior*, 1E. © 2012 South-Western, a part of Cengage Learning, Inc. Reproduced by permission. www.cengage.com/permissions.

Hersey-Blanchard Situational Leadership® Model

The Situational Leadership® model, developed by Paul Hersey and Kenneth Blanchard, suggests that the leader's behaviour should be adjusted to the maturity level of the followers.[24] The model uses the two dimensions of leader behaviour that have been established by behavioural research (task and relationship oriented) and contrasts leadership styles against follower readiness, which is determined using the follower's ability and willingness to complete a given task. Follower readiness is broken down into four levels depending on the follower's ability and willingness to complete the task: low, where group members are unwilling and unable; low-moderate, where employees are willing but unable; moderate where members are unwilling but able; and high, where members are both willing and able. These levels of readiness are shown in Figure 12.3. According to the Situational Leadership® model, a leader should use a *telling* style when a follower is unable and unwilling to do a certain task. This style involves providing instructions and closely monitoring performance. As such, the telling style involves considerable task behaviour and low relationship behaviour. When a follower is unable but willing to do a task, the leader can use the *selling* style in which there is high task behaviour and high relationship behaviour. In this case, the leader explains decisions and provides opportunities for the employee to seek clarification or help. Sometimes a follower will be able to complete a task but may seem unwilling or insecure about doing so. In these cases, a *participating* style is warranted, which involves high relationship but low task behaviour. The leader in this case encourages the follower to participate in decision making. Finally, for tasks in which a follower is able and willing, the leader is able to use a *delegating* style, characterized by low task behaviour and low relationship behaviour. In this case, follower readiness is high, and low levels of leader involvement (task or relationship) are needed.

The Situational Leadership® model is simple and easy to apply, which makes it a useful assessment tool when deciding what leadership style to use. Maturity and competence of group members are often overlooked in discussions of leadership yet have critical implications for the leader's effectiveness. The model, however, does not have a central hypotheses that can be tested, which could make it a more valid, reliable theory of leadership.[25]

12-5 TRANSACTIONAL THEORIES

Leader–Member Exchange (LMX)

Leader–member exchange theory, or LMX, is a descriptive theory of leadership that focuses on how people

relate to and interact with one another. LMX recognizes that leaders may form different relationships with followers, and do not treat each subordinate the same way. The fundamental idea behind LMX is that leaders form two groups of followers: in-groups and out-groups. In-group members have a better relationship with the leader, often based on trust and respect that extends beyond the work environment.[26] In-group members tend to be more similar to the leader, and are typically given greater responsibilities, more rewards, and more attention. They work within the leader's inner circle of communication. As a result, in-group members are more satisfied, have lower turnover, and have higher organizational commitment. In contrast, out-group members are outside the circle and receive less attention and fewer rewards. They are managed by formal rules and policies.[27]

Research on LMX shows that in-group members are more likely to engage in organizational citizenship behaviour, while out-group members are more likely to retaliate against the organization.[28] One interesting finding is that more frequent communication with the boss may either help or hurt a worker's performance ratings, depending on whether the worker is in the in-group or the out-group. Among the in-group, more frequent communication generally leads to higher performance ratings, while members of the out-group who communicate more often with the superior tend to receive lower performance ratings.[29]

Employees who enjoy more frequent contact with the boss also have a better understanding of the boss's expectations. Such agreement tends to lead to better performance by the employee and fewer misunderstandings between employer and employee.[30] In-group members are also more likely to support the values of the organization and to become models of appropriate behaviour. If the leader, for example, wants to promote safety at work, in-group members model safe work practices, which in turn lead to a climate of workplace safety.[31]

In-group members are more likely to engage in organizational citizenship behaviour.

12-6 INSPIRATIONAL LEADERSHIP THEORIES

Leadership is an exciting area of organizational behaviour, one in which new research is constantly emerging. Three new developments are important to understand. These are transformational leadership, charismatic leadership, and authentic leadership. These three theories can be called *inspirational leadership theories* because in each one, followers are inspired by the leader to perform well.

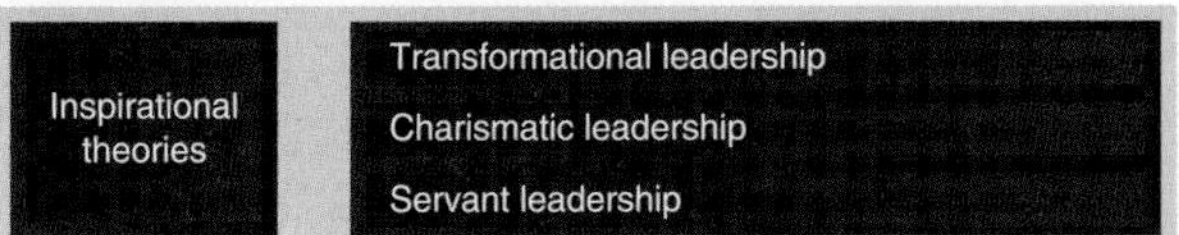

TRANSFORMATIONAL LEADERSHIP Transactional leaders are those who use rewards and punishment to strike deals with followers and shape their behaviour. In contrast, transformational leaders inspire and excite followers to high levels of performance.[32] Transformational leaders appeal to ideals and moral values such as justice, equality, peace, and humanitarianism. They rely on their personal attributes instead of their official position to manage followers, and there is some evidence that transformational leadership can be learned.[33]

Transformational leadership requires trust on the part of followers, who must respect and admire their leader. The leader is charged with developing a vision, establishing trust and commitment, making followers aware of the importance and value of organizational outcomes, and inspiring members to forgo their own self-interest for the sake of the team.[34]

As North American organizations increasingly operate in a global economy, and as organizations move beyond command and control style management, there is a greater demand for leaders who can practise transformational leadership by converting their visions into reality and by inspiring followers to perform above and beyond the call of duty.[35]

Leaders can be both transformational and transactional.[36] Transformational leadership adds to the effects of transactional leadership, but exceptional transactional leadership cannot substitute for transformational

IN ACTION

Starbucks' Transformational Leadership

Howard Schultz, founder and chairman of Starbucks Coffee, is the transformational leader and visionary heart of Starbucks. He has grown his firm from a small specialty coffee bar into one of the best-known brands in the world. With the firm hoping to continue its rapid growth pace of 25–30 percent per year, Schultz's ability to develop new leaders within the firm (which helped Starbucks get where it is today) will be sorely tested. But given the enormous market for coffee worldwide (Starbucks currently has less than 10 percent of the market), the potential for further growth exists if the company can develop the people to tap it.

SOURCE: K. Taylor, "From Brooklyn to Billionaire: The Story of How Howard Schultz Transformed Starbucks Into an $84 Billion Business," *Inc.*, December 13, 2017, https://www.inc.com/business-insider/howard-schultz-chairman-former-ceo-starbucks-successful-billionaire-coffee.html, accessed May 20, 2018.

leadership.[37] Transformational leadership encourages followers to set goals congruent with their authentic interests and values. As a result, followers see their work as important and their goals as aligned with who they are.[38]

CHARISMATIC LEADERSHIP Steve Jobs, the late pioneer behind the Macintosh computer, the music download market, iPods, iPads, and iPhones, had an uncanny ability to create a vision and convince others to become part of it. This was evidenced by Apple's success despite its major blunders in the desktop computer wars. Jobs's unique ability was so powerful that Apple employees coined a term in the 1980s for it—the *reality-distortion field*. This expression is used to describe the persuasive ability and peculiar charisma of managers like Steve Jobs. This reality-distortion field allowed Jobs to convince even skeptics that his plans were worth supporting, no matter how unworkable they appeared. Those close to such managers become passionately committed to possibly "insane" projects, without regard to the practicality of their implementation or competitive forces in the marketplace.[39]

> "You have to be burning with an idea, or a problem, or a wrong that you want to right. If you're not passionate enough from the start, you'll never stick it out.
>
> —Steve Jobs

Charismatic leadership occurs when a leader uses the force of personal abilities and talents to have profound and extraordinary effects on followers.[40] Charismatic leaders articulate ideological goals that are very different from the status quo, but still closely aligned to the mission of the group, as well as to shared values and aspirations of followers. They communicate high expectations of subordinate performance, and at the same time, express confidence in follower abilities. By creating a compelling vision of what the future could look like, charismatic leaders inspire enthusiasm and dedication among followers. Some scholars classify transformational leadership and charismatic leadership together, but charisma goes beyond leadership qualities, to inspire major changes in attitude, assumptions, and commitment.[41]

Seven attributes contribute to charismatic leadership[42]: (1) Extremity of vision—charismatic leaders are more likely to inspire visions that are very different from the status quo; (2) High personal risk—a leader who makes self-sacrifices and incurs high costs to achieve the vision they support is more likely to be viewed as charismatic; (3) Use of unconventional strategies—in order to achieve drastic change, unusual steps must be taken; (4) Accurate assessment of the situation—the inherent risks associated with drastic changes require that the leader have the skills and expertise to make a realistic assessment of the constraints and opportunities they are confronted with; (5) Communication of self-confidence—leaders must be confident about their vision and their paths to achieving it; (6) Use of personal power—leaders must influence followers with power based on expert and referent power in order to be considered charismatic; and (7) Follower disenchantment—charismatic leaders emerge when there is a crisis situation, or when followers are dissatisfied with the status quo. It is this disenchantment that makes the leader's vision and unconventional strategies appealing.

Organizational behaviourists debate whether charisma is a trait that one is born with, or a skill that can be learned and developed.

Charismatic leadership is not always a force for good. Researchers have attempted to demystify charismatic leadership and distinguish

charismatic leadership A leader's use of personal abilities and talents in order to have profound and extraordinary effects on followers.

its two faces.[43] The ugly face of charisma is revealed in the personalized power motivations of Adolf Hitler in Nazi Germany and James Jones of the People's Temple cult; both men led their followers to struggle, conflict, and death. The positive face of charisma can be seen in Prime Minister Justin Trudeau's movement toward equality and former U.S. President Barack Obama's "rock-star quality" that inspired a nation to hope for change. In each case, followers perceived the leader as imbued with a unique vision and unique abilities to lead.

Despite the sometimes warm emotions charismatic leaders can evoke, some charismatic leaders are narcissists who listen only to those who agree with them and do not seek advice from those who disagree.[44] Although charismatic leaders with socialized power motivation are concerned about the collective well-being of their followers, charismatic leaders with a personalized power motivation are driven by the need for personal gain and glorification.[45]

Charismatic leadership styles are associated with several positive outcomes. One study reported that firms headed by more charismatic leaders outperformed other firms, particularly in difficult economic times. Perhaps even more important, charismatic leaders were able to raise more outside financial support for their firms than noncharismatic leaders, meaning that charisma at the top may translate to greater funding at the bottom.[46]

SERVANT LEADERSHIP Robert Greenleaf was director of management research at AT&T for many years. He believed that leaders should serve employees, customers, and the community, and his essays are the basis for today's view called *servant leadership*. His personal and professional philosophy was that leaders lead by serving others. Other tenets of servant leadership are that work exists for the person as much as the person exists for work, and that servant leaders try to find out the will of the group and lead based on that. Servant leaders are also stewards who consider leadership a trust and desire to leave the organization in better shape for future generations.[47] Although Greenleaf's writings were completed 30 years ago, many have now been republished and are becoming more popular.

12-7 IMPORTANT CONCEPTS IN LEADERSHIP

Theories of leadership have thus far been unable to completely and accurately describe the process of leadership in all situations, but essential components that contribute to effective leadership have been discovered.

Emotional Intelligence

It has been suggested that effective leaders possess high levels of emotional intelligence, which is the ability to recognize and manage emotions in oneself and in others. (See Chapter 4 for a complete discussion.) Emotional intelligence is made up of several competencies, including self-awareness, empathy, adaptability, and self-confidence. Emotional intelligence affects the way leaders make decisions. Under high stress, leaders with higher emotional intelligence tend to keep their cool and make better decisions, while leaders with low emotional intelligence make poor decisions and lose their effectiveness.[48] While most people gain emotional intelligence as they age, not everyone starts with an equal amount. Fortunately, emotional intelligence can be learned. With honest feedback from coworkers and ongoing guidance, almost any leader can improve emotional intelligence and, with it, the ability to lead in times of adversity.[49]

Some researchers argue that emotional intelligence is more important for effective leadership than either IQ or technical skills,[50] though others insist that claims about the importance of emotional intelligence are "hyperbolic" and unwarranted.[51] Research on emotional intelligence is only 20 years old, so much more work needs to be done to determine the nature of the relationship between leadership and emotional intelligence, though there appears to be a correlation.

Trust

Trust is an essential element in leadership. Trust is the willingness to be vulnerable to the actions of another.[52] This means that followers believe that their leader will act with the followers' welfare in mind. Trustworthiness is also one of the competencies in emotional intelligence. Trust among top management team members facilitates strategy implementation; that means that if team members trust each other, they have a better chance of getting "buy-in" from employees on the direction of the company.[53] And if employees trust their leaders, they will buy in more readily.

Leaders must not only come to trust their subordinates, but also express that trust. Research has shown that workers who believe their boss trusts them (called "felt trustworthiness") enjoy their work more, are more productive, and are more likely to "go the extra mile" at work and perform organizational citizenship behaviours.[54]

Effective leaders also understand both *whom* to trust and *how* to trust. At one extreme, leaders often

Hans Neleman/Stone/Getty Images

trust a close circle of advisors, listening only to them and gradually cutting themselves off from dissenting opinions. At the opposite extreme, lone-wolf leaders may trust nobody, leading to preventable mistakes. Wise leaders carefully evaluate both the competence and the position of those they trust, seeking out a variety of opinions and input.[55]

Ethics

The leaders of any organization, whether a community sports team or a multinational corporation, directly influence the behaviour of members. Leaders set the tone for the organization's culture and are the embodiment of how members are expected to behave (see Chapter 13 for a more complete discussion of how leaders create culture). Business leaders are often required to make decisions that involve conflicting interests, and in order to encourage a strong and moral culture, they must consistently display transparent, ethical behaviour and avoid abusing their power.

Ethical leadership requires attention not only to business practices, but also to relationships. From accounting scandals to abusive management practices, leaders must actively strive to ensure that what happens within the organization consistently aligns with organizational values. Leaders who show concern for employee rights and treat their employees fairly are perceived as ethical. When leaders are perceived as ethical, followers are more ethical, and organizational commitment is greater.[56]

Gender and Leadership

Historical stereotypes persist, and people frequently characterize successful managers as having more masculine attributes than feminine attributes.[57] Although legitimate gender differences may exist, it is more likely that the same leadership traits may be interpreted differently in a man and a woman because of preconceived notions and perceptual biases. For instance, women are judged as less confident than they actually are because of their tone of voice and word choice when speaking.[58]

Evidence suggests that feminine personalities tend to use a more people-oriented style that is inclusive and empowering, and feminine managers excel in positions that demand strong interpersonal skills.[59] Though more and more women are assuming positions of leadership in organizations, much of what we know about leadership is based on studies that were conducted on men, by male researchers, which implies that our current understanding of leadership is undoubtedly gendered. Organizational researchers have begun to investigate how women lead and the reasons for their under-representation in senior leadership roles, but this research is in its infancy, and much more needs to be done before conclusions and resolutions can be presented.

Recent research has identified the phenomenon of the *glass cliff* (as opposed to the *glass ceiling* discussed in Chapter 2). The *glass cliff* represents a trend in organizations where women appear to be more likely to achieve leadership roles during periods of crisis when the likelihood of failure is highest.[60] Several theories have attempted to explain this phenomenon ranging from the view that women are offered poor opportunities because they are considered expendable and better scapegoats,[61] to people believing that

FAST FACT

Companies with Female CEOs Outperform Those Led by Men

As more women rise to the rank of CEO, the natural question arises as to whether companies led by female or male CEOs fare better. Researchers at Quantopian, a trading platform, used a crowdsourced algorithm to compare the performance of Fortune 1000 companies with female CEOs between 2002 and 2014 with the S&P 500's performance during the same time. The result: Companies led by females produced equity returns 226% better than the S&P 500.

SOURCES: P. Wechsler, "Women-Led Companies Perform Three Times Better Than the S&P 500," *Fortune*, March 3, 2015, http://fortune.com/2015/03/03/women-led-companies-perform-three-times-better-than-the-sp-500/, accessed May 20, 2018.

women are better suited to lead in unsuccessful times because they are more nurturing, caring, and creative.[62] Another theory suggests that women are more likely than men to accept glass cliff positions due to the lack of alternative opportunities combined with male in-group favouritism.[63]

12-8 FOLLOWERSHIP

While theories of leadership continue to be researched, and new dimensions of leadership are being investigated and refined, the concept of **followership**, which is the actions and behaviours of those being led, is gaining ground in organizational behaviour research. Much of the leadership literature suggests that leader and follower roles are highly differentiated, yet that same research has focused only on the leader's role in goal attainment, completely ignoring the follower's (arguably more important) role in that relationship. The traditional view casts followers as passive, but a more contemporary view casts the follower role as an active participant in organizational behaviours, and an integral component to the leadership process. It must be acknowledged that followers play a critical role within the organization, because ultimately, it is the followers, their behaviour, and their work that either establishes a leader's success or rejects their efforts to lead.

> "He who cannot be a good follower cannot be a leader.
> —Aristotle"

followership The process of being guided and directed by a leader in an organizational environment.

Much like leadership, there are trait, behavioural, and constructionist theories devoted to understanding and explaining follower behaviour, though these theories are in their infancy. Much of the early work in the research has set itself to exploring the myths and misunderstandings about followership. The traditional concept that leaders are active while followers are passive is demonstrably incorrect, and yet this misconception persists.[64] Followers influence their leaders at every level of the hierarchy[65]—not only through formal channels of communication, but also through the organization's culture (see Chapter 13); impression management and organizational citizenship behaviours (see Chapter 3); through leader–member exchange (see "Leader–Member Exchange (LMX)" in this chapter); and in all the myriad ways that empowered followers interact with their leaders. One organization that recognizes the active role of followers is the U.S. Army, which has a military doctrine called *mission command* that states "that the commander in the field is always right and the rear echelon is wrong, unless proven otherwise."[66] This means that the "front line" is assumed to be correct, and the "control centre" is assumed to be wrong, until proven otherwise.[67]

As organizations move toward empowerment and as they embrace self-directed work teams, the follower role can be seen as one of self-leadership in which the follower assumes responsibility for influencing their own performance.[68] Good followers are desirable employees: They are not only technically capable, but also comply with orders and requests, and act appropriately when not being directly supervised. They are self-aware, they seek improvement, and they accept responsibility for their actions.

Michael Shake/Shutterstock.com

Followers are active participants in organizational behaviours.

Types of Followers

Contemporary work environments are ones in which followers recognize their interdependence with leaders and learn to challenge them while at the same time respecting the leaders' authority.[69] Effective followers are active, responsible, and autonomous in their behaviour and critical in their thinking without being insubordinate or disrespectful; in essence, they are highly engaged at work.

Followers can be categorized in two dimensions: (1) activity versus passivity, and (2) independent, critical thinking versus dependent, uncritical thinking.[70] These two dimensions create a grid that identifies five types of follower, as shown in Figure 12.4.

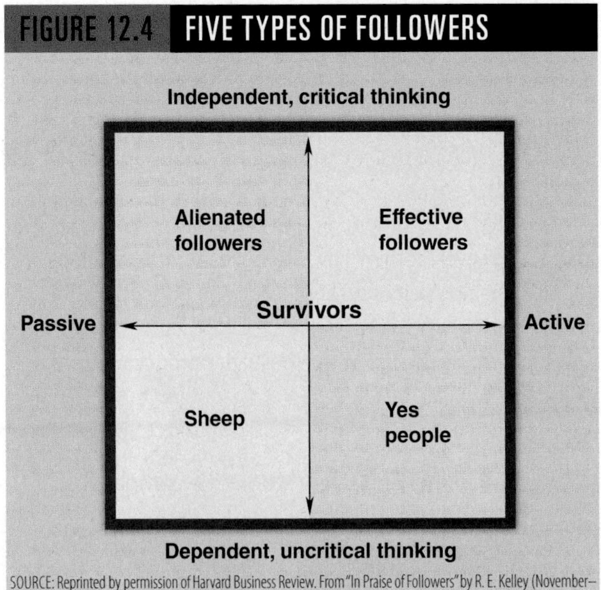

SOURCE: Reprinted by permission of Harvard Business Review. From "In Praise of Followers" by R. E. Kelley (November–December 1988): 145. Copyright © 1988 by Harvard Business School Publishing Corporation; all rights reserved.

Alienated followers think independently and critically, yet are very passive in their behaviour. As a result, they become psychologically and emotionally distanced from their leaders. Alienated followers are potentially disruptive and a threat to the health of the organization.

Sheep are followers who do not think independently or critically and are passive in their behaviour. They simply do as they are told by their leaders.

Yes people are followers who also do not think independently or critically, yet are very active in their behaviour. They uncritically reinforce the thinking and ideas of their leaders with enthusiasm, never questioning or challenging the wisdom of the leaders' ideas and proposals. Yes people are the most dangerous to a leader because they are the most likely to give a false positive reaction and give no warning of potential pitfalls.

Survivors are the least disruptive and the lowest-risk followers in an organization. They perpetually sample the wind, and their motto is "better safe than sorry."

Effective followers are the most valuable to a leader and an organization because of their active contributions. Effective followers share four essential qualities. First, they practise self-management and self-responsibility. A leader can delegate to an effective follower without undue anxiety about the outcome. Second, they are committed both to the organization and a purpose, principle, or person outside themselves. Effective followers are not self-centred or self-aggrandizing. Third, effective followers invest in their own competence and professionalism and focus their energy for maximum impact. Effective followers look for challenges and ways in which to add to their talents or abilities. Fourth, they are courageous, honest, and credible.[71]

12-9 GUIDELINES FOR LEADERSHIP

Leadership is a key to influencing organizational behaviour and achieving organizational effectiveness. When external artifacts are eliminated, studies of leadership succession show a moderately strong leader influence on organizational performance.[72] With this said, it is important to recognize that other factors also influence organizational performance. These include environmental factors (such as general economic conditions) and technological factors (such as efficiency).

Leaders play a central role in setting the ethical tone and moral values for their organizations. Five useful guidelines have emerged from the extensive leadership research of the past 60 years:

1. Leaders and organizations should appreciate the unique attributes, predispositions, and talents of each leader. No two leaders are the same, and there is value in this diversity.
2. Although there appears to be no single best style of leadership, there are organizational preferences in terms of style. Leaders should be chosen who challenge the organizational culture when necessary, without destroying it.
3. Participative, considerate leader behaviours that demonstrate a concern for people appear to enhance the health and well-being of followers in the work environment. This does not imply, however, that a leader must ignore the team's work tasks.
4. Different leadership situations call for different leadership talents and behaviours. This may result in different individuals taking the leader role, depending on the specific situation in which the team finds itself.
5. Good leaders are likely to be good followers. Although there are distinctions between their social roles, the attributes and behaviours of leaders and followers may not be as different as is sometimes thought.

IN ACTION

Leadership Factories

Some of North America's best-known companies seem to have perfected the art of grooming and producing exceptional leaders. Companies such as General Electric, Johnson & Johnson, PepsiCo, and several others have strong leadership development programs in place that help them identify and groom employees for leadership positions. These leaders in turn are instrumental in guiding the organization to the goal of delivering on its promises.

One research study examined the internal processes of leadership development across 150 of the top leader-producing firms and identified five key principles that were common to all the organizations.

What do top leader-producing firms do? They:

- Identify leaders who are proficient at setting organizational strategy and identifying talent within the company.
- Focus on customer expectations of the firm and ensure that leadership never loses sight of those expectations.
- Evaluate leader performance and effectiveness against these customer expectations.
- Develop leadership training that includes skill development specific to meeting customer expectations.
- Periodically evaluate the success of leadership development, including asking customers for feedback on company leadership.

SOURCE: D. Ulrich and N. Smallwood, "Building a Leadership Brand," *Harvard Business Review* 85(7, 8) (2007): 92–100.

STUDY TOOLS 12

IN THE BOOK YOU CAN ...

- ☐ Rip out the **Chapter Review card** at the end of the book to review Key Concepts and Key Terms.
- ☐ Take a "What about You?" Quiz related to material in the chapter.
- ☐ Read additional cases in the Mini Case and Shopify Running Case sections.

ONLINE YOU CAN ...

NELSON.COM/STUDENT

- ☐ Take a "What about You?" Quiz related to material in the chapter.
- ☐ Test your understanding with a quick Multiple-Choice Pre-Test quiz.
- ☐ Read the eBook, which includes discussion points for questions posed in the Cases.
- ☐ Watch Videos related to chapter content.
- ☐ Use the available Flashcards and Matching Quizzes to test your understanding of key terms and concepts.
- ☐ See how much you've learned by taking a Post-Test.

WHAT ABOUT YOU?

How Does Your Supervisor Lead?

Answer the following 16 questions concerning your supervisor's (or professor's) leadership behaviours using the seven-point Likert scale below. Then complete the summary to examine your supervisor's (or professor's) behaviours.

NOT AT ALL					VERY MUCH	
1	2	3	4	5	6	7

Is your superior strict about observing regulations?
1 2 3 4 5 6 7

To what extent does your superior give you instructions and orders?
1 2 3 4 5 6 7

Is your superior strict about the amount of work you do?
1 2 3 4 5 6 7

Does your superior urge you to complete your work by the time he or she has specified?
1 2 3 4 5 6 7

Does your superior try to make you work to your maximum capacity?
1 2 3 4 5 6 7

When you do an inadequate job, does your superior focus on the inadequate way the job was done instead of on your personality?
1 2 3 4 5 6 7

Does your superior ask you for reports about the progress of your work?
1 2 3 4 5 6 7

Does your superior work out precise plans for goal achievement each month?
1 2 3 4 5 6 7

Can you talk freely with your superior about your work?
1 2 3 4 5 6 7

Generally, does your superior support you?
1 2 3 4 5 6 7

Is your superior concerned about your personal problems?
1 2 3 4 5 6 7

Do you think your superior trusts you?
1 2 3 4 5 6 7

Does your superior give you recognition when you do your job well?
1 2 3 4 5 6 7

When a problem arises in your workplace, does your superior ask your opinion about how to solve it?
1 2 3 4 5 6 7

Is your superior concerned about your future benefits like promotions and pay raises?
1 2 3 4 5 6 7

Does your superior treat you fairly?
1 2 3 4 5 6 7

Add up your answers to Questions 1 through 8. This total indicates your supervisor's (or professor's) performance orientation:

Task orientation = ________

Add up your answers to Questions 9 through 16. This total indicates your supervisor's (or professor's) maintenance orientation:

People orientation = ________

A score above 40 is high, and a score below 20 is low.

SOURCE: Reprinted from "The Performance-Maintenance Theory of Leadership: Review of a Japanese Research Program" by J. Misumi and M. F. Peterson published in *Administrative Science Quarterly* 30 (1985): 207 by permission of *Administrative Science Quarterly* © 1985.

MINI CASE

Dwane Casey and the Toronto Raptors

Dwane Casey is the winningest coach in the history of the Toronto Raptors basketball franchise. When Casey first joined the team in 2011, the Raptors were one of the worst teams in the league, and had consistent losing seasons (where they lost more games than they won). But only two years later, in 2013, the Raptors made it to the playoffs, and they have returned every year since. Dwane Casey is credited with overhauling the Raptors' culture, and developing top-rated talent for the Raptors, by holding all players accountable to the same high standards, from star players to relative unknowns. He is known as a coach who enforces strict team rules that are clearly communicated to all players at the start of the season.

He focused the team's efforts on strength and conditioning, by challenging each player to reduce their body fat to less than 10 percent (which all but one player achieved), and he assigned all players specific goals in the off-season and monitored their progress through summer. Players who failed to reach their targets were given extra workouts. He required players to have their shirts tucked during practice; if a player was late for a practice or a team meeting, they were fined; if players failed to pick up after themselves, they were fined. Casey has been quoted as saying "If a guy's not disciplined off the floor he's not going to be disciplined on the floor."

Casey also enforced team building and cohesion. The Raptors had one of the youngest rosters in the NBA, with approximately two-thirds of the team being young players, while one-third were veterans. Casey actively promoted unity between the groups by requiring all team members to put in the same amount of time on the court, and then leaving together on the team bus when practice was over.

The 2017–2018 season was Toronto's most successful year. The team finished first in the Eastern Conference with a franchise record 59 wins in the regular season. On May 9, Casey was named the NBA's Coach of the Year by his peers. However, on May 11, Casey was fired by the Raptors.

After finishing at the top of their division, and beating the Washington Wizards in the first round of playoffs, the Raptors were favoured to win round two against the Cleveland Cavaliers, but the team didn't win a game, and were swept 0–4. This is the second year in a row that the Raptors have been eliminated from the Eastern Conference semifinal playoffs without winning a game against the Cavaliers. It seems that what worked in the regular season hasn't worked for the Raptors in the post season, and while Dwane Casey received his share of credit for the Raptors' regular season, he is receiving all of the blame for the Raptors' post-season performance.

Apply Your Understanding

1. Is Dwane Casey a leader or a manager for the Toronto Raptors?
2. Describe how Dwane Casey was able to change the Raptors' culture.
3. How does the Leader–Member Exchange (LMX) theory of leadership apply to this case?

RUNNING CASE **SHOPIFY**

GROWING THE BRAND

In May 2018, Shopify executives spent two days at the company's annual Unite Conference for developers ad partners discussing ways to grow the Shopify brand. Shopify CEO Tobias Lütke wants to grow the company by creating new services and products that can help secure Shopify's position within the global market, and he's asking his team to come up with the best way to accomplish that goal.

Amazon is currently the leader in global market e-commerce, accounting for 44 percent of all US digital sales in 2017, with a market cap of US$784 billion. Valued at almost $20 billion, Shopify is looking to take some of that market share. The company markets itself to small businesses as a platform with tools to be successful in whatever way works best for the small businesses, whether in physical, digital, or increasingly hybrid retail locations.

At the conference, Shopify announced that it would be opening a physical location for its merchants to get in-person support to help them develop their merchant sites, an unusual step for a digital company. Shopify also described new infrastructure for retailers that have physical locations including debit and credit card tap readers; support for foreign currencies and digital payment methods; and products and services in languages other than English to help attract new merchants and expand their global market.

Justin Trudeau attended the Unite Conference and said, "What you're doing is really creating opportunities for individuals, for small businesses, for entrepreneurs to succeed in very real tangible ways. That's one of the real differences [between] the stereotypical view of the American Dream versus the Canadian dream."

SOURCE: https://www.theglobeandmail.com/business/technology/article-shopify-looks-to-offer-more-services-products-as-part-of-growth/

Apply Your Understanding

1. What type of leadership does Tobias Lütke use?
2. What type of followers most likely make up the Shopify executive team?
3. Given your answer to question 2, and using the Hersey-Blanchard Situational Leadership® model, what type of leadership style could Tobias Lütke use?

THE CANADIAN PRESS/Nathan Denette

© iStockphoto.com/Besjunior

13 Organizational Culture

LEARNING OUTCOMES

After reading this chapter, you should be able to do the following:

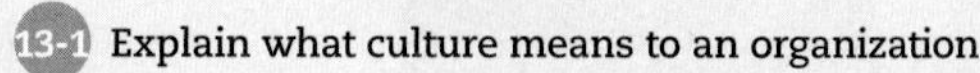

13-1 Explain what culture means to an organization.

13-2 Identify and evaluate the levels of culture.

13-3 Describe how culture is started, shaped, and reinforced.

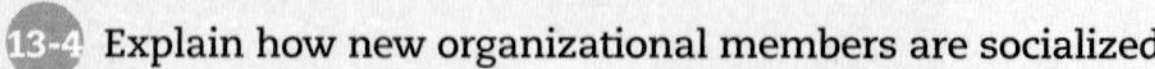

13-4 Explain how new organizational members are socialized.

13-5 Discuss how leaders can change organizational culture.

13-6 Describe how culture relates to organizational performance.

See the end of this chapter for a list of available Study Tools, a "What about You?" Quiz, Mini Case, and the Shopify Running Case.

Most of the communities to which we belong have their own culture: our racial, religious, and political affiliations; our workplace; even recreational clubs have their own culture. Many times, the culture is so ingrained in our behaviours that we don't even recognize that our actions are being affected. Organizational culture affects every interaction between members of an organization, and every individual, in turn, affects the culture. Considering culture's impact on individuals and organizations, it is important to be able to recognize cultural symbols and behaviours, and know how to manage and direct them.

> "Our culture is friendly and intense, but if push comes to shove we'll settle for intense."
> —Jeff Bezos

 WHAT IS ORGANIZATIONAL CULTURE?

An organization's culture explains why it operates the way it does, and why its employees behave the way they do. It is the fundamental component of the organizational identity, yet, even though organizational culture impacts every decision and every interaction within an organization, many people become aware of their culture only when they have the opportunity to compare it against another. The word *culture* encompasses the values, norms, beliefs, and customs of a group, every organization has its own unique culture.

Organizational culture is the consistent, shared, observable patterns of behaviour in organizations.[1] Organizational culture describes the expectations and perceptions that affect decisions and behaviours within an organization, and defines what behaviours are appropriate and expected (and what behaviours are not) for members. Culture is a very broad concept and includes the norms, values, customs, traditions, habits, skills, knowledge, and beliefs of a group of people. Because every group has a unique makeup of norms, values, habits etc., culture can be used to distinguish between groups.[2]

The most basic function of a culture is that it serves as a control mechanism for shaping behaviour. Norms that guide behaviour are an important part of culture, and norms can be both prescriptive (describing what one *should* do) and proscriptive (describing what one should *not* do).[3] This control mechanism provides a sense of identity and belonging to members and increases their commitment to the organization.[4] When employees internalize the values of the company, they find their work intrinsically rewarding and identify with their fellow workers. Motivation is enhanced, and employees are more committed.[5] Culture also provides an element of stability and predictability to an organization. Culture shapes the way employees respond to stress and conflict, and helps to provide direction when the unexpected occurs.

Components of Organizational Culture

Organizational culture has three different components[6]:

1. The *structural* system of an organization. This describes the formal structures, policies, strategies, and management processes that an organization uses to enact its day-to-day operations. These include its formal goals and objectives, its authority and power structure, reward mechanisms, recruitment and training operations, and other managerial processes.
2. The *expressive and affective* systems of an organization. This defines how organizations assign and share meanings and values among members. It is this system that unifies and legitimizes member beliefs and provides standards for organizational behaviours. This system is shaped by many factors including society at large, the history of the organization, and the environment in which the organization operates.
3. The *individuals* who make up the organization. As individuals are influenced by their external environment, internalizing norms and aligning themselves with the values that surrounded them, they also affect that environment. It follows then, that a group of individuals, with their myriad attitudes, values, and personalities, who interact frequently, will likely develop an internal identity that reflects a consistent set of values. People within an organization become contributors and fabricators of organizational meaning and values.

Impact of Culture on Organizational Members

Perception of how well one fits with an organization's culture influences whether a person is attracted to the organization, whether it be a

organizational culture Consistent, shared, observable patterns of behaviour that distinguish between groups.

community sports team or a potential employer.[7] Studies indicate that there are small but consistent links between culture and personality, and people are attracted to organizations with features similar to their own personalities.[8] Research shows, for example, that highly extraverted students were attracted to aggressive and team-oriented cultures and less interested in supportive cultures. Those who ranked high on *openness to experience* (see Chapter 3 for a discussion on components of personality) were attracted to innovative cultures, while students with high neuroticism were less attracted to innovative cultures.[9]

Perception of how well an employee fits in with the organization's culture also influences the decision to offer employment.[10] How closely aligned individual values are with organizational culture is a good predictor of job satisfaction and organizational commitment,[11] as well as coworker satisfaction, trust in managers, indicators of strain, and intention to quit.[12]

Differentiation of Culture

Culture affects all interactions within an organization. It affects the way people address each other, how much status influences interactions, whether information is shared and with whom, how much people "joke around," and whether employees are likely to see each other socially and consider each other friends or as simply colleagues. When we discuss an organization's culture as a whole, what we are truly referencing is its dominant culture. The **dominant culture** describes the overarching core values that are shared by most members of the organization. It is the amalgamation of all of the different components of culture used to describe the organization's personality as a whole. But many organizations, especially large ones, often have regionalized subcultures.

A **subculture** is a unique microculture created within a subset unit of the organization. Subcultures typically evolve in identifiable units within the organization in response to external problems, or situations that members experience. Often, subcultures are the result of an organization's divisions, so functional departments will often have their own subculture. Engineering, marketing, production, and planning are four common organizational divisions that typically have their own unique subcultures. Even management may be considered a subculture with its own set of values in contrast to non-managers.[13] Different organizational teams also share a culture that is somewhat different than the organization's dominant culture. (Consider Chapter 9's discussion of group norms to understand how and why this occurs.) Subcultures are not limited to business organizations; consider the offensive and defensive lines of a sports team—though united by the teams dominant culture, the offense and the defense often have different "personalities."

dominant culture The overarching core values shared by most members of the organization.

subculture A microculture created within a subset unit of the organization.

counterculture Subcultures with values that oppose the dominant culture.

Individual departments or functional units within an organization often have a subculture that is unique to that particular unit, but these subcultures normally include the core values of the dominant culture. Sometimes, however, some groups have values that oppose the dominant culture, making them a **counterculture**. Organizations, then, are collections of various subcultures that operate within the larger whole. That is not to say that organizational subcultures always get along; subcultures often compete for power, control, and resources. Subcultures, including countercultures, can increase stress and conflict within the organization; however, they also challenge the status quo and can identify ways in which the organization needs to change to adapt to dynamic business environments.[14]

Advantages and Disadvantages of Organizational Culture

ADVANTAGES Organizational culture can provide significant benefits to an organization. It can increase the organization's marketability, improve productivity, decrease conflict, increase employee satisfaction, and provide stability. In addition to being one of the prime factors that determines who chooses to apply to the organization, and hence what type of talent the organization can attract, culture serves to reinforce the way the company does business. Cultures can encourage creativity, problem solving, and innovation (which can be critical for tech or development companies) or they can reinforce punctuality and rigid adherence to policy and schedules, (which is equally important for manufacturing companies). The beliefs, norms, and values that a culture promotes can guide members' behaviours, and to the degree that the culture helps the organization fit into, and respond to, its environment, then culture is a powerful tool for directing and focusing members and increasing organizational productivity.[15]

At the same time, the culture provides unspoken cues for how organizational members communicate, what is expected of them, and who they can turn to for help, which can help reduce internal conflict.

Some cultures encourage open, and casual behaviour, with jeans and T-shirt dress codes, open-concept work spaces, wall-less offices, team orientation, and breakrooms with games or free food; this culture serves to encourage open, casual communication among all levels of employees. Other cultures are more suit-and-tie oriented, maintaining strict hierarchical divisions between managers and employees with offices whose doors remain closed, and with expectations that meetings will be scheduled, through assistants, well in advance. This culture sets clear expectations that casual conversation is not welcome, and in-office discussions will concern work topics, not social pleasantries.

Providing organizational members with cues about what types of behaviour are acceptable; what types of conversation are expected and when, and where; and what the core values of the organization are acts to reduce member uncertainty and provides a framework for the day-to-day operations of the organization. When members know what to expect, they are better able to fulfill their role within the organization.

DISADVANTAGES Organizational culture is not always the answer to organizational problems. Often, organization culture is the *source* of an organization's problems.[16] If an organization's culture is very weak, then every change to the organization will result in a change to the culture. This instability means that members don't know what to expect from day to day, which can be stressful, and can also result in increased political behaviours, as individuals seeks to gain what power and resources they can.

Too-weak cultures are a liability, but so are cultures that are too strong: Strong cultures are often resistant to change, which can cause the organizational culture to stagnate—that is, they fail to change with the environment.[17] The stability that started as an advantage turns into a disadvantage when it becomes intractable and prevents the culture from adapting and developing. Strong but stubborn cultures become barriers to diversity as employees who do not fit the cultural expectation will choose to leave the organization, further reinforcing the strong culture. Stagnant cultures allow the organization to become out of sync with customers, competitors, and other important stakeholders.[18]

Finally, cultures can become misaligned with organizational values. The company can say that it values one thing, but the culture may show that it values the opposite. One common occurrence of misaligned culture is unethical culture. Because culture is dynamic and responsive to many factors, if the organization allows its ethical code to slip, without swift corrective action, it may find that all employees begin to act in ways that are not in keeping with the stated ethical values.[19] If one employee cheats but gets away with it, or worse gets rewarded, soon all employees will cheat and the culture will erode quickly. Similarly, some cultures seem to reward bullying behaviours either by not adequately punishing transgressors and allowing the behaviour to continue, or by outright promoting the behaviour through rewards and accolades.[20]

13-2 LEVELS OF ORGANIZATIONAL CULTURE

Organizational culture has three distinct levels (see Figure 13.1), which broadly categorize how easily an observer can identify the cultural component. The upper level, called artifacts, encompasses the most visible and recognizable components of culture. The middle level describes shared and espoused values within the organization, and the lowest level describes the subconscious underlying assumptions that are embedded within the organization's culture.[21]

Artifacts

Artifacts are the visible expressions of a culture, and include the way people behave; stories; rituals; and symbols, which can include everything from how people dress to physical attributes, such as the use of space and interior design.[22] Artifacts are the most visible and accessible level of culture, though their meanings are not consistent across organizations, or even across time, so interpreting artifacts is not always straightforward.

Behavioural artifacts describe the consistent pattern of behaviour within the organization. Any organizational behaviour that can be observed is a behavioural artifact. How polite are people within the organization? How deferential are they to customers or authority figures? How do people speak to one another in meetings or in the breakroom? Behavioural artifacts are powerful learning tools for employees,[23] because individuals often learn by observing others' behaviour and patterning their own behaviour similarly. Managerial behaviour can clarify what is important and coordinate the work of employees, in effect negating the need for close supervision.[24]

Ceremonies and rites are any relatively elaborate sets of activities that are enacted on important occasions.[25] These occasions provide organizations with the opportunity to encourage

artifacts The visible expressions of a culture.

FIGURE 13.1 LEVELS OF ORGANIZATIONAL CULTURE

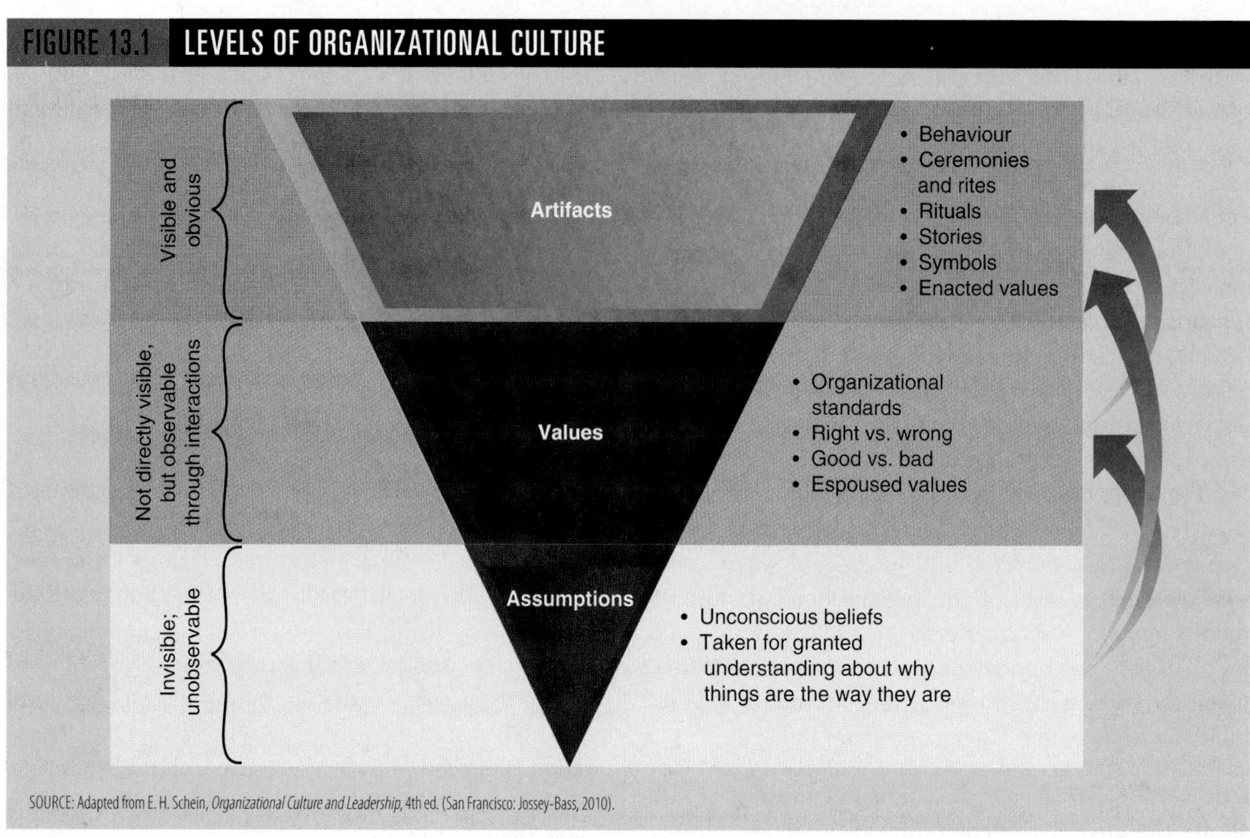

SOURCE: Adapted from E. H. Schein, *Organizational Culture and Leadership*, 4th ed. (San Francisco: Jossey-Bass, 2010).

desired behaviours by rewarding and recognizing employees whose behaviour is preferred. Ceremonies and rites send a message that individuals who both espouse and exhibit certain values are to be admired and emulated. Ceremonies and rites also bond organizational members together. Edmonton-based Intuit Canada creates financial and tax preparation software, including the popular TurboTax. This means that during tax season the whole company must pull together to meet the intense demand to field calls from customers. To make this annual challenge more palatable, during the last week of tax season, employees are treated to free ice cream sundaes in the lobby, juggling lessons, and other games.[26] Six types of rites in organizations (see Table 13.1) have been identified.[27]

Japan Considers Making Vacations Mandatory

Japanese workers often work long days of 13 hours or more and sleep as little as 35 hours a week—a schedule that leads sometimes to *karoshi*, which means death by overwork. When *karoshi* is paired with the concept of *kaizen*, or continuous improvement, workers seldom if ever take a vacation. The Japanese government is considering legislation that would make five days of paid vacation mandatory each year. There is growing evidence that young people work long and intense hours and die young. Grieving families have started non-profit organizations to influence business and government to change the culture of overwork.

SOURCE: A. Peters, "In Japan, It Soon May Be Illegal Not to Take Vacation," *Fast Company*, March 11, 2015, accessed at http://www.fastcoexist.com/3043444/in-japan-it-soon-may-be-illegal-not-to-take-vacation.

Rituals are the repetitive organizational practices that occur consistently and reliably within an organizational setting. Unlike rites, which are formalized and orchestrated, rituals are informal and unwritten, but they send a clear message about "the way we do things around here." Do members take coffee breaks together? Do people eat lunch at their desk? Do they share personal information and plans for the upcoming weekend? Some organizations require that people address each other formally by their titles to reinforce a professional image (Mr., Mrs., Dr., Your Honour) while others prefer to operate on a first-name basis.

Stories are one of the most effective ways to reinforce organizational values.[28] As they are retold, stories personalize the organization and are especially helpful in orienting new employees. To be effective cultural artifacts, stories must be credible: A story about a flat corporate hierarchy in an organization with reserved parking

TABLE 13.1 RITES IN ORGANIZATIONS

Rite	Effect	Ceremony
Rites of passage	Show that an individual's status within the organization has changed	Promotion celebrations
Rites of enhancement	Reinforce the achievement of individuals	Awarding certificates to sales contest winners
Rites of renewal	Emphasize change in the organization and commitment to learning and growth	Professional development activities
Rites of integration	Unite diverse groups or teams within the organization and renew commitment to the larger organization	Company functions such as annual picnics or Christmas parties
Rites of conflict reduction	Deal with conflicts or disagreements that arise naturally in organizations	Grievance hearings and the negotiation of union contracts
Rites of degradation	Visibly punish persons who fail to adhere to values and norms of behaviour	Publicly replacing a CEO for unethical conduct or for failure to achieve organizational goals

SOURCE: H.M. Trice, and J. Beyer, "Studying Organizational Cultures through Rites and Ceremonials," *Academy of Management Review* 9 (1984): 653–669.

spaces for managers (a distinctly hierarchical reward) can lead to cynicism and mistrust. Certain themes commonly appear in stories across different types of organizations[29]:

1. *Stories about how the company started.* These stories often serve to reflect the work ethic or intelligence of the founder.
2. *Stories about a particular instance of great customer satisfaction.* These stories serve to remind employees about the values of the organization.
3. *Stories about the boss.* These stories may reflect whether the boss is "human" or how the boss reacts to mistakes.
4. *Stories about getting fired.* Events leading to employee firings are often recounted.
5. *Stories about whether lower-level employees can rise to the top.* Often, these stories describe a person who started out at the bottom and eventually became the CEO.
6. *Stories about how the company deals with crisis situations.* These stories show how the company overcomes obstacles.
7. *Stories about what happens when rules are broken.* These stories convey information about what is actually important to the organization.

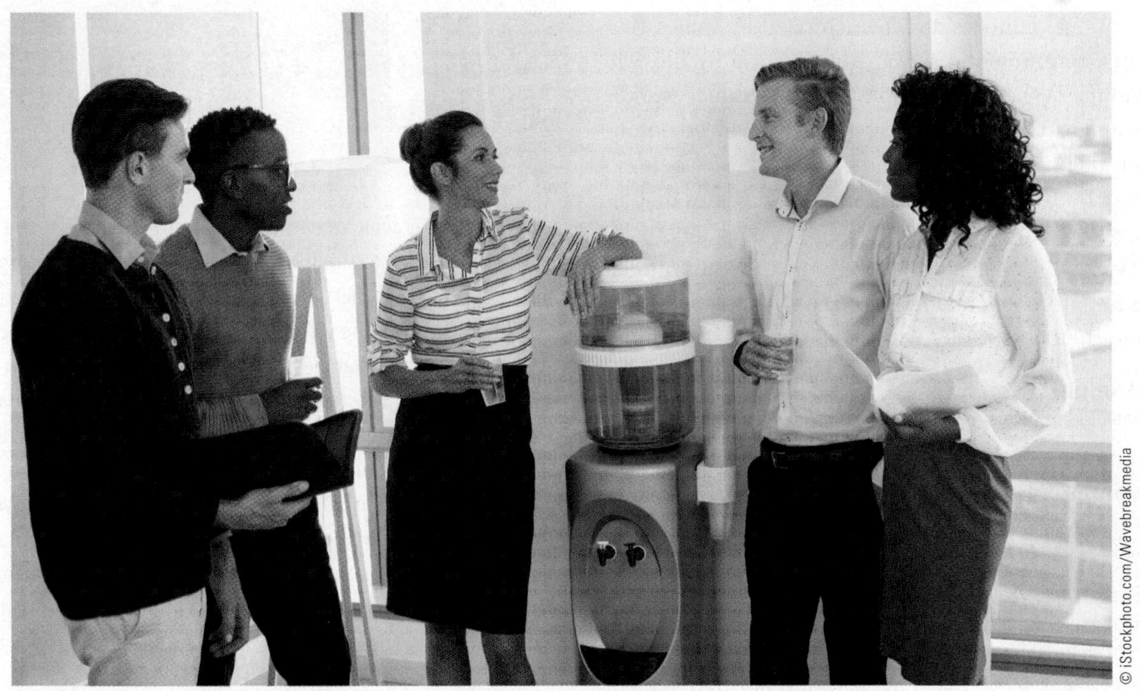
© iStockphoto.com/Wavebreakmedia

The way we do things around here.

Symbols communicate organizational culture through unspoken messages. The organizational chart quickly communicates its emphasis on hierarchy and status. The company dress code represents its relative concern with formality. The location, design, and size of the boss's office, especially in relation to everyone else's offices, can convey a great deal of information about company culture.[30] Symbols can also be literal in the illustrative symbols an organization chooses to represent itself. Graphic symbols are representative of organizational identity and membership to employees. Nike's trademark "swoosh" is proudly tattooed above the ankles of some Nike employees, and the Iron Ring is worn by many Canadian engineers on the pinky finger of their dominant hand. Symbols are used to build solidarity in the organizational culture.[31]

Shared and Espoused Values

Shared values represent the middle level of organizational culture. This level of culture cannot be seen just by looking, but can still be observed through interactions and in discussions with organizational members. Cultural values encompass organizational standards, conscious beliefs about what is right and wrong, and judgments about what is good or bad. Values are often consciously articulated, both in conversation and in a company's mission statement or annual report.

Some organizational cultures are characterized by values that support innovation[32]; others value prestige and income generation above all other attributes.[33] Other organizational cultures are characterized by values that support environmental stewardship or healthy lifestyle behaviours.[34] When the workplace culture values worker health and psychological needs, there is enhanced potential for high performance and improved well-being[35]; however, there are few restrictions on the values that an organization can promote, and there is no standard by which values are evaluated as good or bad. Organizational values are promoted and internalized by employees, and become the standard by which actions and behaviours are assessed as either good or bad. Behaviours that conform to organizational values will be judged as good, and behaviours that do not conform to, or oppose, organizational values will be judged as bad.

espoused values What members of an organization say they value.

enacted values Values reflected in the way individuals actually behave.

assumptions Deeply held beliefs that guide behaviour and tell members of an organization how to perceive and think about things.

There may, however, be a difference between a company's espoused values and its enacted values.[36] **Espoused values** are written or vocalized beliefs about the nature of the relationship between members, or between the organization and its community. Espoused values describe the worldview shared by the members of the organization; however, it is possible that espoused values are only aspirations or rationalizations. In contrast, **enacted values** are the observable behaviours of individuals (and because they are directly visible, they are artifacts of culture). It is not uncommon for organizations to experience discrepancies between their espoused values and their enacted values; that is, for organizations to say one thing, but to do another.[37] For instance, many organizations espouse values of equality and fairness, but their hiring practices or promotion systems favour a particular gender or race. These discrepancies affect employees' perception of organizational integrity and reduce employee commitment.[38]

Assumptions

Assumptions are the deeply held and often unconscious beliefs that guide behaviour and tell members of an organization how to perceive situations and people. These beliefs are so fundamental to an organization's culture that they are often taken-for-granted conditions about why the company exists and what it does. These assumptions become the organization's reality. For most

IN ACTION

WestJet Nurtures Fun Culture

WestJet is well known for its April Fool's jokes. The company invests significant time and effort producing viral marketing videos that serve as both advertising and a culture-building exercise. The videos act as rites of integration and help reinforce the idea that WestJet is a fun and casual place to work. The company's most famous April Fool's video was back in 2012, when it introduced Kargo Kids, a service in which children could be checked in as baggage to allow passengers to enjoy child-free flights. In 2014, the company claimed that WestJet would be converting to metric time, and in 2017, it rebranded itself as Canada Air, the #MostCanadian airline ever. Customers look forward to the annual April Fool's video and WestJet is able to market the company and reinforce its corporate culture annually.

SOURCE: https://onemileatatime.boardingarea.com/2018/04/01/swoop-duty-not-free

organizations, and their employees, it is inconceivable to consider creating a product that is unsafe, because product safety is a fundamental taken-for-granted belief about how products should be created. Asking someone why they don't design and market a patently unsafe product would get you a sputtering, indignant response. Assumptions are often unconsciously held, and they are so strongly held that a member behaving in a fashion that would violate them is unthinkable. Questioning basic assumptions results in defensiveness and anxiety, because individuals may not even be aware of their assumptions and may be reluctant or unable to discuss them or change them.

Cultural artifacts are difficult to interpret and decipher, and espoused values may be ideals or goals, rather than true values. In order to be able to accurately interpret and understand culture, an organization's assumptions must be examined carefully. As the deepest, most fundamental level of an organization's culture, assumptions are the essence of culture from which all values and artifacts flow.

13-3 HOW CULTURE IS STARTED, SHAPED, AND REINFORCED

Leaders play crucial roles in shaping and reinforcing culture.[39] The process of creating a culture begins with the idea for the new enterprise. The new organization is already a part of an existing environment with operational conditions that set expectations and limits on its cultural potential. Next, a founding group is created, made up of like-minded individuals who believe that the organization has the potential to succeed. Organizational founders often share a common vision and goal for the organization, and this lays the foundation for the organization's operational culture. As the organization takes shape, the founding group creates the internal structure, by incorporating, purchasing retail or manufacturing space, and finding customers and suppliers. By this early point in the organization, a culture has already developed, and is changing as the organization grows and develops. Finally, others are brought into the group according to what the founding group considers necessary, and the group

"Determine what behaviours and beliefs you value as a company, and have everyone live true to them. These behaviours and beliefs should be so essential to your core that you don't even think of it as culture.

—Brittany Forsyth

Alexander Supertramp/Shutterstock.com

Culture is started and maintained by organizational leaders.

begins to function, developing its own history.[40] Companies are built in the image of their founders, and it is the founders who set down the original cultural blueprint. If the founder is competitive, the company will be more aggressive and results oriented. If the founders are analytical and data driven, the resulting culture is likely to be systematic as well.

Eventually, if the company gets big enough, the founder will have to relinquish control over every aspect of the business. Many founders become the CEOs of their organization. Then the management of the culture becomes an organizational responsibility, where the leaders are responsible for maintaining, reinforcing, and shaping the culture as needed. The five most important elements in managing culture are (1) what leaders pay attention to; (2) how leaders react to crises; (3) how leaders behave; (4) how leaders allocate rewards; and (5) how leaders hire and fire individuals. These categories are common areas where discrepancies arise between espoused and enacted values.

What Leaders Pay Attention to

Leaders in an organization communicate their priorities, expectations, values, and beliefs in what they notice, comment on, measure, and control. If leaders are consistent in their focus, employees receive clear signals about what is important in the organization. If, however, leaders are inconsistent, employees spend a lot of time trying to decipher and find meaning in the inconsistent signals.

How Leaders React to Crises

The way that a leader deals with watershed moments communicates a powerful message about culture because crisis situations highlight the underlying assumptions of culture that are normally impossible to see. When emotions are heightened, true priorities are often revealed. For instance, most companies claim to value employees, (espoused values), but underlying assumptions and values are revealed when some organizations make every effort to avoid laying off workers during a recession, while others quickly institute major layoffs at the first sign of an economic downturn.

How Leaders Behave

Employees observe the behaviour of leaders to find out what the organization values. Through role modelling, teaching, and coaching, leaders teach and reinforce the values of the organizational culture. Members of an organization often emulate the leaders' behaviour, and look to leaders for cues to appropriate behaviour. Studies show that if managers want employees to be more entrepreneurial and use more initiative and innovation, they must demonstrate such behaviours themselves.[41]

How Leaders Allocate Rewards

Organizations must ensure that reward systems establish and reinforce consistent cultural values. Some companies claim to reward performance but offer raises according to length of service with the company. Other companies say they value teamwork, forming cross-functional teams and empowering these teams to make important decisions, yet when performance is appraised, the criterion for rating employees focuses on individual performance.

How Leaders Hire and Fire Individuals

Finally, a powerful way that leaders shape and reinforce culture is through the selection of newcomers to the organization. Leaders often unconsciously look for individuals who are similar to current organizational members in terms of values and assumptions. Some companies hire individuals on the recommendation of a current employee, which tends to perpetuate the culture as the new employee will typically hold similar values.

The way a company fires an employee and the rationale behind the firing also communicate culture. Some companies deal with poor performers by trying to find a place within the organization where they can perform better and make a contribution. Other companies fire employees who fail to live up to performance expectations. Similarly, rationales for keeping employees who have committed organizational infractions share a great deal of information about what the organization truly values. An employee who engages in behaviour that is clearly against the organization's stated values but is lightly reprimanded sends an important message to other employees. While some employees may view this as a failure to reinforce the values within the organization, others may view it as tacit permission or encouragement to engage in that behaviour.

socialization The process by which newcomers are transformed from outsiders to participating, effective members of the organization.

IN ACTION

How WestJet Hires

WestJet emphasizes personality in its flight staff and other employees who deal with clients, yet the company's impersonal panel interviews did not allow those personalities to show through. So WestJet changed its one-on-three panel interviews to three-hour sessions with groups of 20 to 30 applicants. Potential hires engage in games, team tasks, individual tasks, and presentations, and WestJet looks for the personalities revealed in the interactions. This approach is used for flight attendants, call centre and counter employees, and luggage handlers.

SOURCE: P. Brent, "WestJet Culture Gets Employees On-Board," *Workopolis*, http://www.workopolis.com/work.aspx?action=Transfer&View=Content/Common/ArticlesDetailView&lang=EN&articleId=brent20071128File1Article1.

Leaders play a critical role in shaping and reinforcing organizational culture. They need to actively create and model culture through what they pay attention to, how they react to crises, how they behave, the way they allocate rewards, and how they hire and fire employees. See Figure 13.2 for a graphical representation of the formation and maintenance of an organization's culture.

13-4 ORGANIZATIONAL SOCIALIZATION

Culture is learned and shared. It is not instinctual nor is it individual.[42] Culture, and all of its components, is transmitted and learned through the process of **socialization**, which is how an individual comes to understand and appreciate the abilities, values, expected behaviours, and social knowledge required to

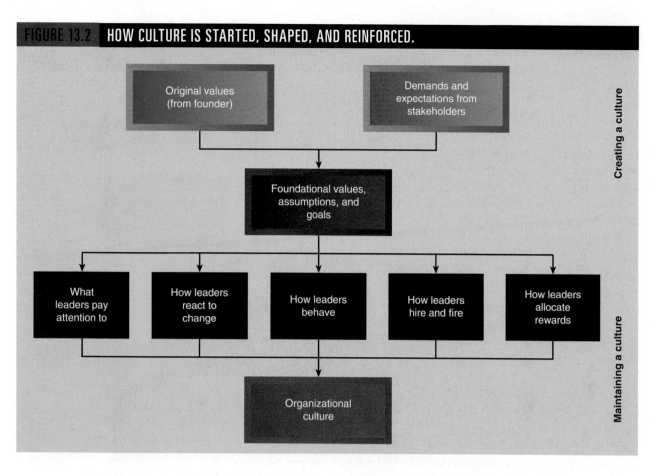

FIGURE 13.2 HOW CULTURE IS STARTED, SHAPED, AND REINFORCED.

Creating a culture

Original values (from founder)

Demands and expectations from stakeholders

Foundational values, assumptions, and goals

Maintaining a culture

What leaders pay attention to

How leaders react to change

How leaders behave

How leaders hire and fire

How leaders allocate rewards

Organizational culture

assume an organizational role and for participating as an organizational member.[43] In other words, it's how newcomers are transformed from *outsiders* into *members*,[44] and it's how culture is passed on from generation to generation. Even individuals who move to a new position within the same organization must be socialized to the new subculture.

The Socialization Process

Typically, an individual will be successful in their new role to the extent that their expectations about the new role are realistic, and to the extent that their abilities and values conform to the job requirements and the organizational culture.[45] There are three stages of the

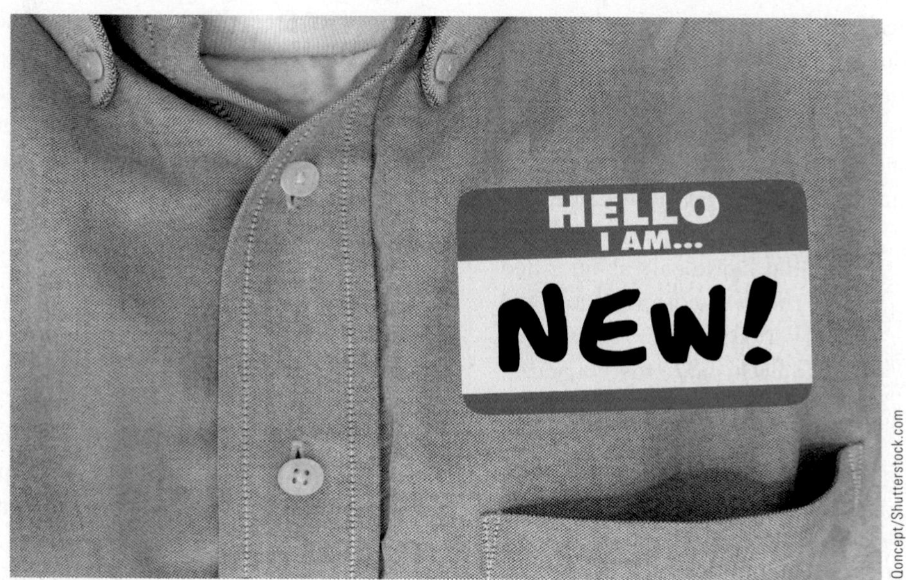

Socialization is how outsiders become members.

socialization process: anticipatory socialization, encounter, and change. Figure 13.3 presents a model of the process and the key concerns at each stage of it.

FIGURE 13.3 **THE ORGANIZATIONAL SOCIALIZATION PROCESS: STAGES AND OUTCOMES**

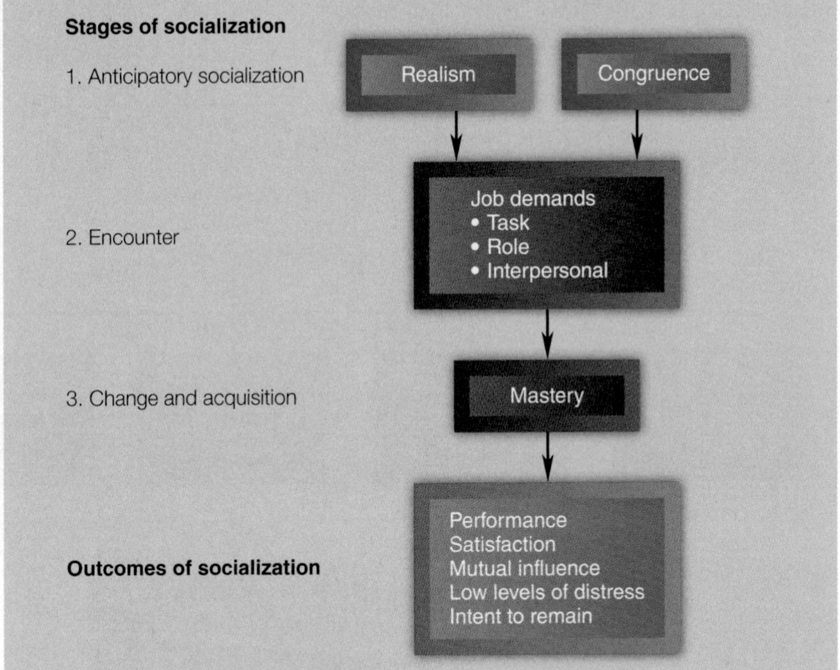

SOURCE: Reprinted from *Organizational Dynamics*, Autumn 1989, "An Ethical Weather Report: Assessing the Organization's Ethical Climate" by John B. Cullen et al. Copyright © 1989, with permission from Elsevier Science.

ANTICIPATORY SOCIALIZATION **Anticipatory socialization** encompasses all of the learning that takes place prior to the newcomer's first day on the job. Before an individual joins a new organization, or assumes a new role within an organization, they actively seek information about that new role. This information includes expectations about what tasks will be required to function in the new role (role clarity), expectations of how well the newcomer believes they will be able to perform (self-efficacy), and expectations about their social acceptance within the group. The information that is collected at this stage about all facets of the new role can help newcomers begin to construct a scheme for interpreting their experiences within the organization. Organizations provide information about many aspects of their operations through web pages, annual reports, and recruitment brochures, but it is important for newcomers to realistically and accurately assess that information.

Realism is the degree to which the newcomer has realistic expectations about the job and the organization, and this is a critical component for successful transitions. If an individual's expectations about the new role are drastically different than reality, they will experience higher levels of dissatisfaction and will have to make greater changes to accommodate and acclimate to their role requirements.[46] *Congruence* describes the level of "fit" between both the individual's abilities and the demands of the job, and between the individual's values and the organization's values. Newcomers whose values match the company's values are more satisfied with their new jobs, adjust more quickly, and say they intend to remain with the firm longer.[47]

anticipatory socialization The first socialization stage, which encompasses all of the learning that takes place prior to the newcomer's first day on the job.

encounter The second socialization stage in which the newcomer learns the tasks associated with the job, clarifies roles, and establishes new relationships at work.

ENCOUNTER The second stage of socialization, known as the **encounter** stage, is where organizational socialization tactics begin. It is when newcomers learn the actual tasks associated with the job, clarify their roles, and establish new relationships at work. The encounter stage is where individuals discover how realistic and congruent their expectations were with respect to the position as they discover whether the expectations formed in anticipatory socialization align, or clash, with the realities of the job. This stage commences on the first day at work and is thought to encompass the first six to nine months on the new job. Newcomers face task demands, role demands, and interpersonal demands during this period and organizational socialization tactics begin.

Task demands involve the actual work performed. How individuals learn to perform tasks is directly related to the organization's culture. In some organizations, where creativity is valued, newcomers are given considerable latitude to experiment with new ways to do their job. In others, newcomers are expected to learn the established procedures for their tasks with little deviation.

Role demands involve the expectations placed on newcomers. Newcomers often do not know exactly what is expected of them (role ambiguity) or may receive conflicting expectations from other individuals (role conflict). The way the organization approaches role demands is greatly affected by the organization's culture. Some organizations offer limited training and newcomers are expected to operate with considerable uncertainty, while others offer significant and detailed training, perhaps even mentoring, in order to clarify the newcomer's roles.

Interpersonal demands arise from relationships at work. The organization's political climate, leadership styles, and group pressure are interpersonal demands that newcomers must adapt and adjust to.

FIGURE 13.4 HOW ANTICIPATORY SOCIALIZATION AND ORGANIZATIONAL SOCIALIZATION IN TASK, ROLE, AND INTERPERSONAL DEMANDS CONTRIBUTE TO SOCIALIZATION OUTCOMES

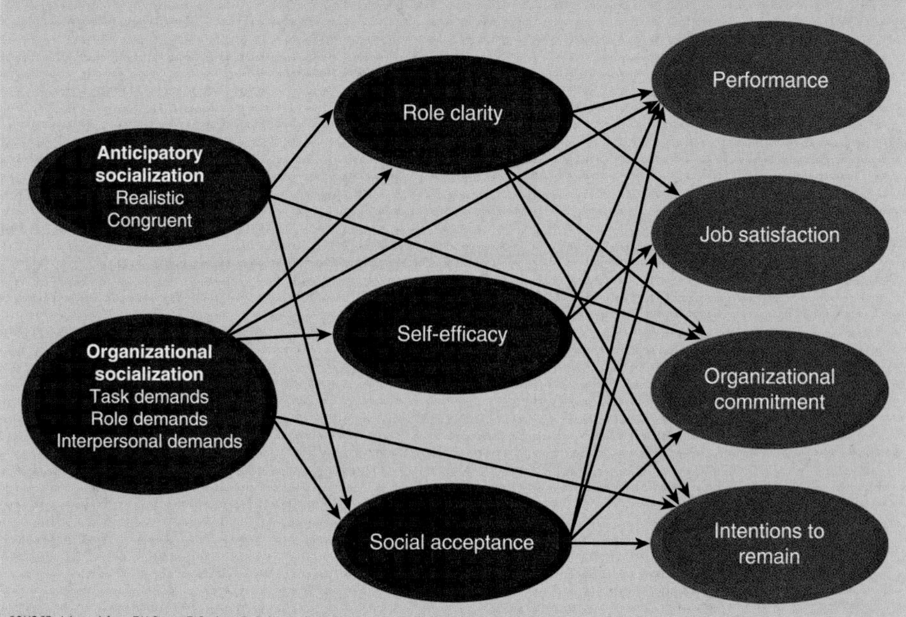

SOURCE: Adapted from T.N Bauer, T. Bodner, B. Erdogan, D. M. Truxillo and J. S. Tucker, "Newcomer Adjustment During Organizational Socialization: A Meta Analytic Review of Antecedents, Outcomes, and Methods," *Journal of Applied Psychology* 92(3) (2007): 707–721.

CHANGE AND ACQUISITION In the third and final stage of socialization, **change and acquisition**, newcomers begin to master the demands of the job. They become proficient at managing their tasks, clarifying and negotiating their roles, and engaging in relationships at work. The time when the socialization process is completed varies widely, depending on the individual, the job, and the organization. The end of the socialization process is signalled when newcomers identify as a member of the group, and when they are considered insiders by others within the group.

Outcomes of Socialization

Newcomers who are successfully socialized should exhibit good performance, high job satisfaction, high levels of organizational commitment, and the intention to stay with the organization.[48] In addition, they should exhibit low levels of distress symptoms.[49] When socialization is effective, newcomers understand and adopt the organization's values and norms. This ensures that the company's culture, including its core values, survives. It also provides employees a context for interpreting and responding to things that happen at work, and it ensures a shared framework of understanding.[50]

Successful socialization is also signalled by mutual influence. Recall from earlier that individuals affect and are affected by the culture in which they operate. As individuals grow comfortable in their new roles, they will make adjustments to those roles that accommodate and showcase their knowledge and personalities, which, in turn, will leave their mark on the organization. See Figure 13.4 for a graphical representation of how new employees are socialized.

13-5 CHANGING ORGANIZATIONAL CULTURE

Organizational culture *is* dynamic. As new members join the organization and as old members retire from it, as the political, social, and economic landscape changes, the culture will change. But that change is fluid—it occurs in infinitesimally small measures, and it occurs in any and every direction. Because organizational cultures are responsive to many different variables, they are notoriously difficult to pin down, and often take on a life of their own. Further, the components of culture are mutually reinforcing, and the same way that culture

change and acquisition The third stage of socialization, where the newcomer begins to master the demands of the job.

#HOT TREND

GE Changes Its Culture by Crowdsourcing Its Employees

General Electric realized that cultures have a life cycle and that its culture needed to shift with the times. Employees felt that GE needed to become more decentralized and easier to do business with. The company simplified its operating mantra and created a new culture template called "GE Beliefs," including *stay lean to go fast, learn and adapt to win,* and *empower and inspire each other*, among other beliefs. For the first time in company history, these beliefs were crowdsourced from GE employees. Management wanted to drive a culture that employees wanted to see. One of the changes resulting from the culture shift is that annual events are now passé at GE. Strategic planning processes and employee appraisals have moved from yearly events to more continuous, real-time processes. The changes reinforce the new culture characterized by speed, simplicity, and customer focus.

SOURCE: R. Krishnamoorthy, "GE's Culture Challenge After Welch and Immelt," *Harvard Business Review*, January 26, 2015, accessed from https://hbr.org/2015/01/ges-culture-challenge-after-Welch-and-Immelt.

provides stability to an organization, it resists attempts to direct or manage it. This means that changing an organization's culture is feasible but can be very difficult.[51] (For a more comprehensive examination of organizational change, see Chapter 17.)

One reason that directing changes to organizational culture is so difficult is that assumptions—the deepest level of culture—are often unconscious. As such, they are often non-confrontable and non-debatable. Having strong subcultures and countercultures can help change the dominant culture, but changing assumptions cannot be done directly, and in some situations, may not even be possible. Culture is deeply ingrained and behavioural norms and rewards are well learned.[52] In a sense, employees must unlearn the old norms before they can learn new ones, and this requires first identifying and recognizing those old norms, some of which may be so embedded in the organizational routine that they are automatic and subconscious. Anyone who wants to change culture must first look to the many ways the current culture is being maintained.

A model for cultural change that summarizes the interventions leaders can use is presented in Figure 13.5. There are two approaches to changing an existing culture: The first is helping current members buy into a new set of values (which corresponds to points 1 and 2 in Figure 13.5); while the other is adding newcomers, socializing them into the desired culture, and removing older members who are failing to change (which corresponds to points 3 and 4 in Figure 13.5).[53]

> “If you want to change the culture, you will have to start by changing the organization.”
>
> —Mary Douglas

The first action that leaders must take when attempting to change culture is to replace the artifacts of the old culture with artifacts representing the new culture (point 1 in Figure 13.5). Recall that artifacts of culture include all of the components that can be seen, including behaviours, rites and ceremonies, rituals, stories, and symbols. The new artifacts must send a consistent message about the new values and beliefs. Simply changing cultural artifacts, however, does not change culture. Individuals may change their behaviour or their symbols, but not the values and beliefs that drive underlie those behaviours. They may rationalize, "I'm only doing this because my manager wants me to."

Changing cultural artifacts serves as a notice that cultural change is on the horizon, but real change cannot begin until the espoused and shared values within the organization are changed (point 2, in Figure 13.5). All communication must be revised to ensure that it is consistent with the new values, and it is crucial that the communication be credible; that is, managers must live the new values and not just talk about them. This chapter showed how leaders play crucial roles in shaping and reinforcing culture.[54] The five most important elements in managing culture are (1) what leaders pay attention to; (2) how leaders react to crises; (3) how leaders behave; (4) how leaders allocate rewards; and (5) how leaders hire and fire individuals. These categories are common areas for discrepancy between espoused and enacted values. The leader's role within these five elements must be carefully examined to ensure that the message being communicated is consistent with the new culture.

Leaders should also pay more attention to the informal social networks within the organization than to structural positions when leading organizational change. These informal network communication channels combined with employees' values, and employee beliefs that managers are truly committed to the change effort, can go a long way in making the change a success.[55]

The remaining two actions (points 3 and 4 in Figure 13.5) involve reshaping the workforce to fit the intended culture. First, the organization can revise its selection strategies to more accurately reflect the new culture by hiring new employees who have the desired values and attitudes (point 3 in Figure 13.5). Alternatively, the organization can identify individuals who are resisting the cultural change or who no longer embody the values of the organization and help them move on to other opportunities (point 4 in Figure 13.5). Reshaping the workforce should not involve a ruthless pursuit of nonconforming employees; it should be a gradual and subtle change that takes considerable time. Changing culture is a difficult and drawn-out process, and employees must be given adequate opportunity to come around to the new way of things. Changing personnel adds instability to the organization; adding too many new employees all at once can change culture in unintended ways.

FIGURE 13.5 INTERVENTIONS FOR CHANGING ORGANIZATIONAL CULTURE

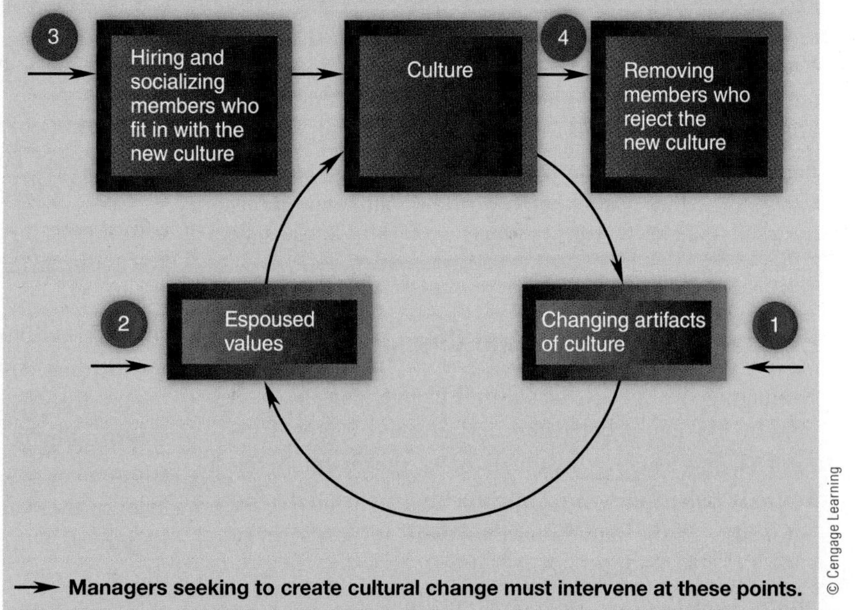

SOURCE: From Vijay Sathe, "How to Decipher and Change Corporate Culture," Chap. 13 in *Gaining Control of the Corporate Culture* (R. H. Kilmann et al., eds.), Fig. 1, p. 245. Copyright © 1985 Jossey-Bass Inc. Reprinted with permission of John Wiley & Sons, Inc.

IN ACTION

Dos and Don'ts for Implementing Cultural Change

Organizational change is possible, but difficult. When attempting organization change:

- Do have a *very* clear vision of what you want to achieve, and what the new culture should look like. Share that vision forcefully.
- Do define the role of managers and draw on the full capabilities of staff.
- Do develop and implement systems and processes to support and reinforce the new vision.
- Do communicate horizontally in conversations and stories, not through top-down commands.
- Don't start by re-organizing. Give people the opportunity to adjust.

SOURCE: S. Denning, *The Leader's Guide to Radical Management: Reinventing the Workplace for the 21st Century* (San Francisco: Jossey-Bass, 2010).

Developing an Ethical Organizational Culture

The organizational culture can have profound effects on the ethical behaviour of organization members.[56] When a company's culture promotes ethical norms, individuals behave accordingly. Managers can encourage ethical behaviour by being good role models for employees. Managers can institute the philosophy that ethical behaviour makes good business sense and puts the company in congruence with the larger values of society.[57] Managers can also communicate that rationalizations for unethical behaviour are not tolerated.

Many companies have implemented a code of ethics to help their employees discern right from wrong, but the impact of these codes is not always as positive as might be expected. The implementation of formal ethics guidelines might be expected to improve ethical behaviour, yet some studies have shown the exact opposite—institution of formal ethics codes can actually lead to less ethical behaviour among employees. There appear to be two main reasons for this: in some cases employees see the code of ethics as simply a management showpiece, leading to cynicism and resentment. In other cases, a heavy reliance on a strict set of rules may reduce the perceived need for employees to think about and be involved in ethical decision making, leading to inferior choices in the long run.[58]

Developing a Culture of Empowerment and Quality

Throughout this text, we have seen that successful organizations promote a culture that empowers employees. Empowerment serves to unleash employees' creativity and productivity by eliminating traditional hierarchical notions of power. Cultures that emphasize empowerment and quality are preferred by Canadian employees. Companies that value empowerment and continuous improvement have cultures that promote high product and service quality.[59]

Evaluating Organizational Change

Evaluating the success of cultural change can be done only by looking at behaviour and enacted values. Cultural change can be assumed to be successful if the desired behaviours are intrinsically motivated and automatic: If the new behaviour were to persist even if rewards were not present, and if the employees have internalized the new value system, then the behaviour is probably intrinsically motivated. When new employees, ideally hired with the desired values and beliefs, maintain these beliefs after being socialized, it can be a good indication that the desired culture has permeated the organization; otherwise, the socialization process would subtly shift employees toward the undesired norms and values. Further, if employees automatically respond to a crisis in ways consistent with the new culture, then the change effort can be deemed successful.

13-6 THE RELATIONSHIP OF CULTURE TO CORPORATE PERFORMANCE

strong culture An organizational culture with a consensus on the values that drive the company and with an intensity that is recognizable even to outsiders.

adaptive culture An organizational culture that encourages confidence and risk taking among employees, has leadership that produces change, and focuses on the changing needs of customers.

The effects of organizational culture are hotly debated by organizational behaviourists and researchers. Because culture is so nebulous and difficult to quantify, and because it is markedly different between industries, between organizations, and even between time periods, its effects on performance are difficult to measure with any reliability or consensus. There are two main theories about how culture relates to organizational performance: the *strong culture perspective* and the *adaptation perspective*.[60]

The Strong Culture Perspective

The strong culture perspective states that organizations with "strong" cultures perform better than other organizations.[61] A **strong culture** is an organizational culture with a consensus on the values that drive the company and with an intensity that is recognizable even to outsiders. Thus, a strong culture is deeply held and widely shared. It also is highly resistant to change.

Strong cultures are thought to facilitate performance for three reasons. First, these cultures are characterized by goal alignment; that is, all employees share common goals. Second, strong cultures create a high level of motivation because of the values shared by the members. Third, strong cultures provide control without the oppressive effects of a bureaucracy.

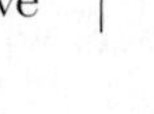

100 years of tradition unimpeded by progress.

—Unknown

There is evidence to support this model. Organizations in a variety of industries were examined over a 10-year period, and those with have strong cultures had greater average levels of return on investment, net income growth, and change in share price.[62] Analysis showed that the link between culture and performance was particularly strong in highly competitive markets and could be attributed to the increased efficiency of routine execution.[63]

There are two concerns with the strong culture perspective: First, there is some evidence indicating that strong economic performance creates strong cultures, rather than the culture being responsible for the economic performance. Second, because strong cultures are notoriously difficult to change, there are countless examples of what happens when the industry or environment changes, and the organizational culture does not. Organizations with unadaptable and inflexible strong cultures often take so long to adjust to changes in their environment that performance suffers, sometimes irreparably.[64]

The Adaptation Perspective

The adaptation perspective states that only cultures that help organizations adapt to environmental change are associated with excellent performance. An **adaptive culture** is a culture that encourages confidence and risk taking among employees,[65] has leadership that produces change,[66] and focuses on the changing needs of customers.[67]

Adaptive cultures facilitate change to meet the needs of three groups of constituents—stockholders, customers, and employees—and showed significantly better long-term economic performance than non-adaptive cultures. Analysis of data from 339 Canadian corporate bankruptcies supports the adaptation perspective: Young firms tended to fail due to a lack of managerial knowledge or financial management abilities, failure among older firms seems to be due to an inability to adapt to environmental change.[68]

STUDY TOOLS 13

IN THE BOOK YOU CAN ...

- ☐ Rip out the **Chapter Review card** at the end of the book to review Key Concepts and Key Terms.
- ☐ Take a "What about You?" Quiz related to material in the chapter.
- ☐ Read additional cases in the Mini Case and Shopify Running Case sections.

ONLINE YOU CAN ... NELSON.COM/STUDENT

- ☐ Take a "What about You?" Quiz related to material in the chapter.
- ☐ Test your understanding with a quick Multiple-Choice Pre-Test quiz.
- ☐ Read the eBook, which includes discussion points for questions posed in the Cases.
- ☐ Watch Videos related to chapter content.
- ☐ Use the available Flashcards and Matching Quizzes to test your understanding of key terms and concepts.
- ☐ See how much you've learned by taking a Post-Test.

WHAT ABOUT YOU?

Organizational Culture and Ethics

Think about the organization you currently work for or one you know something about and complete the following Ethical Climate Questionnaire.

Use the scale below and write the number that best represents your answer in the space next to each item.

To what extent are the following statements true about your company?

COMPLETELY FALSE	MOSTLY FALSE	SOMEWHAT FALSE	SOMEWHAT TRUE	MOSTLY TRUE	COMPLETELY TRUE
0	1	2	3	4	5

____ **1.** In this company, people are expected to follow their own personal and moral beliefs.

____ **2.** People are expected to do anything to further the company's interests.

____ **3.** In this company, people look out for each other's good.

____ **4.** It is very important here to follow the company's rules and procedures strictly.

____ **5.** In this company, people protect their own interests above other considerations.

____ **6.** The first consideration is whether a decision violates any law.

____ **7.** Everyone is expected to stick by company rules and procedures.

____ **8.** The most efficient way is always the right way in this company.

____ **9.** Our major consideration is what is best for everyone in the company.

____ **10.** In this company, the law or ethical code of the profession is the major consideration.

____ **11.** It is expected at this company that employees will always do what is right for the customer and the public.

To score the questionnaire, first add up your responses to questions 1, 3, 6, 9, 10, and 11. This is subtotal number 1. Next, reverse the scores on questions 2, 4, 5, 7, and 8 (5 = 0, 4 = 1, 3 = 2, 2 = 3, 1 = 4, 0 = 5). Add the reverse scores to form subtotal number 2. Add subtotal number 1 to subtotal number 2 for an overall score.

Subtotal 1 ______ + Subtotal 2 ______ = Overall Score ______.

Overall scores can range from 0 to 55. The higher the score, the more the organization's culture encourages ethical behaviour.

SOURCE: Republished with permission of Elsevier Science and Technology Journals, from *Organizational Dynamics*, "An Ethical Weather Report: Assessing the Organization's Ethical Climate" by John B. Cullen et al., Autumn 1989. Copyright © 1989; permission conveyed through Copyright Clearance Center, Inc.

MINI CASE

The Great Little Box Company

The Great Little Box Company (GLBC) is an award-winning Canadian company that manufactures and distributes custom and stock packaging solutions. The company produces more than several hundred thousand boxes and more than a million labels every day. The corporate culture of GLBC is apparent in the facility on Mitchell Island, Richmond, BC, that houses its head office, manufacturing, and warehouse activities: Open-concept offices are arranged in a horseshoe design so employees have a view of the Fraser River; there's a gym open 24 hours a day; the manufacturing and warehouse facilities are clean, with abundant natural light; and there's even an outdoor gazebo, volleyball and basketball courts, horseshoe pitch and dock for kayaking commuters. The company also offers employees a nap room for quiet time, and free coffee, tea, and snacks.

But GLBC offers more to its 300 employees than just amenities: The company sets a production goal each year and then uses "open-book management" where, once a month, it share their financial data with employees so employees know precisely how the company is performing. If the company's performance surpasses its original target, every employee goes on an all-expenses-paid vacation to a sunny destination.

As if that's not enough, the company-subsidized social committee organizes many events (e.g., golf tournament, paintball competition, summer barbeques, summer cruises on the president's boat), and the social calendar reflects the cultural diversity of the firm with its annual celebrations of the Chinese New Year and the Sikh festival of Baisakhi. Employees receive individual performance reviews every three months, 360-degree feedback is invited, and exceptional performance and cost-saving ideas are rewarded. Benefits include full tuition subsidies for courses completed at outside institutions, academic scholarships for employees' children, flexible working hours, reduced summer hours, compressed work weeks, and phased-in retirement. GLBC donates and matches employee donations to numerous charitable and community initiatives, with employees helping to select the charitable groups assisted each year. The company planted over 4,000 trees and shrubs on its new site and is reducing its carbon footprint through an internal scrap recovery program and shipping pallet repair program. The artifacts at GLBC reinforce the notion that GLBC cares about excellence but at the same time cares about employees and the environment, seeking a balance that creates a fine quality of life for all.

SOURCE: R. Yerema and R. Caballero, 2010. "Great Little Box Company," Canada's Top 100 Employers competition; P. DeVries, 2014. "Robert Meggy: Manufacturer puts people first," *Business Insider*, https://biv.com/article/2014/11/robert-meggy-manufacturer-puts-people-first, accessed May 11, 2018.

Apply Your Understanding

1. Identify the levels of organizational culture described in this case.
2. Describe how new employees might be socialized.
3. What is the cultural significance of the open-book management technique?

RUNNING CASE **SHOPIFY**

CULTURE OF OPTIMISM AND CREATIVITY

Shopify is currently one of Canada's most valuable public technology companies, and founder and CEO Tobias Lütke has explained that they got there not because of their knowledge but by being as creative as possible: "We are all here because of how we react when we don't know what to do."

The whole focus of the Shopify model is to make commerce better and easier for vendors to sell their goods online, so the company's business focus is heavily invested in responding to its customers and improving its technology. Like many tech companies, Shopify fosters innovation and development through a culture that encourages optimism and creativity. Shopify has a director of culture whose responsibility it is to bridge the gap between the executive team and the rest of the company, and she says "My team and I are obsessed about not losing our culture but balancing that with the fact that it does need to evolve and change in some ways. At the core, it's about maintaining whatever culture we're trying to embody, because if it goes in a direction that we don't want it to, it's a lot harder to reign in."

Shopify actively recruits employees who are ambitious, driven, and like to be challenged by their work, and those employees are granted a very high level of autonomy. The company focuses on employee health and offers benefits like self-directed budgets to support learning and growth, and even offers employees catered meals and housecleaning services to save them time and stress and help them focus on staying positive, creative, and optimistic. Shopify is alert to the future, and has identified virtual reality and cryptocurrencies as technologies that will surely influence how Shopify does business. Shopify plans to stay on top of these trends—they've pledged to be a 100-year business.

SOURCES: https://www.cbc.ca/news/canada/ottawa/shopify-cynicism-optimism-1.3261379; http://wayswework.io/interviews/konval-matin-director-of-culture-at-shopify

Apply Your Understanding

1. How do the many different departments at Shopify differentiate the culture?
2. How is Shopify's culture affected by its current CEO also being its founder?
3. Explain the significance of Shopify's director of culture saying, "My team and I are obsessed about not losing our culture but balancing that with the fact that it does need to evolve and change in some ways."

Carlos Osorio/Toronto Star via Getty Images

ColorBlind Images/Getty Images

14 Learning and Performance Management

LEARNING OUTCOMES

After reading this chapter, you should be able to do the following:

14-1 Describe classical conditioning and reinforcement theory's approach to learning.

14-2 Describe Bandura's social learning theory.

14-3 Describe evidence showing that thinking about learning seems to influence the learning process.

14-4 Explain the aspects of performance management.

14-5 Explain the importance of performance feedback and how it can be delivered effectively.

14-6 Identify ways managers can reward performance.

14-7 Describe how to correct poor performance.

See the end of this chapter for a list of available Study Tools, a "What about You?" Quiz, Mini Case, and the Shopify Running Case.

MODELS OF LEARNING IN ORGANIZATIONS

A lot of managerial work involves facilitating learning, motivating performance, and using feedback to improve performance. A large organization like the federal government can provide a great career, but if it is to be a productive one, you'll need to manage yourself, set your own work goals, reward yourself when you do well, and penalize yourself when you do a poor job. Setting your own goals lets you set up measures and feedback systems to tell you if you are making positive progress toward these goals. Don't worry about being overly self-critical concerning performance problems; think more about rewarding yourself. Praise breeds confidence, leading to better performance.

> "Learning is a change in behaviour acquired through experience ... it helps guide and direct motivated behaviour."

Learning is a change in behaviour acquired through experience. Learning helps guide and direct motivated behaviour. Learning may begin with the cognitive activity of developing knowledge about a subject, which then leads to a change in behaviour. We will examine cognitive and social theories of learning. Alternatively, other approaches to learning assume that observable behaviour is a result of conditioning or is a function of its consequences. This is where we begin our discussion of models of learning.

14-1 CLASSICAL CONDITIONING

Classical conditioning is the process of modifying behaviour by pairing a conditioned stimulus with an unconditioned stimulus to elicit an unconditioned response. Its discovery is largely the result of Russian physiologist Ivan Pavlov's experimentation on animals (primarily dogs).

Classical conditioning builds on the natural reaction of an unconditioned response to an unconditioned stimulus. In dogs, this might be the natural production of saliva (unconditioned response) in response to the presentation of meat (unconditioned stimulus). By presenting a conditioned stimulus (for example, a ringing bell) simultaneously with the unconditioned stimulus (meat), the researcher made the dog develop a conditioned response (salivation). After enough trials, the dog salivated at the sound of a bell, even when no meat was presented.

As demonstrated by B.F. Skinner, classical conditioning may occur similarly in humans.[1]

For example, people working at a computer terminal may get lower back tension (unconditioned response) from poor posture (unconditioned stimulus). If they become aware of that tension only when the manager appears (conditioned stimulus), then they may develop a conditioned response (lower back tension) to the appearance of the manager.

But classical conditioning has limited applicability to human behaviour in organizations for three reasons. First, humans are more complex than dogs and less amenable to simple cause-and-effect conditioning. Second, the behavioural environments in organizations are complex and not very amenable to single stimulus–response manipulations. Third, the human capacity for decision making can override simple conditioning.

Reinforcement Theory

Reinforcement theory focuses on the power of consequences to influence behaviour. Recall the concepts of instrumentality and valence from expectancy theory, discussed in Chapter 5, and expectancy theory's contention that we are motivated if we see a connection between our actions and valued outcomes. Reinforcement theory focuses on the power of those outcomes and can be applied to the motivation to learn new tasks as well as to perform known ones. Reinforcement theory emerged from Skinner's work on **operant conditioning** with animals. Skinner's animal subjects learned to "operate" on their environment in response to the consequences Skinner provided. For example, rats learned to press levers a specific number of times to release food pellets, not a natural way for them to get food. Skinner and others extended the work to humans, providing reinforcements in response to specific behaviour and watching the results. Humans have used consequences in the form of rewards and punishments to try to modify others' behaviour for a long time (e.g., gold stars for schoolwork, imprisonment for committing crimes). Reinforcement

learning A change in behaviour acquired through experience.

classical conditioning Modifying behaviour by pairing a conditioned stimulus with an unconditioned stimulus to elicit an unconditioned response.

operant conditioning Modifying behaviour through the use of positive or negative consequences following specific behaviours.

theory and its research systematically examine the motivational effect of consequences on all aspects of human behaviour. Many of the findings from Skinner's animal research also apply to people: timing of consequences is important (the closer an outcome is to the behaviour, the more impact it has); the consistency of reinforcement affects how fast something is learned and how quickly it is "unlearned" once reinforcement stops; performers will learn behaviours in order to avoid unpleasant consequences as well as achieve desirable consequences; learning is faster when the reinforcement is more valued (when the person is "hungrier" for it); learning can be accidental and unintended when outcomes just happen to coincide with behaviours (the origin of many superstitions); people will work at less desirable activities in order to get the opportunity of working on highly desirable activities; and people can learn complex tasks by a shaping process of reinforcing first only crude attempts and then requiring performance closer and closer to the ideal before reinforcement is given.[2]

Reinforcement theory is central to the design and implementation of organizational reward systems (e.g., paying sales commissions) and many aspects of performance management, like disciplinary approaches. The underlying premise is that people develop or strengthen behaviours that are followed by positive consequences and weaken or eliminate behaviours that are not.

Organizations applying reinforcement theory can use four basic strategies: positive reinforcement, negative reinforcement (both of which serve to encourage more of the behaviour), punishment, and extinction (both of which discourage the repetition of the behaviour). Table 14.1 shows these approaches.

REINFORCEMENT Reinforcement is the attempt to develop or strengthen desirable behaviour by either bestowing positive consequences or withholding negative consequences. **Positive reinforcement** occurs when a positive consequence (like a bonus) follows a desirable behaviour (like a successful business year).

The Pressure Pipe Inspection Company based in Mississauga, Ontario, has instituted a "going to the moon" philosophy as its theme, aiming to double its revenues over the next year and quintuple it over the next five. To motivate staff to work toward this common goal, employees who best represent the company and pull their weight are rewarded with an all-expenses-paid trip to Cape Canaveral.

positive reinforcement Attempting to strengthen desirable behaviour by bestowing positive consequences.

negative reinforcement Attempting to strengthen desirable behaviour by withholding negative consequences.

TABLE 14.1 USING CONSEQUENCES TO CHANGE BEHAVIOUR

Increase Behaviour Via ...	**Positive reinforcement** e.g., Top salesperson earns car
	Negative reinforcement e.g., Top salesperson's paperwork is completed by other person for next month
Decrease Behaviour Via ...	**Punishment** e.g., Poorest salesperson gets moved to less promising sales territory and has to go for (disliked) sales training
	Extinction e.g., Ignore the salesperson when they whine and complain

Negative reinforcement occurs when there is an attempt to strengthen desirable behaviour by withholding a negative consequence. For example, if an instructor says to students that an 80 percent or higher on all term work before the final will mean they do not need to write the final exam, the instructor is using negative reinforcement to motivate student effort and learning. The same approach is being used by a manager who promises an employee that, if they figure out how to resolve a tough debugging problem, the manager will take the employee's place at the committee meeting this week, the one the employee dislikes attending so much. In a less deliberate example of negative reinforcement, an employee might learn to come in early each day to avoid the manager's critical look when arriving after the manager.

Managers can use either continuous or intermittent schedules of positive reinforcement. Table 14.2 describes both. When managers design organizational reward systems, they consider not only the type of reinforcement but also how often to provide it. Research results indicate that ratio schedules of reinforcement that link reinforcement to specific responses are more effective than interval ones based on time passed.[3] Unsurprisingly, this suggests pay-for-performance schemes will motivate greater effort than fixed salaries. Research also suggests that variable, unpredictable schedules of reinforcement motivate a steadier high rate of response than fixed schedules. Not knowing the likely outcome of the next move and knowing it could be important will trigger a more motivated employee than knowing exactly when and how one will be reinforced. Of course, all reinforcement schedules have to be created within the constraints of what is fair and reasonable in the organizational context.

TABLE 14.2 SCHEDULES OF REINFORCEMENT

Schedule	Description	Effects on Responding
Continuous	Reinforcer follows every response.	**1.** Steady high rate of performance as long as reinforcement follows every response **2.** High frequency of reinforcement may lead to early satiation **3.** Behaviour weakens rapidly (undergoes extinction) when reinforcers are withheld **4.** Appropriate for newly emitted, unstable, low-frequency responses
Intermittent	Reinforcer does not follow every response.	**1.** Capable of producing high frequencies of responding **2.** Low frequency of reinforcement precludes early satiation **3.** Appropriate for stable or high-frequency responses
Fixed Ratio	A fixed number of responses must be emitted before reinforcement occurs. Example: bonus for every 50 trees planted	**1.** A fixed ratio of 1:1 (reinforcement occurs after every response) is the same as a continuous schedule **2.** Tends to produce a high rate of response that is vigorous and steady
Variable Ratio	A varying or random number of responses must be emitted before reinforcement occurs. Example: salesperson rewarded with sale after unpredictable number of calls	Capable of producing a high rate of response that is vigorous, steady, and resistant to extinction
Fixed Interval	The first response after a specific period of time has elapsed is reinforced. Example: salary given every two weeks for continued performance	Produces an uneven response pattern varying from a very slow, unenergetic response immediately following reinforcement to a very fast, vigorous response immediately preceding reinforcement
Variable Interval	The first response after varying or random periods of time have elapsed is reinforced. Example: promotion based on seniority occurs when space becomes available	Tends to produce a high rate of response that is vigorous, steady, and resistant to extinction

SOURCE: Table from *Organizational Behavior Modification and Beyond*, by Fred Luthans and Robert Kreitner. Copyright © 1985, p. 58, by Scott Foresman and Company and the authors. Reprinted by permission of the authors.

PUNISHMENT **Punishment** is the attempt to eliminate or weaken undesirable behaviour. One way to punish a person is to follow an undesirable behaviour with a negative consequence. For example, a professional athlete who is excessively offensive to an official (undesirable behaviour) may be ejected from a game (negative consequence). The other way to punish a person is to withhold a positive consequence following an undesirable behaviour. For example, a salesperson who makes few visits to potential clients (undesirable behaviour) will likely receive a very small commission cheque (positive consequence).

Punishment sometimes has unintended results. Because punishment is discomforting to the individual being punished, it can bring about negative psychological, emotional, performance, or behavioural consequences (such as workplace deviance). Some managers use the threat of punishment to scare workers into greater effort.[4]

EXTINCTION An alternative to punishing undesirable behaviour is **extinction**—the attempt to weaken a behaviour by attaching no consequences (either positive or negative) to it. Extinction may require time and patience, but the absence of consequences eventually weakens a behaviour.

Extinction may be most effective when used in conjunction with the positive reinforcement of desirable behaviours; for example, by complimenting a colleague for constructive comments (reinforcing desirable behaviour) while ignoring sarcastic comments (extinguishing undesirable behaviour).

Extinction is not always the best strategy, however. In cases of dangerous, or seriously undesirable, behaviour, punishment might better deliver a swift, clear lesson.

Note that extinction can happen unintentionally, with unwanted results. Imagine you are a keen new employee who works hard yet gets no praise and attention. Eventually you stop trying so hard. Your manager believes she has been showing her faith in you by leaving you alone. She has no idea that her lack of response has extinguished your eagerness.

punishment Attempting to eliminate or weaken undesirable behaviour by bestowing negative consequences or withholding positive consequences.

extinction Attempting to eliminate or weaken undesirable behaviour by attaching no consequences to it.

14-2 SOCIAL AND COGNITIVE THEORIES OF LEARNING

Reinforcement theory is not the only model of learning. Albert Bandura's social learning theory offers an alternative and complement to Skinner's behaviourist approaches.[5] Cognitive theory draws on the theories of Carl Jung discussed in Chapter 3. Recent research has emphasized the importance of learners thinking about what and how they are learning.

Bandura's Social Learning Theory

Bandura believes learning occurs when we observe other people and model their behaviour. Since employees look to their supervisors for acceptable norms of behaviour, they are likely to pattern their own actions after the supervisor's.

Central to Bandura's social learning theory is the notion of **task-specific self-efficacy**, an individual's beliefs and expectancies about their ability to perform a specific task effectively. Individuals with high self-efficacy believe that they have the ability to get things done. Self-efficacy is higher in a learning context than in a performance context, especially for individuals with a high learning orientation.[6] There are four sources of task-specific self-efficacy: prior experiences, behaviour models (witnessing the success of others), persuasion from other people, and assessment of current physical and emotional capabilities.[7] Evidence suggests that self-efficacy leads to high performance on a wide variety of physical and mental tasks.[8] Conversely, success can enhance your self-efficacy. For example, women who trained in physical self-defence increased their self-efficacy in self-defence and new tasks.[9]

task-specific self-efficacy An individual's beliefs and expectancies about their ability to perform a specific task effectively.

Bandura saw the power of social reinforcement, recognizing that financial and material rewards often occur following or in conjunction with the approval of others, whereas punishments often follow social disapproval. Thus, self-efficacy and social reinforcement influence behaviour and performance at work.

bikeriderlondon/Shutterstock

Managers can empower employees and help them develop self-efficacy by providing job challenges, coaching and counselling for improved performance, and rewarding employees' achievements. Given the increasing diversity of the workforce, managers may want to target their efforts toward women and other disadvantaged groups, who tend to have lower than average self-efficacy.[10]

Cognitive Theories of Learning

The cognitive approach to learning is based on the *Gestalt* school of thought and draws on Jung's theory of personality differences.

Recall the distinction between introverts (who need to study, concentrate, and reflect) and extraverts (who need to interact with other people). Introverts learn best alone, and extraverts learn best by exchanging ideas with others. The personality functions of intuition, sensing, thinking, and feeling all have learning implications, which are listed in Table 14.3.

TABLE 14.3 PERSONALITY FUNCTIONS AND LEARNING

Personality Preference	Implications for Learning by Individuals
Information Gathering	
Intuitors	Prefer theoretical frameworks. Look for the meaning in material. Attempt to understand the grand scheme. Look for possibilities and interrelations.
Sensors	Prefer specific, empirical data. Look for practical applications. Attempt to master details of a subject. Look for what is realistic and doable.
Decision Making	
Thinkers	Prefer analysis of data and information. Work to be fair-minded and even-handed. Seek logical, just conclusions. Do not like to be too personally involved.
Feelers	Prefer interpersonal involvement. Work to be tender-hearted and harmonious. Seek subjective, merciful results. Do not like objective, factual analysis.

SOURCE: O. Kroeger and J. M. Thuesen, *Type Talk: The 16 Personality Types That Determine How We Live, Love, and Work* (New York: Dell Publishing Co., 1989).

IN ACTION

Andy Byford and the TTC

Andy Byford joined the Toronto Transit Commission (TTC) in 2012 at its CEO. His goal was to modernize the TTC from top to bottom. After five years, he believed that he had accomplished his goal. In June 2017, his work was recognized when the TTC received the best transit agency award. The chair of the TTC, Josh Colle, commented that "Mr. Byford has been no less than superb when it comes to taking the tens of millions of additional dollars city council has given the TTC ..." Colle also praised Byford's "relentless focus on customer service," which he said had made the transit system "cleaner, safer and more reliable for our customers."

Byford left the TTC to become the CEO of the New York City Transit Authority (NYCTA). The NYCTA is the largest public transit system in North America; eight million people a day use it! It is in a state of operational and financial crisis. For example, trains are delayed 70,000 times a month now, while in 2012, the rate was 28,000. The on-time rate has decreased from 90 percent in 2012 to 58 percent in 2018. Early in his tenure as CEO in New York, Byford spent time on the platforms to learn directly from passengers and to observe the conditions of the stations. Byford has concluded that the NYCTA has a "coercive attitude" to its employees, which has resulted in many problems. Byford has a massive performance challenge in front of him.

SOURCES: W. Finnegan, "Tunnel Vision: Can Andy Byford Fix New York's Disastrous Subways? "*The New Yorker*, July 9 and 16, 2018: 36–49; B. Spurr, "Andy Byford Leaving the TTC for a Job with New York City Transit," *Toronto Star*, November 21, 2017, accessed from https://www.thestar.com/news/gta/transportation/2017/11/21/andy-byford-stepping-down-as-head-of-ttc.html, July 1, 2018.

Managers can help employees develop self-efficacy. Each employee has a preferred mode of gathering information and a preferred mode of evaluating and making decisions about that information. For example, an intuitive thinker may want to skim research reports about implementing total quality programs and then, based on hunches, decide how to apply the research findings to the organization. A sensing feeler may prefer viewing videotaped interviews with people in companies that implemented total quality programs and then identify people in the organization most likely to be receptive to the approaches presented.

> "Managers can help employees develop self-efficacy."

14-3 THE VALUE OF THINKING ABOUT LEARNING

Regardless of an individual's personality, the success of several learning approaches emphasizes the value of getting learners to reflect on what and how they are learning. These approaches are self-regulation prompts in online training, error management training, and after-events reviews.

Self-regulation prompting is a technique that was developed for online training, an increasingly popular approach for organizational training because it can be cost-effective and convenient. Online training means the learning is essentially self-controlled and no teacher can easily keep an eye on how the learner is doing. Self-regulation prompting puts the learner into the role of monitoring their own learning. In this technique, learners are prompted at regular intervals to reflect on their learning through questions interspersed in the online delivery of material, e.g., am I concentrating on learning the training material? Are the study tactics I have been using effective for learning the training material? Which main points haven't I understood yet? Do I need to continue to review before taking the final exam?[11] Research shows that the prompting not only increases learning (compared to participants not given the prompts) but learners are also less likely to disengage after failures and are less likely to drop out of the course. The prompts to self-regulate lead to more time spent on task and may create more internal attributions and a sense of personal control so learners are less likely to give up.[12]

Error management training suggests that when it comes to learning, the more errors you make, the better. In error management training, the learner is immersed in a safe training environment where errors are likely to occur, is given minimum guidance, and is encouraged to explore and make mistakes. The errors are positively framed as learning experiences. Research shows that not only is learning more effective than in a proceduralized

self-regulation prompting Questions that encourage learners to reflect on what and how they are learning.

error management training Immersion in a safe training environment where learners are encouraged to deliberately make mistakes and see what happens.

approach, but also after the training the learners are more likely to transfer their learning to new situations.[13] This seems to be because they have had so much feedback and had a chance to develop rich mental models of their actions and the consequences. Error management training also seems to help participants learn to deal less emotionally with errors and setbacks in general and to plan, monitor, and evaluate their progress during task completion.[14]

The **after-events review** (AER, also known as after-action review, post-event review, or incident review) is a training procedure that gives the individual the chance to systematically analyze their decisions and behaviours after a learning activity or real performance. For example, after a first project management experience, employees may be asked to reconstruct their actions in the project and suggest which of their behaviours supported the project's success and which hindered the project's progress, trying to figure out their mistakes and why they occurred, and determine their successful decisions or actions, and what they can learn from their mistakes to improve future performance.[15] There is no sense of blame and there is no reward offered; the focus is on the task and analyzing what worked and what did not. AERs advance learning from experience because they direct learners to analyze their experience, create rich mental models of the events,[16] and produce more internal and specific attributions. After successful events, the most effective way to gain lessons is from reviewing wrong actions. After failed experience, any kind of review (correct or wrong actions) is effective, though focusing on correct actions is slightly less effective in improving later performance.[17] Interestingly, watching an AER of another person whose performance is relevant can be just as effective as a personal AER if the video models a thorough, systematic analysis because watching still triggers self-reflection.[18] AERs seem to enhance learning not only through increased information but also through increased self-efficacy. Because learners have a deeper understanding of the reasons for their success or failure, there is a greater sense of mastery. AERs have been used in organizations as different as the World Meteorological Organization, Chrysler, British Petroleum and GE.[19] General Electric's legendary reputation for talent management owes much to one person, William J. Conaty, who retired in 2007 after 13 years as head of human resources and 40 years at GE. Conaty had seven keys to nurture leaders so they could achieve great performance.

after-events review Procedure where, following an experience, learners systematically analyze how their actions and decisions contributed to the success and failure of the performance.

performance management A process of defining, measuring, appraising, providing feedback on, and responding to performance.

1. Dare to differentiate the best from the rest by constantly judging, ranking, rewarding, and punishing employees for their performance.
2. Constantly raise the bar to improve performance, which leaders do both among their own team members and for themselves.
3. Do not be friends with the boss but establish your own trustworthiness and integrity as a confidant to all.
4. Become easy to replace by developing great succession plans, especially when you do not need them, and mentoring the next generation.
5. Be inclusive and do not favour people that you know because it can undermine your success.
6. Free up others to do their jobs, especially by taking things off your boss's desk that are better done by you or others.
7. Keep it simple by being consistent and straightforward because most organizations require simple, focused, and disciplined communications.[20]

FAST FACT

Based on a content analysis of individual annual performance reviews, women are 1.4 times more likely to receive critical subjective feedback rather than positive feedback or critical objective feedback. As well, women get less constructive critical feedback and get less specific feedback than men do.

SOURCE: Paola Cecchi-Dimeglio, How Gender Bias Corrupts Performance Reviews, and What to Do About It, *Harvard Business Review*, April 12 2017, accessed from https://hbr.org/2017/04/how-gender-bias-corrupts-performance-reviews-and-what-to-do-about-it, December 10 2018.

14-4 PERFORMANCE MANAGEMENT

Ultimately, an organization is concerned with the performance or task accomplishments of the individuals and teams within it. The organization's success and survival depend on that performance. Research has shown that the more people know what to do, why, and how, and care about it, the more likely their performance will be successful. This is the underlying premise of performance management.

Performance management is a process of defining, measuring, appraising, providing feedback on, and responding to performance.[21] Defining performance in behavioural terms is an essential first step in the process. Once defined, performance can be measured and assessed so that workers can receive feedback and managers can set goals to improve performance. Positive performance behaviours should be rewarded, and poor performance behaviours should be corrected.

IN ACTION

Deloitte's Performance Management Redesign

TonyV3112/Shutterstock.com

Ask any company which HRM process has the most significant impact on employee performance, and it will likely point to its performance management system. Companies use performance management systems to evaluate the work of their employees, then train, promote, and pay them based on the outcomes. Big 4 consulting firm Deloitte is no different.

For years, Deloitte has used a performance management process that is similar to the process used by many companies, one characterized by once-a-year rankings of employees, cascading goals and objectives, backward-looking assessments, and 360-degree surveys to capture multiple impressions of employee performance. Recently, Deloitte announced a major overhaul of its performance management system. Why? Three discoveries. First, the once-a-year "batch" process of evaluating employee performance against goals did not reflect the need to evaluate real-time employee performance. The process needed to allow for more agility. Next, Deloitte realized that 62 percent of an employee's evaluation on certain criteria actually reflected the idiosyncrasies of the rater. For instance, how tough a rater evaluated an employee's strategic thinking skills depended on how much of a strategic thinker the rater was. Finally, a study of their own work teams found that employees who believed they had a chance to use their strengths at work were the highest performers. Deloitte's redesigned performance management is characterized by compensation decisions that are separate from daily performance, regular or per-project "performance snapshots," and weekly check-ins with managers to help keep performance on track.

SOURCE: M. Buckingham and A. Goodall, "Reinventing Performance Management," *Harvard Business Review* (April 2015): 40–50.

Defining Performance

Managers must clearly define performance if their employees are to perform well at work. Most work performance is multidimensional. For example, a sales executive's performance will require administrative, financial, and interpersonal skills. Defining performance (listing the skills and behaviours needed to perform) is a prerequisite to measuring and evaluating job performance.

One of the reasons goal setting (see Chapter 5) can be effective is that it clarifies task–role expectations for employees. Goal setting typically involves a discussion between supervisor and employee about what goals are relevant, what levels and deadlines are reasonable, and how varying goals compare in importance. The process of goal setting therefore improves communication between managers and employees[22] and reduces the role of stress associated with confusing and conflicting expectations. A 14-month evaluation found that goal setting reduced conflict, confusion, and absenteeism.[23]

Goals Improve Performance Evaluation

Goal setting is effective for not only motivational purposes but also improving the accuracy and validity of performance evaluation. One of the best methods for this is **management by objectives (MBO)**—a goal-setting program based on interaction and negotiation between employees and managers.

According to Peter Drucker, who developed the concept of MBO over 50 years ago, the objectives-setting process begins with the employee writing an "employee's letter" to the manager. The letter explains the employee's general understanding of the scope of the manager's job, as well as the scope of the employee's own job, and lays out a set of specific objectives to be pursued over the next six to 12 months. After some discussion and negotiation, the manager and the employee finalize the items into a performance plan.

Drucker considers MBO a participative and interactive process. This does not mean that goal setting begins at the bottom of the organization. It means that goal setting is applicable to all employees, even lower-level organizational members and professional staff having influence in the goal-setting process.[24] Most goal-setting programs are designed to enhance performance, especially when incentives are associated with goal achievement.[25]

management by objectives (MBO) A goal-setting program based on interaction and negotiation between employees and managers.

The two central ingredients in goal-setting programs are planning and evaluation.

The planning component consists of organizational and individual goal setting, two essential and interdependent processes.[26]

In planning, individuals and departments usually have discretionary control to develop operational and tactical plans to support the organizational objectives. The idea is to formulate a clear, consistent, measurable, and ordered set of goals to articulate *what* to do. Operational support planning then determines *how* to do it. The concept of intention encompasses both the goal *(what)* and the set of pathways that lead to goal attainment *(how)*.[27]

The evaluation component consists of interim reviews of goal progress (conducted by managers and employees) and formal performance evaluation. The reviews are mid-term assessments designed to help employees take self-corrective action. The formal performance evaluation occurs at the close of a reporting period, usually once a year. Effective performance reviews must be tailored to the business, capture what goes on in the business, and be easily adapted to business changes.[28]

Because goal-setting programs are somewhat mechanical by nature, they are most easily implemented in stable, predictable industrial settings and less useful at unpredictable organizations. Finally, individual, gender, and cultural differences do not appear to threaten the success of goal-setting programs, making them useful tools for a diverse workforce.[29]

Measuring Performance

Ideally, actual performance matches measured performance. Practically, this is seldom the case. Since operational performance generates more quantifiable data, it is easier to measure than managerial performance. Goal setting is applicable to all employees, even lower-level organizational members and professional staff.

Because quantifiable data is easier to discuss and respond to, there is a temptation to focus only on it. That means that other behaviour, equally important but harder to measure, gets ignored in performance measurement. For example, employees may have high productivity numbers and a low reject rate but at the same time not follow safety practices, refuse to assist others in the team environment when there are difficulties, and not maintain their equipment. As a result, the company has to pay for new equipment that wears out prematurely, there is enhanced safety risk for all, and morale in the team is damaged. Yet, if only the employees' production rate and reject rate are measured, the problems will not be flagged or addressed. What gets measured is what gets done, so it is important that all the important behaviours are addressed in performance measurement.

Performance appraisal systems should improve the accuracy of measured performance and increase its agreement with actual performance. The extent of agreement is called the *true assessment*, as Figure 14.1 shows. The performance measurement problems, including deficiency, unreliability, and invalidity, contribute to inaccuracy. Deficiency occurs when important aspects of a person's actual performance are overlooked. Unreliability results from poor-quality performance measures. Invalidity stems from inaccurate definition of the expected job performance.

Many performance-monitoring systems use modern electronic technology to measure the performance of vehicle operators, computer technicians, and customer service representatives. For example, such systems might record the rate of keystrokes or the total number of keystrokes for a computer technician, or how long the employee was at the work station.[30]

FIGURE 14.1 ACTUAL AND MEASURED PERFORMANCE

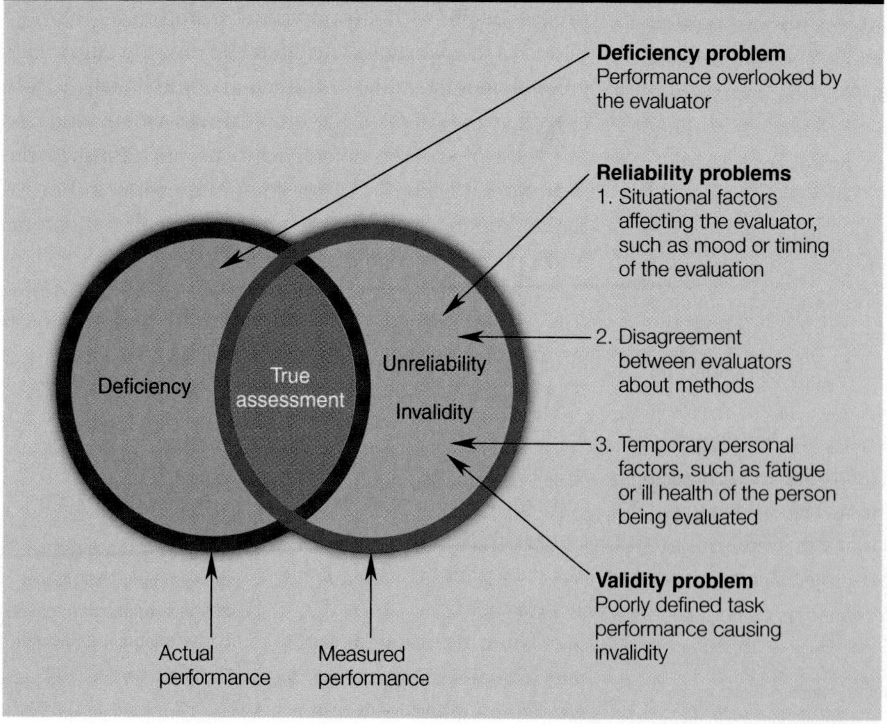

When is electronic monitoring spying and when is it acceptable to employees? Employees who show strong commitment and identification with the organization are more likely to accept electronic monitoring and surveillance and those with low commitment are most likely to find innovative ways to circumvent the monitoring system. This creates an interesting paradox in that committed individuals are unlikely to need monitoring anyway because their goals align with the organization's goals, whereas the uncommitted employees may need monitoring yet are more likely to undermine its success. Monitoring seems to be more accepted where employees know what is being monitored and the rationale behind it (enhancing procedural justice), and how the information will be used (and not abused). If the company has an ethical culture that clearly practices and rewards ethical behaviour, electronic monitoring is more accepted.[31]

Measuring the performance is one step and sharing the performance appraisal with the employee is another step, also fraught with potential difficulties. The value and challenges of giving performance feedback are addressed next.

14-5 PERFORMANCE FEEDBACK

Feedback sessions create stress for both supervisors and employees. Early research at General Electric found employees responded constructively to positive feedback, but often responded defensively to critical or negative feedback, by shifting responsibility for the problem, denying it outright, or providing a wide range of excuses for it.[32] However, although it is easier to give and accept positive feedback, negative feedback is typically more effective in improving subsequent performance.[33] Sometimes performance actually decreases after feedback, particularly positive feedback because people feel they have achieved their aim and do not need to continue to work so hard.[34] The earlier discussion of AERs emphasized the value of discussing errors even within the context of success.

Both supervisor and employee should try to make performance feedback a constructive learning experience because feedback has long-term implications for the employee's performance and for their working relationship. The following three guidelines are useful for providing evaluative feedback.[35] First, refer to specific, verbatim statements and specific, observable behaviours displayed by the employee. This enhances the acceptance of the feedback while discouraging denial. Second, focus on changeable behaviours, not intrinsic or personality-based attributes. Third, plan the session ahead of time, notifying the person who will receive the feedback so that both parties can be ready.

Supervisors should start coaching and counselling sessions with something positive. Once the session is under way and rapport is established, then the evaluator can introduce more difficult and negative material. No one is perfect, so everyone can learn and grow through performance feedback sessions. Critical feedback is the basis for improvement. It is especially challenging to give feedback in times of stress because employees are less likely to make good use of the feedback, reacting emotionally rather than focusing on systematically determining what happened.[36] Because evaluation itself can be stressful, it is advisable to let employees know beforehand when it will happen but not to emphasize it, to avoid comparisons with others and focus strictly on the tasks, and not to emphasize the negative consequences, especially for employees who are high in trait anxiety.[37]

360-Degree Feedback

Many organizations use **360-degree feedback**, which is based on multiple sources of information, to improve the accuracy of performance appraisals. Evidence suggests that including self-evaluations in this process makes evaluation interviews more satisfying, more constructive, and less defensive.[38] Some dislike the fact that self-evaluations often disagree with supervisory evaluations.[39] However, these disagreements are part of the full picture of the person's performance. The 360-degree feedback method provides a well-rounded view of performance from superiors, peers, followers, and customers.[40] It has high reliability and validity, and individuals usually improve after receiving the feedback, although not by a large amount. Interestingly, the ones who improve the most are the ones who originally overrate their performance, and receive negative feedback indicating they are out of line with how others see them.[41]

360-degree feedback can be improved by adding a systematic coaching component.[42] By focusing on enhanced self-awareness and behavioural management, feedback-coaching improves performance, satisfaction, and commitment, and reduces intent to turnover. Separating the performance feedback component from the management development component also improves the 360-degree method.[43] The feedback component contains quantitative feedback and performance measures, while the management development

360-degree feedback A process of self-evaluation and evaluations by a manager, peers, direct reports, and possibly customers.

component emphasizes qualitative feedback and competencies for development.

Developing People and Enhancing Careers

Good performance appraisal systems develop people and enhance careers. Developmentally, performance appraisals should explore individual growth needs and future performance. The supervisor must establish mutual trust to coach and develop employees. The supervisor must be vulnerable and open to challenge from the subordinate while maintaining responsibility for the subordinate's best interests.[44] Good supervisors are skilled, empathic listeners who encourage employees to discuss their aspirations.[45]

Employees must also take active responsibility for future development and growth. This might mean challenging the supervisor's ideas about future development and expressing their own goals. Passive, compliant employees cannot accept responsibility for themselves nor achieve full emotional development.

FedEx has incorporated a novel and challenging approach to evaluation in its blueprint for service quality. All managers at FedEx are evaluated by their employees through a survey–feedback–action system. Employees evaluate their managers using a five-point scale on 29 standard statements and 10 local option ones. Low ratings suggest problem areas requiring management attention. One year the survey revealed that employees thought upper management was not paying attention to ideas and suggestions from people at their level. CEO Fred Smith developed a biweekly employee newsletter to correct the problem.

Key Characteristics of an Effective Appraisal System

Effective performance appraisal systems have five key characteristics: validity, reliability, responsiveness,

© Susan Van Etten

IN ACTION

American Express

American Express (AmEx), a company with operations around the world, was founded in 1850 to provide freight forwarding and delivery services. Since then AmEx has evolved into a global financial services company, perhaps best known for its American Express charge card. With about 65,000 employees worldwide, enhancing the performance capabilities of employees is an important concern at AmEx, and this concern is addressed through the activities of the American Express Learning Network (AELN). Jeanette Harrison, vice president of AELN, explains the importance of superior employee performance in the financial services industry. She says, "Anytime you're touching your own money—let alone anyone else's—you want control and compliance to be top of mind. That includes privacy of data, data integrity and ensuring appropriate adherence to all regulations and legislation. That has always been fundamental to the learning network's curriculum."

The stated mission of AELN is to "ready all those who serve"—a mission that is very close to the "approximately 15,000 customer-care professionals within the company's Service Delivery Network, which is responsible for assisting card members and merchants with needs ranging from processing new accounts to card remittance."

According to Harrison, the initial learning for customer-care employees focuses on ensuring that "everyone has a solid understanding of how they introduce themselves, how they ensure the appropriate privacy and security levels for all of our customers and how they proceed into the interaction." Harrison explains further that employees' interaction with customers is about solving problems, whether it's a customer's question, a request for a replacement credit card, a request for information, or some other issue. Consequently, customer service learning is oriented toward training scenarios that involve problem resolution.

AELN provides both technical training and soft skills training. Technical training focuses on learning the specific job, how to use different software applications, and how to process forms, among other skills. Soft skills training addresses topics such as customer care principles, speaking and listening skills, dispute resolution, and others.

In summarizing the desired outcomes of AELN's customer service training, Harrison emphasizes, "We're not looking for service—we're looking for extraordinary service."

SOURCES: Anonymous, "Our Story—About American Express," American Express, http://home3.americanexpress.com/corp/os/history.asp, accessed July 10, 2009; R. Hill, "Analysis for the American Express Learning Network (AELN)," November 3, 2008, http://www.robertphill.com/portfolio/media/artifacts/AELN_analysis.pdf, accessed July 9, 2009; B. Summerfield, "American Express' Jeanette Harrison: Learning as a Service," Chief Learning Officer, March 2008: 28, www.clomedia.com.

flexibility, and equitability. Validity means capturing multiple dimensions of a person's job performance. Reliability means collecting evaluations from multiple sources and at different times throughout the evaluation period. Responsiveness means allowing the person being evaluated some input. Flexibility means staying open to modification based on new information, such as situational demands. Equitability means evaluating fairly against established criteria, regardless of individual differences.

14-6 REWARDING PERFORMANCE

Performance appraisals can provide input for reward decisions. If organizations celebrate "teamwork," "values," and "customer focus," then they must reward behaviours demonstrating these ideas. Despite their importance, reward decisions are among the most difficult and complicated decisions managers make. While pay and rewards for performance have value, so too do trust, fun, and meaningful work.

Reward and punishment decisions affect entire organizations, not just the individuals receiving the consequence. Reward allocation involves sequential decisions about which people to reward, how to reward them, and when to reward them. These decisions shape all employees' behaviour, either directly or through vicarious learning especially when new programs are implemented. People watch what happens to peers who succeed and who make mistakes; then they adjust their own behaviour accordingly.

Individual versus Team Reward Systems

Although some say it is a myth that people work for money,[46] evidence shows that money is a powerful reward that can trigger dramatic improvements. Meta-analytic reviews comparing different motivational approaches showed individual pay incentives increased productivity on average by 30 percent, far beyond any other approaches (e.g., job enrichment achieves gains of 9–17 percent; enhanced employee participation less than one percent).[47] This is because money is not simply an extrinsic motivator but also a form of recognition, providing information on competence. Besides an incentive effect, pay-for-performance plans can have a sorting effect, influencing who applies to a job and who stays with the organization.[48] Less productive workers may quit when switched from salary to an incentive system[49] whereas incentive plans are attractive to those higher in need for achievement[50] and self-efficacy.[51] Individual incentive plans may create problems by undermining cooperative behaviour and encouraging dysfunctional competition. They may also be seen as unfair when factors out of the control of the employee affect performance (e.g., employees assigned to "bad" shifts selling less because there are simply fewer customers walking through the door).

Team reward systems solve the problems caused by individual competitive behaviour by encouraging joint effort, cooperation, and the sharing of information and expertise. For example, incentives or merit pay can be based on group performance rather than individual performance. Gainsharing plans emphasize collective cost reduction by allowing workers to share in the gains achieved by reducing production costs. Profit sharing encourages everyone in the organization to support each other as they all play a role in contributing to the organization's ultimate success and their pay-offs. However, group-based plans also have their drawbacks. One is the fact that, in a rather individualistic society like Canada, many prefer their pay to be based on individual performance,[52] and this preference is strongest among the most productive and achievement-oriented employees who may feel frustrated at "carrying" weaker workers. Group size is a moderator of any group plan effectiveness. Expectancy effects weaken as the employee sees less impact of their own effort on group output. For example, doubling the number of employees involved in a gainsharing plan can cut the productivity gain in half.[53]

A third option is to use a hybrid approach to rewarding employees. With interdependent teams, higher performance can result from the use of both individual and shared rewards, recognizing individual contributions while also encouraging cooperation. Hybrid reward systems lead to increased sharing of information and reduced social loafing.[54]

Organizations get the performance they reward, not the performance they say they want.

”

The Power of Earning

Both individual and team reward systems shape productive behaviour. Effective performance management boosts individual and team achievements in an organization. Performance management and reward systems assume a demonstrable connection between performance and rewards. Organizations get the performance they reward, not the performance they say they want.[55] Further, when there is no apparent link between performance and rewards, people may begin to believe they are entitled to rewards regardless of their performance.

Jupiter Images. Bank notes image used with the permission of the Bank of Canada.

The notion of entitlement at work is counterproductive when it counteracts the power of earning.[56] People who believe they are entitled to rewards are not motivated to behave constructively. Merit raises in some organizations, for example, have come to be viewed as entitlements, thus reducing their positive value in the organizational reward system. Entitlement engenders passive, irresponsible behaviour, whereas earning engenders active, responsible, adult behaviour. The power of earning rests on a direct link between performance and rewards.

14-7 CORRECTING POOR PERFORMANCE

Often a challenge for supervisors, correcting poor performance is a three-step process. First, supervisors must identify the cause or primary responsibility for the poor performance. Second, if the primary responsibility is a person's, supervisors must determine the source of the personal problem. Third, they must develop a plan for correcting the poor performance. The Self-Assessment at the end of the Chapter helps you examine one of your own poor performances.

A number of problems trigger poor performance. These include poorly designed work systems, poor selection processes, inadequate training and skills development, lack of personal motivation, and personal problems intruding on the work environment. Not all poor performance is self-motivated; some is induced by the work system. Therefore, a good diagnosis should precede corrective action. For example, it may be that an employee is subject to a work design or resources issue that keeps the employee from exhibiting good performance.

If the poor performance can't be attributed to work design or organizational process problems, then supervisors should examine the employee. The problem may lie in (1) some aspect of the person's relationship to the organization or supervisor, (2) some area of the employee's personal life, or (3) a training or developmental deficiency. In the latter two cases, poor performance may be treated as a symptom rather than a motivated consequence. In such cases, identifying financial problems, family difficulties, or health disorders may help the employee solve problems before they become too extensive.

Poor performance may also stem from an employee's displaced anger or conflict with the organization or supervisor. In such cases, the employee may be unaware of the internal reactions causing the problem. Such angry motivations can generate sabotage, work slowdowns, and work stoppages. The supervisor may attribute the cause of the problem to the employee, while the employee attributes it to the supervisor or organization. Supervisors must treat the poor performance as a symptom with a deeper cause and resolve the underlying anger or conflict.

However, there is a danger that supervisors will tend to leap prematurely to the conclusion that performance problems are to be blamed on the employee. It is important for a supervisor to think through the consensus, consistency, and distinctiveness aspects of the situation: how have others done in a similar situation? How has this employee performed in similar situations in the past? How is this employee performing in very different tasks?

Coaching, Counselling, and Mentoring

Supervisors have important coaching, counselling, and mentoring responsibilities to their subordinates. Supervisors and coworkers are often more effective guides than formally assigned mentors from higher up in the organizational hierarchy.[57] Success in the mentoring relationship depends on openness and trust.[58] This relationship may help address performance-based deficiencies or personal problems.[59] In either case, the supervisors can play a helpful role in employee problem-solving activities without accepting responsibility for the employees' problems. They may also refer the employee to trained professionals.

Coaching and counselling are among the career and psychosocial functions of a mentoring relationship.[60] **Mentoring** is a work relationship that encourages development and career enhancement. Mentor relationships typically go through four phases: initiation, cultivation, separation, and redefinition. Mentoring offers protégés many career benefits.[61] The relationship can significantly enhance the early development of a newcomer and the mid-career development of an experienced employee. Some organizations, such as IBM, offer mentoring at all levels of employment.[62] One study found that good performance by newcomers increased delegation from leaders.[63] Peer relationships can also enhance career development.[64] Executive coaching is increasingly used to outsource the business mentoring functions.[65] Informational, collegial, and special peers aid the individual's development by sharing information, career strategizing, job-related feedback, emotional support, and friendship. (Chapter 18 explores mentoring further.)

mentoring A work relationship that encourages development and career enhancement for people moving through the career cycle.

Positive Feedback

Today, more organizations are asking their managers to "accentuate the positive" and urged to use praise and emphasize small victories rather than focus on what workers do wrong. For example, it was once the conventional practice for BCG managers to evaluate employee performance by calling attention to their missteps and areas for improvement. According to Michelle Russell, a BCG partner, "We would bring them in and beat them down a bit." After the feedback session, the company noticed that some employees would not return. Rather than motivate them to improve their performance, the harsh feedback resulted in employees feeling disheartened and shaken, with reduced confidence. Now BCG managers are expected to focus on a particular worker's strength and to mention no more than one or two areas that require improvement. While overly positive feedback may lead to managers overlooking serious performance problems; however, people tend to perform better when they're encouraged and inspired.

SOURCE: R. Feintzeig, "You're Awesome! Firms Scrap Negative Feedback—Managers Ease Up on Harsh Reviews; in Past, 'We'd Beat Them Down a Bit," *Wall Street Journal*, February 11, 2015: B1.

STUDY TOOLS 14

IN THE BOOK YOU CAN ...

- ☐ Rip out the **Chapter Review card** at the end of the book to review Key Concepts and Key Terms.
- ☐ Take a "What about You?" Quiz related to material in the chapter.
- ☐ Read additional cases in the Mini Case and Shopify Running Case sections.

ONLINE YOU CAN ...

NELSON.COM/STUDENT

- ☐ Take a "What about You?" Quiz related to material in the chapter.
- ☐ Test your understanding with a quick Multiple-Choice Pre-Test quiz.
- ☐ Read the eBook, which includes discussion points for questions posed in the Cases.
- ☐ Watch Videos related to chapter content.
- ☐ Use the available Flashcards and Matching Quizzes to test your understanding of key terms and concepts.
- ☐ See how much you've learned by taking a Post-Test.
- ☐ Watch Videos related to chapter content.
- ☐ Use the available Flashcards and Matching Quizzes to test your understanding of key terms and concepts.
- ☐ See how much you've learned by taking a Post-Test.

WHAT ABOUT YOU?

How Do You Correct Poor Performance?

At one time or another, each of us has had a poor performance of some kind. It may have been a poor test result in school, a poor presentation at work, or a poor performance in an athletic event. Think of a poor performance event that you have experienced and work through the following three steps.

Step 1. Briefly describe the specific event in some detail. Include why you label it a poor performance (bad score? someone else's evaluation?).

Step 2. Analyze the poor performance.

a. List all the possible contributing causes to the poor performance. Be specific, such as the room was too hot, you did not get enough sleep, you were not told how to perform the task, etc. You might ask other people for possible ideas, too.

____

____

____

____

____

____

b. Is there a primary cause for the poor performance? What is it?

Step 3. Plan to correct the poor performance.

Develop a step-by-step plan of action that specifies what you can change or do differently to improve your performance the next time you have an opportunity. Include seeking help if it is needed. Once your plan is developed, look for an opportunity to execute it.

MINI CASE

Murder–Suicide at BC Government Office

Gunshots close by. You have to pass the source of the shots to get out of the building so, instead, you run to the washroom, lock yourself in, and call emergency services. You wait anxiously, not knowing what has happened. Four hours later, RCMP officers knock on the door and tell you it is safe to come out. You learn three are dead—the union steward, the office manager, and his director. This could have been your experience if you had been an employee of the Kamloops office of BC's Ministry of Water, Land and Air Protection on October 15, 2002.

The Kamloops Incident

On the previous day's Thanksgiving holiday, Dick Anderson, the Regional Pollution Protection Manager, drove to Penticton so he could have an early morning meeting next day with staff there and still make the three-hour journey back to Kamloops for an afternoon meeting. Anderson had the unenviable task of announcing that layoffs meant their jobs would be ending in several months. He was not happy about having to deliver the message, but he was optimistic about the meeting planned for later, anticipating that the discussion with the regional director would address increasing resources and possibly save one of the Penticton jobs after all. Anderson drove back to his Kamloops office to meet with Jim McCracken at 2:00. The meeting was a brief five minutes. Anderson was handed two letters: one in which McCracken recommended to the Deputy Minister that Anderson's employment be terminated, the other from the Deputy Minister saying Anderson had the chance to respond to the termination recommendation. Anderson was relieved of his duties as of that moment. He walked out of the building, commenting to staff that he had been fired because he could not "get along with people." Fifteen minutes later he returned to the building and entered the office where McCracken was meeting with Rick Mardon, the union steward. He fired two shots, killing McCracken and Mardon. The office employees scrambled to find refuge, several being injured in the panicked evacuation. Anderson went to his office and fired one more shot, killing himself.

Why Was It a Surprise?

Anderson had no idea of the impending dismissal. The shock and humiliation were likely a major trigger for his violent response. A forensic psychiatrist who spoke at the coroner's inquest said that in his experience the biggest trigger for interpersonal violence is disrespect or perceived disrespect. It is not the discipline that causes the problem but how the process was handled. Anderson thought he was doing a good job and then was suddenly told he was not. How is it possible that a senior manager can be completely unaware that he is in danger of losing his job because of issues with his performance?

Background

Anderson had been hired in 1989 and had several performance appraisals over the next few years which noted that he was hardworking and loyal but his communication style could benefit from greater tact and diplomacy. Anderson accepted these early appraisals and took them as an opportunity to improve. His last formal performance appraisal, in 1995, noted that Anderson had taken steps to reduce stress and manage his emotions when dealing with staff but that the situation should be monitored. Between 1995 and 2002 there is no documentation about Anderson's performance—no performance appraisals, no formal complaints. Does that mean his performance improved? No. At the coroner's inquest coworkers and staff testified that through most of his career with the ministry his management of people was an issue. His main problems were an inability to delegate, micromanagement, "extreme negativity and assumption of the worst-case scenario, lack of anger and stress control and a tendency to bully staff into compliance." The former regional director noted that he had anticipated complaints from staff because of Anderson's managerial style so when he received them he did not formally document them because he thought they were not credible. Apparently there were several verbal coaching sessions but no record of date and content. At the time of the crisis in 2002 Anderson was having difficulty finding people who would work for him and morale in his office was low. He accepted McCracken's suggestion to hire an outside facilitator to do a stress/change workshop for his staff. Anderson was not aware that the facilitator was reporting to his senior manager, had concluded that Anderson was the problem, and recommended Anderson's immediate removal. Days later, the termination occurred. Ironically, although McCracken had arranged for security personnel to attend an event occurring the day after Anderson's termination in case he disrupted it, McCracken did not think to take similar precautions for the termination itself.

Recommendations from Investigators

Could the violence have been avoided if things had been handled differently? Could similar events be prevented in future? This was the focus of investigations by several groups. Investigation reports by the Workman's Compensation Board, a coroner's jury and a joint union management workplace committee yielded recommendations to the ministry, many around issues of performance management:

- Ensure that people have positive, effective leadership skills when hired into supervisory roles, and that they understand the use of constructive and progressive discipline. (p. 4)
- All employees should receive annual performance reviews and performance plans. (p. 6)
- Performance reviews for managers should be 360-degrees (input by coworkers, subordinates, and the employee's supervisor) and include a review of staff interaction and management styles. (p. 6)
- New supervisors should review all staff appraisals. (p. 6)
- The performance review process within the ministry should be reviewed for effectiveness. (p. 6)

As a result, BC took a number of steps, adding units on violence prevention and trust to its leadership training program, modifying its hiring practices, ensuring performance appraisals are held regularly, requiring supervisors to provide feedback on employee interactions with staff and supervisors, and developing a 360-degree assessment program.

The irony is that, instead of killing the others and himself, if Anderson had charged the ministry with wrongful dismissal, he would likely have won. There is no evidence that Anderson had ever been disciplined nor warned of any misconduct, and his personnel file showed no concerns with his leadership abilities. Unaware of the issues, how could he have changed his behaviour?

Apply Your Understanding

1. Explain what performance management is and how the ministry failed to apply the process in Anderson's case.
2. Discuss how the principles of feedback should have been followed in Anderson's case.
3. Explain how Anderson's manager could have applied the three steps for correcting poor performance.

SHOPIFY RUNNING CASE

CONTINUED LEARNING AS A PATH TO SUCCESS

Shopify emphasizes hard work and learning as the path to success at the company. One reviewer, who has worked at Shopify for more than a year, notes on Glassdoor, "Shopify is a great place to learn and grow[;] you will experience situations that are challenging and exciting." However, the same reviewer also notes, "Communication between leadership and workers need[s] to be ironed out. There's a lack of training resources available to teach new leads." Without the necessary training, Shopify's employees will not be able to achieve their performance goals. Another reviewer describes Shopify's commitment to developing a learning culture. The reviewer observes that "I've learned more than I thought I would, and developed professionally and personally more than any other job I've had. You get the opportunity to work with a diverse group of colleagues who all bring something to the table."

"Guru" is a critical role at Shopify. Gurus are Shopify's front-line support; they provide the point of contact for merchants on a day-to-day basis. They support shop owners and communicate through various means such as e-mails, phones, and chats. Gurus need to be resourceful. Gurus are placed in Squads. Squads are teams of 10 people that work the same shifts. Gurus learn that being a guru is a stepping stone position but, according to another Glassdoor reviewer, "[It is next] to impossible to get promoted within the company—the bottlenecks at every position are astounding."

SOURCES: Shopify, "Guru 101—About the Role," accessed from https://supporthiring.shopify.com/pages/guru-101-the-customer-success-guru-role, September 28, 2018; Glassdoor, https://www.glassdoor.ca/Reviews/Shopify-Reviews-E675933_P2.htm and https://www.glassdoor.ca/Reviews/Shopify-Reviews-E675933_P3.htm, accessed September 28, 2018.

Apply Your Understanding

1. How important is the Guru role to Shopify's mission?
2. How could Shopify use the goal-setting process to drive performance?
3. Why is training so important for effective performance management?

Kevin Van Paassen/Bloomberg via Getty Images

4 PART

kate_sept2004/E+/Getty Images

Jobs and the Design of Work

LEARNING OUTCOMES

After reading this chapter, you should be able to do the following:

15-1 Differentiate between *job* and *work*.

15-2 Explain how job enlargement and job rotation counter Taylor's scientific management concepts.

15-3 Explain the job characteristics model, and how it has been expanded by subsequent research.

15-4 Describe the concepts of social information processing (SIP), ergonomics, and job crafting.

15-5 Identify and describe contemporary issues facing organizations in the design of work.

See the end of this chapter for a list of available Study Tools, a "What about You?" Quiz, Mini Case, and the Shopify Running Case.

The design of jobs and work is a central issue in organizations. A poorly designed job can have significant demotivating impacts on managers and employees. On the other hand, jobs designed well can result in engaged employees. We know engaged employees can make significant contributions to organizational outcomes, as they are motivated to work with enthusiasm and commitment. There is evidence that individual engagement can have measurable business outcomes—"[we] conclude ... that employee satisfaction and engagement are related to meaningful business outcomes at a magnitude that is important to many organizations. ..."[1]

Through work, people become securely attached to reality and securely connected in human relationships.

 WORK IN ORGANIZATIONS

Work is effortful, productive activity resulting in a product or a service. A **job** is defined as an employee's set of specific task activities in an organization, assigned pieces of work to be done in a specified time period. Work is an especially important human endeavour because it has a powerful effect in binding a person to reality. Through work, people become securely attached to reality and securely connected in human relationships. *Work* has different meanings for different people. For all people, work is organized into jobs, and jobs fit into the larger structure of an organization. The structure of jobs is the concern of this chapter, and the structure of the organization is the concern of the next chapter. Both chapters emphasize organizations as sets of task and authority relationships through which people get work done.

The Meaning of Work

Many big lottery winners choose to continue working. Work does not simply fulfill financial needs; it is an important element of most people's lives. It contributes to their identity, their self-esteem, social interaction and status, and the fulfillment of personal needs as well as practical ones.[2]

In a study of lottery winners, the majority (85 percent) chose to continue working, even though the average win in that group was $2.59 million. The choice to quit was certainly related to the amount won, but also strongly related to the centrality of work in the lives of the winners. Those to whom work was important chose to continue working despite no longer having the financial incentive. For example, a 64-year-old bus driver who won $20 million stated that the "lottery is just a bonus that came my way; it has not or will not affect my work habits and goals in life."[3]

work Mental or physical activity that has productive results.

job A set of specified work and task activities that engage an individual in an organization.

The key role of work in our lives is demonstrated by the impact on both physical and psychological health when work is lost. One longitudinal study followed meat-processing workers after their plants closed and compared them to similar workers in a neighbouring community who had not lost their jobs. It found a significant difference in mental distress leading to serious self-harm.[4] Other studies link involuntary job loss to the risk of stroke,[5] heart disease and arthritis,[6] depression, substance abuse, and anxiety.[7] Several international studies assess the importance of work as compared with other aspects of people's lives and show that work is typically ranked second in importance to family in most countries.[8] One study examined 5,550 people across 10 occupational groups in 20 different countries, asking them to complete the Work Value Scales (WVS),[9] which consists of 13 items measuring various aspects of the work environment, such as responsibility and job security. The study found two common basic work dimensions across cultures. Work content is one dimension, measured by items such as "the amount of responsibility on the job." Job content is the other dimension, measured by items such as "the policies of my company." This finding suggests that people in many cultures distinguish between the nature of the work itself and elements of the context in which the work is done. This supports Herzberg's two-factor theory of motivation and his job enrichment approach discussed later in this chapter.

Jobs in Organizations

Task and authority relationships define an organization's structure. Jobs are the basic building blocks of this task–authority structure and are considered the microstructural element to which employees most directly relate. Jobs are usually designed to complement and support other jobs in the organization. Isolated jobs are rare.

Jobs in organizations are interdependent and designed to make a contribution to the organization's overall mission and goals. For salespeople to be successful, the production people must be effective. For production people to be effective, the materials department must be effective. These interdependencies require careful planning and design so that all of the "pieces of work" fit together into a whole. For example, an envelope salesperson who wants to take an order for one million envelopes from Canadian Tire Financial Services must coordinate with the production department to establish

IN ACTION

The Call of the Wild

Jupiter Images

A study of Canadian and American zookeepers illustrated the impact of work centrality so deeply personal that work is seen as a personal calling. Those zookeepers with a sense of calling found their work more significant and important. At the same time, they were more willing to sacrifice money, time, and physical comfort for their work, and were more vulnerable to exploitation by management. Devotion to the job permeated their lives, giving them great meaning but it came at a price.

SOURCE: "The Call of the Wild: Zookeepers, Callings and the Double-Edged Sword of Deeply Meaningful Work," *Administrative Science Quarterly* 54 (2009): 32–57.

an achievable delivery date. The failure to incorporate this interdependence into their planning could create conflict and doom the company to failure in meeting Canadian Tire's expectations. The central themes of this chapter are designing work and structuring jobs to prevent such problems and to ensure employee well-being. Inflexible jobs that are rigidly structured have an adverse effect and lead to stressed-out employees.

© James W. Porter/Corbis

A multi-tasker in action!

The larger issues in the design of organizations are the competing processes of differentiation and integration in organizations (see Chapter 16). Differentiation is the process of subdividing and departmentalizing the work of an organization. Jobs result from differentiation, which is necessary because no one can do it all. Even small organizations must divide work so that each person is able to accomplish a manageable piece of the whole. At the same time the organization divides up the work, it must also integrate those pieces back into a whole. Integration is the process of connecting jobs and departments into a coordinated, cohesive whole. For example, if the envelope salesperson had coordinated with the production manager before finalizing the order with Canadian Tire, the company could have met the customer's expectations as integration had occurred.

15-2 TRADITIONAL APPROACHES TO JOB DESIGN

The balance of integration and differentiation—decisions about who does what—can have a significant impact on behaviour in organizations. People can respond to their work positively or negatively, with consequences for the organization. We saw in Chapter 6 how excessive demands and lack of control are major sources of stress for workers. Job design underlies demands and control and, consequently, stress. Job design also offers the opportunity to create work that engages people. Many managers underestimate the importance of job design characteristics in motivating employee performance.[10] This is ironic considering managers often have more control over the design features of their employees' jobs than over technology, organizational culture, relationships, or people themselves. We will examine how approaches to job design have changed over time, starting with the traditional approaches from the 20th century.

Scientific Management

Scientific management, an approach to work design first advocated by Frederick Taylor, emphasized work simplification. This emphasis on simplification is rooted in the idea of division of labour advocated by early economists Smith[11] and Babbage,[12] who believed productivity would increase if work could be broken down into simple tasks. **Work simplification** is the standardization and the narrow, explicit specification

work simplification
Standardization and the narrow, explicit specification of task activities for workers.

of task activities for workers.[13] Jobs designed through scientific management have a limited number of tasks, and each task is specified so that the worker is not required to think or deliberate. According to Taylor, the role of management—and the industrial engineer, in particular—is to calibrate and define each task carefully. The role of the worker is to execute the task. Work simplification is the underlying principle of assembly-line work. The elements of scientific management, such as offering breaks for workers (which were not common in Taylor's time), differential piece-rate systems of pay, the careful selection and training of workers, and time-and-motion studies all focus on the efficient use of labour to the economic benefit of the corporation. Many of Taylor's approaches persist because they were and are successful. The time-and-motion studies have not seen continuing popularity, however, despite their contribution to scientifically reshaping work to be more effective.

job enlargement A method of job design that increases the number of activities in a job to overcome the boredom of overspecialized work.

job rotation A variation of job enlargement in which workers are exposed to a variety of specialized jobs over time.

© iStockphoto.com/Dusko Jovic

Work simplification is the underlying principle of assembly-line work.

Work simplification has some benefits but it also has significant drawbacks. Its *benefits* include (1) low skill requirements mean lower wages, ease in replacing absent workers, and speed in training; (2) allowing people of diverse backgrounds to work together in a systematic way; which (3) leads to production efficiency and higher profits. Its *drawbacks* include (1) undervaluing worker capacity for thought and ingenuity; underutilization means loss of opportunity for the organization to gain from employee creativity and problem solving; (2) boring, repetitive work for employees, leading to problems such as repetitive strain injuries, absenteeism, turnover, substance abuse; and (3) dehumanization.

Scientific management triggered a reactionary focus on the importance of people and their feelings about work conditions. This human relations movement launched the Hawthorne studies described in Chapter 1 that examined how people's work changed under varying conditions. Worker satisfaction and motivation were seen as key to the organization's success.

Job Enlargement/Job Rotation

Recognizing the problems created by oversimplification of work led to the use of job rotation and job enlargement.[14] **Job enlargement** is a method of job design that increases the number of tasks in a job. **Job rotation**, a variation of job enlargement, exposes a worker to a variety of specialized job tasks over time. The reasoning behind these approaches to the problems of overspecialization is as follows. First, the core problem with overspecialized work was believed to be lack of variety. That is, jobs designed by scientific management were too narrow and limited in the number of tasks and activities assigned to each worker. Second, a lack of variety led to understimulation and underutilization of the worker. Third, the worker would be more stimulated and better utilized by increasing the variety in the job. Variety could be increased by increasing the number of activities or by rotating the worker through different jobs. For example, job enlargement for a lathe operator in a steel plant might include selecting the steel pieces to be turned and performing all of the maintenance work on the lathe. As an example of job rotation, an employee at a small bank might take new accounts one day, serve as a teller another day, and process loan applications on a third day.

One of the first studies of the problem of repetitive work was conducted at IBM after World War II. The company implemented a job enlargement program during the war and evaluated the effort after six years.[15] The two most important results were a significant increase in product quality and a reduction in idle time, both for people and for machines. Less obvious and measurable were the benefits of job enlargement to IBM through enhanced worker status and improved manager–worker communication. IBM concluded that job enlargement countered the problems of work specialization.

More recent work suggests that enlargement may create problems. A study with employees of an English glass manufacturer showed that job enlargement had a negative impact on self-efficacy.[16] Although work variety can be welcome, if people are given a wider range of tasks without also getting more influence over the situation, it can feel like greater pressure.

Job rotation and **cross-training** programs are variations of job enlargement. Job rotation can be a proactive means for enhancing work experiences for career development and can have tangible benefits for employees in the form of salary increases and promotions.[17] In cross-training, workers are trained in different specialized tasks or activities. All three kinds of programs horizontally enlarge jobs; that is, the number and variety of an employee's tasks and activities are increased.

IN ACTION

Job Rotation at TCS

TCS is a software services and consulting company based in India that has offices in 42 countries globally and customers throughout the world. TCS implemented an overseas program of job rotation for employees native to India, believing that sending skilled Indian employees abroad is essential to employee development. The program allows TCS to provide better service by drawing on the strength of its entire workforce rather than only employee talent found in the office located closest to the customer. TCS overseas assignments usually span 18 to 24 months, with employees learning both from their work with the customer and from fellow TCS employees who are based permanently at that location.

SOURCE: https://www.glassdoor.ca/Benefits/Tata-Consultancy-Services-Singapore-Benefits-EI_IE13461.0,25_IL.26,35_IN217.htm?countryRedirect=true, accessed August 12, 2018.

Job Enrichment

Although job enlargement refers to expanding the scope of the job by adding tasks at the same level,[18] job enrichment refers to incorporating motivational factors into the design of the job. Job enrichment emerged from Herzberg's two-factor theory of motivation. Recall Herzberg's claim that job satisfaction is a result of motivational factors characteristic of the work itself and that job dissatisfaction results from poor hygiene factors. **Job enrichment** recommends increasing the recognition, responsibility, and opportunity for achievement. For example, enlarging the lathe operator's job means adding maintenance activities, whereas enriching the job could mean having the operator meet with customers who buy the products.

Herzberg believes that only certain jobs should be enriched and that the first step is to select the jobs appropriate for job enrichment.[19] He recognizes that some people prefer simple jobs. Once jobs are selected for enrichment, management should brainstorm about possible changes, revise the list to include only specific changes related to motivational factors, and screen out generalities and suggestions that would simply increase activities or numbers of tasks. Those whose jobs are to be enriched should not participate in this process because of a conflict of interest.

A seven-year implementation study of job enrichment found the approach beneficial.[20] Job enrichment required a big change in management style, and the company found that it could not ignore hygiene factors in the work environment just because it was enriching existing jobs. Although its experience with job enrichment was positive,

cross-training A variation of job enlargement in which workers are trained in different specialized tasks or activities.

job enrichment Designing or redesigning jobs by incorporating motivational factors into them.

iQoncept/Shutterstock

a critical review of job enrichment did not find that to be the case generally.[21] One problem with job enrichment as a strategy for work design is that it is based on an oversimplified motivational theory. Another problem is the lack of consideration for individual differences among employees. Job enrichment, like scientific management's work specialization and job enlargement/job rotation, is a universal approach to the design of work and thus does not differentiate among individuals. There are two key cautions when implementing job enrichment: (1) an initial drop in performance can be expected as workers accommodate to the change, and (2) first-line supervisors may experience some anxiety or hostility as a result of employees' increased responsibility.

FIGURE 15.1 THE JOB CHARACTERISTICS MODEL

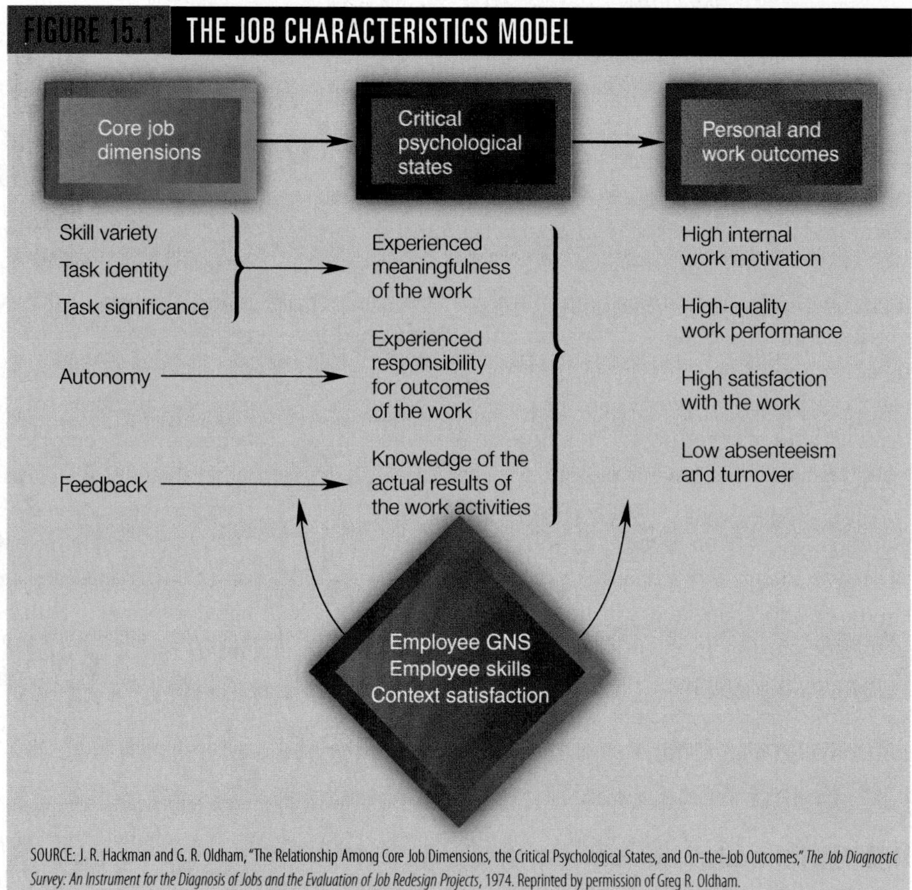

SOURCE: J. R. Hackman and G. R. Oldham, "The Relationship Among Core Job Dimensions, the Critical Psychological States, and On-the-Job Outcomes," *The Job Diagnostic Survey: An Instrument for the Diagnosis of Jobs and the Evaluation of Job Redesign Projects*, 1974. Reprinted by permission of Greg R. Oldham.

15-3 JOB CHARACTERISTICS THEORY

In the mid-1960s, Hackman and Oldham created job characteristics theory, a job design approach that came to dominate the field for decades. It made a significant departure from the earlier approaches in that it emphasized the interaction between the individual and the specific attributes of the job. It is a person–job fit model rather than a universal job design model.

According to the **job characteristics model (JCM)**, desirable work behaviours and attitudes are a result of employees experiencing three critical psychological states: they experience their work as meaningful, they feel responsible for their work actions, and they know how well they are doing (see Figure 15.1). Five core dimensions of job design feed directly into those critical psychological states. A job is more meaningful if it requires a variety of skills, if it has an impact on others (task significance), and if it involves completing a whole or identifiable piece of work (task identity) that one can take pride in. Employees need a level of autonomy in order to feel personally responsible for their work. Feedback is required for employees to know how they are doing. The **Job Diagnostic Survey (JDS)**, the most commonly used design measure, was developed to diagnose jobs by measuring the core job dimensions shown in the model. It allows the calculation of the Motivating Potential Score of a job by combining the specific core dimension scores with the following equation:

$$\text{MPS} = \frac{\begin{bmatrix}\text{Skill}\\ \text{variety}\end{bmatrix} \times \begin{bmatrix}\text{Task}\\ \text{identity}\end{bmatrix} \times \begin{bmatrix}\text{Task}\\ \text{significance}\end{bmatrix}}{3} \times \left[\text{Autonomy}\right] \times \left[\text{Feedback}\right]$$

job characteristics model (JCM) A framework for understanding person–job fit through the interaction of core job dimensions with critical psychological states within a person.

Job Diagnostic Survey (JDS) The survey instrument designed to measure the elements in the Job Characteristics Model.

Hackman and his colleagues created norms for the JDS by administering it to almost 7,000 employees in 876 different jobs.[22] These norms established a baseline for comparison, allowing organizations to see whether the JDS scores of their jobs indicated a need for redesign. Using the JDS could lead immediately to suggestions for redesign by indicating which core job dimensions were weak. Hackman and Oldham suggested a number of implementing concepts to address design problems: (1) combining tasks into larger jobs, (2) forming natural work units to increase task identity and task significance, (3) establishing relationships with customers, (4) loading jobs vertically by giving more responsibility and authority, and (5) opening feedback channels for the job incumbent. For example, if an auto mechanic received little feedback on the quality of repair work performed, one redesign strategy would be to solicit customer feedback one month after each repair.

As noted earlier, the JCM is not a universal design. It does not suggest one size fits all. Note the moderator variables at the bottom of the job characteristics model in Figure 15.1: growth need strength, skills, and context satisfaction. These three factors influence whether an employee will respond positively to the five core dimensions. They must be considered before deciding to redesign a job. One of the moderators relates directly to Herzberg's theory—satisfaction with work context. It suggests that an organization cannot forget the impact of the hygiene factors. So the JDS measures satisfaction with security, pay, relations with supervisors, and relations with others. If an organization sees issues in these areas, it knows they must be addressed. An employee may quit a perfectly designed job if fed up with an unreasonable supervisor or feeling drastically underpaid. Skills and abilities also moderate the relationship between core job dimensions and outcomes. Highly motivated employees will still be limited in their productivity if lacking the necessary skills to achieve successful performance. The third moderator is an employee's growth need strength (GNS), the desire to grow and fully develop one's abilities. Employees with low GNS will not respond favourably to jobs with a high motivating potential. On the other hand, employees with high GNS will thrive in a job with variety and challenge.

Research shows general support for the JCM in that the core job characteristics are moderately correlated with favourable attitudes and behaviours, mediated by the three psychological states.[23] Interestingly, meta-analysis indicates that feedback influences all three critical psychological states, not just knowledge of results.[24] Feedback also contributes to experienced meaningfulness and a sense of greater autonomy, emphasizing its key role in proposed job redesign.

Importance of Experienced Meaningfulness

One of the most interesting aspects of JCM research is the evidence of the importance of experienced meaningfulness of work.[25] Meaningfulness has a closer link to attitudinal and behavioural outcomes than the other critical psychological states, and all five core job dimensions contribute to it. Other research supports the apparent impact of perceived meaningfulness. For example, a Swedish study of patients with chronic pain found that the perceived meaningfulness of their job was a significant influence on their motivation to return to work.[26] Manipulation of task significance in a series of experiments with lifeguards and fundraising callers demonstrated the link between significance and performance. Callers in the task significance condition earned more pledges; lifeguards in the task significance condition showed increased dedication and helping behaviour.[27]

This work also indicates how organizations can enhance the task significance of a job and, subsequently, the experienced meaningfulness: by providing opportunities for employees to have a positive impact on others and by putting workers in contact with those who benefit from their work.[28] For example, when fundraisers had one 15-minute interaction with a student explaining how the funds made an impact in her life, it resulted in more than five times the weekly donation money a full month later.[29] A medical study provides similar findings. When radiologists saw the photographs of patients whose imaging scans they were evaluating, they reported stronger empathy for the patients and they were more accurate in diagnosing medical problems.[30] Consider how unusual it is for radiologists to see patient photographs and for fundraisers to meet fund recipients, yet how relatively easy it is for the organization to take this step and make a significant difference.

How else can we increase experienced meaningfulness? JCM research suggests that giving feedback, autonomy, skill variety, and task identity will each contribute to meaningfulness. A study of Canadian health care workers, funeral directors, and dental hygienists demonstrated that transformational leadership enhances the psychological well-being of workers through adding meaning to their work.[31] This is to be expected, since transformational leaders inspire and excite their employees (see Chapter 12).

Expanding the Job Characteristics Model

Criticism of the JCM's narrow focus on five task attributes has prompted research into complementary areas. As a result, some researchers created the Work Design Questionnaire (WDQ) as their version of the JDS measure.[32] The expanded model still includes the JCM original core dimensions but adds task variety, and divides autonomy into three types: work scheduling autonomy, work methods autonomy, and decision-making autonomy.

The original autonomy was a vague concept that could be interpreted differently. The three specific types of autonomy capture different employee experiences more accurately. The expanded model adds three broad categories to the JCM's original task grouping: social characteristics, knowledge characteristics, and work context characteristics (see Table 15.1).

We saw the critical impact of social factors on workers in Chapter 6's discussion of how social support prevents stress, and acts as an important buffer in times of high demands and low control. The expanded JCM posits four specific social characteristics of importance: the degree of interdependence between an employee's job and the jobs of others, the extent of interaction outside the organization, the degree of social support, and feedback from others. Research shows that all play an important role in employees' attitudes and experiences. They are strongly linked to job satisfaction, turnover intentions, subjective performance, and organizational commitment.[33] A discussion in Chapter 14 described the key role of feedback, particularly negative feedback, in changing behaviour. Whereas managers have tended to ignore social aspects of a job, it is clear that the ways in which a job's design causes workers to interact with others is a critical element in their experience of work.

TABLE 15.1 MORGESON AND HUMPHREY'S EXPANSION OF THE JCM

WORK DESIGN CHARACTERISTICS	CRITICAL PSYCHOLOGICAL STATES AS MEDIATORS	OUTCOMES
Task Characteristics		**Behaviours**
• Task significance	Experiences meaningfulness	• Performance
• Task identity	Experiences responsibility	• Absenteeism
• Task variety	Knowledge of results	• Turnover
• Autonomy:		**Attitudes**
– Work scheduling – Work methods – Decision making		• Satisfaction with job
• Feedback from job		• Satisfaction with supervisor
Knowledge Characteristics		• Organizational commitment
• Job complexity		• Job involvement
• Information processing		• Internal work motivation
• Specialization		**Role Perceptions**
• Problem solving		• Role ambiguity
• Skill variety		• Role conflict
Social Characteristics		**Well-Being**
• Interdependence		• Anxiety
• Feedback from others		• Stress
• Social support		• Burnout/exhaustion
• Interaction outside organization		• Overload
Work Context Characteristics		
• Physical demands		
• Work conditions		
• Ergonomics		

SOURCE: Adapted from S. E. Humphrey, J. D. Nahrgang and F. P. Morgeson, Integrating Motivational, Social and Contextual Work Design Features: A Meta-Analytic Summary and Theoretical Extension of the Work Design Literature, *Journal of Applied Psychology* 92 (2007): 1332–1356. Copyright © 2007 by the American Psychological Association. Reproduced with permission.

Jobs also vary in their knowledge demands—complexity, information processing, problem solving, and specialization. Initial research suggests that high knowledge demands promote satisfaction but may also lead to perceptions of overload. Therefore, these high knowledge demands can be both engaging and overwhelming.[34] A study of Danish managers showed that cognitively challenging activities (e.g., problem solving) are linked to the experience of "flow," an engrossing and enjoyable immersion in an activity.[35]

The physical characteristics of a job are critical in an employee's perception of their work[36]; e.g., what are the hazards, what does the workspace look like, how fatiguing is the work? The WDQ focuses on ergonomics, physical demands, work conditions, and equipment use. Humphrey and Morgeson's[37] meta-analysis showed that these physical characteristics strongly correlate with stress, separately from all the other job characteristics, and also link to job satisfaction.

Task uncertainty was shown to have an adverse effect on morale in a study of 629 employment security work units.[38] More importantly, the study showed that morale was better predicted by considering both the overall design of the work unit and the task uncertainty. This study suggests that if one work design parameter, such as task uncertainty, is a problem in a job, its adverse effects on people may be mitigated by other work design parameters. For example, higher pay may offset an employee's frustration with a difficult coworker, or a friendly, supportive working environment may offset frustration with low pay. See Table 15.2 for more information on increasing control, reducing uncertainty, and managing conflict.

Go to the Self-Assessment at the end of the chapter to diagnose your current job or one you've had.

15-4 ALTERNATIVE APPROACHES TO JOB DESIGN

This section examines alternative work design approaches that have emerged. First, it discusses the social information-processing model and a recent variation that focuses on the subjective social experience of the worker. Then we look at job crafting and i-deals, assertions that employees actually shape their own jobs to a great extent. Finally, we examine how the changing parameters of the work world are influencing job design, and how perspectives on the design of work vary internationally.

Social Information Processing

Traditional approaches to the design of work focus on the objective characteristics of a job. The **social information-processing (SIP) model** emphasizes a job's subjective characteristics. Specifically, the SIP model says that what others tell us about our jobs is important.[39] The SIP model has four basic premises about the work environment.[40] First, other people provide cues we use to understand the work environment. Second, other people help us judge what is important in our jobs. Third, other people tell us how they see our jobs. Fourth, other people's positive and negative feedback helps us understand our feelings about our jobs. This is consistent with the dynamic model of the job design process that views it as a social one involving job holders, supervisors, and peers.[41]

People's perceptions and reactions to their jobs are shaped by information

social information-processing (SIP) model A model that suggests that the important job factors depend in part on what others tell a person about the job.

TABLE 15.2 ADJUSTING WORK DESIGN PARAMETERS

INCREASE CONTROL BY	REDUCE UNCERTAINTY BY	MANAGE CONFLICT THROUGH
Giving workers the opportunity to control several aspects of the work and the workplace	Providing employees with timely and complete information needed for their work	Participative decision making
Designing machines and tasks with optimal response times and/or ranges	Making clear and unambiguous work assignments	Supportive supervisory styles
Implementing performance-monitoring systems as a source of relevant feedback to workers	Improving communication at shift change time	Having sufficient resources available to meet work demands, thus preventing conflict
	Increasing employee access to information sources	

from other people in the work environment.[42] In other words, what others believe about a person's job may be important to understanding the person's perceptions of, and reactions to, the job. This does not mean that objective job characteristics are unimportant; rather, it means that others can modify the way these characteristics affect us. For example, one study of task complexity found that the objective complexity of a task must be distinguished from the subjective task complexity experienced by the employee.[43] Although objective task complexity may be a motivator, the presence of others in the work environment, social interaction, or even daydreaming may be important additional sources of motivation. The SIP model makes an important contribution to the design of work by emphasizing the importance of other people and the social context of work. For example, relational job design may motivate employees to take prosocial action and make a positive difference in other people's lives.[44] In addition, the relational aspects of the work environment may be more important than objective core job characteristics. Therefore, the subjective feedback of other people about how difficult a particular task is may be more important to a person's motivation to perform than an objective estimate of the task's difficulty.

Research for the SIP model's validity is mixed. Although some lab experiments have shown that positive social cues can improve productivity,[45] field experiments have not been so supportive.[46] Positive changes in task perceptions do not consistently result in performance improvement. The effect of social cues is considerably weaker than objective characteristics of job design, in contrast to SIP's contention.

> "The subjective feedback of other people about how difficult a particular task is may be more important to a person's motivation to perform than an objective estimate of the task's difficulty."

The SIP model has been updated by a model of interpersonal sense making.[47] Rather than seeing the employee as the SIP passive recipient of social cues about job tasks, the updated model sees the employee as actively seeking out cues far beyond the task. Employees want to understand the meaning and value of their work and their performance, so they actively construct that meaning through noticing cues from others and interpreting those cues. The words and actions of others are interpreted as either affirming (communicating regard, worth, care) or disaffirming (communicating a derogatory attribute). These interpretations shape the employees' sense of the meaning of their job, their role in the organization, and themselves. That, in turn, will influence attitudes such as job satisfaction and behaviours such as absenteeism and OCB. This model fits closely with the discussion earlier in the chapter about the importance of work's meaningfulness.

ergonomics The science of adapting work and working conditions to the employee or worker.

ERGONOMICS AND INTERDISCIPLINARY FRAMEWORK Michael Campion and Paul Thayer used **ergonomics** based on engineering, biology, and psychology to develop an interdisciplinary framework for the design of work. Actually, they say that four approaches—the mechanistic, motivational, biological, and perceptual/motor approaches—are necessary because no one approach can solve all performance problems caused by poorly designed jobs. We will take a closer look at the biological and perceptual/motor approaches below. One ergonomic study of 87 administrative municipal employees found lower levels of upper body pain along with other positive outcomes thanks to the workstation redesign.[48]

The interdisciplinary framework allows the job designer or manager to consider trade-offs and alternatives among the approaches based on desired outcomes. If a manager finds poor performance a problem, for example, the manager should analyze the job to ensure a design aimed at improving performance. The interdisciplinary framework is important because badly designed jobs cause far more performance problems than managers realize.[49]

The *biological approach* to job design emphasizes the person's interaction with physical aspects of the work environment and is concerned with the amount of physical exertion, such as lifting and muscular effort, required by the position. For example, an analysis of medical claims at TXI Chaparral Steel Company identified lower back pain as the most common physical problem experienced by steel workers and managers alike. As a result, the company instituted an education and exercise program under expert guidance to improve employees' lower back care. Program graduates received back cushions for their chairs.[50]

The *perceptual/motor approach* to job design also emphasizes the person's interaction with physical aspects of the work environment and is based on engineering that considers human factors such as strength or coordination, ergonomics, and experimental psychology. It places an important emphasis on human interaction with computers, information, and other operational systems. This approach addresses how people mentally process information acquired from the physical work environment through perceptual and motor skills. The approach emphasizes perception and fine motor skills as opposed to the gross motor skills and muscle strength emphasized in the *mechanistic approach*. The perceptual/motor approach is more likely to be relevant to operational and technical work, such as keyboard operations and data entry jobs, which may tax a person's concentration and attention, than to managerial, administrative, and custodial jobs, which are less likely to strain concentration and attention.

One study using the interdisciplinary framework to improve jobs evaluated 377 clerical, 80 managerial, and 90 analytical positions.[51] The jobs were improved by combining tasks and adding ancillary duties. The improved jobs provided greater motivation for the incumbents and were better from a perceptual/motor standpoint. The jobs were poorly designed from a mechanical engineering standpoint, however, and they were unaffected from a biological standpoint. Again, the interdisciplinary framework considers trade-offs and alternatives when evaluating job redesign efforts.

Job Crafting and I-deals

Although job design approaches have typically seen job design as something an organization creates for an employee, the **job crafting** concept sees employees as the active architects of their jobs.[52] Employees take the initiative to redefine their jobs, changing the boundaries of their job in terms of how they interact with others, how they think about and approach their work, and exactly what they do. Why do they do it? Job crafting can be motivated by a desire for some control, a desire for a positive self-image (by focusing on activities in which the employee excels), and a desire for connection with others. For example, a hospital cleaner may choose to engage in interactions with patients, finding pleasure in it, and believing he is contributing to the well-being of sick and lonely patients.[53] Job crafting is more common in jobs with high autonomy and low interdependence because these jobs offer more opportunity for crafting.[54] In a study of outside salespeople, 75 percent of them reported engaging in job crafting, shaping the job to their own preferences, in ways largely unknown to management.[55] Both collaborative and individual job crafting were observed in a study of childcare workers. The collaborative job crafting led to higher performance.[56] A study of employees at different ranks yielded the unexpected result that higher ranked employees, despite having more "power," actually felt more constrained in crafting their jobs and tended to alter their own expectations and behaviours. Lower-ranked employees were more likely to alter others' expectations and behaviours. The constraint felt by higher ranks may be due to the greater interdependence of their jobs and their visibility.[57]

The redefinition or shaping of an employee's job can be a process in which both employee and supervisor participate. Employees often negotiate changes in roles,[58] which are described as idiosyncratic deals, or "**i-deals**." They are customized employment terms negotiated between employees and their supervisors. They can be formed before hiring or after and typically emerge because the employee has special life circumstances (such as a need for flexible hours) or unique skills. A study with German government employees showed that i-deals tended to focus on either scheduling or personal development, were more common in departments with individualized work arrangements already (such as telecommuting and part-time work), and were more likely to be negotiated by employees who had a personality highlighting personal initiative.[59] A further study of i-deals in German and American hospitals showed that employees were more likely to negotiate successful i-deals when they had high quality leader–member exchange relationships with their supervisors[60] (see Chapter 12).

Job Design in the Changing World of Work

Many of today's changes have implications for job design—the movement from an economy based on manufacturing to a service base, globalization, new technology, the increasing numbers of knowledge workers, organizations remaking themselves or merging in response to competition, and the increasing use of teams. Jobs are increasingly characterized by uncertainty and complexity. There is more interdependence, and greater relations with others. Organizations are looking to employees for more initiative and creativity.

Autonomy is particularly important under such conditions. When we are working in uncertain, ambiguous environments, a feeling of control within our work helps us cope. People react more positively to getting

job crafting Employees take the initiative to redefine their jobs.

i-deals Customized employment terms negotiated between employees and their supervisors.

autonomy in uncertain conditions than they do in certain ones.[61] The combination of high interdependence and uncertainty in many jobs supports the use of self-managed work teams (Chapter 9), so the autonomy is given to a group in order to deal with uncertain conditions. Employees are more likely to be proactive in implementing ideas and solving problems when they are given autonomy and control.[62] The autonomy enhances their self-efficacy by signalling they are capable of handling responsibilities.[63] The autonomy also leads employees to define their role in a more flexible way.[64] A longitudinal study of German employees found that initial levels of autonomy and complexity in their jobs predicted higher levels of personal initiative. Exercising personal initiative, in turn, predicted perceptions of increased autonomy and complexity over time.[65]

Andresr/Shutterstock.com

Scheduling shifts for employees in a clockwise manner (1st, 2nd, 3rd) rather than a counterclockwise manner (1st, 3rd, 2nd) is more compatible with human biology.

IN ACTION

Telstra Corporation

Australian telecommunications and information services firm Telstra Corporation employs more than 34,000 employees in more than 15 countries including the UK, the United States, Hong Kong, New Zealand, and China. Like other organizations, Telstra has had to respond to the changing workplace demographics and increasing employee requests for flexible work arrangements. Like other organizations, Telstra met employee requests with empathy yet reiterated the stark reality that certain jobs had to be performed during specific hours during the workday. That was before Telstra piloted its "All Roles Flex" job design approach in 2013. "All Roles Flex" assumes that every job can be performed with flexibility built in. In fact, Telstra expects its managers to use the assumption that all job roles can flex as the starting point for job design. Rather than provide reasons that a job cannot be performed flexibly, Telstra's managers are asked to demonstrate why a job cannot be done flexibly. Telstra's unconventional approach to flexible work arrangements has resulted in increased employee engagement and 84 percent of its employees saying they have the flexibility they need in their jobs. Telstra's job design approach has also been good for diversifying its workforce. Since implementing "All Roles Flex," Telstra has seen an increase in its ability to recruit women into mid- and senior-level positions.

SOURCE: D. Thodey, "All Roles Flex," *McKinsey Quarterly* 4 (2014): 108; "Telstra Corporation Limited," *MarketLine Company Profile* (March 2015): 1–33.

Interpersonal feedback is also critical in many of today's jobs. Uncertainty means that the task feedback in many jobs is ambiguous.[66] The majority of the population now works in service jobs where they rely on interpersonal feedback to interpret the success of their performance.[67] Feedback has a key role in all three critical psychological states of the JCM, yet is often not built into jobs, so the organization must find a way to design feedback into the workday.

Creativity is a valuable resource and increasingly needed. There is evidence that job enrichment provides the foundation for greater creativity. Oldham and Cummings found employees working in enriched jobs (high on JCM attributes) were rated as more creative, produced more patents, and offered more suggestions.[68] Job complexity can encourage initiative and creativity[69] but is related to higher stress.[70] This had led some to suggest that routinized or "mindless" work may be a welcome break for those in complex, challenging jobs.[71] Intertwining routinized tasks within a complex job would provide a balance, allowing workers to relax, and may even stimulate greater proactivity and creativity by freeing up psychological resources.[72]

INTERNATIONAL PERSPECTIVES ON THE DESIGN OF WORK

Each nation or ethnic group has a unique way of understanding and designing work.[73] As organizations become more global and international, an appreciation of the perspectives of other nations is increasingly important. The Japanese, Germans, and Scandinavians in particular have distinctive perspectives on the design and organization of work.[74] Each country's perspective is forged within its unique cultural and economic system, and each is distinct from the approaches used in North America.

The Japanese Approach

The Japanese began harnessing their productive energies during the 1950s by drawing on the product quality ideas of W. Edwards Deming.[75] In addition, the central government became actively involved in the economic resurgence of Japan, and it encouraged companies to conquer industries rather than to maximize profits.[76] Such an industrial policy, which built on the Japanese cultural ethic of collectivism, has implications for how work is done. Although Frederick Taylor and his successors in the United States emphasized the job of an individual worker, the Japanese work system emphasizes the strategic level and encourages collective and cooperative working arrangements.[77] The Japanese emphasize performance, accountability, and other- or self-directedness in defining work, whereas North Americans emphasize the positive affect, personal identity, and social benefits of work.

The Japanese have had success with lean production methods, an approach that focuses on using committed employees with ever-expanding responsibilities to achieve zero waste, 100 percent good product, delivered on time, every time. This "do more with less" approach has drawn the attention of North American and European managers and spread rapidly. However, its use outside Japan has been less successful. For example, one three-year evaluation of lean teams, assembly lines, and workflow formalization as lean production practices was conducted in Australia.[78] Employees in all production groups were negatively affected, and the assembly-line employees the most.

Telecommuting and alternative work patterns such as job sharing can increase flexibility for employees.

The German Approach

The German approach to work has been shaped by Germany's unique educational system, cultural values, and economic system. The Germans are a highly educated and well-organized people. For example, their educational system has a multi-track design with technical and university alternatives. The German economic system puts a strong emphasis on free enterprise, private property rights, and management–labour cooperation. A comparison of voluntary and mandated management–labour cooperation in Germany found that productivity was superior under voluntary cooperation.[79] The Germans value hierarchy and authority relationships and, as a result, are generally disciplined.[80] Germany's workers are highly unionized, and their discipline and efficiency have enabled Germany to be highly productive while its workers labour substantially fewer hours than do North Americans.

The traditional German approach to work design was **technocentric**, an approach that placed technology and engineering at the centre of job design decisions. Recently, German industrial engineers have moved to a more **anthropocentric** approach, which places human considerations at the centre of job design decisions.

The Scandinavian Approach

The Scandinavian cultural values and economic system stand in contrast to the German system. The social democratic tradition in Scandinavia has emphasized social concern rather than industrial efficiency. The Scandinavians place great emphasis on a work design model that encourages a high degree of worker control and good social support systems for workers.[81] Lennart Levi believes that circumstantial and inferential scientific evidence provides a sufficiently strong basis for legislative and policy actions for redesigns aimed at enhancing worker well-being. An example of such an action for promoting good working environments and occupational health was the Swedish Government Bill 1976/77:149, which stated, "Work should be safe both physically and mentally *and also* provide opportunities for involvement, job satisfaction, and personal development." In 1991, the Swedish Parliament set up the Swedish Working Life Fund to fund research, intervention programs, and demonstration projects in work design. For example, a study of Stockholm police on shift schedules found that going from a daily, counterclockwise rotation to a clockwise rotation was more compatible with human biology and resulted in improved sleep, less fatigue, lower systolic blood pressure, and lower blood levels of triglycerides and glucose.[82] The work redesign improved the police officers' health.

technocentric Placing technology and engineering at the centre of job design decisions.

anthropocentric Placing human considerations at the centre of job design decisions.

A Morneau Shepell 2017 survey of 1,081 Canadian employees found that 46 percent had taken time off work or had noticed others taking sick leave because of changes to the nature of their work. To the researchers' surprise, job redesign was most likely to result in employee sick leave. "Employers generally recognize the need for communication and support around the major moves, but not so much the need for support around changes that directly affect employees' day-to-day work lives." Job redesign has a direct and personal impact that is essentially out of the employees' control and therefore adds to their stress.

SOURCE: V. Galt, "Sudden Change in Job Functions Can Take Toll on Employees' Mental Health," *The Globe and Mail*, February 11, 2017, accessed from https://www.theglobeandmail.com/report-on-business/careers/career-ad...functions-can-take-toll-on-employees-mental-health/article33985344, August 6, 2018.

15-5 CONTEMPORARY ISSUES IN THE DESIGN OF WORK

A number of contemporary issues related to specific aspects of the design of work have an effect on increasing numbers of employees. Rather than addressing job design or worker well-being in a comprehensive way, these issues address one or another aspect of a job. The issues include telecommuting, alternative work patterns, technology at work, and skill development. Telecommuting and alternative work patterns such as job sharing can increase flexibility for employees. Companies use these and other approaches to the design of work as ways to manage a growing business while contributing to a better balance of work and family life for employees.

Telecommuting

Telecommuting is when employees work away from the company (typically at home) through the use of technology. Telecommuting may entail working in a combination of home, satellite office, and main office locations. This flexible arrangement is designed to achieve a better fit between the needs of the individual employee and the organization's task demands.

Telecommuting has been around since the 1970s but was slower to catch on than some expected.[83] There is reluctance in some managers and employers to break the traditional visibility of work—if you cannot see them, how do you know they are actually working? Telecommuting requires a focus on performance outcomes rather than "face time." In Canada, telecommuting is not typically an all-or-nothing arrangement. Approximately 10 percent of Canadian workers telecommute, with 71 percent of them doing so one day a week and only 3 percent doing so for a 40-hour week.[84]

telecommuting Employees work away from the company (typically at home) through the use of technology.

Advocates of telecommuting point to the many benefits. It is easier to recruit and maintain employees, who find telecommuting appealing. Employers save overhead costs because less organizational space may be required. From the employees' point of view, telecommuting saves them time and money through less commuting time, and gives them more autonomy and flexibility in how their day is spent, thereby reducing work–family conflict.[85]

Environmental benefits add weight to the list of telecommuting's advantages. The City of Calgary held its first Telework Week in 2010 to highlight the many benefits of telecommuting and encourage more employers to adopt it.[86] In an address advocating Telework Week, Councillor Diane Colley-Urquhart reported that the City of Calgary's own telework program, in less than a year, had already produced a reduction of 7,440 commuter trips and 183,000 vehicle kilometres travelled, conserving 16,000 litres of fuel and reducing carbon dioxide emissions by 42,000 kilograms.[87] This is good news to a city rated by the UN as one of the worst carbon dioxide producers in the world.[88] As part of Calgary's telework initiative, organizations—including TELUS, ATB Financial, SAIT Polytechnic, Calgary Police Services, ENMAX and Calgary Economic Development—have signed the Calgary Telework Charter.[89]

Research supports the value of telecommuting. Telecommuting is correlated with improved satisfaction, performance, turnover intent, and role stress as well as increased autonomy and lower work–family conflict.[90] Some have feared that the social isolation of telecommuting would damage relationships and career prospects. Ironically, research suggests that telecommuting is actually associated with a higher quality of employee–supervisor relationship.[91] This could be because telecommuting is more likely to be granted to workers who are already performing well or are favoured by the supervisor, or it may be that awareness of the potential for damage in the relationship triggers a focus on ensuring the relationship is maintained.[92] Coworker relationships are also maintained under most telecommuting. It is only when the telecommuting becomes more intensive (over 2.5 days a week) that coworker relationships are harmed.[93] Meta-analysis showed that telecommuting had no adverse effects on employees' perceived career prospects.[94] Not all forms of work are amenable to telecommuting. For example, firefighters and police officers must be at their duty stations to be successful in their work. Employees for whom telecommuting is not a viable option within a company may feel jealous of those able to telecommute. In addition, telecommuting may have the potential to create the sweatshops of the 21st century.

Alternative Work Patterns

Job sharing is a permanent work arrangement where two or more employees voluntarily share or split one full-time position. A written agreement outlines the terms and each employee's salary and benefits are pro-rated for the hours worked. Typical job sharing means either splitting the work day with each employee working half or splitting the work week with each employee working 2.5 days. These arrangements are usually initiated by employees who want the time to deal with other life commitments (e.g., education, young children) but sometimes by employers to deal with recessionary conditions, allowing employees to keep their full-time status while saving the company money.[95]

The **compressed work week** (CWW) is an arrangement where employees work longer shifts in exchange for a reduction in the number of working days in their work cycle. For example, they may work four 10-hour days rather than five days a week. Compressed work weeks may be a standard work schedule set by the employer or an employee option. The Yukon government allows employees to request a compressed work arrangement that allows them regular days off by working longer days.[96] For instance, if an employee's schedule is normally 7.5 daily hours of work, the employee may take two days off in every two-week period and work 9.38 hours on a daily basis spread over the other eight working days. For Yukon government employees, this scheduling is a longer-term arrangement that requires the agreement of the other workers in the work area and the concurrence of the employee's deputy minister or designate. A CWW arrangement can be attractive for balancing work and family life and saving commute time and money, but regular long days can be fatiguing.

Flextime is the most common form of alternative work arrangement. Thirty-five percent of Canadian workers[97] have the freedom to set their daily start and stop times as long as they are present within specified core operational hours. It can lead to reduced absenteeism. Companies in highly concentrated urban areas, such as Vancouver, Toronto, and Montreal, may allow employees to set their own daily work schedules as long as they start their eight hours at any thirty-minute interval from 6:00 A.M. to 9:00 A.M. This arrangement is designed to ease traffic and commuting pressures. It also is somewhat responsive to individual biorhythms, allowing early risers to go to work early and nighthawks to work late. Even in companies without formal flextime programs, flextime may be an individual option arranged between supervisor and subordinate. For example, a first-line supervisor who wants to complete a university degree may negotiate a work schedule accommodating both job requirements and course schedules at the university. Flextime options may be more likely for high performers who assure their bosses that work quality and productivity will not suffer.[98] On the cautionary side, one study found that a woman on a flexible work schedule was perceived to have less job/career dedication and less advancement motivation, though no less ability.[99]

Research shows flexible and compressed workweek schedules have positive effects.[100] Flexible work schedules are correlated with higher employee productivity and job satisfaction, and lower employee absenteeism. However, these effects apply only to general employees, not to professionals or managers. And the positive effects with flextime may diminish over time as employees become accustomed to it. Compressed work weeks are associated with higher job satisfaction but do not seem to significantly affect productivity or absenteeism.[101] Though telecommuting helps employees and companies save time and money, it can cause managers anxiety. Since employees are not physically in the office, managers have few ways of keeping track of how employees are spending their working hours. To help solve this problem, one software company has created oDesk, a program that will take frequent snapshots of a worker's computer screen and record all of their keystrokes and mouse clicks. Using this information, managers can get a better sense of whether an employee is actually working.[102] Such technology does raise questions about the role of excessive workplace surveillance, however.

Technology at Work

New technologies and electronic commerce are here to stay and are changing the face of work environments—dramatically in some cases. Many government jobs expect to change, and even disappear, with the advent of e-government using

job sharing A permanent work arrangement where two or more employees voluntarily share or split one full-time position.

compressed work week Employees work longer shifts in exchange for a reduction in the number of working days.

flextime An alternative work pattern that enables employees to set their own daily work schedules outside core operational hours.

Internet technology. As forces for change, new technologies are a double-edged sword that can be used to improve job performance or to create stress. On the positive side, modern technologies are helping to revolutionize the way jobs are designed and the way work gets done. The **virtual office** is a mobile platform of computer, telecommunication, and information technology and services that allows mobile workforce members to conduct business virtually anywhere, anytime, globally. While virtual offices have benefits, they may also lead to a lack of social connection or to technostress.

Technostress is stress caused by new and advancing technologies in the workplace, most often information technologies.[103] For example, the widespread use of electronic bulletin boards as a forum for rumours of layoffs may cause feelings of uncertainty and anxiety (technostress). However, the same electronic bulletin boards can be an important source of information and thus reduce uncertainty for workers.

New information technologies enable organizations to monitor employee work performance, even when the employee is not aware of the monitoring.[104] These new technologies also allow organizations to tie pay to performance because performance is electronically monitored.[105] Three guidelines can help make electronic workplace monitoring, especially of performance, less distressful. First, workers should participate in the introduction of the monitoring system. Second, performance standards should be seen as fair. Third, performance records should be used to improve performance, not to punish the performer. In the extreme, new technologies that allow for virtual work in remote locations take employees beyond such monitoring.[106]

virtual office A mobile platform of computer, telecommunication, and information technology and services.

technostress The stress caused by new and advancing technologies in the workplace.

#HOT TREND Artificial Intelligence

Artificial intelligence (AI) has gained traction recently and is expected to change the nature of work. Ontario is now a hot spot for AI companies. Started in 2014, Blue J Legal built its first prototype by 2015 and then established a partnership with Thomson Reuters to bring its offering to the wider market.

Blue J Legal's mission is to make law more accessible and to help legal professionals to become more efficient. Blue J Legal uses machine learning for its predictive capabilities; for example, to predict how a court might rule in their client's case. Blue J Legal has developed Tax Foresight, which uses machine learning algorithms to predict how courts will rule on tax and employment law issues.

SOURCES: "10 AI Companies to Watch for in 2018," January 9, 2018, https://www.investinontario.com/spotlights/10-ai-companies-watch-2018 accessed August 6 2018; Blue J Legal, News, https://www.bluejlegal.com/news, accessed August 12, 2018.

Skill Development

Problems in work system design are often seen as the source of frustration for those dealing with technostress.[107] However, system and technical problems are not the only sources of technostress in new information technologies. Some experts see a growing gap between the skills demanded by new technologies and the skills possessed by employees in jobs using these technologies.[108] Although technical skills are important and are emphasized in many training programs, the largest sector of the economy is actually service oriented, and service jobs require interpersonal skills. Managers also need a wide range of nontechnical skills to be effective in their work.[109] Therefore, any discussion of jobs and the design of work must recognize the importance of incumbent skills and abilities to meet the demands of the work. Organizations must consider the talents and skills of their employees when they engage in job design efforts. The two issues of employee skill development and job design are interrelated. The knowledge and information requirements for jobs of the future are especially high.

STUDY TOOLS 15

IN THE BOOK YOU CAN ...

- ☐ Rip out the **Chapter Review card** at the end of the book to review Key Concepts and Key Terms.
- ☐ Take a "What about You?" Quiz related to material in the chapter.
- ☐ Read additional cases in the Mini Case and Shopify Running Case sections.

ONLINE YOU CAN ...

NELSON.COM/STUDENT

- ☐ Take a "What about You?" Quiz related to material in the chapter.
- ☐ Test your understanding with a quick Multiple-Choice Pre-Test quiz.
- ☐ Read the eBook, which includes discussion points for questions posed in the Cases.
- ☐ Watch Videos related to chapter content.
- ☐ Use the available Flashcards and Matching Quizzes to test your understanding of key terms and concepts.
- ☐ See how much you've learned by taking a Post-Test.

WHAT ABOUT YOU?

Diagnosing Your Job

This questionnaire challenges you to examine the motivating potential in your job. If you are not currently working, complete the questionnaire for any job you have ever held for which you want to examine the motivating potential. For each of the following five questions, circle the number of the most accurate description of the job. Be as objective as you can in describing the job by answering these questions.

1. How much *autonomy* is there in the job? That is, to what extent does the job permit a person to decide *on his or her own* how to go about doing the work?

1	2	3	4	5	6	7
Very little; the job gives a person almost no personal say about how and when the work is done.		Moderate autonomy; many things are standardized and not under the control of the person, but he or she can make some decisions about the work.			Very much; the job gives the person almost complete responsibility for deciding how and when the work is done.	

2. To what extent does the job involve doing a *"whole"* and *identifiable piece of work*? That is, is the job a complete piece of work that has an obvious beginning and end? Or is it a small part of the overall piece of work, which is finished by other people or by automatic machines?

1	2	3	4	5	6	7
The job is only a tiny part in the overall piece of work; the results of the person's activities cannot be seen in the final product or service.		The job is a moderate-sized "chunk" of the overall piece of work; the person's own contribution can be seen in the final outcome.			The job involves doing the whole piece of work, from start to finish; the results of the person's activities are easily seen in the final product or service.	

3. How much *variety* is there in the job? That is, to what extent does the job require a person to do many different things at work, using a variety of his or her skills and talents?

1	2	3	4	5	6	7
Very little; the job requires the person to do the same routine things over and over again.		Moderate variety.			Very much; the job requires the person to do many different things, using a number of different skills and talents.	

4. In general, how *significant* or *important* is the job? That is, are the results of the person's work likely to affect significantly the lives or well-being of other people?

1	2	3	4	5	6	7
Not at all significant; the outcome of the work is *not* likely to affect anyone in any important way.		Moderately significant.			Highly significant; the outcome of the work can affect other people in very important ways.	

5. To what extent *does doing the job itself* provide the person with information about his or her work performance? That is, does the actual work itself provide clues about how well the person is doing—aside from any feedback coworkers or supervisors may provide?

1	2	3	4	5	6	7
Very little; the job itself is set up so a person could work forever without finding out how well he or she is doing.		Moderately; sometimes doing the job provides feedback to the person; sometimes it does not.			Very much; the job is set up so that a person gets almost constant feedback as he or she works about how well he or she is doing.	

To score your questionnaire, place your responses to Questions 3, 2, 4, 1, and 5, respectively, in the blank spaces in the following equation:

Q3 Q2 Q4 Q1 Q5

Motivating Potential = [ ] + [ ] + [ ] × [ ] × [ ] = ______.

SOURCE: J. R. Hackman and G. R. Oldham, "The Job Diagnostic Survey: An Instrument for the Diagnosis of Jobs and the Evaluation of Job Redesign Projects," Technical Report No. 4, 1974, 2–3 of the Short Form.

MINI CASE

CKCK (CTV) Regina: Job Design Changes for the Newsroom Journalist

The newsroom at CKCK Television in Regina has transformed in the past 25 years, changing the daily lives of the professionals within it. CKCK was the first privately owned television station in western Canada and, from its first broadcast on July 28, 1954, providing the local news was a foundation of its existence. By 1985 CKCK was a medium-sized but still locally owned firm. Through the sale to Baton Broadcasting in 1987, the later merging of Baton and other players into a new CTV structure and the 2000 purchase of CTV by Bell Globemedia, the Regina station eventually became a small part in the television division of a multi-billion dollar media empire.

The 1980s

The station of the 1980s was run by a general manager whose management team included a news director, a sales manager, a manager of promotions, and a community liaison manager. The newsroom had 15 full-time editorial staff: a news producer and assignment editor reporting to the news director; six reporters working with both the producer and editor; three news anchors who wrote and presented newscasts for noon, 6 pm, and 11:30 pm; a weather person who doubled as a community affairs contact; and three sports reader/reporters. Technical crew complemented the editorial work: photojournalists, camera operators, videotape editors, audioboard technicians, video switchers, character generators, and others. In all, the CKCK of the late 80s employed 122 full-time staff and 10 part-time and freelance staff, 31 of whom were dedicated to the news operation. CKCK was an integral part of the community, proud of its reputation for vigilantly reporting events of local significance fairly and accurately. It took pains to ensure that, while still operating as a for-profit business, it acted for the public good. As a trusted source of local information with a reputation for "truth seeking," the six o'clock newscast was watched by literally half the city's population.

In this setting, newsroom journalists worked with photographers who would operate the cameras and videotape editors who would edit their reports. They were given stories to cover by the assignment editor but also encouraged to come up with their own ideas. The station welcomed investigative "enterprise stories" that had a large impact on the community.

In the 21st Century

Today's CKCK journalist works within a different work structure and set of expectations. The newsroom that had 31 dedicated employees in 1987 has only 15 now. There is only one news camera operator and there are no more videotape editors. The loss of the assignment editor means journalists now come up with their own stories and resources and shape the editorial content with less guidance from others. There are few enterprise reports these days—producing them is time consuming, expensive, and risky (due to the possibility of lawsuits). And the absentee corporate owners have less interest in performing a watchdog role in the community. Now known as video-journalists, today's reporters research, shoot, and edit their own reports. Each person essentially takes on the responsibilities of three previously separate positions. Mobile phones have given reporters much greater mobility in their work, allowing them to do research and make arrangements while on the go. But the mobile phones have also created more room for close monitoring. Reporters are now always accessible.

What has stayed the same? Deadlines continue to structure the day—the news must be produced for show times. There are still daily meetings for reporters and management to exchange views and information. The news director remains in charge of the content of the daily newscasts. There also still remains the pressure to get good stories and get them in on time. Some fear that the complex multitasking required of current journalists under these pressured conditions has led to a drop in the quality of the news produced. "The temptation, more than ever, is to settle for the workable sound bite, the useable quote, then move on as quickly as possible to gather the remaining elements—illustrative pictures, cutaway shots, stand-ups, and reaction quotes—in order to make the assigned deadline. It is … part of a move toward greater superficiality and greater manipulation of the audience."

SOURCES: J.S. McLean, "When Head Office Was Upstairs: How Corporate Concentration Changed a Television Newsroom," *Canadian Journal of Communication* 30 (2005), accessed from http://www.cjc-online.ca/index.php/journal/article/viewArticle/1613/1770 September 24, 2018; Canadian Communications Foundation History of Canadian Broadcasting— Television Stations: CKCK-TV Regina, http://www.broadcasting-history.ca/index3.html?url=http%3A//www.broadcasting-history.ca/listings_and_histories/television/histories.php%3Fid%3D93%26historyID%3D72, accessed January 1, 2011.

Apply Your Understanding

1. Apply the core job dimensions of the job characteristics model to explain how the journalist position has changed.
2. Use the job characteristics model to explain whether the journalist's job has become more or less meaningful and why.
3. Use the job characteristics model to explain why, despite the high motivating potential of the journalist job design, a specific journalist may not show strong personal and work outcomes.

SHOPIFY RUNNING CASE

FLEXIBLE WORK ARRANGEMENTS

Shopify provides flexibility for its employees; there are many work and job options for employees. Shopify has many employees working remotely because it wants to create a "connected Remote culture." (Many tech companies do provide opportunities for remote work although some have reconsidered the benefits of remote work.) At the moment, there are about 1,400 remote employees at Shopify. As Shopify notes, "Shopifolk solve problems with us, from all over the world." There are remote employees from around the world—from New Zealand to Canada to Denmark to Vietnam, to name a few.

One of its remote employees does talent acquisition for the support team from her camper van from various places in BC. She noted that she was grateful she could work from a location that enabled her to thrive and enjoy nature's beauty. Among the some of the remote roles are production engineer, support front-end developer, customer success guru, and Asia-Pacific benefits specialist.

Shopify also is on the leading edge of using AI in its work. Shopify was an early adopter of AI and is expected to develop its AI use further. As well, it is a founding member of the Vector Institute, a non-profit organization dedicated to researching deep learning and machine learning. Shopify is funding research into new technologies to apply "recommender systems" to personalize the Shopify experience for merchants and their customers. One assessment about Shopify's use of AI concludes that "[as] more AI capability is added to its platform … [there should be benefits such as] … incremental new services and revenue streams, reduced merchant churn levels, and additional competitive differentiation in the e-commerce platform market."

SOURCES: "Careers," Shopify, accessed from https://www.shopify.com/careers/locations/remote, September 28, 2018; B. Abernethy, "Shopify Is Canada's Artificial Intelligence Leader: Industrial Alliance," October 10, 2017, accessed from https://www.cantechletter.com/2017/10/shopify-is-canadas-artificial-intelligence-leader-industrial-alliance, September 28, 2018.

Apply Your Understanding

1. How does Shopify benefit from providing remote work opportunities?
2. What are the risks to Shopify and its remote workers of such opportunities?
3. How is AI central to Shopify's business case?

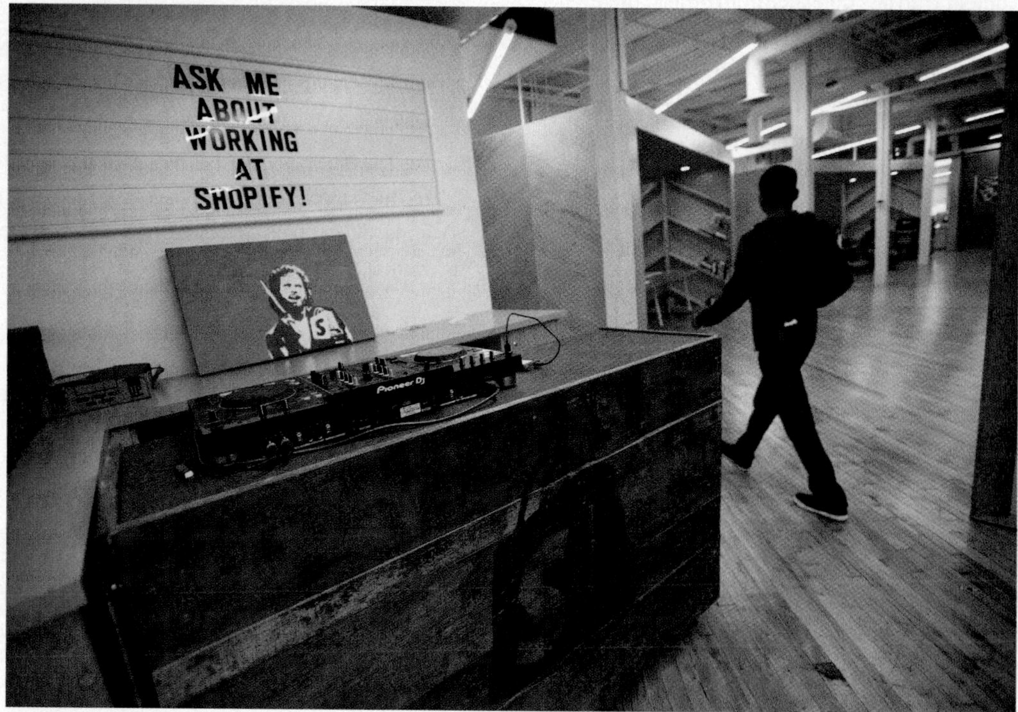

Kevin Van Paassen/Bloomberg via Getty Images

Raywoo/Shutterstock.com

Organizational Design and Structure

16

LEARNING OUTCOMES

After reading this chapter, you should be able to do the following:

16-1 Explain what aspects of organizational structure are represented on an organizational chart.

16-2 Discuss the basic design dimensions managers must consider in structuring an organization.

16-3 Describe the basic organizational structures: simple, functional, divisional, matrix.

16-4 Describe four contextual variables that influence organizational structure.

16-5 Explain the forces reshaping organizations.

16-6 Identify and describe emerging organizational structures.

16-7 Identify the consequences of an inappropriate structure.

See the end of this chapter for a list of available Study Tools, a "What about You?" Quiz, Mini Case, and the Shopify Running Case.

We spend a lot of time interacting with organizations—whether universities, colleges, banks, co-ops, and non-profits, to name a few. Each is likely to be designed in a different way, depending on its goals, strategies and external environments. As organizations have such a profound impact on our daily lives, it important to understand how they are structured and why. Such understanding is perhaps even more important in your workplaces. You become better able to navigate your organizations the more you know about organizational design. Should you want to start your organization, it is even more important for you to think through the design choices you have. In short, a rich understanding of organizations and their structure will make you a more informed organizational decision maker.

Organizational design is the process of constructing and adjusting an organization's structure to achieve its goals. The design process begins with the organization's goals. These goals are broken into tasks as the basis for jobs, as discussed in Chapter 15. Jobs are grouped into departments, and departments are linked to form the **organizational structure**.

The most visible representation of an organization's structure is the organizational chart. Most organizations have a series of organizational charts showing reporting relationships throughout the system. An organizational chart does not show the informal relationships that occur between people. The underlying components are (1) formal lines of authority and responsibility (the organizational structure designates reporting relationships by the way jobs and departments are grouped) and (2) formal systems of communication, coordination, and integration (the structure designates the expected patterns of formal interaction among employees). The organizational structure is designed to prevent chaos through an orderly set of reporting relationships and communication channels.[1]

organizational design The process of constructing and adjusting an organization's structure to achieve its goals.

organizational structure The linking of departments and jobs within an organization.

16-1 IMPACT OF STRUCTURE ON EMPLOYEES

The way an organization is structured has an impact on the daily lives of the people within it. It influences what people do and what skills are needed in their position. It determines who they interact with, what information they have access to, and who they are accountable to. It influences leadership behaviour and organizational culture. Employees may "craft" their job (see Chapter 15) to create a better fit for themselves, but the organizational structure will put boundaries on just how far an employee can modify the job and its interactions. There is no ideal structure—different organizations achieve success within the same industry with different structures. But a poor structure can cause economic and social difficulties for the organization, holding it back from achieving its goals and frustrating its employees. And no structure will appeal to everyone. As in every other topic discussed in this book, individual differences play a role.

The organizational structure is designed to prevent chaos through an orderly set of reporting relationships and communication channels.

Thinking of the experiences of students in different educational structures helps us to reflect on the interaction between structure and individual differences. High school students and university students are all educated within structures that include classes, courses, timetables, and rules. But the experience is vastly different. Consider someone you know who was highly successful in high school but found the transition to university difficult and whose grades showed it. Consider another person who did not perform well in high school but blossomed within the university context. High school is a highly structured environment with small classes, extensive contact with school staff, lots of rules, and little autonomy for students. University offers much more freedom to students and relative anonymity within the large-class setting. Some students feel stifled by the high school context and thrive in the opportunities provided by university. Other students feel safe and connected in the earlier structure and find the flexible, more open structure of university cold and overwhelming. The two structures are necessarily different as they are dealing with different age groups and have different goals. Neither one is "better." But individuals have different levels of comfort with the different types of structure, which can affect their performance. A parallel occurs in work settings. In some organizations, employees know exactly what they are expected to do, when and how; their activities are predictable, and their relations with others are defined. This may provide security and low stress on the one hand, or boredom on the other. Other employees work in a context of ill-defined duties and are expected to work to changing expectations with a varying group of people, resources, and deadlines. This may be exciting and stimulating, or it may be stressful. This chapter examines how and why organizational structures vary, and the interplay with employee behaviour and attitudes.

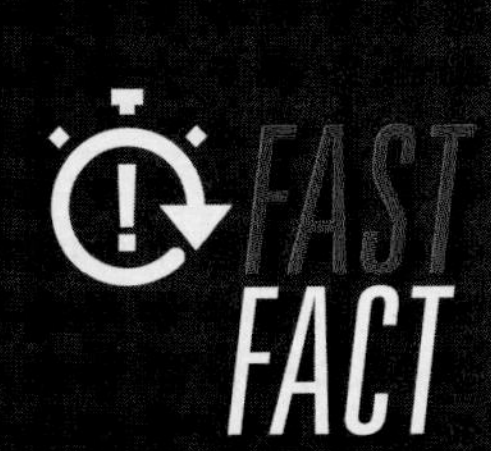

The pyramid of King Cheops of Egypt could not have been built without a well-conceived organization. The pyramid contains 2.3 million blocks of stone, each of which had to be quarried, cut to precise size and shape, cured (hardened in the sun), transported by boat for two to three days, moved on to the construction site, numbered to identify where it would be placed, and then shaped and smoothed so that it would fit perfectly into place. It took 20,000 workers 23 years to complete this pyramid; more than 8,000 were needed just to quarry the stones and transport them.

SOURCE: A. Erman, *Life in Ancient Egypt* (London: Macmillan & Co., 1984); C. Williams, Management (Mason, OH: Cengage Learning, 2008).

16-2 DESIGN DIMENSIONS

At the core of organization design are the division of labour and the coordination of work activities. The appropriate structure to meet an organization's goals will mean an appropriate combination of differentiation and integration. **Differentiation** refers to the process of deciding how to divide the work in an organization. The organization exists because no one person can achieve all the demands, so the work must be spread among organizational members. At the same time, the various parts of the organization must work together to achieve organizational success. Thus integration must be created; the different parts of the organization must be coordinated to form a structure that supports goal accomplishment. Every manager and organization looks for the best combination of differentiation and **integration** for accomplishing the goals of the organization. There are many ways to divide work and coordinate the various work activities. In order to understand the underlying characteristics of the various organizational structures, it is important that we begin by considering the basic structural dimensions.

In addition to *differentiation* and *integration* as key ways to describe organizations, there are several other key variables that are used to describe the characteristics of organizations. They are

1. **Formalization:** The degree to which an employee's role is defined by formal documentation (procedures, job descriptions, manuals, and regulations).
2. **Centralization:** The extent to which decision-making authority has been delegated to lower levels of an organization. An organization is centralized if the decisions are made at the top of the organization and decentralized if decision making is pushed down to lower levels in the organization.
3. **Specialization:** The degree to which organizational tasks are subdivided into separate jobs. The division of labour and the degree to which formal job descriptions spell out job requirements indicate the level of specialization in the organization.
4. **Standardization:** The extent to which work activities are described and performed routinely in the same way. Highly standardized organizations have little variation in the defining of jobs.
5. **Complexity:** The number of activities within the organization and the amount of differentiation needed within the organization.
6. **Hierarchy of authority:** The degree of vertical differentiation through reporting relationships and the span of control within the structure of the organization.[2]

These concepts relate closely to differentiation and integration. The more specialization occurs, the greater the differentiation. Differentiation can occur

differentiation The process of deciding how to divide work in the organization.

integration The process of coordinating the different parts of the organization.

formalization The degree to which the organization has official rules, regulations, and procedures.

centralization The degree to which decisions are made at the top of the organization.

specialization The degree to which jobs are narrowly defined and depend on unique expertise.

standardization The degree to which work activities are accomplished in a routine fashion.

complexity The degree to which many different types of activities occur in the organization.

hierarchy of authority The degree of vertical differentiation across levels of management.

horizontally so different units at the same level have jobs with different training and scope (e.g., an engineer and accountant in different departments with similar levels of responsibility but specialized jobs). Differentiation can also occur vertically (through creating differences in hierarchy and authority) and spatially (through locating parts of the organization in different places). The greater the differentiation is, the greater the complexity will be and the greater the need for integration. Formalization, centralization, standardization, and authority are all potential ways of achieving integration. The organization can ensure employee behaviours are aligned with organizational goals by creating explicit rules and procedures (formalization) or by standardizing activities so there is seldom any variation. Top management could insist on making all important decisions (centralization), leaving few decisions to employees. The organization could ask supervisors to monitor and guide employee behaviours (using their authority). These are not the only ways in which to achieve integration. Others include using the management information system, liaison roles (such as a project manager), task forces, or teams. One of the interesting research results on authority is that the **span of control** (number of people reporting to a supervisor) is related to integration in opposite ways in different circumstances. A large span of control can mean improved performance in some situations because employees feel less monitored and appreciate the freedom to do their job.[3] Their activities are coordinated through other means, such as routine and procedures or teamwork. However, for groups that are interdependent and for whom coordination is critical, a smaller span of control supports the group coordination.[4] The manager is more available to staff and is more likely to work alongside the staff, to offer coaching and feedback, and to have frequent and timely communication with staff, thereby creating shared goals.[5] A study with cross-functional flight departure teams (e.g., baggage handlers,

span of control The number of employees reporting to a supervisor.

IN ACTION

Deloitte

Deloitte Touche Tohmatsu (Deloitte) has a single brand name that spans the world. It is a global network of independent member firms that provide audit, tax, consulting, and financial advisory services. About 165,000 professionals in 140 countries work for separate member partnerships coordinated under the Deloitte brand. This is true of the other "Big Four" auditing firms: Ernst & Young, PricewaterhouseCoopers and KPMG. These firms are comprised of hundreds of smaller organizations linked by knowledge, economics, and brand, each with one coordinating firm. The individual firms within the Deloitte structure are owned by partners who become co-owners or shareholders as they go on to become senior members of the organization.

The individual firms within the "one firm" design structure are largely unlimited liability partnerships doing auditing and/or accounting work. Even if some of the individual firms are limited liability companies, the senior members who become shareholders are still designated as partners. This design becomes a double-edged sword when a local affiliate is cited for accounting wrongdoing. For instance, PricewaterhouseCoopers would have to face regulatory and possibly judicial review if an individual firm in India was involved in fraud. The power and global reach of this organizational design are therefore offset by the risk of financial and material liability.

The differentiation process within Deloitte is accomplished in a relatively straightforward manner based upon independent firms and partnership structure under a single umbrella. The more difficult task in a naturally differentiated structure is one of integration. Deloitte has accomplished these critical tasks of coordination and integration through video. The company has been able to reach more employees and keep its costs down through visual media.

Deloitte made a strategic decision to launch a video department in 2005 for three reasons. First, the demand for online video is increasing. Second, video can be a critical communication tool that actually saves money. For the 50 videos that Deloitte produced during 2008, they estimated a 300 percent return on investment (ROI), excluding savings on travel. Third, online communication skills have evolved dramatically in the past decade, both in consumption and production. Companies may already have professional staff with necessary skills for video communication without fully realizing that they do. Ultimately, organization design and structure is about getting lots of people well connected and working together.

SOURCE: K. Frankola, "How Deloitte Build Video into the Corporate Strategy," *Strategic Communication Management* 13 (2009): 28–31.

pilots, cabin cleaners, ticketing agents) at a variety of airlines demonstrated that those with smaller spans of control achieved better performance in terms of gate time per departure, staff time per departure, customer complaints, and late arrivals.[6] When span of control increases, managers have less opportunity for interacting with individual subordinates,[7] tend to become more autocratic in their decision making,[8] and are more likely to handle problems with subordinates in a formalized, impersonal way, using warnings and punishments instead of coaching and feedback.[9]

Henry Mintzberg, the pre-eminent Canadian management thinker, argues that the following questions can guide managers in designing formal structures that fit an organization's unique set of circumstances:

1. How many tasks should a given position in the organization contain, and how specialized should each task be?
2. How standardized should the work content of each position be?
3. What skills, abilities, knowledge, and training should be required for each position?
4. What should be the basis for the grouping of positions within the organization into units, departments, divisions, and so on?
5. How large should each unit be, and what should the span of control be (that is, how many individuals should report to each manager)?
6. How much standardization should be required in the output of each position?
7. What mechanisms should be established to help individuals in different positions and units to adjust to the needs of other individuals?
8. How centralized or decentralized should decision-making power be in the chain of authority? Should most of the decisions be made at the top of the organization (centralized) or be made down in the chain of authority (decentralized)?[10]

The manager who can answer these questions has a good understanding of how the organization should implement the basic structural dimensions. These basic design dimensions act in combination with one another and are not entirely independent characteristics of an organization.

16-3 BASIC STRUCTURES

Most organizations begin their existence as a simple structure. All power rests in the entrepreneur (centralization) whose few staff do whatever is needed. There are no job descriptions or written procedures. The owner decides what will be done and how as the need arises. An example of a **simple structure** would be a small computer consulting company. The owner works with three technicians to help small businesses fix computer applications and to make decisions regarding computer hardware and software that meet their needs (Figure 16.1). The owner supervises the work and works alongside the technicians as needed. Some specialized functions, such as the bookkeeping and advertising, are contracted out rather than done in-house.

FIGURE 16.1 SIMPLE STRUCTURE

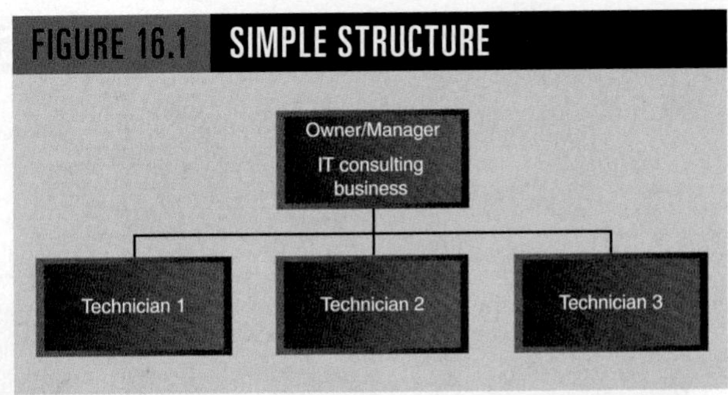

As an organization grows, it adds people, including middle managers, to relieve the pressure on the owner. The staff becomes more specialized, dividing up the duties rather than jointly doing whatever is needed. Staff are grouped (or departmentalized) for the purpose of supervision and resource sharing. This grouping can take several forms: functional, divisional, or matrix.

A **functional structure** groups people according to their function in the organization. The computer consulting company expands and takes back the functions it had outsourced when it was small. It groups people into consulting, finance, and marketing (Figure 16.2).

Divisional structures create self-contained units

simple structure A centralized form of organization that emphasizes direct supervision and low formalization.

functional structure A form of organization that groups people according to the function they perform.

divisional structure A form of organization that groups employees according to product, service, client, or geography.

FIGURE 16.2 FUNCTIONAL STRUCTURE

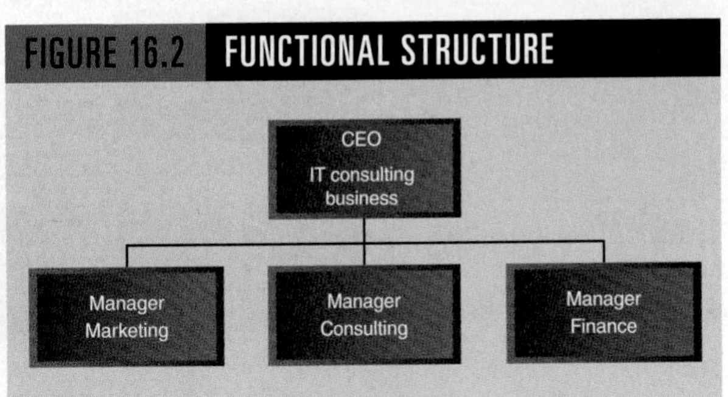

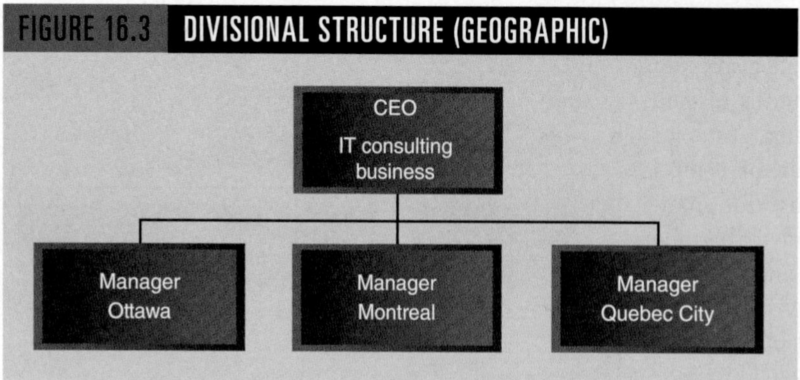

FIGURE 16.3 DIVISIONAL STRUCTURE (GEOGRAPHIC)

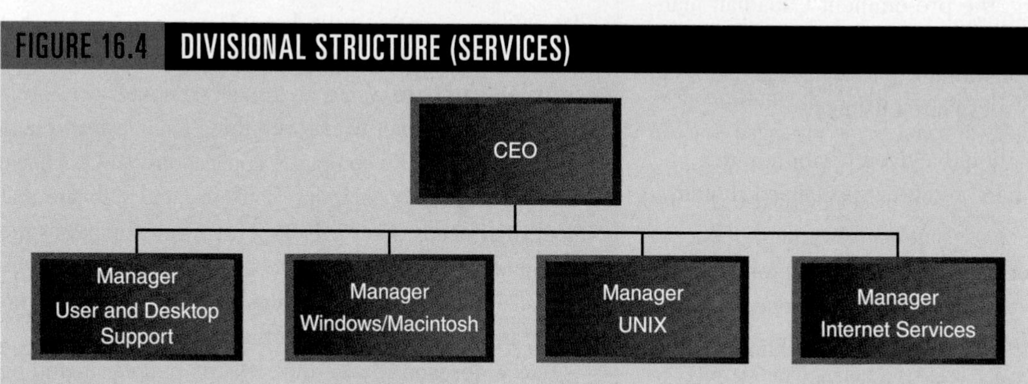

FIGURE 16.4 DIVISIONAL STRUCTURE (SERVICES)

that focus on products, services, clients, or geographical regions. One way in which the computer consulting company could divisionalize is by opening up several offices that provide services within particular geographical areas (Figure 16.3). Other divisional structures would see the company structured according to specific specialty services, e.g., computer applications, web design, IT training (Figure 16.4) or according to clients (Figure 16.5).

matrix structure A dual-authority form of structure that combines functional and divisional structures, typically through project teams.

Matrix structures are dual-authority structures that combine functional and divisional approaches. For example, an employee in Internet services could be assigned as a web designer to a project team working on a major project for Client A (Figure 16.6). That web designer would work with a multidisciplinary team pulled together to meet these particular project needs and would report on a daily basis to the project manager (who reports to the person in charge of Client A). The web designer is also under the supervision of the Internet services manager, who can provide technical facilitation that the project manager could not. When this project is completed, the web designer will be assigned to another project. A matrix design can also be more permanent. For example, the human resources manager of a large manufacturing plant can report both to the plant manager and to the corporate human resources director (who oversees human resources at the company's six plants to ensure consistency and quality).

Once an organizational structure grows beyond a simple structure, it often combines several structural designs rather than following one, thereby creating a hybrid structure. For instance, the sales force is likely to be grouped on a geographical basis, whereas headquarters may have a functional structure for the staff functions contained there (e.g., human resources, finance), and the plants may be divided according to product.

Experiences with Structure

To give you a sense of what each structure is like, its pros and cons, and the experience for an employee within it, let's look at an employee who gets the opportunity to work in each of the structures. Shay is hired as a marketing assistant in a start-up promotional company. Besides the owner, there are three staff members. Shay is hired to manage client promotion campaigns but also finds herself helping with client pitches and client management, office accounting, and the

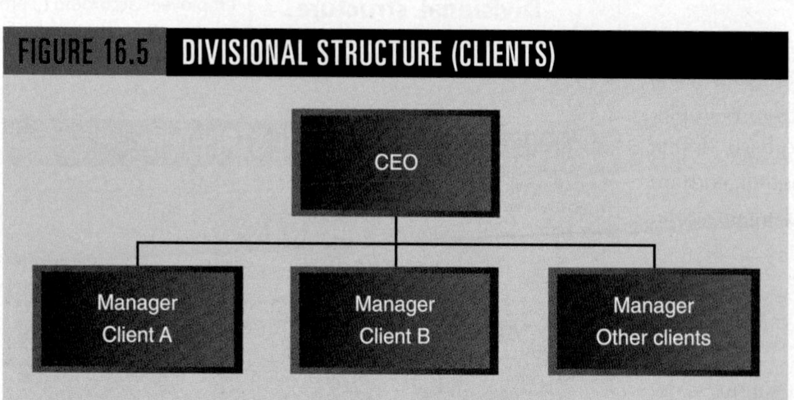

FIGURE 16.5 DIVISIONAL STRUCTURE (CLIENTS)

FIGURE 16.6 MATRIX STRUCTURE

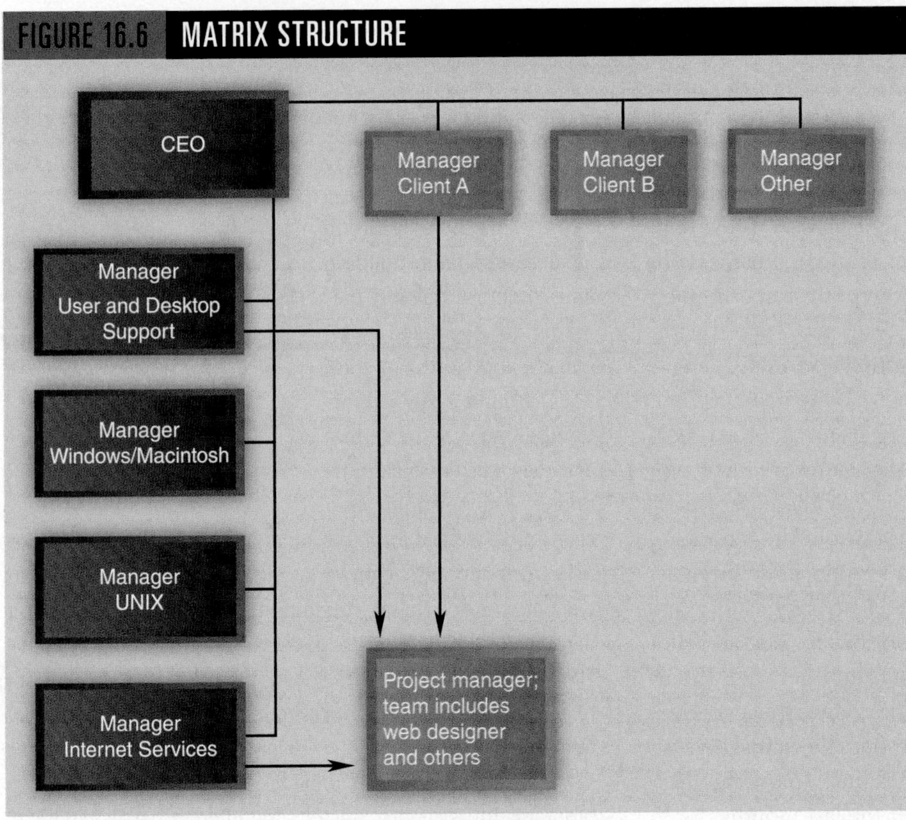

hiring of contract workers. Because it is a simple structure there are few rules, no job description, and her work varies daily; all major decisions are made by the owner but the frequent office interaction means Shay has input into many decisions. There is no bureaucracy to deal with. She sees that the company is very adaptable, able to move quickly when a need is identified. Her future career depends on the success and direction of the company—she may end up doing far more complex work, she may enter management as it grows, or she may lose her job if the company has difficulties. Shay likes the variety in her activities and the close atmosphere of the small group. She knows her contribution to the company's success. She gets to stretch her skills and is learning constantly. On the other hand, Shay is frustrated at the hours. The owner expects long hours from all staff and it is difficult to say no. There is no one to complain to when she is annoyed with her boss. Shay sees the risks with this structure: the owner is good at many things but not everything, yet he has the final say, and, if he is absent, the organization is handicapped because no one else has full information or power.

Looking for experience with a much larger, established organization, Shay takes a job as a marketing assistant in a functional structure. Now, working in a marketing department separated from the other parts of the organization, she is managed by a supervisor who is a marketer. Shay works only with marketers, works within clear procedures and defined activities, has specified tasks and responsibilities, and ends up specializing in labelling. She is able to learn from the experts in her area, watching them handle more challenging assignments than she is ready to deal with. Her career direction is a clear progression through marketing positions. It is comforting to be with people similar to her but she also misses the variety of interaction from her old job and being stretched to undertake roles that are outside her expertise. Also, she does not get the same sense of being close to the action because corporate decisions are far removed from her. She realizes, because of her experience at the small company, that the disadvantage of the functional structure is the narrow focus of each department—each one seems to focus more on its own success than the success of the company as a whole and there seems to be competitiveness among them. She sees a lack of coordination and communication between the departments, which she has heard, is called a "silo" mentality.

Reorganization and layoffs led to Shay once again looking for a job, this time in a company divisionalized according to product. She now works for a large consumer products company within a self-contained subunit that is focused on a particular product line. So now she specializes in marketing that particular product. She finds that the various functions in the large subunit are well coordinated and focused on jointly making the product successful. There is a sensitivity to the needs of its market, with a willingness to adapt as needed. But she has limited contact with the other functional people in her subunit (such as production and finance) and usually interacts only with marketers. She sees the silo mentality again here, but in a different form. This time the conflict lies between the product divisions. It seems to generate a lot of politicking. She also sees some duplication between product divisions; for example, why do they each have a human resources function when it would probably be more efficient to have a central human resource department supporting all parts of the company? In terms of Shay's future career, she can move up within the marketing group assigned to this product division but would like to ultimately get a broader experience.

When, once again, Shay changes employment, she moves to a matrix organization. She is now providing marketing expertise within a series of project teams with others of different functional backgrounds. For example, in a recent new product project team she worked with operations people (e.g., production planning, engineering design, and product design). Shay now has two supervisors: one is the marketing manager and the other is the project manager. She likes the teamwork involved, the range of projects she works on over the course of a year, and the variety of people with whom she interacts, as well as the security of having an expert in her area as backup. But sometimes her project manager and marketing manager have different priorities for her, and she wishes there was closer communication between them when it comes to doing her performance review. Her functional manager (the marketer) does the actual review even though the project manager is much more familiar with what she has been doing over the last months.

IN ACTION

Delta Synergy Group

The Delta Synergy Group delivers team-building and corporate training programs to clientele across Canada and North America, and around the globe. Compelling experiential activities (such as building a bridge or rappelling down a cliff) form the basis for reflection on interaction and leadership, risk, trust, support, teamwork, and communication. From its creation in 1994, Delta's structure has evolved to a geographic divisionalization with offices in Calgary, Vancouver, and Toronto. This was partially to meet the needs of local clients and partially to take advantage of the local training resources (e.g., mountains and lakes).

Photo courtesy of Delta Synergy Group

Delta Synergy Group provides detailed evaluation of its programs to its clients. Since its founding, it has worked with 637 clients, completed 974 projects and provided 46,752 hours of training experiences.

SOURCE: Delta Synergy, 2018, About, accessed from https://deltasynergy.com/about/, September 9, 2018.

Mechanistic and Organic Structures

The six basic structural dimensions can be combined into two broad and contrasting descriptive categories: mechanistic and organic organizations.[11] **Mechanistic structures** have a cluster of formalization, centralization, standardization, hierarchy, and specialization. As in a machine, every part has a specific, well-defined role and no room for variation. Communication is mostly top down. The traditional automobile-manufacturing facility with an assembly line setup fits this description. Organic organizations act more like living things than machines. As living things survive through adaptation to their environment, organic organizations continuously adjust their operations as needed and can do so because they have a flat structure with decentralization, low formalization, low standardization, and low specialization. They emphasize open communication and de-emphasize hierarchy. Decisions are linked more to expertise than formal authority. A consulting firm that uses its staff interchangeably on project teams tends to have a more **organic structure**. Activities are not bound by job descriptions, rules, or standardized procedures. Each project is a new challenge and handled jointly by team members, with support rather than interference coming from the top. In fact, no organization is purely organic or mechanistic, with a more varied combination of the six basic dimensions likely. But these contrasting concepts are useful short forms for the typical clustering of characteristics that have implications for efficiency and innovation (to be discussed later).

mechanistic structure An organizational design that emphasizes structured activities, specialized tasks, and centralized decision making.

organic structure An organizational design that emphasizes teamwork, open communication, and decentralized decision making.

Organizations are not often pure forms of the various structures. They often use a hybrid structure that combines characteristics of various structures that are necessary to achieve a particular strategic outcome. Rogers Communication Inc., for example, has three business units—wireless, cable, and telecom—as well as functional support across the organization.[12]

16-4 CONTEXTUAL VARIABLES

The basic design dimensions and the resulting structural configurations play out in the context of the organization's internal and external environments. Four **contextual variables** influence the success of an organization's design: size, technology, environment, and strategy and goals. These variables provide a manager with key considerations for the right organizational design, although they do not determine the structure. The amount of change in the contextual variables throughout the life of the organization influences the amount of change needed in the basic dimensions of the organization's structure. For example, competitive pressures in many industries have led to outsourcing, one of the greatest shifts in organizational structure in a century.[13]

Size

In organizational structure, size is defined as the total number of employees. This is logical, because people and their interactions are the building blocks of structure. Other measures, such as net assets, production rates, and total sales, are usually highly correlated with the total number of employees but may not reflect the actual number of interpersonal relationships that are necessary to effectively structure an organization.

When exploring structural alternatives, what should the manager know about designing structures for large and small organizations?

Formalization, specialization, and standardization all tend to be greater in larger organizations because they are necessary to control activities within the organization. For example, larger organizations are more likely to use documentation, rules, written policies and procedures, and detailed job descriptions than to rely on personal observation by the manager. McDonald's has several volumes that describe how to make all its products, how to greet customers, how to maintain the facilities, and so on. This level of standardization, formalization, and specialization helps McDonald's maintain the same quality of product no matter where a restaurant is located. In contrast, at a small, locally owned café, your hamburger and French fries may taste a little different every time you visit. This is evidence of a lack of standardization.

Formalization and specialization also help a large organization decentralize decision making. Because of the complexity and number of decisions in a large organization, formalization and specialization are used to set parameters for decision making at lower levels. By decentralizing decision making, the larger organization adds horizontal and vertical complexity, but not necessarily spatial complexity. However, it is more common for a large organization to have more geographic dispersion.

Although some have argued that the future belongs to small, agile organizations, others argue that size continues to be an advantage. To take advantage of size, organizations must become centreless corporations with a global core.[14] These concepts were pioneered by Booz Allen Hamilton based on its worldwide technology and management consulting. The global core provides strategic leadership, helps distribute and provide access to the company's capabilities and knowledge, creates the corporate identity, ensures access to low-cost capital, and exerts control over the enterprise as a whole.

Hierarchy of authority is another dimension of design related to complexity. As size increases, complexity increases; thus, more levels are added to the hierarchy of authority. This keeps the span of control from getting too large. However, there is a balancing force, because formalization and specialization are added. The more formalized, standardized, and specialized the roles within the organization, the wider the span of control can be.

Technology

An organization's technology is an important contextual variable in determining the organization's structure.[15] Technology is defined as the tools, techniques, and actions used by an organization to transform inputs into outputs.[16] The inputs of the organization include human resources, machines, materials, information, and money. The outputs are the products and services that the organization offers to the external environment. Determining the relationship between technology and structure is complicated because different departments may employ very different technologies. As organizations become larger, there is greater variation in technologies across units in the organization. Joan Woodward, Charles Perrow, and James Thompson have developed ways to understand traditional organizational technologies.

Woodward introduced one of the best-known classification schemes for technology, identifying three types: unit, mass, or process production. Unit technology is small-batch manufacturing technology and, sometimes, made-to-order production. Examples include Island View Design, a custom furniture and cabinet-making shop near Halifax, and Vancouver's KIMBO Design, a full-service design firm specializing in branding and website design. Mass technology is large-batch manufacturing technology. Examples include automotive assembly lines and latex glove production. Process production is continuous-production processes. Examples include oil refining and beer making. Woodward

contextual variables A set of characteristics that influence the organization's design processes.

#HOT TREND

Retailers Respond to Declining Sales with Downsizing

Staples, one of North America's largest retailers, plans to close up to 225 stores over the next two years, and will shrink the floor space for those stores that remain. Like other retailers, Staples' decision to downsize is in response to increased online purchases and declining foot traffic in brick-and-mortar stores and other retail establishments. Retailers of electronics, appliances, and office supplies have been hit especially hard by the shift to online shopping since these items tend to move more quickly than other goods. Nearly half of Staples' $23 billion annual revenue was the result of Internet sales. By reducing the size of its stores, Staples expects to improve its overall profitability through reduced rents in addition to maintenance, wages, and other operating expenses.

SOURCE: D. Fitzgerald, "Staples' Solution: Smaller Stores," *Wall Street Journal* (March 7, 2014): B1.

classified unit technology as the least complex, mass technology as more complex, and process technology as the most complex. The more complex the organization's technology, the more complex the administrative component or structure of the organization needs to be.

Perrow proposed an alternative to Woodward's scheme based on two variables: task variability and problem analyzability. Task variability considers the number of exceptions encountered in doing the tasks within a job. Problem analyzability examines the types of search procedures followed to find ways to respond to task exceptions. For example, for some exceptions encountered while doing a task, the appropriate response is easy to find. If you are driving down a street and see a sign that says, "Detour—Bridge Out," it is very easy to respond to the task variability, so analyzability is low (i.e., limited analysis is needed). By contrast, when Alexander Graham Bell was designing the first telephone, the problem analyzability was very high for his task.

Perrow went on to identify the four key aspects of structure that could be modified to the technology. These structural elements are (1) the amount of discretion that an individual can exercise to complete a task, (2) the power of groups to control the unit's goals and strategies, (3) the level of interdependence among groups, and (4) the extent to which organizational units coordinate work using either feedback or planning. Figure 16.7 summarizes Perrow's findings about types of technology and basic design dimensions.[17]

technological interdependence The degree of interrelatedness of the organization's various technological elements.

Thompson offered yet another view of technology and its relationship to organizational design. This view is based on the concept of **technological interdependence** (i.e., the degree of interrelatedness of the organization's various technological elements) and the pattern of an organization's work flows. Thompson's research suggests that greater technological interdependence leads to greater organizational complexity and that the problems of this greater complexity may be offset by decentralized decision making.[18]

The research of these three early scholars on the influence of technology on organizational design can be combined into one integrating concept—routineness in the process of changing inputs into outputs in an organization. This routineness has a very strong relationship with organizational structure. The more routine and repetitive the tasks of the organization, the higher the degree of formalization that is possible; the more centralized, specialized, and standardized the organization can be; and the more hierarchical levels with wider spans of control that are possible.

Essentially, the more routine the technology, the more effective a mechanistic structure will be in supporting organizational success. The less routine the technology, the more likely an organic structure is appropriate.

FIGURE 16.7 SUMMARY OF PERROW'S FINDINGS ABOUT THE RELATIONSHIP BETWEEN TECHNOLOGY AND BASIC DESIGN DIMENSIONS

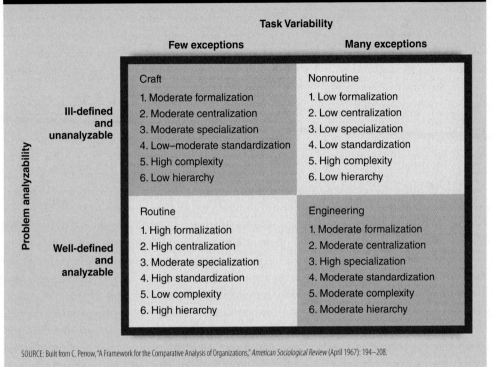

Problem analyzability	Task Variability: Few exceptions	Task Variability: Many exceptions
Ill-defined and unanalyzable	Craft 1. Moderate formalization 2. Moderate centralization 3. Moderate specialization 4. Low–moderate standardization 5. High complexity 6. Low hierarchy	Nonroutine 1. Low formalization 2. Low centralization 3. Low specialization 4. Low standardization 5. High complexity 6. Low hierarchy
Well-defined and analyzable	Routine 1. High formalization 2. High centralization 3. Moderate specialization 4. High standardization 5. Low complexity 6. High hierarchy	Engineering 1. Moderate formalization 2. Moderate centralization 3. High specialization 4. Moderate standardization 5. Moderate complexity 6. Moderate hierarchy

SOURCE: Built from C. Perrow, "A Framework for the Comparative Analysis of Organizations," *American Sociological Review* (April 1967): 194–208.

Environment

The third contextual variable for organizational design is **environment**. The environment of an organization is most easily defined as anything outside the boundaries of that organization. Different aspects of the environment have varying degrees of influence on the organization's structure. The general environment includes all conditions that may have an impact on the organization. These conditions could include economic factors, political considerations, ecological changes, sociocultural demands, and governmental regulation.

The level of **environmental uncertainty** is the contextual variable of environment that most influences organizational design. Some organizations have relatively static and simple environments with little uncertainty, whereas others are so dynamic and complex that no one is sure what tomorrow may bring. Binney & Smith, for example, has made relatively the same product for more than 50 years, with very few changes in the product design or packaging. The environment for its Crayola products is relatively static. In fact, customers rebelled when the company tried to get rid of some old colours and add new ones. In contrast, in the last two decades, competitors in the airline industry have encountered deregulation, mergers, bankruptcies, safety changes, changes in cost and price structures, changes in customer and employee demographics, and changes in global competition. In such uncertain conditions, fast-response organizations must use expertise coordination practices to ensure that distributed expertise is managed and applied in a timely manner.[19]

The degree of uncertainty in the environment influences the structural dimensions. A functional structure is superior in a predictable environment because it enhances efficiencies, but a divisional structure's (e.g., geography/product) customized focus allows it to respond more quickly in an unpredictable environment.[20]

If the organization's environment is uncertain, dynamic, and complex, and resources are scarce, the manager needs an organic structure that is better able to adapt to its environment. Such a structure allows the manager to monitor the environment from a number of internal perspectives, thus helping the organization maintain flexibility in responding to environmental changes.[21]

environment Anything outside the boundaries of an organization.

environmental uncertainty The number of different elements and the rate of change in the organization's environment.

© Photodisc/Getty Images

This finding has been replicated recently in Chinese companies.[22] Although an organic structure's flexibility makes it suitable to meet the need for timely responsiveness, research suggests that there remains a need for some structure and it may be better to err on the side of too much structure rather than too little.[23] Some suggest the use of a "simple rules" structure that can be robust in a number of environments.[24]

Dess and Beard defined three dimensions of environment that should be measured in assessing the degree of uncertainty: capacity, volatility, and complexity.[25] The capacity of the environment reflects the abundance or scarcity of resources. If resources abound, the environment supports expansion, mistakes, or both. In contrast, in times of scarcity, the environment demands survival of the fittest. Volatility is the degree of instability. The airline industry is in a volatile environment. This makes it difficult for managers to know what needs to be done. The complexity of the environment refers to the differences and variability among environmental elements.

The organization's perceptions of its environment and the actual environment may not be the same. The environment that the manager perceives is the environment that the organization responds to and organizes for.[26] Therefore, two organizations may be in relatively the same environment from an objective standpoint, but if the managers perceive differences, the organizations may enact very different structures to deal with this same environment. For example, one company may decentralize and use monetary incentives for managers that lead it to be competitively aggressive while another company may centralize and use incentives for managers that lead it to be less intense in its rivalry.[27]

Strategy and Goals

The fourth contextual variable that influences how the design dimensions of structure should be enacted is the strategies and goals of the organization. Strategies and goals provide legitimacy to the organization, as well as employee direction, decision guidelines, and criteria for performance.[28] In addition, strategies and goals help the organization fit into its environment.

Different strategies will lead to different emphases on efficiency versus innovation. If a company follows a cost leadership strategy, aiming at selling more because its products are the least expensive, it needs efficiency to lower its costs. It will typically lean toward a mechanistic structure in order to gain this efficiency. On the other hand, if it emphasizes differentiation from the competition through a unique or innovative product, an organic structure with decentralization and low formalization will encourage the creativity and quick responsiveness needed.[29]

For example, when Apple Computer introduced personal computers to the market, its strategies were very innovative. The structure of the organization was relatively flat and very informal. Apple had Friday afternoon beer and popcorn discussion sessions, and eccentric behaviour was easily accepted. As the personal computer market became more competitive, however, the structure of Apple changed to help it control costs. The innovative strategies and structures devised by Steve Jobs, one of Apple's founders, were no longer appropriate. The board of directors recruited John Scully, a marketing expert from PepsiCo, to help Apple better compete in the market it had created. In 1996 and 1997, Apple reinvented itself again and brought back Jobs to try to restore its innovative edge. After his return, Apple became a major player in the digital music market with its introduction of several models of the iPod, iPhone, and iPad.

Limitations exist, however, on the extent to which strategies and goals influence structure. Because the structure of the organization includes the formal information-processing channels in the organization, it stands to reason that the need to change strategies may not be communicated throughout the organization. In such a case, the organization's structure influences its strategic choice. Changing the organization's structure may not unlock value but rather drive up costs and difficulties. Therefore, strategic success may hinge on choosing an organization design that works reasonably well, and then fine tuning the structure through a strategic system.[30]

The inefficiency of the structure to perceive environmental changes may even lead to organizational failure. Examples of how different design dimensions can affect the strategic decision process are listed in Table 16.1.

The four contextual variables—size, technology, environment, and strategy and goals—combine to influence the design process. However, the existing structure of the organization influences how the organization interprets and reacts to information about each of the variables. Each of the contextual variables has management researchers who claim that it is the most important variable in determining the best structural design. Because of the difficulty in studying the interactions of the four contextual dimensions and the complexity of organizational structures, the argument about which variable is most important continues.

What is apparent is that there must be some level of fit between the structure and the contextual dimensions

TABLE 16.1 EXAMPLES OF HOW STRUCTURE AFFECTS THE STRATEGIC DECISION PROCESS

Formalization
As the level of formalization increases, so does the probability of the following:
1. The strategic decision process will become reactive to crisis rather than proactive through opportunities.
2. Strategic moves will be incremental and precise.
3. Differentiation in the organization will not be balanced with integrative mechanisms.
4. Only environmental crises that are in areas monitored by the formal organizational systems will be acted upon.
Centralization
As the level of centralization increases, so does the probability of the following:
1. The strategic decision process will be initiated by only a few dominant individuals.
2. The decision process will be goal-oriented and rational.
3. The strategic process will be constrained by the limitations of top managers.
Complexity
As the level of complexity increases, so does the probability of the following:
1. The strategic decision process will become more politicized.
2. The organization will find it more difficult to recognize environmental opportunities and threats.
3. The constraints on good decision processes will be multiplied by the limitations of each individual within the organization.

SOURCE: Republished with permission of Academy of Management, "The Strategic Decision Process and Organizational Structure" (Table), J. Fredrickson, *Academy of Management Review* (1986): 284. Reproduced by permission conveyed through Copyright Clearance Center, Inc.

of the organization. The better the fit, the more likely the organization will achieve its short-run goals. In addition, the better the fit, the more likely the organization will process information and design appropriate organizational roles for long-term prosperity, as indicated in Figure 16.8.

Interaction Between Structure and People

One can also apply the idea of fit between structures and people. Studies of Americans show they were more attracted to organizations with decentralized structures,[31] and their job satisfaction was inversely related to the level of bureaucracy in the work. Individual differences showed that the low job satisfaction–bureaucracy link was particularly pronounced in those individuals who place a high value on individuality, freedom, and independence.[32] In contrast, research investigating the high failure rate of development projects in developing countries attributed many of the difficulties in the Nepalese projects to the mismatch between the high bureaucratic orientation of the Nepalese and the Western project-management structure.[33] Finnish research showed that individuals with a high personal need for structure experience more job strain in highly complex work circumstances.[34] An individual's level of self-esteem seems related to the influence of organization structural dimensions, with low-self-esteem people more sensitive to those cues.[35]

FIGURE 16.8 THE RELATIONSHIP AMONG KEY ORGANIZATIONAL DESIGN ELEMENTS

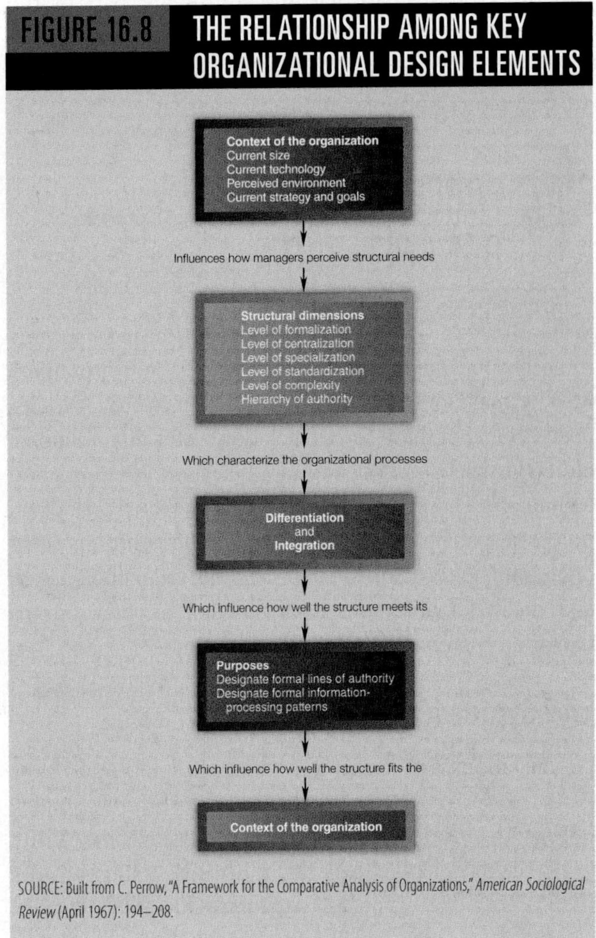

SOURCE: Built from C. Perrow, "A Framework for the Comparative Analysis of Organizations," *American Sociological Review* (April 1967): 194–208.

Structure influences leadership. Charismatic leaders are more likely to emerge in organic structures than in mechanistic ones.[36] Flat structures reward those managers who favour sharing information and objectives with employees by promoting them faster than those managers who do not believe in making information and objectives explicit to those below them. The opposite was observed in tall structures.[37] Leadership also influences structure. CEOs with a high need for achievement are more likely to use centralization, formalization, and integration. Because they want to meet standards of excellence and want to have control over events affecting performance, they try to accomplish their work in an interactive way (because they like feedback) and an analytical/rational way (suggesting a focus on good procedures and linking mechanisms).[38]

“Organizations are dynamic entities; they ebb and flow through different stages.”

Structure also influences justice expectations and perceptions. Decentralized organizations are seen as more procedurally fair than centralized.[39] Individuals are more sensitive to procedural justice in mechanistic structures because formal procedures are part of the daily work landscape. Individuals are more sensitive to interactional justice in organic structures because they are based on interpersonal interactions.[40]

16-5 FORCES RESHAPING ORGANIZATIONS

Several forces reshaping organizations are causing managers to go beyond the traditional frameworks and to examine ways to make organizations more responsive to customer needs. Some of these forces include shorter organizational life cycles, globalization, and rapid changes in information technology. These forces together increase the demands on process capabilities within the organization and emerging organizational structures. To successfully retain their health and vitality, organizations must function as open systems that are responsive to their task environment.[41]

Life Cycles in Organizations

Organizations are dynamic entities; they ebb and flow through different stages. Usually, researchers think of these stages as **organizational life cycles**. The total organization has a life cycle that begins at birth, moves through growth and maturity to decline, and possibly experiences revival.[42]

organizational life cycles The differing stages of an organization's life from birth to death.

Organizational subunits may have very similar life cycles. Because of changes in technology and product design, many organizational subunits, especially those that are product based, are experiencing shorter life cycles. Hence, the subunits that compose the organization are changing more rapidly than in the past. These shorter life cycles enable the organization to respond quickly to external demands and changes.

When a new organization or subunit is born, the structure is organic and informal. If the organization or subunit is successful, it grows and matures. This usually leads to formalization, specialization, standardization, complexity, and a more mechanistic structure. If the environment changes, however, the organization must be able to respond. A mechanistic structure is not able to respond to a dynamic environment as well as an organic one. If the organization or subunit does respond, it becomes more organic and revives; if not, it declines and possibly dies.

Shorter life cycles put more pressure on the organization to be both flexible and efficient at the same time. Further, as flexible organizations use design to their competitive advantage, discrete organizational life cycles may give way to a kaleidoscope of continuously emerging, efficiency-seeking organizational designs.[43] The manager's challenge in this context becomes one of creating congruency among various organizational design dimensions to fit continuously changing markets and locations.

Globalization

Another force that is reshaping organizations is the process of globalization. In other words, organizations operate worldwide rather than in just one country or region. Global corporations can become pitted against sovereign nations when rules and laws conflict across national borders. Globalization makes spatial differentiation even more of a reality for organizations. Besides the obvious geographic differences, there may be deep cultural and value system differences. This adds another type of complexity to the structural design process and necessitates the creation of integrating mechanisms so that people are able to understand and interpret one another, as well as coordinate with one another.

The choice of structure for managing an international business is generally based on choices concerning the following three factors:

1. *The level of vertical differentiation.* A hierarchy of authority must be created that clarifies the responsibilities of both domestic and foreign managers.
2. *The level of horizontal differentiation.* Foreign and domestic operations should be grouped in such a way that the company effectively serves the needs of all the customers.
3. *The degree of formalization, specialization, standardization, and centralization.* The global structure must allow decisions to be made in the most appropriate area of the organization. However, controls must be in place that reflect the strategies and goals of the parent firm.[44]

Changes in Information-processing Technologies

Many of the changes in information-processing technologies have allowed organizations to move into new product and market areas more quickly. However, just as shorter life cycles and globalization have caused new concerns for designing organizational structures, so has the increased availability of advanced information-processing technologies.

Organizational structures are already feeling the impact of advanced information-processing technologies. More integration and coordination are evident because managers worldwide can be connected through computerized networks. The basic design dimensions have also been affected as follows:

1. The hierarchy of authority has been flattened.
2. The basis of centralization has been changed. Now managers can use technology to acquire more information and make more decisions, or they can use technology to push information and decision making lower in the hierarchy and thus decrease centralization. In fact, decentralized structures do make greater use of information technology than do centralized structures.[45]
3. Less specialization and standardization are needed because people using advanced information-processing technologies have more sophisticated jobs that require a broader understanding of how the organization gets work done.[46]

Advances in information processing are leading to knowledge-based organizations that incorporate virtual enterprising, dynamic teaming, and knowledge networking.[47]

Demands on Organizational Processes

Because of the forces reshaping organizations, managers find themselves trying to meet what seem to be conflicting goals: an efficiency orientation that results in on-time delivery *and* a quality orientation that results in customized, high-quality goods or services.[48] Traditionally, managers have seen efficiency and customization as conflicting demands.

To meet these conflicting demands, organizations need to become "dynamically stable."[49] To do so, an organization must have managers who see their roles as architects who clearly understand the "how" of the organizing process. Managers must combine long-term thinking with flexible and quick responses that help improve process and know-how (see Table 16.2). The organizational structure must help define, at least to some degree, roles for managers who hope to successfully address the conflicting demands of dynamic stability. Go to the Self-Assessment to assess your organization.

IN ACTION

La Presse

La Presse, one of Canada's best-known papers, started a significant restructuring in 2018. It is moving from a for-profit unit of the Demarais' Power Corporation to a stand-alone non-profit. The goal of the change in structure is to enable La Presse to get government grants and to receive donations. The Demarais family will make an initial donation of $50 million to the new entity and then will not have any role in the French-language paper. "The new structure is designed to be a modern approach adapted to the realities of today's written media," according to La Presse. Further, La Presse president Pierre-Elliott Levasseur noted, "I don't think there's a person in Quebec or in the rest of Canada who's going to give money to La Presse in the form of a donation knowing that Power Corp. is the owner."

La Presse first published in 1884 and was created by conservatives who did not support John A. MacDonald. In 2017, La Presse made headlines by no longer printing paper copies of the newspaper and went fully digital. La Presse employs 585 people.

SOURCES: S. Rukavina, "Montreal's La Presse is to Become Non-profit Entity," *CBC News*, May 8, 2018, accessed from https://www.cbc.ca/news/canada/montreal/montreal-s-la-presse-to-become-non-profit-entity-1.4653138, September 26, 2018; The Canadian Press, "Bill to Make La Presse a Not for Profit Passes after Quebec Invoked Closure," June 15, 2018, accessed from https://globalnews.ca/news/4277310/bill-to-make-la-presse-a-not-for-profit-passes-after-quebec-invoked-closure, September 9, 2018.

TABLE 16.2 STRUCTURAL ROLES OF MANAGERS TODAY VERSUS MANAGERS OF THE FUTURE

Roles of Managers Today	**1.** Strictly adhering to boss–employee relationships. **2.** Getting things done by giving orders. **3.** Carrying messages up and down the hierarchy. **4.** Performing a prescribed set of tasks according to a job description. **5.** Having a narrow functional focus. **6.** Going through channels, one by one. **7.** Controlling subordinates.
Roles of Future Managers	**1.** Having hierarchical relationships subordinated to functional and peer relationships. **2.** Getting things done by negotiating. **3.** Solving problems and making decisions. **4.** Creating the job by developing entrepreneurial projects. **5.** Having broad cross-functional collaboration. **6.** Emphasizing speed and flexibility. **7.** Coaching their workers.

SOURCE: Republished with permission of American Management Association, from T. R. Horton and P. C. Reid (1991). "What Fate for Middle Managers?" *Management Review,* 80(1), 22. © 1991. Thomas R. Horton; permission conveyed through Copyright Clearance Center, Inc.

16-6 EMERGING ORGANIZATIONAL STRUCTURES

The demands on managers and on process capabilities place demands on structures. The emphasis in organizations is shifting to organizing around processes. This process orientation emerges from the combination of three streams of applied organizational design: high-performance, self-managed teams; managing processes rather than functions; and the evolution of information technology. Information technology and advanced communication systems have led to internetworking. For example, Procter & Gamble increased its level of innovation by creating teams dedicated to conducting market research, developing technology, creating business plans, and testing assumptions for specific projects.[50]

In a study of 469 firms, deeply inter-networked firms were found to be more focused and specialized, less hierarchical, and more engaged in external partnering.[51] Three emerging organizational structures associated with these changes are network organizations, virtual organizations, and the circle organization.

Network organizations are weblike structures that contract some or all of their operating functions to other organizations and then coordinate their activities through managers and other employees at their headquarters. Information technology is the basis for building the weblike structure of the network organization and business unit managers that are essential to the success of these systems. This type of organization has arisen in the age of electronic commerce and brought into practice transaction cost economics, interorganizational collaborations, and strategic alliances. Network organizations can be global in scope.[52] For example, the focus of the Canadian Forces changed with the end of its Afghan mission and its redeployment in other parts of the world. This triggered reorganization in 2011. Lieutenant-General Andrew Leslie, former chief of land staff, had the task of transforming the military's organizational structure to cope with the changing demands on the military.[53]

Virtual organizations are temporary network organizations consisting of independent enterprises. Many dot-coms were virtual organizations designed to come together swiftly to exploit an apparent market opportunity. They may function much like a theatrical troupe that comes together for a "performance."[54] Trust can be a challenge for virtual organizations because it is a complex phenomenon involving ethics, morals, emotions, values, and natural attitudes. However, trust and trustworthiness are important connective issues in virtual environments. Three key ingredients for the development of trust in virtual organizations are technology that can communicate emotion; a sharing of values, vision, and organizational identity; and a high standard of ethics.[55] Virtuality in organizations is often broken down into four interlocking components: geographic dispersion, electronic interdependence, dynamic structure, and national diversity.[56]

The circle organization is a third emerging structure, crafted by Harley-Davidson in its drive to achieve teamwork without teams.[57] The three organizational parts are those that (1) create demand, (2) produce product, and (3) provide support. The three parts are linked by the leadership and strategy council (LSC). The circle organization is a more open system than most and an organic structure for customer responsiveness. One innovation in this organizational scheme is the "circle coach," who possesses acute communication, listening, and influencing skills so as to be highly respected.

Other new structures do not fit these models. Precision Biologic of Dartmouth, Nova Scotia, was named one of the best employers in Canada for 2010. The developer and manufacturer of medical lab products has an unusual hub-and-spokes organizational structure that de-emphasizes hierarchy and promotes collaboration in a working relationship approach that resembles a molecular structure (see Figure 16.9). More organizations will be experimenting with unusual structures like this in order to meet demands for responsiveness, flexibility, and innovation.

The demands placed on managers and on process capabilities in turn place demands on structures. Consequently, the emphasis in organizations is shifting to organizing around processes.

Disruptive Organizational Designs

The following are examples of disruptive organizational designs that can help organizations become efficient, innovative, adaptable, and reactive, especially during times of change and uncertainty.

1. *Self-management and self-organization*—First tested in the 1960s, this design is characterized by increased autonomy and responsibility of employees and teams for all organizational processes. Whole Foods and W. L. Gore are examples.
2. *Intrapreneurship*—A subset of the organization functions autonomously from a budgetary, process, and operational standpoint until it gains recognition in the marketplace, after which the unit will either rejoin the organization or become a separate branch. Cisco used a form of this design to inject agility into its organization.
3. *Virtual ephermal structures*—These are interim structures made up of dedicated virtual teams that use a collaborative platform to support promising niche markets and jumpstart new businesses.
4. *The neuroscienced organization*—This design uses a neurocognitive approach to manage human capital by developing an understanding of how people behave in unplanned situations. Success depends on each employee's ability to be open-minded, view situations differently, and adapt accordingly. Juniper Networks is an example.
5. *The acculturated organization*—Built on the premise that culture isn't created; culture happens by focusing on operating the organization using practical principles of fostering creativity, adaptability, collaboration, trust, and keeping things simple. S7Signals, the startup that developed the top cloud-based project management platform, is an example.
6. *The transparent organization*—This type of organization is based on the notion that a high degree of transparency throughout the organization increases the quality of insights since individuals know that their contributions will be seen. In that way, executives support and assist lower-level employees instead of vice versa. HCL Technologies uses this design.
7. *The Agora organization*—More fluid than self-management, this perpetually changing structure is fuelled by creativity and long-lasting values instilled by its founders. Google is the most well-known example.[58]
8. *The holocracy*—"A form of self-management that confers decision power on fluid teams, or "circles," and roles rather than individuals."[59] The best-known advocate for and example of a holocracy is Zappos. In 2015, CEO Tony Hsieh offered severance packages to employees for whom self-management was not a good fit. Some recent research has shown that self-management works for some people in some organizations, but that fully adopting holocracy does not. For example, Medium, a social medium company, restructured from holocracy as the coordination costs were significant.[60]

FIGURE 16.9 PRECISION BIOLOGIC ORGANIZATIONAL FRAMEWORK

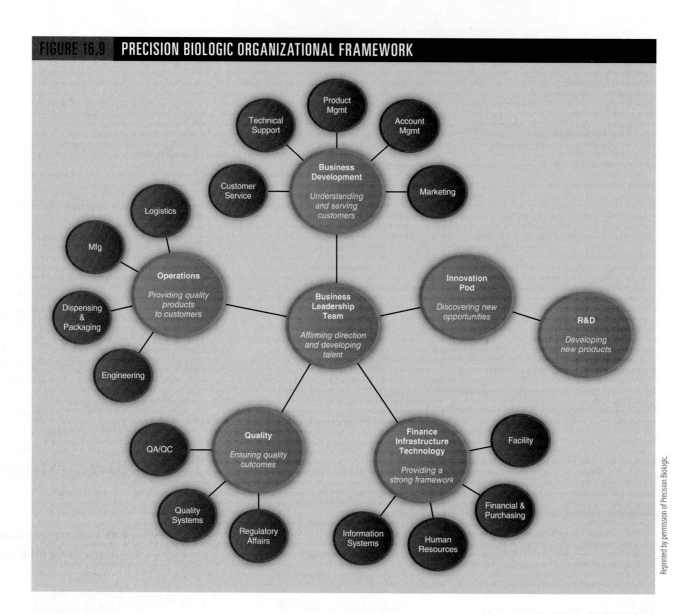

Reprinted by permission of Precision Biologic.

16-7 CONSEQUENCES OF A POOR STRUCTURE

This chapter has identified the purposes of structure, the processes of organizational design, and the dimensions and contexts that must be considered in structure. In addition, it has looked at forces and trends in organizational design. A cautionary note is important for the student of organizational behaviour. An organizational structure may be weak or deficient. In general, if the structure is out of alignment with its contextual variables, one or more of the following symptoms of structural deficiency appear.

- Decision making is delayed because the hierarchy is overloaded and too much information is being funnelled through one or two channels.
- Decision making lacks quality because information linkages are not providing the correct information to the right person in the right format.
- The organization does not respond innovatively to a changing environment, especially when coordinated effort is lacking across departments.
- A great deal of conflict is evident when departments are working against one another rather than working for the strategies and goals of the organization as a whole; then the structure is often at fault.

Second, the personality of the chief executive may adversely affect the structure of the organization.[61] Managers' personal, cognitive biases and political ideologies may affect their good judgment and decision making.[62] Five dysfunctional combinations of personality and organization have been identified: the paranoid, the depressive, the dramatic, the compulsive, and the schizoid.[63] Each of these personality–organization constellations can create problems for the people who work in the organization. For example, in a paranoid constellation, people are suspicious of each other; hence, distrust in working relationships may interfere with effective communication and task accomplishment. In a depressive constellation, people feel depressed and inhibited in their work activities, which can lead to low levels of productivity and task accomplishment.

STUDY TOOLS 16

IN THE BOOK YOU CAN ...

- ☐ Rip out the **Chapter Review card** at the end of the book to review Key Concepts and Key Terms.
- ☐ Take a "What about You?" Quiz related to material in the chapter.
- ☐ Read additional cases in the Mini Case and Shopify Running Case sections.

ONLINE YOU CAN ... NELSON.COM/STUDENT

- ☐ Take a "What about You?" Quiz related to material in the chapter.
- ☐ Test your understanding with a quick Multiple-Choice Pre-Test quiz.
- ☐ Read the eBook, which includes discussion points for questions posed in the Cases.
- ☐ Watch Videos related to chapter content.
- ☐ Use the available Flashcards and Matching Quizzes to test your understanding of key terms and concepts.
- ☐ See how much you've learned by taking a Post-Test.

WHAT ABOUT YOU?

Managers of Today and the Future

Are the roles for managers in your organization more oriented toward today or toward the future? (If you do not work, think of an organization where you have worked or talk with a friend about managerial roles in their organization.)

Roles of Managers Today

1. Strictly adhering to boss–employee relationships.
2. Getting things done by giving orders.
3. Carrying messages up and down the hierarchy.
4. Performing a prescribed set of tasks according to a job description.
5. Having a narrow functional focus.
6. Going through channels, one by one by one.
7. Controlling subordinates.

Roles of Future Managers

1. Having hierarchical relationships subordinated to functional and peer relationships.
2. Getting things done by negotiating.
3. Solving problems and making decisions.
4. Creating the job by developing entrepreneurial projects.
5. Having broad cross-functional collaboration.
6. Emphasizing speed and flexibility.
7. Coaching their workers.

Step 1. Check which orientation (today or future) predominates in your organization for each of the following seven characteristics:

	Today	Future
1. Boss–employee relationships	____	____
2. Getting work accomplished	____	____
3. Messenger versus problem solver	____	____
4. Basis for task accomplishment	____	____
5. Narrow versus broad functional focus	____	____
6. Adherence to channels of authority	____	____
7. Controlling versus coaching subordinates	____	____

Step 2. Examine the degree of consistency across all seven characteristics. Could the organization make one or two structural changes to achieve a better alignment of the manager's role today or in the future?

Step 3. Identify one manager in your organization who fits very well into the organization's ideal-manager role. What does this manager do that creates a good person–role fit?

Step 4. Identify one manager in your organization who does not fit very well into the organization's ideal-manager role. What does this manager do that creates a poor person–role fit?

MINI CASE

Great Little Box Company

Robert Meggie bought the Great Little Box Company (GLBC) in 1982 from a receiver; the box-manufacturing company had struggled since its creation in 1981. An accountant who had worked in the packaging industry, Meggie started with a 5,000 square feet plant in Burnaby and three employees: two machine operators and a sales representative. He himself did everything at the beginning from "taking orders to making sales calls to running one of the machines and shipping out the completed orders." That first year was made more difficult by the tough economic recession. So Meggie approached one of his largest customers, a shipping-supplies firm, with a partnership offer: he would be responsible for administration and production and they would look after sales and marketing. They liked the idea and brought back a recently laid-off salesperson to work with GLBC. The partnership never materialized but the connection between GLBC and the new sales rep was so successful that the rep decided to stay with GLBC. This sales rep was a revelation to Meggie. "He upped our business 80 percent overnight" and taught Meggie the value of a strong sales force.

After that first year, growth was steady. Within five years a sales manager was needed. Then sales and distribution offices were opened in Victoria (1992), Kelowna (1998), and Everett, Washington (1998). The head office and production facility went through several moves to larger quarters in the Vancouver area until the company finally built its own 250,000 square foot facility on Mitchell Island in Richmond, British Columbia, in 2006.

GLBC's main business is designing and manufacturing corrugated boxes and displays. The corrugated-packaging industry is dominated by a few large multinational companies. This means that GLBC cannot get the same economies of scale so competes on the basis of speed and customer service, turning orders around much faster. Striving to become a "one-stop shop" for customer packaging and shipping needs, GLBC has also expanded its services. It established a moving supplies division in 2004 and a label division in 2006 (through the acquisition of C. Davis Enterprises' assets). The 2007 acquisition of Boxster led to the creation of the folding cartons and rigid boxes division. While the recent recession created difficulties for other manufacturers, it led to opportunities for Meggie and GLBC. Since 2009 GLBC has acquired more companies: Parrot Label (which has increased GLBC's label capabilities), Vanisle Packaging (making GLBC the premier packaging provider on Vancouver Island), and Action Box Company (making GLBC the lead provider of protective packaging in BC). Despite the recession, GLBC's revenue has increased from $30 million in 2009 to $36 million in 2010 and is anticipated to reach $45 million to $50 million in 2011. In the effort to meet its one-stop-shop goal, GLBC now manufactures boxes of all sizes, foam protective packaging, and folding cartons and labels, and distributes a full range of shipping and moving supplies.

Meggie's expansion of the business has been aggressive but careful and has involved his employees at each step of the way. At monthly meetings GLBC shares its corporate and financial information with all employees. These meetings are also forums for employee input and for rewarding employees. "It's important to share the financials with everyone. It makes people feel more a part of the company ... It instils a sense of trust. Regardless of whether the news is good or bad, people want to know and, ultimately, will try harder to make the company more profitable." Daily production meetings and weekly departmental meetings provide a steady flow of information with opportunities for employees to ask questions and give input. Meggie meets with everyone in the company twice a year, in small groups of 10 to 12. There he provides a "state-of-the-nation" report, discusses issues like quality or production, and then opens up the meeting for questions and feedback. Strategic planning meetings held every two months invite employees representing each department to review the plan, measure progress, share ideas, and make adjustments. An idea recognition program gives monetary rewards to employees who submit ideas to improve a work process or resolve a problem. GLBC supports teamwork through its profit-sharing plan, paying out 15 percent of its profit monthly, with all eligible employees receiving the same amount regardless of their position or wage rate, whether they are truck drivers or plant supervisors.

GLBC now has over 200 employees. Most of its clients are in BC and there is a lot of potential growth in the state of Washington. There are no plans to expand beyond this western region. GLBC has been on *Maclean's* Top 100 employers each year between 2005 and 2017.

SOURCES: Leadership and Management Development Council of British Columbia, "Great Little Box Company: A team approach to success," December 2005, http://www.leadershipmanagement.bc.ca/pdf/GreatLittleBox_Company_Eng%5B1%5D.pdf, accessed December 31, 2010; B. Morton, "Recession can't box in Richmond firm's growth," *Vancouver Sun*, September 15, 2010, http://www.vancouversun.com/business/Recession+Richmond+firm+growth/3526982/story.html, accessed December 31, 2010; Great Little Box company – History, http://www.greatlittlebox.com/about/history/, accessed December 31, 2010; R. Yerema & K. Leung, Great Little Box Company, http://www.eluta.ca/top-employer-great-little-box-company, accessed December 31, 2010.

Apply Your Understanding

1. Apply the concepts of differentiation and integration to this case.
2. Describe the idea of "fit" between structure and people. Discuss what types of people you see as "fitting" the GLBC structure and why.
3. Discuss where GLBC seems to be in its life cycle.

SHOPIFY RUNNING CASE

SHOPIFY'S GLOBAL STRUCTURE

Shopify's board of directors consists of six people, including the CEO, Tobi Lütke. The board has a lead independent director whose responsibilities include helping the board to follow good governance practices in meeting its obligations which are described in the board's charter. The six each sit on at least one of the board's committees, i.e., the compensation, the audit, and the nominating/governance committees. The leadership team consists of nine people. In addition to the CEO, there is the chief operating officer; chief product officer; chief financial officer; chief marketing officer; general counsel; and senior vice-presidents of human relations, engineering, and support.

Shopify has a global structure. Under Shopify Inc, there are four key units: Payments Canada, Shopify US, Shopify Ireland, and Shopify Holdings US. Shopify Holdings includes US Data Processing and Payments.

Shopify has its own code of conduct that applies to everyone in the organization. It states that everyone—including contractors—must read, understand, and act on the organization's code. Shopify will provide training about its code so that there is no misunderstanding about its content. As well, Shopify has a "no asshole" rule. (In 2007, Robert Sutton first addressed the issue of assholes in his important book, *The No Asshole Rule: Building a Civilized Workplace and Surviving One That Isn't.* Sutton comments the most important reason he wrote the book is "that demeaning people does terrible damage to others and to their companies." He goes on to note that even winners who are assholes are still assholes!) In short, Shopify expects everyone to work in the interests of Shopify.

Apply Your Understanding

1. Is the size of the board too small for the company?
2. As Shopify grows, what structural changes would you expect and why?
3. How can Shopify enforce its code of conduct?

© Paul Mckinnon | Dreamstime.com

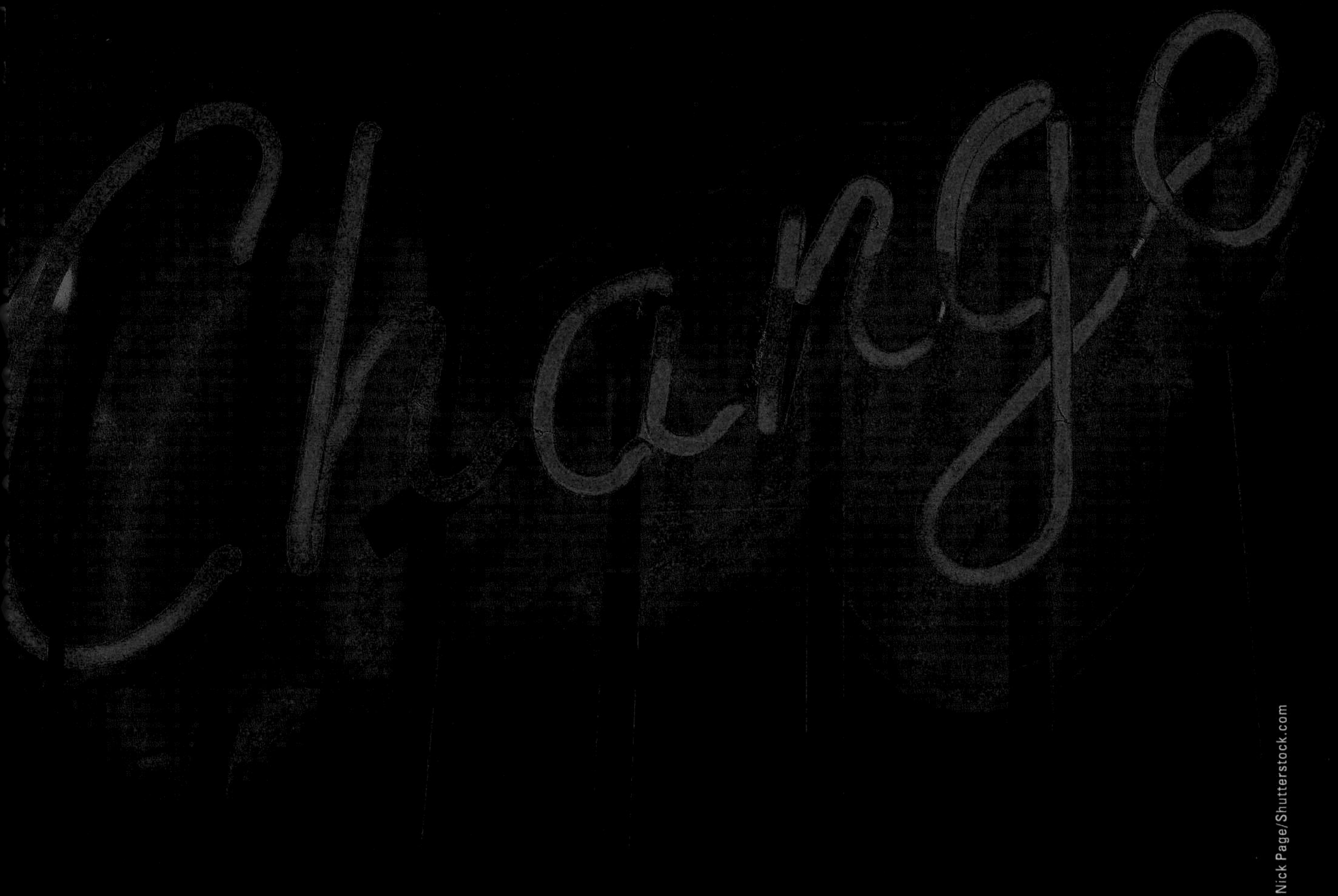

Nick Page/Shutterstock.com

17 Managing Change

LEARNING OUTCOMES

After reading this chapter, you should be able to do the following:

17-1 Identify the major external and internal forces for change in organizations.

17-2 Describe how different types of change vary in scope.

17-3 Discuss methods organizations can use to manage resistance to change.

17-4 Explain Lewin's and Kotter's organizational change models.

17-5 Explain how companies determine the need to conduct an organizational development intervention.

17-6 Discuss the major group-focused techniques for organization development intervention.

17-7 Discuss the major individual-focused techniques for organization development intervention.

See the end of this chapter for a list of available Study Tools, a "What about You?" Quiz, Mini Case, and the Shopify Running Case.

17-1 FORCES FOR CHANGE IN ORGANIZATIONS

Change has become the norm in most organizations. Many Canadian companies have experienced plant closings, business failures, mergers and acquisitions, or downsizing. *Adaptiveness, flexibility,* and *responsiveness* are characteristics of the organizations that will succeed in meeting the competitive challenges.[1] In the past, organizations could succeed by claiming excellence in one area—quality, reliability, or cost, for example—but this is not the case today. The current environment demands excellence in all areas and vigilant leaders. A recent survey of CEOs who were facing crises found that 50 percent of them said they believed the problems arrived "suddenly" and that they had not prepared adequately for them. More than 10 percent said they were, in fact, the last to know about the problems.[2]

> "Managers must be prepared to handle both planned and unplanned forms of change in organizations."

Change has become the norm, and yet successful change can be elusive. Some estimate that 50 to 75 percent of mergers fail their financial objectives and the success rate of large-scale change interventions is at best 50 percent.[3]

As we saw in Chapter 1, change is what's on managers' minds. The pursuit of organizational effectiveness through downsizing, restructuring, reengineering, productivity management, cycle-time reduction, and other efforts is paramount. Organizations are in a state of turmoil and transition, and all members are affected. Continued downsizings may have left firms leaner but not necessarily richer. Though downsizing can increase shareholder value by better aligning costs with revenues, firms may suffer from public criticism for their actions. Laying off employees may be accompanied by increases in CEO pay and stock options, linking the misery of employees with the financial success of owners and management.[4]

Organizations must also deal with ethical, environmental, and other social issues. Competition is fierce, and companies can no longer afford to rest on their laurels. General Electric (GE) holds off-site WorkOut sessions with groups of managers and employees whose goal is to make GE a faster, less complex organization that can respond effectively to change. In the WorkOut sessions, employees recommend specific changes, explain why they are needed, and propose ways the changes can be implemented. Top management must make an immediate response: an approval, a disapproval (with an explanation), or a request for more information. The GE WorkOut sessions try to eliminate the barriers that keep employees from contributing to change. Even so, GE is struggling in 2018 and is engaged in large-scale change efforts.[5]

planned change Change resulting from a deliberate decision to alter the organization.

unplanned change Change that is imposed on the organization and is often unforeseen.

There are two basic forms of change in organizations. **Planned change** results from a deliberate decision to alter the organization. Organizations that wish to move from a traditional hierarchical structure to one that facilitates self-managed teams, for example, must use a proactive, carefully orchestrated approach. **Unplanned change** is imposed on the organization and is often unforeseen. Changes in government regulations and changes in the economy, for example, are unplanned. Responsiveness to unplanned change requires tremendous flexibility and adaptability on the part of organizations. Managers must be prepared to handle both planned and unplanned forms of change in organizations.

Forces for change can come from many sources. Some of these are external, arising from outside the organization, whereas others are internal, arising from sources within.

External Forces

The four major managerial challenges we have described throughout the book are major external forces for change. Globalization, workforce diversity, technological change, and managing ethical behaviour are challenges that often precipitate change in organizations.

GLOBALIZATION Globalization brings the opportunities of new markets, the threat of new competition, and the necessity of adaptive response. Canadian businesses have been affected in varying ways. The Canadian clothing industry has seen huge job losses.[6] Even there, the survivors are the ones that learned to play the global game. Gildan Activewear Inc., headquartered in Montreal, strategically anticipated the changing global competition and searched out the various trade agreements to place its plants where they could ship duty-free into North America, the EU countries, and Australia. The combination of advanced technology and relatively low wages in Honduras, Dominican Republic, Haiti, Mexico, and Nicaragua has meant Gilden has been able to survive the threat from low-cost Chinese labour.[7] Canadian industries based in knowledge or commodities have also done well in the new economic circumstances. For example, Montreal-based CGI Group is one of the world's largest independent IT and business process services firms, employing 26,000 people around the world.[8] Also based in Montreal, SNC-Lavalin remains one of the world's largest engineering companies, even though its reputation was hurt by its 2013 bribery scandal. Globalization means its expertise now finds wider markets.

Tube-Mac, out of Stoney Creek, Ontario, wanted to take its nonwelded hydraulic piping systems global, but to do so had to earn new certifications, such as those from Lloyd's Registry, American Bureau of Shipping, and Chinese Classification Society. Tube-Mac built a test lab in Ontario and invited the associations to audit its product testing.[9] The company hasn't looked back. Choosing to embrace global opportunities rather than let globalization destroy you requires a different mindset. Brad Miller, CEO of IMW Industries Ltd., demonstrates this mindset. Although the poor economy and soaring Canadian dollar suggested he should lay off staff at his natural gas equipment company in Chilliwack, BC, he chose to "rethink the business and dramatically lower the costs and get aggressive and go after the global market in a much bigger way."[10] IMW invested in redesigns and more efficient machinery instead of downsizing, bought a larger factory in Chilliwack, built another in China, and aggressively marketed to developing markets. "Pack your Pepto Bismol, get on a plane and meet the people. The world is full of good people eager to do business with Canadian companies."[11]

IN ACTION

Jazz.FM

Jazz.FM began as CJRT.FM, and was an early innovator in providing strong jazz, blues, and soul playlists and educational programming. It started in 1949 and evolved from a university radio station to a stand-alone registered charity relying on donations for its revenue. However, Jazz.FM has found itself embroiled in controversy. A group known as the Collective, a mix of 13 past and present on-air and behind-the-scenes employees, wrote a letter to the board making allegations of sexual harassment against CEO Ross Porter. The Collective accused Porter of creating a culture of "us-versus-them management style, a climate of fear and intimidation, and a lack of vision in programming and day-to-day operations at the station." Soon after an independent review, Porter resigned but continues to host a radio show.

The controversy shows no sign of abating and the fallout of this unplanned change is considerable. Revenues are down, as are the number of shows and artists. Jazz.FM expects to lose several hundred thousand dollars by the end of 2018. Further, its donors are angry and are trying to replace the board. Marie Slaight is one of the donors attempting to have the entire board replaced but was not successful at the radio station's annual general meeting in August 2018. According to the interim CEO, Charles Cutts, three large for-profit corporations have expressed interest in forging some sort of relationship with Jazz.FM.

SOURCES: D. Vincent, "Jazz.FM Workers Say the CEO Harassed Them. Now, They're Accused of Plotting a Coup," *The Spec*, July 29, 2018, https://www.thespec.com/whatson-story/8768841-jazz-fm-workers-say-the-ceo-harassed-them-now-theyre-accused-of-plotting-a-coup/, accessed August 31, 2018; D. Vincent, "Angry Donors Pack Jazz.FM Meeting amid Corporate Interest in Deal with Station," *Toronto Star*, August 31, 2018, https://www.thestar.com/news/gta/2018/08/31/angry-donors-pack-jazzfm-meeting-amid-corporate-interest-in-deal-with-station.html, accessed August 31, 2018.

WORKFORCE DIVERSITY Related to globalization is the challenge of workforce diversity. As we have seen throughout this book, workforce diversity is a powerful force for change in organizations. Changes in Canadian demographics mean the labour force is aging and becoming more culturally diverse. Census figures from 2016 show that the Canadian workforce has slipped into middle age, with a median age of 42.6.[12] Population projections indicate that Canada may have more people at the age where they can leave the labour force than at the age where they can enter it.[13] Labour shortages are anticipated, as is a shortage of entrepreneurs.[14] Statistics Canada predicts substantial increases in the number of foreign-born and visible-minority citizens in metropolitan areas. For example, from 2006 to 2031, it predicts the percentage of visible minorities in Ottawa will rise from 19 percent to 36 percent, in Calgary from 22 percent to 38 percent, and in Toronto from 43 percent to 63 percent.[15] Current statistics on Toronto show a surprisingly rich multicultural diversity. Residents come from over 200 distinct ethnic origins. Toronto is home to 20 percent of all immigrants living in Canada and 23 percent of all visible minorities living in Canada.[16] Toronto hotels provide an example of the benefits and complexities of this diversity for employers. Immigrant groups provide a large source of potential labour that meets the needs of a diverse group of customers. Also, new market segments are attracted to culturally diverse hotels. However, cultural groups tend to cluster in certain departments, which can lead to communication problems and conflict and can create less incentive for the employees to learn English. These concentrations are counterproductive to diversity goals. Differences in cultural styles have implications for management, since subordinates with varying degrees of power distance (see Chapter 2) interact differently with their supervisors. Differences in behavioural style also influence how the employees get along.[17] The hotels have learned that providing "English as Another Language" courses, paying for at least partial attendance, and rewarding successful completion leads to a more skilled and flexible immigrant workforce. Fostering a culture that is inclusive and supportive also helps.

Many Canadian companies are taking steps to welcome and integrate new Canadians. For example, Canadian Imperial Bank of Commerce was selected as one of the Best Employers for New Canadians because of its initiatives. These include providing career-track internships for foreign professionals, hiring newcomers with international credentials in finance through a five-week job readiness training program, participating in a unique "speed mentoring" program where new Canadians meet one-on-one with employee mentors, and seeking out immigrant job seekers through job fairs, online channels, information sessions, and partnerships with community organizations.[18]

TECHNOLOGICAL CHANGE Rapid technological innovation is another force for change in organizations, and those that fail to keep pace can quickly fall behind. Pressures to remain competitive push organizations to find cost savings and improve productivity where possible. Table 17.1 describes some significant changes brought in by General Motors of Canada and their impact on the design and quality of cars. The idea of the car has changed from that of a rural horseless carriage to an urban vehicle that transports people between cities.[19] Agreements such as the North American Free Trade Agreement and general worldwide tariff reductions resulted in greater competition which, in turn, requires greater technological innovation. Canadian Pacific Railway (and many Canadian companies) has been dramatically altered, accelerating the pace of change.[20]

TABLE 17.1 SIGNIFICANT TECHNOLOGICAL CHANGES AT GM CANADA (MID-1800s–1970s)

DATES	INNOVATION	IMPACT
Mid-1800s–1918	Robert McLaughlin opened a carriage plant in Oshawa to build sleighs for farming	Set quality standard of "one grade only and that is the best"
1901	McLaughlin's sons convinced their father to build a horseless carriage	154 cars, named McLaughlins with Buick engines, built in 1908 in Oshawa
1915	McLaughlin sold his carriage business to make way for production of Chevrolets	Superior finish for cars developed by McLaughlin plant
1918–1972	Family business sold to GM but McLaughlins continued as executives	GM Canada became major contributor to GM

SOURCE: Detailed GM History, History of GM Canada, http://www.gm.ca/gm/english/corporate/about/ourhistory/detail.

Technological innovations bring about profound change because the innovation process promotes associated changes in work relationships and organizational structures.[21] The team approach to innovation adopted by many organizations leads to flatter structures, decentralized decision making, and more open communication between leaders and team members.

The Oxford English Dictionary (OED), one of the best-known resources in the world, turned 90 years old in 2018. In 2000, the OED was launched online and started to record words from various "Englishes" such as Indian and Singaporean ones.

Traditional dictionaries are under threat of obsolescence as more and more users go to online sources to learn about words. To stay current, the OED updates its word list every three months. Here are some recent additions to the OED: (1) *twerk* added in 2015, (2) *retweet* added in 2015, (3) *femcee* added in 2012, and *lepak* added in 2016; it means to hang out in Singaporean and Malaysian English.

SOURCES: H. Richler, "The Last Word," *The Globe and Mail*, September 1, 2018, p. 8 and "A Modern Dictionary," ibid.

MANAGING ETHICAL BEHAVIOUR Recent scandals have brought ethical behaviour in organizations to the forefront of public consciousness. Ethical issues, however, are not always public and monumental. Employees face ethical dilemmas in their daily work lives. The need to manage daily ethical behaviour has brought about several changes in organizations. Most centre around the idea that an organization must create a culture that encourages ethical behaviour.

All public companies issue annual financial reports. Gap Inc. has gone a step further by issuing an annual ethics report. The clothing industry is almost synonymous with the use of sweatshops, but what sets Gap apart is its candid admission that none of its 3,000 suppliers fully complies with the firm's ethical code of conduct. But rather than retreat from these problems, Gap has chosen to work with its suppliers to improve conditions overseas. The firm has more than 90 full-time employees charged with monitoring supplier operations around the world.[22]

The annual report includes extensive descriptions of workers' activities, including which factories were monitored, violations that were found, and which factories are no longer used by Gap because of the violations. It also addresses media reports critical of Gap and its operations.

Gap tries to improve worker conditions by providing training and encouraging suppliers to develop their own conduct codes. For example, in China, it has encouraged lunchtime sessions in which workers are advised of their rights. While most facilities respond positively to these efforts, some don't, and Gap pulled its business from 136 factories it concluded were not going to improve. It also terminated contracts with two factories that had verifiable use of child labour. Gap's approach to overseas labour offers a model for other garment firms.[23]

> "Society expects organizations to maintain ethical behaviour both internally and in relationships with other organizations, as well as with customers, the environment, and society."

The Canadian Centre for Ethics and Corporate Policy notes many specific steps that an organization can take to guide ethical behaviour in addition to the code of conduct. These include ethics training, creating decision aids for likely ethical dilemmas, appointing an ethics officer or ombudsperson, and creating a protected whistle-blowing program.[24] For example, Magna International, the automotive parts supplier headquartered in Aurora, Ontario, has created a "Good Business Line." Stakeholders are encouraged to use this confidential communications tool to report any concerns about questionable business practices.[25]

Lynn Amaral/Shutterstock.com

Adult workers in a garment factory.

Society expects organizations to maintain ethical behaviour both internally and in relationships with other organizations, as well as with customers, the environment, and society. These expectations may be informal, or they may come in the form of increased regulation. In addition to the pressure from societal expectations, legal developments, changing stakeholder expectations, and shifting consumer demands can also lead to change.[26] And some companies change simply because others are changing.[27] Other powerful forces for change originate from within the organization.

Internal Forces

Pressures for change that originate inside the organization are generally recognizable. A decline in effectiveness is a pressure to change. A company that experiences its third quarterly loss within a fiscal year is undoubtedly motivated to do something about it. Some companies react by instituting layoffs and massive cost-cutting programs, whereas others look at the bigger picture, view the loss as symptomatic of an underlying problem, and seek the cause of the problem.

A crisis may also stimulate change in an organization. Strikes or walkouts may lead management to change the wage structure. The resignation of a key decision maker may cause the company to rethink the composition of its management team and its role in the organization.

Changes in employee expectations can also trigger change in organizations. A company that hires a group of young newcomers may find that their expectations are very different from those expressed by older workers. The workforce is more educated than ever before. Although this has its advantages, workers with more education demand more of employers. Today's workers are also concerned with career and family balance issues, such as dependant care. The many sources of workforce diversity hold potential for a host of differing expectations among employees.

Changes in the work climate at an organization can also stimulate change. A workforce that seems lethargic, unmotivated, and dissatisfied is showing symptoms of larger problems that must be addressed. Such symptoms are common in organizations that have

IN ACTION

McDonald's Europe

In response to market pressures, McDonald's Europe has implemented several socially responsible business practices. The company buys all of its coffee from the world's poorest farmers and from farms sanctioned by the Rainforest Alliance. McDonald's Europe mostly buys locally raised beef and meat that is not genetically altered. The chain has also introduced more organic products to its menu. Surprisingly, a large chicken nuggets and French fries in the United States contains almost ten times the trans fat as the same meal in Denmark, so McDonald's Europe committed to matching Denmark's trans fat content throughout the organization. Such proactive strategies to addressing change have made McDonald's Europe very profitable.

SOURCE: K. Capell, "McDonald's Offers Ethics with Those Fries," *BusinessWeek*, January 9, 2007, http://www.businessweek.com/ globalbiz/content/jan2007/gb20070109_958716.htm.

experienced layoffs. Workers who have escaped a layoff may grieve for those who have lost their jobs and may find it hard to continue to be productive. They may fear that they will be laid off as well, and many feel insecure in their jobs.

17-2 THE SCOPE OF CHANGE

Change can be of a relatively small scope, such as a modification in a work procedure (an **incremental change**). Such changes are a fine-tuning of the organization. Schweitzer-Mauduit Canada, a flax straw processing company, is receiving financial support from the federal and Manitoba governments to upgrade and expand its plants in Winkler and Carman, Manitoba. With this new equipment, it will be able to produce a line of renewable, sustainable biomaterials to serve the growing bio-economy, expanding its current business.[28] While radical change is more exciting and interesting to discuss, much research on change has focused on evolutionary (incremental) rather than revolutionary change.[29] Change can also be of a larger scale, such as the restructuring of an organization (a **strategic change**).[30] In strategic change, the organization moves from an old state to a known new state during a controlled period of time. Strategic change usually involves a series of transition steps. For example, Sleep Country, while being challenged by Casper and Endy, continues to grow incrementally by adding 10 to 12 stores each year. Sleep Country was once "... the original disrupter in the mattress industry."[31]

incremental change Change of a relatively small scope, such as making small improvements.

strategic change Change of a larger scale, such as organizational restructuring.

transformational change Change in which the organization moves to a radically different, and sometimes unknown, future state.

The most massive scope of change is **transformational change**, in which the organization moves to a radically different, and sometimes unknown, future state.[32] In transformational change, the organization's mission, culture, goals, structure, and leadership may all change dramatically.[33] Several industries are undergoing transformational change due to the Internet, including financial services, publishing, and the music industry. The digital environment, easy access to inexpensive recording equipment, ease of distribution through the Internet, widespread practices of illegal copying, and the new ways in which audiences access music mean that the power of the major record companies has been challenged. They cannot stop the technological developments and must design a business model that responds appropriately to the new environment.[34] Record labels are transforming themselves from vendors of physical goods to licensors of digital media.[35] The organization must shift from a command and control approach focused on low costs to a loop of connections and collaboration with consumers and partners.[36]

One of the toughest decisions faced by leaders is the proper pace of change. Some scholars argue that rapid change is more likely to succeed, since it creates momentum,[37] while others argue that these short, sharp changes are actually rare and not experienced by most firms.[38] Still others observe that change in a large organization may occur incrementally in parts of the firm and quickly in others.[39] In summary, researchers agree that the pace of change is important, but they can't quite agree on which pace of change is most beneficial.

Very little long-term research has looked at change over a significant time period. One 12-year study looked at change in the structure of Canadian National Sports Organizations (NSOs). It found that within NSOs, radical transition did not always require a fast pace of change. It also found that successful transitions often involve changing the high-impact elements of an organization (in this case, their decision-making structures) early in the process.[40]

The Change Agent's Role

The individual or group that introduces and manages change in an organization is known as a **change agent**. Change agents can be internal, such as managers or employees who are appointed to oversee the change process.

Internal change agents have certain advantages in managing the change process. They know the organization's past history, its political system, and its culture. Because they must live with the results of their change efforts, internal change agents are likely to be very careful about managing change. There are disadvantages, however, to using internal change agents. They may be associated with certain factions within the organization, be accused of favouritism, or be too close to the situation to have an rigorous view of what needs to be done.

Change leaders within organizations tend to be creative people with positive self-concepts and high risk tolerance.[41] In fact, a study of Israeli firms found that risk aversion and self-centredness in leaders are both associated with resistance to change and, consequently, organizational decline.[42] A transformational leadership style is particularly effective at gaining employee commitment to a change when the impact on employees is high.[43] A high number of change leaders are women such as Mary Barra of GM. Change managers are more flexible than ordinary general managers and much more people-oriented. Using a balance of technical and interpersonal skills, they are tough decision makers who focus on performance results. They also know how to energize people and get them aligned in the same direction. In addition, they have the ability to operate in more than one leadership style and can shift from a team mode to command and control, depending on the situation. They are also comfortable with uncertainty.[44] If change is large scale or strategic in nature, it may take a team of leaders to make change happen. A team assembling leaders with a variety of skills, expertise, and influence that can work together harmoniously may be needed to accomplish change of large scope.[45]

External change agents bring an outsider's objective view to the organization. They may be preferred by employees because of their impartiality. When an organization wants a new approach and a fresh perspective, it is important that it choose a change leader who has no psychological connection to the previous decision maker(s). In Chapter 7 you learned that one way in which to minimize escalation of commitment is to separate project decisions so different people make the decisions at different stages. However, intriguing research has recently demonstrated that if the subsequent decision maker has any psychological connection to that initial person, they are likely to get trapped in repeating and justifying that person's errors. This suggests that an internal change leader may be unconsciously tied to the previous leader's actions. Perhaps only an outsider can truly make a clean break with the past.[46] External change agents face certain problems, however; not only is their knowledge of the organization's history limited, but they may also be viewed with suspicion by organization members. External change agents have more power in directing changes if employees perceive the change agents as being trustworthy, possessing important expertise, having a track record that establishes credibility, and being similar to them.[47]

Different change agent competencies are required at different stages of the change process. Leadership, communication, training, and participation have varying levels of impact as the change proceeds, meaning change agents must be flexible in how they work through the different phases of the process.[48] Effective change leaders build strong relationships within their leadership team, between the team and organizational members, and between the team and key environmental players. Maintaining all three relationships simultaneously is quite difficult, so successful leaders are continually "coupling" and "uncoupling" with the different groups as the change process proceeds. Adaptability is a key skill for both internal and external change leaders.[49]

17-3 RESISTANCE TO CHANGE

Resistance to change is an expected human response. As Mark Smith, a change specialist at KPMG Canada says, "Nobody likes change except a wet baby."[50] The resistance can be quite rational, motivated by self-interest or by the best interests of the organization. A change that seems the exciting start of something new for the change leader can mean an end to the employee—an end to the way he or she is used to doing things. The change proposal can be interpreted as indicating that the employee was somehow failing.[51]

Employee resistance is a natural response, so preventing it is unlikely. Instead, knowing resistance will occur, organizations need to deal with it and work toward gaining employee commitment and support for the change. Employees emotionally opposed to a change may not only undermine the change implementation but also are likely to withdraw and lose trust in both management and the organization.[52]

change agent The individual or group that undertakes the task of introducing and managing a change in an organization.

Major Reasons People Resist Change

There are several common reasons people resist change. They include the following.

FEAR OF THE UNKNOWN Change often brings with it substantial uncertainty. Employees facing a technological change may resist the change because it introduces ambiguity into what was once a comfortable situation for them. We know from Chapter 6 how stressful uncertainty is. Research shows that employees who feel uncertain because the change seems poorly planned or there seems to be a high frequency of changes have lower job satisfaction and are more likely to consider quitting.[53]

FEAR OF LOSS Some employees may fear losing their jobs with impending change, especially when an advanced technology like robotics is introduced. Employees may also fear losing their status because of a change.[54] Computer systems experts, for example, may feel threatened when they feel their expertise is eroded by the installation of a more user-friendly networked information system. Another common fear is that changes may diminish the positive qualities the individual enjoys in the job.

FEAR OF FAILURE Some employees fear changes because they fear their own failure. Employees may fear that changes will result in increased workloads or increased task difficulty, and subsequently may question their own competencies. They may also fear that performance expectations will be elevated following the change, and that they may not measure up.[55]

Anticipating that a change (even a positive one) will increase demands is quite justified. A study of over 2,000 working Norwegians showed that organizational change increased stress, principally through increasing job demands, no matter how well the change was implemented or how desirable the change was.[56] Employees resist even changes with favourable outcomes if they require significant personal adaptation.[57]

DISRUPTION OF INTERPERSONAL RELATIONSHIPS Employees may resist change that threatens to limit meaningful interpersonal relationships on the job. Librarians facing automation feared that once the computerized system was implemented, they would not be able to interact as they did when they had to go to another floor of the library to get help finding a resource.

PERSONALITY AND JUSTICE ISSUES When the change agent's personality creates negativity, employees may resist the change. A change agent who appears insensitive to employee concerns may meet considerable resistance because employees perceive that their needs are not being taken into account. Resistance to change can also derive from a perception that the outcomes are unfair or the way it is being implemented is unfair.[58] In fact, resistance can arise long before the change from the simple anticipation that it will not be handled fairly, based on employees' past experiences with management.[59]

POLITICS Organizational change may also shift the existing balance of power in the organization. Individuals or groups empowered under the current arrangement may be threatened with losing these political advantages in the advent of change.

CULTURAL ASSUMPTIONS AND VALUES Sometimes cultural assumptions and values can be impediments to change, particularly if the assumptions underlying the change are alien to employees. Other times, employees might interpret strategic change initiatives from the standpoint of the organization's value system and ideologies of the management team. What an organization chooses to change and how it implements the change both express something about the company's values. How well an employee's values match those of the organization during change influences the employee's perceptions of how well they fit into that organization.[60] Resistance based on cultural values can be very difficult to overcome because some cultural assumptions are unconscious. As we discussed in Chapter 2, some cultures tend to avoid uncertainty. In Mexican and Greek cultures, for example, change that creates a great deal of uncertainty may be met with great resistance.

We have described several sources of resistance to change. The reasons for resistance are as diverse as the workforce itself and vary with different individuals and organizations. The challenge for managers is introducing change in a positive manner and managing employee resistance.

Managing Resistance to Change

The traditional view of resistance to change treated it as something to be overcome, and many organizational attempts to reduce the resistance have served only to intensify it. The contemporary view holds that resistance is simply a form of feedback and that this feedback can be used very productively to manage the change process.[61] One key to managing resistance is to plan for it and to be ready with a variety of strategies for using the resistance as feedback and helping employees negotiate the transition. Three key strategies for managing resistance to change are

TABLE 17.2	CHARACTERISTICS OF AN EFFECTIVE CHANGE MESSAGE
Appropriateness:	The desired change is right for the organization.
Discrepancy:	We need to change.
Self-efficacy:	We have the capability to successfully change.
Personal valence:	It is in our best interest to change.
Principle support:	Those affected are behind the change.

SOURCE: A. A. Armenakis and A. G. Bedeian, "Organizational Change: A Review of Theory and Research in the 1990s," *Journal of Management* 25 (1999): 293–315.

communication, participation, and empathy and support.[62] Table 17.2 highlights some of the key elements of an effective change message. The messages need to be adapted to employees at different levels in the organization.

Much of the previous research done on resistance to change assumes that those who resist encourage dysfunction. In a recent study, researchers found that resistance to change can, in fact, be a valuable organizational resource on three levels: existence, engagement, and strengthening.

1. Existence: While it is often difficult to disseminate new ideas, resistance provides an opportunity to repeat, clarify, and keep a change topic or idea in existence long enough to garner support.
2. Engagement: Individuals who resist are typically more invested in a change's impact. Change agents should listen to engaged individuals and consider altering the pace, scope, or sequencing of the change based on their arguments.
3. Strengthening: Countering resistance effectively may actually be beneficial to the change process. Resistance can strengthen communication and participation, which often leads to better working relationships.[63]

Communication about impending change is essential if employees are to adjust effectively.[64] The details and, equally importantly, the rationale of the change should be provided. Accurate and timely information can help prevent unfounded fears and potentially damaging rumours from developing. Conversely, announcement delay and witholding information can serve to fuel the rumour mill. Open communication in a culture of trust is a key ingredient for successful change.[65] Managers should pay attention to the informal communication networks in an organization because they can serve as power channels for disseminating change-related information.[66] All employees (especially those high in organizational identification) want information about a change that will affect them—not only what will happen and why but also how the change will be implemented.[67] This will influence their perception of fairness and reduce feelings of uncertainty. A study looking at employees voluntarily adopting a new self-service technology found that, before the change, information on ease of use affected their support for the change. Both before and after the change, information on the usefulness of the change was important to get support.[68] In a merger situation, the information provided in realistic merger previews can help employees prepare for the change, giving a greater sense of certainty and control and reducing the stress.[69] A change message gives the manager the opportunity to influence employee perception of the change, to see it as an opportunity rather than a threat,[70] to see the benefits in the change, and to have confidence in dealing with the change.[71]

There is substantial research support underscoring the importance of participation in the change process. Employees must be engaged and involved in order for change to work—as supported by the notion "That which we create, we support." Participation helps employees become involved in the change and establishes a feeling of ownership in the process. It also guarantees they will become more informed on the what, how, and why of the change, thereby reducing uncertainty.

Another strategy for managing resistance is to provide empathy and support to employees who have trouble dealing with the change. Active listening is an excellent tool for identifying the reasons behind resistance and for uncovering fears. An expression of concern about the change can provide important feedback that managers can use to improve the change process. Emotional support and encouragement can help an employee deal with the anxiety that is a natural response to change. Supportive leadership actually changes employee perceptions of the change so they experience less uncertainty, less frequency of change, and a greater sense that the change is well planned.[72]

Management patience is an important aspect of support. Relapses are typical. People often slide back into old habits several times before they maintain the new behaviour.[73] The stress of a change affects management as well as employees, and supervisors may not always feel up to supporting their employees. In fact, research indicates that middle managers tend to withdraw during large-scale change processes in an attempt to get the situation under control for themselves.[74] Managers responsible for downsizing often engage in avoidance tactics to avoid needy or upset employees.[75] Yet manager availability is a key component in an effective change management process.[76]

FIGURE 17.1 FORCE-FIELD ANALYSIS OF A DECISION TO ENGAGE IN EXERCISE

Forces for change		Forces for status quo
Weight gain		Lack of time
Minimally passing treadmill test		No exercise facility at work
Feeling lethargic; having no energy	→ Equilibrium ←	Spouse/partner hates to exercise
Family history of cardiovascular disease		No interest in physical activity or sports
New, physically demanding job		Made a grade of D in a physical education class

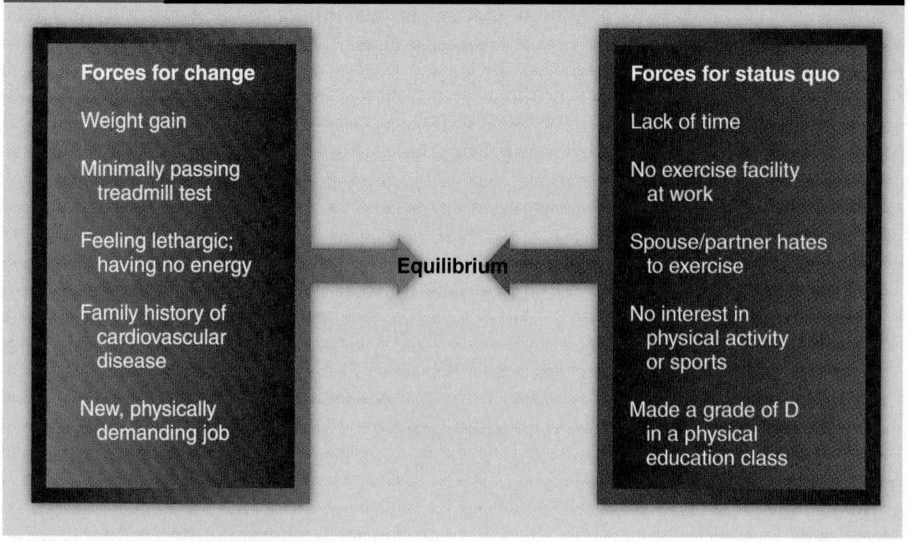

The employee–supervisor relationship in general is critical to how the employee reacts to a specific change. In a high-quality relationship, the employee is more accepting of supervisor change influence tactics, believing they must be justified. In a poor-quality relationship, the employee is more suspicious and resistant.[77] Past experience with a supervisor shapes employee expectations of how fairly a change will be handled and colours their actual experience of fairness when the change occurs.[78] When employees trust their supervisors, it serves as a social support mechanism and they are more committed to the organization even if they feel they can't control the change process.[79]

These approaches to managing change have actually been made into law in Norway. The Working Environment Act, implemented in Norway in 2006, ensures the rights of employees during a reorganization process. In a reorganization that involves significant changes to employees' working situation, the employer must ensure provision of necessary information to employees, participation of the employees in the process, and competence development to meet the requirements of a fully satisfactory working environment.[80] Sponsored research to guide the labour inspection authorities in dealing with these change situations found that a healthy change process cannot prevent adaptation demands but it can reduce stress and increase perceptions of support and control (in line with Karasek's job demand-control-support model of stress in Chapter 6).[81]

unfreezing The first step in Lewin's change model, in which individuals are encouraged to discard old behaviours by shaking up the equilibrium state that maintains the status quo.

17-4 LEWIN'S MODEL FOR MANAGING CHANGE

Kurt Lewin developed a model of the change process that has stood the test of time and continues to influence the way organizations manage planned change. Lewin's model is based on the idea of force-field analysis.[82] Figure 17.1 shows a force-field analysis of a decision to engage in exercise behaviour.

This model contends that a person's behaviour is the product of two opposing forces: One force pushes toward preserving the status quo, and the other force pushes for change. When the two opposing forces are approximately equal, current behaviour is maintained. For behavioural change to occur, the forces maintaining the status quo must be overcome. This can be accomplished by increasing the forces for change, by weakening the forces for the status quo, or by a combination of these actions. Use the Self-Assessment at the end of the chapter to enact a personal change process.

Lewin's change model is a three-step process, as shown in Figure 17.2. The process begins with **unfreezing**, which is a crucial first hurdle in the change process. Unfreezing involves encouraging individuals to discard old behaviours by shaking up the equilibrium state that maintains the status quo. Change management literature has long advocated that certain individuals have personalities that make them more resistant to change. However, recent research indicates that only a small portion of a study's respondents (23 percent) displayed consistency in their reactions to three different kinds of change: structural, technological, and office relocation. The majority of respondents (77 percent) reacted differently to these differing kinds of change, suggesting that reactions to change might be more situationally driven than was previously thought.[83] Organizations often accomplish unfreezing by eliminating the rewards for current behaviour and showing that current behaviour is not valued. In essence, individuals surrender by allowing the boundaries of their status quo to be opened in preparation for change.[84]

FIGURE 17.2 LEWIN'S CHANGE MODEL

Unfreezing	Moving	Refreezing
Reducing forces for status quo	Developing new attitudes, values, and behaviours	Reinforcing new attitudes, values, and behaviours

The second step in the change process is **moving**. In the moving stage, the change is implemented and new attitudes, values, and behaviours are substituted for old ones. Adapting to the change at this second stage is much easier if unfreezing was effective. Employees know what is changing and why, and what their role is to be.

Refreezing is the final step in the change process. In this step, new attitudes, values, and behaviours are established as the new status quo. The new ways of operating are cemented in and reinforced. Managers should ensure that the organizational culture and formal reward systems encourage the new behaviours. Changes in the reward structure may be needed to ensure that the organization is not rewarding the old behaviours and merely hoping for the new behaviours. A study by Exxon Research and Engineering showed that framing and displaying a mission statement in managers' offices may eventually change the behaviour of 2 percent of the managers. In contrast, changing managers' evaluation and reward systems will change the behaviour of 55 percent of the managers almost overnight.[85]

The approach used by Monsanto to increase opportunities for women within the company is an illustration of how to use Lewin's model effectively. First, Monsanto emphasized unfreezing by helping employees debunk negative stereotypes about women in business. This also helped overcome resistance to change. Second, Monsanto moved employees' attitudes and behaviours by diversity training in which differences were emphasized as positive, and supervisors learned ways of training and developing female employees. Third, Monsanto changed its reward system so that managers were evaluated and paid according to how they coached and promoted women, which helped refreeze the new attitudes and behaviours.

Following through all three stages of Lewin's model is not easy or typical. A review of change management practices at the Correctional Services of Canada examined four specific change initiatives. It found that the early stages of change initiatives were well handled (for example, making the case for change, and articulating and communicating the vision). However, there was mixed success in sustaining the change. There was inconsistency in continuing the communications, generating early wins to build momentum, and keeping the focus needed to institutionalize the change.[86]

One frequently overlooked issue is whether or not the change is consistent with the company's deeply held core values. Value consistency is critical to making a change "stick." Organizations whose members perceive the changes to be consistent with the firm's values adopt the changes much more easily and fully. Conversely, organizations whose members' values conflict with the changes may display "superficial conformity," in which members pay lip service to the changes but ultimately revert to their old behaviours.[87]

John Kotter has developed a model of change based on his research into the causes for change failures. His work is currently seen as the one of the best ways to think about and to implement change. Kotter's ideas continue to evolve and his model itself is now less linear than in its original formulation.

moving The second step in Lewin's change model, in which new attitudes, values, and behaviours are substituted for old ones.

refreezing The final step in Lewin's change model, in which new attitudes, values, and behaviours are established as the new status quo.

IN ACTION

Warby Parker

The popular eyewear brand Warby Parker started on the Internet, and the company's success has looked easy. But according to co-CEOs Dave Gilboa and Neil Blumenthal, it is actually painstaking and deliberate. They have produced disruptive change in the eyewear industry by being carefully focused on execution and brand. By designing and making their own frames, sold to consumers on the Internet for as little as US$95, they have taken a bite out of the luxury eyewear business. Prices include prescription lenses, shipping, and donations to a not-for-profit organization. They're now opening up retail stores and plan to add children's frames and thinner lenses. There's also an investment in future technology that conducts eye exams online, which may render traditional optical stores obsolete. Warby Parker is a company that has changed the way consumers think about buying eyewear.

SOURCE: M. Chafkin, "Most Innovative Companies 2015: 1, Warby Parker," *Fast Company*, March 2015, 69–144.

FIGURE 17.3 KOTTER'S CHANGE MODEL

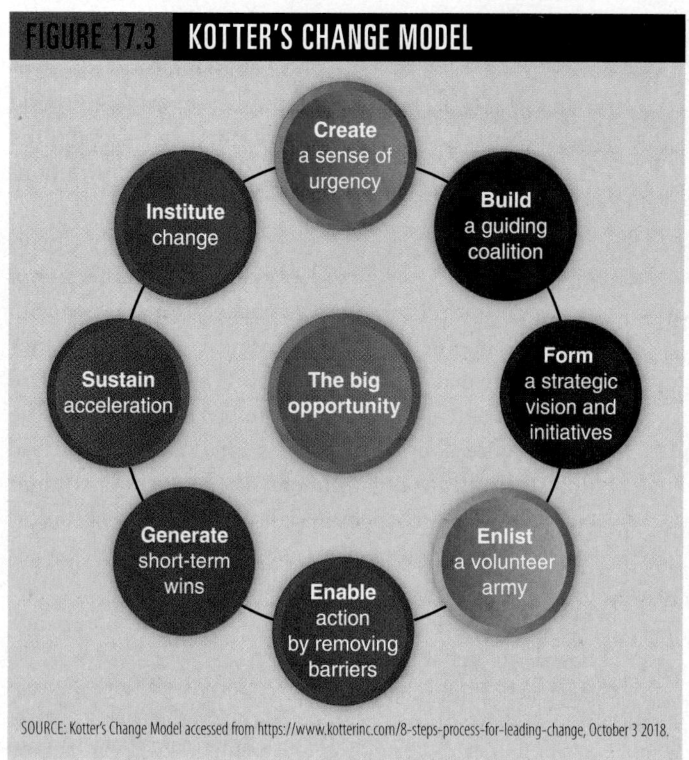

SOURCE: Kotter's Change Model accessed from https://www.kotterinc.com/8-steps-process-for-leading-change, October 3 2018.

According to Kotter, to implement change well, we need to work through a series of stages. We must go through each stage in the change process in order and we cannot skip any stages. His change model has eight stages: (1) create urgency, (2) build a powerful coalition, (3) create a vision, (4) communicate the vision and enlist supporters, (5) remove obstacles, (6) generate short-term wins, (7) create the change, and (8) anchor the change in the culture. Kotter's observation about the importance of creating urgency as the first step in change is notable as sometimes change agents create a change vision without establishing a compelling need for change.[88] (Kotter's books are required reading for change agents. They include *The Heart of Change, Buy-in, A Sense of Urgency,* and *Our Iceberg Is Melting.*)

17-5 DETERMINING THE NEED FOR ORGANIZATION DEVELOPMENT INTERVENTIONS

organization development (OD)
A systematic approach to organizational improvement that applies behavioural science theory and research in order to increase individual and organizational well-being and effectiveness.

Organization development (OD) is a systematic approach to organizational improvement that applies behavioural science theory and research in order to increase individual and organizational well-being and effectiveness.[89] This definition implies certain characteristics. First, OD is a systematic approach to planned change. It is a structured cycle of diagnosing organizational problems and opportunities and then applying expertise to them. Second, OD is grounded in solid research and theory. It involves the application of behavioural science knowledge to the challenges that organizations face. Third, OD recognizes the reciprocal relationship between individuals and organizations. It acknowledges that for organizations to change, individuals must change. Finally, OD is goal oriented. It is a process that seeks to improve both individual and organizational well-being and effectiveness.

Prior to deciding on a method of intervention, managers must carefully diagnose the problem they are attempting to address. Diagnosis and needs analysis is a critical first step in any OD intervention. An intervention method is then chosen and applied. Finally, a thorough follow-up of the OD process is conducted.

Diagnosis and Needs Analysis

Before any intervention is planned, a thorough organizational diagnosis should be conducted. Diagnosis is an essential first step for any organization development intervention.[90] The term *diagnosis* comes from *dia* (through) and *gnosis* (knowledge of). Thus, the diagnosis should pinpoint specific problems and areas in need of improvement. Six areas to examine carefully are the organization's purpose, structure, reward system, support systems, relationships, and leadership.[91]

Levinson's diagnostic approach asserts that the process should begin by identifying where the pain (the problem) in the organization is, what it is like, how long it has been happening, and what has already been done about it.[92] Then a four-part, comprehensive diagnosis can begin. The first part of the diagnosis involves achieving an understanding of the organization's history. In the second part, the organization as a whole is analyzed to obtain data about its structure and processes. In the third part, interpretive data about attitudes, relationships, and current organizational functioning are gathered. In the fourth part of the diagnosis, the data are analyzed and conclusions are reached. In each stage of the diagnosis, the data can be gathered using a variety of methods, including observation, interviews, questionnaires, and archival records.

A needs analysis is another crucial step in managing change. This is an analysis of the skills and competencies that employees must have to achieve the goals of the change. A needs analysis is essential because interventions such as training programs must target these skills and competencies.

Hundreds of alternative OD intervention methods exist. One way of classifying these methods is by the target of change. The target of change may be the organization, groups within the organization, or individuals.

The diagnostic process may yield the conclusion that change is necessary. As part of the diagnosis, it is important to address the following issues:

- What are the forces for change?
- What are the forces preserving the status quo?
- What are the most likely sources of resistance to change?
- What are the goals to be accomplished by the change?

This information constitutes a force-field analysis, as discussed earlier in the chapter.

17-6 GROUP-FOCUSED TECHNIQUES FOR OD INTERVENTION

Some OD intervention methods emphasize changing the organization itself or changing the work groups within the organization. Intervention methods in this category include survey feedback, management by objectives, product and service quality programs, team building, and process consultation.

Survey Feedback

Survey feedback is a widely used intervention method whereby employee attitudes are solicited using a questionnaire. Once the data are collected, they are analyzed and fed back to the employees to diagnose problems and plan other interventions. Survey feedback is often used as an exploratory tool and then is combined with some other intervention. The effectiveness of survey feedback in actually improving outcomes (absenteeism or productivity, for example) increases substantially when this method is combined with other interventions.[93] The effectiveness of this technique is contingent on trust between management and subordinates, and this can be reinforced through the anonymity and confidentiality of survey responses.

For survey feedback to be an effective method, certain guidelines should be used. Employees must be assured that their responses to the questionnaire will be confidential and anonymous. Feedback should be reported in a group format. Employees must be able to trust that negative repercussions will not result from their responses. Employees should be informed of the purpose of the survey. Failing to do this can set up unrealistic expectations about the changes that might come from the surveys.

In addition, management must be prepared to follow up on the survey results. If some things cannot be changed, the rationale (for example, prohibitive cost) must be explained to the employees. Without appropriate follow-through, employees will not take the survey process seriously the next time.

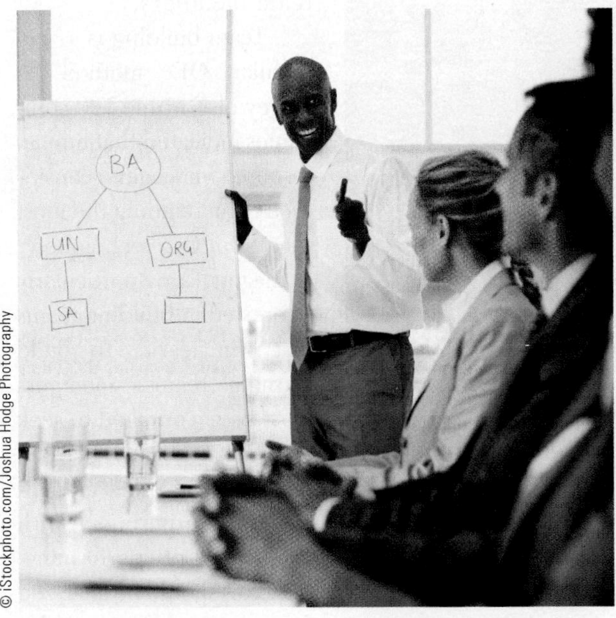

© iStockphoto.com/Joshua Hodge Photography

Using a participative process to collect data for an initial diagnosis.

Management by Objectives

As an organization-wide technique, **management by objectives (MBO)** involves joint goal setting between employees and managers. The MBO process (discussed in Chapter 14) includes the setting of initial objectives, periodic progress reviews, and problem solving to remove any obstacles to goal achievement.[94] All these steps are joint efforts between managers and employees.

survey feedback A widely used method of intervention whereby employee attitudes are solicited using a questionnaire.

management by objectives (MBO) An organization-wide intervention technique that involves joint goal setting between employees and managers.

MBO is a valuable intervention because it meets three needs. First, it clarifies what is expected of employees. This reduces role conflict and ambiguity. Second, MBO provides knowledge of results, an essential ingredient in effective job performance. Finally, MBO provides an opportunity for coaching and counselling by the manager. The problem-solving approach encourages open communication and discussion of obstacles to goal achievement.[95]

One company that has used MBO successfully is General Electric. The success of MBO in effecting organizational results hinges on the linking of individual goals to the goals of the organization.[96] MBO programs should be used with caution, however. An excessive emphasis on goal achievement can result in cutthroat competition among employees, falsification of results, and striving for results at any cost.

Product and Service Quality Programs

Quality programs—programs that embed product and service quality excellence in the organizational culture—are assuming key roles in the organization development efforts of many companies. For example, the success or failure of a service company may depend on the quality of customer service it provides.[97]

quality program A program that embeds product and service quality excellence in the organizational culture.

team building An intervention designed to improve the effectiveness of a work group.

Toyota Motor Corporation constantly finds ways to integrate cutting-edge technological innovations with the growing pains of global expansion. The famed "Toyota Way" of doing business is focused on two key principles: continuous improvement focused on innovation and respect for people.[98] Interestingly, Toyota does not seem to use reengineering. Business process engineering involves the redesign of the work processes by examining times that it takes to make a product or deliver a service.[99]

Some suggest that Toyota's recent problems with defective parts and major recalls arose because Toyota had been focusing on growth instead of its traditional devotion to quality.[100] Hyundai, on the other hand, has turned around its fortunes and reputation because of its focus on quality. Once the butt of jokes in the 1980s with its poorly made compact cars, Hyundai committed itself to quality. In 2000, it adopted the Six Sigma management discipline, using intense statistical analysis to identify flaws in the manufacturing process. The Korean company has now surpassed Ford to become the fourth-largest car manufacturer in the world.[101]

Team Building

Team building programs can improve the effectiveness of work groups. Team building usually begins with a diagnostic process through which team members identify problems, and continues with the team planning actions to take in order to resolve those problems. The OD practitioner in team building serves as a facilitator, and the work itself is completed by team members.[102]

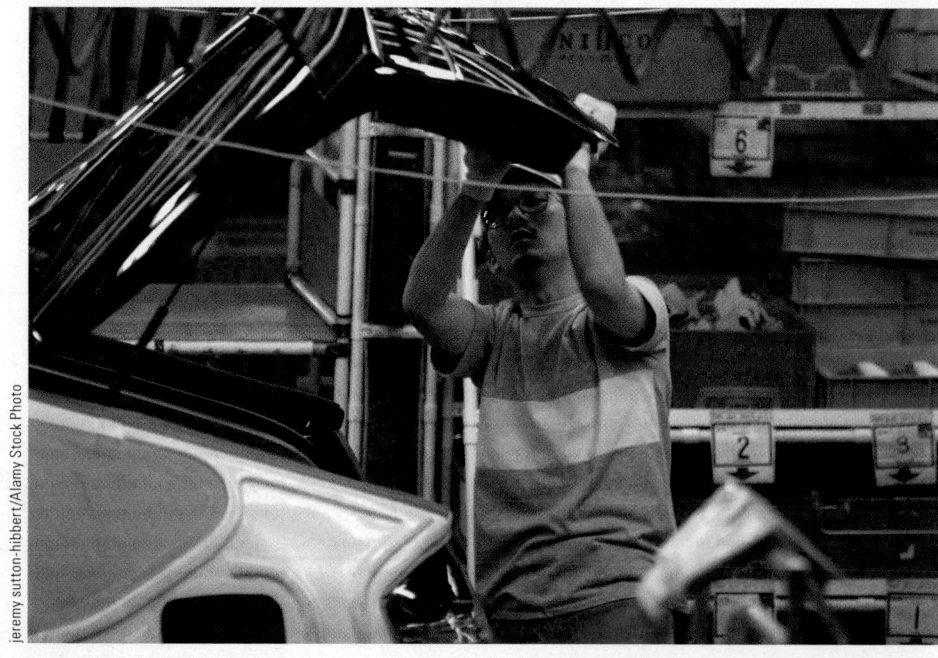

jeremy sutton-hibbert/Alamy Stock Photo

The andon cord is a cord that runs the length of every Toyota assembly line, and any worker who encounters a quality problem is allowed to pull it and stop the line.

Team building is a very popular OD method. A survey of Fortune 500 companies indicated that human resource managers considered team building the most successful OD technique.[103] Managers are particularly interested in building teams that can learn. To build learning teams, members must be encouraged to seek feedback, discuss errors, reflect on successes and failures, and experiment with new ways of performing. Mistakes should be analyzed for ways to improve, and a climate of mutual support should be developed. Leaders of learning teams are good coaches who promote a climate of psychological safety so that team members feel comfortable discussing problems.[104]

One popular technique for team building is the use of outdoor challenges. Participants go through a series of outdoor activities, such as climbing a four-metre wall. Similar physical challenges require the participants to work as a team and focus on trust, communication, decision making, and leadership. GE and Weyerhaeuser use outdoor challenges at the beginning of their team-building courses, and later in the training, team members apply what they have learned to actual business situations.[105] One innovative firm called Teambuilding Inc. uses rowing as team building exercise. It enlisted the services of an Olympic gold medalist to design a seminar focused on team building using rowing as the central organizing theme. This activity encourages participants to practise leadership, communication, goal setting, conflict management, and motivation. GE Healthcare, ING Direct, and Wyeth Corporate Communications have all used this technique for their team-building programs.[106] Preliminary studies indicate that team building can improve group processes.[107]

Process Consultation

Pioneered by Edgar Schein, **process consultation** is an OD method that helps managers and employees improve the processes that are used in organizations.[108] The processes most often targeted are communication, conflict resolution, decision making, group interaction, and leadership.

One of the distinguishing features of the process consultation approach is that an outside consultant is used. The role of the consultant is to help employees help themselves. In this way, the ownership of a successful outcome rests with the employees.[109] The consultant guides the organization members in examining the processes in the organization and in refining them. The steps in process consultation are entering the organization, defining the relationship, choosing an approach, gathering data and diagnosing problems, intervening, and gradually leaving the organization.

Process consultation is an interactive technique between employees and an outside consultant, so it is seldom used as a sole OD method. Most often, it is used in combination with other OD interventions.

All the preceding OD methods focus on changing the organization or the work group. The following OD methods are aimed toward individual change.

17-7 INDIVIDUAL-FOCUSED TECHNIQUES FOR OD INTERVENTION

Organization development efforts that are targeted toward individuals include skills training, leadership training and development, executive coaching, job redesign, health promotion programs, and career planning.

Skills Training

The key question addressed by **skills training** is, "What knowledge, skills, and abilities are necessary to do this job effectively?" Skills training is accomplished either in formal classroom settings or on the job. The challenge is integrating skills training into organization development in today's rapidly changing environments that most organizations face. The job knowledge in many positions requires continual updates to keep pace with rapid change.

Leadership Training and Development

Companies invest millions of dollars in **leadership training and development**, a term that encompasses a variety of techniques that are designed to enhance individuals' leadership skills. One popular technique is sending future leaders to off-site training classes. Research shows that this type of education experience can have some impact, but participants' enthusiastic return to work may be short lived due to the challenges and realities of work life. Classroom learning alone thus has a limited effect on leadership skills.

The best leadership training and development programs combine classroom learning with on-the-job experiences. One way of accomplishing development is through the use of action learning, a technique that was pioneered in Europe.[110] In action learning, leaders take on unfamiliar problems or familiar problems in unfamiliar settings. The leaders work on the problems and meet weekly in small groups made up of individuals from different parts of the organizations. The outcome of action learning is that leaders learn about themselves through the challenges of their colleagues.

process consultation An OD method that helps managers and employees improve the processes that are used in organizations.

skills training Increasing the job knowledge, skills, and abilities that are necessary to do a job effectively.

leadership training and development A variety of techniques that are designed to enhance individuals' leadership skills.

Other techniques that provide active learning for participants are simulations, business games, role-playing, and case studies.[111]

Eli Lilly has an action learning program that pulls together 18 future company leaders and gives them a strategic business issue to resolve. For six weeks, the trainees meet with experts, best-practices organizations, and customers, and then present their recommendations to top brass. One action learning team was charged with coming up with an e-business strategy; their plan was so good that executives immediately implemented it. At Eli Lilly and other firms, action learning programs provide developmental experiences for leaders and result in useful initiatives for the company.[112]

> "Leadership training and development is an ongoing process that takes considerable time and effort. There are no quick fixes."

Leadership training and development is an ongoing process that takes considerable time and effort. There are no quick fixes. At IBM, managers are held accountable for leadership development. In fact, IBM's managers will not be considered for promotion into senior executive positions unless they have a record of developing leaders. Top management must be committed to the process of leadership training and development if they want to create a pipeline of high-potential employees to fill leadership positions.[113]

Executive Coaching

Executive coaching is a technique in which managers or executives are paired with a coach in a partnership to help the executive perform more effectively at work. Although coaching is usually done in a one-on-one manner, it is sometimes attempted in groups. The popularity of executive coaching has increased dramatically in recent years. The International Coach Federation, a group that trains and accredits executive coaches, in just two years of existence doubled its membership, which is now at 7,000 members in 35 countries.[114]

executive coaching A technique in which managers or executives are paired with a coach in a partnership to help the executive perform more efficiently.

job redesign An OD intervention method that alters jobs to improve the fit between individual skills and the demands of the job.

Coaching is typically a special investment in top-level managers. Coaches provide another set of eyes and ears and help executives see beyond their own blinders. Coaches elicit solutions and ideas from the client rather than making suggestions; thus, they develop and enhance the talents and capabilities within the client. Many coaching arrangements focus on developing the emotional intelligence of the client executive and may use a 360-degree assessment in which the executive, their boss, peers, subordinates, and even family members rate the executive's emotional competencies.[115] This information is then fed back to the executive, and along with the coach, a development plan is put in place.

Good coaches form strong connections with clients, exhibit professionalism, and deliver thoughtful, candid feedback. The top reasons executives seek out coaches are to make personal behaviour changes, enhance their effectiveness, and foster stronger relationships. Does executive coaching pay off? Evidence suggests that successful coaching can result in sustained changes in executives' behaviour, increased self-awareness and understanding, and more effective leadership competencies.[116] In one study, for example, executives who worked with executive coaches were more likely to set specific goals, ask for feedback from their supervisors, and rated as better performers by their supervisors and subordinates when compared to executives who simply received feedback from surveys.[117] Effective coaching relationships depend on a professional, experienced coach, an executive who is motivated to learn and change, and a good fit between the two.

Job Redesign

As an OD intervention method, **job redesign** emphasizes the fit between individual skills and the demands of the job. Chapter 15 outlined several approaches to job design. Many of these methods are used as OD techniques for realigning task demands and individual capabilities or for redesigning jobs to fit new techniques or organizational structures better.

Ford Motor Company has redesigned virtually all of its manufacturing jobs, shifting workers from individual to team-based roles in which they have greater control of their work and can take the initiative to improve products and production techniques. Ford began trying this technique more than a decade ago and found that it improved not only employee job satisfaction but also productivity and product quality.

Another form of job redesign is telecommuting. Companies including Telus, Bell Canada, and IBM Canada have significant numbers of employees who work this way. Research reported by the Canadian Telework

Association indicates that 1.5 million Canadians telecommute at least one day a week and 77 percent of them claim it increases job satisfaction.[118]

Health Promotion Programs

As organizations have become increasingly concerned with the costs of distress in the workplace, health promotion programs have become a part of larger organization development efforts. Companies that have successfully integrated health promotion programs into their organizations include both large and small firms. KPMG, an established accounting and professional services firm with over 5,000 full-time employees in Canada, helps employees with a generous fitness participation subsidy (up to 1.25 percent of salary) that can be used for health-club memberships, weight-loss support, and home equipment purchases. KPMG also supports a number of employee sports teams, from cricket to hockey.[119] With only 96 employees, Digital Extremes, a London, Ontario–based company offering custom computer programming services, also recognizes the benefits of a healthy workforce; it offers fitness club subsidies as well as a bonus (up to $450) to encourage employees to get fit and stay fit.[120] Hershey's Nova Scotia plant (makers of Pot of Gold chocolates) introduced a comprehensive wellness program. It started with over 500 employees completing a voluntary health risk assessment that provided data for developing wellness programs, and benchmarks to note improvements. This led to the creation of weight management, smoking cessation, and fitness programs.[121]

Although organizations have long recognized the importance of maintenance of their machinery, many are only recently learning that their human assets need maintenance as well, in the form of employee wellness and health promotion activities. All are focused on helping employees manage their stress and health in a preventive manner.

Career Planning

Matching an individual's career aspirations with the opportunities in the organization is career planning. This proactive approach to career management is often part of an organization's development efforts. Career planning is a joint responsibility of organizations and individuals.

Career-planning activities benefit both the organization and its individuals. Through counselling sessions, employees identify their skills and skill deficiencies. The organization then can plan its training and development efforts based on this information. In addition, the process can be used to identify and nurture talented employees for potential promotion.

Managers can choose from a host of organization development techniques to facilitate organizational change.

© Juice Images—Fotolia.com

Organizational wellness programs often include gym access.

Large-scale changes in organizations require the use of multiple techniques. For example, implementing a new technology such as robotics may require simultaneous changes in the structure of the organization, the configuration of work groups, and individual attitudes.

We should recognize at this point that the organization development methods just described are a means to an end. Programs do not drive change; business needs do. The OD methods are merely vehicles for moving the organization and its employees in a more effective direction.

Are Organization Development Efforts Effective?

Since organization development is designed to help organizations manage change, it is important to evaluate the effectiveness of these efforts. The success of any OD intervention depends on a host of factors, including the technique used, the competence of the change agent, the organization's readiness for change, and top management commitment. No single method of OD is effective in every instance. Instead, multiple-method OD approaches are recommended because they allow organizations to capitalize on the benefits of several approaches.[122]

Efforts to evaluate OD effects have focused on outcomes such as productivity. One review of more than 200 interventions indicated that worker productivity improved in 87 percent of the cases.[123] We can conclude that when properly applied and managed, organization development programs have positive effects on performance.[124]

STUDY TOOLS 17

IN THE BOOK YOU CAN ...

- ☐ Rip out the **Chapter Review card** at the end of the book to review Key Concepts and Key Terms.
- ☐ Take a "What about You?" Quiz related to material in the chapter.
- ☐ Read additional cases in the Mini Case and Shopify Running Case sections.

ONLINE YOU CAN ...

NELSON.COM/STUDENT

- ☐ Take a "What about You?" Quiz related to material in the chapter.
- ☐ Test your understanding with a quick Multiple-Choice Pre-Test quiz.
- ☐ Read the eBook, which includes discussion points for questions posed in the Cases.
- ☐ Watch Videos related to chapter content.
- ☐ Use the available Flashcards and Matching Quizzes to test your understanding of key terms and concepts.
- ☐ See how much you've learned by taking a Post-Test.
- ☐ Watch Videos related to chapter content.
- ☐ Use the available Flashcards and Matching Quizzes to test your understanding of key terms and concepts.
- ☐ See how much you've learned by taking a Post-Test.

WHAT ABOUT YOU?

Applying the Force-Field Analysis Tool

Think of a problem you are currently facing. An example would be trying to increase the amount of study time you devote to a particular class.

1. Describe the problem, as specifically as possible.
2. List the forces driving change on the arrows at the left side of the diagram. Weight their importance.
3. List the forces restraining change on the arrows at the right side of the diagram. Weight their importance.

FORCES DRIVING CHANGE	FORCES RESTRAINING CHANGE
→	←
→	←
→	←

Questions

1. What can you do, specifically, to remove the obstacles to change?
2. What can you do to increase the forces driving change?
3. What benefits can be derived from breaking a problem down into forces driving change and forces restraining change?

MINI CASE

TD and Canada Trust

In 2000, TD acquired Canada Trust. The acquisition at the time was the largest change management initiative that Canada had ever experienced. The TD bank was established in 1869 and had gone through various changes long before the acquisition of Canada Trust.

At the time of the acquisition, Canada Trust customers were concerned that their trust company would lose its personalized retail focus. The number of bank branches and the size of the workforce would be reduced by the acquisition. The takeover would make TD the third largest bank in Canada, known as TD Canada Trust.

The change was rolled out across the country and the best elements from each company were implemented. The changes for the Canada Trust customers were more significant than those for TD customers so a help line was established. Even so, TD was pleased with the merger roll-out as it had very few or significant logistical issues.

According to the first CEO of the new organization, there were clear complementarities between TD and Canada Trust as each had what the other did not. Tim Hockey noted, "The complementary element was that TD had a strong commercial banking presence and sales culture but its service culture wasn't as strong. Canada Trust had a very strong service culture; it had no business banking presence to speak of, and its sales culture (as is usual with service organizations) was probably a little less strong." He also noted that selecting the best people from both organizations to create new teams was very challenging. (It is interesting to note that increasingly the name Canada Trust is not part of the TD's official name.)

SOURCES: TD, "Historical Fast Facts," https://www.td.com/about-tdbfg/corporate-information/tds-history/historical-fast-facts.jsp, accessed September 2, 2018; K. Noble, J. Geddes, J. Hunter and D. Hawaleshka, "TD Bids for Canada Trust," 2013, https://www.thecanadianencyclopedia.ca/en/article/td-bids-for-canada-trust/, August 31, 2018; M. Nelson, "TD, Canada Trust Finish Merger of Retail Branches," *The Globe and Mail*, August 7, 2001, https://www.theglobeandmail.com/report-on-business/td-canada-trust-finish-merger-of-retail-branches/article4151090/, accessed August 12, 2018; D. Ovsey, "Behind the Scenes of TD Canada Trust's Cultural Evolution," *Financial Post*, November 20, 2012, https://business.financialpost.com/executive/behind-the-scenes-of-td-canada-trusts-cultural-evolution, accessed August 12 2018; D. Martin, "Why TD Bank Is Losing Me As A Customer After 30 Years," Huffington Post, March 17, 2017, https://www.huffingtonpost.ca/david-martin/td-bank-sales-tactics_b_15411962.html, accessed September 1, 2018.

Apply Your Understanding

1. What are the change management challenges in such a large change?
2. What would be the customers' concerns about the merger?
3. Why is it so hard to blend organizational cultures?

SHOPIFY RUNNING CASE

DISRUPTING THE RETAIL STATUS QUO

Shopify has changed the nature of commerce by creating a new retail ecosystem that combines technology and personalization. It provides a service that lets small entrepreneurs have access to a global reach of customers and transaction security. It also enables customers to have greater confidence in the security of their financial transactions. In short, Shopify disrupted both bricks-and-mortar commerce as well as earlier e-commerce approaches such as F-commerce.

Shopify has not only disrupted the retail ecosystem but also challenges conventional wisdom. CEO Tobi Lütke attributes some of its success to ignoring academic credentials in the hiring process. Academic credentials are seen more as a signal rather than as a predictor of future performance. Some very senior positions do seem to require academic credentials but most do not. Shopify joins other firms such as Google, Apple, and IBM in dropping the requirement of a college degree. Again, Shopify is having a significant impact on the external environment and causing significant change.

SOURCES: T. Lütke, Twitter Post, August 28, 2018, and C. Connley, "Google, Apple and 13 Other Companies That No Longer Require Employees to Have a College Degree, CNBC, August 16, 2018, accessed from https://www.cnbc.com/2018/08/16/15-companies-that-no-longer-require-employees-to-have-a-college-degree.html?__source=facebook%7Cmain, September 28, 2018.

Apply Your Understanding

1. How and why is Shopify innovative?
2. What are the advantages of its recruitment and selection strategy?
3. What are the disadvantages?

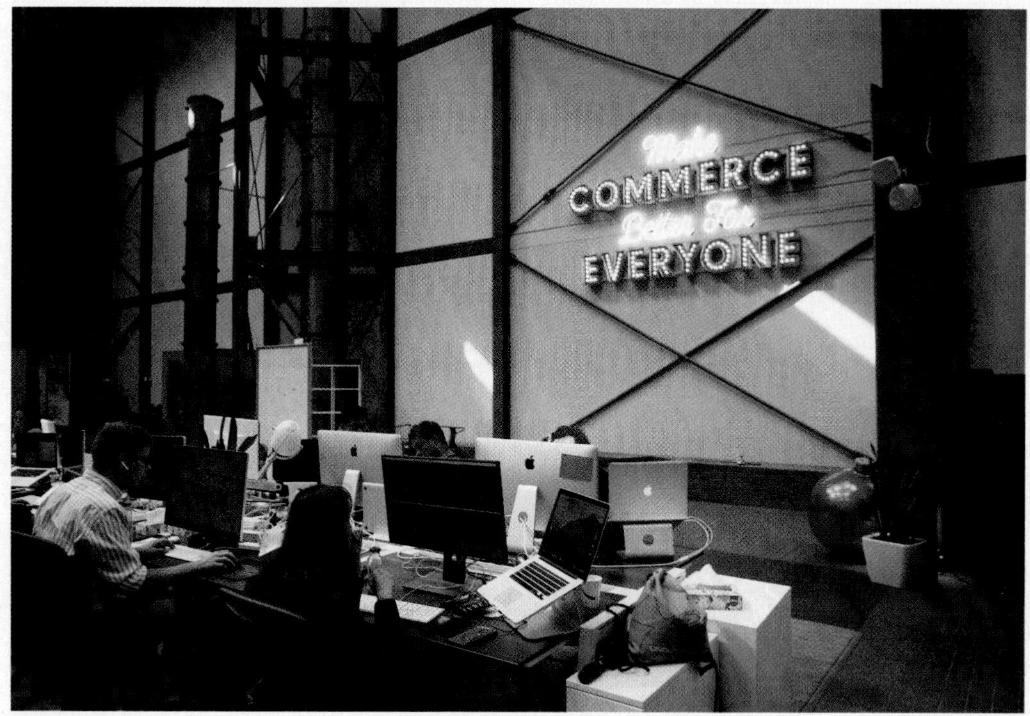

Cole Burston/Bloomberg via Getty Images

Career Management

18

LEARNING OUTCOMES

After reading this chapter, you should be able to do the following:

18-1 Explain occupational and organizational choice decisions.

18-2 Identify foundations for a successful career.

18-3 Explain the career-stage model.

18-4 Explain the major tasks facing individuals in the establishment stage of the career model.

18-5 Identify the issues confronting individuals in the advancement stage of the career model.

18-6 Describe how individuals can navigate the challenges of the maintenance stage of the career model.

18-7 Explain how individuals withdraw from the workforce.

18-8 Explain how career anchors help form a career identity.

18-9 Become familiar with some current tools and practices that will help you develop your own career.

See the end of this chapter for a list of available Study Tools, a "What about You?" Quiz, Mini Case, and the Shopify Running Case.

As you get closer to graduation, you will need to appreciate how you can apply the concepts from the discipline of organizational behaviour. In this chapter, you will learn about navigating your career as you progress through your life stages. As well, you will learn about the importance of mentoring and what behaviours will help you have a successful career. You need to be proactive in managing your career; appreciate that career management is a journey and not an end-state.

A **career** is a pattern of work-related experiences that span the course of a person's life.[1] A career is more a journey than a destination. The two elements in a career are the objective element and the subjective element.[2] The objective element of the career is the observable, concrete environment. For example, you can manage a career by getting training to improve your skills. In contrast, the subjective element involves your perception of the situation. Rather than getting training (an objective element), you might change your aspirations (a subjective element). Therefore, both objective events and the individual's perception of those events are important in defining a career.

Career management is a lifelong process of learning about self, jobs, and organizations; setting personal career goals; developing strategies for achieving the goals; and revising the goals based on work and life experiences.[3] Whose responsibility is career management? It is tempting to place all the responsibility on individuals, and it is appropriate. However, it is also the organization's responsibility to form partnerships with individuals in managing their careers. Careers are made up of exchanges between individuals and organizations. Inherent in these exchanges is the idea of reciprocity, or give and take.

> "Careers are made up of exchanges between individuals and organizations."

Whether we approach it as managers or as employees, career management is an integral activity in our lives. There are three reasons it is important to understand careers:

- If we know what to look forward to over the course of our careers, we can take a proactive approach to planning and managing them.
- As managers, we need to understand the experiences of our employees and colleagues as they pass through the various stages of careers over their life spans.
- Career management is good for business. It makes good financial sense to have highly trained employees keep up with their fields so that organizations can protect valuable investments in human resources.

career The pattern of work-related experiences that span the course of a person's life.

career management A lifelong process of learning about self, jobs, and organizations; setting personal career goals; developing strategies for achieving the goals, and revising the goals based on work and life experiences.

18-1 OCCUPATIONAL AND ORGANIZATIONAL CHOICE DECISIONS

The time of the fast track to the top of the hierarchical organization is past. Also gone is the idea of lifetime employment in a single organization. Today's environment often demands leaner and flexible organizations. The paternalistic attitude that organizations take care of employees no longer exists. Individuals now take on more responsibility for managing their own careers. The concept of the career is undergoing a paradigm shift, as shown in Table 18.1.

The old career paradigm is giving way to a new career characterized by discrete exchange, occupational excellence, organizational empowerment, and project allegiance.[4] One study found that both individuals and organizations are actively involved in the management of the new career of employees. As such, the new career involves a type of participatory management technique on the part of the individual; the organization responds to each individual's needs and thus is more flexible in its career development programs.[5] As shown in Figure 18.1, the skills that we will need in the future are "soft" skills, better described as essential skills. The interaction of effective communication, critical thinking, and collaboration will result in creativity and innovation.

Discrete exchange occurs when an organization gains productivity while a person gains work experience. It is a short-term arrangement that recognizes that job skills change in value and that renegotiation of the relationship must occur as conditions change. This contrasts sharply with the mutual loyalty contract of the old career paradigm in which employee loyalty was exchanged for job security.

Occupational excellence means continually honing skills that can be marketed across organizations.

TABLE 18.1 THE NEW VERSUS THE OLD CAREER PARADIGMS

NEW CAREER PARADIGM	OLD CAREER PARADIGM
Discrete exchange means:	**The mutual loyalty contract meant:**
• Explicit exchange of specified rewards in return for task performance	• Implicit trading of employee compliance in return for job security
• Basing job rewards on the current market value of the work being performed	• Allowing job rewards to be routinely deferred into the future
• Engaging in disclosure and renegotiation on both sides as the employment relationship unfolds	• Treating the mutual loyalty assumptions as a political barrier to renegotiation
• Exercising flexibility as each party's interests and market circumstances change	• Assuming employment and career opportunities are standardized and prescribed by the organization
Occupational excellence means:	**The one-employer focus meant:**
• Performance of current jobs in return for developing new occupational expertise	• Relying on the organization to specify jobs and their associated occupational skill base
• Employees identifying with and focusing on what is happening in their adopted occupation	• Employees identifying with and focusing on what is happening in their particular organization
• Emphasizing occupational skill development over the local demands of any particular firm	• Forgoing technical or functional development in favour of firm-specific learning
• Getting training in anticipation of future job opportunities; having training lead jobs	• Doing the job first to be entitled to new training: making training follow jobs
Organizational empowerment means:	**The top-down firm meant:**
• Strategic positioning is dispersed to separate business units	• Strategic direction is subordinated to "corporate headquarters"
• Everyone is responsible for adding value and improving competitiveness	• Competitiveness and added value are the responsibility of corporate experts
• Business units are free to cultivate their own markets	• Business-unit marketing depends on the corporate agenda
• New enterprise, spinoffs, and alliance building are broadly encouraged	• Independent enterprise is discouraged, and likely to be viewed as disloyalty
Project allegiance means:	**Corporate allegiance meant:**
• Shared employer and employee commitment to the overarching goal of the project	• Project goals are subordinated to corporate policy and organizational constraints
• A successful outcome of the project is more important than holding the project team together	• Being loyal to the work group can be more important than the project itself
• Financial and reputational rewards stem directly from project outcomes	• Financial and reputational rewards stem from being a "good soldier" regardless of results
• Upon project completion, organization and reporting arrangements are broken up	• Social relationships within organizational boundaries are actively encouraged

FIGURE 18.1 21st-CENTURY SKILLS

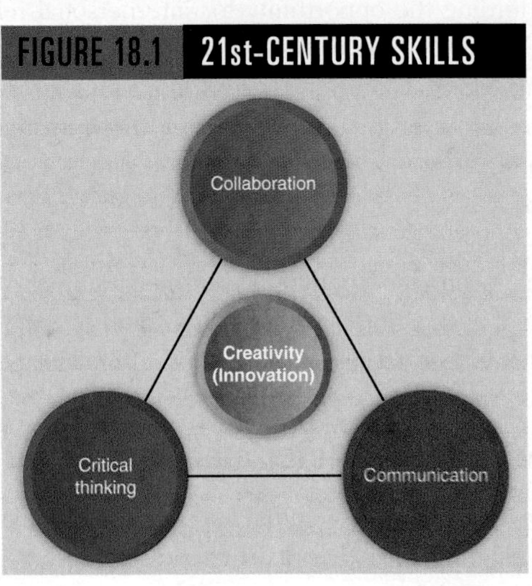

The individual identifies more with the occupation (*I am an engineer*) than the organization (*I am a IBMer*). In contrast, the old one-employer focus meant that training was company specific rather than preparation for future job opportunities. A research study that focused on ethnographic data (interviews and stories) was conducted among software engineers in three European firms and two North American firms. Software engineers did not have much regard for their immediate supervisors, the organization, or formal dress codes. The only thing they did believe in was occupational excellence so that they could be better at what they do. In this regard, the authors of the study note that software engineers represent a unique group

Super Skills

There are five key skills that individuals need to be successful in the future. The five "super skills" are (1) *Personal brand* which involves building a reputation, trust, and a following; (2) *Digital fluency* to assemble teams of people, robots, and bots to accomplish work; (3) *Networking* to create your own "tribe"; (4) *Managing complexity* to be adaptable; and (5) *Resilience* to deal with setbacks.

Careers should be seen not as ladders, but "lattices."

SOURCE: S. Vozza, "These are the 5 'Super Skills' You Need for the Jobs of the Future," *Fast Company*, June 20, 2018, https://www.fastcompany.com/40584248/these-are-the-5-super-skills-you-need-for-jobs-of-the-future, accessed September 16, 2018.

in terms of career development and that they fit well within the model of the "new career."[6]

Organizational empowerment means that power flows down to subunits and in turn to employees. Employees are expected to add value and help the organization remain competitive by being innovative and creative. The old top-down approach meant that control and strategizing were done only by the top managers, and individual initiative might be viewed as disloyalty or disrespect.

Project allegiance means that both individuals and organizations are committed to the successful completion of a project. The organization's gain is the project outcome; the individual's gain is experience and shared success. On project completion, the project team breaks up as individuals move on to new projects. Under the old paradigm, organizational allegiance was paramount. The needs of projects were overshadowed by policies and procedures. Work groups were long term, and keeping the group together was often as important a goal as project completion.

Preparing for the World of Work

When viewed from one perspective, you might say that we spend our youth preparing for the world of work. Educational experiences and personal life experiences help an individual develop the skills and maturity needed to enter a career. Preparation for work is a developmental process that gradually unfolds over time.[7] As the time approaches for beginning a career, individuals face two difficult decisions: the choice of occupation and the choice of organization.

Occupational Choice

In choosing an occupation, individuals assess their needs, values, abilities, and preferences and attempt to match them with an occupation that provides a fit. Personality plays a role in the selection of occupation. Holland's theory of occupational choice contends that there are six types of personalities and that each personality is characterized by a set of interests and values.[8]

Holland also states that occupations can be classified using his typology. The six types are:

1. *Realistic:* stable, persistent, and materialistic
2. *Artistic:* imaginative, emotional, and impulsive
3. *Investigative:* curious, analytical, and independent
4. *Enterprising:* ambitious, energetic, and adventurous
5. *Social:* generous, cooperative, and sociable
6. *Conventional:* efficient, practical, and obedient

For example, realistic occupations include mechanic, restaurant server, and mechanical engineer. Artistic occupations include architect, voice coach, and interior designer. Investigative occupations include physicist, surgeon, and economist. Real estate agent, human resource manager, and lawyer are enterprising occupations. The social occupations include counsellor, social worker, and religious leader. Conventional occupations include word processor, accountant, and data entry operator.

Holland's typology has been used to predict career choices with a variety of international participants, including Mexicans, Australians, Indians, New Zealanders, Taiwanese, Pakistanis, South Africans, and Germans.[9] An assumption that drives Holland's theory is that people choose occupations that match their own personalities. People who fit Holland's social types are those who prefer jobs that are highly interpersonal in nature. They may see careers in physical and math sciences, for example, as not affording the opportunity for interpersonal relationships.[10] To fulfill the desire for interpersonal work, they may instead gravitate toward jobs in customer service or counselling in order to better match their personalities. Although personality is a major influence on occupational choice, it is not the only influence. There are a host of other influences, including social class, parents' occupations, economic conditions, and geography.[11] Once a choice of occupation has been made, another major decision that individuals face is the choice of organizations.

Organizational Choice and Entry

Several theories of how individuals choose organizations exist, ranging from theories that postulate very logical and rational choice processes to those that suggest seemingly irrational processes. Expectancy theory, which we discussed in Chapter 5, can be applied to organizational choice.[12] According to the expectancy theory view, individuals choose organizations that maximize positive outcomes and avoid negative outcomes. Job candidates calculate the probability that an organization will provide a certain outcome and then compare the probabilities across organizations.

Other theories propose that people select organizations in a much less rational fashion. Job candidates may satisfice, that is, select the first organization that meets one or two important criteria and then justify their choice by distorting their perceptions.[13] The method of selecting an organization varies greatly among individuals and may reflect a combination of the expectancy theory and theories that postulate less rational approaches.

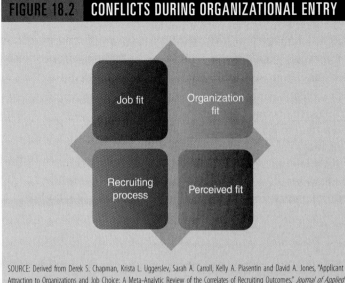

FIGURE 18.2 CONFLICTS DURING ORGANIZATIONAL ENTRY

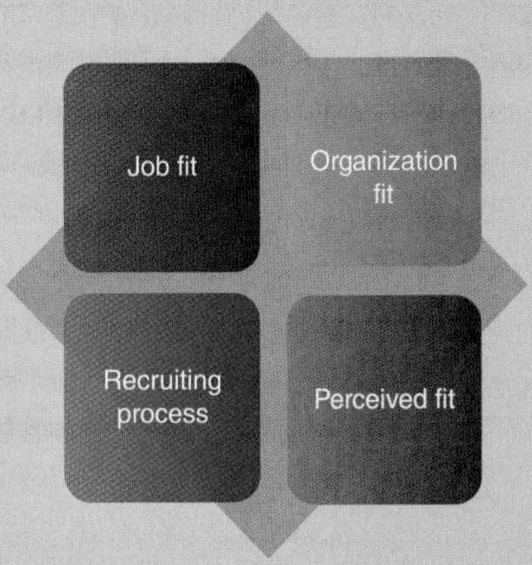

SOURCE: Derived from Derek S. Chapman, Krista L. Uggerslev, Sarah A. Carroll, Kelly A. Piasentin and David A. Jones, "Applicant Attraction to Organizations and Job Choice: A Meta-Analytic Review of the Correlates of Recruiting Outcomes," *Journal of Applied Psychology*, 90, 5 (2005): 928–944.

Entry into an organization is further complicated by the conflicts that occur between individuals and organizations during the process. The first is a conflict between the organization's effort to attract candidates and the individual's choice of an organization. The individual needs complete and accurate information to make a good choice, but the organization may not provide it. The organization is trying to attract a large number of qualified candidates, so it presents itself in an overly attractive way.

The second conflict is between the individual's attempt to attract several organizations and the organization's need to select the best candidate. Individuals want good offers, so they do not disclose their faults. They describe their preferred job in terms of the organization's opening instead of describing a job they would really prefer. Also, there are conflicts internal to the two parties. The third is a conflict between the organization's desire to recruit a large pool of qualified applicants and the organization's need to select and retain the best candidate.[14]

In recruiting, organizations tend to give only positive information, and this results in mismatches between the individual and the organization. The fourth conflict is internal to the individual; it is between the individual's desire for several job offers and the need to make a good choice. When individuals present themselves as overly attractive, they risk being offered positions that are poor fits in terms of their skills and career goals.[15]

Figure 18.2 highlights some key determinants of organizational entry. Characteristics of the job and the organization are key considerations. As well, the recruiting process itself has an impact on individuals' choices. Perception of fit—a subjective factor—was found to be a particularly important predictor of applicants' attraction to a particular organization.[16] The organizational choice and entry process is very complex due to the nature of such conflicts. Partial responsibility for preventing these conflicts rests with the individual. Individuals should conduct thorough research of the organization through published reports and industry analyses. Individuals also should conduct a careful self-analysis and be as honest as possible with organizations to ensure a good match. The job interview process can be stressful, but also informative.

Partial responsibility for good matches also rests with the organization. One way of avoiding the conflicts and mismatches is to use a realistic job preview.

REALISTIC JOB PREVIEWS The conflicts just discussed may result in unrealistic expectations on the part of the candidate. People entering the world of work may expect, for example, that they will receive explicit directions from their boss, only to find that they are left with ambiguity about how to do the job. They may expect that promotions will be based on performance and find that promotions are based mainly on political considerations. Some new hires expect to be given managerial responsibilities right away; however, this is not often the case.

Giving potential employees a realistic picture of the job they are applying for is known as a **realistic job preview (RJP)**. When candidates are given both positive and negative information, they can make more effective job choices.

realistic job preview (RJP) Both positive and negative information given to potential employees about the job they are applying for, thereby giving them a more realistic picture of the job.

Traditional recruiting practices produce unrealistically high expectations, which produce low job satisfaction when these unrealistic expectations meet the reality of the job situation. RJPs tend to create expectations that are much closer to reality, and they increase the numbers of candidates who withdraw from further consideration.[17] This occurs because candidates with unrealistic expectations tend to look for employment elsewhere. TD's website provides a realistic job preview through a series of videos and photo stories. A potential applicant can watch employees talking about a day in the life of their particular role. Ontario Power Generation has created a booklet that provides RJP information for new graduates who want to work as engineering/applied science trainees. The booklet covers topics such as life as a new trainee, continuing training requirements, rewards and challenges of the work, and critical success factors.[18]

RJPs can also be thought of as inoculation against disappointment. If new recruits know what to expect in the new job, they can prepare for the experience. Newcomers who are not given RJPs may find that their jobs don't measure up to their expectations. They may then believe that their employer was deceitful in the hiring process, become unhappy and mishandle job demands, and ultimately leave the organization.[19] Reverse résumé viewing is an intriguing additional process that organizations might consider to enhance their RJPs.[20] It involves the job candidate reviewing the résumés of current employees such as their supervisor, peers, and/or subordinates. That way, the job candidate can make a more informed decision about their fit with the organization. There are, of course, significant privacy issues to address and résumés could not be used without the employee's consent.

Job candidates who receive RJPs view the organization as honest and also have a greater ability to cope with the demands of the job.[21] RJPs perform another important function: they reduce uncertainty.[22] Knowing what to expect, both good and bad, gives a newcomer a sense of control that is important to job satisfaction and performance. With today's emphasis on ethics, organizations need to do all they can to be seen as operating consistently and honestly. Realistic job previews are one way in which companies can provide ethically required information to newcomers. Ultimately, RJPs result in more effective matches, lower turnover, and higher organizational commitment and job satisfaction.[23] There is much to gain, and little to risk, in providing realistic job information.[24]

In summary, the needs and goals of individuals and organizations can clash during entry into the organization. To avoid potential mismatches, individuals should conduct a careful self-analysis and provide accurate information about themselves to potential employers. Organizations should present realistic job previews to show candidates both the positive and negative aspects of the job, along with the potential career paths available to the employee.

18-2 FOUNDATIONS FOR A SUCCESSFUL CAREER

In addition to planning and preparation, building a career takes attention and self-examination. One way you can build a successful career is by becoming your own career coach; another is by developing your emotional intelligence, which is an important attribute if you want to succeed in your organization. Do the Self-Assessment at the end of the chapter now to measure the current state of your flexibility skills.

Becoming Your Own Career Coach

The best way to stay employed is to see yourself as being in business for yourself, even if you work for someone else. Know what skills you can package for other employers and what you can do to ensure that your skills are current. Organizations need employees who have acquired multiple skills and are adept at more than one job. Employers want employees who have demonstrated competence in dealing with change.[25] To be successful, think of organizational change not as a disruption to your work but instead as the central focus of your work, as we discussed in Chapter 17. You will also need to develop self-reliance, to deal effectively with the stress of change. Self-reliant individuals take an interdependent approach to relationships and are comfortable both giving and receiving support from others.

The people who will be most successful in the new career paradigm are individuals who are flexible, team oriented (rather than hierarchical), energized by change, and tolerant of ambiguity. Those who will become frustrated in the new career paradigm are individuals who are rigid in their thinking and learning styles and who have high needs for control. A commitment to continuous, lifelong learning will prevent you from becoming a professional dinosaur.[26] An intentional and purposeful commitment to taking charge of your professional life will be necessary in managing the new career paradigm.

Behaving in an ethical manner, standing by your values, and building a professional image of integrity is also very important. Major organizations conduct extensive reference checks on their applicants—not only with the references supplied by the applicants, but also with friends of such references. Behaving ethically is not only a benefit to your job application but also can help you withstand pressures that might endanger your career. One study suggests that executives succumb to the temptation of fraud because they feel pressure to keep up with inflated expectations and changes in cultural norms, short-term versus long-term orientations, board of directors' composition, and senior leadership in the organization.[27]

Emotional Intelligence and Career Success

Almost 40 percent of new managers fail within the first 18 months on the job.[28] What are the reasons for the failure? Newly hired managers flame out because they fail to build good relationships with peers and subordinates (82 percent of failures), are confused or uncertain about what their bosses expect (58 percent of failures), lack political skills (50 percent of failures), and are unable to achieve the two or three most important objectives of the new job (47 percent of failures).[29] You'll note that these failures are all due to a lack of human (rather than technical) skills.

Emotional intelligence is important to career success in many cultures.

We have discussed the concept of emotional intelligence (EI) as an important determinant of conflict management skills. Daniel Goleman argues that emotional intelligence is a constellation of the qualities that mark a star performer at work. These attributes include self-awareness, self-control, trustworthiness, confidence, and empathy, among others. Goleman's belief is that emotional competencies are twice as important to people's success today as raw intelligence or technical know-how. He also argues that the further up the ranks you go, the more important emotional intelligence becomes.[30] Employers, either consciously or unconsciously, look for emotional intelligence during the hiring process. In addition to traditionally recognized competencies such as communication and social skills, interns with higher levels of emotional intelligence are rated as more hireable by their host firms than those with lower levels of EI.[31] Neither gender seems to have cornered the market on EI. Both men and women who can demonstrate high levels of EI are seen as particularly gifted and may be promoted more rapidly.[32] For example, organizations such as Wrigley, CIBC, Canada Life, and McDonnell Douglas use EI in hiring and training.[33] L'Oréal has found emotional intelligence to be a profitable selection tool. Salespeople selected on the basis of emotional competence outsold those selected using the old method by an average of $91,370 per year. As an added bonus for the firm, these salespeople also had 63 percent less turnover during the first year than those selected in the traditional way.

Emotional intelligence is important to career success in many cultures. A recent study in Australia found that high levels of emotional intelligence are associated with job success. EI improves your ability to work with other team members and to provide high-quality customer service, and workers with high EI are more likely to take steps to develop their skills. This confirms North American studies that portray high emotional intelligence as an important attribute for the upwardly mobile worker.[34]

The good news is that emotional intelligence can be developed and does tend to improve throughout life. Some companies are providing training in emotional intelligence competencies. American Express began sending managers through an emotional competence training program. It found that trained managers outperformed those who lacked this training. In the year after completing the course, managers trained in emotional competence grew their businesses by an average of 18.1 percent compared to 16.2 percent for those businesses whose managers were untrained.[35]

 18-3 THE CAREER STAGE MODEL

A common way of understanding careers is viewing them as a series of stages through which individuals pass during their working lives.[36] Figure 18.3 presents the career stage model, which will form the basis for our discussion in the remainder of this chapter.[37] The career-stage model shows that individuals pass through four stages in their careers: establishment, advancement, maintenance, and withdrawal. It is important to note that the age ranges shown are approximations; that is, the timing of the career transitions varies greatly among individuals.

Establishment is the first stage of a person's career. The activities that occur in this stage centre around learning the job and fitting into the

establishment The first stage of a person's career in which the person learns the job and begins to fit into the organization and occupation.

FIGURE 18.3 THE CAREER STAGE MODEL

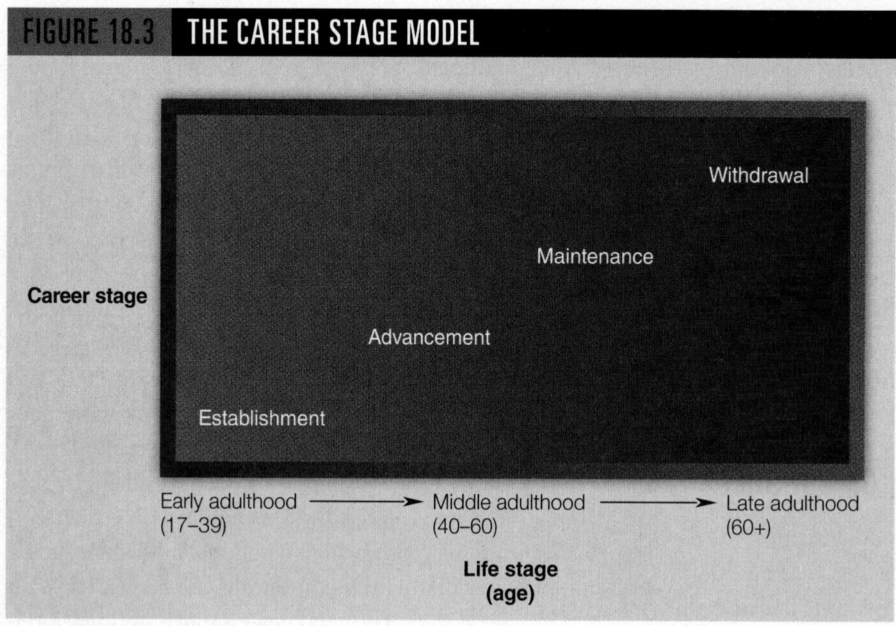

advancement The second, high achievement–oriented career stage in which people focus on increasing their competence.

maintenance The third stage in an individual's career in which the individual tries to maintain productivity while evaluating progress toward career goals.

withdrawal The final stage in an individual's career in which the individual contemplates retirement or possible career changes.

organization and occupation. **Advancement** is a high achievement–oriented stage in which people focus on increasing their competence. The **maintenance** stage finds the individual trying to maintain productivity while evaluating progress toward career goals. The **withdrawal** stage involves contemplation of retirement or possible career change.

Along the horizontal axis in Figure 18.2 are the corresponding life stages for each career stage. These life stages are based on the pioneering research on adult development conducted by Levinson and his colleagues. Levinson conducted extensive biographical interviews to trace the life stages of men and women. He interpreted his research in two books, *The Seasons of a Man's Life* and *The Seasons of a Woman's Life*.[38] Levinson's life stages are characterized by an alternating pattern of stability and transition.[39] Throughout the discussion of career stages that follows, we weave in the transitions of Levinson's life stages. Work and personal life are inseparable, and to understand a person's career experiences, we must also examine the unfolding of the person's own experiences.

You can see that adult development provides unique challenges for the individual and that there may be considerable overlap between the stages. Now let us examine each career stage in detail.

18-4 THE ESTABLISHMENT STAGE

During the establishment stage, the individual begins a career as a newcomer to the organization. This is a period of great dependence on others, as the individual is learning about the job and the organization. The establishment stage usually occurs during the beginning of the early adulthood years (ages 18 to 25). During this time, Levinson notes, an important personal life transition into adulthood occurs: the individual begins to separate from their parents and becomes less emotionally and financially dependent. Following this period is a fairly stable time of exploring the adult role and settling down. The transition from school to work is a part of the establishment stage. Many graduates find the transition to be a memorable experience. The following description was provided by a newly graduated individual who went to work at a large public utility:

> We all tried to one-up each other about jobs we had just accepted . . . bragging that we had the highest salary, the best management training program, the most desirable coworkers, the most upward mobility . . . and

IN ACTION

KPMG

Many workers in the sandwich generation find themselves caught between taking care of their children and their elderly parents. KPMG offers a backup childcare service for employees whose babysitting arrangements fall through and has a shared-leave program in which employees can donate personal time to colleagues experiencing a family emergency. Most unique of KPMG's work–life balance initiatives is its three-part eldercare benefit. This benefit consists of an online information and referral service to connect employees with eldercare organizations, up to 20 days of backup care for elderly relatives per year, and paid time off or a leave of absence to care for elderly relatives. These programs have reduced turnover and improved morale for KPMG.

believed we were destined to become future corporate leaders. . . . Every Friday after work we met for happy hour to visit and relate the events of the week. It is interesting to look at how the mood of those happy hours changed over the first few months . . . at first, we jockeyed for position in terms of telling stories about how great these new jobs were, or how weird our bosses were. . . . Gradually, things quieted down at happy hour. The mood went from "Wow, isn't this great?" to "What in the world have we gotten ourselves into?" There began to be general agreement that business wasn't all it was cracked up to be.[40]

Establishment is thus a time of big transitions in both personal and work life. At work, two major tasks face the newcomer: negotiating effective psychological contracts and managing the stress of socialization.

Psychological Contracts

A **psychological contract** is an implicit agreement between the individual and the organization that specifies what each is expected to give and to receive in the relationship.[41] Individuals expect to receive salary, status, advancement opportunities, and challenging work to meet their needs. Organizations expect to receive time, energy, talents, and commitment in order to meet their goals. Working out the psychological contract with the organization begins with entry, but the contract is modified as the individual proceeds through the career.

Psychological contracts can also form and exist between individuals.[42] During the establishment stage, newcomers form attachment relationships with many people in the organization. Working out effective psychological contracts within each relationship is important. Newcomers need social support in many forms and from many sources. Table 18.2 shows the type of psychological contracts, in the form of social support, that newcomers may work out with key insiders in the organization.

Socialization Stress

One common newcomer concern, for example, is whose behaviour to watch for cues to appropriate behaviour. Senior colleagues can provide modelling support by displaying behaviour that the newcomer can emulate. This is only one of many types of support that newcomers need. Newcomers should contract with others to receive each of the needed types of support so that they can adjust to the new job. Organizations can also help newcomers form relationships early and should encourage the psychological contracting process between newcomers and insiders. Broken or breached psychological contracts can have detrimental outcomes. The influence of a broken psychological contract is often felt even after an employee leaves a job. Laid-off employees who feel that a psychological contract breach has occurred are not only unhappy with their former firms but also may be both more cynical and less trusting of their new employers.[43]

THE ADVANCEMENT STAGE

The advancement stage is a period when many individuals strive for achievement. They seek greater responsibility and authority and strive

psychological contract An implicit agreement between an individual and an organization that specifies what each is expected to give and receive in the relationship.

TABLE 18.2 NEWCOMER–INSIDER PSYCHOLOGICAL CONTRACTS FOR SOCIAL SUPPORT

TYPE OF SUPPORT	FUNCTION OF SUPPORTIVE ATTACHMENTS	NEWCOMER CONCERN	EXAMPLES OF INSIDER RESPONSE/ ACTION
Protection from stressors	Direct assistance in terms of resources, time, labour, or environmental modification	What are the major risks/ threats in this environment?	*Supervisor* cues newcomer to risks/threats
Informational	Provision of information necessary for managing demands	What do I need to know to get things done?	*Mentor* provides advice on informal political climate in organization
Evaluative	Feedback on both personal and professional role performances	How am I doing?	*Supervisor* provides day-to-day performance feedback during first week on new job
Modelling	Evidence of behavioural standards provided through modelled behaviour	Whom do I follow?	Newcomer is apprenticed to *senior colleague.*
Emotional	Empathy, esteem, caring, or love	Do I matter? Who cares if I'm here or not?	*Other newcomers* empathize with and encourage individual when reality shock sets in.

SOURCE: Table from D. L. Nelson, J. C. Quick, and J. R. Joplin, "Psychological Contracting and Newcomer Socialization: An Attachment Theory Foundation," *Journal of Social Behavior and Personality* 6 (1991): 65. Reprinted with permission.

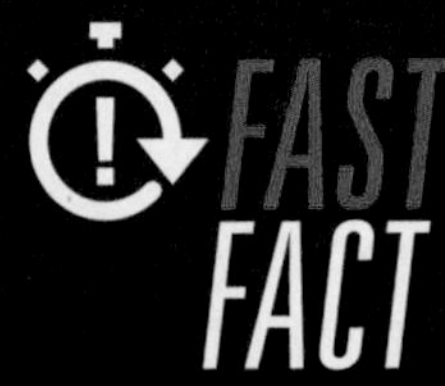

Unemployment and Immigration

Immigrants face higher unemployment than Canadian-born individuals. In the GTA, the unemployment rate between 2006 and 2011 for working-age recent immigrants was 10.92 percent compared to 5.56 percent for Canadian born. The unemployment/underemployment of immigrants in Canada costs more than $30 billion annually—about 2 percent of GDP—in lost income for immigrants.

To address such talent waste, programs such as the Rotman School of Management's Business Edge for Internationally Educated Professionals provide coaching and training.

By 2031, one in three workers across the country will be born outside Canada.

SOURCES: "Immigrant Employment: Facts and Figures, TRIEC," accessed from https://triec.ca/about-us/focus-on-immigrant-employment, October 5, 2018; "Immigrant Labour Market Outcomes in Canada: The Benefits of Addressing Wage and Employment Gaps," RBC Economics, 2011, accessed from http://www.rbc.com/newsroom/pdf/1219-2011-immigration.pdf, September 15, 2018.

for upward mobility. Usually around age 30, an important life transition occurs.[44] Individuals reassess their goals and feel the need to make changes in their career dreams. The transition at age 30 is followed by a period of stability during which the individual tries to find a role in adult society and wants to succeed in a career. During this stage, several issues are important: exploring career paths, finding a mentor, working out dual-career partnerships, and managing conflicts between work and personal life.

Career Paths and Career Ladders

Career paths are sequences of job experiences along which employees move during their careers. [45] At the advancement stage, individuals examine their career dreams and the paths they must follow to achieve those dreams. For example, suppose a person's dream is to become a top executive in the pharmaceutical industry. She majors in chemistry in undergraduate school and takes a job with a nationally recognized firm.

After she has adjusted to her job as a quality control chemist, she reevaluates her plan and decides that further education is necessary. She plans to pursue an MBA degree part-time, hoping to gain expertise in management. From there, she hopes to be promoted to a supervisory position within her current firm. If this does not occur within five years, she will consider moving to a different pharmaceutical company. An alternate route would be to try to transfer to a sales position, from which she might advance into management.

A **career ladder** is a structured series of job positions through which an

career path A sequence of job experiences that an employee moves along during their career.

career ladder A structured series of job positions through which an individual progresses in an organization.

IN ACTION

Mike Smith, Co-founder No. 22 Bicycle Company

Mike Smith completed a B.Comm. degree and then went on to do a combined Law/MBA degree. During his undergraduate studies, he worked at Pieriks Cycle Shop. Although Smith was successful in his articling and was asked back, he felt that his entrepreneurial spirit might not make him a good long-term fit in a large law firm.

Instead, he co-founded No. 22 Bicycle Company, having already made titanium bicycles for personal use. The number *22* comes from the periodic table for titanium. The bicycles cost between $7,000 and $10,000 and "are viewed in a unique way by the cycling community—as objects of beauty that also happen to be beautiful to ride." The mission of the company is that it "strives to create forward-thinking, feature-rich titanium frames tempered by a legacy of experience."

The company opened up its own titanium factory in 2014. It is staffed by skilled staff who have considerable experience in frame building. Smith notes that 2018 is a year of change for the company. He comments, "We've always tried to err on the side of setting ourselves up for growth. I'm sure we'll continue that by maybe not paying ourselves as much now to make it easier to grow for tomorrow."

SOURCE: C. Gillespie, "MBA and law graduate changes career gears to launch a bicycle company," *The Globe and Mail*, August 15, 2018, https://www.theglobeandmail.com/business/careers/business-education/article-mba-and-law-graduate-changes-career-gears-to-launch-a-bicycle-company/

individual progresses in an organization. For example, a person may go through a series of alternating line and staff supervisory assignments to advance toward upper management. Supervisors in customer service might be assigned next to the training staff and then rotate back as line supervisors in network services to gain experience in different departments.

Some companies use the traditional concept of career ladders to help employees advance in their careers. Other organizations take a more contemporary approach to career advancement. Sony encourages creativity from its engineers by using nontraditional career paths. At Sony, individuals have the freedom to move on to interesting and challenging job assignments without notifying their supervisors. If they join a new project team, their current boss is expected to let them move on. This self-promotion philosophy at Sony is seen as a key to high levels of innovation and creative new product designs.

There has been heightened interest in international assignments by multinational corporations in response to globalization and global staffing issues. One challenge in this regard has been that most expatriate assignments are not successful and organizations have been facing the challenge of properly training and preparing individuals for such assignments. Alternative international work assignments (e.g., commuter work assignments, virtual assignments, short-term assignments, etc.) can be used to help individuals gain international work experience in preparation for higher levels in the organization.[46]

Another approach used by some companies to develop skills is the idea of a "career lattice"—an approach to building competencies by moving laterally through different departments in the organization or by moving through different projects. Top management support for the career lattice is essential because in traditional firms an employee who has made several lateral moves might not be viewed with favour. However, the career lattice approach is an effective way to develop an array of skills to ensure one's employability.[47]

The career paths of many women have moved from working in large organizations to starting their own businesses. Currently, there are about one million women-owned businesses in Canada. Women are at the forefront of two primary drivers of current small business growth: the rise in one-person operations and "seniorpreneurs" (small business owners over the age of 55).[48] The main reasons for this exodus to entrepreneurship are to seek additional challenge and self-fulfillment and to have more self-determination and freedom.[49]

Exploring career paths is one important activity in advancement. Another crucial activity during advancement is finding a mentor.

Finding a Mentor

A **mentor** is an individual who provides guidance, coaching, counselling, and friendship to a protégé. Mentors are important to career success because they perform both career and psychosocial functions.[50]

The career functions provided by a mentor include sponsorship, facilitating exposure and visibility, coaching, and protection. Sponsorship means actively helping the individual get job experiences and promotions. Facilitating exposure and visibility means providing opportunities for the protégé to develop relationships with key figures in the organization in order to advance. Coaching involves providing advice in both career and job performance. Protection is provided by shielding the protégé from potentially damaging experiences. A more positive strategy is to focus on career functions through career coaching. One study found that the amount of career coaching received by protégés was related to more promotions, and higher salaries four years later.[51] Career functions are particularly important to the protégé's future success. While it may be tempting to go after the "top dog" as your mentor, personality compatibility is also an important factor in the success or failure of a mentoring relationship.

The mentor also performs psychosocial functions. Role modelling occurs when the mentor displays behaviour for the protégé to emulate. This facilitates social learning. Acceptance and confirmation is important to both the mentor and protégé. When the protégé feels accepted by the mentor, it fosters a sense of pride. Likewise, positive regard and appreciation from the junior colleague provide a sense of satisfaction for the mentor. Counselling by a mentor helps the protégé explore personal issues that arise and require assistance. Friendship is another psychosocial function that benefits both mentor and protégé alike.

In effective mentoring relationships, there is regular contact between mentor and protégé that has clearly specified purposes. Mentoring should be consistent with the organization's goals and culture. Both mentors and protégés alike should be trained in ways to manage the relationship. Mentors should be held accountable and rewarded for their role. Mentors should be perceived (accurately) by protégés as having considerable influence within the organization.[52] Mentors who are similar to their protégés

mentor An individual who provides guidance, coaching, counselling, and friendship to a protégé.

in terms of personality traits such as extraversion, and whose expectations are largely met by the relationship, are more likely to show interest in continuing the arrangement.[53] RBC, for example, has a mentoring program called RBC Diversity Dialogues. It is a reciprocal mentoring program currently involving 180 employees. The program connects two people with different professional experiences and backgrounds to learn about leadership and diversity from each other.[54]

Mentoring programs are also effective ways of addressing the challenge of workforce diversity. The mentoring process, however, presents unique problems, including the availability of mentors, issues of language and acculturation, and cultural sensitivity. Negative stereotypes can limit racialized members' access to mentoring relationships and the benefits associated with mentoring.[55] To address this problem, organizations can facilitate access to mentors. Informal mentoring programs identify pools of mentors and protégés, provide training in the development of effective mentoring and diversity issues, and then provide informal opportunities for the development of mentoring relationships.

Network groups are another avenue for mentoring. Network groups help members identify with those few others who are like them within an organization, build relationships with them, and build social support. Network groups enhance the chance that minorities will find mentors.[56] IBM Canada, for example, has an Aboriginal Peoples Network Group, Black IBM Network Group, Blue Q (Gay, Lesbian, Bisexual, and Transgender employees), East Asian Diversity Network Group, Latin American Network Group, South Asian Network Group, Men's Association, and a People Enablement Network Group focused on Persons with Disabilities.[57]

Networks also increase the likelihood that individuals will have more than one mentor. Individuals with multiple mentors, such as those gained from mentoring networks, have even greater career success than those with only one mentor.[58]

Some companies have formal mentoring programs. PricewaterhouseCoopers (PwC) uses the mentoring model to help its interns. Each intern is assigned both a peer mentor to help with day-to-day questions and an experienced mentor to help with larger issues such as career path development. As an international firm, PwC also employs similar methods overseas. In PwC's Czech Republic operations, a team of two mentors—one of whom is called a "counsellor"—fills the same guidance role as the two mentors generally fill for its other employees.[59]

Mentoring has had a strong impact in shaping the identities of the major accounting firms. In one study, every partner who was interviewed reported having at least one mentor who played a critical role in their attainment of the partnership and beyond. Protégés' identities are shaped through mentoring, and their work goals, language, and even lifestyles reflect the imperatives of the firm.[60] Protégés are schooled on partners' "hot buttons" (what not to talk about), what to wear, to "tuck in the tie," and not to cut the grass without wearing a shirt (!).

Although some organizations have formal mentoring programs, junior employees more often are left to negotiate their own mentoring relationships. The barriers to finding a mentor include lack of access to mentors, fear of initiating a mentoring relationship, and fear that supervisors or coworkers might not approve of the mentoring relationship. Individuals may also be afraid to initiate a mentoring relationship because it might be misconstrued as a sexual advance by the potential mentor or others. This is a fear of potential mentors as well. Some are unwilling to develop a relationship because of their own or because of the protégé's gender. Women report more of these barriers than men, and individuals who lack previous experience report more barriers to finding a mentor.[61]

Organizations can encourage junior workers to approach mentors by providing opportunities for them to interact with senior colleagues. The immediate supervisor is not often the best mentor for an individual, so exposure to other senior workers is important. Seminars, multilevel teams, and social events can serve as vehicles for bringing together potential mentors and protégés.

Mentoring relationships go through a series of phases: initiation, cultivation, separation, and redefinition. There is no fixed time length for each phase because each relationship is unique. In the initiation phase, the mentoring relationship begins to take on significance for both the mentor and the protégé. In the cultivation phase, the relationship becomes more meaningful, and the protégé shows rapid progress because of the career and psychosocial support provided by the mentor. Protégés influence mentors as well.

In the separation phase, the protégé feels the need to assert independence and work more autonomously. Separation can be voluntary, or it can result from an involuntary change (the protégé or mentor may be promoted or transferred). The separation phase can be difficult if it is resisted, either by the mentor (who is reluctant to let go of the relationship) or by the protégé (who resents the mentor's withdrawal of support).

The redefinition phase occurs if separation has been successful. In this phase, the relationship takes on a new identity as both parties consider themselves colleagues or friends. The mentor feels pride in the protégé, and the protégé develops a deeper appreciation for the support from the mentor.

Why are mentors so important? Aside from the support they provide, the research shows that mentors are important to the protégé's future success. For example, studies have demonstrated that individuals with mentors have higher promotion rates and higher incomes than individuals who do not have mentors.[62] Professionals who have mentors earn between $5,600 and $22,000 more per year than those who do not.[63] Individuals with mentors also are better decision makers.[64] It is not just the presence of the mentor that yields these benefits; the quality of the relationship is most important.[65]

Dual-Career Partnerships

During the advancement stage, many individuals face another transition: they settle into a relationship with a life partner. This lifestyle transition requires adjustment in many respects: learning to live with another person, being concerned with someone else, dealing with an extended family, and many other demands. The partnership can be particularly stressful if both members are career oriented.

The two-career lifestyle has increased in recent years due in part to the need for two incomes to maintain a preferred standard of living. **Dual-career partnerships** are relationships in which both people have important career roles. This type of partnership can be mutually beneficial, but it can also be stressful. Often these stresses centre around lingering stereotypes that providing income is a man's responsibility and taking care of the home is the woman's domain. Among married couples, working women's satisfaction with the marriage is affected by how much the husband shares childcare. Men who adhere to traditional gender beliefs may be threatened if the wife's income exceeds their own. Beliefs about who should do what in the partnership complicate the dual-career issue.[66]

One stressor in a dual-career partnership is time pressure. When both partners work outside the home, there may be a time crunch fitting in work, family, and leisure time. Another potential problem is jealousy. When one partner's career blooms before the other's, the partner may feel threatened.[67] Another issue to work out is whose career takes precedence. For example, what happens if one partner is transferred to another city? Must the other partner make a move that might threaten their own career in order to be with the individual who was transferred? Who, if anyone, will stay home and take care of a new baby?

Working out a dual-career partnership takes careful planning and consistent communication between the partners. Each partner must serve as a source of social support for the other. Couples can also turn to other family members, friends, and professionals for support if the need arises.

IN ACTION

Women's Executive Network (WXN)

WXN is a member-based organization to support the advancement, development, and recognition of professional women in Canada. Its core value is that "[e]quity and inclusion make industry stronger and society better. Through engaging topics and remarkable speakers, WXN is able to bring inspiration and intellect to the podium." It is part of the Phasenyne Network of Companies, which includes the Canadian Board Diversity Council.

Among its programs, WXN offers Wisdom Mentoring™. The program matches up-and-coming successful women with mentors from the community of Canada's Most Powerful Women: Top 100™ Award Winners. The women have the opportunity to have four one-hour mentoring sessions with the Top 100™. They participate in classes as well and learn about how to have a mutually beneficial mentor–mentee relationship.

SOURCE: WXN, Wisdom Mentoring™, https://wxnetwork.com/wxn/mentoring/, accessed September 16, 2018.

Work–Home Conflicts

An issue related to dual-career partnerships that is faced throughout the career cycle, but often first encountered in the advancement phase, is the conflicts that occur between work and personal life. Experiencing a great deal of work–home conflict negatively affects an individual's overall quality of life. Work–home conflicts can lead to emotional exhaustion. Dealing with customer complaints all day, failed sales calls, and missed deadlines can magnify negative events at home, and vice versa.[68] Responsibilities at home can clash with responsibilities at work, and these conflicts must be planned for. For example, suppose a child gets sick at school. Who will pick up and stay home with the child? Couples must work together to resolve these conflicts. Even at Eli Lilly and Co., only 36 percent of workers said it is possible to get ahead in their careers and still devote sufficient time to family. This is surprising, because Lilly has a reputation as one of the world's most family-friendly workplaces.[69]

dual-career partnership A relationship in which both people have important career roles.

People in the advancement stage are also dealing with developmental and life-stage changes. The midlife transition, which takes place approximately between ages 40 and 45, is often a time of crisis. Levinson points out three major changes that contribute to the midlife transition:

1. People realize that their lives are half over and that they are mortal.
2. Age 40 is considered by people in their 20s and 30s to be "over the hill" and not part of the youthful culture.
3. People reassess their dreams and evaluate how close they have come to achieving their dreams.

Midlife transition can add a layer of stress to the challenges employees face during the advancement stage.

Work–home conflicts are particular problems for working women.[70] Women have been quicker to share the provider role than men have been to share responsibilities at home.[71] When working women experience work–home conflict, their performance declines, and they suffer more strain.

Work–home conflict is a broad topic. It can be narrowed further into work–family conflict, in which work interferes with family, versus family–work conflict, in which family or home life interferes with work.[72] Cultural differences arise in these types of conflicts. One study showed that while North Americans experience more family–work conflict, Chinese experience more work–family conflict.[73] For example, women in management positions in China were very positive about future advancements and carried a strong belief in their ability to succeed. This, in turn, caused them to reevaluate their personal and professional identities. Such an identity transformation is marked by happiness associated with career advancement, even though many women foresaw emotional costs with such career advancement. This study indicated that female Chinese managers experience work–family conflict in part because the Chinese culture emphasizes close social ties and *guanxi*.[74]

WAYS TO MANAGE WORK–HOME CONFLICT To help individuals deal with work–home conflict, companies can offer **flexible work schedules**.[75] Programs such as flextime give employees freedom to take care of personal concerns while still getting their work done. Organization-sponsored childcare is another way to help. Organizations with on-site daycare centres include Johnson & Johnson, University of Toronto, and Campbell Soup. Syscon Justice Systems, a software firm located in Richmond, BC, has an onsite daycare centre. According to Syscon's CEO, Floyd Sully, "[childcare] is not a women's issue, it's a business issue. . . . It's a parental issue. . . . The fact that women have to go out and work puts it into stark relief."[76] While large organizations may offer corporate daycare, small ones can also assist their workers by providing referral services for locating the type of childcare the workers need. For smaller organizations, this can be a cost-effective alternative.[77] At the very least, organizations need to be sensitive to work–home conflicts and handle them on a case-by-case basis with flexibility and concern.

flexible work schedule A work schedule that allows employees discretion in order to accommodate personal concerns.

eldercare Assistance in caring for elderly parents and/or other elderly relatives.

A program of increasing interest that organizations can provide is **eldercare**. Often workers find themselves part of the sandwich generation as they are expected to care for both their children and their elderly parents. Approximately one million Canadians care for both their children and their parents.[78] This extremely stressful role is reported more often by women than men.[79] The impact of caring for an aging loved one is often underestimated. But 17 percent of those who provide care eventually quit their jobs due to time constraints, and another 15 percent cut back their work hours for the same reason.[80] Caring for an elderly relative at home can create severe work–home conflicts for employees and also takes a toll on the employee's own well-being and performance at work. This is especially the case if the organization is not one that provides a supportive climate for discussion of eldercare issues.[81] Harvard University has taken steps to help its faculty and staff deal with eldercare issues by contracting with Parents In A Pinch, a firm that specializes in nanny services and now also offers eldercare.[82] Catholic Children's Aid Society of Greater Toronto offers compassionate top-up leave payments (to 70 percent for eight weeks) for employees taking time off to care for a loved one.[83]

John Beatrice is one of a handful of men making work fit their family, rather than trying to fit family around career. John remembers his father working most of the night so he could be at John's athletic events during the day, and John wants the same for his family. So while job sharing, flexible scheduling, and telecommuting have traditionally been viewed as meeting the needs of working mothers, John and other men are increasingly taking advantage of such opportunities. In John's case, flexible work hours at Ernst & Young allow him to spend part of his mornings and afternoons coaching a high school hockey team. In John's assessment, flexible work hours actually led him to work more hours than he would otherwise, and he's happier about doing it. Not surprisingly, John's employer also benefits from the arrangement; after 19 years, John is more loyal than ever and still loves what he does.[84]

Alternative work arrangements such as flextime, compressed workweeks, work-at-home arrangements, part-time hours, job sharing, and leave options can help employees manage work–home conflicts. Managers must not let their biases get in the way of these benefits. Top managers may be less willing to grant alternative work arrangements to men than to women, to supervisors than to subordinates, and to employees caring for elderly parents rather than children. It is important that family-friendly policies be applied fairly.[85]

18-6 THE MAINTENANCE STAGE

Maintenance may be a misnomer for this career stage, because some people continue to grow in their careers, although the growth is usually not at the rate it was earlier. A career crisis at midlife may accompany the midlife transition. A senior product manager at Borden found himself in such a crisis and described it this way: "When I was in college, I had thought in terms of being president of a company. ... But at Borden I felt used and cornered. Most of the guys in the next two rungs above me had either an MBA or fifteen to twenty years of experience in the food business. My long-term plans stalled."[86]

Some individuals who reach a career crisis are burned out, and a month's vacation will help, according to Carolyn Smith Paschal, who owns an executive search firm. She recommends that organizations give employees in this stage sabbaticals instead of bonuses to help rejuvenate them.

Some individuals reach the maintenance stage with a sense of achievement and contentment, feeling no need to strive for further upward mobility. Whether the maintenance stage is a time of crisis or contentment, however, there are two issues to grapple with: sustaining performance and becoming a mentor.

Sustaining Performance

Remaining productive is a key concern for individuals in the maintenance stage. This becomes challenging when you reach a **career plateau**, a point where the probability of moving further up the hierarchy is low. Some people handle career plateauing fairly well, but others may become frustrated, bored, and dissatisfied with their jobs.

To keep employees productive, organizations can provide challenges and opportunities for learning. Lateral moves are one option. Another option is to involve the employee in project teams that provide new tasks and skill development. The key is to keep the work stimulating and involving. Individuals at this stage also need continued affirmation of their value to the organization. They need to know that their contributions are significant and appreciated.[87]

Becoming a Mentor

During maintenance, individuals can make a contribution by sharing their wealth of knowledge and experience with others. Opportunities to be mentors to new employees can keep senior workers motivated and involved in the organization. It is important for organizations to reward mentors for the time and energy they expend. Some employees adapt naturally to the mentor role, but others may need training on how to coach and counsel junior workers.

Maintenance is a time of transition, like all career stages. It can be managed by individuals who know what to expect and plan to remain productive, as well as by organizations that focus on maximizing employee involvement in work. According to Levinson, during the latter part of the maintenance stage, another life transition occurs. The age-50 transition is another time of reevaluating the dream and working further on the issues raised in the midlife transition. Following the age-50 transition is a fairly stable period. During this time, individuals begin to plan seriously for withdrawing from their careers. It is important for organizations to reward mentors for the time and energy they expend. Kram notes that there are four keys to the success of a formal mentoring program: (1) participation should be voluntary. No one should be forced to enter a mentoring relationship, and careful matching of mentors and protégés is important; (2) support from top executives is needed to convey the intent of the program and its role in career development; (3) training should be provided to mentors so they understand the functions of the relationship and (4) a graceful exit should be provided for mismatches or for people in mentoring relationships who have fulfilled their purpose.[88]

18-7 THE WITHDRAWAL STAGE

The withdrawal stage usually occurs later in life and signals that a long period of continuous employment

career plateau A point in an individual's career in which the probability of moving further up the hierarchy is low.

will soon come to a close. Older workers may face discrimination and stereotyping. They may be viewed by others as less productive, more resistant to change, and less motivated. However, older workers are one of the most undervalued groups in the workforce. They can provide continuity in the midst of change and can serve as mentors and role models to younger generations of employees.

Discrimination against older workers is prohibited by law. Organizations must create a culture that values older workers' contributions. With their level of experience, strong work ethic, and loyalty, these workers have much to contribute. In fact, older workers have lower rates of tardiness and absenteeism, are more safety conscious, and are more satisfied with their jobs than are younger workers.[89]

Planning for Change

The decision to retire is an individual one, but the need for planning is universal. A retired sales executive from Boise Cascade said that the best advice is to "plan no unplanned retirement."[90] This means carefully planning not only the transition but also the activities an individual will be involved in once the transition is made. All the options should be open for consideration. One recent trend is the need for temporary top-level executives. Some companies are hiring senior managers from the outside on a temporary basis. The qualities of a good temporary executive include substantial high-level management experience, financial security that allows the executive to choose only assignments that really interest them, and a willingness to relocate.[91] Some individuals at the withdrawal stage find this an attractive option.

Planning for retirement should include not only financial planning but also a plan for psychologically withdrawing from work. The pursuit of hobbies and travel, volunteer work, or more time with extended family can all be part of the plan. The key is to plan early and carefully, as well as to anticipate the transition with a positive attitude and a full slate of desirable activities.

phased retirement An arrangement that allows employees to reduce their hours and/or responsibilities in order to ease into retirement.

bridge employment Employment that takes place after a person retires from a full-time position but before the person's permanent withdrawal from the workforce.

Retirement

There are several retirement trends right now, ranging from early retirement to phased retirement to never retiring. Some adults are choosing a combination of these options, leaving their first career for some time off before reentering the workforce either part-time or full-time doing something they enjoy. For more and more North Americans, the idea of a retirement spent sitting beside a swimming pool sounds—for lack of a better word—boring. Factors that influence the decision of when to retire include company policy, financial considerations, family support or pressure, health, and opportunities for other productive activities.[92]

During the withdrawal stage, the individual faces a major life transition that Levinson refers to as the late adulthood transition (ages 60 to 65). A person's own mortality becomes a major concern and the loss of family members and friends becomes more frequent. The person works to achieve a sense of integrity in life—that is, the person works to find the encompassing meaning and value in life.

Retirement need not be a complete cessation of work. Many alternative work arrangements can be considered, and many organizations offer flexibility in these options. **Phased retirement** is a popular option for retirement-age workers who want to gradually reduce their hours and/or responsibilities. There are many forms of phased retirement, including reduced workdays or workweeks, job sharing, and consulting and mentoring arrangements. Many organizations cannot afford the loss of large numbers of experienced employees at once. This means there is an increase in **bridge employment**, which is employment that takes place after a person retires from a full-time position but before the person's permanent withdrawal from the workforce. Bridge employment is related to retirement satisfaction and overall life satisfaction.[93]

Some companies are helping employees transition to retirement in innovative ways. Retired individuals can continue their affiliation with the organization by serving as mentors to employees who are embarking on retirement planning or other career transitions. This helps diminish the fear of loss some people have about retirement because the retiree has an option to serve as a mentor or consultant to the organization.

Some retirement-agers may go through a second midlife "crisis." Vickie Ianucelli, for example, bought a condo on a Mexican beach, celebrated a birthday in Paris, bought herself a 9.5-karat ring, and got plastic surgery. She's a psychologist who is also a 60-plus grandmother of two.[94]

Lawrence Livermore National Labs (LLNL) employs some of the best research minds in the world. And when these great minds retire from full-time work, they have numerous opportunities to continue contributing. LLNL's retiree program website lists a wide variety of requests, ranging from guiding tours and making phone calls to providing guidance on current research and helping researchers make contact with other researchers.[95] Programs like this one help LLNL avoid the typical knowledge drain that takes place when seasoned veteran employees retire.

18-8 CAREER ANCHORS

Much of an individual's self-concept rests upon a career. Over the course of the career, career anchors are developed. **Career anchors** are self-perceived talents, motives, and values that guide an individual's career decisions.[96] Schein developed the concept of career anchors based on a 12-year study of MBA graduates from the Massachusetts Institute of Technology (MIT). Schein found great diversity in the graduates' career histories but great similarities in the way they explained the career decisions they had made.[97] From extensive interviews with the graduates, Schein developed the career anchors.

There are five career anchors.

1. *Technical/functional competence.* Individuals who hold this career anchor want to specialize in a given functional area (for example, finance or marketing) and become competent. The idea of general management does not interest them.
2. *Managerial competence.* Adapting this career anchor means individuals want general management responsibility. They want to see their efforts have an impact on organizational effectiveness.
3. *Autonomy and independence.* Freedom is the key to this career anchor, and often these individuals are uncomfortable working in large organizations. Autonomous careers such as writer, professor, or consultant attract these individuals.
4. *Creativity.* Individuals holding this career anchor feel a strong need to create something. They are often entrepreneurs.
5. *Security/stability.* Long-term career stability, whether in a single organization or in a single geographic area, fits people with this career anchor. Some government jobs provide this type of security.

Career anchors emerge over time and may be modified by work or life experiences.[98] The importance of knowing your career anchor is that it can help you find a match between you and an organization. For example, individuals with creativity as an anchor may find themselves stifled in bureaucratic organizations. Textbook sales may not be the place for an individual with a security anchor because of the frequent travel and seasonal nature of the business.

18-9 CAREER RESOURCES

In the last section of the book, the focus will move from the theoretical to the applied. There are some key individual, team, and organizational skills required to manage your career well. As Figure 18.4 shows, there are some key drivers today that will shape the sorts of skills that you will need in a very few years.

First, you need to develop a good understanding of who you are, what you value, what you do well, and what you need to improve. In addition to the material in Part 2 of the book, there are many tools to help you. The most popular is Richard N. Bolles's *What Color Is My Parachute? A Practical Manual for Job-Hunters and Career-Changers*. It was originally self-published in 1970, is updated annually, and now sells 20,000 copies monthly! Another valuable resource is Daniel Pink's *The Adventures of Johnny Bunko—The Last Career Guide You'll Ever Need*, a manga-style business book that has been translated into more than 10 languages and received many awards. As well, here are some useful career management websites:

1. https://www.glassdoor.com
2. https://www.talentegg.com
3. https://www.vault.com
4. https://www.workopolis.com
5. http://www.canadastop100.com/national
6. https://www.tenthousandcoffees.com

As much of your work will be done in teams, it is vital that you understand team dynamics and team decision making, discussed in Chapters 7 and 9. In addition, there are many books on teams. One that has become popular for its storytelling style, coupled with its rich insights, is Patrick M. Lencioni's *The Five Dysfunctions of a Team: A Leadership Fable*. He identifies five significant and typical problems in teams and then suggests way to address them.

In Chapter 13, you learned about organizational culture and its impact on shaping behaviour in organizations. It is vitally important that you understand the nuances of organizational life so that you don't make career-limiting errors or

career anchors A network of self-perceived talents, motives, and values that guide an individual's career decisions.

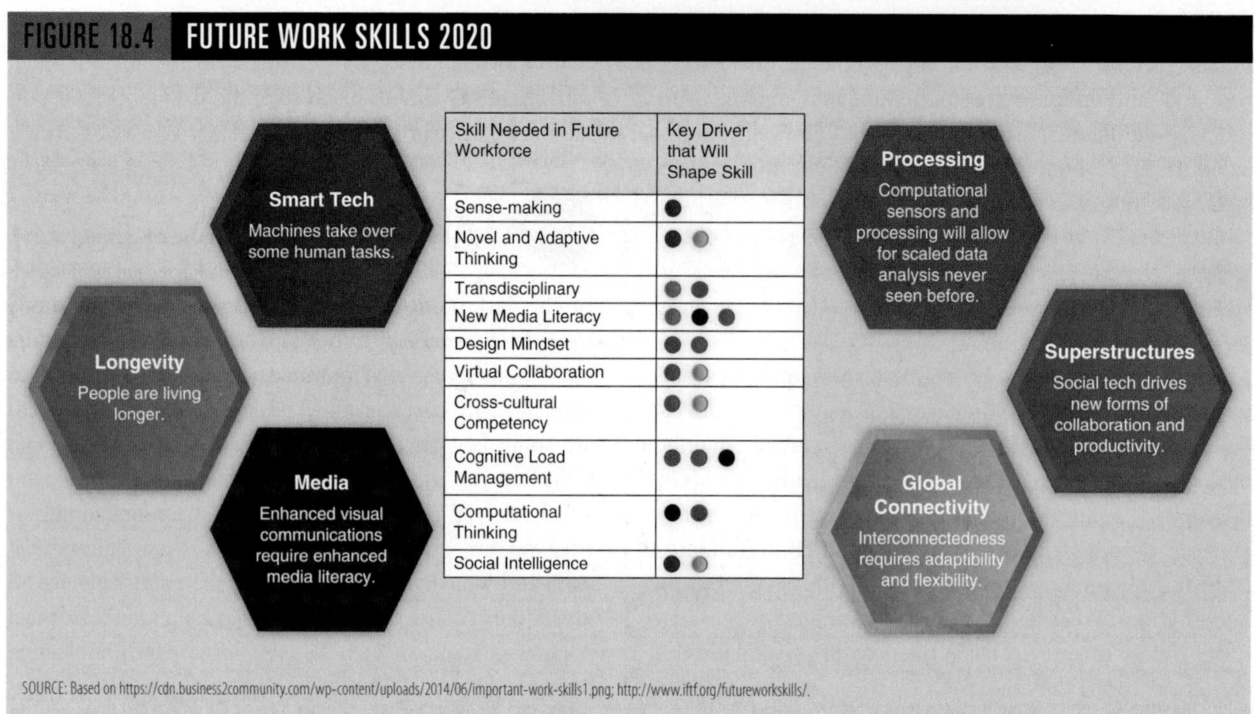
Smart Tech
Machines take over some human tasks.
Longevity
People are living longer.
Media
Enhanced visual communications require enhanced media literacy.
Skill Needed in Future Workforce
Key Driver that Will Shape Skill
Sense-making
Novel and Adaptive Thinking
Transdisciplinary
New Media Literacy
Design Mindset
Virtual Collaboration
Cross-cultural Competency
Cognitive Load Management
Computational Thinking
Social Intelligence
Processing
Computational sensors and processing will allow for scaled data analysis never seen before.
Superstructures
Social tech drives new forms of collaboration and productivity.
Global Connectivity
Interconnectedness requires adaptibility and flexibility.

FIGURE 18.4 FUTURE WORK SKILLS 2020

SOURCE: Based on https://cdn.business2community.com/wp-content/uploads/2014/06/important-work-skills1.png; http://www.iftf.org/futureworkskills/.

engage in career-killer behaviours. To address career-limiting or -killing behaviour, you have to be brutally honest with yourself to assess, for example, if you are self-absorbed, needy, boring, mechanical, judgmental, insensitive, or overly self-promoting.[99]

As you prepare for the world of work, take time for self-assessment, work on your team skills, and research in detail the organizations you are interested in and then determine the extent to which you fit. Remember, your career is a journey and there will be many good times if you work hard at managing your career. Throughout your career, be sure to have regular discussions with your mentor and/or your boss about your career path and your progress on the path.[100]

STUDY TOOLS 18

IN THE BOOK YOU CAN ...

- ☐ Rip out the **Chapter Review card** at the end of the book to review Key Concepts and Key Terms.
- ☐ Take a "What about You?" Quiz related to material in the chapter.
- ☐ Read additional cases in the Mini Case and Shopify Running Case sections.

ONLINE YOU CAN ...

NELSON.COM/STUDENT

- ☐ Take a "What about You?" Quiz related to material in the chapter.
- ☐ Test your understanding with a quick Multiple-Choice Pre-Test quiz.
- ☐ Read the eBook, which includes discussion points for questions posed in the Cases.
- ☐ Watch Videos related to chapter content.
- ☐ Use the available Flashcards and Matching Quizzes to test your understanding of key terms and concepts.
- ☐ See how much you've learned by taking a Post-Test.

WHAT ABOUT YOU?

Assess Your Flexibility Skills

Use the following scale to rate the frequency with which you perform the behaviours described in each question. Place the corresponding number (1–7) in the blank preceding the statement.

RARELY	1
IRREGULARLY	2
OCCASIONALLY	3
USUALLY	4
FREQUENTLY	5
ALMOST ALWAYS	6
CONSISTENTLY	7

____ **1.** I manage a variety of assignments with varying demands and complexities.

____ **2.** I adjust work plans to account for new circumstances.

____ **3.** I modify rules and procedures in order to meet operational needs and goals.

____ **4.** I work with ambiguous assignments when necessary and use these when possible to further my goals and objectives.

____ **5.** I rearrange work or personal schedules to meet deadlines.

____ **6.** In emergencies, I respond to the most pressing needs first.

____ **7.** I change my priorities to accommodate unexpected events.

____ **8.** I manage my personal work overload by seeking assistance or by delegating responsibility to others.

____ **9.** I vary the way I deal with others according to their needs and personalities.

____ **10.** I help others improve their job performance, or I assign tasks that will further their development.

____ **11.** I accept the authority of my manager but continue to demonstrate my initiative and assertiveness.

____ **12.** I work well with all types of personalities.

____ **13.** I measure my performance on the job against the feedback I receive.

____ **14.** I correct performance deficits that have been brought to my attention.

____ **15.** When I disagree with my manager's appraisal of my work, I discuss our differences.

____ **16.** I seek training and assignments that can help me improve my job-related skills.

____ **17.** In disagreements concerning work-related issues, I look at matters impersonally and concentrate on the facts.

____ **18.** I make compromises to get problems moving toward resolution.

____ **19.** I look for new and better ways to accomplish my duties and responsibilities.

____ **20.** I offer to negotiate all the areas of disagreement.

Figure A: Flexible Behaviours Questionnaire (FBQ) Scoring

SKILL AREA	ITEMS	SCORE
Working with new, changing, and ambiguous situations	1, 2, 3, 4	
Working under pressure	5, 6, 7, 8	
Dealing with different personal styles	9, 10, 11, 12	
Handling feedback	13, 14, 15, 16	
Resolving conflicts	17, 18, 19, 20	
TOTAL SCORE		

FBQ Scoring

The scoring sheet in Figure A summarizes your responses for the FBQ. It will help you identify your existing strengths and pinpoint areas that need improvement.

FBQ Evaluation

Figure B shows score lines for your total score and for each category measured on the FBQ. Each line shows a continuum from the lowest score to the highest.

The score lines in Figure B show graphically where you stand with regard to the five flexible behaviours. If you have been honest with yourself, you now have a better idea of your relative strengths and weaknesses in the categories that make up the skills of flexibility.

Figure B: Flexible Behaviours Questionnaire (FBQ) Evaluation

TOTAL SCORE

Lowest score	20	50	80	110	140	Highest score

CATEGORY SCORES

Working with new, changing, and ambiguous situations

4	10	16	22	28

Working under pressure

4	10	16	22	28

Dealing with different personality styles

4	10	16	22	28

Handling feedback

4	10	16	22	28

Resolving conflicts

4	10	16	22	28

SOURCE: From Fandt. *Management Skills*, 1E. © 1994 Custom Solutions, a part of Cengage Inc. Reproduced by permission. www.cengage.com/permissions

MINI CASE

My Friend Morgan

You have just hung up from speaking with your friend Morgan and your supervisor is due in your office any time now.

You have known Morgan for many years. You attended the same high school and knew Morgan as an acquaintance but wouldn't say the two of you were friends. Whereas you enjoyed academic and athletic pursuits, Morgan was rebellious and often in trouble. During high school, it was a known fact that Morgan had been caught shoplifting but didn't suffer any real consequences. You saw Morgan cheat on exams in high school on more than one occasion. You also know that Morgan had confessed to often stealing money from their parents and would arrive late and leave early from a part-time job at the local McDonald's but would write in the full shift on time sheets.

You and Morgan both attended the same university nearly 500 miles away. You each majored in business, had a couple of classes together, and began sharing rides home. You got to know Morgan, and you were even glad to see a familiar face while you were so far from home. You were both accepted into the university's MBA program, and over the course of these university years, you became very good friends with Morgan; you were even in Morgan's wedding following graduation. Coincidentally, you both received attractive job offers (in separate departments) from the major employer in your hometown; you both accepted the offers and returned home.

Morgan and their spouse frequently socialize with you and your spouse. They often come over on weekends, and you usually meet for lunch at least once a week. Although Morgan has matured and "straightened out" for the most part, you believe that Morgan's ethical and moral standards are sometimes questionable. For example, last fall Morgan was caught being unfaithful. Thankfully, they were able to repair their marriage, and this has never happened again. Morgan has also confessed to you that they recently lied to a supervisor to gain additional time to finish an assignment. Morgan often copies and mails personal items at the company's expense and even failed to report to payroll that a personal expenditure had not been deducted from the last paycheque. Furthermore, Morgan cheated on income taxes a few years ago. You don't mean to be keeping an ethics balance sheet on Morgan, but you have had several private discussions with Morgan regarding the questionable nature of these types of behaviours. You believe that these conversations have helped Morgan to see things in a new light and have positively impacted their behaviour.

You've recently been promoted to District 4 manager. Your regional manager is on her way to meet with you to get your recommendation for filling the District 3 manager position.

Morgan has just phoned to ask for your support and recommendation for this position. To Morgan's benefit, they have been a hard worker for this company, has always had positive evaluations, and is well liked. Although you feel loyalty to Morgan and know that Morgan is a good employee, you also want to make a good impression in your new position and wonder if Morgan is really the best (and safest) person to recommend for the job.

Your regional manager has just arrived at your office. She gets right to the point, asking if you have any recommendations for the District 3 manager's position. Do you recommend Morgan?

Apply Your Understanding

1. What responsibilities or obligations do the reader and Morgan owe to themselves, the organization, their profession, their peers, and the business community?
2. What are the implications of their behaviour and decisions?
3. Does a company have the right to know about employees' off-work behaviour? At what point does personal life spill over into work life?

SHOPIFY RUNNING CASE

DEV DEGREE ADDRESSING BRAIN GAIN

Shopify is expanding and has many openings. It is interested in candidates who have impact and are ambitious. There are many roles from internships to UX developers to director of datastores. As described elsewhere in this book, it would seem that people enjoy working at Shopify. Its overall rating is 4.1 out of 5 from 312 reviewers on Glassdoor.ca. Seventy-nine percent of the reviewers would recommend Shopify to their friends while 90 percent approved of the CEO, Tobias Lutke. Here is a small sample of the comments on Glassdoor: (1) "Finally a place for me"; (2) "Great place to work"; and (3) "No better place for growth."

Shopify recognizes that there is a "brain gain" in Canada. The company has created a program called Dev Degree, which integrated work and learning. It combines a degree from Carleton University with a co-op experience. Students work with mentors to gain essential skills and address real workplace technological challenges. Shopify recently was recognized as the Top Toronto Employer Brand in Hired's Brand Health Report. Hired's 2017 list of organizations' brand positivity placed Shopify third, after SpaceX in Los Angeles and Google in the San Francisco area.

Michael Nagle/Bloomberg via Getty Images

Shopify seems to be addressing the issue of how to make the organization more diverse and inclusive. According to Satish Kanwar, VP & GM of Channels, Shopify is intentional about its diversity and inclusion work. He has noted that diverse teams in inclusive environments have clear bottom-line results—better organizations, happier employees, and stronger financial outcomes.

SOURCES: "Shopify," accessed from https://www.glassdoor.ca/Benefits/Shopify-Canada-Benefits-EI_IE675933.0,7_IL.8,14_IN3.htm, September 28, 2018; J-M. Lemieux, B. Dorland, and I. Givoni, "How to Sustain Canada's Brain Gain," *The Globe and Mail*, May 31, 2018, accessed from https://www.theglobeandmail.com/business/commentary/article-how-to-sustain-canadas-brain-gain, September 28, 2018; "2017 Global Brand Health Report," *Hired*, accessed from https://hired.com/blog/highlights/hired-brand-health-report-2017, September 28, 2018; E. Blaskie, "Satish Kanwar, Shopify, on the Importance of Diversity and Inclusivity," September 18, 2018, accessed from https://www.l-spark.com/satish-kanwar-shopify-on-the-importance-of-diversity-and-inclusivity, September 28, 2018.

Apply Your Understanding

1. What accounts for Shopify's positive ratings?
2. Would you like to work there? Why or why not?
3. Should other organization develop programs like Dev Degree? Why? Why not?

NOTES

1

1. H. Schwartz, "The Clockwork or the Snakepit: An Essay on the Meaning of Teaching Organizational Behavior," *Organizational Behavior Teaching Review* 11, No. 2 (1987): 19–26.

2. Ibid.

3. L. G. Bolman and T. E. Deal, *Reframing Organizations: Artistry, Choice, and Leadership*, 6th ed. (Hoboken, New Jersey: John Wiley & Sons, 2017).

4. H. G. Barkem, J.A.C. Baum and E.A. Mannix, "Management Challenges in a New Time," *Academy of Management Journal*, 45 (2002): 916–930.

5. K. Lewin, "Field Theory in Social Science," selected theoretical papers (edited by Dorin Cartwright) (New York: Harper, 1951).

6. N. Schmitt, ed., *Industrial/Organizational Section in Encyclopedia of Psychology* (Washington, D.C.: American Psychological Association, and New York: Oxford University Press, 2000).

7. "Personality in the Workplace: Why It's Important & 5 Tests to Measure It," accessed from https://tech.co/personality-workplace-important-5-tests-measure-2015-07.

8. R. L. Daft and A. Armstrong, *Organization Theory and Design*, 3rd CE (Toronto: Nelson, 2015).

9. F. W. Taylor, *The Principles of Scientific Management* (New York: Norton, 1911).

10. E. A. Locke and G. P. Latham, *A Theory of Goal Setting and Task Performance* (Englewood Cliffs, NJ: Prentice-Hall, 1990).

11. A. L. Wilkins and W. G. Ouchi, "Efficient Cultures: Exploring the Relationship between Culture and Organizational Performance," *Administrative Science Quarterly* 28 (1983): 468–481.

12. M. F. R. Kets de Vries and D. Miller, "Personality, Culture, and Organization," *Academy of Management Review* 11 (1986): 266–279.

13. T. Kelly and D. Kelly, "Why Designers Need Empathy," Slate, November 8, 2013, accessed from http://www.slate.com/blogs/the_eye/2013/11/08/empathize_with_your_end_user_creative_confidence_by_tom_and_david_kelley.html, May 4, 2018.

14. IDEO, Work Blog Tools, accessed from https://www.ideo.com, June 22, 2018.

15. H. B. Elkind, *Preventive Management: Mental Hygiene in Industry* (New York: B. C. Forbes, 1931).

16. J. C. Quick, "Occupational Health Psychology: Historical Roots and Future Directions," *Health Psychology* 18 (1999).

17. V. Graham, Hershey Canada Inc. "Fit For Life" Worksite Wellness Program, presented at Canadian Labour and Business Centre (CLBC) Workplace Health Works, November 18–19, 2003.

18. D. R. Ilgen, "Health Issues at Work," *American Psychologist* 45 (1990): 273–283.

19. "Meaning and Definition of Economics" accessed from https://www.newagepublishers.com/samplechapter/001983.pdf, May 4, 2018.

20. Sherman, M., "Canadian Businesses Jumping on Behavioural Economics Bandwagon," *The Globe and Mail*, February 13, 2016, accessed from https://www.theglobeandmail.com/report-on-business/rob-commentary/canadian-business-jumping-on-the-behavioural-economics-bandwagon/article28747073/, May 4, 2018.

21. B. M. Staw, L. E. Sandelands, and J. E. Dutton, "Threat-Rigidity Effects in Organizational Behavior: A Multilevel Analysis," *Administrative Science Quarterly* 26 (1981): 501–524.

22. D. Kirkpatrick, "The Net Makes It All Easier—Including Exporting U.S. Jobs," *Fortune* (May 26, 2003): 146.

23. E. V. Brown, Vice President of Global Business Development, Alberto Culver, Inc., "Commencement Address—College of Business Administration, the University of Texas at Arlington" (December 2003).

24. T. Reay, K. Golden-Biddle, and K. Germann, "Legitimizing a New Role: Small Wins and Microprocesses of Change," *Academy of Management Journal* 49 (2006): 977–998.

25. R. L. A. Sterba, "The Organization and Management of the Temple Corporations in Ancient Mesopotamia," *Academy of Management Review* 1 (1976): 16–26; S. P. Dorsey, *Early English Churches in America* (New York: Oxford University Press, 1952).

26. Sir I. Moncreiffe, *The Highland Clans: The Dynastic Origins, Chiefs, and Background of the Clans and of Some Other Families Connected to Highland History*, rev. ed. (New York: C. N. Potter, 1982); D. Shambaugh, "The Soldier and the State in China: The Political Work System in the People's Liberation Army," *Chinese Quarterly* 127 (1991): 527–568.

27. L. L'Abate, ed., *Handbook of Developmental Family Psychology and Psychopathology* (New York: Wiley, 1993); J. A. Hostetler, *Communitarian Societies* (New York: Holt, Rinehart & Winston, 1974).

28. J. M. Lewis, "The Family System and Physical Illness," *No Single Thread: Psychological Health in Family Systems* (New York: Brunner/Mazel, 1976).

29. J. D. Thompson, *Organizations in Action* (New York: McGraw-Hill, 1967).

30. "Businesses Say They're Worried about Future after GreenON Rebate Program Cancellation," June 20, 2018, accessed from https://globalnews.ca/video/4287029/businesses-say-theyre-worried-about-future-after-greenon-rebate-program-cancellation, August 30, 2018.

31. F. J. Roethlisberger and W. J. Dickson, *Management and the Worker* (Cambridge, MA: Harvard University Press, 1939).

32. G. Wickstrom and T. Bendix, The "Hawthorne Effect"—What Did the Original Hawthorne Studies Actually Show?, *Scandinavian Journal of Work, Environment & Health* 26, No. 4 (August 2000) 363–367.

33. W. L. French and C. H. Bell, *Organization Development*, 4th ed. (Englewood Cliffs, NJ: Prentice-Hall, 1990).

34. S. G. Barsade and D. E. Gibson, "Why Does Affect Matter in Organizations?" *Academy of Management Perspectives* 21 (2007): 36–59.

35. J. P. Kotter, "Managing External Dependence," *Academy of Management Review* 4 (1979): 87–92.

36. H. K. Steensma and D. G. Corley, "Organizational Context as a Moderator of Theories on Firm Boundaries for Technology Sourcing," *Academy of Management Journal* 44 (2001): 271–291.

37. T. B. Lawrence and V.Corwin, "Being There: The Acceptance and Marginalization of Part-time Professional Employees," *Journal of Organizational Behavior* 24 (2003): 923–943.

38. M. K. Gowing, J. D. Kraft, and J. C. Quick, *The New Organizational*

Reality: Downsizing, Restructuring and Revitalization (Washington, D.C.: American Psychological Association, 1998); T. Tang and R. M. Fuller, "Corporate Downsizing: What Managers Can Do to Lessen the Negative Effects of Layoffs," *SAM Advanced Management Journal* 60 (1995): 12–15, 31.

39. L. R. Offermann and M. K. Gowing, "Organizations of the Future," *American Psychologist* 45 (1990): 95–108.

40. J. Chatman, J. Polzer, S. Barsade, and M. Neale, "Being Different Yet Feeling Similar: The Influence of Demographic Composition and Organizational Culture on Work Processes and Outcomes," *Administrative Science Quarterly* 43 (1998): 749–780.

41. L. E. Thurow, *Head to Head: The Coming Economic Battle among Japan, Europe, and America* (New York: William Morrow, 1992).

42. J. E. Patterson, *Acquiring the Future: America's Survival and Success in the Global Economy* (Homewood, IL: Dow Jones-Irwin, 1990); H. B. Stewart, *Recollecting the Future: A View of Business, Technology, and Innovation in the Next 30 Years* (Homewood, IL: Dow Jones-Irwin, 1989).

43. D. Ciampa, *Total Quality* (Reading, MA: Addison-Wesley, 1992).

44. Aguntuk, "Toyota President Akio Toyoda Tearful After Congressional Hearing, Vows to Regain Customer Trust," *The Tech Journal*, February 25, 2010, https://thetechjournal.com/off-topic/toyota-president-akio-toyoda-tearful-after-congressional-hearing-vows-to-regain-customer-trust.xhtml. Reprinted by permission.

45. T. J. Douglas and W. Q. Judge, Jr., "Total Quality Management Implementation and Competitive Advantage: The Role of Structural Control and Exploration," *Academy of Management Journal* 44 (2001): 158–169.

46. American Management Association, *Blueprints for Service Quality: The Federal Express Approach* (New York: American Management Association, 1991); P. R. Thomas, L. J. Gallace, and K. R. Martin, *Quality Alone Is Not Enough* (New York: American Management Association, 1992).

47. "2009 Canada Awards for Excellence Recipients," http://www.nqi.ca/galadinner/2009CAEVideos.aspx.

48. J. de Mast, "A Methodological Comparison of Three Strategies for Quality Improvement," *International Journal of Quality & Reliability Management* 21 (2004): 198–213.

49. M. Barney, "Motorola's Second Generation," *Six Sigma Forum Magazine* 1(3) (May 2002): 13.

50. J. A. Edosomwan, "Six Commandments to Empower Employees for Quality Improvement," *Industrial Engineering* 24 (1992): 14–15.

51. "What Is Six Sigma?" accessed from https://www.isixsigma.com/new-to-six-sigma/getting-started/what-six-sigma, June 22, 2018.

52. L. Proserpio and D. A. Gioia, "Teaching the Virtual Generation," *Academy of Management Learning & Education* 6 (2007): 69–80.

53. R. M. Steers, L. W. Porter, and G. A. Bigley, *Motivation and Leadership at Work* (New York: McGraw-Hill, 1996).

54. H. Levinson, *Executive Stress* (New York: New American Library, 1975).

55. Government of Canada, "Understanding Essential Skills," accessed form https://www.canada.ca/en/employment-social-development/programs/essential-skills/definitions.html

56. C. Argyris and D. A. Schon, *Organizational Learning: A Theory of Action Perspective* (Reading, MA: Addison-Wesley, 1978).

57. A. Y. Kolb and D. A. Kolb, "Learning Styles and Learning Spaces: Enhancing Experiential Learning in Higher Education" *Academy of Management Learning & Education* 4 (2005): 193–212.

58. D. A. Kolb, *Experiential Learning: Experience as the Source of Learning and Development* (Englewood Cliffs, N.J.: Prentice Hall, 1984).

59. B. Breen, "The Business of Design," *Fast Company* (April 1, 2005) http://www.fastcompany.com/magazine/93/design.html.

60. Ibid.

61. "The Academic: Roger Martin," *BusinessWeek* (August 1, 2005), accessed from http://www.businessweek.com/magazine/content/05_31/b3945417.htm.

62. C. Atkinson, "Software Firm Provides Time for 'Personal Pet Projects,'" *Report on Business* (June 2, 2010) accessed from http://www.theglobeandmail.com/report-on-business/your-business/grow/new-product-development/fusenet-creates-friday-labs-to-spur-enterprising-staffers/article1589169/ ?cmpid=rss1.

2

1. M. A. Hitt, R. E. Hoskisson, and J. S. Harrison, "Strategic Competitiveness in the 1990s: Challenges and Opportunities for U.S. Executives," *Academy of Management Executive* 5 (1991): 7–22.

2. H. G. Barkem, J. A. C. Baum, and E. A. Mannix, "Management Challenges in a New Time," *Academy of Management Journal* 45 (2002): 916–930.

3. Business Council of Canada, "Business Council calls on federal government to address Canada's competitiveness challenges," December 14 2017, accessed from http://thebusinesscouncil.ca/news/budget2018/, July 1 2018.

4. "The Post-Recession Outlook: Canada's Key Economic Strengths and Challenges," remarks prepared for the Honourable John Manley, CEO of CCCE, http://www.ceocouncil.ca/en/view/?area_id=1&document_id=1396.

5. C. Wong. "Pace of Economic Growth Slowed in First Quarter: Statistics Canada," *Toronto Star*, May 31, 2018, accessed from https://www.thestar.com/business/economy/2018/05/31/pace-of-economic-growth-slowed-in-first-quarter-statistics-canada.html, July 1, 2018.

6. Business Council of Canada, "Business Council Calls on Federal Government to Address Canada's Competitiveness Challenges,' December 14 2017, accessed from http://thebusinesscouncil.ca/news/budget2018/, July 1, 2018.

7. K. Sera, "Corporate Globalization: A New Trend," *Academy of Management Executive* 6 (1992): 89–96.

8. K. Ohmae, *Borderless World: Power and Strategies in the Interlinked Economy* (New York: Harper & Row, 1990).

9. C. A. Bartlett and S. Ghoshal, *Managing across Borders: The Transnational Solution* (Boston, MA: Harvard Business School Press, 1989).

10. H. W. Arthurs, "The Hollowing Out of Corporate Canada?" (n.d.), http://www.yorku.ca/robarts/archives/pub_domain/pdf/apd_arthurs.pdf.

11. F. Warner, "Learning How to Speak to Gen Y," *Fast Company* 72 (July 2003): 36–37.

12. K. R. Xin and J. L. Pearce, "Guanxi: Connections as Substitutes for Formal Institutional Support," *Academy of Management Journal* 39 (1996): 1641–1658.

13. P. S. Chan, "Franchise Management in East Asia," *Academy of Management Executive* 4 (1990): 75–85.

14. H. Weihrich, "Europe 1992: What the Future May Hold," *Academy of Management Executive* 4 (1990): 7–18.

15. E. H. Schein, "Coming to a New Awareness of Organizational Culture," *MIT Sloan Management Review* 25 (1984): 3–16.

16. S. S. Sarwano and R. M. Armstrong, "Microcultural Differences and Perceived Ethical Problems: An International Business Perspective," *Journal of Business Ethics* 30 (2001): 41–56.

17. R. Sharpe, "Hi-Tech Taboos," *The Wall Street Journal* (October 31, 1995): A1.

18. G. Hofstede, *Culture's Consequences: International Differences in Work-related Values* (Beverly Hills, Calif.: SAGE Publications, 1980).

19. G. Hofstede, "Motivation, Leadership, and Organization: Do American Theories Apply Abroad?" *Organizational Dynamics* (Summer 1980): 42–63.

20. G. M. Spreitzer, M. W. McCall, Jr., and J. D. Mahoney, "Early Identification of International Executive Potential," *Journal of Applied Psychology* 82 (1997): 6–29.

21. M. A. Hitt, L. Bierman, K. Uhlenbruck, and K. Shimizu, "The Importance of Resources in the Internationalization of Professional Service Firms: The Good, the Bad, and the Ugly," *Academy of Management Journal* 49 (2006): 1137–1157.

22. A. J. Michel, "Goodbyes Can Cost Plenty in Europe," *Fortune* (April 6, 1992): 16.

23. "Hofstede's Cultural Dimensions, Understanding Workplace Values Around the World," http://www.mindtools.com/pages/article/newLDR_66.htm.

24. G. Hofstede, "Gender Stereotypes and Partner Preferences of Asian Women in Masculine and Feminine Countries," *Journal of Cross Cultural Psychology* 27 (1996): 533–546.

25. G. Hofstede, "Cultural Constraints in Management Theories," *Academy of Management Executive* 7 (1993): 81–94.

26. Indulgence Vs. Restraint—The 6th Dimension, November 1, 2013, accessed from https://www.communicaid.com/cross-cultural-training/blog/indulgence-vs-restraint-6th-dimension/, July 1, 2018.

27. E. Brandt, "Global HR," *Personnel Journal* 70 (1991): 38–44.

28. L. Hartley, "The Roots of Conflict: A Conversation with Michelle LeBaron," *Fieldnotes* (April 1–4, 2005): 9.

29. G. Lubin, "These 8 Scales Reveal Everything You Should Know About Different Cultures," June 20, 2015, accessed from http://www.businessinsider.com/the-culture-map-8-scales-for-work-2015-1, July 1, 2018.

30. Country Mapping Tool, Canada, accessed from https://www.erinmeyer.com/culturemap/, July 1, 2018.

31. P. Chattopadhyay, "Can Dissimilarity Lead to Positive Outcomes: The Influence of Open versus Closed Minds," *Journal of Organizational Behavior* 24 (2003): 295–312.

32. R. Caballero and R. Yerema (2010). "Agrium," http://www.eluta.ca/diversity-at-agrium.

33. S. Block, "How Do Race and Gender Factor into Income Inequality?" 2010, accessed from http://www.policyalternatives.ca/sites/default/files/uploads/publications/reports/docs/The%20Role%20of%20Race%20Ontario%20Growing% 20Gap.pdf.

34. S. Caudron, "Task Force Report Reveals Coke's Progress on Diversity," *Workforce* 82 (2003): 40, accessed from http://www.workforceonline.com/section/03/ feature/23/42/44/234246.html.

35. T. Perkins, "How RBC Became a Champion of Diversity," *Report on Business* (March 24, 2010), accessed from http://www.theglobeandmail.com/report-on-business/managing/how-rbc-became-a-champion-of-diversity/article1508812.

36. D. Tencer, "Look How Much Smaller Canada's Economy Would Be Without Women," Huffpost, March 8, 2018, accessed from https://www.huffingtonpost.ca/2018/03/08/women-workforce-canada_a_23380416/, July 2, 2018.

37. Rosenzweig & Company, "Women in Canada's Top Corporate Jobs Still Less Than 10 Per Cent," March 7, 2018, accessed from https://www.newswire.ca/news-releases/women-in-canadas-top-corporate-jobs-still-less-than-10-per-cent-676121373.html, July 2, 2018.

38. A. M. Morrison, R. P. White, E. Van Velsor, and the Center for Creative Leadership, *Breaking the Glass Ceiling: Can Women Reach the Top of America's Largest Corporations?* (Reading, Mass.: Addison-Wesley, 1987).

39. HR Reporter, "How HR Can Move the Needle and Get Women on Boards," November 6, 2017, accessed from http://www.hrreporter.com/columnist/the-c-suite/archive/2017/11/06/how-hr-can-move-the-needle-and-get-women-on-boards, July 2, 2018.

40. S. Whawell, "Women Are Shattering the Glass Ceiling Only to Fall Off the Glass Cliff," The Conversation, April 12, 2018, accessed from http://theconversation.com/women-are-shattering-the-glass-ceiling-only-to-fall-off-the-glass-cliff-94071, July 2, 2018.

41. "Women CEOs who Broke the Glass Ceiling in India," December 1, 2009, accessed from http://business.rediff.com/slide-show/2009/dec/01/slide-show-1-more-women-ceos-in-india-than-abroad.htm#contentTop, August 30, 2018.

42. Ibid.

43. L. L. Martins and C. K. Parsons, "Effects of Gender Diversity Management on Perceptions of Organizational Attractiveness: The Role of Individual Differences in Attitudes and Beliefs," *Journal of Applied Psychology* 92 (2007): 865–875.

44. A. Eyring and B. A. Stead, "Shattering the Glass Ceiling: Some Successful Corporate Practices," *Journal of Business Ethics* 17 (1998): 245–251.

45. Catalyst, *Advancing Women in Business: The Catalyst Guide* (San Francisco, CA: Jossey-Bass, 1998).

46. D. L. Nelson and M. A. Hitt, "Employed Women and Stress: Implications for Enhancing Women's Mental Health in the Workplace," in J. C. Quick, L. R. Murphy, and J. J. Hurrell, Jr., eds., *Stress and Well-Being at Work* (Washington, D.C.: American Psychological Association, 1992): 164–177.

47. Statistics Canada, "Same-Sex Couples and Sexual Orientation … By the Numbers," The Daily, June 20, 2014, accessed from https://www150.statcan.gc.ca/n1/dai-quo/smr08/2014/smr08_189_2014-eng.htm, August 15, 2018.

48. "Great Place to Work and Pride at Work Canada, Beyond Diversity: An LGBT Best Practice Guide for Employers, 2015," accessed from https://prideatwork.ca/wp-content/uploads/2017/09/Beyond-Diversity-LGBT-Guide.pdf, July 2, 2018.

49. Ibid.

50. "The Challenges and Opportunities of Being Out and a Leader at Work," accessed from https://www.gendereconomy.org/the-challenges-and-opportunities-of-being-out-and-a-leader-at-work/, July 2, 2018.

51. "IBM Commitment to Diversity," accessed from http://prideatwork.ca/partner/ibm/, July 2, 2018.

52. StatsCan, "A Portrait of Canadian Youth," February 7, 2018, accessed from https://www150.statcan.gc.ca/n1/pub/11-631-x/11-631-x2018001-eng.htm, July 2, 2018.

53. W. B. Johnston, "Global Workforce 2000: The New World Labor Market," *Harvard Business Review* 69 (1991): 115–127.

54. S. E. Jackson and E. B. Alvarez, "Working through Diversity as a Strategic Imperative," in S. E. Jackson, ed., *Diversity in the Workplace: Human Resources Initiatives* (New York: Guilford Press, 1992), 13–36.

55. "Managing Generational Diversity," *HR Magazine* 36 (1991): 91–92.

56. K. Tyler, "The Tethered Generation," *HR Magazine* (May 2007): 41–46.

57. S. R. Rhodes, "Age-related Differences in Work Attitudes and Behavior: A Review and Conceptual Analysis," *Psychological Bulletin* 93 (1983): 338–367.

58. B. L. Hassell and P. L. Perrewe, "An Examination of Beliefs about Older Workers: Do Stereotypes Still Exist?" *Journal of Organizational Behavior* 16 (1995): 457–468.

59. StatsCan, "A Profile of Persons with Disabilities among Canadians Aged 15

Years or Older, 2012," accessed from https://www150.statcan.gc.ca/n1/pub/89-654-x/89-654-x2015001-eng.htm#a1, July 1, 2018.

60. J. J. Laabs, "The Golden Arches Provide Golden Opportunities," *Personnel Journal* (July 1991): 52–57.

61. J. E. Rigdon, "PepsiCo's KFC Scouts for Blacks and Women for Its Top Echelons," *The Wall Street Journal* (November 13, 1991): A1.

62. P. A. Galagan, "Tapping the Power of a Diverse Workforce," *Training and Development Journal* 26 (1991): 38–44.

63. C. L. Holladay, J. L. Knight, D. L. Paige, and M. A. Quinones, "The Influence of Framing on Attitudes Toward Diversity Training," *Human Resource Development Quarterly* 14 (2003): 245–263.

64. Ibid.

65. R. Thomas, "From Affirmative Action to Affirming Diversity," *Harvard Business Review* 68 (1990): 107–117.

66. T. H. Cox, Jr., *Cultural Diversity in Organizations: Theory, Research and Practice* (San Francisco, CA: Berrett-Koehler, 1994).

67. Six Degrees-RBC, "All of Us: What We Mean When We Talk About Inclusion, 2017," accessed from https://www.icc-icc.ca/site/site/uploads/2016/10/6Degrees-RBC-Report-All-of-Us-What-we-mean-when-we-talk-about-inclusion-Sarmishta-Subramanian-September-2017.pdf, July 2, 2018.

68. Merck Annual Report 2000, http://www.anrpt2000.com/18.htm.

69. M. R. Fusilier, C. D. Aby, Jr., J. K. Worley, and S. Elliott, "Perceived Seriousness of Business Ethics Issues," *Business and Professional Ethics Journal* 15 (1996): 67–78.

70. J. S. Mill, Utilitarianism, Liberty, and Representative Government (London: Dent, 1910).

71. K. H. Blanchard and N. V. Peale, *The Power of Ethical Management* (New York: Morrow, 1988).

72. A. Smith, *An Inquiry into the Nature and Causes of the Wealth of Nations,* vol. 10 of The Harvard Classics, ed. C. J. Bullock (New York: P. F. Collier & Son, 1909).

73. C. Fried, *Right and Wrong* (Cambridge, Mass.: Harvard University Press, 1978).

74. I. Kant, *Groundwork of the Metaphysics of Morals,* trans. H. J. Paton (New York: Harper & Row, 1964).

75. R. C. Solomon, "Corporate Roles, Personal Virtues: Aristotelean Approach to Business Ethics," *Business Ethics Quarterly* 2 (1992): 317–339; R. C. Solomon, *A Better Way to Think about Business: How Personal Integrity Leads to Corporate Success* (New York: Oxford University Press, 1999).

76. D. Kemp, "Employers and AIDS: Dealing with the Psychological and Emotional Issues of AIDS in the Workplace," *American Review of Public Administration* 25 (1995): 263–278.

77. J. J. Koch, "Wells Fargo's and IBM's HIV Policies Help Protect Employees' Rights," *Personnel Journal* (April 1990): 40–48.

78. "Global Business Coalition Member Profiles," http://www.gbcimpact.org/itcs_type/9/506/member_profiles.

79. U.S. EEOC, "Discrimination Because of Sex under Title VII of the 1964 Civil Rights Act as Amended: Adoption of Interim Guidelines—Sexual Harassment," *Federal Register* 45 (1980): 25024–25025; S. J. Adler, "Lawyers Advise Concerns to Provide Precise Written Policy to Employees," *The Wall Street Journal* (October 9, 1991): B1.

80. L. F. Fitzgerald, F. Drasgow, C. L. Hulin, M. J. Gelfand, and V. J. Magley, "Antecedents and Consequences of Sexual Harassment in Organizations: A Test of an Integrated Model," *Journal of Applied Psychology* 82 (1997): 578–589.

81. E. Felsenthal, "Rulings Open Way for Sex-Harass Cases," *The Wall Street Journal* (June 29, 1998): A10.

82. Canadian Human Rights Commission, Anti-Harassment Policies for the Workplace: An Employer's Guide, March 2006, accessed from http://www.chrc-ccdp.ca/publications/anti_harassment_toc-en.asp#23.

83. K. T. Schneider, S. Swan, and L. F. Fitzgerald, "Job-related and Psychological Effects of Sexual Harassment in the Workplace: Empirical Evidence from Two Organizations," *Journal of Applied Psychology* 82 (1997): 401–415.

84. A. M. O'Leary-Kelly, R. L. Paetzold, and R. W. Griffin, "Sexual Harassment as Aggressive Behavior: An Actor-based Perspective," *Academy of Management Review* 25 (2000): 372–388.

85. B. Marsh, B. ICN, Chairman Settle 2nd Sexual Harassment Case, *Los Angeles Times*, July 2, 1996, accessed from http://articles.latimes.com/1996-07-02/business/fi-20479_1_sexual-harassment.

86. L. M. Goldenhar, N. G. Swanson, J. J. Hurrell, Jr., A. Ruder, and J. Deddens, "Stressors and Adverse Outcomes for Female Construction Workers," *Journal of Occupational Health Psychology* 3 (1998): 19–32; C. S. Piotrkowski, "Gender Harassment, Job Satisfaction and Distress Among Employed White and Minority Women," *Journal of Occupational Health Psychology* 3 (1998): 33–42.

87. R. A. Posthuma, C. P. Maertz, Jr., and J. B. Dworkin, "Procedural Justice's Relationship with Turnover: Explaining Past Inconsistent Findings," *Journal of Organizational Behavior* 28 (2007): 381–398.

88. D. Fields, M. Pang, and C. Chio, "Distributive and Procedural Justice as Predictors of Employee Outcomes in Hong Kong," *Journal of Organizational Behavior* 21 (2000): 547–562.

89. H. L. Laframboise, "Vile Wretches and Public Heroes: The Ethics of Whistleblowing in Government," *Canadian Public Administration* (Spring 1991): 73–78.

90. D. B. Turban and D. W. Greening, "Corporate Social Performance and Organizational Attractiveness to Prospective Employees," *Academy of Management Journal* 40 (1996): 658–672.

91. Task Force on Management of Innovation, *Technology and Employment: Innovation and Growth in the U.S. Economy* (Washington, D.C.: U.S. Government Research Council, 1987).

92. C. H. Ferguson, "Computers and the Coming of the U.S. Keiretsu," *Harvard Business Review* 68 (1990): 55–70.

93. J. Collins, *Good to Great: Why Some Companies Make the Leap ... and Others Don't* (New York: HarperCollins, 2001).

94. J. A. Senn, *Information Systems in Management,* 4th ed. (Belmont, Calif.: Wadsworth, 1990).

95. D. K. Sorenson, O. Bouhaddou, and H. R. Warner, *Knowledge Engineering in Health Informatics* (New York: Springer, 1999).

96. M. T. Damore, "A Presentation and Examination of the Integration of Unlawful Discrimination Practices in the Private Business Sector with Artificial Intelligence" (Thesis, Oklahoma State University, 1992).

97. IEEE Robotics and Automation Society, "IFR Statistics Report Optimistic About Robotics Industry Growth in 2011–12."

98. E. Fingleton, "Jobs for Life: Why Japan Won't Give Them Up," *Fortune* (March 20, 1995): 119–125.

99. M. Iansitu, "How the Incumbent Can Win: Managing Technological Transitions in the Semiconductor Industry," *Management Science* 46 (2000): 169–185.

100. M. B. W. Fritz, S. Narasimhan, and H. Rhee, "Communication and Coordination in the Virtual Office," *Journal of Management Information Systems* 14 (1998): 7–28.

101. "Telus Finds Telecommuting Good for Planet and the Bottom Line," *The*

Vancouver Sun, June 25, 2007, accessed from http://www.working.com/vancouver/story.html?id=bc7b53a1-4cf4-4624-9c23-b28c6ee8e559&k=31069.

102. M. Apgar, IV, "The Alternative Workplace: Changing Where and How People Work," *Harvard Business Review* (May–June 1998): 121–136.

103. D. L. Nelson, "Individual Adjustment to Information-driven Technologies: A Critical Review," *MIS Quarterly* 14 (1990): 79–98.

104. S. Armour, "Hi, I'm Joan and I'm a Workaholic," *USA Today* (May 23, 2007).

105. M. Allen, "Legislation Could Restrict Bosses from Snooping on Their Workers," *The Wall Street Journal* (September 24, 1991): B1–B8.

106. K. D. Hill and S. Kerr, "The Impact of Computer-integrated Manufacturing Systems on the First Line Supervisor," *Journal of Organizational Behavior Management* 6 (1984): 81–87.

107. J. Anderson, "How Technology Brings Blind People into the Workplace," *Harvard Business Review* 67 (1989): 36–39.

108. D. L. Nelson and M. G. Kletke, "Individual Adjustment during Technological Innovation: A Research Framework," *Behavior and Information Technology* 9 (1990): 257–271.

109. D. Mankin, T. Bikson, B. Gutek, and C. Stasz, "Managing Technological Change: The Process Is the Key," *Datamation* 34 (1988): 69–80.

3

1. K. Lewin, "Formalization and Progress in Psychology," in D. Cartwright, ed., *Field Theory in Social Science* (New York: Harper, 1951).

2. N. S. Endler and D. Magnusson, "Toward an Interactional Psychology of Personality," *Psychological Bulletin* 83 (1976): 956–974.

3. J. R. Terborg, "Interactional Psychology and Research on Human Behavior in Organizations," *Academy of Management Review* 6 (1981): 561–576.

4. U. Neisser, G. Boodoo, T. J. Bouchard Jr., A. W. Boykin, N. Brody, et al., "Intelligence: Knowns and Unknowns," *American Psychologist* 51(2) (1996): 77– 101.

5. F. L. Schmidt and J. Hunter, "General Mental Ability in the World of Work: Occupational Attainment and Job Performance," *Journal of Personality and Social Psychology* 86(1) (2004): 162–173; C. Bertua, N. Anderson, and J. F. Salgado, "The Predictive Validity of Cognitive Ability Tests: A UK Meta-Analysis," *Journal of Occupational and Organizational Psychology* 78 (2004): 387–409.

6. T. J. Bouchard, Jr., "Twins Reared Together and Apart: What They Tell Us about Human Diversity," in S. W. Fox, ed., *Individuality and Determinism* (New York: Plenum Press, 1984); R. D. Arvey, T. J. Bouchard, Jr., N. L. Segal, and L. M. Abraham, "Job Satisfaction: Environmental and Genetic Components," *Journal of Applied Psychology* 74 (1989): 235–248.

7. T. A. Judge, C. Hurst, and L. S. Simon, "Does It Pay to Be Smart, Attractive or Confident (or All Three)? Relationships Among General Mental Ability, Physical Attractiveness, Core Self-Evaluations, and Income," *Journal of Applied Psychology* 94(3) (2009): 742–755.

8. O. P John, "The 'Big Five' Factor Taxonomy: Dimensions of Personality in the Natural Language and in Questionnaires," *Handbook of Personality: Theory and Research* (New York: Guilford, 1990): 66–100.

9. J. M. Digman, "Personality Structure: Emergence of a Five-Factor Model," *Annual Review of Psychology* 41 (1990): 417–440.

10. T. A. Judge, J. J. Martocchio, and C. J. Thoresen, "Five-Factor Model of Personality and Employee Absence," *Journal of Applied Psychology* 82 (1997): 745–755.

11. H. J. Bernardin, D. K. Cooke, and P. Villanova, "Conscientiousness and Agreeableness as Predictors of Rating Leniency," *Journal of Applied Psychology* 85 (2000): 232–234.

12. S. E. Seibert and M. L. Kraimer, "The Five-Factor Model of Personality and Career Success," *Journal of Vocational Behavior* 58 (2001): 1–21.

13. T. A. Judge and R. Ilies, "Relationships of Personality to Performance Motivation: A Meta-Analytic Review," *Journal of Applied Psychology* 87 (2002): 797–807.

14. G. M. Hurtz and J. J. Donovan, "Personality and Job Performance: The Big Five Revisited," *Journal of Applied Psychology* 85 (2000): 869–879.

15. S. T. Bell, "Deep-Level Composition Variables as Predictors of Team Performance: A Meta-Analysis," *Journal of Applied Psychology* 92(3) (2007): 595–615.

16. D. P. Schmitt, J. Allik, R. R. McCrae, and V. Benet-Martinez, "The Geographic Distribution of Big Five Personality Traits: Patterns and Profiles of Human Self-Description across 56 Nations," *Journal of Cross-Cultural Psychology* 38(2) (2007): 173–212.

17. M. R. Barrick and M. K. Mount, "The Big Five Personality Dimensions and Job Performance: A Meta-Analysis," *Personnel Psychology* 44 (1991): 1–26.

18. P. K. Jonason, and G. D. Webster, "The Dirty Dozen: A Concise Measure of the Dark Triad," *Psychological Assessment* 22(2) (2010): 420–432.

19. P. K. Jonason, S. B. Kaufman, G. D. Webster, and G. Geher, "What Lies Beneath the Dark Triad Dirty Dozen: Varied Relations with the Big Five," *Individual Differences Research* 11(2013): 81–90.

20. M. C. Ashton, K. Lee, M. Perugini, P. Szarota, R. E. de Vries, et al., "A Six-Factor Structure of Personality-Descriptive Adjectives: Solutions from Psycholexical Studies in Seven Languages," *Journal of Personality and Social Psychology* 86 (2) (2004): 356–366.

21. T. A., Judge, E. A. Locke, and C. C. Durham, "The Dispositional Causes of Job Satisfaction: A Core Self-Evaluation Approach," *Research in Organizational Behavior* 19 (1997): 151–188.

22. B. A. Scott and T. A. Judge, "The Popularity Contest at Work: Who Wins, Why, and What Do They Receive?" *Journal of Applied Psychology* 94(1) (2009): 20–33.

23. T. A. Judge and C. Hurst, "How the Rich (and Happy) Get Richer (and Happier): Relationship of Core Self-Evaluations to Trajectories in Attaining Work Success," *Journal of Applied Psychology* 93(4) (2008): 849–863.

24. J. B. Rotter, "Generalized Expectancies for Internal vs. External Control of Reinforcement," *Psychological Monographs* 80 (1966): 1–28.

25. T. W. H. Ng, K. L. Sorensen, and L. T. Eby, "Locus of Control at Work: A Meta-Analysis," *Journal of Organizational Behavior* 27 (2006): 1057–1087.

26. G. Chen, S. M. Gully, J. Whiteman, and R. N. Kilcullen, "Examination of Relationships Among Trait-Like Individual Differences, State-Like Individual Differences, and Learning Performance," *Journal of Applied Psychology* 85 (2000): 835–847; G. Chen, S. M. Gully, and D. Eden, "Validation of a New General Self-Efficacy Scale," *Organizational Research Methods* 4 (2001): 62–83.

27. A. Bandura, *Self-Efficacy: The Exercise of Control* (San Francisco, CA: Freeman, 1997).

28. D. R. Avery, "Personality as a Predictor of the Value of Voice," *The Journal of Psychology* 137 (2003): 435–447.

29. T. A. Judge and J. E. Bono, "Relationship of Core Self-Evaluations

Traits—Self-Esteem, Generalized Self-Efficacy, Locus of Control, and Emotional Stability—with Job Satisfaction and Job Performance: A Meta-Analysis," *Journal of Applied Psychology* 86 (2001): 80–92.

30. B. W. Pelham and W. B. Swann, Jr., "From Self-Conceptions to Self-Worth: On the Sources and Structure of Global Self-Esteem," *Journal of Personality and Social Psychology* 57 (1989): 672–680.

31. A. H. Baumgardner, C. M. Kaufman, and P. E. Levy, "Regulating Affect Interpersonally: When Low Esteem Leads to Greater Enhancement," *Journal of Personality and Social Psychology* 56 (1989): 907–921.

32. P. Tharenou and P. Harker, "Moderating Influences of Self-Esteem on Relationships between Job Complexity, Performance, and Satisfaction," *Journal of Applied Psychology* 69 (1984): 623–632.

33. R. A. Ellis and M. S. Taylor, "Role of Self-Esteem within the Job Search Process," *Journal of Applied Psychology* 68 (1983): 632–640.

34. J. Brockner and T. Hess, "Self-Esteem and Task Performance in Quality Circles," *Academy of Management Journal* 29 (1986): 617–623.

35. B. R. Schlenker, M. F. Weingold, and J. R. Hallam, "Self-Serving Attributions in Social Context: Effects of Self-Esteem and Social Pressure," *Journal of Personality and Social Psychology* 57 (1990): 855–863.

36. M. K. Duffy, J. D. Shaw, and E. M. Stark, "Performance and Satisfaction in Conflicted Interdependent Groups: When and How Does Self-Esteem Make a Difference?" *Academy of Management Journal* 43 (2000): 772–782.

37. P. T. Costa, and R. R. McCrae, "Personality in Adulthood: A Six-Year Longitudinal Study of Self-Reports and Spouse Ratings on the NEO Personality Inventory." *Journal of Personality and Social Psychology* 54 (5) (1988): 853–863.

38. M. Erez and T. A. Judge, "Relationship of Core Self-Evaluations to Goal Setting, Motivation and Performance," *Journal of Applied Psychology* 86 (2001): 1270– 1279.

39. M. Snyder and S. Gangestad, "On the Nature of Self-Monitoring: Matters of Assessment, Matters of Validity," *Journal of Personality and Social Psychology* (1986): 125–139.

40. A. H. Church, "Managerial Self-Awareness in High-performing Individuals in Organizations," *Journal of Applied Psychology* 82 (1997): 281–292.

41. A. Mehra, M. Kilduff, and D. J. Brass, "The Social Networks of High and Low Self-Monitors: Implications for Workplace Performance," *Administrative Science Quarterly* 46 (2001): 121–146.

42. C. Douglas and W. L. Gardner, "Transition to Self-Directed Work Teams: Implications of Transition Time and Self-Monitoring for Managers' Use of Influence Tactics," *Journal of Organizational Behavior* 25 (2004): 45–67.

43. M. Kilduff and D. V. Day, "Do Chameleons Get Ahead? The Effects of Self-Monitoring on Managerial Careers," *Academy of Management Journal* 37 (1994): 1047–1060.

44. W. H. Turnley and M. C. Bolino, "Achieving Desired Images While Avoiding Undesired Images: Exploring the Role of Self-Monitoring in Impression Management," *Journal of Applied Psychology* 86 (2001): 351–360.

45. A. M. Isen and R. A. Baron, "Positive Affect and Organizational Behavior," in B. M. Staw and L. L. Cummings, eds., *Research in Organizational Behavior,* vol. 12 (Greenwich, Conn.: JAI Press, 1990).

46. D. Watson and L. A. Clark, "Negative Affectivity: The Disposition to Experience Aversive Emotional States," *Psychological Bulletin* 96 (1984): 465–490.

47. S. Lyubormirsky, L. King, and L. E. Diener, "The Benefits of Frequent Positive Affect: Does Happiness Lead to Success?" *Psychological Bulletin* 131(6) (2005): 803–855.

48. R. Ilies and T. Judge, "On the Heritability of Job Satisfaction: The Mediating Role of Personality," *Journal of Applied Psychology* 88 (2003): 750–759.

49. J. M. George, "State or Trait," *Journal of Applied Psychology* 76 (1991): 299–307.

50. J. M. George, "Mood and Absence," *Journal of Applied Psychology* 74 (1989): 287–324.

51. S. Barsade, A. Ward, J. Turner, and J. Sonnenfeld, "To Your Heart's Content: A Model of Affective Diversity in Top Management Teams," *Administrative Science Quarterly* 45 (2000): 802–836.

52. W. Mischel, "The Interaction of Person and Situation," in D. Magnusson and N. S. Endler, eds., *Personality at the Crossroads: Current Issues in Interactional Psychology* (Hillsdale, N.J.: Erlbaum, 1977).

53. R. M. Kaplan and D. P. Saccuzzo, *Psychological Testing*, 9 ed. (Boston, MA: Cengage, 2018).

54. R. Benfari and J. Knox, *Understanding Your Management Style* (Lexington, MA: Lexington Books, 1991).

55. C. G. Jung, *Psychological Types* (New York: Harcourt & Brace, 1923).

56. "Myers-Briggs Type Indicator ® (MBTI®) Instrument in French and English Canada" *Research Department Psychometrics Canada*, (2008), https://www.psychometrics.com/wpcontent/uploads/2015/02/mbti-in-canada.pdf

57. S. Hirsch and J. Kummerow, *Life Types* (New York: Warner Books, 1989).

58. "Myers-Briggs Type Indicator ® (MBTI®) Instrument in French and English Canada" *Research Department Psychometrics Canada*, (2008), https://www.psychometrics.com/wpcontent/uploads/2015/02/mbti-in-canada.pdf

59. Ibid.

60. Ibid.

61. G. P Macdaid, M. H. McCaulley, and R. I Kainz, *Myers-Briggs Type Indicator: Atlas of Type Tables* (Gainesville, FL.: Center for Application of Psychological Type, 1987).

62. https://www.cpp.com/en-US/Products-and-Services/Myers-Briggs

63. https://www.psychometrics.com/wp-content/uploads/2015/02/vanoc-cs.pdf

64. F. P. Morgeson, M. C. Campion, R. L. Dipboye, J. R. Hollenbeck, K. Murphy, and N. Schmitt, "Reconsidering the Use of Personality Tests in Personnel Selection Contexts," *Personnel Psychology* 60 (2007): 683–729.

65. J. Hunsley, C.M. Lee, and J. M. Wood, "Controversial and Questionable Assessment Techniques," *Science and Pseudoscience in Clinical Psychology* (2003): 39–76. New York: Guilford.

66. J. Michael, "Using the Myers-Briggs Indicator as a Tool for Leadership Development: Apply with Caution," *Journal of Leadership & Organizational Studies* 10 (2003): 68–78.

67. Gustave Flaubert.

68. S. Kassin, S. Fein, and H.R. Markus, *Social Psychology* 7e. (Belmont, CA: Wadsworth, Cengage Learning. (2008): 93–127.

69. J. Park and M. R. Banaji, "Mood and Heuristics: The Influence of Happy and Sad States on Sensitivity and Bias in Stereotyping," *Journal of Personality and Social Psychology* 78 (2000): 1005–1023.

70. R. L. Dipboye, H. L. Fromkin, and K. Willback, "Relative Importance of Applicant Sex, Attractiveness, and Scholastic Standing in Evaluations of Job Applicant Resumes," *Journal of Applied Psychology* 60 (1975): 39–43; I. H. Frieze, J. E. Olson, and J. Russell, "Attractiveness and Income for Men and Women in Management," *Journal of Applied Social Psychology* 21 (1991): 1039–1057.

71. J. H. Langlois, L. Kalakanis, A. J. Rubenstein, A. Larson, M. Hallam, et al., "Maxims or Myths of Beauty? A Meta-Analytic and Theoretical Review,"

Psychological Bulletin 126(3) (2000): 390–423.

72. M. W. Levine and J. M. Shefner, *Fundamentals of Sensation and Perception* (Reading, Mass.: Addison-Wesley, 1981).

73. J. E. Rehfeld, "What Working for a Japanese Company Taught Me," *Harvard Business Review* (November–December 1990): 167–176.

74. M. W. Morris and R. P. Larrick, "When One Cause Casts Doubt on Another: A Normative Analysis of Discounting in Causal Attribution," *Psychological Review* 102 (1995): 331–355.

75. F. Heider, *The Psychology of Interpersonal Relations* (New York: Wiley, 1958).

76. B. Weiner, "An Attributional Theory of Achievement Motivation and Emotion," *Psychological Review* (October 1985): 548–573.

77. P. D. Sweeney, K. Anderson, and S. Bailey, "Attributional Style in Depression: A Meta-Analytic Review," *Journal of Personality and Social Psychology* 51 (1986): 974–991.

78. P. Rosenthal, D. Guest, and R. Peccei, "Gender Differences in Managers' Causal Explanations for Their Work Performance," *Journal of Occupational and Organizational Psychology* 69 (1996): 145–151.

79. M. J. Martinko and W. L. Gardner, "The Leader/Member Attributional Process," *Academy of Management Review* 12 (1987): 235–249.

80. K. N. Wexley, R. A. Alexander, J. P. Greenawalt, and M. A. Couch, "Attitudinal Congruence and Similarity as Related to Interpersonal Evaluations in Manager-Subordinate Dyads," *Academy of Management Journal* 23 (1980): 320–330.

81. H. H. Kelley, *Attribution in Social Interaction* (New York: General Learning Press, 1971); H. H. Kelley, "The Processes of Causal Attribution," *American Psychologist* 28 (1973): 107–128.

82. E. Aronson, T. D. Wilson, and R. M. Akert, *Social Psychology* 7th ed.. (Upper Saddle River, NJ: Pearson Education, Inc., 2010): 83–115.

83. J. A. Bargh and T. L Chartrand, "The Unbearable Automaticity of Being," *American Psychologist* 54(7) (1999): 462–479.

84. L. Winter, and J. S. Uleman, "When Are Social Judgments Made? Evidence for the Spontaneousness of Trait Inferences," *Journal of Personality and Social Psychology* 47(2) (1984): 237–252.

85. N. Ambady and R. Rosenthal, "Half a Minute: Predicting Teacher Evaluations from Thin Slices of Nonverbal Behavior and Physical Attractiveness," *Journal of Personality and Social Psychology* 64(3) (1993): 431–441.

86. J. Willis and A. Todorov, "First Impressions: Making Up Your Mind After a 100-Ms Exposure to a Face," *Psychological Science* 17 (7) (2006): 592–598.

87. G. B. Sechrist and C. Stangor, "Perceived Consensus Influences Intergroup Behavior and Stereotype Accessibility," *Journal of Personality and Psychology* 80 (2001): 645–654; A. Lyons and Y. Kashima, "How Are Stereotypes Maintained through Communication? The Influence of Stereotype Sharedness," *Journal of Personality and Social Psychology* 85 (2003): 989–1005.

88. L. Copeland, "Learning to Manage a Multicultural Workforce," *Training* (May 1988): 48–56.

89. L. Ross, "The Intuitive Psychologist and His Shortcomings: Distortions in the Attribution Process," in L. Berkowitz, ed., *Advances in Experimental Social Psychology* (New York: Academic Press, 1977); M. O'Sullivan, "The Fundamental Attribution Error in Detecting Deception: The Boy-Who-Cried-Wolf Effect," *Personality & Social Psychology Bulletin* 29 (2003): 1316–1327.

90. D. T. Miller and M. Ross, "Self-serving Biases in the Attribution of Causality: Fact or Fiction?" *Psychological Bulletin* 82 (1975): 313–325.

91. J. G. Miller, "Culture and the Development of Everyday Causal Explanation," *Journal of Personality and Social Psychology* 46 (1984): 961–978.

92. G. Si, S. Rethorst, and K. Willimczik, "Causal Attribution Perception in Sports Achievement: A Cross-Cultural Study on Attributional Concepts in Germany and China," *Journal of Cross-Cultural Psychology* 26 (1995): 537–553.

93. R. L. Gross and S. E. Brodt, "How Assumptions of Consensus Undermine Decision Making," *MIT Sloan Management Review* 42 (Winter 2001): 86–94.

94. E. Burnstein and Y. Schul, "The Informational Basis of Social Judgments: Operations in Forming an Impression of Another Person," *Journal of Experimental Social Psychology* 18 (1982): 217–234.

95. G. L. Stewart, S. L. Dustin, M. R. Barrick, and T. C. Darnold, "Exploring the Handshake in Employment Interviews," *Journal of Applied Psychology* 93(5) (2008): 1139–1146.

96. M. Snyder, "When Belief Creates Reality," *Advances in Experimental Social Psychology* 18 (1984): 247–305.

97. J. H. Langlois, L. Kalakanis, A. J. Rubenstein, A. Larson, M. Hallam, et al., "Maxims or Myths of Beauty? A Meta-Analytic and Theoretical Review," *Psychological Bulletin* 126(3) (2000): 390–423.

98. R. Rosenthal and L. Jacobson, *Pygmalion in the Classroom: Teacher Expectations and Pupils' Intellectual Development* (New York: Holt, Rinehart & Winston, 1968).

99. R. A. Giacolone and P. Rosenfeld, eds., *Impression Management in Organizations* (Hillsdale, NJ: Erlbaum, 1990); J. Tedeschi and V. Melburg, "Impression Management and Influence in the Organization," in S. Bacharach and E. Lawler, eds., *Research in the Sociology of Organizations* (Greenwich, CT: JAI Press, 1984), 31–58.

100. R. Sikveland and E. Stokoe, "Dealing with Resistance in Initial Intake and Inquiry Calls to Mediation: The Power of 'Willing,'" *Conflict Resolution Quarterly* 33 (2016): 235–254.

101. D. C. Gilmore and G. R. Ferris, "The Effects of Applicant Impression Management Tactics on Interviewer Judgments," *Journal of Management* (December 1989): 557–564; C. K. Stevens and A. L. Kristof, "Making the Right Impression: A Field Study of Applicant Impressions Management during Job Interviews," *Journal of Applied Psychology* 80 (1995): 587–606; S. J. Wayne and R. C. Liden, "Effects of Impression Management on Performance Ratings: A Longitudinal Study," *Academy of Management Journal* 38 (1995): 232–260.

102. M. R. Barrick, J. A. Shaffer, and S. W. DeGrassi, "What You See May Not Be What You Get: Relationships Among Self-Presentation Tactics and Ratings of Interview and Job Performance," *Journal of Applied Psychology* 94(6) (2009): 1394–1411.

4

1. N. H. Frijda, "Moods, Emotion Episodes, and Emotions," in M. Lewis and J. M. Haviland, eds., *Handbook of Emotions* (New York: Guilford Press, 1993), 381–403.

2. A. Ortony, G. L. Clore, and A. Collins, "The Cognitive Structure of Emotions (Cambridge: Cambridge University Press, 1988).

3. A. Öhman, A. Flykt, and F. Esteves, "Emotion Drives Attention: Detecting the Snake in the Grass," *Journal of Experimental Psychology: General* 130(3) (2001): 466–478.

4. R. J. Dolan, "Emotion, Cognition, and Behavior," *Science* 298 (2002): 1191–1194.

5. W. James, *The Principles of Psychology* (New York: Holt, 1890).

6. J. A. Russell, "Is There Universal Recognition of Emotion from Facial Expression? A Review of the Cross-Cultural Studies," *Psychological Bulletin* 115 (1) (1994): 102–141.

7. R. S. Lazarus, *Emotion and Adaptation* (New York: Oxford University Press, 1991).

8. B. L. Fredrickson and C. Brannigan, "Positive Emotions," in G. Bonnano and T. Mayne, eds., *Emotions: Current Issues and Future Directions* (New York: Guilford Press, 2001), 123–152.

9. A. M. Isen and R. A. Baron, "Positive Affect as a Factor in Organizational Behavior," *Research in Organizational Behavior* 13 (1991): 1–53.

10. S. G. Barsade and D. E. Gibson, "Why Does Affect Matter in Organizations?" *The Academy of Management Perspectives* 21 (2007): 36–59.

11. M. M. Pillutla and J. K. Murnighan, "Unfairness, Anger, and Spite: Emotional Rejections of Ultimatum Offers," *Organizational Behavior Human Decision Processes* 68 (1996): 208–224.

12. A. A. Grandey, "Emotion Regulation in the Workplace: A New Way to Conceptualize Emotional Labor." *Journal of Occupational Health Psychology* 5 (1) (2000): 59–100.

13. A. Grandey, "When 'The Show Must Go On': Surface and Deep Acting as Predictors of Emotional Exhaustion and Service Delivery," *Academy of Management Journal* 46 (2003): 86–96.

14. A. R. Hochschild, *The Managed Heart: Commercialization of Human Feeling*. (Berkeley, CA: University of California Press, 1983).

15. D. L. Joseph and D. A. Newman, "Emotional Intelligence: An Integrative Meta-analysis and Cascading Model," *Journal of Applied Psychology* 95 (2010): 54–78.

16. D. Matsumoto, S. H. Yoo, and J. Fontaine, "Mapping Expressive Differences Around the World: The Relationship between Emotional Display Rules and Individualism versus Collectivism," *Journal of Cross-Cultural Psychology* 39 (2008): 55–74.

17. S. Safdar, W. Friedlmeier, D. Matsumoto, S. H. Yoo, C. T. Kwantes, et al., "Variations of Emotional Display Rules Within and Across Cultures: A Comparison between Canada, USA and Japan," *Canadian Journal of Behavioural Science* 41 (2009): 1–10.

18. E. Palagi, V. Nicotra, and G. Cordoni, "Rapid Mimicry and Emotional Contagion in Domestic Dogs," *Royal Society Open Science* 2 (12)(2015): http://rsos.royalsocietypublishing.org/content/2/12/150505.

19. J. E. Dutton, P. J. Frost, M. C. Worline, J. M. Lilius, and J. M. Kanov, eds., "Leading in Times of Trauma," *Harvard Business Review* 80 (1) (2002): 54–61, 125.

20. A. H. Eagly and S. Chaiken, *The Psychology of Attitudes* (Orlando, FL: Harcourt Brace Jovanovich, 1993).

21. M. J. Rosenberg, C. I. Hovland, W. J. McGuire, R. P. Abelson, and J. H. Brehm, *Attitude Organization and Change* (New Haven, CT: Yale University Press, 1960).

22. R. H. Fazio and M. P. Zanna, "On the Predictive Validity of Attitudes: The Roles of Direct Experience and Confidence," *Journal of Personality* 46 (1978): 228–243.

23. A. Tversky and D. Kahneman, "Judgment under Uncertainty: Heuristics and Biases," in D. Kahneman, P. Slovic, and A. Tversky, eds., *Judgment under Uncertainty* (New York: Cambridge University Press, 1982), 3–20.

24. I. Ajzen and M. Fishbein, "Attitude–Behavior Relations: A Theoretical Analysis and Review of Empirical Research," *Psychological Bulletin* 84 (1977): 888–918.

25. M. A. Adam and D. Rachman-Moore, "The Methods Used to Implement an Ethical Code of Conduct and Employee Attitudes," *Journal of Business Ethics* 54 (2004): 225–244.

26. A. B. Frymier and M. K. Nadler, "The Relationship between Attitudes and Behaviours," in *Persuasion: Integrating Theory, Research and Practice* (Dubuque, Iowa: Kendall Hunt Publishing, 2017).

27. Ajzen and Fishbein, "Attitude–Behavior Relations": 888–918.

28. B. T. Johnson and A. H. Eagly, "Effects of Involvement on Persuasion: A Meta-Analysis," *Psychological Bulletin* 106 (1989): 290–314.

29. K. G. DeBono and M. Snyder, "Acting on One's Attitudes: The Role of History of Choosing Situations," *Personality and Social Psychology Bulletin* 21 (1995): 629–636.

30. I. Ajzen and M. Fishbein, *Understanding Attitudes and Predicting Social Behavior* (Englewood Cliffs, NJ: Prentice-Hall, 1980).

31. I. Ajzen, "From Intentions to Action: A Theory of Planned Behavior," in J. Kuhl and J. Beckmann, eds., *Action-Control: From Cognition to Behavior* (Heidelberg: Springer, 1985); I. Ajzen, "The Theory of Planned Behavior," *Organizational Behavior and Human Decision Processes* 50 (1991): 1–33.

32. L. Festinger, *A Theory of Cognitive Dissonance* (Evanston, IL: Row, Peterson, 1957).

33. J. Cooper, *Cognitive Dissonance: 50 Years of a Classic Theory* (London: SAGE Publications, 2007).

34. L. M. Saari and T. A. Judge, "Employee Attitudes and Job Satisfaction," *Human Resource Management* 43 (2004): 395–407.

35. J. W. Harter, F. L. Schmidt, and T. L. Hayes, "Business-Unit-Level Relationship between Employee Satisfaction, Employee Engagement, and Business Outcomes: A Meta-Analysis," *Journal of Applied Psychology* 87 (2002): 268–279.

36. A. Sagie and M. Krausz, "What Aspects of the Job Have Most Effect on Nurses?" *Human Resource Management Journal* 13 (2003): 46–62.

37. C. P. Parker, B. B. Baltes, S. A. Young, J. W. Huff, R. A. Altman, et al., "Relationships between Psychological Climate Perceptions and Work Outcomes: A Meta-Analytic Review," *Journal of Organizational Behavior* 24 (2003): 389–416.

38. J. Lemmick and J. Mattsson, "Employee Behavior, Feelings of Warmth and Customer Perception in Service Encounters," *International Journal of Retail & Distribution Management* 30 (2002): 18–44.

39. E. A. Locke, "The Nature and Causes of Job Satisfaction," in M. Dunnette, ed., *Handbook of Industrial and Organizational Psychology* (Chicago, IL: Rand McNally, 1976).

40. P. C. Smith, L. M. Kendall, and C. L. Hulin, *The Measurement of Satisfaction in Work and Retirement* (Skokie, IL: Rand McNally, 1969).

41. A. Sousa-Poza and A. A. Sousa-Poza, "Well-being at Work: A Cross-national Analysis of the Levels and Determinants of Job Satisfaction," *Journal of Socio-Economics* 29 (2000): 517–538.

42. D. Chiaburu and D. A. Harrison, "Do Peers Make the Place? Conceptual Synthesis and Meta-Analysis of Coworker Effects on Perceptions, Attitudes, OCB's and Performance," *Journal of Applied Psychology* 93 (2008): 1082–1103.

43. P. Warr, "Work Values: Some Demographic and Cultural Correlates," *Journal of Occupational and Organizational Psychology* 81 (2008): 751–775.

44. Ibid.

45. T. A. Judge and J. E. Bono, "Relationship of Core Self-Evaluation

Traits—Self-esteem, Generalized Self-Efficacy, Locus of Control, and Emotional Stability—with Job Satisfaction and Job Performance: A Meta-Analysis," *Journal of Applied Psychology* 86 (2001): 80–92.

46. R. Ilies and T. A. Judge, "On the Heritability of Job Satisfaction: The Mediating Role of Personality," *Journal of Applied Psychology* 88 (2003): 750–759; I. Levin and J. P. Stokes, "Dispositional Approach to Job Satisfaction: Role of Negative Affectivity," *Journal of Applied Psychology* 74 (1989): 752–758.

47. B. M. Staw, N. E. Bell, and J. A. Clausen, "The Dispositional Approach to Job Attitudes: A Lifetime Longitudinal Test," *Administrative Science Quarterly* 31 (1986): 56–77.

48. T. A. Judge, C. J. Thoresen, J. E. Bono, and G. K. Patton, "The Job Satisfaction–Job Performance Relationship: A Qualitative and Quantitative Review," *Psychological Bulletin* 127 (2001): 376–407.

49. C. Ostroff, "The Relationship between Satisfaction, Attitudes and Performance: An Organizational Level Analysis," *Journal of Applied Psychology* 77 (1992): 963–974.

50. R. Griffin and T. Bateman, "Job Satisfaction and Organizational Commitment," in C. Cooper and I. Robertson, eds., *International Review of Industrial and Organizational Psychology* (New York: Wiley, 1986).

51. L. A. Bettencourt, K. P. Gwinner, and M. L. Meuter, "A Comparison of Attitude, Personality, and Knowledge Predictors of Service-oriented Organizational Citizenship Behaviors," *Journal of Applied Psychology* 86 (2001): 29–41.

52. D. W. Organ, *Organizational Citizenship Behavior: The Good Soldier Syndrome* (Lexington, MA: Lexington Books, 1988).

53. P. M. Podsakoff, S. B. Mackenzie, and C. Hui, "Organizational Citizenship Behaviors and Managerial Evaluations of Employee Performance: A Review and Suggestions for Future Research," in G. Ferris, ed., *Research in Personnel and Human Resources Management* (Greenwich, CT: JAI Press, 1993), 1–40.

54. O. Christ, R. Van Dick, and U. Wagner, "When Teachers Go the Extra Mile: Foci of Organizational Identification as Determinants of Different Forms of Organizational Citizenship Behavior among Schoolteachers," *British Journal of Educational Psychology* 73 (2003): 329–341.

55. G. L. Blakely, M. C. Andrews, and J. Fuller, "Are Chameleons Good Citizens: A Longitudinal Study of the Relationship between Self-Monitoring and Organizational Citizenship Behavior," *Journal of Business & Psychology* 18 (2003): 131–144.

56. W. H. Bommer, E. W. Miles, and S. L. Grover, "Does One Good Turn Deserve Another? Coworker Influences on Employee Citizenship," *Journal of Organizational Behavior* 24 (2003): 181–196.

57. N. P. Podsakoff, S. W. Whiting, P. M. Podsakoff, and B. D. Blume, "Individual- and Organizational-Level Consequences of Organizational Citizenship Behaviors: A Meta-Analysis," *Journal of Applied Psychology* 94 (2009): 122–141.

58. T. D. Allen, J. D. Facteau, and C. L. Facteau, "Structured Interviewing for OCB: Construct Validity, Faking and the Effects of Question Type," *Human Performance* 17 (2004): 247–260.

59. D. W. Organ, P. M. Podsakoff, and S. B Mackenzie, *Organizational Citizenship Behavior: Its Nature, Antecedents and Consequences* (Thousand Oaks, CA: SAGE. 2006).

60. S. L. Robinson, and R. J. Bennett, "A Typology of Deviant Workplace Behaviors: A Multidimensional Scaling Study," *Academy of Management Journal* 38(2) (1995): 555.

61. M. E. Heilman and V. B. Alcott, "What I Think You Think of Me: Women's Reactions to Being Viewed as Beneficiaries of Preferential Selection," *Journal of Applied Psychology* 86 (2001): 574–582; M. E. Heilman, C. J. Block, and P. Stathatos, "The Affirmative Action Stigma of Incompetence: Effects of Performance Information Ambiguity," *Academy of Management Journal* 40 (1997): 603–625.

62. R. T. Mowday, L. W. Porter, and R. M. Steers, *Employee–Organization Linkages: The Psychology of Commitment* (New York: Academic Press, 1982).

63. H. S. Becker, "Notes on the Concept of Commitment," *American Journal of Sociology* 66 (1960): 32–40.

64. J. P. Meyer, N. J. Allen, and C. A. Smith, "Commitment to Organizations and Occupations: Extension and Test of a Three-Component Model," *Journal of Applied Psychology* 78 (1993): 538–551.

65. J. P. Meyer, D. S. Stanley, L. Herscovitch, and L. Topolnytsky, "Affective, Continuance and Normative Commitment to the Organization: A Meta-Analysis of Antecedents, Correlates and Consequences," *Journal of Vocational Behavior* 61 (2002): 20–52.

66. F. Stinglhamber and C. Vandenberghe, "Organizations and Supervisors as Sources of Support and Targets of Commitment," *Journal of Organizational Behavior* 24 (2003): 251–270.

67. R. Eisenberger, et al., "Reciprocation of Perceived Organizational Support," *Journal of Applied Psychology* 86 (2001): 42–51; J. E. Finegan, "The Impact of Person and Organizational Values on Organizational Commitment," *Journal of Occupational and Organizational Psychology* 73 (2000): 149–169.

68. E. Snape and T. Redman, "Too Old or Too Young? The Impact of Perceived Age Discrimination," *Human Resource Management Journal* 13 (2003): 78–89.

69. J. A. Conger, "The Necessary Art of Persuasion," *Harvard Business Review* 76 (1998): 84–96.

70. R. M. Perloff, *The Dynamics of Persuasion: Communication and Attitudes in the 21st Century.* (New Jersey: Lawrence Erlbaum Associates, Inc., 2003).

71. J. Cooper and R. T. Croyle, "Attitudes and Attitude Change," *Annual Review of Psychology* 35 (1984): 395–426.

72. S. Chaiken, "Communicator Physical Attractiveness and Persuasion," *Journal of Personality and Social Psychology* 37(8) (1979): 1387–1397.

73. K. M. Kniffen and D. S. Wilson, "The Effect of Nonphysical Traits on the Perception of Physical Attractiveness: Three Naturalistic Studies," *Evolution and Human Behavior* 25 (2004): 88–101.

74. D. Albarracin and R. S. Wyer, Jr., "Elaborative and Nonelaborative Processing of a Behavior-related Communication," *Personality and Social Psychology Bulletin* 27(6) (2001): 691–705.

75. N. Rhodes and W. Wood, "Self-Esteem and Intelligence Affect Influenceability: The Mediating Role of Message Reception," *Psychological Bulletin* 111 (1992): 156–171.

76. D. M. Mackie and L. T. Worth, "Processing Deficits and the Mediation of Positive Affect in Persuasion," *Journal of Personality and Social Psychology* 57 (1989): 27–40.

77. L. C. Levitan, and P. S. Visser, "The Impact of the Social Context on Resistance to Persuasion: Effortful versus Effortless Responses to Counter-attitudinal Information," *Journal of Experimental Social Psychology* 44 (2008): 640–649.

78. R. E. Petty and J. T. Cacioppo, "The Elaboration Likelihood Model of Persuasion," *Communication and Persuasion* (New York: Springer, 1986).

79. J. W. Brehm, *Responses to Loss of Freedom: A Theory of Psychological Reactance* (New York: General Learning Press, 1972).

80. R. E. Petty, and J. T. Cacioppo, "The Effects of Involvement on Responses to Argument Quantity and Quality: Central and Peripheral Routes to Persuasion," *Journal of Personality and Social Psychology* 46 (1984): 69–81.

81. D. DeSteno, R. E. Petty, and D. D. Rucker, "Discrete Emotions and Persuasion: The Role of Emotion-induced Expectancies," *Journal of Personality & Social Psychology* 86 (2004): 43–56.

82. R. Petty, D. T. Wegener, and L. R. Fabrigar, "Attitudes and Attitude Change," *Annual Review of Psychology* 48 (1997): 609–647.

83. P. Brinol and R. E. Petty, "Overt Head Movements and Persuasion: A Self-Validation Analysis," *Journal of Personality & Social Psychology* 84 (2003): 1123–1139.

84. R. E. Petty, and J. T. Cacioppo, "The Elaboration Likelihood Model of Persuasion," *Advances in Experimental Social Psychology* 19 (1986): 123–205.

85. K. Miller, "Theories of Message Processing," *Communication Theories: Perspectives, Processes, and Contexts* (Boston, MA: McGraw-Hill, 2005): 129.

86. W. Wood, "Attitude Change: Persuasion and Social Influence," *Annual Review of Psychology* 51 (2000): 539–570.

87. F. Navran, "Your Role in Shaping Ethics," *Executive Excellence* 9 (1992): 11–12.

88. C. H. J. Schwepker, "Ethical Climate's Relationship to Job Satisfaction, Organizational Commitment and Turnover in the Sales Force," *Journal of Business Research* 54 (2001): 39–52.

89. D. B. Turban and D. M. Cable, "Firm Reputation and Applicant Pool Characteristics," *Journal of Organizational Behavior* 24 (2003): 733–751.

90. L. S. Paine, *Value Shift: Why Companies Must Merge Social and Financial Imperatives to Achieve Superior Performance* (New York: McGraw-Hill, 2003).

91. Ibid.; J. O. Cherrington and D. J. Cherrington, "A Menu of Moral Issues: One Week in the Life of *The Wall Street Journal*," *Journal of Business Ethics* 11 (1992): 255–265.

92. M. Easwaramoorthy, C. Barr, M. Runte, and D. Basil, *Business Support for Employee Volunteers in Canada: Results of a National Survey* (Imagine Canada, 2006).

93. B. L. Flannery and D. R. May, "Environmental Ethical Decision Making in the U.S. Metal-Finishing Industry," *Academy of Management Journal* 43 (2000): 642–662.

94. K. R. Andrews, "Ethics in Practice," *Harvard Business Review* (September–October 1989): 99–104.

95. M. Rokeach, *The Nature of Human Values* (New York: Free Press, 1973).

96. S. P. Eisner, "Managing Generation Y," S.A.M. *Advanced Management Journal* 70(4) (2005): 4–15.

97. R. H. Doktor, "Asian and American CEOs: A Comparative Study," *Organizational Dynamics* 18 (1990): 46–56.

98. R. L. Tung, "Handshakes across the Sea: Cross-cultural Negotiating for Business Success," *Organizational Dynamics* (Winter 1991): 30–40.

99. C. Gomez, B. L. Kirkman, and D. L. Shapiro, "The Impact of Collectivism and In-Group/Out-Group Membership on the Evaluation Generosity of Team Members," *Academy of Management Journal* 43 (2000): 1097–1106; J. Zhou and J. J. Martocchio, "Chinese and American Managers' Compensation Award Decisions: A Comparative Policy-capturing Study," *Personnel Psychology* 54 (2001): 115–145.

100. A. J. Ali and M. Amirshahi, "The Iranian Manager: Work Values and Orientations," *Journal of Business Ethics* 40 (2002): 133–143.

101. R. Neale and R. Mindel, "Rigging up Multicultural Teamworking," *Personnel Management* (January 1992): 27–30.

102. G. W. England, "Organizational Goals and Expected Behavior of American Managers," *Academy of Management Journal* 10 (1967): 107–117.

103. B. M. Meglino, E. C. Ravlin, and C. L. Adkins, "A Work Values Approach to Corporate Culture: A Field Test of the Value Congruence Process and Its Relationship to Individual Outcomes," *Journal of Applied Psychology* 74 (1989): 424–432.

104. D. R. Avery, M. Hernandez, and M. R. Hebl, "Who's Watching the Race? Racial Salience in Recruitment Advertising," *Journal of Applied Social Psychology* 34 (2004): 146–161.

105. P. F. McKay and D. R. Avery, "Warning! Diversity Recruitment Could Backfire," *Journal of Management Inquiry* 14 (2005): 330–336.

106. J. B. Rotter, "Generalized Expectancies for Internal versus External Control of Reinforcement," *Psychological Monographs* 80 (1966): 1–28.

107. L. K. Trevino and S. A. Youngblood, "Bad Apples in Bad Barrels: A Causal Analysis of Ethical Decision-making Behavior," *Journal of Applied Psychology* 75 (1990): 378–385.

108. H. M. Lefcourt, *Locus of Control: Current Trends in Theory and Research*, 2nd ed. (Hillsdale, NJ: Erlbaum, 1982).

109. N. Machiavelli, *The Prince*, trans. George Bull (Harmondsworth, England: Penguin Books, 1961).

110. R. Christie and F. L. Geis, *Studies in Machiavellianism* (New York: Academic Press, 1970).

111. R. A. Giacalone and S. B. Knouse, "Justifying Wrongful Employee Behavior: The Role of Personality in Organizational Sabotage," *Journal of Business Ethics* 9 (1990): 55–61.

112. S. B. Knouse and R. A. Giacalone, "Ethical Decision Making in Business: Behavioral Issues and Concerns," *Journal of Business Ethics* 11 (1992): 369–377.

113. L. Kohlberg, "Stage and Sequence: The Cognitive Developmental Approach to Socialization," in D. A. Goslin, ed., *Handbook of Socialization Theory and Research* (Chicago, IL: Rand McNally, 1969), 347–480.

114. C. I. Malinowski and C. P. Smith, "Moral Reasoning and Moral Conduct: An Investigation Prompted by Kohlberg's Theory," *Journal of Personality and Social Psychology* 49 (1985): 1016–1027.

115. M. Brabeck, "Ethical Characteristics of Whistleblowers," *Journal of Research in Personality* 18 (1984): 41–53.

116. W. Y. Penn and B. D. Collier, "Current Research in Moral Development as a Decision Support System," *Journal of Business Ethics* 4 (1985): 131–136; Trevino and Youngblood, "Bad Apples in Bad Barrels."

5

1. U. Klehe and N. Anderson, "Working Hard and Working Smart: Motivation and Ability During Typical and Maximum Performance," *Journal of Applied Psychology* 92 (2007): 978–999.

2. C. C. Pinder, *Work Motivation in Organizational Behavior*, 2nd ed. (New York: Psychology Press, 2008.)

3. L. W. Porter, G. Bigley, and R. M. Steers, *Motivation and Leadership at Work*, 7th ed. (New York: McGraw-Hill, 2002).

4. K. Rhee and T. Sigler, "Science versus Humankind: The Yin and Yang of Motivation Theory," *International Journal of Organization Theory and Behavior* 8 (3) (2005): 313–342.

5. A. Smith, *An Inquiry into the Nature and Causes of the Wealth of Nations*, Vol. 10. of *The Harvard Classics*, C. J. Bullock, ed. (New York: Collier, 1909).

6. F. Taylor, *The Principles of Scientific Management* (New York: Harper & Row, 1911).

7. S. Befort and J. Budd, *Invisible Hands, Invisible Objectives: Bringing Workplace Law and Public Policy into Focus* (Stanford University Press, 2009).

8. J. French, "Field Experiments: Changing Group Productivity," *Experiments in Social Process: A Symposium on Social Psychology* (New York: McGraw-Hill, 1950).

9. J. Muldoon, "The Hawthorne Legacy: A Reassessment of the Impact of the Hawthorne Studies on Management Scholarship, 1930–1958," *Journal of Management History*18(1), (2012): 105–119.

10. A. H. Maslow, "A Theory of Human Motivation," *Psychological Review* 50 (1943): 370–396.

11. W. C. Compton, "Self-Actualization Myths: What Did Maslow Really Say?" *Journal of Humanistic Psychology, 2018.*

12. M.A. Wahba, and L.G. Bridwell, "Maslow Reconsidered: A Review of Research on the Need Hierarchy Theory," *Organizational Behavior and Human Performance*, 15(1976): 212–240.

13. D. M. McGregor, *The Human Side of Enterprise* (New York: McGraw-Hill, 1960).

14. V. Hattangadi, "Theory X & Theory Y," *International Journal of Recent Research Aspects* 2(2015): 20–21.

15. E. E. Lawler, G. R. Lawford, S. A. Mohrman, and G.E Ledford, Jr., *Strategies for High Performance Organizations—The CEO Report: Employee Involvement, TQM, and Reengineering Programs in Fortune 1000 Corporations* (San Francisco: Jossey-Bass, Inc. 1998).

16. C. P. Alderfer, *Human Needs in Organizational Settings* (New York: Free Press, 1972).

17. B. Schneider and C. P. Alderfer, "Three Studies of Need Satisfactions in Organizations," *Administrative Science Quarterly* 18 (1973): 489–505.

18. D. C. McClelland, *Motivational Trends in Society* (Morristown, N.J.: General Learning Press, 1971).

19. J. P. Chaplin and T. S. Krawiec, *Systems and Theories of Psychology* (New York: Holt, Rinehart & Winston, 1960).

20. D. C. McClelland, "Achievement Motivation Can Be Learned," *Harvard Business Review* 43 (1965): 6–24.

21. E. A. Ward, "Multidimensionality of Achievement Motivation among Employed Adults," *Journal of Social Psychology* 134 (1997): 542–544.

22. A. Sagie, D. Elizur, and H. Yamauchi, "The Structure and Strength of Achievement Motivation: A Cross-cultural Comparison," *Journal of Organizational Behavior* 17 (1996): 431–444.

23. D. C. McClelland and D. Burnham, "Power Is the Great Motivator," *Harvard Business Review* 54 (1976): 100–111; J. Hall and J. Hawker, *Power Management Inventory* (The Woodlands, Tex.: Telemetrics International, 1988).

24. S. Schachter, *The Psychology of Affiliation* (Stanford, Calif.: Stanford University Press, 1959).

25. G. G. Alpander and K. D. Carter, "Strategic Multi-National Intra-Company Differences in Employee Motivation," *Journal of Managerial Psychology* 6 (1991): 25–32.

26. J. S. Adams, "Inequity in Social Exchange," in L. Berkowitz, ed., *Advances in Experimental Social Psychology,* vol. 2 (New York: Academic Press, 1965), 267–299; J. S. Adams, "Toward an Understanding of Inequity," *Journal of Abnormal and Social Psychology* 67 (1963): 422–436.

27. Pay Equity Legislation in Canada, Human Resources and Skills Development Canada (March 28, 2010), http://www.hrsdc.gc.ca/eng/labour/labour_law/esl/pay_equity.shtml

28. P. D. Sweeney, D. B. McFarlin, and E. J. Inderrieden, "Using Relative Deprivation Theory to Explain Satisfaction with Income and Pay Level: A Multistudy Examination," *Academy of Management Journal* 33 (1990): 423–436.

29. D. van Dierendonck, W. B. Schaufeli, and H. J. Sixma, "Burnout among General Practitioners: A Perspective from Equity Theory," *Journal of Social and Clinical Psychology* 13 (1994): 86–100.

30. J. Greenberg, "Approaching Equity and Avoiding Inequity in Groups and Organizations," in J. Greenberg and R. L. Cohen, eds., *Equity and Justice in Social Behavior* (New York: Academic Press, 1982), 337–351.

31. R. C. Huseman, J. D. Hatfield, and E. A. Miles, "A New Perspective on Equity Theory: The Equity Sensitivity Construct," *Academy of Management Review* 12 (1987): 222–234.

32. K. E. Weick, M. G. Bougon, and G. Maruyama, "The Equity Context," *Organizational Behavior and Human Performance* 15 (1976): 32–65.

33. O. H. Akan, R. S. Allen, and C. S. White, "Equity Sensitivity and Organizational Citizenship Behavior in a Team Environment," *Small Group Research* 40 (2009): 94–112.

34. R. Coles, *Privileged Ones* (Boston, MA: Little, Brown, 1977).

35. W. C King, E. W. Miles, and D. D. Day, "A Test and Refinement of the Equity Sensitivity Construct," *Journal of Organizational Behavior* 14 (1993): 301–317.

36. L. Y. Fok, S. J. Hartman, M. F. Villere, and R. C. Freibert, "A Study of the Impact of Cross Cultural Differences on Perceptions of Equity and Organizational Citizenship Behavior," *International Journal of Management* 13 (1996): 3–14.

37. J. Greenberg, "Who Stole the Money, and When? Individual and Situational Determinants of Employee Theft," *Organizational Behavior and Human Decision Processes* 89 (2002): 985–1003.

38. M. L. Ambrose, M. A. Seabright, and M. Schminke, "Sabotage in the Workplace: The Role of Organizational Justice," *Organizational Behavior and Human Decision Processes* 89 (2002): 947–965.

39. D. P. Skarlicki and R. Folger, "Retaliation in the Workplace: The Roles of Distributive, Procedural and Interactional Justice," *Journal of Applied Psychology* 82 (1997): 434–443.

40. K. Zimmerman, "This Company Is Letting Its Employees Choose Their Rewards," *Forbes,* May 2, 2018.

41. R. Oliver, "Expectancy Theory Predictions of Salesmen's Performance," *Journal of Marketing Research* 11 (1974): 243–253.

42. R. J. Sanchez, D. M. Truxillo, and T. N. Bauer, "Development and Examination of an Expectancy-based Measure of Test-taking Motivation," *Journal of Applied Psychology* 85 (2000): 739–750.

43. V. H. Vroom, *Work and Motivation* (New York: Wiley, 1964/1970).

44. C. F. Chiang, S. Jang, "An Expectancy Theory Model for Hotel Employee Motivation," *Journal of Hospitality Management* 27(2) (2008): 313–322.

45. M. C. Kernan and R.G. Lord, "Effects of Valence, Expectancies, and Goal Performance Discrepancies in Single and Multiple Goal environments," *Journal of Applied Psychology* 75 (1990):194–203.

46. U. R. Larson, "Supervisor's Performance Feedback to Subordinates: The Effect of Performance Valence and Outcome Dependence," *Organizational Behavior and Human Decision Processes* 37 (1986): 391–409.

47. W. VanEerde and H. Thierry, "Vroom's Expectancy Models and Work-related Criteria: A Meta-Analysis," *Journal of Applied Psychology* 81 (1996): 575–586.

48. E. D. Pulakos and N. Schmitt, "A Longitudinal Study of a Valence Model

Approach for the Prediction of Job Satisfaction of New Employees," *Journal of Applied Psychology* 68 (1983): 307–312; F. J. Landy and W. S. Becker, "Motivation Theory Reconsidered," in L. L. Cummings and B. M. Staw, eds., *Research in Organizational Behavior* 9 (Greenwich, CT: JAI Press, 1987), 1–38.

49. L. Kohlberg, "The Cognitive-developmental Approach to Socialization," in D. A. Goslin, ed., *Handbook of Socialization Theory and Research* (Chicago, IL: Rand McNally, 1969).

50. E. Locke, K. Shaw, L. Saari, and G. Latham, "Goal Setting and Task Performance: 1969–1980," *Psychological Bulletin* 90 (1981): 125–152.

51. E. A. Locke and G. P. Latham, "Building a Practically Useful Theory of Goal Setting and Task Motivation: A 35-year Odyssey," *American Psychologist* 57 (2002): 705–717.

52. Ibid.

53. Ibid.

54. Ibid.

55. J. Hollenbeck, C. Williams, and H. Klein, "An Empirical Examination of the Antecedents of Commitment to Difficult Goals," *Journal of Applied Psychology* 74 (1989): 18–23.

56. E. A. Locke and G. P. Latham, "Building a Practically Useful Theory of Goal Setting and Task Motivation: A 35-year Odyssey," *American Psychologist* 57 (2002): 705–717.

57. C. Pinder, *Work Motivation* (Glenview IL: Scott, Foresman, 1984)

58. E. Locke, "Motivation through Conscious Goal Setting," *Applied and Preventive Psychology* 5 (1996): 117–124.

59. N. J. Adler, *International Dimensions of Organizational Behavior*, 4th ed. (Mason, OH: South-Western, 2001).

60. M. Erez, "A Culture-based Approach to Work Motivation," in C. P. Early and M. Erez, eds., *New Perspectives on International Industrial/Organizational Psychology* (San Francisco, CA: Jossey-Bass, 1997), 192–242.

61. H. Thierry, "Payment by Results: A Review of Research 1945–1985," *Applied Psychology: An International Review* 36 (1987): 91–108.

62. K. Y. Thornblum, D. Jonsson, and U. G. Foa, "Nationality Resource Class, and Preferences among Three Allocation Rules: Sweden vs. USA," *International Journal of Intercultural Relations* 9 (1985): 51–77.

63. J. J. Berman and P. Singh, "Cross-cultural Similarities and Differences in Perceptions of Fairness," *Journal of Cross-cultural Psychology* 16 (1985): 55–67.

64. U. M. Gluskinos, "Cultural and Political Considerations in the Introduction of Western Technologies: The Mekorot Project," *Journal of Management Development* 6 (1988): 34–46.

65. M. Erez and C. P. Earley, "Comparative Analysis of Goal-setting Strategies across Cultures," *Journal of Applied Psychology* 71 (1987): 658–665.

6

1. D.- E. Dube, "Stress Is the Reason 1 in 4 Canadians Quit Their Job," August 16, 2017, accessed from https://globalnews.ca/news/3672298/stress-is-the-reason-1-in-4-canadians-quit-their-job, September 6, 2018.

2. J. Park, "Work Stress and Job Performance," *Perspectives on Labour and Income*, Statistics Canada, December 2007, catalogue no. 75–001-XIE, http://www.statcan.gc.ca/pub/75-001-x/75-001-x2007112-eng.htm.

3. D.- E. Dube, Stress Is the Reason 1 in 4 Canadians Quit their Job, August 16, 2017, accessed from https://globalnews.ca/news/3672298/stress-is-the-reason-1-in-4-canadians-quit-their-job, September 6, 2018.

4. C. Higgins, L. Duxbury, and S. Lyons, "Reducing Work–Life Conflict: What Works? What Doesn't?" Health Canada, 2008, http://www.hc-sc.gc.ca/ ewh-semt/pubs/occup-travail/balancing-equilibre/sum-res-eng.php.

5. OECD Better Life Index Canada, accessed from http://www.oecdbetterlifeindex.org/countries/canada, September 6, 2018.

6. Cited in C. Williams, "Sources of Workplace Stress," *Perspectives on Labour and Income*, Statistics Canada, June 2003, accessed from http://www.statcan.gc.ca/pub/75-001-x/00603/6533-eng.html, September 6, 2018.

7. A. Ostry, S. Maggi, J. Tansey, J. Dunn, R. Hershler, L. Chen, and C. Hertzman., "The Impact of Psychosocial and Physical Work Experience on Mental Health: A Nested Case Control Study," *Canadian Journal of Community Mental Health* 25 (2006): 59–70.

8. L. Duxbury, C. Higgins, and S. Lyons, "The Etiology and Reduction of Role Overload in Canada's Health Care Sector, 2010," http://www.sprott.carleton .ca/news/2010/docs/complete-report.pdf.

9. S. A. Murphy, L. Duxbury, and C. Higgins, "The Individual and Organizational Consequences of Stress, Anxiety and Depression in the Workplace: A Case Study," *Canadian Journal of Community Mental Health* 25 (2006): 143–157.

10. European Foundation for the Improvement of Living and Working Conditions, Work-Related stress, 2007, http://www.eurofound.europa.eu/ewco/reports/TN0502TR01/TN0502TR01.pdf

11. F. Green and S. McIntosh, "The Intensification of Work in Europe," *Labour Economics* 8 (2001): 291–308.

12. M. Dollard, N. Skinner, M. R. Tuckey, and T. Bailey, "National Surveillance of Psychosocial Risk Factors in the Workplace: An International Overview," *Work and Stress* 21 (2007): 1–29.

13. J. Sun, S. Wang, J. Zhang, and W. Li, "Assessing the Cumulative Effects of Stress: The Association between Job Stress and Allostatic Load in a Large Sample of Chinese Employees," *Work and Stress* 21 (2007): 333–347.

14. K. Peltzer, O. Shisana, K. Zuma, B. Van Wyk, and N. Zungu-Dirwayi, "Job Stress, Job Satisfaction and Stress-Related Illnesses among South African Educators," *Stress and Health* 25 (2009): 247–257.

15. European Social Partners, "Implementation of the European Autonomous Framework Agreement on Work-related Stress," June 2008, http://www.etuc.org/IMG/pdf_Final_Implementation_report.pdf.

16. Health and Safety Executive, "Managing the Causes of Work-related Stress," United Kingdom, 2007, http://www.hse.gov.uk/pubns/priced/hsg218.pdf.

17. BBC News, "'Stress Code' for Firms Launched," *BBC News*, June 16, 2003, accessed from http://news.bbc.co.uk/go/pr/fr/-/2/hi/health/2993116.stm, September 6, 2018.

18. S. Leka, A. Griffiths, and T. Cox (Institute of Work, Health and Organizations; World Health Organization), *Work Organization and Stress: Systematic Problem Approaches for Employers, Managers and Trade Union Representatives*, World Health Organization, 2003.

19. S. Sri Kantha, "Productivity Drive," *Nature* (April 30, 1992): 738; S. Sri Kantha, "Clues to Prolific Productivity among Prominent Scientists," *Medical Hypotheses* 39 (1992): 159–163.

20. H. Selye, *The Stress of Life* (New York: McGraw-Hill, 1956).

21. W. B. Cannon, "Stresses and Strains of Homeostasis," *American Journal of the Medical Sciences* 189 (1935): 1–14.

22. W. B. Cannon, *The Wisdom of the Body* (New York: Norton, 1932).

23. R. S. Lazarus, *Psychological Stress and the Coping Process* (New York: McGraw-Hill, 1966).

24. T. R. Schneider, "The Role of Neuroticism on Psychological and Physiological Stress Responses," *Journal of Experimental Social Psychology* 40 (2004): 795–804.

25. D. Katz and R. L. Kahn, *The Social Psychology of Organizations*, 2nd ed. (New York: Wiley, 1978), 185–221.

26. H. Levinson, "A Psychoanalytic View of Occupational Stress," *Occupational Mental Health* 3 (1978): 2–13.

27. S. Cohen, D. Janicki-Deverts, and G. E. Miller, "Psychological Stress and Disease," *Journal of the American Medical Association* 298 (2007): 1685–1687.

28. T. L. Friedman, *The Lexus and the Olive Tree* (New York: Vintage Anchor, 2000).

29. S. Zuboff, *In the Age of the Smart Machine: The Future of Work and Power* (New York: Basic Books, 1988).

30. D. T. Hall and J. Richter, "Career Gridlock: Baby Boomers Hit the Wall," *Academy of Management Executive* 4 (1990): 7–22.

31. N. P. Podsakoff, J. A. LePine, and M. A. LePine, "Differential Challenge Stressor-Hindrance Stressor Relationships with Job Attitudes, Turnover Intentions, Turnover, and Withdrawal Behavior: A Meta-Analysis," *Journal of Applied Psychology* 92 (2007): 438–454.

32. R. L. Kahn, D. M. Wolfe, R. P. Quinn, J. D. Snoek, and R. A. Rosenthal, *Organizational Stress: Studies in Role Conflict and Ambiguity* (New York: Wiley, 1964).

33. L. B. Hammer, T. N. Bauer, and A. A. Grandey, "Work-Family Conflict and Work-Related Withdrawal Behaviors," *Journal of Business and Psychology* 17 (2003): 419–436.

34. R. B. Reid, "Mental Stress in the Workplace," Lancaster, Brooks and Welch (2004), http://www.lbwlawyers.com/publications/mentalstressintheworkplace.php.

35. Quoted in J. Burton, *The Business Case for a Healthy Workplace*, Industrial Accident Prevention Association (2008), http://www.iapa.ca/pdf/fd_business_case_healthy_workplace.pdf.

36. P. J. Frost, *Toxic Emotions at Work: How Compassionate Managers Handle Pain and Conflict* (Boston, MA: Harvard Business School Press, 2003).

37. S. Grebner, N. K. Semmer, L. L. Faso, S. Gut, W. Kalin, and A. Elfering, "Working Conditions, Well-being, and Job-related Attitudes among Call Centre Agents," *European Journal of Work and Organizational Psychology* 12 (2003): 341–365.

38. M. P. Bell, J. C. Quick, and C. Cycota, "Assessment and Prevention of Sexual Harassment: An Applied Guide to Creating Healthy Organizations," *International Journal of Selection and Assessment* 10 (2002): 160–167.

39. L. T. Hosmer, "Trust: The Connecting Link between Organizational Theory and Philosophical Ethics," *Academy of Management Review* 20 (1995): 379–403; V. J. Doby and R. D. Caplan, "Organizational Stress as Threat to Reputation: Effects on Anxiety at Work and at Home," *Academy of Management Journal* 38 (1995): 1105–1123.

40. R. T. Keller, "Cross-functional Project Groups in Research and New Product Development: Diversity, Communications, Job Stress, and Outcomes," *Academy of Management Journal* 33 (2001): 547–555.

41. R. Sharp, "How Your Office Makes You Sick," *The Independent*, London (March 3, 2009).

42. J. Burton, *The Business Case for a Healthy Workplace* (Industrial Accident Prevention Association, 2008).

43. M. F. Peterson and P. B. Smith, "Does National Culture or Ambient Temperature Explain Cross-national Differences in Role Stress? No Sweat!" *Academy of Management Journal* 40 (1997): 930–946.

44. K. K. Gillingham, "High-G Stress and Orientational Stress: Physiologic Effects of Aerial Maneuvering," *Aviation, Space, and Environmental Medicine* 59 (1988): A10–A20.

45. R. S. DeFrank, "Executive Travel Stress: Perils of the Road Warrior," *Academy of Management Executive* 14 (2000): 58–72; M. Westman, "Strategies for Coping with Business Trips: A Qualitative Exploratory Study," *International Journal of Stress Management* 11 (2004): 167–176.

46. Open Offices Make People Talk Less and Email More, BBC Capital, July 20, 2018, accessed from http://www.bbc.com/capital/story/20180718-open-offices-make-people-talk-less-and-email-more, September 6, 2018.

47. https://www.fastcompany.com/90170941/the-subtle-sexism-of-your-open-plan-office

48. R. S. Bhagat, S. J. McQuaid, S. Lindholm, and J. Segovis, "Total Life Stress: A Multimethod Validation of the Construct and Its Effect on Organizationally Valued Outcomes and Withdrawal Behaviors," *Journal of Applied Psychology* 70 (1985): 202–214.

49. J. C. Quick, J. R. Joplin, D. A. Gray, and E. C. Cooley, "The Occupational Life Cycle and the Family," in L. L'Abate, ed., *Handbook of Developmental Family Psychology and Psychopathology* (New York: John Wiley, 1993).

50. S. A. Lobel, "Allocation of Investment in Work and Family Roles: Alternative Theories and Implications for Research," *Academy of Management Review* 16 (1991): 507–521.

51. G. Porter, "Organizational Impact of Workaholism: Suggestions for Researching the Negative Outcomes of Excessive Work," *Journal of Occupational Health Psychology* 1 (1996): 70–84.

52. R. A. Karasek, "Job Demands, Job Decision Latitude, and Mental Strain: Implications for Job Redesign," *Administrative Science Quarterly* 24 (1979): 285–310.

53. T. Theorell, A. Tsutsumi, J. Hallquist, C. Reuterwall, C. Hagstedt, P. Fredlund, N. Emlund, and J. V. Johnson, "Decision Latitude, Job Strain, and Myocardial Infarction: A Study of Working Men in Stockholm," *American Journal of Public Health* 88 (1998): 382–388.

54. C. Aboa-Eboule, C. Brisson, E. Maunsell, B. Masse, R. Bourbonnais, et al., "Job Strain and Risk of Recurrent Coronary Heart Disease Events," *Journal of the American Medical Association* 298 (2007): 1652–1660.

55. H. Kuper and M. Marmot, "Job Strain, Job Demands, Decision Latitude, and Risk of Coronary Heart Disease within the Whitehall II Study," *Journal of Epidemiology and Community Health* 57 (2003): 147–153.

56. A. Ostry, S. Maggi, J. Tansey, J. Dunn, R. Hershler, L. Chen, and C. Hertzman, "The Impact of Psychosocial and Physical Work Experience on Mental Health: A Nested Case Control Study," *Canadian Journal of Community Mental Health* 25 (2006): 59–70.

57. J. L. Wang, A. Lesage, N. Schmitz, and A. Drapeau, "The Relationship between Work Stress and Mental Disorders in Men and Women: Findings from a Population-based Study," *Journal of Epidemiology and Community Health* 62 (2008): 42–47.

58. J. J. Hakanen, W. B. Schaufeli, and K. Ahola, "The Job Demands–Resources Model: A Three-Year Cross-lagged Study of Burnout, Depression, Commitment, and Work Engagement," *Work and Stress* 22 (2008): 224–241.

59. D. G. J. Beckers, D. van der Linden, P. G. W. Smulders, M. A. J. Kompier, T. W. Taris, and S. A. E. Geurts, "Voluntary or Involuntary? Control over Overtime

and Rewards for Overtime in Relation to Fatigue and Work Satisfaction," *Work and Stress* 22 (2008): 33–50.

60. H. K. Knudsen, L. J. Ducharme, and P. M. Roman, "Turnover Intention and Emotional Exhaustion 'At the Top': Adapting the Job Demands–Resources Model to Leaders of Addiction Treatment Organizations," *Journal of Occupational Health Psychology* 14 (2009): 84–95.

61. S. B. Bacharach, P. A. Bamberger, and E. Doveh, "Firefighters, Critical Incidents, and Drinking to Cope: The Adequacy of Unit-Level Performance Resources as a Source of Vulnerability and Protection," *Journal of Applied Psychology* 93 (2008): 155–169.

62. D. de Bacquer, E. Pelfrene, E. Clays, R. Mak, M. Moreau, et al., "Perceived Job Stress and Incidence of Coronary Events: 3-Year Follow-up of the Belgian Stress Project Cohort," *American Journal of Epidemiology* 161 (2005): 434–441.

63. N. W. Van Yperen and M. Hagedoorn, "Do High Job Demands Increase Intrinsic Motivation or Fatigue or Both? The Role of Job Control and Job Social Support," *Academy of Management Journal* 46 (2003): 339–348.

64. V. Rousseau, S. Salek, C. Aube, and E. M. Morin, "Distributive Justice, Procedural Justice, and Psychological Distress: The Moderating Effect of Coworker Support and Work Autonomy," *Journal of Occupational Health Psychology* 14 (2009): 305–317.

65. J. Siegrist, "Adverse Health Effects of High Effort/Low Reward Conditions," *Journal of Occupational Health Psychology* 1 (1996): 27–41.

66. K. Schmidt, B. Neubach, and H. Heuer, "Self-Control Demands, Cognitive Control Deficits, and Burnout, *Work and Stress* 21 (2007): 142–154.

67. I. Godin, F. Kittel, Y. Coppieters, and J. Siegrist, "A Prospective Study of Cumulative Job Stress in Relation to Mental Health," *BMC Public Health* 5 (2005): 67.

68. H. Kuper, A. Singh-Manoux, J. Siegrist, and M. Marmot, "When Reciprocity Fails: Effort–Reward Imbalance in Relation to Coronary Heart Disease and Health Functioning in the Whitehall II Study," *Occupational and Environmental Medicine* 59 (2002): 777–784.

69. R. Rugulies and N. Krause, "Effort–Reward Imbalance and Incidence of Low Back and Neck Injuries in San Francisco Transit Operators," *Occupational and Environmental Medicine* 65 (2008): 525–533.

70. A. S. Ostry, S. Kelly, P. A. Demers, C. Mustard, and C. Hertzman, "A Comparison between the Effort–Reward Imbalance and Demand Control Models," *BMC Public Health* 3 (2003): 10.

71. C. Maslach and M. P Leiter, "Early Predictors of Job Burnout and Engagement," *Journal of Applied Psychology* 93 (2008): 498–512.

72. Health Canada, "Best Advice for Stress Risk Management," Cat. No.: H39-546/2000E, 2000, http://www.hc-sc.gc.ca/ewh-semt/pubs/occup-travail/stress-part-1/index-eng.php.

73. J. Loehr and T. Schwartz, "The Making of a Corporate Athlete," *Harvard Business Review* 79 (2001): 120–129.

74. J. D. Quick, R. S. Horn, and J. C. Quick, "Health Consequences of Stress," *Journal of Organizational Behavior Management* 8 (1986): 19–36.

75. R. M. Yerkes and J. D. Dodson, "The Relation of Strength of Stimulus to Rapidity of Habit-Formation," *Journal of Comparative Neurology and Psychology* 18 (1908): 459–482.

76. J. D. Cresswell, W. T. Welch, S. E. Taylor, D. K. Sherman, T. L. Gruenewald, and T. Mann., "Affirmation of Personal Values Buffers Neuroendocrine and Psychological Stress Responses," *Psychological Science* 16 (2005): 846–851.

77. M. B. Ford and N. L. K. Collins, "Self-Esteem Moderates Neuroendocrine and Psychological Responses to Interpersonal Rejection," *Journal of Personality and Social Psychology* 98 (2010): 405–419.

78. Y. E. Shen, "Relationships between Self-Efficacy, Social Support and Stress Coping Strategies in Chinese Primary and Secondary School Teachers," *Stress and Health* 25 (2009): 129–138.

79. J. L. Xie, J. Schaubroeck, and S. S. K. Lam, "Theories of Job Stress, and the Role of Traditional Values: A Longitudinal Study in China," *Journal of Applied Psychology* 93 (2008): 831–848.

80. K. L. Zellars, J. A. Meurs, P. L. Perrewe, C. J. Kacmar, and A. M. Rossi, "Reacting to and Recovering from a Stressful Situation: The Negative Affectivity–Physiological Arousal Relationship," *Journal of Occupational Health Psychology* 14 (2009): 11–22.

81. N. A. Bowling and K. J. Eschleman, "Employee Personality as a Moderator of the Relationships between Work Stressors and Counterproductive Work Behavior," *Journal of Occupational Health Psychology* 15 (2010): 91–103.

82. Ibid.

83. M. D. Friedman and R. H. Rosenman, *Type A Behavior and Your Heart* (New York: Knopf, 1974).

84. L. Wright, "The Type A Behavior Pattern and Coronary Artery Disease," *American Psychologist* 43 (1988): 2–14.

85. J. M. Ivancevich and M. T. Matteson, "A Type A–B Person–Work Environment Interaction Model for Examining Occupational Stress and Consequences," *Human Relations* 37 (1984): 491–513.

86. S. O. C. Kobasa, "Conceptualization and Measurement of Personality in Job Stress Research," in J. J. Hurrell, Jr., L. R. Murphy, S. L. Sauter, and C. L. Cooper, eds., *Occupational Stress: Issues and Developments in Research* (New York: Taylor & Francis, 1988), 100–109.

87. Psychology Today, "About Resilience," accessed from https://www.psychologytoday.com/ca/basics/resilience, September 6, 2018.

88. J. Borysenko, "Personality Hardiness," *Lectures in Behavioral Medicine* (Boston, MA: Harvard Medical School, 1985).

89. J. S. House, K. R. Landis, and D. Umberson, "Social Relationships and Health," *Science* 241 (1988): 540–545.

90. J. Bowlby, *A Secure Base* (New York: Basic Books, 1988).

91. C. Hazan and P. Shaver, "Love and Work: An Attachment-Theoretical Perspective," *Journal of Personality and Social Psychology* 59 (1990): 270–280.

92. J. C. Quick, D. L. Nelson, and J. D. Quick, *Stress and Challenge at the Top: The Paradox of the Successful Executive* (Chichester, England: Wiley, 1990).

93. J. C. Quick, J. R. Joplin, D. L. Nelson, and J. D. Quick, "Self-Reliance for Stress and Combat," in *Proceedings of the 8th Combat Stress Conference,* U.S. Army Health Services Command, Fort Sam Houston, Texas, September 23–27, 1991, 1–5.

94. L. Duxbury, C. Higgins, and D. Coghill, "Voices of Canadians: Seeking Work–Life Balance," Human Resources Canada, Cat. No. RH54-12, 2003.

95. S. D. Tvedt, P. O. Saksvik, and K. Nytro, "Does Change Process Healthiness Reduce the Negative Effects of Organizational Change on the Psychosocial Environment?" *Work and Stress* 23 (2009): 80–98.

96. M. Fugate, A. J. Kinicki, and G. E. Prussia, "Employee Coping with Organizational Change: An Examination of Alternative Theoretical Perspectives and Models," *Personnel Psychology* 61 (2008): 1–36.

97. L. Duxbury, C. Higgins, and S. Lyons, "The Etiology and Reduction of Role

Overload in Canada's Health Care Sector, 2010," http://www.sprott.carleton .ca/news/2010/docs/complete-report.pdf.

98. J. Halpern, M. Gurevich, B. Schwartz, and P. Brazeau, "Interventions for Critical Incident Stress in Emergency Medical Services: A Qualitative Study," *Stress and Health* 25 (2009): 139–149.

99. Health and Safety Executive, "Managing the Causes of Work-related Stress," United Kingdom, 2007, http://www.hse.gov.uk/pubns/priced/hsg218.pdf.

100. M. Fugate, A. J. Kinicki, and G. E. Prussia, "Employee Coping with Organizational Change: An Examination of Alternative Theoretical Perspectives and Models," *Personnel Psychology* 61 (2008): 1–36.

101. J. C. Wallace, B. D. Edwards, T. Arnold, M. L. Frazier, and D. M. Finch, "Work Stressors, Role-based Performance and the Moderating Influence of Organizational Support," *Journal of Applied Psychology* 94 (2009): 254–262.

102. M. A. Glynn, "Effects of Work Task Cues and Play Task Cues on Information Processing, Judgment and Motivation," *Journal of Applied Psychology* 79 (1994): 34–45.

103. R. Bourbonnais, C. Brisson, A. Vinet, M. Vezina, B. Abdous, and M. Gaudet, "Effectiveness of a Participative Intervention on Psychosocial Work Factors to Prevent Mental Health Problems in a Hospital Setting," *Occupational and Environmental Medicine* 63 (2006): 335–342; C. Maslach and M. P Leiter, "Early Predictors of Job Burnout and Engagement," *Journal of Applied Psychology* 93 (2008): 498–512.

104. R. Bourbonnais, C. Brisson, A. Vinet, M. Vezina, B. Abdous, and M. Gaudet, "Effectiveness of a Participative Intervention on Psychosocial Work Factors to Prevent Mental Health Problems in a Hospital Setting," *Occupational and Environmental Medicine* 63 (2006): 335–342.

105. S. Leka, A. Griffiths, and T. Cox (Institute of Work, Health and Organizations; World Health Organization), *Work Organization and Stress: Systematic Problem Approaches for Employers, Managers and Trade Union Representatives*, World Health Organization, 2003.

106. WorksafeBC, "Coping with Critical Incident Stress at Work," Workers Compensation Board, BC, 2002, http://www.worksafebc.com/publications/health_and_safety/by_topic/assets/pdf/critical_incident_stress.pdf.

107. J. C. Quick and C. L. Cooper, *FAST FACTS: Stress and Strain*, 2nd ed. (Oxford: Health Press, 2003).

108. M. E. P. Seligman, *Learned Optimism* (New York: Knopf, 1990).

109. W. T. Brooks and T. W. Mullins, *High-Impact Time Management* (Englewood Cliffs, NJ: Prentice-Hall, 1989).

110. M. Westman and D. Eden, "Effects of a Respite from Work on Burnout: Vacation Relief and Fade-Out," *Journal of Applied Psychology* 82 (1997): 516–527.

111. C. P. Neck and K. H. Cooper, "The Fit Executive: Exercise and Diet Guidelines for Enhancing Performance," *Academy of Management Executive* 14 (2000): 72–84.

112. M. Davis, E. R. Eshelman, and M. McKay, *The Relaxation and Stress Reduction Workbook*, 3rd ed. (Oakland, CA: New Harbinger, 1988).

113. H. Benson, "Your Innate Asset for Combating Stress," *Harvard Business Review* 52 (1974): 49–60.

114. J. W. Pennebaker, *Opening Up: The Healing Power of Expressing Emotions* (New York: Guilford, 1997).

115. M. E. Francis and J. W. Pennebaker, "Putting Stress into Words: The Impact of Writing on Physiological, Absentee, and Self-Reported Emotional Well-Being Measures," *American Journal of Health Promotion* 6 (1992): 280–287.

116. Z. Solomon, B. Oppenheimer, and S. Noy, "Subsequent Military Adjustment of Combat Stress Reaction Casualties: A Nine-Year Follow-Up Study," in N. A. Milgram, ed., *Stress and Coping in Time of War: Generalizations from the Israeli Experience* (New York: Brunner/Mazel, 1986), 84–90.

117. D. Wegman and L. Fine, "Occupational Health in the 1990s," *Annual Review of Public Health* 11 (1990): 89–103; J. C. Quick, "Occupational Health Psychology: Historical Roots and Future Directions," *Health Psychology* 17 (1999): 82–88.

118. D. Gebhardt and C. Crump, "Employee Fitness and Wellness Programs in the Workplace," *American Psychologist* 45 (1990): 262–272.

119. T. Wolf, H. Randall, and J. Faucett, "A Survey of Health Promotion Programs in U.S. and Canadian Medical Schools," *American Journal of Health Promotion* 3 (1988): 33–36.

120. S. Weiss, J. Fielding, and A. Baum, *Health at Work* (Hillsdale, NJ: Erlbaum, 1990).

121. J. B. Bennett, R. F. Cook, and K. R. Pelletier, "Toward an Integrated Framework for Comprehensive Organizational Wellness: Concepts, Practices, and Research in Workplace Health Promotion," in J. C. Quick and L. E. Tetrick, eds., *Handbook of Occupational Health Psychology* (Washington, D.C.: American Psychological Association, 2003): 69–95.

7

1. H. A. Simon, *The New Science of Management Decision* (New York: Harper & Row, 1960).

2. G. Huber, *Managerial Decision Making* (Glenview, IL: Scott, Foresman, 1980).

3. H. A. Simon, *Administrative Behavior* (New York: Macmillan, 1957).

4. E. F. Harrison, *The Managerial Decision-Making Process* (Boston, MA: Houghton Mifflin, 1981).

5. V. H. Vroom and P. W. Yetton, *Leadership and Decision Making* (Pittsburgh: University of Pittsburgh, 1973).

6. V. H. Vroom, "Leadership and the Decision-making Process," *Organizational Dynamics* 28 (2000): 82–94.

7. R. L. Ackoff, "The Art and Science of Mess Management," *Interfaces* (February 1981): 20–26.

8. R. M. Cyert and J. G. March, eds., *A Behavioral Theory of the Firm* (Englewood Cliffs, NJ: Prentice-Hall, 1963).

9. M. D. Cohen, J. March, and J. P. Olsen, "A Garbage Can Model of Organizational Choice," *Administrative Science Quarterly* 17 (1) (1972): 1–25.

10. "'Garbage Can' Models: Multiple Stream Theory" (n.d.), http://faculty.chass.ncsu.edu/parson?PA/65?garbagecan.htm.

11. M. Lipson, *A Garbage Can Model of UN Peacekeeping* (2004), http://www.allacademic.com/meta/p_mla_apa_research_citation/0/7/3/1/5/p73159_index.html.

12. B. M. Staw, "Knee-Deep in the Big Muddy: A Study of Escalating Commitment to a Chosen Course of Action," *Organizational Behavior and Human Performance* 16 (1976): 27–44; B. M. Staw, "The Escalation of Commitment to a Course of Action," *Academy of Management Review* 6 (1981): 577–587.

13. B. M. Staw and J. Ross, "Understanding Behavior in Escalation Situations," *Science* 246 (1989): 216–220.

14. T. Freemantle and M. Tolson, "Space Station Had Political Ties in Tow," *Houston Chronicle* (August 4, 2003), http://www.chron.com/cs/CDA/ssistory.mpl/space/2004947.

15. R. Walker, "Is The International Space Station The Most Expensive Single Item Ever Built?" Science 2.0, August 22, 1015, accessed from https://www.science20.com/robert_inventor/is_the_international_space_station_the_most_expensive_single_item_ever_built-156922, September 7, 2018.

16. L. Festinger, *A Theory of Cognitive Dissonance* (Evanston, IL: Row, Peterson, 1957).

17. B. M. Staw, "The Escalation of Commitment: An Update and Appraisal," in Z. Shapira, ed., *Organizational Decision Making* (Cambridge: Cambridge University Press, 1997).

18. D. M. Boehne and P. W. Paese, "Deciding Whether to Complete or Terminate an Unfinished Project: A Strong Test of the Project Completion Hypothesis," *Organizational Behavior and Human Decision Processes* 81 (2000): 178–194; H. Moon, "Looking Forward and Looking Back: Integrating Completion and Sunk Cost Effects within an Escalation-of-Commitment Progress Decision," *Journal of Applied Psychology* 86 (2000): 104–113.

19. D. M. Rowell, "*Concorde*: An Untimely and Unnecessary Demise" (April 11, 2003), http://www.thetravelinsider.info/2003/0411.htm.

20. G. McNamara, H. Moon, and P. Bromiley, "Banking on Commitment: Intended and Unintended Consequences of an Organization's Attempt to Attenuate Escalation of Commitment," *Academy of Management Journal* 45 (2002): 443–452.

21. G. Whyte, "Diffusion of Responsibility: Effects on the Escalation Tendency," *Journal of Applied Psychology* 76 (1991): 408–415.

22. D. Kahneman, *Thinking, Fast and Slow* (Toronto: Doubleday Canada, 2011); Online Learning Center, "Glossary," http://highered.mcgrawhill.com/sites/0072413875/student_view0/glossary.html; Shell liveWire, "What Can Go Wrong with the Appraisal Process?" http://www.shell-livewire.org/home/business-library/employing-people/delegation-and-staff-appraisal/what-can-go-wrong-with-the-appraisal-process/; "The Halo Effect," *The Economist,* October 14, 2009, accessed from http://www.economist.com/node/14299211, September 7, 2018.

23. S. Pratt, "9 Types of Unconscious Bias and the Shocking Ways They Affect Your Recruiting Efforts," November 3, 2016, accessed from https://www.socialtalent.com/blog/recruitment/9-types-of-unconscious-bias, September 7, 2018.

24. NPR, "Bias Isn't Just a Police Problem, It's A Preschool Problem," September 28, 2016, accessed from http://www.npr.org/sections/ed/2016/09/28/495488716/bias-isnt-just-a-police-problem-its-a-preschool-problem, September 7, 2018.

25. Kirwan Institute for the Study of Race and Ethnicity, http://kirwaninstitute.osu.edu/research/understanding-implicit-bias, accessed September 7, 2018.

26. NPR, "Bias Isn't Just a Police Problem, It's A Preschool Problem," September 28, 2016, accessed from http://www.npr.org/sections/ed/2016/09/28/495488716/bias-isnt-just-a-police-problem-its-a-preschool-problem, September 7, 2018.

27. D. van Knippenberg, B. van Knippenberg, and E. van Dijk, "Who Takes the Lead in Risky Decision Making? Effects of Group Members' Risk Preferences and Prototypicality," *Organizational Behavior and Human Decision Processes* 83 (2000): 213–234.

28. J. A. Nelson, "Are Women Really More Risk-Averse Than Men? A Re-Analysis of the Literature Using Expanded Methods," *Journal of Economic Surveys* 29 (3) (2015): 566–585.

29. K. R. MacCrimmon and D. Wehrung, *Taking Risks* (New York: Free Press, 1986).

30. T. S. Perry, "How Small Firms Innovate: Designing a Culture for Creativity," *Research Technology Management* 28 (1995): 14–17.

31. "Cognitive Style," Psychology Research and Reference, accessed from http://psychology.iresearchnet.com/developmental-psychology/cognitive-development/cognitive-style, October 3, 2018.

32. A. Y. Nozari and H. Siamian, "The Relationship between Field Dependent-Independent Cognitive Style and Understanding English Text Reading and Academic Success," *MateriaSocioMedica* 27 (1) (2015): 39–41.

33. T. Gallén, "Managers and Strategic Decisions: Does the Cognitive Style Matter?" *The Journal of Management Development* 25 (2) (2006): 118–133.

34. A. Saleh, "Brain Hemisphericity and Academic Majors: A Correlation Study," *College Student Journal* 35 (2001): 193–200.

35. N. Khatri, "The Role of Intuition in Strategic Decision Making," *Human Relations* 53 (2000): 57–86.

36. H. Mintzberg, "Planning on the Left Side and Managing on the Right," *Harvard Business Review* 54 (1976): 51–63.

37. D. J. Isenberg, "How Senior Managers Think," *Harvard Business Review* 62 (1984): 81–90.

38. Ibid.

39. K. G. Ross, G. A. Klein, P. Thunholm, J. F. Schmitt, and H. C. Baxter, "The Recognition-primed Decision Model," *Military Review, Fort Leavenworth* 84 (2004): 6–10.

40. C. I. Barnard, *The Functions of the Executive* (Cambridge, MA: Harvard University Press, 1938).

41. R. Rowan, *The Intuitive Manager* (New York: Little, Brown, 1986).

42. W. H. Agor, *Intuition in Organizations* (Newbury Park, CA: SAGE, 1989).

43. Isenberg, "How Senior Managers Think," 81–90.

44. H. A. Simon, "Making Management Decisions: The Role of Intuition and Emotion," *Academy of Management Executive* 1 (1987): 57–64.

45. J. L. Redford, R. H. McPhierson, R. G. Frankiewicz, and J. Gaa, "Intuition and Moral Development," *Journal of Psychology* 129 (1994): 91–101.

46. W. H. Agor, "How Top Executives Use Their Intuition to Make Important Decisions," *Business Horizons* 29 (1986): 49–53.

47. R. Wild, "Naked Hunch; Gut Instinct Is Vital to Your Business," *Success* (June 1998), http://www.findarticles.com/cf_dls/m3514/n6_v45/20746158/p1/article.html.

48. O. Behling and N. L. Eckel, "Making Sense out of Intuition," *Academy of Management Executive* 5 (1991): 46–54.

49. L. R. Beach, *Image Theory: Decision Making in Personal and Organizational Contexts* (Chichester, England: Wiley, 1990).

50. E. Bonabeau, "Don't Trust Your Gut," *Harvard Business Review* 81 (2003): 116–126.

51. L. Livingstone, "Person–Environment Fit on the Dimension of Creativity: Relationships with Strain, Job Satisfaction, and Performance" (Ph.D. diss., Oklahoma State University, 1992).

52. G. Wallas, *The Art of Thought* (New York: Harcourt Brace, 1926).

53. H. Benson and W. Proctor, *The Break-out Principle* (Scribner: New York, 2003); G. L. Fricchione, B. T. Slingsby, and H. Benson, "The Placebo Effect and the Relaxation Response: Neural Processes and Their Coupling to Constitutive Nitric Oxide," *Brain Research Reviews* 35 (2001): 1–19.

54. M. D. Mumford and S. B. Gustafson, "Creativity Syndrome: Integration, Application, and Innovation," *Psychological Bulletin* 103 (1988): 27–43.

55. T. Poze, "Analogical Connections—The Essence of Creativity," *Journal of Creative Behavior* 17 (1983): 240–241.

56. I. Sladeczek and G. Domino, "Creativity, Sleep, and Primary Process Thinking in Dreams," *Journal of Creative Behavior* 19 (1985): 38–46.

57. F. Barron and D. M. Harrington, "Creativity, Intelligence, and Personality," *Annual Review of Psychology* 32 (1981): 439–476.

58. R. J. Sternberg, "A Three-faced Model of Creativity," in R. J. Sternberg, ed., *The Nature of Creativity* (Cambridge: Cambridge University Press, 1988), 125–147.

59. A. M. Isen, "Positive Affect and Decision Making," in W. M. Goldstein and R. M. Hogarth, eds., *Research on Judgment and Decision Making* (Cambridge: Cambridge University Press, 1997).

60. G. L. Clore, N. Schwartz, and M. Conway, "Cognitive Causes and Consequences of Emotion," in R. S. Wyer, and T. K. Srull, eds., *Handbook of Social Cognition* (Hillsdale, NJ: Erlbaum, 1994), 323–417.

61. B. L. Frederickson, "What Good Are Positive Emotions?" *Review of General Psychology* 2 (1998): 300–319; B. L. Frederickson, "The Role of Positive Emotions in Positive Psychology," *American Psychologist* 56 (2001): 218–226.

62. T. M. Amabile, S. G. Barsade, J. S. Mueller, and B. M. Staw, "Affect and Creativity at Work," *Administrative Science Quarterly* 50 (3) (2005): 367–403.

63. J. Zhou, "When the Presence of Creative Coworkers Is Related to Creativity: Role of Supervisor Close Monitoring, Developmental Feedback, and Creative Personality," *Journal of Applied Psychology* 88 (2003): 413–422.

64. C. Axtell, D. Holman, K. Unsworth, T. Wall, and P. Waterson, "Shopfloor Innovation: Facilitating the Suggestion and Implementation of Ideas," *Journal of Occupational Psychology* 73 (2000): 265–285.

65. B. Kijkuit and J. van den Ende, "The Organizational Life of an Idea: Integrating Social Network, Creativity and Decision-making Perspectives," *Journal of Management Studies* 44 (6) (2007): 863–882.

66. T. M. Amabile, R. Conti, H. Coon, J. Lazenby, and M. Herron, "Assessing the Work Environment for Creativity," *Academy of Management Journal* 39 (1996): 1154–1184.

67. T. Tetenbaum and H. Tetenbaum, "Office 2000: Tear Down the Wall," *Training* (February 2000): 58–64.

68. Livingstone, "Person–Environment Fit."

69. R. L. Firestein, "Effects of Creative Problem-Solving Training on Communication Behaviors in Small Groups," *Small Group Research* (November 1989): 507–521.

70. D. M. Harrington, "Creativity, Analogical Thinking, and Muscular Metaphors," *Journal of Mental Imagery* 6 (1981): 121–126; R. M. Kanter, *The Change Masters* (New York: Simon & Schuster, 1983); T. M. Amabile, B. A. Hennessey, and B. S. Grossman, "Social Influences on Creativity: The Effects of Contracted-for Reward," *Journal of Personality and Social Psychology* 50 (1986): 14–23.

71. R. Von Oech, *A Whack on the Side of the Head* (New York: Warner, 1983).

72. A. G. Robinson and S. Stern, *How Innovation and Improvement Actually Happen* (San Francisco, CA: Berrett Koehler, 1997).

73. K. Unsworth, "Unpacking Creativity," *Academy of Management Review* 26 (2001): 289–297.

74. P. Burns, "Case Studies in Entrepreneurship," accessed from http://www.efos.unios.hr/korporacijsko-poduzetnistvo/wp-content/uploads/sites/245/2017/04/Case-study-3M.pdf, October 9, 2018.

75. M. F. R. Kets de Vries, R. Branson, and P. Barnevik, "Charisma in Action: The Transformational Abilities of Virgin's Richard Branson and ABBS's Percy Barnevik," *Organizational Dynamics* 26 (1998): 7–21.

76. G. Stasser, L. A. Taylor, and C. Hanna, "Information Sampling in Structured and Unstructured Discussion of Three- and Six-Person Groups," *Journal of Personality and Social Psychology* 57 (1989): 67–78.

77. E. Kirchler and J. H. Davis, "The Influence of Member Status Differences and Task Type on Group Consensus and Member Position Change," *Journal of Personality and Social Psychology* 51 (1986): 83–91.

78. R. F. Maier, "Assets and Liabilities in Group Problem Solving," *Psychological Review* 74 (1967): 239–249.

79. M. E. Shaw, *Group Dynamics: The Psychology of Small Group Behavior*, 3rd ed. (New York: McGraw-Hill, 1981).

80. P. W. Yetton and P. C. Bottger, "Individual versus Group Problem Solving: An Empirical Test of a Best Member Strategy," *Organizational Behavior and Human Performance* 29 (1982): 307–321.

81. W. Watson, L. Michaelson, and W. Sharp, "Member Competence, Group Interaction, and Group Decision Making: A Longitudinal Study," *Journal of Applied Psychology* 76 (1991): 803–809.

82. I. Janis, *Victims of Groupthink* (Boston: Houghton Mifflin, 1972); M. Kostera, M. Proppe, and M. Szatkowski, "Staging the New Romantic Hero in the Old Cynical Theatre: On Managers, Roles, and Change in Poland," *Journal of Organizational Behavior* 16 (1995): 631–646.

83. M. A. Hogg and S. C. Hains, "Friendship and Group Identification: A New Look at the Role of Cohesiveness in Groupthink," *European Journal of Social Psychology* 28 (1998): 323–341.

84. P. E. Jones and H. M. P. Roelofsma, "The Potential for Social Contextual and Group Biases in Team Decision Making: Biases, Conditions, and Psychological Mechanisms," *Ergonomics* 43 (2000): 1129–1152; J. M. Levine, E. T. Higgins, and H. Choi, "Development of Strategic Norms in Groups," *Organizational Behavior and Human Decision Processes* 82 (2000): 88–101.

85. A. L. Brownstein, "Biased Predecision Processing," *Psychological Bulletin* 129 (2003): 545–568.

86. C. P. Neck and G. Moorhead, "Groupthink Remodeled: The Importance of Leadership, Time Pressure, and Methodical Decision-making Procedures," *Human Relations* 48 (1995): 537–557.

87. J. Schwartz and M. L. Ward, "Final Shuttle Report Cites 'Broken Safety Culture' at NASA," *New York Times* (August 26, 2003), http://www.nytimes.com/2003/08/26/national/26CND-SHUT.html?ex=1077253200&en=882575f2c17ed8ff&ei=5070; C. Ferraris and R. Carveth, "NASA and the *Columbia* Disaster: Decision Making by Groupthink?" in Proceedings of the 2003 Convention of the Association for Business Communication Annual Convention, http://www.businesscommunication.org/conventions/Proceedings/2003/PDF/03ABC03.pdf.

88. A. C. Homan, D. van Knippenberg, G. A. Van Kleef, and K. W. C. De Dreu, "Bridging Faultlines by Valuing Diversity: Diversity Beliefs, Information Elaboration, and Performance in Diverse Work Groups," *Journal of Applied Psychology* 92 (5) (2007):1189–1199.

89. G. Moorhead, R. Ference, and C. P. Neck, "Group Decision Fiascoes Continue: Space Shuttle Challenger and a Revised Groupthink Framework," *Human Relations* 44 (1991): 539–550.

90. J. R. Montanari and G. Moorhead, "Development of the Groupthink Assessment Inventory," *Educational and Psychological Measurement* 49 (1989): 209–219.

91. P. T. Hart, "Irving L. Janis' Victims of Groupthink," *Political Psychology* 12 (1991): 247–278.

92. A. C. Mooney, P. J. Holahan, and A. C. Amason, "Don't Take It Personally: Exploring Cognitive Conflict as a Mediator of Affective Conflict," *Journal of Management Studies* 44 (5) (2007): 733–758.

93. J. A. F. Stoner, "Risky and Cautious Shifts in Group Decisions: The Influence of Widely Held Values," *Journal of Experimental Social Psychology* 4 (1968): 442–459.

94. S. Moscovici and M. Zavalloni, "The Group as a Polarizer of Attitudes," *Journal of Personality and Social Psychology* 12 (1969): 125–135.

95. G. R. Goethals and M. P. Zanna, "The Role of Social Comparison in Choice of Shifts," *Journal of Personality and Social Psychology* 37 (1979): 1469–1476.

96. A. Vinokur and E. Burnstein, "Effects of Partially Shared Persuasive Arguments on Group-induced Shifts: A Problem-solving Approach," *Journal of Personality and Social Psychology* 29 (1974): 305–315; J. Pfeffer, "Seven Practices of Successful Organizations," *California Management Review* 40 (1998): 96–124.

97. L. Armstrong, "Toyota's Scion: A Siren to Young Buyers?" *BusinessWeek* (March 4, 2002).

98. G. Pitts, "Daniel Lamarre: Cirque du Soleil," *The Globe and Mail* (August 27, 2007), http://www.theglobeandmail.com/report-on-business/article778263.ece.

99. K. Dugosh, P. Paulus, E. Roland, and H. Yang, "Cognitive Stimulation in Brainstorming," *Journal of Personality and Social Psychology* 79 (2000): 722–735.

100. A. Van de Ven and A. Delbecq, "The Effectiveness of Nominal, Delphi and Interacting Group Decision-making Processes," *Academy of Management Journal* 17 (1974): 605–621.

101. R. A. Cosier and C. R. Schwenk, "Agreement and Thinking Alike: Ingredients for Poor Decisions," *Academy of Management Executive* 4 (1990): 69–74.

102. D. M. Schweiger, W. R. Sandburg, and J. W. Ragan, "Group Approaches for Improving Strategic Decision Making: A Comparative Analysis of Dialectical Inquiry, Devil's Advocacy, and Consensus," *Academy of Management Journal* 29 (1986): 149–159.

103. G. Whyte, "Decision Failures: Why They Occur and How to Prevent Them," *Academy of Management Executive* 5 (1991): 23–31.

104. E. E. Lawler, III, and S. A. Mohrman, "Quality Circles: After the Honeymoon," *Organizational Dynamics* (Spring 1987): 42–54.

105. T. L. Tang and E. A. Butler, "Attributions of Quality Circles' Problem-solving Failure: Differences among Management, Supporting Staff, and Quality Circle Members," *Public Personnel Management* 26 (1997): 203–225.

106. L. Scholten, D. van Knippenberg, B. A. Nijstad, and K. W. C. De Dreu, "Motivated Information Processing and Group Decision-making: Effects of Process Accountability on Information Processing and Decision Quality," *Journal of Experimental Social Psychology* 43 (4) (2007): 539–552.

107. R. E. Silverman, "Who's the Boss? There Isn't One," *The Wall Street Journal*, June 19, 2012, accessed from http://online.wsj.com/article/SB100014240527 02303379204577474953586383604.html, September 7, 2018.

108. L. I. Glassop, "The Organizational Benefits of Teams," *Human Relations* 55 (2002): 225–249.

109. C. J. Nemeth, "Managing Innovation: When Less Is More," *California Management Review* 40 (1997): 59–68.

110. N. Adler, *International Dimensions of Organizational Behavior*, 3rd ed. (Mason, OH: South-Western, 1997).

111. K. W. Phillips and D. L. Lloyd, "When Surface- and Deep-Level Diversity Collide: The Effects on Dissenting Group Members," *Organizational Behavior and Human Decision Processes* 99 (2) (2006): 143–160.

112. T. Simons, L. H. Pelled, and K. A. Smith, "Making Use of Difference: Diversity, Debate, and Decision Comprehensiveness in Top Management Teams," *Academy of Management Journal* 42 (6) (1999): 662–673.

113. S. Elbanna and J. Child, "The Influence of Decision, Environmental and Firm Characteristics on the Rationality of Strategic Decision-Making," *Journal of Management Studies* 44 (4) (2007): 561–591.

114. J. Pfeffer, "Seven Practices of Successful Organizations," *California Management Review* 40 (1998): 96–124.

115. L. A. Witt, M. C. Andrews, and K. M. Kacmar, "The Role of Participation in Decision Making in the Organizational Politics—Job Satisfaction Relationship," *Human Relations* 53 (2000): 341–358.

116. J. He and W. R. King, "The Role of User Participation in Information Systems Development: Implications from a Meta-Analysis," *Journal of Management Information Systems* 25 (2008): 301–331.

117. C. R. Leana, E. A. Locke, and D. M. Schweiger, "Fact and Fiction in Analyzing Research on Participative Decision Making: A Critique of Cotton, Vollrath, Froggatt, Lengnick-Hall, and Jennings," *Academy of Management Review* 15 (1990): 137–146; J. L. Cotton, D. A. Vollrath, M. L. Lengnick-Hall, and K. L. Froggatt, "Fact: The Form of Participation Does Matter—A Rebuttal to Leana, Locke, and Schweiger," *Academy of Management Review* 15 (1990): 147–153.

118. T. W. Malone, "Is Empowerment Just a Fad? Control, Decision Making, and Information Technology," *Sloan Management Review* 38 (1997): 23–35.

119. IBM Customer Success Stories, "City and County of San Francisco Lower Total Cost of Ownership and Build on Demand Foundation" (February 3, 2004), http://www-306.ibm.com/software/success/cssdb.nsf/cs/LWRT-5VTLM2?OpenDocument&Site=lotusmandc.

120. T. L. Brown, "Fearful of 'Empowerment': Should Managers Be Terrified?" *IndustryWeek* (June 18, 1990): 12.

121. L. Hirschhorn, "Stresses and Patterns of Adjustment in the Postindustrial Factory," in G. M. Green and F. Baker, eds., *Work, Health, and Productivity* (New York: Oxford University Press, 1991), 115–126.

122. P. G. Gyllenhammar, *People at Work* (Reading, MA: Addison-Wesley, 1977).

123. R. Tannenbaum and F. Massarik, "Participation by Subordinates in the Managerial Decision-making Process," *Canadian Journal of Economics and Political Science* 16 (1950): 408–418.

124. H. Levinson, *Executive* (Cambridge, MA: Harvard University Press, 1981).

125. J. S. Black and H. B. Gregersen, "Participative Decision Making: An Integration of Multiple Dimensions," *Human Relations* 50 (1997): 859–878.

8

1. D. Deming, "The Growing Importance of Social Skills in the Labor Market," *The Quarterly Journal of Economics* 132 (2017): 1593–1640.

2. *Richness* is a term originally coined by W. D. Bodensteiner, "Information Channel Utilization under Varying Research and Development Project Conditions" (Ph.D. diss., University of Texas at Austin, 1970).

3. S. Covey, *The Seven Habits of Highly Effective People* (New York: Free Press, 1998).

4. E. Rautalinko and H. O. Lisper, "Effects of Training Reflective Listening in a Corporate Setting," *Journal of Business and Psychology* 18 (2004): 281–299.

5. A. D. Mangelsdorff, "Lessons Learned from the Military: Implications for Management" (Distinguished Visiting Lecture, University of Texas at Arlington, January 29, 1993).

6. J. W. Gilsdorf, "Organizational Rules on Communicating: How Employees Are—and Are Not—Learning the Ropes," *Journal of Business Communication* 35 (1998): 173–201.

7. R. Kelly Garrett, "Echo Chambers Online?: Politically Motivated Selective Exposure among Internet News Users," *Journal of Computer-Mediated Communication* 14 (2009): 265–285.

8. D. Tannen, *That's Not What I Mean! How Conversational Style Makes or Breaks Your Relations with Others* (New York: Morrow, 1986); D. Tannen, *You Just Don't Understand* (New York: Ballantine, 1990).

9. C. Goman, *The Silent Language of Leaders: How Body Language Can Help—or Hurt—How you Lead* (San Francisco, CA: Jossey-Bass, 2011).

10. K. L. Ashcraft, "Empowering 'Professional' Relationships," *Management Communication Quarterly* 13 (2000): 347–393.

11. G. Hofstede, *Culture's Consequences: International Differences in Work-related Values* (Beverly Hills, CA: SAGE Publications, 1980).

12. G. Hofstede, "Motivation, Leadership, and Organization: Do American Theories Apply Abroad?" *Organizational Dynamics* 9 (1980): 42–63.

13. H. Levinson, *Executive* (Cambridge, MA: Harvard University Press, 1981).

14. J. Neuliep, *Intercultural Communication: A Contextual Approach* (Los Angeles, CA: SAGE Publications, 2009).

15. C. D. Mortensen, *Communication Theory* (New York: Routledge, 2007).

16. R. D. Laing, *The Politics of the Family and Other Essays* (New York: Pantheon, 1971).

17. T. Wells, *Keeping Your Cool under Fire: Communicating Nondefensively* (New York: McGraw-Hill, 1980).

18. H. S. Schwartz, *Narcissistic Process and Corporate Decay: The Theory of the Organizational Ideal* (New York: New York University Press, 1990).

19. J. Buckland, S.Wiebe, S. Stobbe, and J. Schmidt, *Building Managers and Staff Members' Capacity to Communicate About Work Performance* (SSRN: 2017).

20. W. R. Forrester and M. F. Maute, "The Impact of Relationship Satisfaction on Attribution, Emotions, and Behaviors Following Service Failure," *Journal of Applied Business Research* (2000): 1–45.

21. M. L. Knapp, *Nonverbal Communication in Human Interaction* (New York: Holt, Rinehart & Winston, 1978); J. McCroskey and L. Wheeless, *Introduction to Human Communication* (New York: Allyn & Bacon, 1976).

22. A. M. Katz and V. T. Katz, eds., *Foundations of Nonverbal Communication* (Carbondale, IL: Southern Illinois University Press, 1983).

23. M. D. Lieberman, "Intuition: A Social Cognitive Neuroscience Approach," *Psychological Bulletin* (2000): 109–138.

24. M. Eaves and D. Leathers, *Successful Nonverbal Communication* (New York: Routledge, 2017).

25. R. L. Birdwhistell, *Kinesics and Context* (Philadelphia, PA: University of Pennsylvania Press, 1970).

26. M. Eaves and D. Leathers, *Successful Nonverbal Communication* (New York: Routledge, 2017).

27. M. G. Frank and P. Ekman, "Appearing Truthful Generalizes across Different Deception Situations," *Journal of Personality and Social Psychology* 86 (2004): 486–495.

28. M. Eaves and D. Leathers, *Successful Nonverbal Communication* (New York: Routledge, 2017).

29. H. H. Tan, M. D. Foo, C. L. Chong, and R. Ng, "Situational and Dispositional Predictors of Displays of Positive Emotions," *Journal of Organizational Behavior* 24 (2003): 961–978.

30. C. Barnum and N. Wolniansky, "Taking Cues from Body Language," *Management Review* 78 (1989): 59.

31. Katz and Katz, *Foundations of Nonverbal Communication,* 181.

32. E. T. Hall, *The Hidden Dimension* (Garden City, NY: Doubleday Anchor, 1966).

33. E. T. Hall, "Proxemics," in A. M. Katz and V. T. Katz, eds., *Foundations of Nonverbal Communication* (Carbondale, IL: Southern Illinois University Press, 1983).

34. R. T. Barker and C. G. Pearce, "The Importance of Proxemics at Work," *Supervisory Management* 35 (1990): 10–11.

35. F. Salajan, D. Schonwetter, and B. Cleghorn. "Student and Faculty Inter-generational Digital Divide: Fact or Fiction?" *Computers and Education* 53 (2010): 1393–403.

36. J. Constine, "Facebook Now Has 2 Billion Monthly Users … and Responsibility," accessed from https://techcrunch.com/2017/06/27/facebook-2-billion-users," October 3, 2018.

37. L. Salm, "70% of Employers Are Snooping Candidates' Social Media Profiles," Careerbuilder, June 15, 2017, accessed from https://www.careerbuilder.com/advice/social-media-survey-2017, October 3, 2018.

38. "Among Affluents, Millennials Spend the Most Time Online" October 19, 2016, accessed from https://www.emarketer.com/Article/Among-Affluents-Millennials-Spend-Most-Time-Online/1014618, October 3, 2018.

39. How Millennials Get News: Inside the Habits of America's First Digital Generation, conducted by the Media Insight Project: An initiative of the American Press Institute and The Associated Press (NORC Center for Public Affairs Research: 2015).

40. S. Flaxman, S. Goel, and J. M. Rao; "Filter Bubbles, Echo Chambers, and Online News Consumption," *Public Opinion Quarterly* 80 (2016): 298–320.

41. W. Phillips, *This Is Why We Can't Have Nice Things. Mapping the Relationship Between Online Trolling and Mainstream Culture* (Cambridge, MA: MIT Press, 2015).

42. S. Kiesler, "Technology and the Development of Creative Environments," in Y. Ijiri and R. L. Kuhn, eds., *New Directions in Creative and Innovative Management* (Cambridge, MA: Ballinger Press, 1988).

43. B. L. Ott, "The Age of Twitter: Donald J. Trump and the Politics of Debasement," *Critical Studies in Media Communication* 34(2016): 59–68.

44. C. Brod, *Technostress: The Human Cost of the Computer Revolution* (Reading, MA: Addison-Wesley, 1984).

45. D. Derks, A. E. R. Bos, and J. V. Grumbkow, "Emoticons and Online Message Interpretation. *Social Science Computer Review* (2007).

46. A. B. Fox, D. Bukatko, M. Hallahan, and M. Crawford, "The Medium Makes a Difference: Gender Similarities and Differences in Instant Messaging," *Journal of Language and Social Psychology* 26 (2007): 389–397.

47. S. Kiesler, J. Siegel, and T. W. McGuire, "Social Psychological Aspects of Computer-mediated Communication," *American Psychologist* 39 (1984): 1123–134.

48. D. A. Morand, "Language and Power: An Empirical Analysis of Linguistic Strategies Used in Superior–Subordinate

Communication," *Journal of Organizational Behavior* 21 (2000): 235–249.

49. R. Beck, and J. Harter, "Why Great Managers Are So Rare," *Harvard Business Review,* March 13, 2014, accessed from https://hbr.org/2014/03/why-good-managers-are-so-rare, October 4, 2018.

50. F. Luthans, "Successful versus Effective Real Managers," *Academy of Management Executive* 2 (1988): 127–132.

51. F. M. Jablin, "Superior–Subordinate Communication: The State of the Art," *Psychological Bulletin* 86 (1979): 1201–222; W. C. Reddin, *Communication within the Organization: An Interpretive Review of Theory and Research* (New York: Industrial Communication Council, 1972).

52. B. Barry and J. M. Crant, "Dyadic Communication Relationships in Organizations: An Attribution Expectancy Approach," *Organization Science* 11 (2000): 648–665.

53. S. Baral, "Role of Emotional Intelligence to Handle Conflicts and Team Building: An Analytical Study," *Splint International Journal of Professionals* 4 (2017): 85–95.

54. K. Mishra, L. Boynton and A. Mishra, "Driving Employee Engagement: The Expanded Role of Internal Communications," *International Journal of Business Communications* 51(2014): 183–202.

9

1. J. R. Katzenbach and D. K. Smith, "The Discipline of Teams," *Harvard Business Review* 71 (1993): 111–120.

2. D. L. Fields and T. C. Bloom, "Employee Satisfaction in Work Groups with Different Gender Composition," *Journal of Organizational Behavior* 18 (1997): 181–196.

3. G. Parker, *Team Players and Teamwork* (San Francisco, CA: Jossey-Bass, 1990).

4. N. R. F. Maier, "Assets and Liabilities in Group Problem Solving: The Need for an Integrative Function," *Psychological Review* 74 (1967): 239–249.

5. B. Tuckman, "Developmental Sequence in Small Groups," *Psychological Bulletin* 63 (1965): 384–399; B. Tuckman and M. Jensen, "Stages of Small-Group Development," *Group and Organizational Studies* 2 (1977): 419–427.

6. C. J. G. Gersick, "Time and Transition in Work Teams: Toward a New Model of Group Development," *The Academy of Management Journal* 31 (1988): 9–41.

7. G. A. Okhuysen, and M. J. Waller, "Focusing on Midpoint Transitions: An Analysis of Boundary Conditions," *Academy of Management Journal*, 45 (2002): 1056–1065.

8. A. Chang, P. Bordia, and J. Duck, "Punctuated Equilibrium and Linear Progression: Toward a New Understanding of Group Development," *Academy of Management Journal* 46 (2003): 106–112.

9. K. L. Bettenhausen and J. K. Murnighan, "The Emergence of Norms in Competitive Decision-making Groups," *Administrative Science Quarterly* 30 (1985): 350–372; K. L. Bettenhausen, "Five Years of Groups Research: What We Have Learned and What Needs to Be Addressed," *Journal of Management* 17 (1991): 345–381.

10. J. E. McGrath, *Groups: Interaction and Performance* (Englewood Cliffs, NJ: Prentice-Hall, 1984).

11. I. Adarves-Yorno, T. Postmes, and S. A. Haslam, "Creative Innovation or Crazy Irrelevance? The Contribution of Group Norms and Social Identity to Creative Behavior," *Journal of Experimental Social Psychology* 43 (2007): 410–416.

12. D. Tjosvold and Z. Yu, "Goal Interdependence and Applying Abilities for Team In-Role and Extra-Role Performance in China," *Group Dynamics: Theory, Research, and Practice* 8 (2004): 98–111.

13. V. U. Druskat and S. B. Wolff, "Building the Emotional Intelligence of Groups," *Harvard Business Review* 79 (2001): 80–90.

14. I. Summers, T. Coffelt, and R. E. Horton, "Work-Group Cohesion," *Psychological Reports* 63 (1988): 627–636.

15. D. C. Man and S. S. K. Lam, "The Effects of Job Complexity and Autonomy on Cohesiveness in Collectivistic and Individualistic Work Groups: A Cross-cultural Analysis," *Journal of Organizational Behavior* 24 (2003): 979–1001.

16. S. M. Klein, "A Longitudinal Study of the Impact of Work Pressure on Group Cohesive Behaviors," *International Journal of Management* 12 (1996): 68–75.

17. L. Hirschhorn, *Managing in the New Team Environment* (Upper Saddle River, NJ: Prentice-Hall, 1991), 521A.

18. B. Beersma, J. R. Hollenbeck, S. E. Humphrey, H. Moon, D. E. Conlon, and D. R. Ilgen, "Cooperation, Competition, and Team Performance: Toward a Contingency Approach," *Academy of Management Journal* 46 (2003): 572–590.

19. W. R. Lassey, "Dimensions of Leadership," in W. R. Lassey and R. Fernandez, eds., *Leadership and Social Change* (La Jolla, CA.: University Associates, 1976), 10–15.

20. W. J. Duncan and J. P. Feisal, "No Laughing Matter: Patterns of Humor in the Workplace," *Organizational Dynamics* 17 (1989): 18–30.

21. P. F. Drucker, "There's More than One Kind of Team," *The Wall Street Journal* (February 11, 1992): A16.

22. A. Taylor and H. R. Greve, "Superman or the Fantastic Four? Knowledge Combination and Experience in Innovative Teams," *Academy of Management Journal* 49 (2006): 723–740.

23. J.R. Hollenbeck, B. Beersma, and M.E. Schouten, "Beyond Team Types and Taxonomies: A Dimensional Scaling Conceptualization for Team Description," *Academy of Management Review* 37 (2012): 82–106.

24. L. J. Krajewski, and L. P. Ritzman. *Operations Management: Processes and Value Chains* (Upper Saddle River, NJ: Pearson Education, 2005).

25. C. Douglas and W. L. Gardner, "Transition to Self-directed Work Teams: Implications of Transition Time and Self-monitoring for Managers' Use of Influence Tactics," *Journal of Organizational Behavior* 25 (2004): 47–65.

26. S. I. Tannenbaum, J. I. Mathieu, E. Salas, and D. Cohen, "Teams Are Changing: Are Research and Practice Evolving Fast Enough? *Industrial and Organisational Psychology* 5 (2011): 2–24.

27. B. Weber, and G. Hertel, "Motivation Gains of Inferior Group Members: A Meta-Analytical Review," *Journal of Personality and Social Psychology* 93 (2007): 973–993.

28. P. Shaver and D. Buhrmester, "Loneliness, Sex-Role Orientation, and Group Life: A Social Needs Perspective," in P. Paulus, ed., *Basic Group Processes* (New York: Springer-Verlag, 1985), 259–288.

29. B. Weber, and G. Hertel, "Motivation Gains of Inferior Group Members: A Meta-analytical Review," *Journal of Personality and Social Psychology* 93 (2007): 973–993.

30. K. H. Price, "Working Hard to Get People to Loaf," *Basic and Applied Social Psychology* 14 (1993): 329–344.

31. M. Schippers, "Social Loafing Tendencies and Team Performance: The Compensating Effect of Agreeableness and Conscientiousness," *Academy of Management Learning & Education* 13 (2014): 62–81.

32. E. Diener, "Deindividuation, Self-Awareness, and Disinhibition," *Journal of Personality and Social Psychology* 37 (1979): 1160–1171.

33. C. H. Farnsworth, "Torture by Army Peacekeepers in Somalia Shocks Canada," *The New York Times* (November 27, 1994), http://www.nytimes.com/1994/11/27/world/torture-by-army-peacekeepers-in-somalia-shocks-canada.html?pagewanted=1.

34. S. Prentice-Dunn and R. W. Rogers, "Deindividuation and the Self-Regulation of Behavior," in P. Paulus, ed., *Psychology of Group Influence* (Hillsdale, NJ: Erlbaum, 1989), 87–109.

10

1. Definition adapted from D. Hellriegel, J. W. Slocum, Jr., and R. W. Woodman, *Organizational Behavior* (St. Paul: West, 1992) and from R. D. Middlemist and M. A. Hitt, *Organizational Behavior* (St. Paul: West, 1988).

2. D. Tjosvold, *The Conflict-Positive Organization* (Reading, MA: Addison-Wesley, 1991).

3. R. A. Cosier and D. R. Dalton, "Positive Effects of Conflict: A Field Experiment," *International Journal of Conflict Management* 1 (1990): 81–92.

4. M. Rahim, *Managing Conflict in Organizations* (New York: Routledge, 2010).

5. D. Cahn, and R. Abigail, *Managing Conflict through Communication*, 3rd ed. (Boston, MA: Allyn and Bacon, 2007).

6. Tjosvold, D. (2008). The conflict-positive organization: It depends upon us. *Journal of Organizational Behavior*, 29 (1), 19–28.

7. A. C. Amason, W. A. Hochwarter, K. R. Thompson, and A. W. Harrison, "Conflict: An Important Dimension in Successful Management Teams," *Organizational Dynamics* 24 (1995): 25–35.

8. C. K. De Dreu, "The Virtue and Vice of Workplace Conflict: Food for (Pessimistic) Thought," *Journal of Organizational Behavior* 29 (2008): 5–18.

9. E. Brahm, "Conflict Stages," *Beyond Intractability* (University of Colorado, Boulder: Conflict Research Consortium, 2003).

10. E. Martínez- Moreno, P. González-Navarro, A. Zornoza, and P. Ripoll, "Relationship, Task and Process Conflicts on Team Performance: The Moderating Role of Communication Media," *International Journal of Conflict Management* 20 (2009): 251–268.

11. E. K. Wayne, "Two Kinds of Conflict Means Two Kinds of Response," *Washington Business Journal*, January 26, 2005, accessed from http://www.bizjournals.com/washington/stories/2005/01/31/smallb13.html?page=all, October 15, 2012.

12. C. A. Insko, J. Scholper, L. Gaertner, et al., "Interindividual–Intergroup Discontinuity Reduction through the Anticipation of Future Interaction," *Journal of Personality and Social Psychology* 80 (2001): 95–111.

13. K. W. Thomas, "Conflict and Conflict Management," in M. D. Dunnette, ed., *Handbook of Industrial and Organizational Psychology* (Chicago, IL: Rand McNally, 1976), 900.

14. L. A. Dechurch, K. L. Hamilton, and C. Haas, "Effects of Conflict Management Strategies on Perceptions of Intragroup Conflict," *Group Dynamics: Theory, Research, and Practice* 11 (1) (2007): 66–78.

15. S. Alper, D. Tjosvold, and K. S. Law, "Conflict Management, Efficacy, and Performance in Organizational Teams," *Personnel Psychology* 53 (2000): 625–642.

16. W. King and E. Miles, "What We Know and Don't Know about Measuring Conflict," *Management Communication Quarterly* 4 (1990): 222–243.

17. M. Chan, "Intergroup Conflict and Conflict Management in the R&D Divisions of Four Aerospace Companies," *IEEE Transactions on Engineering Management* 36 (1989): 95–104.

18. S. L. Phillips and R. L. Elledge, *The Team Building Source Book* (San Diego, CA: University Associates, 1989).

19. S. Steinberg, "Airbus Workers in France, Germany Strike against Massive Job Cuts," March 1, 2007, http://www.wsws.org/articles/2007/mar2007/airb-m01.shtml.

20. C. K. W. De Dreu and A. E. M. Van Vianen, "Managing Relationship Conflict and the Effectiveness of Organizational Teams," *Journal of Organizational Behavior* 22 (2001): 309–328.

21. R. A. Baron, S. P. Fortin, R. L. Frei, L. A. Hauver, and M. L. Shack, "Reducing Organizational Conflict: The Role of Socially Induced Positive Affect," *International Journal of Conflict Management* 1 (1990): 133–152.

22. K. W. Thomas, "Toward Multidimensional Values in Teaching: The Example of Conflict Behaviors," *Academy of Management Review* 2 (1977): 484–490.

23. A. Tyerman and C. Spencer, "A Critical Text of the Sheriff's Robber's Cave Experiments: Intergroup Competition and Cooperation between Groups of Well-Acquainted Individuals," *Small Group Behavior* 14 (1983): 515–531; R. M. Kramer, "Intergroup Relations and Organizational Dilemmas: The Role of Categorization Processes," in B. Staw and L. Cummings, eds., *Research in Organizational Behavior* 13 (Greenwich, CT: JAI Press, 1991), 191–228.

24. A. Carmeli, "The Relationship between Emotional Intelligence and Work Attitudes, Behavior and Outcomes: An Examination among Senior Managers," *Journal of Managerial Psychology* 18 (2003): 788–813.

25. M. Stan, and P. Puranam, "The Role of Integrators in Organizational Adaptation to Interdependence Shocks: Evidence from Fertility Clinics," Working paper, 2014.

26. R. Blake and J. Mouton, "Overcoming Group Warfare," *Harvard Business Review* 64 (1984): 98–108.

27. M. A. Cronin and L. R. Weingart, "Representational Gaps, Information Processing and Conflict in Functionally Diverse Teams," *Academy of Management Review* 32 (3) (2007): 761–773.

28. D. Cahn and R. Abigail, *Managing Conflict through Communication*, 3rd ed. (Boston, MA: Allyn and Bacon, 2007) .

29. R. J. Lewicki, J. A. Litterer, J. W. Minton, and D. M. Saunders, *Negotiation*, 2nd ed. (Burr Ridge, IL: Irwin, 1994).

30. C. K. W. De Dreu, S. L. Koole, and W. Steinel, "Unfixing the Fixed Pie: A Motivated Information-Processing Approach to Integrative Negotiation," *Journal of Personality and Social Psychology* 79 (2000): 975–987.

31. R. Fisher, W. Ury, and B. Patton, *Getting to Yes: Negotiating Agreement without Giving In*, 3rd ed. (New York: Penguin Books, 2011).

32. D. Lax and J. Sebenius, "The Manager as Negotiator: The Negotiator's Dilemma: Creating and Claiming Value," *Dispute Resolution*, 2nd ed., (Boston, MA: Little Brown and Co., 1992), 49–62.

33. M. H. Bazerman, J. R. Curhan, D. A. Moore, and K. L. Valley, "Negotiation," *Annual Review of Psychology* 51 (2000): 279–314.

34. I. Ayers and P. Siegelman, "Race and Gender Discrimination in Bargaining for a New Car," *American Economic Review* 85 (1995): 304–321.

35. R. Fisher, W. Ury, and B. Patton, *Getting to Yes: Negotiating Agreement without Giving In*, 3rd ed. (New York: Penguin Books, 2011).

36. D. Lax and J. Sebenius, "The Power of Alternatives or the Limits to Negotiation,"

Negotiation Theory and Practice (Cambridge: The Program on Negotiation at Harvard Law School, 1991): 97–114.

37. B. *Spangler,* "Zone of Possible Agreement (ZOPA)". beyondintractability.org. (University of Colorado, Boulder, Conflict Information Consortium: June 2003).

38. ADR Institute of Ontario, FAQ, http://www.adrontario.ca/about/faq.cfm.

11

1. L. Munduate and F. J. Medina, "How Does Power Affect Those Who Have It and Those Who Don't? Power Inside Organizations," *An Introduction to Work and Organizational Psychology: An International Perspective,* 3rd ed. (Sussex, UK: John Wiley & Sons, 2017): 176–191.

2. E. N. Kocev, "Modern Concept of Power as a Social and Economic Category," 2002, http://www.ejournalnet.com/Contents/Issue_2/4/4_2002.htm.

3. C. Anderson, O. P. John, and D. Keltner, "The Personal Sense of Power," *Journal of Personality* 80 (2012): 313–344.

4. R. D. Middlemist and M. A. Hitt, *Organizational Behavior: Managerial Strategies for Performance* (St. Paul, MN: West Publishing, 1988).

5. J. R. P. French and B. Raven, "The Bases of Social Power," in D. Cartwright, ed., *Group Dynamics: Research and Theory* (Evanston, IL: Row Peterson, 1962); T. R. Hinkin and C. A. Schriesheim, "Development and Application of New Scales to Measure the French and Raven (1959) Bases of Social Power," *Journal of Applied Psychology* 74 (1989): 561–567.

6. M. A. Rahim, "Relationships of Leader Power to Compliance and Satisfaction with Supervision: Evidence from a National Sample of Managers," *Journal of Management* 15 (1989): 545–556.

7. P. M. Podsakoff and C. A. Schriesheim, "Field Studies of French and Raven's Bases of Power: Critique, Reanalysis, and Suggestions for Future Research," *Psychological Bulletin* 97 (1985): 387–411.

8. C. Cadwalladr, "The Great British Brexit Robbery: How Our Democracy Was Hijacked," *The Observer.* May 7, 2017, accessed from https://www.theguardian.com/technology/2017/may/07/the-great-british-brexit-robbery-hijacked-democracy, October 9, 2018.

9. C. Argyris, "Management Information Systems: The Challenge to Rationality and Emotionality," *Management Science* 17 (1971): 275–292; J. Naisbitt and P. Aburdene, *Megatrends 2000* (New York: Morrow, 1990).

10. J. Pfeffer and G. Salancik, *The External Control of Organizations* (New York: Harper & Row, 1978).

11. T. M. Welbourne and C. O. Trevor, "The Roles of Departmental and Position Power in Job Evaluation," *Academy of Management Journal* 43 (4) (2000): 761–771.

12. D. Hickson, C. Hinings, C. Lee, R. E. Schneck, and J. M. Pennings, "A Strategic Contingencies Theory of Intraorganizational Power," *Administrative Science Quarterly* 14 (1971): 219–220.

13. R. H. Miles, *Macro Organizational Behavior* (Glenview, IL: Scott, Foresman, 1980).

14. P. P. Carson, K. D. Carson, E. L. Knight, and C. W. Roe, "Power in Organizations: A Look through the TQM Lens," *Quality Progress* (November 1995): 73–78.

15. L. Bourne, A. Shelley, and D. H. Walker, "Influence, Stakeholder Mapping and Visualization," *Construction Management and Economics* 26 (6) (2008): 645–658.

16. M. Segalia, "Vision Statement: Find the Real Power in Your Organization," *Harvard Business Review*, May 2010, accessed from http://hbr.org/2010/05/vision-statement-find-the-real-power-in-your-organization/ar/pr, September 15, 2018.

17. S. McShane, S. Steen, and K. Tasa, "Power and Influence in the Workplace," *Canadian Organizational Behaviour* 10Ce (2018): 283–285.

18. The Canadian Human Rights Commission, "What Is Harassment," 2017, accessed from https://www.chrc-ccdp.gc.ca/eng/content/what-harassment-1, September 15, 2018.

19. G. Namie and R. Namie, *The Bully at Work,* 2nd ed. (Naperville, IL: Sourcebooks, 2009), 3.

20. A. Webber, "Danger: Toxic Company," *Fast Company,* October 31, 1998, http://www.fastcompany.com/magazine/19/toxic.html?page=0%2C0.

21. Public Service Alliance of Canada, "Workplace Violence Prevention: Get the Stats," October 19, 2015, accessed from http://psacunion.ca/workplace-violence-prevention-get-stats, October 9, 2018.

22. G. Namie, "WBI U.S. Workplace Bullying Survey June 2017," accessed from http://www.workplacebullying.org/wbiresearch/wbi-2017-survey, September 15, 2018.

23. Ibid., 27.

24. Angus Reid Institute, Public Interest Research, 2014, http://angusreid.org/wp-content/uploads/2014/12/2014.12.05-Sexual-Harassment-at-work.pdf.

25. Pew Research Center, "Online Harassment," *Internet and Technology,* October 22, 2014, accessed from http://www.pewinternet.org/2014/10/22/online-harassment, September 15, 2018.

26. C. Anderson, O. P. John, and D. Keltner, "The Personal Sense of Power," *Journal of Personality* 80 (2012): 313–344.

27. J. Lammers and A.D. Galisnsky, "The Conceptualization of Power and the Nature of Interdependency: The Role of Legitimacy and Culture," *Power and Interdependence in Organizations* (2009): 67–82.

28. M. Velasquez, D. J. Moberg, and G. F. Cavanaugh, "Organizational Statesmanship and Dirty Politics: Ethical Guidelines for the Organizational Politician," *Organizational Dynamics* 11 (1982): 65–79.

29. D. Bhatnagar, "Understanding Political Behaviour in Organizations: A Framework" 17(1992): 15–22.

30. H. Mintzberg, *Power in and around Organizations* (Englewood Cliffs, NJ: Prentice-Hall, 1983), 172.

31. W. A. Hochwarter, "The Interactive Effects of Pro-Political Behavior and Politics Perceptions on Job Satisfaction and Affective Commitment," *Journal of Applied Social Psychology* 33 (2003): 1360–1378.

32. W. A. Hochwarter, K. M. Kacmar, D. C. Treadway, and T. S. Watson, "It's All Relative: The Distinction and Prediction of Political Perceptions across Levels," *Journal of Applied Social Psychology* 33 (2003): 1955–2016.

33. A. Latif, Z. U. Abideen, and M. S. Nazar, "Individual Political Behavior in Organizational Relationships" *Journal of Politics and Law* 4 (2011): 199–210.

34. D. A. Ralston, "Employee Ingratiation: The Role of Management," *Academy of Management Review* 10 (1985): 477–487; D. R. Beeman and T. W. Sharkey, "The Use and Abuse of Corporate Politics," *Business Horizons* (March–April 1987): 25–35.

35. D. L. Madison, R. W. Allen, L. W. Porter, P. R. Renwick, and B. T. Mayes, "Organizational Politics: An Exploration of Managers' Perceptions," *Human Relations* 33 (2) (1980): 79–100.

36. C. O. Longnecker, H. P. Sims, and D. A. Gioia, "Behind the Mask: The Politics of Employee Appraisal," *Academy of Management Executive* 1 (1987): 183–193.

37. M. Valle and P. L. Perrewe, "Do Politics Perceptions Relate to Political Behaviors? Tests of an Implicit Assumption and Expanded Model," *Human Relations* 53 (3) (2000): 359–386.

38. D. Kipnis, S. M. Schmidt, and I. Wilkinson, "Intraorganizational Influence Tactics: Explorations in Getting One's Way," *Journal of Applied Psychology* 65 (1980): 440–452; D. Kipnis, S. Schmidt, C. Swaffin-Smith, and I. Wilkinson, "Patterns of Managerial Influence: Shotgun Managers, Tacticians, and Bystanders," *Organizational Dynamics* (Winter 1984): 60–67; G. Yukl and C. M. Falbe, "Influence Tactics and Objectives in Upward, Downward, and Lateral Influence Attempts," *Journal of Applied Psychology* 75 (1990): 132–140.

39. G. R. Ferris, P. L. Perrewe, W. P. Anthony, and D. C. Gilmore, "Political Skill at Work," *Organizational Dynamics* 28 (2000): 25–37.

40. D. C. Treadway, W. A. Hochwarter, G. R. Ferris, C. J. Kacmar, C. Douglas, A. P. Ammeter, et al., "Leader Political Skill and Employee Reactions," *Leadership Quarterly* 15 (2004): 493–513; K. K. Ahearn, G. R. Ferris, W. A. Hochwarter, C. Douglas, and A. P. Ammeter, "Leader Political Skill and Team Performance," *Journal of Management* 30 (3) (2004): 309–327.

41. G. R. Ferris, D. C. Treadway, R. W. Kolodinsky, W. A. Hochwarter, C. J. Kacmar, C. Douglas, et al., "Development and Validation of the Political Skill Inventory," *Journal of Management* 31 (2005): 126–152.

42. G. R. Ferris, D. C. Treadway, R. W. Kolodinsky, W. A. Hochwarter, C. J. Kacmar, C. Douglas, et al., "Development and Validation of the Political Skill Inventory," *Journal of Management* 31 (2005): 126–152.

43. J. Zhou and G. R. Ferris, "The Dimensions and Consequences of Organizational Politics Perceptions: A Confirmatory Analysis," *Journal of Applied Social Psychology* 25 (1995): 1747–1764.

44. M. L. Seidal, J. T. Polzer, and K. J. Stewart, "Friends in High Places: The Effects of Social Networks on Discrimination in Salary Negotiations," *Administrative Science Quarterly* 45 (2000): 1–24.

45. K. Kumar and M. S. Thibodeaux, "Organizational Politics and Planned Organizational Change," *Group and Organization Studies* 15 (1990): 354–365.

46. D. R Beeman & T. W. Sharkey, (1987). The use and abuse of corporate politics. *Business Horizons*, 30 (2), 26–30.

47. C. P. Parker, R. L. Dipboye, and S. L. Jackson, "Perceptions of Organizational Politics: An Investigation of Antecedents and Consequences," *Journal of Management* 21 (1995): 891–912.

48. S. J. Ashford, N. P. Rothbard, S. K. Piderit, and J. E. Dutton, "Out on a Limb: The Role of Context and Impression Management in Selling Gender-Equity Issues," *Administrative Science Quarterly* 43 (1998): 23–57.

49. J. Conger and R. Kanungo, *Charismatic Leadership: The Elusive Factor in Organizational Effectiveness* (New York: Jossey-Bass, 1988).

50. G. M. Spreitzer, M. A. Kizilos, and S. W. Nason, "A Dimensional Analysis of the Relationship between Psychological Empowerment and Effectiveness, Satisfaction, and Strain," *Journal of Management* 23 (1997): 679–704.

51. M. W. Stander, and S. Rothmann, "Psychological Empowerment, Job Insecurity and Employee Engagement," *Journal of Industrial Psychology* 36 (1) (2010): 849.

52. G. R. Bushe, "Power and the Empowered Organization: The Design of Power in Highly Adaptive Organizations," *The Organization Development Practitioner* 30 (4) (1998): 37.

53. Ibid, 32.

54. J. J. Gabarro and J. P. Kotter, "Managing Your Boss," *Harvard Business Review* (January–February 1980): 92–100.

55. P. Newman, "How to Manage Your Boss," *Peat, Marwick, Mitchell & Company's Management Focus* (May–June 1980): 36–37.

12

1. D. Goleman, "Leadership that gets Results," *Harvard Business Review Classics* (Boston, MA: Harvard Business School Publishing Corporation 2017).

2. J. P. Kotter, "What Leaders Really Do," *Harvard Business Review* 68 (1990): 103–111.

3. D. A. Plowman, S. Solansky, T. E Beck, L. Baker, M. Kulkarni, and D. V. Travis, "The Role of Leadership in Emergent, Self-Organization," *Leadership Quarterly* 18 (4) (2007): 341–356.

4. R. M. Stogdill, "Personal Factors Associated with Leadership: A Survey of the Literature," *Journal of Psychology* 25 (1948): 35–71.

5. R. J. House, and R. Aditya, "The Social Scientific Study of Leadership: Quo Vadis," *Journal of Management* 23 (1997): 409–474.

6. A. W. Halpin and J. Winer, "A Factorial Study of the Leader Behavior Description Questionnaire," in R. M. Stogdill and A. E. Coons, eds., *Leader Behavior: Its Description and Measurement,* research monograph no. 88.

7. E. A. Fleishman, "Leadership Climate, Human Relations Training, and Supervisory Behavior," *Personnel Psychology* 6 (1953): 205–222.

8. R. Kahn and D. Katz, "Leadership Practices in Relation to Productivity and Morale," in D. Cartwright and A. Zander, eds., *Group Dynamics, Research and Theory* (Elmsford, NY: Row, Paterson, 1960).

9. R. R. Blake and J. S. Mouton, *The Managerial Grid III: The Key to Leadership Excellence* (Houston: Gulf, 1985).

10. W. Vandekerckhove and R. Commers, "Downward Workplace Mobbing: A Sign of the Times?" *Journal of Business Ethics* 45 (2003): 41–50.

11. R. J. House, and R. Aditya, "The Social Scientific Study of Leadership: Quo Vadis," *Journal of Management* 23 (1997): 409–474.

12. M. G. Aamodt, *Industrial/Organizational Psychology: An Applied Approach* (Boston, MA: Cengage Learning, 2015).

13. F. E. Fiedler, *A Theory of Leader Effectiveness* (New York: McGraw-Hill, 1964).

14. F. E. Fiedler, *Personality, Motivational Systems, and Behavior of High and Low LPC Persons,* tech. rep. no. 70-12 (Seattle: University of Washington, 1970).

15. F. E. Fiedler and M. M. Chemers, *Improving Leadership Effectiveness: The Leader Match Concept,* 2nd ed. (New York: John Wiley & Sons, 1984).

16. J. T. McMahon, "The Contingency Theory: Logic and Method Revisited," *Personnel Psychology* 25 (1972): 697–710; L. H. Peters, D. D. Hartke, and J. T. Pohlman, "Fiedler's Contingency Theory of Leadership: An Application of the Meta-Analysis Procedures of Schmidt and Hunter," *Psychological Bulletin* 97 (1985): 224–285.

17. D. R. Forsyth, "Leadership," *Group Dynamics* 5th ed. (Belmont: CA, Wadsworth, Cengage Learning, 2006), 245–277.

18. F. E. Fiedler, "The Contingency Model and the Dynamics of the Leadership Process," in L. Berkowitz, ed., *Advances in Experimental and Social Psychology,* vol. 11 (New York: Academic Press, 1978).

19. S. Arin and C. McDermott, "The Effect of Team Leader Characteristics on Learning, Knowledge Application, and Performance of Cross-functional New Product Development Teams," *Decision Sciences* 34 (2003): 707–739.

20. F. E. Fiedler, "Engineering the Job to Fit the Manager," *Harvard Business Review* 43 (1965): 115–122.

21. R. J. House, "A Path–Goal Theory of Leader Effectiveness," *Administrative Science Quarterly* 16 (1971): 321–338; R. J. House and T. R. Mitchell, "Path–Goal Theory of Leadership," *Journal of Contemporary Business* 3 (1974): 81–97; M. Evans, "The Effects of Supervisory Behavior on the Path-Goal Relationship," *Organizational Behavior and Human Performance* 5 (3) (1970): 277–298.

22. R. J. House, "Path-Goal Theory of Leadership: Lessons, Legacy and a Reformulated Theory," *Leadership Quarterly* 7 (1996): 323–352.

23. C. A. Schriescheim and V. M. Von Glinow, "The Path–Goal Theory of Leadership: A Theoretical and Empirical Analysis," *Academy of Management Journal* 20 (1977): 398–405; E. Valenzi and G. Dessler, "Relationships of Leader Behavior, Subordinate Role Ambiguity, and Subordinate Job Satisfaction," *Academy of Management Journal* 21 (1978): 671–678; N. R. F. Maier, *Leadership Methods and Skills* (New York: McGraw-Hill, 1963).

24. P. Hersey and K. H. Blanchard, "Life Cycle Theory of Leadership," *Training and Development* 23 (1969): 26–34; P. Hersey, K. H. Blanchard, and D. E. Johnson, *Management of Organizational Behavior: Leading Human Resources*, 8th ed. (Upper Saddle River, NJ: Prentice-Hall, 2001).

25. B. M. Bass, *Bass and Stogdill's Handbook of Leadership: Theory, Research, and Managerial Applications*, 3rd ed. (New York: Free Press, 1990).

26. T. Bauer, and B. Ergoden, *The Oxford Handbook of Leader–Member Exchange* (New York, Oxford University Press, 2015).

27. G. B. Graen and M. Uhl-Bien, "Relationship-based Approach to Leadership: Development of Leader–Member Exchange (LMX) Theory of Leadership over 25 Years," *Leadership Quarterly* 6 (1995): 219–247; C. R. Gerstner and D. V. Day, "Meta-analytic Review of Leader–Member Exchange Theory: Correlates and Construct Issues," *Journal of Applied Psychology* 82 (1997): 827–844; R. C. Liden, S. J. Wayne, and R. T. Sparrowe, "An Examination of the Mediating Role of Psychological Empowerment on the Relations between the Job, Interpersonal Relationships, and Work Outcomes," *Journal of Applied Psychology* 85 (2001): 407–416.

28. J. Townsend, J. S. Phillips, and T. J. Elkins, "Employee Retaliation: The Neglected Consequence of Poor Leader–Member Exchange Relations," *Journal of Occupational Health Psychology* 5 (2000): 457–463.

29. K. M. Kacmar, L. A. Witt, S. Zivnuska, and S. M. Gully, "The Interactive Effect of Leader–Member Exchange and Communication Frequency on Performance Ratings," *Journal of Applied Psychology* 88 (2003): 764–772.

30. A. G. Tekleab and M. S. Taylor, "Aren't There Two Parties in an Employment Relationship? Antecedents and Consequences of Organization–Employee Agreement on Contract Obligations and Violations," *Journal of Organizational Behavior* 24 (2003): 585–608.

31. D. A. Hoffman, S. J. Gerras, and F. P. Morgeson, "Climate as a Moderator of the Relationship between Leader–Member Exchange and Content Specific Citizenship: Safety Climate as an Exemplar," *Journal of Applied Psychology* 88 (2003): 170–178.

32. J. M. Burns, *Leadership* (New York: Harper & Row, 1978); T. O. Jacobs, *Leadership and Exchange in Formal Organizations* (Alexandria, VA: Human Resources Research Organization, 1971).

33. B. M. Bass, "From Transactional to Transformational Leadership: Learning to Share the Vision," *Organizational Dynamics* 19 (1990): 19–31; B. M. Bass, *Leadership and Performance beyond Expectations* (New York: Free Press, 1985).

34. W. Bennis and B. Nanus, *Leaders: The Strategies for Taking Charge* (New York: Harper and Row, 1985).

35. W. Bennis, "Managing the Dream: Leadership in the 21st Century," *Training* 27 (1990): 43–48; P. M. Podsakoff, S. B. MacKenzie, R. H. Moorman, and R. Fetter, "Transformational Leader Behaviors and Their Effects on Followers' Trust in Leader, Satisfaction, and Organizational Citizenship Behaviors," *Leadership Quarterly* 1 (1990): 107–142.

36. C. P. Egri and S. Herman, "Leadership in the North American Environmental Sector: Values, Leadership Styles, and Contexts of Environmental Leaders and Their Organizations," *Academy of Management Journal* 43 (2000): 571–604.

37. T. A. Judge and J. E. Bono, "Five-Factor Model of Personality and Transformational Leadership," *Journal of Applied Psychology* 85 (2001): 751–765.

38. J. E. Bono and T. A. Judge, "Self-Concordance at Work: Toward Understanding the Motivational Effects of Transformational Leaders," *Academy of Management Journal* 46 (2003): 554–571.

39. The Jargon Dictionary, "The R Terms: Reality-Distortion Field," http://info .astrian.net/jargon/terms/r/reality -distortion_field.html.

40. R. J. House and M. L. Baetz, "Leadership: Some Empirical Generalizations and New Research Directions," in B. M. Staw, ed., *Research in Organizational Behavior*, vol. 1 (Greenwood, CT: JAI Press, 1979), 399–401.

41. G. Yukl, *Leadership in Organizations* 7th ed. (Upper Saddle River, NJ: Pearson Prentice Hall, 2010).

42. W. H. Friedland, "For a Sociological Concept of Charisma," *Social Forces* 43 (1964): 18.

43. J. M. Howell, "Two Faces of Charisma: Socialized and Personalized Leadership in Organizations," in J. A. Conger, ed., *Charismatic Leadership: Behind the Mystique of Exceptional Leadership* (San Francisco, CA: Jossey-Bass, 1988).

44. M. Maccoby, "Narcissistic Leaders: The Incredible Pros, the Inevitable Cons," *Harvard Business Review* 78 (2000): 68–77.

45. D. Sankowsky, "The Charismatic Leader as Narcissist: Understanding the Abuse of Power," *Organizational Dynamics* 23 (1995): 57–71.

46. F. J. Flynn and B. M. Staw, "Lend Me Your Wallets: The Effect of Charismatic Leadership on External Support for an Organization," *Strategic Management Journal* 25 (2004): 309–330.

47. R. K. Greenleaf, L. C. Spears, and D. T. Frick, eds., *On Becoming a Servant-Leader* (San Francisco, CA: Jossey-Bass, 1996).

48. C. L. Gohm, "Mood Regulation and Emotional Intelligence: Individual Differences," *Journal of Personality and Social Psychology* 84 (2003): 594–607.

49. D. Goleman, "Never Stop Learning," *Harvard Business Review* 82 (2004): 28–30.

50. D. Goleman, "What Makes a Leader?" *Harvard Business Review* 82 (2004): 82–91.

51. J. Antonakis, N. M. Ashkanasy, and M. T. Dasborough, "Does Leadership Need Emotional Intelligence?" *The Leadership Quarterly* 20 (2009): 247–261.

52. R. C. Mayer, J. H. Davis, and F. D. Schoorman, "An Integrative Model of Organizational Trust," *Academy of Management Review* 20 (1995): 709–734.

53. R. S. Dooley and G. E. Fryxell, "Attaining Decision Quality and Commitment from Dissent: The Moderating Effects of Loyalty and

Competence in Strategic Decision-making Teams," *Academy of Management Journal* 42 (1999): 389–402.

54. S. W. Lester and H. H. Brower, "In the Eyes of the Beholder: The Relationship between Subordinates' Felt Trustworthiness and Their Work Attitudes and Behaviors," *Journal of Leadership and Organizational Studies* 10 (2003): 17–33.

55. S. A. Joni, "The Geography of Trust," *Harvard Business Review* 82 (2003): 82–88.

56. M. W. Grojean, C. J. Resick, M. W. Dickson, and D. B. Smith, "Leaders, Values, and Organizational Climate: Examining Leadership Strategies for Establishing an Organizational Climate Regarding Ethics," *Journal of Business Ethics* 55 (2004): 223–241.

57. M. E. Heilman, C. J. Block, R. F. Martell, and M. C. Simon, "Has Anything Changed? Current Characteristics of Men, Women, and Managers," *Journal of Applied Psychology* 74 (1989): 935–942.

58. D. Tannen, "The Power of Talk: Who Gets Heard and Why," *Harvard Business Review* (September/October 1995).

59. A. H. Eagly, S. J. Darau, and M. Makhijani, "Gender and the Effectiveness of Leaders: A Meta-Analysis," *Psychological Bulletin* 117 (1995): 125–145.

60. S. Bruckmüller and N. R. Branscombe, "How Women End Up on the 'Glass Cliff'" *Harvard Business Review* 89 (2011): 26.

61. C. Rivers, and R. C. Barnett, "When Wall Street Needs Scapegoats, Women Beware," *Women's eNews,* November 2, 2013, accessed from https://womensenews.org/2013/11/when-wall-street-needs-scapegoats-women-beware, October 8, 2018.

62. S. Haslam, S. Alexander and M. K. Ryan, "The Road to the Glass Cliff: Differences in the Perceived Suitability of Men and Women for Leadership Positions in Succeeding and Failing Organizations," *The Leadership Quarterly* 19 (2008): 530–546.

63. M. K. Ryan, S. A. Haslam, and T. Postmes, "Reactions to the Glass Cliff: Gender Differences in the Explanations for the Precariousness of Women's Leadership Positions," *Journal of Organizational Change Management* 20 (2) (2007): 182–197.

64. B. Kellerman, *Followership: How Followers Are Creating Change and Changing Leaders* (Boston, MA: Harvard Business Press, 2008).

65. B. Shamir, "From Passive Recipients to Active Co-Producers: Followers' Role in the Leadership Process," in *Follower-Centre Perspectives on Leadership: A Tribute to Joseph Meindl* (Greenwich, CT: Information Age Publishing, 2007), xii – xviiii.

66. C. Powell (n.d.)

67. T. Thomas, and P. Berg, "Followership: Exercising Discretion," *Journal of Leadership Education. Special* 4 (2014): 21–35.

68. H. P. Sims, Jr., and C. C. Manz, *Company of Heros: Unleashing the Power of Self-Leadership* (New York: John Wiley & Sons, 1996).

69. L. Hirschhorn, "Leaders and Followers in a Postindustrial Age: A Psychodynamic View," *Journal of Applied Behavioral Science* 26 (1990): 529–542.

70. R. E. Kelley, "In Praise of Followers," *Harvard Business Review* 66 (1988): 142–148.

71. C. C. Manz and H. P. Sims, "SuperLeadership: Beyond the Myth of Heroic Leadership," *Organizational Dynamics* 20 (1991): 18–35.

72. G. A. Yukl, *Leadership in Organizations,* 2nd ed. (Upper Saddle River, NJ: Prentice-Hall, 1989).

13

1. E. H. Schein, *Organizational Culture and Leadership*, 4th ed. (San Francisco, CA: Jossey-Bass, 2010), 18

2. G. Hofstede, G. J. Hofstede, and M. Minkov, *Cultures and Organizations—Software of the Mind: Intercultural Cooperation and Its Importance for Survival.* (New York: McGraw-Hill, 2010), 6.

3. D. D. Van Fleet and R. W. Griffin, "Dysfunctional Organization Culture: The Role of Leadership in Motivating Dysfunctional Work Behaviors," *Journal of Managerial Psychology* 21(8) (2006): 698–708.

4. L. Smircich, "Concepts of Culture and Organizational Analysis," *Administrative Science Quarterly* (1983): 339–358.

5. Y. Weiner and Y. Vardi, "Relationships between Organizational Culture and Individual Motivation: A Conceptual Integration," *Psychological Reports* 67 (1990): 295–306.

6. Y. Allaire, and M. R. Firsitotu, "Theories of Organizational Culture," *Organization Studies* 5 (3)(1984): 193–226.

7. T. A. Judge and D. M. Cable, "Applicant Personality, Organizational Culture, and Organization Attraction," *Personnel Psychology* 50 (1997): 359–394.

8. W. Gardner, B. J. Reithel, C. Cogliser, F. O. Walumbwa, and R. T. Foley, "Matching Personality and Organizational Culture Effects of Recruitment Strategy and the Five-Factor Model on Subjective Person–Organization Fit," *Management Communication Quarterly* 24 (2012): 585–622.

9. P. Warr and A. Pearce, "Preferences for Careers and Organizational Cultures as a Function of Logically Related Personality Traits," *Applied Psychology: An International Review* 53 (2004): 423–435.

10. A. L. Kristof-Brown, R. D. Zimmerman, and E. C. Johnson, "Consequences of Individuals' Fit at Work: A Meta-Analysis of Person–Job, Person–Organization, Person–Group, and Person–Supervisor Fit," *Personnel Psychology* 58 (2005): 281–342.

11. C. A. O'Reilly, J. Chatman, and D. F. Caldwell, "People and Organizational Culture: A Profile Comparison Approach to Assessing Person-Organization Fit," *Academy of Management Journal* 34 (1991): 487–516.

12. A. L. Kristof-Brown, R. D. Zimmerman, and E. C. Johnson, "Consequences of Individuals' Fit at Work: A Meta-Analysis of Person–Job, Person–Organization, Person–Group, and Person–Supervisor Fit," *Personnel Psychology* 58 (2005): 281–342.

13. A. E. M. van Vianen and A. H. Fischer, "Illuminating the Glass Ceiling: The Role of Organizational Culture Preferences," *Journal of Occupational and Organizational Psychology* 75 (2002): 315–337.

14. J. B. Sorensen, "The Strength of Corporate Culture and the Reliability of Firm Performance," *Administrative Science Quarterly* 47 (2002): 70–91.

15. J. W. O'Neill, L. L. Beauvais, and R. W. Scholl, "The Use of Organizational Culture and Structure to Guide Strategic Behavior: An Information Processing Perspective," *Journal of Behavioural Control* 2 (2) (2016): 132–152.

16. T. Rick, "When Organizational Culture Needs to Change Fundamentally," Meliorate, March 13, 2017, accessed from https://www.torbenrick.eu/t/r/wut, September 18, 2018.

17. D. Leipziger, H. Kharas, I. Sud, P. Modan, V. Elliott, and V. Nehru, *The Key Challenges Facing the World Bank President: An Independent Diagnostic* (The 1818 Society, World Bank Group Alumni, 2012).

18. J. A. Chatman, and K. A. Jehn, "Assessing the Relationship between Industry Characteristics and Organizational Culture: How Different Can You Be?" *Academy of Management Journal* 37(1994): 522–553.

19. B. Blackwelder, K.Coleman, S. Colunga-Santoyo, J. S. Harrison, and D. Wozniak. *The Volkswagen Scandal*. Case Study (University of Richmond, BC: Robins School of Business, 2016).

20. H. Miller and C. Rayner, "The Form and Function of 'Bullying' Behaviours in a Strong Occupational Culture: Bullying in a U.K. Police Service," *Group and Organization Management* 37 (2) (2012): 347–375.

21. E.H. Schein, *Organization Development: A Jossey-Bass Reader* (John Wiley & Sons, 2006).

22. C. D. Sutton and D. L. Nelson, "Elements of the Cultural Network: The Communicators of Corporate Values," *Leadership and Organization Development* 11 (1990): 3–10.

23. A. Bandura, *Social Learning Theory* (Englewood Cliffs, NJ: Prentice-Hall, 1977).

24. J. A. Chatman, "Leading by Leveraging Culture," *California Management Review* 45 (2003): 20–34.

25. J. M. Beyer and H. M. Trice, "How an Organization's Rites Reveal Its Culture," *Organizational Dynamics* 16 (1987): 5–24.

26. S. Hasulo, "Workplace Balance: The Intuitive Approach," *Canadian Business Online*, January 8, 2007, http://www.canadianbusiness.com/article.jsp?content=20070108_132428_5568.

27. H. M. Trice and J. M. Beyer, "Studying Organizational Cultures through Rites and Ceremonials," *Academy of Management Review* 9 (1984): 653–669.

28. H. Levinson and S. Rosenthal, *CEO: Corporate Leadership in Action* (New York: *Basic Books*, 1984).

29. J. Martin, M. S. Feldman, M. J. Hatch, and S. B. Sitkin, "The Uniqueness Paradox in Organizational Stories," *Administrative Science Quarterly* 28 (1983): 438–453.

30. Ibid.

31. R. Goffee and G. Jones, "What Holds the Modern Company Together?" *Harvard Business Review* (November–December 1996): 133–148.

32. V. Govindarajan and S. Srinivas, "The Innovation Mindset in Action: 3M Corporation," *Harvard Business Review*, August 2013, https://hbr.org/2013/08/the-innovation-mindset-in-acti-3.

33. M. Moody, *Vault's Top 100 Law Firms for 2018*, accessed from http://www.vault.com/blog/vaults-law-blog-legal-careers-and-industry-news/vaults-top-100-law-firms-for-2018, October 8, 2018.

34. M. Peterson, "Work, Corporate Culture, and Stress: Implications for Worksite Health Promotion," *American Journal of Health Behavior* 21 (1997): 243–252.

35. M. Peterson, "Work, Corporate Culture, and Stress: Implications for Worksite Health Promotion," *American Journal of Health Behavior* 21 (1997): 243–252.

36. C. Argyris and D. A. Schon, *Organizational Learning* (Reading, MA: Addison-Wesley, 1978).

37. R. Cialdini, P. K. Petrova, and N. J. Goldstein, "The Hidden Cost of Organizational Dishonesty," *Sloan Management Review* 45 (2004): 66–74.

38. A, Howell, A. Kirk-Brown, and B. K. Cooper "Does Congruence between Espoused and Enacted Organizational Values Predict Affective Commitment in Australian Organizations?" *The International Journal of Human Resource Management* 23 (2012): 731–747.

39. E. Schein, *Organizational Culture and Leadership*, 5e (San Francisco, CA: Jossey-Bass, 2016).

40. E. Schein, "The Role of the Founder in Creating Organizational Culture," *Family Business Review* 8 (3) (1995): 221–238.

41. J. A. Pearce, II, T. R. Kramer, and D. K. Robbins, "Effects of Managers' Entrepreneurial Behavior on Subordinates," *Journal of Business Venturing* 12 (1997): 147–160.

42. J. Pieterse, *Globalization and Culture: Global Mélange*, 2nd rev. ed. (Lanham, MD: Rowman & Littlefield, 2009).

43. G. Chao, A. M. O'Leary-Kelly, S. Wolf, H. Klein, and P. Gardner, "Organizational Socialization: Its Content and Consequences," *Journal of Applied Psychology* 79 (1994): 730–743.

44. T. N Bauer, T. Bodner, B. Erdogan, D. M. Truxillo, and J. S. Tucker, "Newcomer Adjustment During Organizational Socialization: A Meta Analytic Review of Antecedents, Outcomes, and Methods," *Journal of Applied Psychology* 92 (3) (2007): 707–721.

45. T. N. Bauer, T. Bodner, B. Erdogan, D. M. Truxillo, and J. S. Tucker, "Newcomer Adjustment During Organizational Socialization: A Meta Analytic Review of Antecedents, Outcomes, and Methods," *Journal of Applied Psychology* 92 (3) (2007): 707–721.

46. D. M. Cable, L. Aiman-Smith, P. W. Mulvey, and J. R. Edwards, "The Sources and Accuracy of Job Applicants' Beliefs about Organizational Culture," *Academy of Management Journal* 43 (2000): 1076–1085.

47. J. Chatman, "Matching People and Organizations: Selection and Socialization in Public Accounting Firms," *Administrative Science Quarterly* 36 (1991): 459–484.

48. T. N. Bauer, T. Bodner, B. Erdogan, D. M. Truxillo, and J. S. Tucker, "Newcomer Adjustment During Organizational Socialization: A Meta Analytic Review of Antecedents, Outcomes, and Methods," *Journal of Applied Psychology* 92(3) (2007): 707–721.

49. D. L. Nelson, J. C. Quick, and M. E. Eakin, "A Longitudinal Study of Newcomer Role Adjustment in U.S. Organizations," *Work and Stress* 2 (1988): 239–253.

50. T. N. Bauer, E. W. Morrison, and R. R. Callister, "Organizational Socialization: A Review and Directions for Future Research," *Research in Personnel and Human Resources Management* 16 (1998): 149–214.

51. P. Bate, "Using the Culture Concept in an Organization Development Setting," *Journal of Applied Behavior Science* 26 (1990): 83–106.

52. K. R. Thompson and F. Luthans, "Organizational Culture: A Behavioral Perspective," in B. Schneider, ed., *Organizational Climate and Culture* (San Francisco, CA: Jossey-Bass, 1990).

53. V. Sathe, "How to Decipher and Change Corporate Culture," in R. H. Kilman et al., *Managing Corporate Cultures* (San Francisco, CA: Jossey-Bass, 1985).

54. Schein, *Organizational Culture and Leadership*.

55. M. E. Johnson-Cramer, S. Parise, and R. L. Cross, "Managing Change through Networks and Values," *California Management Review* 49 (3) (2007): 85–109.

56. L. K. Trevino and K. A. Nelson, *Managing Business Ethics: Straight Talk about How to Do It Right* (New York: John Wiley & Sons, 1995).

57. A. Bhide and H. H. Stevenson, "Why Be Honest if Honesty Doesn't Pay?" *Harvard Business Review* (September–October 1990): 121–129.

58. A. Pater and A. van Gils, "Stimulating Ethical Decision Making in a Business Context: Ethics of Ethical and Professional Codes," *European Management Journal* 21 (December 2003): 762–772.

59. J. R. Detert, R. G. Schroeder, and J. J. Mauriel, "A Framework for Linking Culture and Improvement Initiatives in Organizations," *Academy of Management Review* 25 (2000): 850–863.

60. J. P. Kotter and J. L. Heskett, *Corporate Culture and Performance* (New York: Free Press, 1992).

61. Deal and Kennedy, *Corporate Cultures.*

62. J. P. Kotter and J. L. Heskett, *Corporate Culture and Performance* (New York: Free Press, 1992).

63. R. S. Burt, S. S. Gabbay, G. Holt, and P. Moran, "Contingent Organization as a Network Theory: The Culture Performance Contingency Function," *Acta Sociologica* 37 (1994): 345–370.

64. G. Donaldson and J. Lorsch, *Decision Making at the Top* (New York: Basic Books, 1983).

65. R. H. Kilman, M. J. Saxton, and R. Serpa, eds., *Gaining Control of the Corporate Culture* (San Francisco: Jossey-Bass, 1986).

66. J. P. Kotter, *A Force for Change: How Leadership Differs from Management* (New York: Free Press, 1990); R. M. Kanter, *The Change Masters* (New York: Simon & Schuster, 1983).

67. T. Peters and N. Austin, *A Passion for Excellence: The Leadership Difference* (New York: Random House, 1985).

68. S. Thornhill and R. Amit, "Learning about Failure: Bankruptcy, Firm Age, and the Resource-based View," *Organization Science* 14 (2003): 497–509.

14

1. B. F. Skinner, *The Behavior of Organisms: An Experimental Analysis* (New York: Appleton-Century-Crofts, 1938).

2. B. F. Skinner, "Operant Behavior," *American Psychologist* 18 (1963): 503–515; B. F. Skinner, "Reinforcement Today," *American Psychologist* 13 (1958): 94–99; Research summarized in A. Poling and D. Braatz, "Principles of Learning: Respondent and Operant Conditioning and Human Behavior," in C. M. Johnson, W. K. Redmon, and T. C. Mawhinney, eds., *Handbook of Organizational Performance: Behavior Analysis and Management* (Binghampton, NY: The Haworth Press, 2001), 23–50.

3. G. P. Latham and V. L. Huber, "Schedules of Reinforcement: Lessons from the Past and Issues for the Future," *Journal of Organizational Behavior Management* 12 (1991): 125–149.

4. M. Maccoby, J. Hoffer Gittell, and M. Ledeen, "Leadership and the Fear Factor," *Sloan Management Review* 148 (Winter 2004): 14–18.

5. A. Bandura, *Social Learning Theory* (Englewood Cliffs, NJ: Prentice-Hall, 1977); A. Bandura, "Self-Efficacy: Toward a Unifying Theory of Behavioral Change," *Psychological Review* 84 (1977): 191–215.

6. J. J. Martocchio and E. J. Hertenstein, "Learning Orientation and Goal Orientation Context: Relationships with Cognitive and Affective Learning Outcomes," *Human Resource Development Quarterly* 14 (2003): 413–434.

7. A. Bandura, "Regulation of Cognitive Processes through Perceived Self-Efficacy," *Developmental Psychology* (September 1989): 729–735.

8. J. M. Phillips and S. M. Gully, "Role of Goal Orientation, Ability, Need for Achievement, and Locus of Control in the Self-Efficacy and Goal-Setting Process," *Journal of Applied Psychology* 82 (1997): 792–802.

9. J. C. Weitlauf, R. E. Smith, and D. Cervone, "Generalization Effects of Coping-Skills Training: Influence of Self-Defense Training on Women's Efficacy Beliefs, Assertiveness, and Aggression," *Journal of Applied Psychology* 85 (2000): 625–633.

10. V. Gecas, "The Social Psychology of Self-Efficacy," *Annual Review of Sociology* 15 (1989): 291–316.

11. T. Sitzmann, B. Bell, K. Kraiger, and A. Kanar, "A Multilevel Analysis of the Effect of Prompting Self-Regulation in Technology-delivered Instruction," *Personnel Psychology* 62 (2009): 697–734.

12. T. Sitzmann and K. Ely, "Sometimes You Need a Reminder: The Effects of Prompting Self-Regulation on Regulatory Processes, Learning and Attrition," *Journal of Applied Psychology* 95 (2010): 132–144.

13. N. Keith and M. Frese, "Effectiveness of Error Management Training: A Meta-Analysis," *Journal of Applied Psychology* 93 (2008): 59–69.

14. N. Keith and M. Frese, "Self-Regulation in Error Management Training: Emotion Control and Metacognition as Mediators of Performance Effects," *Journal of Applied Psychology* 90 (2005): 677–691.

15. S. Ellis, Y. Ganzach, E. Castle, and G. Sekely, "The Effect of Filmed versus Personal After-Event Reviews on Task Performance: The Mediating and Moderating Role of Self-Efficacy," *Journal of Applied Psychology* 95 (2010): 122–131.

16. S. Ellis and I. Davidi, "After-Event Reviews: Drawing Lessons from Successful and Failed Experience," *Journal of Applied Psychology* 90 (2005): 857–871.

17. S. Ellis, R. Mendel, and M. Nir, "Learning from Successful and Failed Experience: The Moderating Role of Kind of After-Event Review," *Journal of Applied Psychology* 91 (2006): 669–680.

18. S. Ellis, Y. Ganzach, E. Castle, and G. Sekely, "The Effect of Filmed versus Personal After-Event Reviews on Task Performance: The Mediating and Moderating Role of Self-Efficacy," *Journal of Applied Psychology* 95 (2010): 122–131.

19. World Meteorological Organization, *Operational Cooperation of the NMHS and DRM and Service Delivery for MNEWS,* accessed from http://www.wmo.int/pages/prog/drr/events/Barbados/Pres/3-OutcomeA.pdf.

20. D. Brady, "Secrets of an HR Superstar," *Businessweek*, 4029 (9 April 2007): 66.

21. R. L. Cardy, *Performance Management: Concepts, Skills, and Exercises* (Armonk, NY, and London, England: M. E. Sharpe, 2004).

22. G. S. Odiorne, *Management by Objectives: A System of Managerial Leadership* (New York: Pitman, 1965).

23. J. C. Quick, "Dyadic Goal Setting and Role Stress," *Academy of Management Journal* 22 (1979): 241–252.

24. P. F. Drucker, *The Practice of Management* (New York: Harper & Bros., 1954).

25. R. D. Prichard, P. L. Roth, S. D. Jones, P. J. Galgay, and M. D. Watson, "Designing a Goal-setting System to Enhance Performance: A Practical Guide," *Organizational Dynamics* 17 (1988): 69–78.

26. C. L. Hughes, *Goal Setting: Key to Individual and Organizational Effectiveness* (New York: American Management Association, 1965).

27. M. E. Tubbs and S. E. Ekeberg, "The Role of Intentions in Work Motivation: Implications for Goal-setting Theory and Research," *Academy of Management Review* 16 (1991): 180–199.

28. S. Vatave, "Managing Risk," *Supervision* 65 (2004): 6–9.

29. J. R. Hollenbeck and A. P. Brief, "The Effects of Individual Differences and Goal Origin on Goal Setting and Performance," *Organizational Behavior and Human Decision Processes* 40 (1987): 392–414.

30. G. D. Nord, T. F. McCubbins, and J. Horn Nord, "E-monitoring in the Workplace: Privacy, Legislation and Surveillance Software," *Communications of the ACM* 49 (2006): 74–77.

31. C. Spitzmuller and J. M. Stanton, "Examining Employee Compliance with Organizational Surveillance and

Monitoring," *Journal of Occupational and Organizational Psychology* 79 (2006): 245–272.

32. H. H. Meyer, E. Kay, and J. R. P. French, "Split Roles in Performance Appraisal," *Harvard Business Review* 43 (1965): 123–129.

33. S. L. Rynes, B. Gerhart, and L. Parks, "Personnel Psychology: Performance Evaluation and Pay for Performance," *Annual Review of Psychology* 56 (2005): 571–600.

34. A. N. Kluger and A. DeNisi, "The Effects of Feedback Interventions on Performance: A Historical Review, a Meta-Analysis and a Preliminary Feedback Intervention Theory," *Psychological Bulletin* 119 (1996): 254–284.

35. W. A. Fisher, J. C. Quick, L. L. Schkade, and G. W. Ayers, "Developing Administrative Personnel through the Assessment Center Technique," *Personnel Administrator* 25 (1980): 44–46, 62.

36. G. A. Van Kleef, A. C. Homan, B. Beersma, D. Van Knippenberg, and F. Damen, "Searing Sentiment or Cold Calculation? The Effects of Leader Emotional Displays on Team Performance Depend on Follower Epistemic Motivation," *Academy of Management Journal* 52 (2009): 562–580.

37. K. Byron, S. Khazanchi, and D. Nazarian, "The Relationship between Stressors and Creativity: A Meta-Analysis Examining Competitive Theoretical Models," *Journal of Applied Psychology* 95 (2010): 201–212.

38. M. B. DeGregorio and C. D. Fisher, "Providing Performance Feedback: Reactions to Alternative Methods," *Journal of Management* 14 (1988): 605–616.

39. G. C. Thornton, "The Relationship between Supervisory and Self-Appraisals of Executive Performance," *Personnel Psychology* 21 (1968): 441–455.

40. A. S. DeNisi and A. N. Kluger, "Feedback Effectiveness: Can 360-Degree Appraisals Be Improved?" *Academy of Management Executive* 14 (2000): 129–140.

41. S. L. Rynes, B. Gerhart, and L. Parks, "Personnel Psychology: Performance Evaluation and Pay for Performance," *Annual Review of Psychology* 56 (2005): 571–600.

42. F. Luthans and S. J. Peterson, "360-Degree Feedback with Systematic Coaching: Empirical Analysis Suggests a Winning Combination," *Human Resource Management* 42 (2003): 243–256.

43. G. Toegel and J. A. Conger, "360-Degree Assessment: Time for Reinvention," *Academy of Management Learning and Education* 2 (2003): 297–311.

44. L. Hirschhorn, "Leaders and Followers in a Postindustrial Age: A Psychodynamic View," *Journal of Applied Behavioral Science* 26 (1990): 529–542.

45. F. M Jablin, "Superior–Subordinate Communication: The State of the Art," *Psychological Bulletin* 86 (1979): 1201–1222.

46. J. Pfeffer, "Six Dangerous Myths about Pay," *Harvard Business Review* 76 (1998): 108–119.

47. E. A. Locke, D. B. Feren, V. M. McCaleb, K. N. Shaw, and A. T. Denny, "The Relative Effectiveness of Four Ways of Motivating Employee Performance, in K. D. Duncan, M. M. Gruenberg, and D. Wallis, eds., *Changes in Working Life*, (New York: Wiley, 1960), 363–388; D. G. Jenkins, Jr., A. Mitra, N. Gupta, and J. D. Shaw, "Are Financial Incentives Related to Performance? A Meta-Analytic Review of Empirical Research," *Journal of Applied Psychology* 83 (1998): 777–787.

48. J. D. Shaw and N. Gupta, "Pay System Characteristics and Quit Patterns of Good, Average and Poor Performers," *Personnel Psychology* 60 (2007): 903–928.

49. E. P. Lazear, "Salaries and Piece Rates," *Journal of Business* 59 (1986): 405–431.

50. R. D. Bretz, R. A. Ash, and G. F. Dreher, "Do People Make the Place? An Examination of the Attraction-Selection-Attrition Hypothesis," *Personnel Psychology* 42 (1989): 561–581.

51. D. M. Cable and T. A. Judge, "Pay Preferences and Job Search Decisions: A Person-Organization Fit Perspective," *Personnel Psychology* 47 (1994): 317–348.

52. C. B. Cadsby, F. Song, and F. Tapon, "Sorting and Incentive Effects of Pay for Performance: An Experimental Investigation," *Academy of Management Journal* 50 (2007): 387–405.

53. R. T. Kaufman, "The Effects of Improshare on Productivity," *Industrial Labour Relations Review* 45 (1992): 311–322.

54. M. J. Pearsall, M. S. Christian, and A. P. J. Ellis, "Motivating Interdependent Teams: Individual Rewards, Shared Rewards, or Something In-Between," *Journal of Applied Psychology* 95 (2010): 183–191.

55. S. Kerr, "On the Folly of Rewarding A, While Hoping for B," *Academy of Management Journal* 18 (1975): 769–783.

56. J. M. Bardwick, *Danger in the Comfort Zone* (New York: American Management Association, 1991).

57. B. Raabe and T. A. Beehr, "Formal Mentoring versus Supervisor and Coworker Relationships: Differences in Perceptions and Impact," *Journal of Organizational Behavior* 24 (2003): 271–293.

58. A. M. Young and P. L. Perrewe, "What Did You Expect? An Examination of Career-rrelated Support and Social Support among Mentors and Protégés," *Journal of Management* 26 (2000): 611–633.

59. K. Doherty, "The Good News about Depression," *Business and Health* 3 (1989): 1–4.

60. K. E. Kram, "Phases of the Mentor Relationship," *Academy of Management Journal* 26 (1983): 608–625.

61. T. D. Allen, L. T. Eby, M. L. Poteet, E. Lentz, and L. Lima, "Career Benefits Associated with Mentoring for Protégés: A Meta-Analysis," *Journal of Applied Psychology* 89 (2004): 127–136.

62. K. E. Kram and L. A. Isabella, "Mentoring Alternatives: The Role of Peer Relationships in Career Development," *Academy of Management Journal* 28 (1985): 110–132.

63. T. N. Bauer and S. G. Green, "Development of Leader–Member Exchange: A Longitudinal Test," *Academy of Management Journal* 39 (1996): 1538–1567.

64. K. E. Kram and L. A. Isabella, "Mentoring Alternatives: The Role of Peer Relationships in Career Development," *Academy of Management Journal* 28 (1985): 110–132.

65. J. Greco, "Hey, Coach!" *Journal of Business Strategy* 22 (2001): 28–32.

15

1. J. K. Harter, F. L. Schmidt, and T. L. Hayes, "Business-Unit-Level Relationship between Employee Satisfaction, Employee Engagement, and Business Outcomes: A Meta-Analysis," *Journal of Applied Psychology* 87 (2) (2002): 268–279.

2. I. Harpaz and X. Fu, "The Structure of the Meaning of Work: A Relative Stability amidst Change," *Human Relations* 55 (2002): 639–668.

3. R. D. Arvey, I. Harpaz, and H. Liao, "Work Centrality and Post-Award Work Behavior of Lottery Winners," *The Journal of Psychology* 138 (2004): 404–420.

4. V. Keefe, P. Reid, C. Ormsby, B. Robson, G. Purdie, J. Baxter, and Ngäti Kahungunu Iwi Incorporated, "Serious Health Events Following Involuntary Job Loss in New Zealand Meat Processing Workers," *International*

Journal of Epidemiology 31 (2002): 1155–1161.

5. W. T. Gallo, H. M. Teng, T. A. Falba, S. V. Kasl, H. M. Krumholz, and E. H. Bradley, "The Impact of Late Career Job Loss on Myocardial Infarction and Stroke: A 10 Year Follow-up Using the Health and Retirement Survey," *Occupational and Environmental Medicine* 63 (2006): 683–687.

6. K. W. Strully, "Job Loss and Health in the U.S. Labor Market," *Demography* 46 (2009): 221–246.

7. Various research described in D. L. Blustein, "The Role of Work in Psychological Health and Well-Being," *American Psychologist* 63 (2008): 228–240.

8. S. A. Ruiz-Quintanilla and B. Wilpert, "Are Work Meanings Changing?" *European Work and Organizational Psychology* 1 (1991): 91–109; MOW—International Research Team, *The Meaning of Working* (London: Academic Press, 1987); S. H. Harding and F. J. Hikspoors, "New Work Values: In Theory and in Practice," *International Social Science Journal* 47 (1995): 441–455.

9. L. R. Gomez-Mejia, "The Cross-Cultural Structure of Task-related and Contextual Constructs," *Journal of Psychology* 120 (1986): 5–19.

10. A. M. Grant, Y. Fried, and T. Juillerat, "Job Design in Classic and Contemporary Perspectives," *APA Handbook of Industrial and Organizational Psychology* (American Psychological Association, 2010).

11. A. Smith, *An Inquiry into the Nature and Causes of the Wealth of Nations* (London: W. Strahan and T. Cadell, 1776).

12. C. Babbage, *On the Economy of Machinery and Manufacturing* (London: Knight, 1835).

13. F. W. Taylor, *The Principles of Scientific Management* (New York: Norton, 1911).

14. C. R. Walker, "The Problem of the Repetitive Job," *Harvard Business Review* 28 (1950): 54–58.

15. R. P. Steel and J. R. Rentsch, "The Dispositional Model of Job Attitudes Revisited: Findings of a 10-Year Study," *Journal of Applied Psychology* 82 (1997): 873–879; C. S. Wong, C. Hui, and K. S. Law, "A Longitudinal Study of the Job Perception–Job Satisfaction Relationship: A Text of the Three Alternative Specifications," *Journal of Occupational & Organizational Psychology* 71 (Part 2, 1998): 127–146.

16. C. M. Axtell and S. K. Parker, "Promoting Role Breadth Self-Efficacy through Involvement, Work Redesign and Training," *Human Relations* 56 (2003): 113–131.

17. M. A. Campion, L. Cheraskin, and M. J. Stevens, "Career-related Antecedents and Outcomes of Job Rotation," *Academy of Management Journal* 37 (1994): 1518–1542.

18. A. M. Grant, Y. Fried, and T. Juillerat, "Job Design in Classic and Contemporary Perspectives," *APA Handbook of Industrial and Organizational Psychology* (American Psychological Association, 2010).

19. F. Herzberg, "One More Time: How Do You Motivate Employees?" *Harvard Business Review* 46 (1968): 53–62.

20. R. N. Ford, "Job Enrichment Lessons from AT&T," *Harvard Business Review* 51 (1973): 96–106.

21. R. J. House and L. A. Wigdor, "Herzberg's Dual-Factor Theory of Job Satisfaction and Motivation: A Review of the Evidence and a Criticism," *Personnel Psychology* 20 (1967): 369–389.

22. G. R. Oldham, J. R. Hackman, and L. P. Stepina, "Norms for the Job Diagnostic Survey," Technical Report No. 16, School of Organization and Management, Yale University, 1978, http://www.dtic.mil/cgi-bin/GetTRDoc?AD=ADA057268andLocation=U2anddoc=GetTRDoc.pdf.

23. S. E. Humphrey, J. D. Nahrgang, and F. P. Morgeson, "Integrating Motivational, Social and Contextual Work Design Features: A Meta-Analytic Summary and Theoretical Extension of the Work Design Literature," *Journal of Applied Psychology* 92 (2007): 1332–1356; Y. Fried and G. R. Ferris, "The Validity of the Job Characteristics Model: A Review and Meta-Analysis," *Personnel Psychology* 40 (1987): 287–322.

24. Ibid.

25. S. E. Humphrey, J. D. Nahrgang, and F. P. Morgeson, "Integrating Motivational, Social and Contextual Work Design Features: A Meta-Analytic Summary and Theoretical Extension of the Work Design Literature," *Journal of Applied Psychology* 92 (2007): 1332–356.

26. G. Gard and A. C. Sandberg, "Motivating Factors for Return to Work," *Physiotherapy Research International* 3 (2006): 100–108.

27. A. M. Grant, "The Significance of Task Significance: Job Performance Effects, Relational Mechanisms, and Boundary Conditions," *Journal of Applied Psychology* 93 (2008): 108–124.

28. A. M. Grant, "Designing Jobs to Do Good: Dimensions and Psychological Consequences of Prosocial Job Characteristics," *The Journal of Positive Psychology* 3 (2008): 19–39.

29. A. M. Grant, "Employees without a Cause: The Motivational Effects of Prosocial Impact in Public Service," *International Public Management Journal* 11 (2008): 48–66.

30. Y. N. Turner, I. Hadas-Halperin, and D. Raveh, "Patient Photos Spur Radiologist Empathy and Eye for Detail," paper presented at annual meeting of the Radiological Society of North America, November 2008, reported in A. M. Grant and S. K. Parker, "Redesigning Work Theories: The Rise of Relational and Proactive Perspectives," *The Academy of Management Annals* 3 (2009): 317–375.

31. K. A. Arnold, N. Turner, J. Barling, E. K. Kelloway, and M. C. McKee, "Transformational Leadership and Psychological Well-Being: The Mediating Role of Meaningful Work," *Journal of Occupational Health Psychology* 12 (2007): 193–203.

32. F. P. Morgeson and S. E. Humphrey, "The Work Design Questionnaire (WDQ): Developing and Validating a Comprehensive Measure for Assessing Job Design and the Nature of Work," *Journal of Applied Psychology* 91 (2006): 1321–1339.

33. S. E. Humphrey, J. D. Nahrgang, and F. P. Morgeson, "Integrating Motivational, Social and Contextual Work Design Features: A Meta-Analytic Summary and Theoretical Extension of the Work Design Literature," *Journal of Applied Psychology* 92 (2007): 1332–1356.

34. Ibid.

35. K. Nielsen and B. Cleal, "Predicting Flow at Work: Investigating the Activities and Job Characteristics that Predict Flow States at Work," *Journal of Occupational Health Psychology* 15 (2010): 180–190.

36. E. F. Stone and H. G. Gueutal, "An Empirical Derivation of the Dimensions Along Which Characteristics of Jobs Are Perceived," *Academy of Management Journal* 28 (1985): 376–396.

37. S. E. Humphrey, J. D. Nahrgang, and F. P. Morgeson, "Integrating Motivational, Social and Contextual Work Design Features: A Meta-Analytic Summary and Theoretical Extension of the Work Design Literature," *Journal of Applied Psychology* 92 (2007): 1332–1356.

38. C. Gresov, R. Drazin, and A. H. Van de Ven, "Work-Unit Task Uncertainty, Design, and Morale," *Organizational Studies* 10 (1989): 45–62.

39. G. R. Salancik and J. Pfeffer, "A Social Information Processing Approach to Job Attitudes and Task Design,"

Administrative Science Quarterly 23 (1978): 224–253.

40. J. Pfeffer, "Management as Symbolic Action: The Creation and Maintenance of Organizational Paradigms," in L. L. Cummings and B. M. Staw, eds., *Research in Organizational Behavior*, vol. 3 (Greenwich, CT: JAI Press, 1981), 1–5.

41. C. Clegg and C. Spencer, "A Circular and Dynamic Model of the Process of Job Design," *Journal of Occupational & Organizational Psychology* 80 (2007): 321–339.

42. J. Thomas and R. Griffin, "The Social Information Processing Model of Task Design: A Review of the Literature," *Academy of Management Review* 8 (1983): 672–682.

42. D. J. Campbell, "Task Complexity: A Review and Analysis," *Academy of Management Review* 13 (1988): 40–52.

44. A. M. Grant, "Relational Job Design and the Motivation to Make a Prosocial Difference," *Academy of Management Review* 32 (2007): 393–417.

45. S. E. White and T. R. Mitchell, "Job Enrichment versus Social Cues: A Comparison and Competitive Test," *Journal of Applied Psychology* 64 (1979): 1–9; S. E. White, T. R. Mitchell, and C. H. Bell, "Goal Setting, Evaluation Apprehension, and Social Cues as Determinants of Job Performance and Job Satisfaction in a Simulated Organization," *Journal of Applied Psychology* 62 (1977): 665–673.

46. R. W. Griffin, "Objective and Social Sources of Information in Task Redesign: A Field Experiment," *Administrative Science Quarterly* 28 (1983): 184–200; S. M. Jex and P. E. Spector, "The Generalizability of Social Information Processing to Organizational Settings: A Summary of Two Field Experiments," *Perceptual and Motor Skills* 69 (1989): 883–893.

47. A. Wrzesniewski, J. E. Dutton, and G. Debebe, "Interpersonal Sensemaking and the Meaning of Work, *Research in Organizational Behavior* 25 (2003): 93–135.

48. D. R. May, K. Reed, C. E. Schwoerer, and P. Potter, "Ergonomic Office Design and Aging: A Quasi-Experimental Field Study of Employee Reactions to an Ergonomics Intervention Program," *Journal of Occupational Health Psychology* 9 (2004): 123–135.

49. M. A. Campion and P. W. Thayer, "Job Design: Approaches, Outcomes, and Trade-Offs," *Organizational Dynamics* 16 (1987): 66–79.

50. J. Teresko, "Emerging Technologies," *Industry Week* (February 27, 1995): 1–2.

51. M. A. Campion and C. L. McClelland, "Interdisciplinary Examination of the Costs and Benefits of Enlarged Jobs: A Job Design Quasi-Experiment," *Journal of Applied Psychology* 76 (1991): 186–199.

52. A. Wrzesniewski and J. E. Dutton, "Crafting a Job: Revisioning Employees as Active Crafters of their Work," *Academy of Management Review* 26 (2001): 179–201.

53. Ibid.

54. Ibid.

55. P. Lyons, "The Crafting of Jobs and Individual Differences," *Journal of Business and Psychology* 23 (2008): 25–36.

56. C. Leana, E. Appelbaum, and I. Shevchuk, "Work Process and Quality of Care in Early Childhood Education: The Role of Job Crafting," *Academy of Management Journal* 52 (2009): 1169–1192.

57. J. M. Berg, A. Wrzesniewski, and J. E. Dutton, "Perceiving and Responding to Challenges in Job crafting at Different Ranks: When Proactivity Requires Adaptivity," *Journal of Organizational Behavior* 31 (2010): 158–186.

58. D. M. Rouseau, V. T. Ho, and J. Greenberg, "I-deals: Idiosyncratic Terms in Employment Relationships," *Academy of Management Review* 31 (2006): 977–994.

59. S. Hornung, D. M. Rousseau, and J. Glaser, "Creating Flexible Work Arrangements through Idiosyncratic Deals," *Journal of Applied Psychology* 93 (2008): 655–664.

60. S. Hornung, D. M. Rousseau, J. Glaser, P. Angerer, and M. Weigl, "Beyond Top-Down and Bottom-up Work Redesign: Customizing Job Content through Idiosyncratic Deals," *Journal of Organizational Work Behavior* 30 (2009): 187–215.

61. B. M. Wright and J. L. Cordery, "Production Uncertainty as a Contextual Moderator of Employee Reactions to Job Design," *Journal of Applied Psychology* 84 (1999): 456–463.

62. D. Fay and M. Frese, "The Concept of Personal Initiative: An Overview of Validity Studies," *Human Performance* 14 (2001): 97–124.

63. S. K. Parker, "Enhancing Role-Breadth Efficacy: The Roles of Job Enrichment and Other Organizational Interventions," *Journal of Applied Psychology* 83 (1998): 835–852; F. P. Morgeson, K. Delaney-Klinger, and M. A. Hemingway, "The Importance of Job Autonomy, Cognitive Ability, and Job-related Skill for Predicting Role Breadth and Job Performance," *Journal of Applied Psychology* 90 (2005): 399–406.

64. S. K. Parker, T. D. Wall, and P. R. Jackson, "'That's Not My Job': Developing Flexible Employee Work Orientations," *Academy of Management Journal* 40 (1997): 899–929.

65. M. Frese, H. Garst, and D. Fay, "Making Things Happen: Reciprocal Relationships between Work Characteristics and Personal Initiative in a Four-Wave Longitudinal Structural Equation Model," *Journal of Applied Psychology* 92 (2007): 1084–1102.

66. S. J. Ashford, R. Blatt, and D. VandeWalle, "Reflections on the Looking Glass: A Review of Research on Feedback-seeking Behavior in Organizations," *Journal of Management* 29 (2003): 769–799.

67. D. M. Mayer, M. G. Ehrhart, and B. Schneider, "Service Attribute Boundary Conditions of the Service Climate-Customer Satisfaction Link," *Academy of Management Journal* 52 (2008): 1034–1050.

68. G. R. Oldham and A. Cummings, "Employee Creativity: Personal and Contextual Factors at Work," *Academy of Management Journal* 39 (1996): 607–634.

69. M. Frese, H. Garst, and D. Fay, "Making Things Happen: Reciprocal Relationships between Work Characteristics and Personal Initiative in a Four-Wave Longitudinal Structural Equation Model," *Journal of Applied Psychology* 92 (2007): 1084–1102; C. E. Shalley, J. Zhou, and G. R. Oldham, "The Effects of Personal and Contextual Characteristics on Creativity: Where Should We Go from Here?" *Journal of Management* 30 (2004): 933–958.

70. J. L. Xie and G. Johns, "Job Scope and Stress: Can Job Scope Be Too High?" *Academy of Management Journal* 38 (1995): 1288–1309.

71. K. D. Elsbach and A. B. Hargadon, "Enhancing Creativity through 'Mindless' Work: A Framework of Workday Design," *Organization Science* 17 (2006): 470–483.

72. S. Ohly, S. Sonnentag, and F. Pluntke, "Routinization, Work Characteristics and Their Relationships with Creative and Proactive Behaviors," *Journal of Organizational Behavior* 27 (2006): 259–279.

73. B. Kohut, *Country Competitiveness: Organizing of Work* (New York: Oxford University Press, 1993).

74. J. C. Quick and L. E. Tetrick, eds., *Handbook of Occupational Health Psychology* (Washington, DC: American Psychological Association, 2002).

75. W. E. Deming, *Out of the Crisis* (Cambridge, MA: MIT Press, 1986).

76. L. Thurow, *Head to Head: The Coming Economic Battle among Japan, Europe, and America* (New York: Morrow, 1992).

77. M. A. Fruin, *The Japanese Enterprise System—Competitive Strategies and Cooperative Structures* (New York: Oxford University Press, 1992).

78. S. K. Parker, "Longitudinal Effects of Lean Production on Employee Outcomes and the Mediating Role of Work Characteristics," *Journal of Applied Psychology* 88 (2003): 620–634.

79. E. Furubotn, "Codetermination and the Modern Theory of the Firm: A Property-Rights Analysis," *Journal of Business* 61 (1988): 165–181.

80. H. Levinson, *Executive: The Guide to Responsive Management* (Cambridge, MA: Harvard University Press, 1981).

81. B. Gardell, "Scandinavian Research on Stress in Working Life" (Paper presented at the IRRA Symposium on Stress in Working Life, Denver, September 1980).

82. L. Levi, "Psychosocial, Occupational, Environmental, and Health Concepts; Research Results and Applications," in G. P. Keita and S. L. Sauter, eds., *Work and Well-Being: An Agenda for the 1990s* (Washington, DC: American Psychological Association, 1992), 199–211.

83. Y. Baruch, "The Status of Research on Teleworking and an Agenda for Future Research," *International Journal of Management Review* 3 (2000): 113–129.

84. E. B. Akyeampong, "Perspectives on Labour and Income June 2007," Statistics Canada Cat. No. 75-001-XIE.

85. R. S. Gajendran and D. A. Harrison, "The Good, the Bad, and the Unknown about Telecommuting: Meta-Analysis of Psychological Mediators and Individual Consequences," *Journal of Applied Psychology* 92 (2007): 1524–1541.

86. M Toneguzzi, "Initiative Aims to Make Calgary a World Leader in Telework," *The Calgary Herald*, April 20, 2010, http://www.calgaryherald.com/life/Spring+ shootie+blends+fashion+with +function/2729973/Initiative+aims+make + Calgary+world+leader+telework/2924782/story.html.

87. http://www.publicaccess.calgary.ca.

88. CBC News, "Calgary Among World's Highest CO2 Emitters," April 6, 2010, accessed from http://www.cbc.ca/technology/story/2010/04/06/calgary-un-report-carbon-dioxide-greenhouse-emissions.html, September 24, 2018.

89. Calgary Economic Development, April 19, 2010, http://www.calgaryeconomicdevelopment.com/global_news_template.cfm?page=0520200974952.

90. R. S. Gajendran and D. A. Harrison, "The Good, the Bad, and the Unknown about Telecommuting: Meta-Analysis of Psychological Mediators and Individual consequences," *Journal of Applied Psychology* 92 (2007): 1524–1541.

91. Ibid.

92. Ibid.

93. Ibid.

94. Ibid.

95. B. Hill, "Recession Gets Real with Job-Sharing," *Ottawa Citizen* (January 11, 2010), http://www.working.com/national/sectors/Recession+gets+real+with+sharing/1356914/story.html.

96. Yukon Public Service Commission, http://www.psc.gov.yk.ca/services/compressed_work.html.

97. Statistics Canada, 2006, http://www.statcan.gc.ca/pub/71-222-x/2006001/4069843-eng.htm.

98. S. M. Pollan and M. Levine, "Asking for Flextime," *Working Women* (February 1994): 48.

99. S. A. Rogier and M. Y. Padgett, "The Impact of Utilizing a Flexible Work Schedule on the Perceived Career Advancement Potential of Women," *Human Resource Development Quarterly* 15 (2004): 89–106.

100. B. Baltes, T. E. Briggs, J. W. Huff, J. A. Wright, and G. A. Neuman, "Flexible and Compressed Workweek Schedules: A Meta-Analysis of Their Effects on Work-Related Criteria," *Journal of Applied Psychology* 84 (1999): 496–513.

101. Ibid.

102. P. Davidson, "Co-founder of oDesk Helps Employers Monitor Freelancers," *USA Today*, September 13, 2010, http://www.usatoday.com/money/companies/management. /entre/2010-09-12-odesk-tsatalos_N.htm.

103. S. Zuboff, *In the Age of the Smart Machine: The Future of Work and Power* (New York: Basic Books, 1988).

104. B. A. Gutek and S. J. Winter, "Computer Use, Control over Computers, and Job Satisfaction," in S. Oskamp and S. Spacapan, eds., *People's Reactions to Technology in Factories, Offices, and Aerospace: The Claremont Symposium on Applied Social Psychology* (Newbury Park, CA: SAGE, 1990), 121–144.

105. L. M. Schleifer and B. C. Amick, III, "System Response Time and Method of Pay: Stress Effects in Computer-based Tasks," *International Journal of Human-Computer Interaction* 1 (1989): 23–39.

106. K. Voight, "Virtual Work: Some Telecommuters Take Remote Work to the Extreme," *The Wall Street Journal Europe* (February 1, 2001): 1.

107. G. Salvendy, *Handbook of Industrial Engineering: Technology and Operations Management* (New York: John Wiley & Sons, 2001).

108. D. M. Herold, "Using Technology to Improve Our Management of Labor Market Trends," in M. Greller, ed., "Managing Careers with a Changing Workforce," *Journal of Organizational Change Management* 3 (1990): 44–57.

109. D. A. Whetten and K. S. Cameron, *Developing Management Skills*, 6th ed. (Upper Saddle River, NJ: Prentice Hall, 2004).

16

1. J. Child, *Organization* (New York: Harper & Row, 1984).

2. D. Pugh, D. Hickson, C. Hinnings, and C. Turner, "Dimensions of Organization Structure," *Administrative Science Quarterly* 13 (1968): 65–91; B. Reimann, "Dimensions of Structure in Effective Organizations: Some Empirical Evidence," *Academy of Management Journal* 17 (1974): 693–708; S. Robbins, *Organization Theory: The Structure and Design of Organizations,* 3rd ed. (Englewood Cliffs, NJ: Prentice-Hall, 1990).

3. T. D. Wall, N. J. Kemp, P. R. Jockron, and C. W. Clegg, "Outcomes of Autonomous Work Groups: A Long-Term Field Experiment," *Academy of Management Journal* 42 (1986): 127–137; R. I. Beekun, "Assessing the Effectiveness of Sociotechnical Interventions: Antidote or Fad?" *Human Relations* 47 (1989): 877–897.

4. L. Porter and E. Lawler, "The Effects of 'Tall' versus 'Flat' Organization Structures on Managerial Job Satisfaction," *Personnel Psychology* 17 (1964): 135–148.

5. J. H. Gittell, "Supervisory Span, Relational Coordination, and Flight Departure Performance: A Reassessment of Postbureaucracy Theory," *Organization Science* 12 (2001): 468–483.

6. Ibid.

7. J. D. Ford, "Department Context and Formal Structure as Constraints on Leader Behavior," *Academy of Management Journal* 24 (1981): 274–288.

8. F. Heller and G. Yukl, "Participation, Managerial Decision-making and Situational Variables," *Organizational Behavior and Human Performance* 2 (1969): 227–241.

9. D. Kipnis and J. Cosentino, "Use of Leadership Powers in Industry," *Journal of Applied Psychology* 53 (1969): 460–466; D. Kipnis and W. P. Lane, "Self

Confidence and Leadership," *Journal of Applied Psychology* 46 (1962): 291–295.

10. H. Mintzberg, *The Structuring of Organizations* (Englewood Cliffs, NJ: Prentice-Hall, 1979).

11. T. Burns and G. Stalker, *The Management of Innovation* (London: Tavistock, 1961); Mintzberg, *Structuring of Organizations.*

12. R. Daft and A. Armstrong, *Organizational Theory and Design*, 2nd Canadian ed. (Toronto: Nelson Education, 2012).

13. C. B. Clott, "Perspectives on Global Outsourcing and the Changing Nature of Work," *Business and Society Review* 109 (2004): 153–170.

14. B. A. Pasternack and A. J. Viscio, *The Centerless Corporation: A New Model for Transforming Your Organization for Growth and Prosperity* (New York: Simon & Schuster, 1999).

15. J. Woodward, *Industrial Organization: Theory and Practices* (London: Oxford University Press, 1965).

16. C. Perrow, "A Framework for the Comparative Analysis of Organizations," *American Sociological Review* 32 (1967): 194–208; D. Rosseau, "Assessment of Technology in Organizations: Closed versus Open Systems Approaches," *Academy of Management Review* 4 (1979): 531–542.

17. Perrow, "A Framework for the Comparative Analysis of Organizations," 194–208.

18. J. D. Thompson, *Organizations in Action* (New York: McGraw-Hill, 1967).

19. S. Faraj and Y. Xiao, "Coordination in Fast-Response Organizations," *Management Science* 52 (2006): 1155–1169.

20. J. R. Hollenbeck, H. Moon, A. P. J. Ellis, B. J. West, D. R. Ilgen, L. Sheppard, et al., "Structural Contingency Theory and Individual Differences: Examination of External and Internal Person–Team Fit," *Journal of Applied Psychology* 87 (2002): 599–606.

21. J. Courtright, G. Fairhurst, and L. Rogers, "Interaction Patterns in Organic and Mechanistic Systems," *Academy of Management Journal* 32 (1989): 773–802.

22. T. C. Head, "Structural Changes in Turbulent Environments: A Study of Small and Mid-Size Chinese Organizations," *Journal of Leadership and Organizational Studies* 12 (2005): 82–93.

23. J. P. Davis, K. M. Eisenhardt, and C. B. Bingham, "Optimal Structure, Market Dynamism, and the Strategy of Simple Rules," *Administrative Science Quarterly* 54 (1009): 413–452.

24. K. M. Eisenhardt and D. Sull, "Strategy as Simple Rules," *Harvard Business Review* 79 (2001): 107–116.

25. G. Dess and D. Beard, "Dimensions of Organizational Task Environments," *Administrative Science Quarterly* 29 (1984): 52–73.

26. H. Downey, D. Hellriegel, and J. Slocum, Jr., "Environmental Uncertainty: The Construct and Its Application," *Administrative Science Quarterly* 20 (1975): 613–629.

27. G. Vroom, "Organizational Design and the Intensity of Rivalry," *Management Science* 52 (2006): 1689–1702.

28. R. Daft, *Organization Theory and Design,* 7th ed. (Mason, OH: South-Western, 2000).

29. M. Porter, *Competitive Strategy* (New York: The Free Press, 1980).

30. D. Miller, "Configurations of Strategy and Structure," *Strategic Management Journal* 7 (1986): 233–249.

31. R. S. Kaplan and D. P. Norton, "How to Implement a New Strategy without Disrupting Your Organization," *Harvard Business Review* (March 2006): 100–109.

32. D. B. Turban and T. L. Keon, "Organizational Attractiveness: An Interactionist Perspective," *Journal of Applied Psychology* 78 (1993): 184–193.

33. N. Dimarco and S. Norton, "Life Style, Organization Structure, Congruity and Job Satisfaction," *Personnel Psychology* 27 (1974): 581–591.

34. C. Allinson and J. Hayes, "Transferring the Western Model of Project Organisation to a Bureaucratic Culture: The Case of Nepal," *International Journal of Project Management* 14 (1996): 53–57.

35. M. Elovainio and M. Kivimäki, "Personal Need for Structure and Occupational Strain: An Investigation of Structural Models and Interaction with Job Complexity," *Personality and Individual Differences* 26 (1998): 209–222.

36. D. B. Turban and T. L. Keon, "Organizational Attractiveness: An Interactionist Perspective," *Journal of Applied Psychology* 78 (1993): 184–193.

37. B. Shamir and J. M. Howell, "Organizational and Contextual Influences on the Emergence and Effectiveness of Charismatic Leadership," *Leadership Quarterly* 10 (1999): 257–284.

38. E. E. Ghiselli and J. P. Siegel, "Leadership and Managerial Success in Tall and Flat Organization Structures," *Personnel Psychology* 25 (1972): 617–614.

39. D. Miller, C. Droge, and J. M. Toulouse, "Strategic Process and Content as Mediators Between Organizational Context and Structure," *Academy of Management Journal* 31 (1988): 544–569.

40. M. Schminke, M. L. Ambrose, and R. Cropanzano, "The Effect of Organizational Structure on Perceptions of Procedural Fairness," *Journal of Applied Psychology* 85 (2000): 294–304.

41. M. L. Ambrose and M. Schminke, "Organizational Structure as a Moderator of the Relationship Between Procedural Justice, Interactional Justice, Perceived Organizational Support, and Supervisory Trust," *Journal of Applied Psychology* 88 (2003): 295–305.

42. W. R. Scott, *Organizations: Rational, Natural, and Open Systems,* 4th ed. (Upper Saddle River, N.J.: Prentice-Hall, 1997).

43. D. Miller and P. Friesen, "A Longitudinal Study of the Corporate Life Cycle," *Management Science* 30 (1984): 1161–1183.

44. M. H. Overholt, "Flexible Organizations: Using Organizational Design as a Competitive Advantage," *Human Resource Planning* 20 (1997): 22–32; P. W. Roberts and R. Greenwood, "Integrating Transaction Cost and Institutional Theories: Toward a Constrained-Efficiency Framework for Understanding Organizational Design Adoption," *Academy of Management Review* 22 (1997): 346–373.

45. C. W. L. Hill and G. R. Jones, *Strategic Management Theory,* 5th ed. (Boston, MA: Houghton Mifflin, 2000).

46. E. Brynjolfsson and L. Hitt, *Information Technology and Organizational Design: Evidence from Micro Data,* MIT Sloan School Working Paper, 1998, http://www2.dse.unibo.it/santarel/BrynjolfssonHitt1998.pdf.

47. Daft, *Organization Theory and Design.*

48. C. M. Savage, *5th Generation Management, Revised Edition: Co-creating through Virtual Enterprising, Dynamic Teaming, and Knowledge Networking* (Boston, MA: Butterworth-Heinemann, 1996).

49. S. M. Davis, *Future Perfect* (Perseus Publishing, 1997).

50. A. Boynton and B. Victor, "Beyond Flexibility: Building and Managing a Dynamically Stable Organization," *California Management Review* 8 (Fall 1991): 53–66.

51. P. J. Brews and C. L. Tucci, "Exploring the Structural Effects of Internetworking," *Strategic Management Journal* 25 (2004): 429–451.

52. J. Fulk, "Global Network Organizations: Emergence and Future

Prospects," *Human Relations* 54 (2001): 91–100.

53. CBC News, April 30, 2010, "Military Plans Post-Afghanistan Review," http://www.cbc.ca/canada/story/2010/04/30/canadian-military-congo-deployment.html. The Canadian Press/Murray Brewster.

54. The use of the theatrical troupe as an analogy for virtual organizations was first used by David Mack, circa 1995.

55. E. C. Kasper-Fuehrer and N. M. Ashkanasy, "Communicating Trustworthiness and Building Trust in Interorganizational Virtual Organizations," *Journal of Management* 27 (2001): 235–254.

56. C. B. Gibson and J. L. Gibbs, "Unpacking the Concept of Virtuality: Geographic Dispersion, Electronic Dependence, Dynamic Structure, and National Diversity on Team Innovation," *Administrative Science Quarterly* 51 (2006): 451–495.

57. R. Teerlink and L. Ozley, *More Than a Motorcycle: The Leadership Journey at Harley-Davidson* (Boston, MA: Harvard Business School Press, 2000).

58. C. Demailly, "Shaping the Organization of the Future," *People & Strategy* 37 (2014): 54–56.

59. E. Bernstein, J. Bunch, Niko Canner, and Michael Lee, "Beyond the Holacracy Hype," *HBR*, July/August 2016.

60. Ibid.

61. W. A. Cohen and N. Cohen, *The Paranoid Organization and 8 Other Ways Your Company Can Be Crazy: Advice from an Organizational Shrink* (New York: American Management Association, 1993).

62. P. E. Tetlock, "Cognitive Biases and Organizational Correctives: Do Both Disease and Cure Depend on the Politics of the Beholder?" *Administrative Science Quarterly* 45 (2000): 293–326.

63. M. F. R. Kets de Vries and D. Miller, "Personality, Culture, and Organization," *Academy of Management* 11(2) (April 1986): 266–279.

17

1. M. A. Verespej, "When Change Becomes the Norm," *Industry Week* (March 16, 1992): 35–38.

2. P. Mornell, "Nothing Endures but Change," *Inc.* 22 (July 2000): 131–132, http://www.inc.com/magazine/20000701/19555.html.

3. D. Fay and H. Luhrmann, "Current Themes in Organizational Change," *European Journal of Work and Organizational Psychology* 13 (2004): 113–119.

4. H. J. Van Buren, III, "The Bindingness of Social and Psychological Contracts: Toward a Theory of Social Responsibility in Downsizing," *Journal of Business Ethics* 25 (2000): 205–219.

5. 5. M. Egan and D. Wiener-Bronner, The New GE Still Faces Many Old Problems, CNN Money, July 15, 2018, accessed from https://money.cnn.com/2018/07/15/investing/stocks-week-ahead-general-electric-earnings/index.html, October 3, 2018.

6. D. Crane, "Don't Discount the Positive Side of Globalization," *Toronto Star*, December 31, 2006, http://www.thestar.com/article/166599.

7. J. Sanford, "Beat China on Cost: Gildan Taps Other Labour Pool—and Trade Pacts," *Canadian Business Online*, November 7, 2005, http://www.canadianbusiness.com/managing/strategy/article.jsp? content=20060109_155539_4340.

8. The Canadian Press, "CGI Wins US Contract," *The Globe and Mail*, May 18, 2010, accessed from http://www.theglobeandmail.com/globe-investor/cgi-wins-us-contract/article1572757/?utm_source=twitterfeed&utm_medium=twitter, October 3, 2018.

9. "Pipes Done Right," *Canadian Business Journal*, March 2009, www.canadianbusinessjournal.ca/business_in_action/march_09/tube_mac_industries.html.

10. D. Nice, "Brad Miller on Expanding in Lean Times," *The Globe and Mail*, April 9, 2009, http://v1.theglobeandmail.com/servlet/story/RTGAM.20090402.onRecord07/BNStory/breakthrough.

11. Ibid.

12. StatsCan, Census, Canadians in the Workforce, 2016, Catalogue number 11-627.

13. Statistics Canada, "2006 Census: Age and Sex," *The Daily*, July 17, 2007, http://www.statcan.gc.ca/daily-quotidien/070717/dq070717a-eng.htm.

14. B. Doskoch, "Canada Can Adapt to Aging Workforce, Experts Say," http://www.ctv.ca/servlet/ArticleNews/story/CTVNews/20070717/labour_age_070717/20070717.

15. Statistics Canada, "Study: Projections of the Diversity of the Canadian Population," *The Daily*, March 9, 2010, http://www.statcan.gc.ca/daily-quotidien/100309/dq100309a-eng.htm.

16. http://www.toronto.ca/toronto_facts/diversity.htm.

17. J. Gandz, "A Business Case for Diversity," Human Resources and Skills Development Canada, Fall 2001, http://www.hrsdc.gc.ca/eng/lp/lo/lswe/we/special_projects/RacismFreeInitiative/BusinessCase-e.shtml#toronto hotels.

18. R. Caballero and R. Yerema, "Canadian Imperial Bank of Commerce/CIBC," April 7, 2010, http://www.eluta.ca/new-canadians-at-canadian-imperial-bank-of-commerce used with permission from the organizer of the Canada's Top 100 Employers for New Canadians competition, Mediacorp Canada Inc., 2010.

19. Detailed GM History, History of GM Canada, http://www.gm.ca/gm/english/corporate/about/ourhistory/detail.

20. The NAFTA's Impact, http://www.international.gc.ca/trade-agreements-accords-commerciaux/agr-acc/nafta-alena/nafta5_section04.aspx?view=d.

21. R. M. Kanter, "Improving the Development, Acceptance, and Use of New Technology: Organizational and Interorganizational Challenges," in *People and Technology in the Workplace* (Washington, DC: National Academy Press, 1991), 15–56.

22. Gap Inc. press release, "Gap Inc. Joins the Ethical Trading Initiative," *CSRwire*, April 28, 2004, http://www.csrwire.com/article.cgi/2683.html.

23. "Gap Inc. 2003 Social Responsibility Report," *Gap Inc.*, September 17, 2004, http://ccbn.mobular.net/ccbn/7/645/696/index.html.

24. L. J. Brooks and D. Selley, *Ethics and Governance: Developing and Maintaining an Ethical Corporate Culture*, 3rd ed. (Toronto: Canadian Centre for Ethics and Corporate Policy, 2008).

25. www.magna.com/magna/en/employee/foremployees/fyiline/default.aspx.

26. S. A. Mohrman and A. M. Mohrman, Jr., "The Environment as an Agent of Change," in A. M. Mohrman, Jr., et al., eds., *Large-Scale Organizational Change* (San Francisco, CA: Jossey-Bass, 1989), 35–47.

27. T. D'Aunno, M. Succi, and J. A. Alexander, "The Role of Institutional and Market Forces in Divergent Organizational Change," *Administrative Science Quarterly* 45 (2000): 679–703.

28. Agriculture and Agri-Food Canada, "Major Flax Straw Processing Plant Expansion Supported by Federal and Provincial Governments," Canada News Centre, May 21, 2010, http://news.gc.ca/web/article-eng.do?m=/indexandnid=534439.

29. Q. N. Huy, "Emotional Balancing of Organizational Continuity and Radical Change: The Contribution of Middle Managers," *Administrative Science Quarterly* 47 (March 1, 2002): 31–69.

30. D. Nadler, "Organizational Frame-bending: Types of Change in the Complex Organization," in R. Kilmann and T. Covin, eds., *Corporate Transformation* (San Francisco, CA: Jossey-Bass, 1988), 66–83.

31. J. Pachner, "Under Attack from Endy and Casper, Sleep Country Canada Fights Back," *ROB Magazine,* August 28, 2018, accessed from https://www.theglobeandmail.com/business/rob-magazine/article-disrupting-the-disruptor-can-sleep-country-canada-survive-the, October 3, 2108.

32. L. Ackerman, "Development, Transition, or Transformation: The Question of Change in Organizations," *OD Practitioner* (December 1986): 1–8.

33. T. D. Jick, *Managing Change* (Homewood, IL: Irwin, 1993), 3.

34. G. Graham, "Music Industry Supply Chain: A Major Label Perspective, Executive Briefing 2006–06 for Supply Chain Management Research Group, Manchester Business School," http://www.mbs.ac.uk/research/supplychain/documents/MusicIndustry.pdf.

35. A. Bruno, "Digital Entertainment: The Future of Music: Industry Transformation Is Just Getting Started," December 3, 2005, http://www.allbusiness.com/retail-trade/miscellaneous-retail-retail-stores-not/4554798-1.html.

36. http://www.sap.com/about/vision/pdf/FTI1878_evolve_bus_netwrk_wp_v1.pdf.

37. D. Miller and M. J. Chen, "Sources and Consequences of Competitive Inertia. A Study of the U.S. Airline Industry," *Administrative Science Quarterly* 39 (1994): 1–23.

38. S. L. Brown and K. M. Eisenhardt, "The Art of Continuous Change: Linking Complexity Theory and Time-paced Evolution in Relentlessly Shifting Organizations," *Administrative Science Quarterly* 42 (1997): 1–34.

39. J. Child and C. Smith, "The Context and Process of Organizational Transformation: Cadbury Ltd. in Its Sector," *Journal of Management Studies* 12 (1987): 12–27.

40. J. Amis, T. Slack, and C. R. Hinings, "The Pace, Sequence, and Linearity of Radical Change," *Academy of Management Journal* 47 (2004): 15–39.

41. T. A. Judge, C. J. Thoresen, V. Pucik, and T. M. Welbourne, "Managerial Coping with Organizational Change: A Dispositional Perspective," *Journal of Applied Psychology* 84 (1999): 107–122.

42. A. Carmeli and Z. Sheaffer, "How Leadership Characteristics Affect Organizational Decline and Downsizing," *Journal of Business Ethics* 86 (2009): 363–378.

43. D. M. Herold, D. B. Fedor, S. Caldwell, and Y. Liu, "The Effects of Transformational and Change Leadership on Employees' Commitment to a Change: A Multi-Level Study," *Journal of Applied Psychology* 93 (2008): 346–357.

44. J. R. Katzenbach, *Real Change Leaders* (New York: Times Business, 1995).

45. J. L. Denis, L. Lamothe, and A. Langley, "The Dynamics of Collective Leadership and Strategic Change in Pluralistic Organizations," *Academy of Management Journal* 44 (2001): 809–837.

46. B. C. Gunia, N. Sivanathan, and A. D. Galinsky, "Vicarious Entrapment: Your Sunk Costs, My Escalation of Commitment," *Journal of Experimental Social Psychology* 45 (2009): 1238–244.

47. M. Beer, *Organization Change and Development: A Systems View* (Santa Monica, CA: Goodyear, 1980), 78.

48. K. Whalen-Berry and C. R. Hinings, "The Relative Effect of Change Drivers in Large-Scale Organizational Change: An Empirical Study," in W. Passmore and R. Goodman, eds., *Research in Organizational Change and Development* 14 (New York: JAI Press, 2003): 99–146.

49. Denis et al., "The Dynamics of Collective Leadership and Strategic Change in Pluralistic Organizations." Jean-Louis Denis, Lise Lamothe and Ann Langley *The Academy of Management Journal* (44) 4 (Aug., 2001): 809–837.

50. G. Pitts, "The Fine Art of Managing Change," *The Globe and Mail,* January 4, 2010, http://www.kpmg.com/Ca/en/IssuesAndInsights/ArticlesPublications/Documents/The_fine_art_of_managing_change.pdf.

51. K. E. Weick and R. E. Quinn, "Organizational Change and Development," *Annual Review of Psychology* 59 (1999): 361–386.

52. T. Kiefer, "Feeling Bad: Antecedents and Consequences of Negative Emotions in Ongoing Change," *Journal of Organizational Behavior* 26 (2005): 875–897.

53. A. E. Rafferty and M. A. Griffin, "Perceptions of Organizational Change: A Stress and Coping Perspective," *Journal of Applied Psychology* 91 (2006): 1154–162.

54. J. A. Klein, "Why Supervisors Resist Employee Involvement," *Harvard Business Review* 62 (1984): 87–95.

55. B. L. Kirkman, R. G. Jones, and D. L. Shapiro, "Why Do Employees Resist Teams? Examining the 'Resistance Barrier' to Work Team Effectiveness," *International Journal of Conflict Management* 11 (2000): 74–92.

56. S. D. Tvedt, P. O. Saksvik, and K. Nytro, "Does Change Process Healthiness Reduce the Negative Effects of Organizational Change on the Psychosocial Work Environment?" *Work & Stress* 23 (2009): 80–98.

57. D. B. Fedor, S. Caldwell, and D. M. Herold, "The Effects of Organizational Changes on Organizational Commitment: A Multilevel Investigation," *Personnel Psychology* 59 (2006): 1–29.

58. J. Brockner, "Making Sense of Procedural Fairness: How High Procedural Fairness Can Reduce or Heighten the Influence of Outcome Favorability," *Academy of Management Review* 27 (2002): 58–76; J. Brockner, M. Konovsky, R. Cooper-Schneider, R. Folger, C. Martin, and R. J. Bies, "Interactive Effects of Procedural Justice and Outcome Negativity on Victims and Survivors of Job Loss," *Academy of Management Journal* 37 (1994): 397–409; D. B. Fedor, S. Caldwell, and D. M. Herold, "The Effects of Organizational Changes on Organizational Commitment: A Multilevel Investigation," *Personnel Psychology* 59 (2006): 1–29.

59. J. B. Rodell and J. A. Colquitt, "Looking Ahead in Times of Uncertainty: The Role of Anticipatory Justice in an Organizational Change Context," *Journal of Applied Psychology* 94 (2009): 989–1002.

60. S. D. Caldwell, D. M. Herold, and D. B. Fedor, "Toward an Understanding of the Relationships among Organizational Change, Individual Differences, and Changes in Person-Environment Fit: A Cross-Level Study," *Journal of Applied Psychology* 89 (2004): 868–882.

61. D. Klein, "Some Notes on the Dynamics of Resistance to Change: The Defender Role," in W. G. Bennis, K. D. Benne, R. Chin, and K. E. Corey, eds., *The Planning of Change,* 3rd ed. (New York: Holt, Rinehart & Winston, 1969), 117–124.

62. T. G. Cummings and E. F. Huse, *Organizational Development and Change* (St. Paul, MN: West, 1989).

63. J. D. Ford, L. W. Ford, and A. D'Amelio, "Resistance to Change: The Rest of the Story," *Academy of Management Review* 33 (2008): 362–377.

64. N. L. Jimmieson, D. J. Terry, and V. J. Callan, "A Longitudinal Study of Employee Adaptation to Organizational Change: The Role of Change-related

Information and Change-related Self-Efficacy," *Journal of Occupational Health Psychology* 9 (2004): 11–27.

65. N. DiFonzo and P. Bordia, "A Tale of Two Corporations: Managing Uncertainty during Organizational Change," *Human Resource Management* 37 (1998): 295–303.

66. J. de Vries, C. Webb, and J. Eveline, "Mentoring for Gender Equality and Organisational Change," *Employee Relations* 28(6) (2006): 573–587.

67. B. van Knippenberg, L. Martin, and T. Tyler, "Process-Orientation versus Outcome-Orientation during Organizational Change: The Role of Organizational Identification," *Journal of Organizational Behavior* 27 (2006): 685–704.

68. J. H. Marler, S. L. Fisher, and W. Ke, "Employee Self-Service Technology Acceptance: A Comparison of Pre-Implementation and Post-Implementation Relationships," *Personnel Psychology* 62 (2009): 327–358.

69. D. Schweiger and A. DeNisi, "Communication with Employees Following a Merger: A Longitudinal Field Experiment," *Academy of Management Journal* 34 (1991): 110–135.

70. M. Fugate, A. J. Kinicki, and G. E. Prussia, "Employee Coping with Organizational Change: An Examination of Alternative Theoretical Perspectives and Models," *Personnel Psychology* 61 (2008): 1–36.

71. D. M. Herold, D. B. Fedor, and S. D. Caldwell, "Beyond Change Management: A Multilevel Investigation of Contextual and Personal Influences on Employees' Commitment to Change," *Journal of Applied Psychology* 92 (2007): 942–951.

72. M. F. R. Kets de Vries and K. Balazs, "The Downside of Downsizing," *Human Relations* 50 (1997): 11–50.

73. K. E. Weick, and R. E. Quinn, "Organizational Change and Development," *Annual Review of Psychology* 59 (1999): 361–386.

74. M. F. R. Kets de Vries and K. Balazs, "The Downside of Downsizing," *Human Relations* 50 (1997): 11–50.

75. J. A. Clair and R. L. Dufresne, "Playing the Grim Reaper: How Employees Experience Carrying Out a Downsizing," *Human Relations* 57 (2004): 1597–1625.

76. P. O. Saksvik, S. D. Tvedt, K. Nytro, G. R. Andersen, T. K. Andersen, M. P. Buvik, et al., "Developing Criteria for Healthy Organizational Change," *Work and Stress* 21 (2007): 243–263.

77. S. A. Furst and D. M. Cable, "Employee Resistance to Organizational Change: Managerial Influence Tactics and Leader–Member Exchange," *Journal of Applied Psychology* 93 (2008): 453–462.

78. J. B. Rodell and J. A. Colquitt, "Looking Ahead in Times of Uncertainty: The Role of Anticipatory Justice in an Organizational Change Context," *Journal of Applied Psychology* 94 (2009): 989–1002.

79. P. Neves and A. Caetano, "Social Exchange Processes in Organizational Change: The Roles of Trust and Control," *Journal of Change Management* 6 (4) (2006): 351–364.

80. European Working Conditions Observatory, "Key Factors in Successful Organisational Change," http://www.eurofound.europa.eu/ewco/2008/12/NO0812039I.htm.

81. S. D. Tvedt, P. O. Saksvik, and K. Nytro, "Does Change Process Healthiness Reduce the Negative Effects of Organizational Change on the Psychosocial Work Environment?" *Work & Stress* 23 (2009): 80–98.

82. K. Lewin, "Frontiers in Group Dynamics," *Human Relations* 1 (1947): 5–41.

83. C. Bareil, A. Savoie, and S. Meunier, "Patterns of Discomfort with Organizational Change," *Journal of Change Management* 7(1) (2007):13–24.

84. W. McWhinney, "Meta-Praxis: A Framework for Making Complex Changes," in A. M. Mohrman, Jr., et al., eds., *Large-Scale Organizational Change* (San Francisco: Jossey-Bass, 1989), 154–199.

85. B. Bertsch and R. Williams, "How Multinational CEOs Make Change Programs Stick," *Long Range Planning* 27 (1994): 12–24.

86. Correctional Service Canada, Review of Change Management Practices, Internal Audit Branch 378-1-239, April 3, 2008, http://www.csc-scc.gc.ca/text/pa/adt-rvw-chng-mgmnt-378-1-239/rvw-chng-mgmnt-378-1-239-eng.shtml.

87. J. Amis, T. Slack, and C. R. Hinings, "Values and Organizational Change," *Journal of Applied Behavioral Science* 38 (2002): 356–385.

88. J. Kotter, *Leading Change* (Cambridge, MA: Harvard Business Review Press, 2012).

89. W. L. French and C. H. Bell, *Organization Development: Behavioral Science Interventions for Organization Improvement*, 4th ed. (Englewood Cliffs, NJ: Prentice-Hall, 1990); W. W. Burke, *Organization Development: A Normative View* (Reading, MA: Addison-Wesley, 1987).

90. A. O. Manzini, *Organizational Diagnosis* (New York: AMACOM, 1988).

91. M. R. Weisbord, "Organizational Diagnosis: Six Places to Look for Trouble with or without a Theory," *Group and Organization Studies* (December 1976): 430–444.

92. H. Levinson, *Organizational Diagnosis* (Cambridge, MA: Harvard University Press, 1972).

93. J. Nicholas, "The Comparative Impact of Organization Development Interventions," *Academy of Management Review* 7 (1982): 531–542.

94. G. Odiorne, *Management by Objectives* (Marshfield, MA: Pitman, 1965).

95. E. Huse, "Putting in a Management Development Program that Works," *California Management Review* 9 (1966): 73–80.

96. J. P. Muczyk and B. C. Reimann, "MBO as a Complement to Effective Leadership," *Academy of Management Executive* (May 1989): 131–138.

97. L. L. Berry and A. Parasuraman, "Prescriptions for a Service Quality Revolution in America," *Organizational Dynamics* 20 (1992): 5–15.

98. T. A. Stewart and A. P. Raman, "Lessons from Toyota's Long Drive," *Harvard Business Review* 85(7–8) (2007): 74–83.

99. F. Balle and M. Balle, "Lean Development," *Business Strategy Review* (Autumn 2005): 17–22.

100. G. Pitts, "Toyota: Too Big, Too Fast," *The Globe and Mail,* February 5, 2010. http://www.theglobeandmail.com/report-on-business/toyota-too-big-too-fast/article1458221.

101. J. Daley and M. Moxley, "How Hyundai Became the Auto Industry's Pacesetter," *The Globe and Mail,* April 29, 2010, http://www.theglobeandmail.com/report-on-business/rob-magazine/how-hyundai-became-the-auto-industrys-pacesetter/article1548295.

102. W. G. Dyer, *Team Building: Issues and Alternatives,* 2nd ed. (Reading, MA: Addison-Wesley, 1987).

103. E. Stephan, G. Mills, R. W. Pace, and L. Ralphs, "HRD in the Fortune 500: A Survey," *Training and Development Journal* (January 1988): 26–32.

104. A. Edmondson, "Psychological Safety and Learning Behavior in Work Teams," *Administrative Science Quarterly* 44 (1999): 350–383.

105. M. Whitmire and P. R. Nienstedt, "Lead Leaders into the '90s," *Personnel Journal* (May 1991): 80–85.

106. http://www.teambuildinginc.com/services4_teamconcepts.htm; http://www.teambuildinginc.com/services5.htm.

107. E. Salas, T. L. Dickinson, S. I. Tannenbaum, and S. A. Converse, *A Meta-Analysis of Team Performance and Training, Naval Training System Center Technical Reports* (Orlando, FL: U.S. Government, 1991).

108. E. Schein, *Its Role in Organization Development, Vol. 1 of Process Consultation* (Reading, MA: Addison-Wesley, 1988).

109. H. Hornstein, "Organizational Development and Change Management: Don't Throw the Baby Out with the Bath Water," *Journal of Applied Behavioral Science* 37 (2001): 223–226.

110. R. W. Revans, *Action Learning* (London: Blonde & Briggs, 1980).

111. I. L. Goldstein, *Training in Organizations,* 3rd ed. (Pacific Grove, CA: Brooks/Cole, 1993).

112. J. A. Conger and R. M. Fulmer, "Developing Your Leadership Pipeline," *Harvard Business Review* 81 (2003): 76–84.

113. D. A. Ready and J. A. Conger, "Why Leadership Development Efforts Fail," *MIT Sloan Management Review* 44 (2003): 83–89.

114. http://coachfederation.org.

115. M. Jay, "Understanding How to Leverage Executive Coaching," *Organization Development Journal* 21 (2003): 6–13; D. Goleman, R. Boyaysis and A. McKee, *Primal Leadership: Learning to Lead with Emotional Intelligence* (Cambridge, MA: Harvard Business School Press, 2004).

116. K. M. Wasylyshyn, "Executive Coaching: An Outcome Study," *Consulting Psychology Journal* 55 (2003): 94–106.

117. J. W. Smither, M. London, R. Flautt, Y. Vargas, and I. Kucine, "Can Working with an Executive Coach Improve Multisource Feedback Ratings over Time? A Quasi-Experimental Field Study," *Personnel Psychology* 56 (2003): 23–44.

118. "You Might Actually Like This Homework," *Edmonton Journal,* July 7, 2007, http://www.working.com/edmonton/story.html?id= 28132444-c8c3-492c-9670-77786f048147&andk=56195.

119. R. Yerema and R. Caballero, "KPMG," http://www.canadastop100.com/national, used with permission from the organizer of the Canada's Top 100 Employers competition, Mediacorp Canada Inc., 2010.

120. R. Yerema and R. Caballero, "Digital Extremes," http://www.canadastop100.com/national, used with permission from the organizer of the Canada's Top 100 Employers competition, Mediacorp Canada Inc., 2010.

121. V. Graham, Hershey Canada Inc., "Fit for Life" Worksite Wellness Program, presentation to Canadian Labour and Business Centre Workplace Health Works, November 18–19, 2003.

122. A. M. Pettigrew, R. W. Woodman, and K. S. Cameron, "Studying Organizational Change and Development: Challenges for Future Research," *Academy of Management Journal* 44 (2001): 697–713.

123. R. A. Katzell and R. A. Guzzo, "Psychological Approaches to Worker Productivity," *American Psychologist* 38 (1983): 468–472.

124. Goldstein, *Training in Organizations.*

18

1. J. H. Greenhaus, *Career Management* (Hinsdale, IL: CBS College Press, 1987).

2. D. T. Hall, *Careers in Organizations* (Pacific Palisades, CA: Goodyear, 1976).

3. Greenhaus, *Career Management;* T. G. Gutteridge and F. L. Otte, "Organizational Career Development: What's Going on Out There?" *Training and Development Journal* 37 (1983): 22–26.

4. M. B. Arthur, P. H. Claman, and R. J. DeFillippi, "Intelligent Enterprise, Intelligent Careers," *Academy of Management Executive* (November 1995): 7–22.

5. M. Lips-Wiersma and D. T. Hall, "Organizational Career Development Is Not Dead: A Case Study on Managing the New Career During Organizational Change," *Journal of Organizational Behavior* 28 (6) (2007): 771–792.

6. D. Jemielniak, "Managers as Lazy, Stupid Careerists?" *Journal of Organizational Change Management* 20 (4) (2007): 491–508.

7. D. E. Super, *The Psychology of Careers* (New York: Harper & Row, 1957); D. E. Super and M. J. Bohn, Jr., *Occupational Psychology* (Belmont, CA: Wadsworth, 1970).

8. J. L. Holland, *The Psychology of Vocational Choice* (Waltham, MA: Blaisdell, 1966); J. L. Holland, *Making Vocational Choices: A Theory of Careers* (Englewood Cliffs, NJ: Prentice-Hall, 1973).

9. F. T. L. Leong and J. T. Austin, "An Evaluation of the Cross-cultural Validity of Holland's Theory: Career Choices by Workers in India," *Journal of Vocational Behavior* 52 (1998): 441–455.

10. C. Morgan, J. D. Isaac, and C. Sansone, "The Role of Interest in Understanding the Career Choices of Female and Male College Students," *Sex Roles* 44 (2001): 295–320.

11. S. H. Osipow, *Theories of Career Development* (Englewood Cliffs, NJ: Prentice-Hall, 1973).

12. J. P. Wanous, T. L. Keon, and J. C. Latack, "Expectancy Theory and Occupational/Organizational Choices: A Review and Test," *Organizational Behavior and Human Performance* 32 (1983): 66–86.

13. P. O. Soelberg, "Unprogrammed Decision Making," *Industrial Management Review* 8 (1967): 19–29.

14. L. W. Porter, E. E. Lawler, III, and J. R. Hackman, *Behavior in Organizations* (New York: McGraw-Hill, 1975).

15. J. P. Wanous, *Organizational Entry: Recruitment, Selection, and Socialization of Newcomers* (Reading, MA: Addison-Wesley, 1980).

16. D. S. Chapman, K. L. Uggerslev, S. A. Carroll, K. A. Piasentin and D. A. Jones, "Applicant Attraction to Organizations and Job Choice: A Meta-analytic Review of the Correlates of Recruiting Outcomes," *Journal of Applied Psychology,* 90 (5) (2005): 928–944.

17. S. L. Premack and J. P. Wanous, "A Meta-Analysis of Realistic Job Preview Experiments," *Journal of Applied Psychology* 70 (1985): 706–719.

18. Ontario Power Generation, Engineering/Applied Science Trainee A Realistic Job Preview, 2009, http://www.mypowercareer.com/NewGrads/Assets / Engineering_Applied_Science_RJP.pdf.

19. P. W. Hom, R. W. Griffeth, L. E. Palich, and J. S. Bracker, "An Exploratory Investigation into Theoretical Mechanisms Underlying Realistic Job Previews," *Personnel Psychology* 41 (1998): 421–451.

20. G. R. Jones, "Socialization Tactics, Self-Efficacy, and Newcomers' Adjustment to Organizations," *Academy of Management Journal* 29 (1986): 262–279.

21. J. G. Pesek, C. Farinacci, and C. Anderson, "Reverse Resume Viewing: An Overlooked Aspect of Realistic Job Preview," *Review of Business* 17 (2) (Winter 1995): 37–41.

22. J. A. Breaugh, "Realistic Job Previews: A Critical Appraisal and Future Research Directions," *Academy of Management Review* 8 (1983): 612–619.

23. M. R. Buckley, D. B. Fedor, J. G. Veres, D. S. Wiese, and S. M. Carraher, "Investigating Newcomer Expectations

and Job-related Outcomes," *Journal of Applied Psychology* 83 (1998): 452–461.

24. M. R. Buckley, D. B. Fedor, S. M. Carraher, D. D. Frink, and D. Marvin, "The Ethical Imperative to Provide Recruits Realistic Job Previews," *Journal of Managerial Issues* 9 (1997): 468–484.

25. P. Buhler, "Managing in the '90s," *Supervision* (July 1995): 24–26.

26. D. T. Hall and J. E. Moss, "The New Protean Career Contract: Helping Organizations and Employees Adapt," *Organizational Dynamics* (Winter 1998): 22–37.

27. S. A. Zahra, R. L. Priem, and A. A. Rasheed, "Understanding the Causes and Effects of Top Management Fraud," *Organizational Dynamics* 36 (2) (2007): 122–139.

28. A. Fisher, "Don't Blow Your New Job," *Fortune*, June 22, 1998: 159–162.

29. Ibid.

30. D. Goleman, *Working with Emotional Intelligence* (New York: Bantam, 1998); A. Fisher, "Success Secret: A High Emotional IQ," *Fortune* (October 26, 1998): 293–298.

31. M. L. Maynard, "Emotional Intelligence and Perceived Employability for Internship Curriculum," *Psychological Reports* 93 (December 2003): 791–792.

32. K. V. Petrides, A. Furnham, and G. N. Martin, "Estimates of Emotional and Psychometric Intelligence," *Journal of Social Psychology* 144 (April 2004): 149–162.

33. D. M. Lucy, "Leadership Landscape: Expanding Your Leadership Styles to Achieve Organizational Effectiveness," 2008, CMI Consulting Services, http://www.ncsi.gov.tw/NcsiWebFileDocuments/f6ce0676278ad0315a33b84f67f3d41e.pdf.

34. C. Chermiss, "The Business Case for Emotional Intelligence," *The Consortium for Research on Emotional Intelligence in Organizations,* 2003, http://www.eiconsortium.org/research/business_case_for_ei.htm; L. M. Spencer, Jr., and S. Spencer, *Competence at Work: Models for Superior Performance* (New York: John Wiley & Sons, 1993); L. M. Spencer, Jr., D. C. McClelland, and S. Kelner, *Competency Assessment Methods: History and State of the Art* (Boston, MA: Hay/McBer, 1997).

35. Chermiss, "The Business Case for Emotional Intelligence."

36. J. O. Crites, "A Comprehensive Model of Career Adjustment in Early Adulthood," *Journal of Vocational Behavior* 9 (1976): 105–118; S. Cytrynbaum and J. O. Crites, "The Utility of Adult Development in Understanding Career Adjustment Process," in M. B. Arthur, D. T. Hall, and B. S. Lawrence, eds., *Handbook of Career Theory* (Cambridge, UK: Cambridge University Press, 1989), 66–88.

37. D. E. Super, "A Life-Span, Life-Space Approach to Career Development," *Journal of Vocational Behavior* 16 (1980): 282–298; L. Baird and K. Kram, "Career Dynamics: Managing the Superior/Subordinate Relationship," *Organizational Dynamics* 11 (1983): 46–64.

38. D. J. Levinson, *The Seasons of a Man's Life* (New York: Knopf, 1978); D. J. Levinson, *The Seasons of a Woman's Life*, 1997.

39. D. J. Levinson, "A Conception of Adult Development," *American Psychologist* 41 (1986): 3–13.

40. D. L. Nelson, "Adjusting to a New Organization: Easing the Transition from Outsider to Insider," in J. C. Quick, R. E. Hess, J. Hermalin, and J. D. Quick, eds., *Career Stress in Changing Times* (New York: Haworth Press, 1990), 61–86.

41. J. P. Kotter, "The Psychological Contract: Managing the Joining Up Process," *California Management Review* 15 (1973): 91–99.

42. D. M. Rousseau, "New Hire Perceptions of Their Own and Their Employers' Obligations: A Study of Psychological Contracts," *Journal of Organizational Behavior* 11 (1990): 389–400; D. L. Nelson, J. C. Quick, and J. R. Joplin, "Psychological Contracting and Newcomer Socialization: An Attachment Theory Foundation," *Journal of Social Behavior and Personality* 6 (1991): 55–72.

43. S. D. Pugh, D. P. Skarlicki, and B. S. Passell, "After the Fall: Layoff Victims' Trust and Cynicism in Reemployment," *Journal of Occupational and Organizational Psychology* 76 (June 2003): 201–212.

44. Levinson, "A Conception of Adult Development," 3–13.

45. J. W. Walker, "Let's Get Realistic about Career Paths," *Human Resource Management* 15 (1976): 2–7.

46. D. G. Collings, H. Scullion, and M. J. Morley, "Changing Patterns of Global Staffing in the Multinational Enterprise: Challenges to the Conventional Expatriate Assignment and Emerging Alternatives," *Journal of World Business* 42 (2) (2007): 198–213.

47. B. Filipczak, "You're on Your Own," *Training* (January 1995): 29–36.

48. CIBC Small Business, "Women Entrepreneurs: Leading the Charge," 2005, http://www.cibc.com/ca/pdf/women-entrepreneurs-en.pdf.

49. E. H. Buttner and D. P. Moore, "Women's Organizational Exodus to Entrepreneurship: Self-reported Motivations and Correlates," *Journal of Small Business Management* 35 (1997): 34–46; Center for Women's Business Research press release, "Privately Held, 50% or More Women-owned Businesses in the United States," 2004, http://www.nfwbo.org/pressreleases/nationalstatetrends/total.htm.

50. K. E. Kram, *Mentoring at Work: Developmental Relationships in Organizational Life* (Glenview, IL: Scott, Foresman, 1985).

51. C. Orpen, "The Effects of Monitoring on Employees' Career Success," *Journal of Social Psychology* 135 (1995): 667–668.

52. J. Arnold and K. Johnson, "Mentoring in Early Career," *Human Resource Management Journal* 7 (1997): 61–70.

53. B. P. Madia and C. J. Lutz, "Perceived Similarity, Expectation–Reality Discrepancies, and Mentors' Expressed Intention to Remain in the Big Brothers/Big Sisters Programs," *Journal of Applied Social Psychology* 34 (March 2004): 598–622.

54. RBC Diversity Dialogues, http://www.rbc.com/responsibility/workplace/diversity.html.

55. B. R. Ragins, "Diversified Mentoring Relationships in Organizations: A Power Perspective," *Academy of Management Review* 22 (1997): 482–521.

56. R. Friedman, M. Kan, and D. B. Cornfield, "Social Support and Career Optimism: Examining the Effectiveness of Network Groups Among Black Managers," *Human Relations* 51 (1998): 1155–1177.

57. "Diversity & Inclusion @ IBM Frequently Asked Questions," January 2007, http://www-03.ibm.com/employment/ca/en/newhire/diversity_faq.pdf.

58. S. E. Seibert, M. L. Kraimer, and R. C. Liden, "A Social Capital Theory of Career Success," *Academy of Management Journal* 44 (2001): 219–237.

59. PricewaterhouseCoopers Czech Republic, "Graduate Recruitment—FAQs," http://www.pwcglobal.com/cz/eng/car-inexp/main/faq.html.

60. M. A. Covaleski, M. W. Dirsmuth, J. B. Heian, and S. Samuel, "The Calculated and the Avowed: Techniques of Discipline and Struggles over Identity in Big Six Public Accounting Firms," *Administrative Science Quarterly* 43 (1998): 293–327.

61. B. R. Ragins and J. L. Cotton, "Easier Said than Done: Gender Differences in Perceived Barriers to Gaining a Mentor," *Academy of Management Journal* 34 (1991): 939–951; S. D. Phillips and A. R. Imhoff, "Women and Career Development: A Decade of Research," *Annual Review of Psychology* 48 (1997): 31–43.

62. W. Whiteley, T. W. Dougherty, and G. F. Dreher, "Relationship of Career Mentoring and Socioeconomic Origin to Managers' and Professionals' Early Career Progress," *Academy of Management Journal* 34 (1991): 331–351; G. F. Dreher and R. A. Ash, "A Comparative Study of Mentoring among Men and Women in Managerial, Professional, and Technical Positions," *Journal of Applied Psychology* 75 (1990): 539–546; T. A. Scandura, "Mentorship and Career Mobility: An Empirical Investigation," *Journal of Organizational Behavior* 13 (1992): 169–174.

63. G. F. Dreher and T. H. Cox, Jr., "Race, Gender and Opportunity: A Study of Compensation Attainment and Establishment of Mentoring Relationships," *Journal of Applied Psychology* 81 (1996): 297–309.

64. D. D. Horgan and R. J. Simeon, "Mentoring and Participation: An Application of the Vroom-Yetton Model," *Journal of Business and Psychology* 5 (1990): 63–84.

65. B. R. Ragins, J. L. Cotton, and J. S. Miller, "Marginal Mentoring: The Effects of Type of Mentor, Quality of Relationship, and Program Design on Work and Career Attitudes," *Academy of Management Journal* 43 (2000): 1177–194.

66. R. T. Brennan, R. C. Barnett, and K. C. Gareis, "When She Earns More than He Does: A Longitudinal Study of Dual-Earner Couples," *Journal of Marriage and Family* 63 (2001): 168–182.

67. F. S. Hall and D. T. Hall, *The Two-Career Couple* (Reading, MA: Addison-Wesley, 1979).

68. J. S. Boles, M. W. Johnston, and J. F. Hair, Jr., "Role Stress, Work–Family Conflict and Emotional Exhaustion: Inter-Relationships and Effects on Some Work-related Consequences," *Journal of Personal Selling and Sales Management* 17 (1998): 17–28.

69. B. Morris, "Is Your Family Wrecking Your Career? (And Vice Versa)," *Fortune* (March 17, 1997): 70–80.

70. D. L. Nelson, J. C. Quick, M. A. Hitt, and D. Moesel, "Politics, Lack of Career Progress, and Work/Home Conflict: Stress and Strain for Working Women," *Sex Roles* 23 (1990): 169–185.

71. L. E. Duxbury and C. A. Higgins, "Gender Differences in Work–Family Conflict," *Journal of Applied Psychology* 76 (1991): 60–74.

72. R. G. Netemeyer, J. S. Boles, and R. McMurrian, "Development and Validation of Work–Family Conflict and Family–Work Conflict Scales," *Journal of Applied Psychology* 81 (1996): 400–410.

73. N. Yang, C. C. Chen, J. Choi, and Y. Zou, "Sources of Work–Family Conflict: A Sino–U.S. Comparison of the Effects of Work and Family Demands," *Academy of Management Journal* 43 (2000): 113–123.

74. A. Iris Aaltion and H. Jiehua Huang, "Women Managers' Careers in Information Technology in China: High Flyers with Emotional Costs?" *Journal of Organizational Change Management* (2) (2007): 227–244.

75. D. L. Nelson and M. A. Hitt, "Employed Women and Stress: Implications for Enhancing Women's Mental Health in the Workplace," in J. C. Quick, L. R. Murphy, and J. J. Hurrell, eds., *Stress and Well-being at Work: Assessments and Interventions for Occupational Mental Health* (Washington, DC: American Psychological Association, 1992), 164–177.

76. P. Woolley, "Is Workplace Daycare a Workable Solution?" 2007, http://www.straight.com/print/124530.

77. Mitchell Gold Co., "Day Care," http://www.mitchellgold.com/daycare.asp.

78. C. Williams, "The Sandwich Generation," Statistics Canada Catalogue No. 11-008, *Canadian Social Trends* (Summer 2005).

79. E. M. Brody, M. H. Kleban, P. T. Johnsen, C. Hoffman, and C. B. Schoonover, "Work Status and Parental Care: A Comparison of Four Groups of Women," *Gerontological Society of America* 27 (1987): 201–208; J. W. Anastas, J. L. Gibson, and P. J. Larson, "Working Families and Eldercare: A National Perspective in an Aging America," *Social Work* 35 (1990): 405–411.

80. Cincinnati Area Senior Services, "Corporate Elder Care Program," http://www .senserv.org/elder.htm.

81. E. E. Kossek, J. A. Colquitt, and R. A. Noe, "Caregiving, Well-being, and Performance: The Effects of Place and Provider as a Function of Dependent Type and Work–Family Climates," *Academy of Management Journal* 44 (2001): 29–44.

82. Harvard University Office of Human Resources, "Work/Life Support Services—Elder Care Resources," http://atwork.harvard.edu/worklife/eldercare/.

83. The Catholic Children's Society of Greater Toronto, "Canada's Top Family-friendly Employers," http://www.eluta.ca/top-employer-ccas.

84. M. Richards, "'Daddy Track' Is Road Taken More Often," *The Morning Call* (July 28, 2004), http://www.mcall.com/business/local/all-daddyjul28,0, 1869593.story?coll=all-businesslocal-hed.

85. L. J. Barham, "Variables Affecting Managers' Willingness to Grant Alternative Work Arrangements," *Journal of Social Psychology* 138 (1998): 291–302.

86. M. B. Arthur and K. E. Kram, "Reciprocity at Work: The Separate Yet Inseparable Possibilities for Individual and Organizational Development," in M. B. Arthur, D. T. Hall, and B. S. Lawrence, eds., *Handbook of Career Theory* (Cambridge, UK: Cambridge University Press, 1989).

87. K. E. Kram, "Phases of the Mentoring Relationship," *Academy of Management Review* 26 (1983): 608–625.

88. B. Rosen and T. Jerdee, *Older Employees: New Roles for Valued Resources* (Homewood, IL: Irwin, 1985).

89. J. W. Gilsdorf, "The New Generation: Older Workers," *Training and Development Journal* (March 1992): 77–79.

90. J. F. Quick, "Time to Move On?" in J. C. Quick, R. E. Hess, J. Hermalin, and J. D. Quick, eds., *Career Stress in Changing Times* (New York: Haworth Press, 1990), 239–250.

91. D. Machan, "Rent-an-Exec," *Forbes* (January 22, 1990): 132–133.

92. E. McGoldrick and C. L. Cooper, "Why Retire Early?" in J. C. Quick, R. E. Hess, J. Hermalin, and J. D. Quick, eds., *Career Stress in Changing Times* (New York: Haworth Press, 1990), 219–238.

93. S. Kim and D. C. Feldman, "Working in Retirement: The Antecedents of Bridge Employment and Its Consequences for Quality of Life in Retirement," *Academy of Management Journal* 43 (2000): 1195–210.

94. E. Daspin, "The Second Midlife Crisis," *The Baltimore Sun* (originally published in *The Wall Street Journal*), May 10, 2004, http://www.baltimoresun.com/business/bal-crisis051004,0,614944.story?coll=bal-business-headlines.

95. Lawrence Livermore Retiree Program, "Tasks Requested by Lab Programs," http://www.llnl.gov/aadp/retiree/tasks.html.

96. E. Schein, *Career Anchors* (San Diego, CA: University Associates, 1985).

97. G. W. Dalton, "Developmental Views of Careers in Organizations," in M. B. Arthur, D. T. Hall, and B. S. Lawrence, eds., *Handbook of Career Theory* (Cambridge, UK: Cambridge University Press, 1989), 89–109.

98. D. C. Feldman, "Careers in Organizations: Recent Trends and Future Directions," *Journal of Management* 15 (1989): 135–156.

99. B. Moses, "Career Killers: Behavior to Change," *The Globe and Mail*, July 15, 2005, http://www.bbmcareerdev.com/booksarticles_articles_detail.php?article=8.

100. C. Crawshaw, "It's Time to Sit Your Boss Down for a Career Chat," *The Globe and Mail*, May 21, 2010: B15.

INDEX

D

E

H

I

J

K

L

M

N

P

Q

R

S

T

U

V

W

Z

CHAPTER REVIEW 1

Organizational Behaviour and Opportunities

KEY CONCEPTS

1-1

Define organizational behaviour. Organizational behaviour (OB) is individual behaviour and group dynamics in organizations. The foundation of organizational behaviour is human behaviour, so the study of OB involves understanding individuals' behaviour in terms of their history and personal value systems and examining the external factors to which a person is subject. Organizational behaviour has grown out of contributions from psychology, sociology, engineering, anthropology, management, medicine, and economics.

1-2

Identify four action steps for responding positively in times of change. Change is an opportunity when a person has a positive attitude, asks questions, listens, and is committed to succeed. People in change situations often become rigid and reactive, rather than open and responsive. Such behaviour may work well in the face of gradual, incremental change. However, rigid and well-learned behaviour is a counterproductive response to significant change.

1-3

Identify the important system components of an organization. Organizations are open systems composed of people, structures, and technologies committed to achieving a task. The organization as a system also has an external task environment composed of different constituents, such as suppliers, customers, and federal regulators. The organization system takes inputs, converts them into throughputs, and delivers outputs to its task environment.

1-4

Describe the formal and informal elements of an organization. Organizations have formal and informal elements. The *formal organization* is the official, legitimate, and most visible part that enables people to think of organizations in logical and rational ways. The *informal organization* is unofficial and less visible. The informal elements of the organization are often points of diagnostic and intervention activities in organization development.

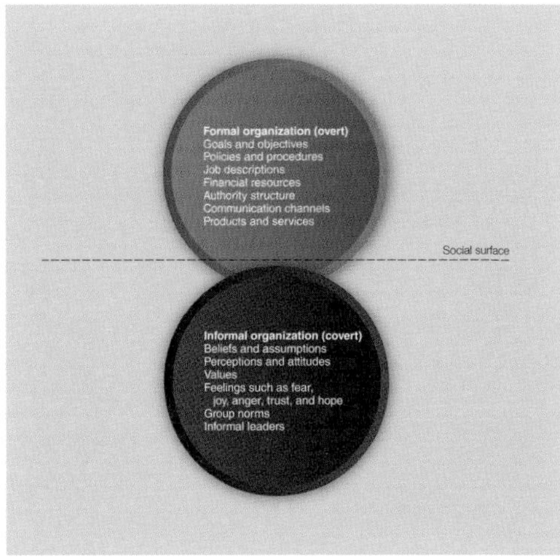

1-5

Understand the diversity of organizations in the economy. Canada's 2016 GDP is worth US$1,529.76 billion or approximately 2.47 percent of the world economy. It is composed of manufacturing organizations, service

KEY TERMS

opportunities Favourable times or chances for progress and advancement.

change The transformation or modification of an organization and/or its stakeholders.

challenge The call to competition, contest, or battle.

organizational behaviour The study of individual behaviour, group dynamics and structural choices in organizations.

psychology The science of human behaviour.

sociology The science of society.

engineering The applied science of energy and matter.

anthropology The science of the learned behaviour of human beings.

management The study of overseeing activities and supervising people in organizations.

medicine The applied science of healing or treatment of diseases to enhance an individual's health and well-being.

economics The study of theories, principles, and models that seek to understand and explain how markets work.

structure The systems of communication, authority, and workflow.

people The human resources of the organization.

task An organization's mission, purpose, or goal for existing.

formal organization The official, legitimate, and most visible part of the system.

CHAPTER REVIEW 1

scientific management An atomistic view of management.

informal organization The unofficial and less visible part of the system.

Hawthorne studies Studies conducted during the 1920s and 1930s that discovered the existence of the informal organization.

objective knowledge Knowledge that results from research and scientific activities.

skill development The mastery of abilities essential to successful functioning in organizations.

organizations, privately owned companies, and non-profit organizations; all contribute to our national well-being. Understanding a variety of organizations will help you develop a greater appreciation for your own organization and for others in the world of private business enterprises and non-profit organizations.

1-6

Evaluate the opportunities that change creates for organizational behaviour. The changes and challenges facing managers are driven by international competition and customer demands. Managers in this environment must be aware of the risks associated with downsizing and marginalization of part-time workers. Organizations also face regular challenges in the areas of globalization, workforce diversity, ethics and character, and technological innovation.

1-7

Demonstrate the value of objective knowledge and skill development in the study of organizational behaviour. Although organizational behaviour is an applied discipline, students are not "trained" in organizational behaviour. Rather, they are "educated" in organizational behaviour and are coproducers in learning. To enrich your study of organizational behaviour, take the learning styles assessment at the end of Chapter 1.

Learning organizational behaviour involves these steps.

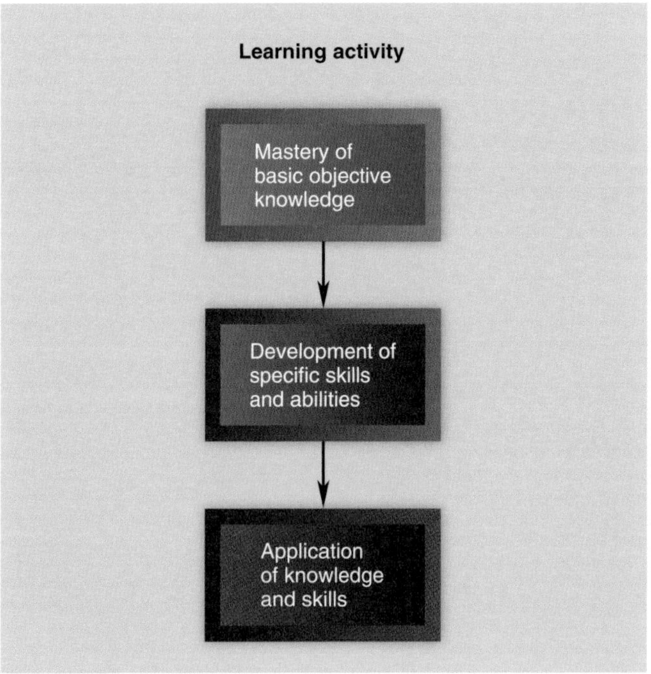

1-8

Explain the process of organizational design thinking. Design thinking is an important new idea and practice. It requires managers to think more like designers when they handle problems. Managers need to use heuristics rather than algorithms when they look at organizational challenges.

CHAPTER REVIEW 2

Organizational Challenges for Today

KEY CONCEPTS

2-1

Describe the factors that affect organizations competing in the global economy. Globalization suggests that the world is free from national boundaries and is borderless. In transnational organizations, the global viewpoint supersedes national issues; organizations operate across long distances and employ a multicultural mix of workers. Social and political issues affect global operations and strategy development.

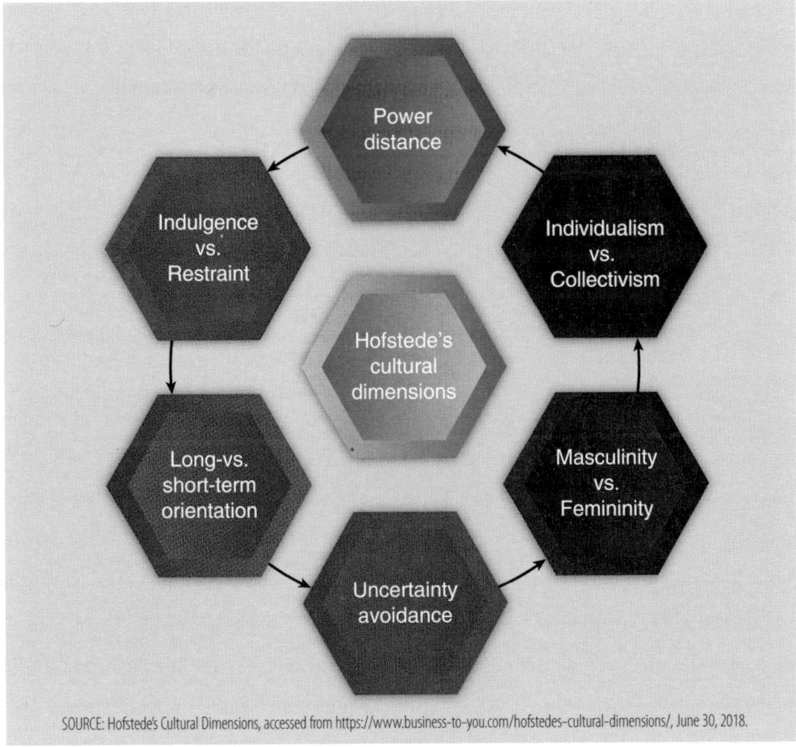

SOURCE: Hofstede's Cultural Dimensions, accessed from https://www.business-to-you.com/hofstedes-cultural-dimensions/, June 30, 2018.

2-2

Explain how cultural differences form the basis of work-related attitudes. Individualistic cultures emphasize and encourage individual achievement, whereas collectivist cultures view group loyalty and unity as paramount. Other factors affecting work-related attitudes are *power distance, uncertainty avoidance, masculinity versus femininity, time orientation, and indulgence.* Developing cross-cultural sensitivity training, cultural task forces, and global human resource management is critical to success.

2-3

Describe the diverse groups that make up today's business environment. *Diversity* encompasses all forms of differences among individuals, including culture, gender, age, ability, religion, personality, social status, and sexual orientation. Benefits from diversity include human talent,

KEY TERMS

transnational organization An organization in which the global viewpoint supersedes national issues.

guanxi The Chinese practice of building networks for social exchange.

expatriate manager A manager who works in a country other than their home country.

individualism A cultural orientation in which people belong to loose social frameworks, and their primary concern is for themselves and their families.

collectivism A cultural orientation in which individuals belong to tightly knit social frameworks, and they depend strongly on large extended families or clans.

power distance The degree to which a culture accepts unequal distribution of power.

uncertainty avoidance The degree to which a culture tolerates ambiguity and uncertainty.

masculinity The cultural orientation in which assertiveness and materialism are valued.

femininity The cultural orientation in which relationships and concern for others are valued.

time orientation Whether a culture's values are oriented toward the future (long-term orientation) or toward the past and present (short-term orientation).

indulgence Indulgent cultures value leisure time, freedom, and personal control.

diversity All forms of individual differences, including culture, gender, age, ability, religion, personality, social status, and sexual orientation.

glass ceiling A transparent barrier that keeps women from rising above a certain level in organizations.

CHAPTER REVIEW 2

glass cliff Senior women finding themselves disproportionately represented in untenable leadership positions.

consequential theory An ethical theory that emphasizes the consequences or results of behaviour.

rule-based theory An ethical theory that emphasizes the character of the act itself rather than its effects.

character theory An ethical theory that emphasizes the character, personal virtues, and integrity of the individual.

distributive justice The fairness of the outcomes that individuals receive in an organization.

procedural justice The fairness of the process by which outcomes are allocated in an organization.

whistle blower An employee who informs authorities of the wrongdoings of their company or coworkers.

social responsibility The obligation of an organization to behave in ethical ways.

technology The intellectual and mechanical processes used by an organization to transform inputs into products or services that meet organizational goals.

expert system A computer-based application that uses a representation of human expertise in a specialized field of knowledge to solve problems.

robotics The use of robots in organizations.

marketing, creativity and innovation, problem solving, and flexibility. Potential problems include resistance to change, lack of cohesiveness, communication, conflicts, and decision making.

2-4

Discuss the role of ethics, character, and personal integrity in the organization. Ethical theories help us understand, evaluate, and classify moral arguments; make decisions; and then defend conclusions about what is right and wrong. Ethical theories can be classified as consequential, rule-based, or character.

2-5

Explain five issues that pose ethical dilemmas for managers and employees. Organizations experience a variety of ethical and moral dilemmas such as employee rights, sexual harassment, organizational justice, whistle blowing, and social responsibility. Managers can use ethical theories to guide them through moral choices and ethical decisions.

2-6

Describe the effects of technological advances on today's workforce. Technological advances have prompted alternative work arrangements, improved working conditions, increased skilled jobs, and brought disadvantaged individuals into the workforce. They have also generated stress, workaholism, and fear of being replaced by technology or being displaced into jobs of lower skill levels.

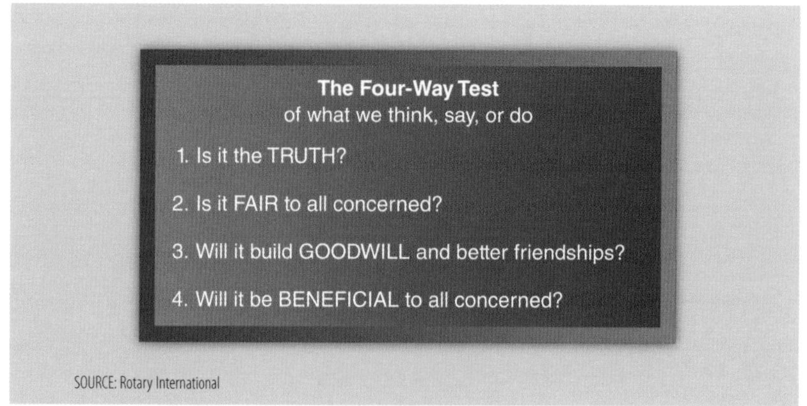

The Four-Way Test
of what we think, say, or do
1. Is it the TRUTH?
2. Is it FAIR to all concerned?
3. Will it build GOODWILL and better friendships?
4. Will it be BENEFICIAL to all concerned?

SOURCE: Rotary International

telecommuting Electronically transmitting work from a home computer to the office.

reinvention The creative application of new technology.

NOTES

CHAPTER REVIEW 3
Personality and Perception

KEY CONCEPTS

3-1
Describe individual differences and their importance in understanding behaviour. Individual differences are skills, abilities, personalities, perceptions, attitudes, emotions, and ethics. (Skills, abilities, personalities, perceptions are discussed in Chapter 3; attitudes, emotions, and ethics discussed in Chapter 4.) To understand human behaviour, we must know something about the person *and* something about the situation and environmental influences.

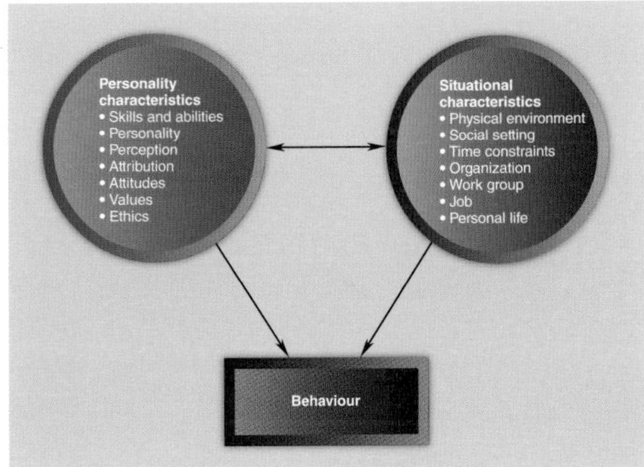

3-2
Explain how personality influences behaviour. Personality is an individual difference that lends consistency to a person's behaviour. The Big Five trait dimensions (or the six HEXACO trait dimensions) as well as core self-evaluation, self-monitoring, and positive/negative affect influence performance and attitudes.

3-3
Discuss the practical assessment of personality theories in organizations. An understanding of personality enhances the understanding of individuals and how they interact with situations and other people. With this knowledge, leaders can choose appropriate ways to interact with others.

3-4
Define *social perception* and explain the factors that affect it. *Social perception* is the process of interpreting information about another person. There are four components of social perception: observation, attribution, integration, and confirmation.

3-5
Identify how biases create barriers to social perception. Each component of social perception (observation, attribution, integration, and

KEY TERMS

individual differences The way in which factors such as skills, abilities, personalities, perceptions, attitudes, values, and ethics differ from one individual to another.

interactional psychology The psychological approach that emphasizes that in order to understand human behaviour, we must know something about the person and about the situation.

abilities Natural capacities that allow an individual to perform a particular task successfully.

skills Talents that have been acquired through deliberate and sustained effort.

***g* factor** A measure of an individual's general mental ability.

personality A relatively stable set of characteristics that influences an individual's behaviour.

traits Distinguishing qualities or features of a person.

core self-evaluation The positiveness of an individual's self-concept; comprised of locus of control, self-esteem, self-efficacy, and neuroticism.

locus of control An individual's generalized belief about internal control (self-control) versus external control (control by the situation or by others).

general self-efficacy An individual's general belief that they are capable of meeting job demands in a wide variety of situations.

self-esteem An individual's general feeling of self-worth.

self-monitoring The extent to which people base their behaviour on cues from other people and situations.

CHAPTER REVIEW 3

positive affect An individual's tendency to accentuate the positive aspects of themselves, other people, and the world in general.

negative affect An individual's tendency to accentuate the negative aspects of themselves, other people, and the world in general.

strong situation A situation that overwhelms the effects of individual personalities by providing strong cues for appropriate behaviour.

projective tests A measure of personality that relies on an individual's interpretation of an ambiguous or abstract image.

behavioural measures A personality assessment that examines behaviour in a controlled environment.

self-report questionnaire A personality assessment tool that analyzes an individual's responses to a series of questions.

Myers-Briggs Type Indicator (MBTI)® instrument A self-report questionnaire personality assessment tool.

Extraversion (E) A preference for interaction with other people.

Introversion (I) A preference for spending time alone.

Sensing (S) Gathering information through the five senses.

Intuition (N) A preference for gathering information through associations and focusing on what "could be" rather than what actually is.

Thinking (T) A preference for making decisions in a logical, objective fashion.

Feeling (F) A preference for making decisions in a personal, value-oriented way.

Judging (J) A preference for closure and completion in making decisions.

Perceiving (P) A preference for exploring many alternatives and maintaining flexibility.

social perception The process of interpreting information about another person.

confirmation) is subject to cognitive biases, which are mistakes in reasoning, evaluating, and remembering, that occur due to heuristics. Some of the most common barriers include selective perception, stereotyping, fundamental attribution error, self-serving bias, projection, first-impression error, the halo effect, recency effect, contrast effect, and self-fulfilling prophecies.

3-6

Describe how individuals manage others' impressions. Though impression management often has negative connotations, individuals engage in impression management in most social interactions. Impression management can be accomplished through self-disclosure, managing appearances, ingratiation, aligning actions, and altercasting. Understanding social perception in organizations may help individuals who compete for jobs, favourable performance evaluations, and salary increases.

discounting principle The assumption that an individual's behaviour is accounted for situational factors, not personality.

attribution theory The process used by individuals to explain the causes of their own behaviour and that of others.

consensus An informational cue indicating the extent to which peers in the same situation behave in a similar fashion.

distinctiveness An informational cue indicating the degree to which an individual behaves the same way in other situations.

consistency An informational cue indicating the frequency of behaviour over time.

perceptual screen The psychological process that evaluates all input.

heuristic Mental shortcuts or information-processing "rules of thumb" to reduce information to manageable levels.

cognitive bias Mistakes in reasoning, evaluating, and remembering as a result of holding on to one's preferences and beliefs.

implicit bias Biases that are subconscious or unrecognized.

selective perception The process of selecting information that supports one's viewpoints while discounting information that threatens those views.

stereotype A generalization about a group of people.

fundamental attribution error The tendency to make attributions to internal causes when focusing on someone else's behaviour.

self-serving bias The tendency to attribute one's own successes to internal causes and one's failures to external causes.

projection Overestimating the number of people who share our own beliefs, values, and behaviours.

first-impression error The tendency to form lasting opinions about an individual based on initial perceptions.

halo effect When one aspect of a person is viewed positively, resulting in all aspects of that person being assumed positive.

recency effect The tendency to weigh recent events more than earlier events.

contrast effect The tendency to diminish or enhance the measure of one target through comparison with another recently observed target.

self-fulfilling prophecy The situation in which our expectations about people affect our interaction with them in such a way that our expectations are fulfilled.

impression management The process by which individuals try to control the impressions others have of them.

CHAPTER REVIEW 4
Emotions, Attitudes, and Ethics

KEY CONCEPTS

4-1
Discuss the definition and importance of emotions. Emotions are mental states including feelings, physiological changes, and the inclination to act and are normal parts of human functioning and decision making. Positive emotions that travel through a work group produce cooperation and task performance. The opposite also occurs when negative emotions destroy morale and performance. Many jobs require emotional labour, expressing particular emotions even if they are not being truly felt. Doing so is easier if one is emotionally intelligent, a set of skills that refer to recognizing and managing both one's own emotions and those of others. Accurate recognition of others' emotions can be difficult if one is not aware of the emotional display rules they are following.

4-2
Explain the ABC model of an attitude. The ABC model says attitudes have three components: the affective (feeling) part, the cognitive (thinking) part, and the behavioural (intention to act) part. The ABC model shows that we must assess all three components to understand a person's attitude.

4-3
Describe how attitudes are formed. Attitudes are learned through direct experience and social learning. Culture also plays a definitive role in attitude development. The relationship between attitude and behaviour depends on five things: attitude specificity, attitude relevance, timing of measurement, personality factors, and social constraints.

4-4
Identify sources and consequences of work attitudes. Attitudes affect work behaviour. Demanding jobs over which employees have little control negatively affect employees' work attitudes. A positive psychological climate can generate positive attitudes and good performance. *Job satisfaction* is a pleasurable or positive emotional state resulting from the appraisal of one's job or job experiences. Job satisfaction correlates with organizational performance, organizational citizenship behaviour, turnover, and attendance.

Individuals who identify strongly with the organization are more likely to perform *organizational citizenship behaviour*—behaviour above and beyond the call of duty. *Workplace deviance behaviour* is a result of negative attitudes and consists of counterproductive behaviour that violates organizational norms and harms others or the organization.

4-5
Describe how characteristics of the source, target, and message affect persuasion. Through persuasion, one individual (the source) tries to change the attitude of another person (the target) in regard to a certain issue (the message). Three major characteristics of the source affect persuasion: expertise, trustworthiness, and attractiveness. Targets with low self-esteem or

KEY TERMS

emotions Mental states that typically include feelings, physiological changes, and the inclination to act.

emotional labour The need to manage emotions in order to perform one's job effectively.

emotional dissonance Conflict between what a person feels and what the person is expected to express.

emotional intelligence The ability to understand and manage of emotions in oneself and others.

emotional display rules Expectations regarding what emotions are appropriate to express in specific situations.

emotional contagion A process through which one person's emotions and related behaviours elicit similar emotions in others.

attitude A set of emotions, beliefs and behaviours expressed when we evaluate a person or an object.

affect The emotional component of an attitude.

cognition The process of understanding through thought, experience, and the senses.

social learning The process of deriving attitudes from family, peer groups, and culture.

cognitive dissonance A state of tension that is produced through conflict between attitudes and behaviour.

job satisfaction A pleasurable or positive emotional state resulting from the appraisal of one's job or job experiences.

organizational citizenship behaviour Behaviour that is above and beyond the call of duty.

CHAPTER REVIEW 4

workplace deviance behaviour Counterproductive behaviour that violates organizational norms and harms others or the organization.

organizational commitment The strength of an individual's identification with an organization.

affective commitment The type of organizational commitment that is based on an individual's desire to remain in an organization.

continuance commitment The type of organizational commitment that is based on the fact that an individual cannot afford to leave.

normative commitment The type of organizational commitment that is based on an individual's perceived obligation to remain with an organization.

ethical behaviour Acting in ways consistent with one's personal values and the commonly held values of the organization and society.

values Enduring beliefs that a specific behaviour or end state of existence is preferable.

cognitive moral development The process of moving through stages of maturity in terms of making ethical decisions.

in a good mood are easier to persuade. Individuals with extreme attitudes or high self-esteem are more resistant. The elaboration likelihood model proposes that persuasion occurs through the central route and the peripheral route differentiated by the amount of elaboration, scrutiny, or motivation in the message.

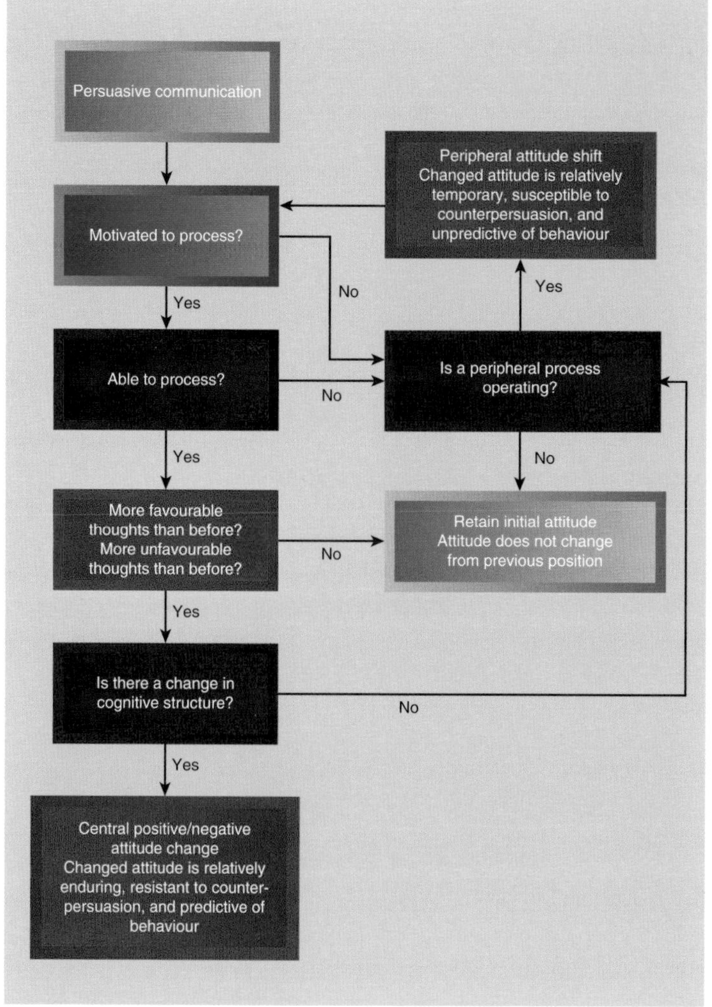

4-6

Describe the consequences of individual and organizational ethical behaviour. *Ethical behaviour* is acting in ways consistent with your personal values and the commonly held values of the organization and society. Firms with better reputations attract more applicants, creating a larger hiring pool, and evidence suggests that respected firms can choose higher-quality applicants. Unethical behaviour by employees can affect individuals, work teams, and even the organization.

4-7

Identify the factors that affect ethical behaviour. Factors that influence an individual's ethical behaviour are values, locus of control, *Machiavellianism* (a willingness to do whatever it takes to get one's own way), and an individual's level of *cognitive moral development.* Organizations can offer guidance by encouraging ethical behaviour through codes of conduct, ethics committees, ethics communication systems, training, norms, modelling, rewards and punishments, and corporate social responsibility programs.

CHAPTER REVIEW 5
Motivation

KEY CONCEPTS

5-1
Define *motivation* and explain the difference between needs theories and process theories of motivation. *Motivation* is the process of arousing and sustaining goal-directed behaviour, and it refers to the forces that influence the direction, intensity, and persistence of a person's efforts. Motivation theories may be broadly classified into needs theories and process theories. Needs theories focus on the variables within an individual and ask "What do people *need* in order to feel motivated?" Process theories focus on external forces and ask "What processes can direct or sustain motivation?"

5.2
Explain how Maslow's need hierarchy is related to Theory X and Theory Y and ERG theory. Maslow's hierarchy of needs sets out five categories of internal needs (physiological, safety, social, esteem, self-actualization), and argues that an unsatisfied need is a motivating need. Maslow's progression hypothesis claims that people progress upward through the levels of needs toward self-actualization.

Theory X and Theory Y explains that managers see employees as either inherently lazy, working only for sustainable income, and motivated by physiological and safety needs (Theory X); or self-directed, internally motivated by love, esteem, and self-actualization needs (Theory Y).

ERG theory groups Maslow's five internal needs into three categories: Existence (physiological, and physical safety needs); Relatedness (interpersonal safety and esteem, and love needs); Growth (self-actualization and self-esteem needs). ERG theory added a regression hypothesis to Maslow's model and explained that individuals who are unable to satisfy the next higher-order needs will intensify their desire to satisfy lower-order needs.

5-3
Discuss the needs for achievement, power, and affiliation. McClelland identified three learned or acquired needs. The *need for achievement* (nAch) encompasses excellence, competition, challenging goals, persistence, and overcoming difficulties. The *need for power* (nPow) includes the desire to influence others, the urge to change people or events, and the wish to make a difference in life. The *need for affiliation* (nAff) means an urge to establish and maintain warm, close, intimate relationships with others.

5-4
Describe the role of inequity in motivation. Equity theory is a process theory of motivation that focuses on perceived fairness: Inequity occurs when a person compares what they have received for their efforts against what someone else has received and perceives that they have received more, or less, than they believe they deserve. Because inequity is uncomfortable, it motivates behaviour to restore equity.

KEY TERMS

motivation The forces that influence the direction, intensity, and persistence of effort.

needs theories Theories of motivation based on the premise that people are motivated by unfulfilled needs.

needs Physiological or psychological insufficiencies that provoke some type of behavioural response.

process theories Theories of motivation that emphasize the nature of the interaction between the individual and their environment.

Theory X Management assumption that workers are lazy and dislike responsibility.

Theory Y Management assumption that workers like work and will seek responsibility.

manifest needs Learned or acquired needs that are subconscious but easily perceived by others.

need for achievement (nAch) Individuals motivated by a manifest need for competition, challenging goals, persistence, and overcoming difficulties.

need for power (nPow) Individuals motivated by a manifest need to make an impact, influence others, change people or events, and make a difference.

need for affiliation (nAff) Individuals motivated by a manifest need to establish and maintain warm, close relationships with other people.

inequity When a person perceives that they are receiving less than they are giving, or is giving less than they are receiving in comparison with another.

CHAPTER REVIEW 5

equity sensitive An individual who prefers an equity ratio equal to that of their comparison other.

benevolent An individual who is comfortable with an equity ratio less than that of their comparison other.

entitled An individual who is comfortable with an equity ratio greater than that of their comparison other.

procedural justice The fairness of the process by which outcomes are allocated in an organization.

interactional justice Fairness in how people are treated.

expectancy The belief that effort leads to performance.

instrumentality The belief that performance is related to outcomes.

valence The value or importance one places on a particular reward.

moral maturity The measure of a person's cognitive moral development.

goal setting The process of establishing desired results that guide and direct behaviour.

5-5

Describe the expectancy theory of motivation. Expectancy theory of motivation focuses on personal perceptions of the performance process. Performers are more motivated (1) if they see a strong link between their efforts and results (expectancy), (2) see that different performance results lead to different outcomes (instrumentality), and (3) value the outcomes or rewards attached to results (valence).

5-6

Explain how goal setting can motivate performance. People with specific challenging goals outperform those with general goals, or no goals at all. Higher goals lead to higher motivation and better performance, as long as the goals are accepted and the performer has the necessary skills. Goal setting directs attention to relevant activities, energizes the performer, and enhances persistence.

5-7

Describe the cultural differences in motivation. Most motivation theories in use today have been developed by and about North Americans. When researchers have examined the universality of these theories, they have found that the studies did not replicate the results found in North America due to cultural differences.

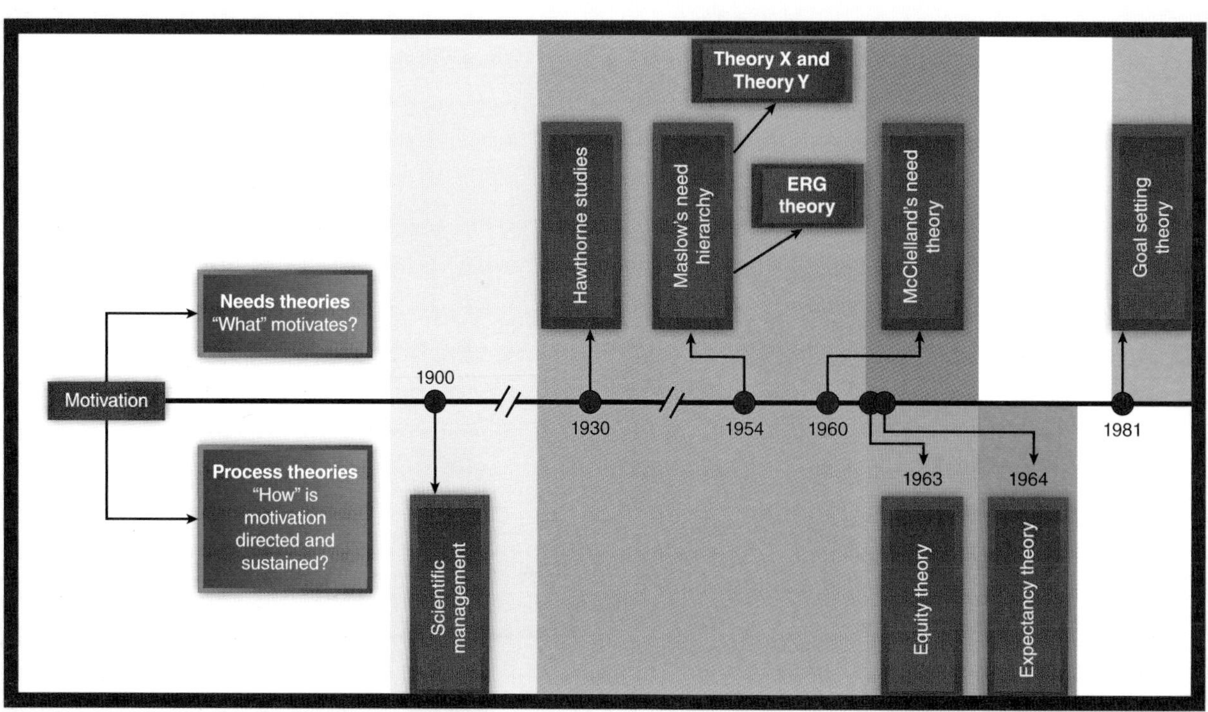

CHAPTER REVIEW 6

Stress and Well-Being at Work

KEY CONCEPTS

6-1

Define *stress, stressor,* and *distress*. *Stress*, or the stress response, is the unconscious preparation to fight or flee experienced when faced with any demand. A *stressor*, or demand, is the person or event triggering the stress response. *Distress* or *strain* refers to adverse psychological, physical, behavioural, and organizational consequences that *may* occur as a result of stressful events.

6-2

Compare four approaches to stress. There are four principal approaches to stress. Cannon developed the homeostatic/medical approach because he believed stress resulted when an external, environmental demand upset the body's balance, or *homeostasis*. Lazarus's cognitive appraisal approach emphasized perception and interpretation in classifying persons or events as stressful. Kahn's person–environment fit approach claimed confusing and conflicting expectations of social roles create stress. Levinson's psychoanalytic approach believed the *ego-ideal* and the *self-image* interact to cause stress.

6-3

Explain the psychophysiology of the stress response. The stress response begins with the release of chemical messengers, primarily adrenaline, into the bloodstream. These messengers activate the sympathetic nervous system and endocrine (hormone) system to trigger mind–body changes to prepare the person for fight or flight. As the body responds, the person shifts from a neutral posture to an offensive posture.

6-4

Identify work and nonwork causes of stress. Major categories of work demands that cause stress are role conflict, role ambiguity, task demands, role demands, interpersonal demands, and physical demands. Nonwork demands may broadly be identified as home demands from an individual's personal life environment and personal demands that are self-imposed.

6-5

Explain the JDCS and ERI models that link stress to negative consequences. The job-demands-control-support (JDCS) model sees stress caused by high demands, low control, and low support. Preventing or alleviating negative stress symptoms (such as anxiety and absenteeism) can be achieved by reducing demands, enhancing control, and offering support. The effort–reward imbalance (ERI) model attributes strain to a combination of high effort and low reward. Consequently, efforts by the organization to reduce the efforts required and improve the rewards offered can right the balance and reduce stress.

6-6

Describe the consequences of stress. Positive stress can create eustress, improving performance. Negative stress creates distress, which can lead to medical, performance, and behavioural problems.

KEY TERMS

stress The unconscious preparation to fight or flee that a person experiences when faced with any demand.

stressor The person or event that triggers the stress response.

distress The adverse psychological, physical, behavioural, and organizational consequences that may arise as a result of stressful events.

strain Distress.

homeostasis A steady state of bodily functioning and equilibrium.

ego-ideal The embodiment of a person's perfect self.

self-image How a person sees themself, both positively and negatively.

workaholism An imbalanced preoccupation with work at the expense of home and personal life satisfaction.

job demand-control-support model (JDCS) This stress model asserts that high demands, low control, and low support all contribute to strain.

effort–reward imbalance model (ERI) This stress model attributes strain to a combination of high effort and low reward.

Type A behaviour pattern A complex of personality and behavioural characteristics, including competitiveness, time urgency, social status insecurity, aggression, hostility, and a quest for achievements.

personality hardiness A personality resistant to distress and characterized by commitment, control, and challenge.

resilience Rather than being knocked down by failure, resilient individuals are able to bounce back.

transformational coping A way of managing stressful events by changing them into less subjectively stressful events.

self-reliance A healthy, secure, interdependent pattern of behaviour related to how people form and maintain supportive attachments with others.

counterdependence An unhealthy, insecure pattern of behaviour that leads to separation in relationships with other people.

overdependence An unhealthy, insecure pattern of behaviour that leads to preoccupied attempts to achieve security through relationships.

preventive stress management An organizational approach that holds that people and organizations should take joint responsibility for promoting health and preventing distress and strain.

primary prevention The stage in preventive stress management designed to reduce, modify, or eliminate the demand or stressor causing stress.

secondary prevention The stage in preventive stress management designed to alter or modify the response to a demand or stressor.

tertiary prevention The stage in preventive stress management designed to heal symptoms of distress and strain.

6-7

Discuss individual factors that influence a person's response to stress and strain. Individual differences, such as negative affectivity and Type A behaviour pattern, enhance vulnerability to strain under stressful conditions. Other individual differences such as personality hardiness, self-esteem, self-efficacy, and self-reliance, reduce vulnerability to strain under stressful conditions.

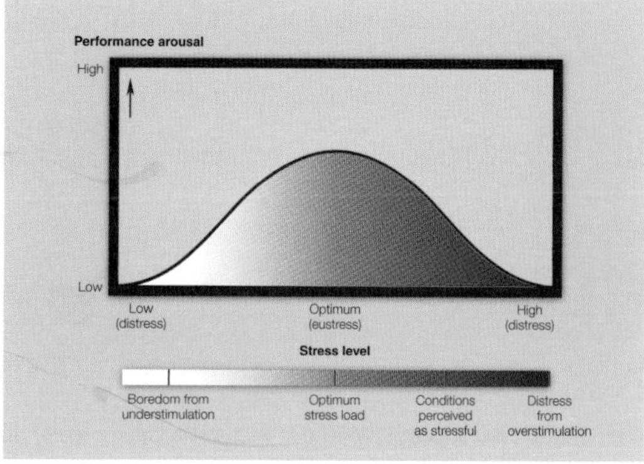

6-8

Identify the stages of preventive stress management. The three stages of prevention are primary, secondary, and tertiary prevention. *Primary prevention* is intended to reduce, modify, or eliminate the demand or stressor causing stress. *Secondary prevention* is intended to alter or modify the response to a demand or stressor. *Tertiary prevention* is intended to heal symptoms of distress and strain.

TABLE 6.2 A FRAMEWORK FOR PREVENTIVE STRESS MANAGEMENT

Focus	Level	Aim
		Prevent the stress:
Organizational stressors	Primary prevention: stressor directed	Reduce work demands Increase control Flexibility Appropriate selection and training Fairness Provide support Management development Clear structure and practices Clear expectations Strong communication Healthy change processes Culture
		Influence the reaction to stressful events:
Stress responses	Secondary prevention: response directed	Encourage challenge appraisal rather than threat appraisal Give employees more control Give employees support
		Help employees deal with stress symptoms:
Distress	Tertiary prevention: symptom directed	Debriefing/defusing sessions EAP Time off Adjust work demands Work with employee to plan changes that will reduce stress

SOURCE: J. D. Quick, R. S. Horn, and J. C. Quick, "Health Consequences of Stress," *Journal of Organizational Behavior Management* 8(2) figure 1 (Fall 1986): 21. Reprinted by permission of the publisher (Taylor & Francis Group, http://www.informaworld.com).

CHAPTER REVIEW 7

Decision Making by Individuals and Groups

KEY CONCEPTS

7-1

Identify the steps in the decision-making process. The decision-making process involves *programmed decisions* and *nonprogrammed decisions.* The first step is recognizing the problem or realizing a decision must be made. Second, the objective of the decision is identified. The third step is gathering information relevant to the problem. The fourth step is listing and evaluating alternative courses of action. Finally, the manager selects the alternative that best meets the decision objective.

7-2

Describe various models of decision making. The *rational model* of decision making contends that the decision maker is completely rational in their approach. *Bounded rationality* theory suggests that constraints force decision makers to be less rational, and assumes that managers satisfice and develop heuristics. The Vroom-Yetton-Jago model is normative and gives managers guidance on the appropriate degree of employee participation in decision making. The Z problem-solving model capitalizes on the strengths of four separate preferences (sensing, intuiting, thinking, and feeling), allowing managers to use preferences and nonpreferences to make decisions. The garbage can model emphasizes the chaotic nature of decision making where problems and solutions are often loosely coupled.

7-3

Discuss the individual influences that affect decision making. Decisions reflect the people who make them. The individual influences that affect decision making are comfort for risk, cognitive style, personality, intuition, and creativity.

7-4

Explain how groups make decisions. Group decisions are utilized for several reasons: *synergy,* to gain commitment to a decision, and to maximize knowledge and experience in problem-solving situations. Seven techniques utilized in group decisions are brainstorming, nominal group technique, devil's advocacy, dialectical inquiry, quality circles, quality teams, and self-managed teams.

7-5

Describe the role culture plays in decision making. Styles of decision making vary greatly among cultures and affect the way people view decisions. The dimensions proposed by Hofstede in Chapter 2 that affect decision making are uncertainty avoidance, power distance, individualist/collectivist, time orientation, masculine/feminine, and indulgence.

7-6

Explain how organizations can improve the quality of decisions through participation. *Participative decision making* can include employees identifying problems, generating alternatives, selecting solutions, planning implementations, and/or evaluating results. Participative management can increase employee creativity, job satisfaction, and productivity, as well as improve an organization's economic performance.

KEY TERMS

programmed decision A simple, routine matter for which a manager has an established decision rule.

nonprogrammed decision A new, complex decision that requires a creative solution.

effective decision A timely decision that meets a desired objective and is acceptable to those individuals affected by it.

rationality A logical, step-by-step approach to decision making, with a thorough analysis of alternatives and their consequences.

blue ocean approach Companies are better off entering new spaces rather than competing with existing companies in the market.

bounded rationality A theory that suggests that there are limits to how rational a decision maker can actually be.

satisfice To select the first alternative that is "good enough" because the costs in time and effort are too great to optimize.

garbage can model Decision making is a process of organizational anarchy.

escalation of commitment The tendency to continue to support a failing course of action.

unconscious or implicit bias Our unconscious, subtle feelings toward others that influence our judgments about them.

cognitive style An individual's preference for gathering information and evaluating alternatives.

risk aversion The tendency to choose options that entail fewer risks and less uncertainty.

intuition A fast, positive force in decision making that is utilized at a level below consciousness and involves learned patterns of information.

CHAPTER REVIEW 7

creativity A process influenced by individual and organizational factors that results in the production of novel and useful ideas, products, or both.

synergy A positive force that occurs in groups when group members stimulate new solutions to problems through the process of mutual influence and encouragement within the group.

social decision schemes Simple rules used to determine final group decisions.

groupthink A deterioration of mental efficiency, reality testing, and moral judgment resulting from pressures within the group.

group polarization The tendency for group discussion to produce shifts toward more extreme attitudes among members.

brainstorming A technique for generating as many ideas as possible on a given subject, while suspending evaluation until all the ideas have been suggested.

nominal group technique (NGT) A structured approach to group decision making that focuses on generating alternatives and choosing one.

devil's advocacy A technique for preventing groupthink in which a group or individual is given the role of critic during decision making.

dialectical inquiry A debate between two opposing sets of recommendations.

quality circle A small group of employees who work voluntarily on company time, typically one hour per week, to address work-related problems such as quality control, cost reduction, production planning and techniques, and even product design.

quality team A team that is part of an organization's structure and is empowered to act on its decisions regarding product and service quality.

participative decision making Decision making in which individuals who are affected by decisions influence the making of those decisions.

TABLE 7.1 20 COGNITIVE BIASES THAT SCREW UP YOUR DECISIONS

Anchoring Bias	Availability Heuristic	Bandwagon Effect	Blind-Spot Bias	Choice-Supportive Bias
People are over-reliant on the first piece of information they hear. In a salary negotiation, whoever makes the first offer establishes a range of reasonable possibilities in each person's mind.	People overestimate the importance of information that is available to them. A person might argue that smoking is not unhealthy because they know someone who lived to 100 years and smoked three packs a day.	The probability of one person adopting a belief increases based on the number of people who hold that belief. This is a powerful form of groupthink and is reason why meetings are often unproductive.	Failing to recognize your own cognitive biases is a bias in itself. People notice cognitive and motivational biases much more in others than in themselves.	When you choose something, you tend to feel positive about it, even if that choice has flaws. Like how you think your dog is awesome – even if it bites people every once in a while.
Clustering Illusion	**Confirmation Bias**	**Conservatism Bias**	**Information Bias**	**Ostrich Effect**
This is the tendency to see patterns in random events. It is key to various gambling fallacies, like the idea that red is more or less likely to turn up on a roulette table after a string of reds.	We tend to listen only to information that confirms our preconceptions – one of the many reasons it's so hard to have an intelligent conversation about climate change.	Where people favour prior evidence over new evidence or information that has emerged. People were slow to accept that the Earth was round because they maintained their earlier understanding that the planet was flat.	The tendency to seek information when it does not affect action. More information is not always better. With less information people can often make more accurate predictions.	The decision to ignore dangerous or negative information by "burying" one's head in the sand, like an ostrich. Research suggests that investors check the value of their holdings significantly less often during bad markets.
Outcome Bias	**Overconfidence**	**Placebo Effect**	**Pro-Innovation Bias**	**Recency**
Judging a decision based on the outcome, rather than how exactly the decision was made in the moment. Just because you won a lot in Vegas doesn't mean gambling your money was a smart decision.	Some of us are too confident about our abilities, and this causes us to take greater risks in our daily lives. Experts are more prone to this bias than laypeople, since they are more convinced they are right.	When simply believing that something will have a certain effect on you causes it to have that effect. In medicine, people given "fake" pills can experience the same physiological effects as people given the real thing.	When a proponent of an innovation tends to overvalue its usefulness and undervalue its limitations. Sound familiar, Silicon Valley?	The tendency to weigh the latest information more heavily than older data. Investors often think the market will always look the way it looks today and make unwise decisions.
Salience	**Selective Perception**	**Stereotyping**	**Survivorship Bias**	**Zero-Risk Bias**
Our tendency to focus on the most easily recognizable features of a person or concept. When you think about dying, you might worry about being mauled by a lion, as opposed to what is more likely, like dying in a car accident.	Allowing our expectations to influence how we perceive the world. An experiment involving a football game between students from two universities showed that one team saw the opposing team commit more infractions.	Expecting a group or person to have certain qualities without having real information about the person. It allows us to quickly identify strangers as friends or enemies, but people tend to overuse and abuse it.	An error that comes from focusing only on surviving examples, causing us to misjudge a situation. For instance, we might think that being an entrepreneur is easy because we haven't heard of all those who have failed.	Sociologists have found that we love certainty – even if it's counterproductive. Eliminating risk entirely means there is no chance of harm being caused.

SOURCE: S. Lee and S. Lebowitz, "20 Cognitive Biases That Screw up Your Decisions," *Business Insider*, August 26 2015, accessed from http://www.businessinsider.com/cognitive-biases-that-affect-decisions-2015-8, September 7, 2018.

CHAPTER REVIEW 8
Communication

KEY CONCEPTS

8-1

Describe the interpersonal communication process. Interpersonal communication is used to evoke shared meaning. The contextual and emotional components of a message are affected by verbal and nonverbal communication and are the key to common understanding. Messages are distorted by perceptual screens but reflective listening enables the listener overcome interpersonal barriers that lead to communication failures.

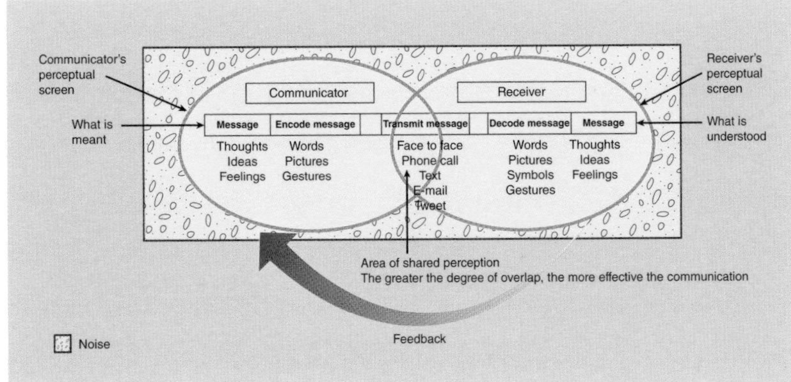

8-2

Explain common communication barriers and gateways through them. Barriers impede successful communication, and can include physical separation, status differences, gender differences, cultural diversity, and language. Awareness and recognition are the first steps in overcoming barriers, but one must also recognize masculine vs. feminine conversation style differences, clarify meaning, understand cultural differences, and avoid technical terms and jargon.

8-3

Distinguish between defensive and nondefensive communication. *Defensive communication* describes posturing intended to avoid communication. It includes aggressive and hostile communication as well as passive, withdrawing communication. *Nondefensive communication* is an assertive and direct form of communication.

8-4

Explain the impact of nonverbal communication. Most meaning in a conversation is conveyed nonverbally. *Nonverbal communication* includes all the elements of communication that do not involve words or do not involve language. The basic categories of nonverbal communication are kinesics, paralanguage, and proxemics.

KEY TERMS

communication The evoking of a shared or common meaning in another person.

interpersonal communication Communication between two or more people in an organization.

communicator The person originating a message.

encode To convert information into a form that may be transmitted.

message The thoughts and feelings that the communicator is attempting to elicit in the receiver.

transmit The way that an encoded message is conveyed to another.

receiver The person receiving a message.

decode To interpret a message that has been received.

feedback Information feedback that completes two-way communication.

language The words, their pronunciation, and the methods of combining them used and understood by a group of people.

data Uninterpreted and unanalyzed facts.

information Data that have been interpreted, analyzed, and have meaning to a user.

richness The ability of a medium or channel to elicit or evoke meaning in the receiver.

reflective listening A skill intended to help the receiver and communicator clearly and fully understand the message sent.

two-way communication A form of communication in which the communicator and receiver interact.

CHAPTER REVIEW 8

one-way communication Communication in which a person sends a message to another person and no feedback, questions, or interaction follows.

barriers to communication Aspects of the communication content and context that can impair effective communication in a workplace.

gateways to communication Pathways through barriers to communication and antidotes to communication problems.

information overload When information provided exceeds our limited capacity for absorbing, sorting, and using it.

culture The pattern of values, beliefs, and behaviours shared by a group.

ethnocentricity The habit of judging other cultures by the standards of our own.

jargon Refers to words or expressions used by a group that have special or unique meanings.

defensive communication Communication that can be aggressive, attacking, and angry, or passive and withdrawing.

nondefensive communication Communication that is assertive, direct, and powerful.

subordinate defensiveness Characterized by meek, submissive, and passive behaviour.

dominant defensiveness Characterized by aggressive and offensive behaviour.

8-5

Identify how social media and communication technologies affect communication. Social media has drastically changed how communities come together; what information they share; and, what information they receive. Technology provides instant exchange of information and renders geographic boundaries and time zones irrelevant. The lack of personal interaction and nonverbal cues alters the social context of exchange and the constant accessibility to work can be detrimental.

8-6

Describe four communication skills of effective managers. Four communication skills that can distinguish a good supervisor from a bad one include being an expressive speaker, an empathic listener, and a persuasive leader, and having an informative managing style.

passive-aggressive behaviour Defensive behaviour that begins as subordinate defensiveness, but ends as dominant defensiveness.

power play Manipulating others through direct use of power.

labelling Using labels out of context to affect how another is perceived.

misleading Deliberately providing inaccurate information in order to manipulate.

hostile jokes Passive-aggressive tactic used to mask aggression.

nonverbal communication All elements of communication that do not involve words.

kinesics The study of gestures, facial expressions, head movement, eye contact, and posture.

paralanguage nonverbal variations in speech, such as pitch, volume, tempo, and tone.

proxemics The study of an individual's use of space in communication.

digital native Someone who has grown up in a digitally connected world.

echo chamber When individuals consume digital content that conforms to their already-held opinions.

trolling posting deliberately provocative material with the aim of eliciting a negative response.

flaming Making excessively rude or provocative comments through digital communication.

information communication technology (ICT) Technologies, such as e-mail, voice mail, teleconferencing, and wireless access, which are used for interpersonal communication.

asynchronous Not coordinated in time.

NOTES

CHAPTER REVIEW 9
Groups and Teams

KEY CONCEPTS

9-1
Define and distinguish between groups and teams. A *group* is two or more people having common interests, objectives, and continuing interaction. A *team* is a type of group that (1) is composed of people with complementary skills, (2) exists to accomplish a goal, (3) includes members who work interdependently, (4) hold each other mutually accountable for their performance.

9-2
Describe how groups form and develop. Diversity is an important consideration in the formation of groups. Ethnic, gender, and culturally diverse groups typically make better decisions, but also have higher levels of conflict. Groups (both formal and informal) go through five stages of development to become mature and productive units. These stages of development are forming, storming, norming, performing, and adjourning, and the progression through these stages is not linear. The punctuated equilibrium model finds that groups alternate between periods of inertia with little visible progress toward goal achievement punctuated by bursts of energy where work is accomplished.

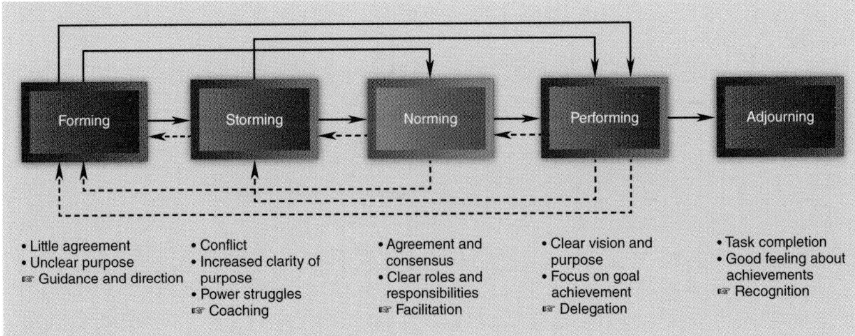

9-3
Identify the factors that influence group behaviour and group effectiveness. Two factors that affect how well groups work together (i.e., behaviour) are *norms of behaviour* and *group cohesion*. Norms of behaviour are the understood standards of behaviour within a group, and *group cohesion* describes how well a group controls its members, and how closely they follow the group norms. Group effectiveness is most affected by *group structure*, which describes the organizational layout of the group (their goals, their composition, and their guidelines); *group process*, which describes how well the group actually performs together; and *task and maintenance behaviours*, which describe the behaviours necessary to ensure the functioning of the group.

9-4
Compare and contrast different types of teams. Teams can have any number of styles depending on their objectives and resources; however, teams can often be grouped by type: (1) production, (2) service, (3) management, (4) project, (5) action and performing, and (6) advisory. Within these types,

KEY TERMS

group Two or more people with common interests, objectives, and continuing interaction.

team A group of people with complementary skills who are committed to common goals, and hold themselves mutually accountable for their performance.

boundary spanning Linking a group's output to the external environment.

norms of behaviour The understood standards of behaviour within a group.

group cohesion How effectively a group ensures adherence to norms of behaviour.

cooperative behaviours Interpersonal teamwork skills.

competitive behaviours Achievement skills.

task function An activity directly related to the effective completion of a team's work.

maintenance function An activity essential to effective, satisfying interpersonal relationships within a team or group.

teamwork Joint action by a team of people in which individual interests are subordinated to team unity.

team permanence How long the team plans to stay together.

skill differentiation How varied the team members' skills are from one another.

authority differentiation How much autonomy and decision-making responsibility is distributed among team members.

cross-functional team People with different expertise and experience working toward a common goal.

CHAPTER REVIEW 9

teams can further be described by their *permanence*, their *skill differentiation*, and their *authority differentiation*. Self-managed teams have the autonomy to plan, organize, and implement work practices as the team decides without managerial oversight, and virtual teams do not meet face to face, and instead rely on digital tools of communication to plan and execute their tasks.

9-5

Explain the advantages and disadvantages of teams. Teams can be very good at performing work that is more complicated and/or more voluminous than one person can handle. When teams work well, they achieve process gains that allow them to make better decisions, develop and deliver better products and services, and create more engaged and committed employees. Disadvantages of teams include process losses, which may be due to the challenges of coordination, social loafing, and group conformity that can lead to groupthink and polarization.

self-managed teams Teams with the autonomy to plan, organize and implement work practices without managerial oversight.

virtual teams Teams that do not meet face to face, and instead rely on digital tools of communication to plan and execute their tasks.

process gain When a group is able to produce more than expected from its members.

social identity A person's sense of who they are based on group membership.

psychological intimacy Emotional and psychological closeness to other team or group members.

integrated involvement Closeness achieved through tasks and activities.

process losses When groups perform worse than expected based on the individual members.

coordination losses Process losses that occur due to challenges associated with coordinating the efforts of a group.

social loafing When one or more group members exert less effort than they would if they were working alone.

loss of individuality A social process in which individual group members lose self-awareness and its accompanying sense of accountability, inhibition, and responsibility for individual behaviour.

NOTES

CHAPTER REVIEW 10
Conflict and Negotiation

KEY CONCEPTS

10-1

Describe the nature of conflicts in organizations. *Conflict* is any situation in which incompatible goals, attitudes, emotions, or behaviours lead to disagreement or opposition between two or more parties. *Functional conflict* is a healthy, constructive disagreement between two or more people that ultimately improves productivity. *Dysfunctional conflict* is an unhealthy, destructive disagreement between two or more people that hinders productivity.

There are four distinct phases for every conflict situation: (1) The *prelude* or latent conflict, where conflict hasn't arisen yet, but the potential for conflict exists; (2) the *trigger* event, where the conflict becomes apparent; (3) the *conflict* stage, where opposing views are expressed and may become entrenched; and finally, (4) (ideally,) *resolution* and dispute settlement.

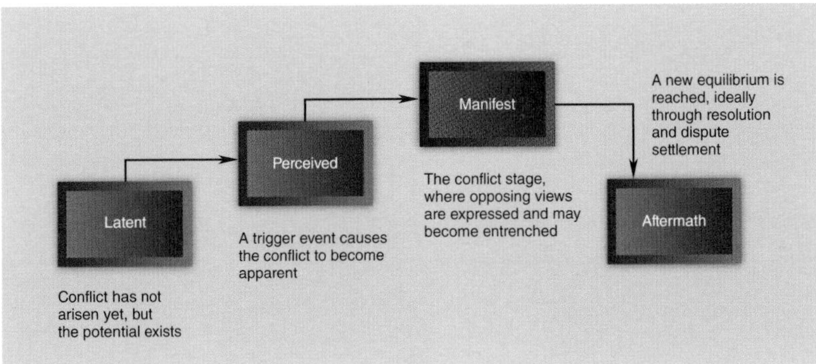

Latent
Conflict has not arisen yet, but the potential exists
Perceived
A trigger event causes the conflict to become apparent
Manifest
The conflict stage, where opposing views are expressed and may become entrenched
Aftermath
A new equilibrium is reached, ideally through resolution and dispute settlement

10-2

Explain the sources of conflict in organizations. There are three sources of conflict in an organization: (1) *Task conflict* arises from differences in perspectives about work details and goals, (2) *Process conflict* describes disagreements about how work will be accomplished, and (3) *Relationship conflict*, which arises due to difficulties in interpersonal interactions. These sources are sometimes referred to as *cognitive conflict*, which groups task and process conflict together, and *affective conflict*, which refers to relationship conflict.

10-3

Discuss different approaches to conflict. The way that a conflict is framed affects how participants think of finding solutions. A *zero-sum* situation describes any time a gain for one side is offset by a corresponding loss for the other side, whereas a *win–win* situation can be resolved with both sides improving their position. The degree of *assertiveness* (the extent to which you want your goals met) and *cooperativeness* (the extent to which you want to see the other party's concerns met) act together to determine the conflict management style that is used in a given situation. (1) *Avoiding* is a deliberate decision to take no action on a conflict or to stay out of a conflict situation. (2) *Accommodating (yielding)* occurs when one party capitulates to the demands

KEY TERMS

conflict When incompatible goals, attitudes, emotions, or behaviours lead to disagreement or opposition between two or more parties.

functional conflict Conflict that improves performance.

dysfunctional conflict An unhealthy, destructive disagreement between two or more people.

task conflict Arises dues to different perspectives about work details and goals.

process conflict Arises due to disagreements about how tasks will be accomplished.

relationship conflict Arises due to challenges in interpersonal interactions.

cognitive conflict Conflict that is task or process oriented.

affective conflict Conflict that is emotional in origin.

zero-sum (win-lose) When gains on one side are offset by losses on the other side.

assertiveness Focused on achieving personal outcomes

win–win When both sides can improve their position.

cooperativeness Focus on satisfying others' concerns.

avoiding A deliberate decision to take no action on a conflict or to stay out of a conflict situation.

accommodating (yielding) When one party gives in to the demands of the other party.

forcing When someone intends to satisfy their own interests at the other party's expense.

compromising When each party gives up something to reach a solution to the conflict.

CHAPTER REVIEW 10

collaborating Arriving at mutually beneficial outcomes.

superordinate goal An organizational goal that is more important to both parties in a conflict than their individual or group goals.

hostility Reacting with antagonism and/or aggression.

retribution When an individual feels justified in taking some course of action, because the other party did it too.

character assassination An attempt to label or discredit an opponent.

coalition building Attempting to shift the balance of power by convincing others of the merits of the position.

negotiation Two parties working toward agreement from different starting positions.

integrative negotiation A cooperative negotiation approach focused on the issues seeking a mutually beneficial solution.

distributive negotiating A competitive negotiation approach where each party seeks to maximize its own outcome.

BATNA **B**est **A**lternative **t**o a **N**egotiated **A**greement.

ZOPA **Z**one **o**f **P**otential **A**greement between parties. Overlap between negotiation limits.

negative bargaining zone When there is no overlap between negotiating parties' minimum limits. No negotiation agreement is possible.

of the other party. (3) *Forcing (competing)* occurs when someone intends to satisfy their own interests and is willing to do so at the other party's expense. (4) In *compromise (or negotiation)* each party gives up something to reach a solution to the conflict. (5) *Collaborating* involves an open and thorough discussion of the conflict to arrive at a solution that is satisfactory to both parties.

10-4

Describe conflict management techniques. Some conflicts can be managed with relatively straightforward techniques to reduce or remove the conflict conditions. These techniques include *appealing to superordinate goals, expanding resources, changing personnel, changing structure, improving communication*, and *negotiating*. Common conflict behaviors that can result in escalating conflict include *avoidance, hostile verbal and nonverbal displays, retribution and retaliation, character assassination*, and *coalition building*.

10-5

Explain the process of negotiation. *Negotiation* involves two parties working toward agreement from different starting positions, and can be cooperative (known as *integrative* negotiation), or competitive (known as *distributive* negotiating). Cultural differences and stereotypes affect the bargaining process. Every negotiator or participant in a negotiation should be aware of, and try to improve their "BATNA," which is the **B**est **A**lternative **t**o a **N**egotiated **A**greement, to avoid negotiating an outcome that is worse than they would have gotten some other way. The **Z**one of **P**otential **A**greement (ZOPA) is the bargaining range.

10-6

Describe third-party conflict interventions. Outside facilitators can help manage hostilities, build trust, open communication, create and implement solutions, and gain commitment to the solutions from participants. Facilitators to conflict (also known as intermediaries) can be *mediators*, or *arbitrators*. When negotiation, mediation, and arbitration fail, the final recourse for conflict is litigation.

mediator Helps conflicting parties negotiate a non-binding agreement.

arbitrator A trusted outsider to the conflict situation who renders a binding decision.

CHAPTER REVIEW 11
Power and Political Behaviour

KEY CONCEPTS

11-1
Describe the concept of power. Power is the ability to influence others. Power relies on dependence and context. Influence is the process of affecting the thoughts, behaviours, and feelings of others. Authority is the right to influence others.

11-2
Identify sources and bases of power in organizations. The source of power in organizations is either positional or personal. Positional sources of power are derived from the hierarchical position within the organization, while personal sources of power reside within the individual. The six bases of power are legitimate, reward, coercive, informational, referent, and expert power.

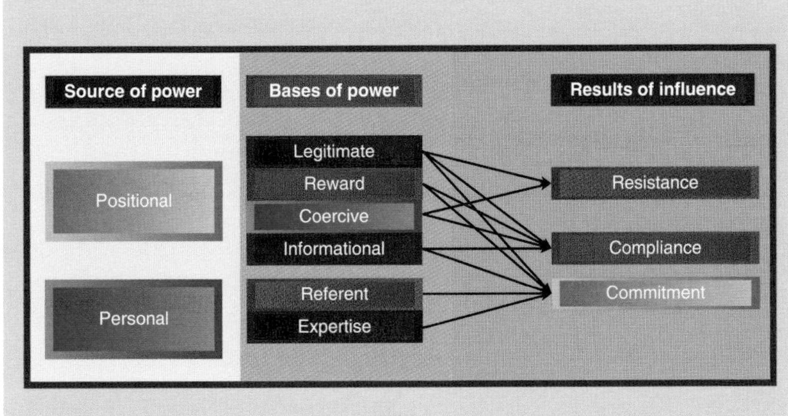

11-3
Describe how people increase their power and abuse their power. Because power is related to dependence and context, changing either of these factors can increase one's power. Factors that increase dependence include substitutability, centrality, and visibility, while factors that influence context include cultivating relationships, coalitions, and authority. Harassment is usually an attempt by one person to exert power over another.

11-4
Explain how to ensure that power is used ethically. Using power appropriately means using it ethically; however, determinations of ethics are often difficult because behaviour depends on perception. To evaluate the ethics of a decision, one can ask three questions: (1) Does the behaviour produce a good outcome for those inside and outside the organization? (2) Does the behaviour respect the rights of all parties? (3) Does the behaviour treat all parties equitably and fairly?

KEY TERMS

power The ability to direct or influence the behaviour of other people or the course of events.

dependence The degree to which someone relies on another to achieve their goals.

context The circumstances that form the setting for an event or an idea.

influence The process of directing behaviour or affecting the outcome of an event.

authority Having the right to influence another person.

legitimate power Power based on position and mutual agreement.

reward power Power based on the ability to control and allocate rewards that a target wants.

coercive power Power based on the ability to punish or cause an unpleasant experience for a target.

informational power The ability to collect and disseminate useful information.

referent power An elusive power that is based on interpersonal attraction.

expert power The power that exists when one has specialized knowledge or skills.

strategic contingencies Activities that other groups depend on in order to complete their tasks.

organizational politics The use of power and influence in organizations.

political behaviour Actions not officially sanctioned by an organization that are taken to influence others in order to meet personal goals.

influence tactics The ways that power is translated into specific actions.

political skill The ability to get things done through favourable interpersonal relationships outside formally prescribed organizational mechanisms.

empowerment Giving employees the authority or power to make their own decisions.

11-5

Describe political behaviour and influence tactics. Political behaviour consists of actions not officially sanctioned that are taken to influence others in order to meet personal goals. Political skill is the ability to get things done through favourable interpersonal relationships outside formally prescribed organizational mechanisms. Political behaviour is typically carried out through influence tactics, including pressure, assertiveness, legitimating, coalition, exchange, upward appeals, ingratiation, rational persuasion, personal appeals, and consultation.

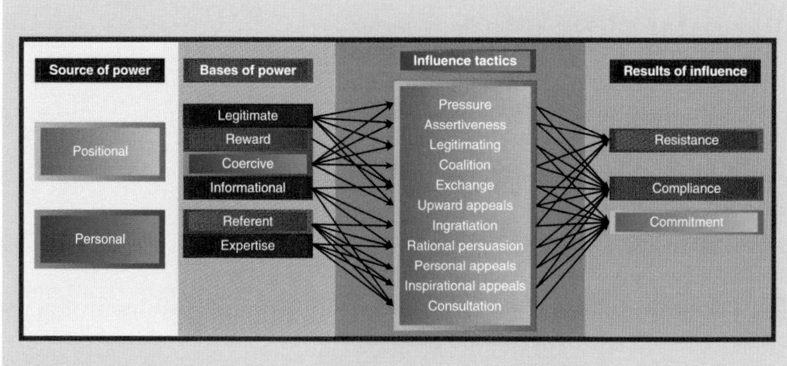

11-6

Identify ways to manage political behaviour in organizations. Politics are unavoidable, but managers can use open communication, clarify expectations regarding employee performance, use participative management techniques, encourage cooperation among work groups, manage scarce resources well, and provide a supportive organizational climate in order to reduce political behaviours. Empowerment can also help reduce unwanted political behaviours, by giving employees authority and autonomy.

NOTES

CHAPTER REVIEW 12
Leadership

KEY CONCEPTS

12-1
Discuss the differences between leadership and management. *Leadership* is the process of motivating, influencing, and enabling others to contribute toward the achievement of organizational goals. *Management* consists of controlling resources to accomplish tasks through (1) planning and budgeting, (2) organizing and staffing, and (3) controlling and problem solving.

12-2
Explain the role of trait theory in describing leaders. The first studies of leadership attempted to identify what physical attributes, personality characteristics, and abilities distinguished leaders from other members of a group. Trait theories have had limited success identifying universal attributes of leaders.

12-3
Describe behavioural research in the development of leadership theories. Behavioural theories address how leaders behave. The Ohio State University measured specific leader behaviours—initiating structure and consideration. The University of Michigan studies suggest two styles of leadership: employee oriented and production oriented. The Leadership Grid® is a graphical representation of how a leader rates in both task and people orientations.

12-4
Describe and compare three contingency theories of leadership. Fiedler's contingency theory proposes that the fit between the leader's need structure and the favourableness of the leader's situation determines the team's effectiveness in work accomplishment. The role of the leader in path–goal theory is to clear the follower's path to the goal. Situational leadership theory suggests that the leader's behaviour should be adjusted to the maturity level of the followers.

12-5
Consider a transactional theory of leadership. With leader–member exchange theory (LMX), leaders are believed to form *in-groups* whose members work within the leader's inner circle and *out-groups* whose members are outside the circle. In-group members receive greater responsibilities, more rewards, and more attention.

12-6
Discuss inspirational leadership styles. Inspirational leadership theories like *transformational leadership, charismatic leadership,* and *servant leadership* can result in positive, productive member behaviour because followers are inspired by the leader to perform.

KEY TERMS

leadership The process of motivating, influencing, and enabling others toward achievement of organizational goals.

management The process of controlling resources to accomplish tasks.

trait A distinguishing quality or characteristic of a person.

initiating structure Task-oriented leader behaviour aimed at defining and organizing work relationships and roles, as well as establishing clear patterns of organization, and communication.

consideration Leader behaviour aimed at nurturing friendly, warm working relationships, as well as encouraging mutual trust and interpersonal respect within the work unit.

Leadership Grid® A graphical representation of a leader's concern for production *and* concern for people.

impoverished (1,1) A leader who exerts just enough effort to get by.

authority-compliance (9,1) A leader who emphasizes efficient production.

middle-of-the-road (5,5) A leader who compromises, meeting neither production nor employee needs fully.

country club (1,9) A leader who creates a happy, comfortable work environment.

team (9,9) A leader who builds a highly productive team of committed people.

least preferred coworker (LPC) The person with whom the leader works the least well.

task structure The degree of clarity, or ambiguity, in the work activities assigned to the group.

position power The authority associated with the leader's formal position in the organization.

leader–member relations The quality of interpersonal relationships among a leader and the group members.

charismatic leadership A leader's use of personal abilities and talents in order to have profound and extraordinary effects on followers.

followership The process of being guided and directed by a leader in the work environment.

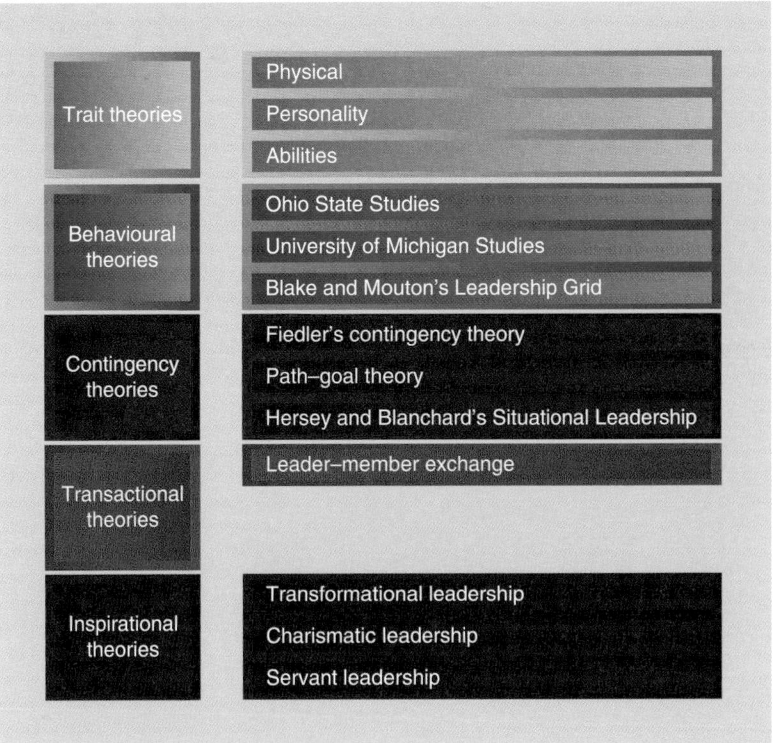

12-7

Discuss how issues of emotional intelligence, trust, ethics, and gender affect leadership. These are essential components that contribute to effective leadership, regardless of the leadership style. Some researchers argue that emotional intelligence, which is the ability to recognize and manage emotions in oneself and in others, is more important for effective leadership than either IQ or technical skills. Trust, the willingness to be vulnerable to the actions of another, is another essential element in leadership. Ethical leadership is important because leaders set the standard of behaviour for the rest of the organization, and finally, though legitimate gender differences may exist, the same leadership traits may be interpreted differently in a man and a woman due to preconceived notions and perceptual biases.

12-8

Define *followership* and identify different types of followers. The follower role is integral to the leadership process. Five types of followers are *effective, alienated, sheep, yes people,* and *survivors*. They are identified based on two dimensions: (1) activity versus passivity and (2) independent, critical thinking versus dependent, uncritical thinking.

12-8

Synthesize historical leadership research into key guidelines for leaders. Leaders and organizations appreciate the unique attributes, predispositions, and talents of each leader. Leaders challenge the organizational culture, when necessary, without destroying it. Participative, considerate leader behaviours demonstrate a concern for people. Different leadership situations call for different leadership talents and behaviours. Good leaders are likely to be good followers.

CHAPTER REVIEW 13
Organizational Culture

KEY CONCEPTS

13-1

Explain what culture means to an organization. Organizational culture is the consistent, shared, observable patterns of behaviour in organizations. Culture is a very broad concept and includes the norms, values, customs, traditions, habits, skills, knowledge, and beliefs of a group of people. Culture serves as a control mechanism for shaping behaviour, which provides a sense of identity and belonging to members. Individuals are attracted to organizations that share their beliefs and values. Culture is made up of (1) *Organizational structures* (goals, power structure, reward mechanisms, etc.), (2) *The expressive systems of an organization* (how beliefs are shared and communicated), and (3) *the individuals* who operate within the organization.

When we speak of an organization's culture, we are talking about its dominant culture, but organizations have subcultures, which are microcultures created within a subset unit of the organization. Organizational culture can provide advantages to organizations by improving the organization's marketability, improving productivity, and increasing employee satisfaction, but culture can also be a detriment to the organization if the culture is too weak, too strong, or misaligned with the organizations values.

13-2

Identify and evaluate the levels of culture. *Artifacts* are visual cues about an organization's culture in the physical and social work environments such as behaviours, ceremonies and rites, stories, rituals, and symbols. Deeper-level *shared and espoused values* reflect inherent beliefs, while the underlying *assumptions* guide behaviour and tell members of an organization how to perceive situations and people.

13-3

Describe how culture is started, shaped, and reinforced. The founders of an organization have the most significant role in shaping its culture. Organizations are created in the image of their founders. When founders leave the organization, leaders play a critical role in shaping and reinforcing organizational culture. Managers influence culture through what they pay attention to, how they react to crises, how they behave, the way they allocate rewards, and how they hire and fire employees.

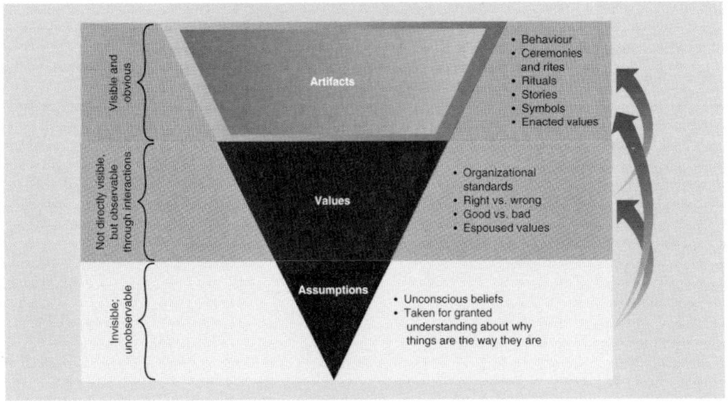

KEY TERMS

organizational culture Consistent, shared, observable patterns of behaviour that distinguish between groups.

dominant culture The overarching core values shared by most members of the organization.

subculture A microculture created within a subset unit of the organization.

counterculture Subcultures with values that oppose the dominant culture.

artifacts The visible expressions of a culture.

espoused values What members of an organization say they value.

enacted values Values reflected in the way individuals actually behave.

assumptions Deeply held beliefs that guide behaviour and tell members of an organization how to perceive and think about things.

socialization The process by which newcomers are transformed from outsiders to participating, effective members of the organization.

anticipatory socialization The first socialization stage, which encompasses all of the learning that takes place prior to the newcomer's first day on the job.

encounter The second socialization stage in which the newcomer learns the tasks associated with the job, clarifies roles, and establishes new relationships at work.

change and acquisition The third stage of socialization, where the newcomer begins to master the demands of the job.

CHAPTER REVIEW 13

strong culture An organizational culture with a consensus on the values that drive the company and with an intensity that is recognizable even to outsiders.

adaptive culture An organizational culture that encourages confidence and risk taking among employees, has leadership that produces change, and focuses on the changing needs of customers.

13-4

Explain how new organizational members are socialized. Newcomers are transformed from outsiders to participating, effective members of the organization through *organizational socialization*. Three stages in the socialization process are *anticipatory socialization, encounter,* and *change and acquisition*. Newcomers learn and adopt values and norms, ensuring the company's culture carries on. Results of successful organizational socialization include good performance, high job satisfaction, and the intention to stay with the organization.

13-5

Discuss how leaders can change organizational culture. Though organizational culture can be changed, it is very difficult because one of the inherent properties of culture is that it provides stability by resisting change. There are two approaches to changing an existing culture: The first is helping current members buy into a new set of values; the other is adding newcomers, socializing them into the desired culture, and removing older members as appropriate. Commonly, organizations attempt to change their culture to become more ethical, or they may attempt to encourage empowerment and equality.

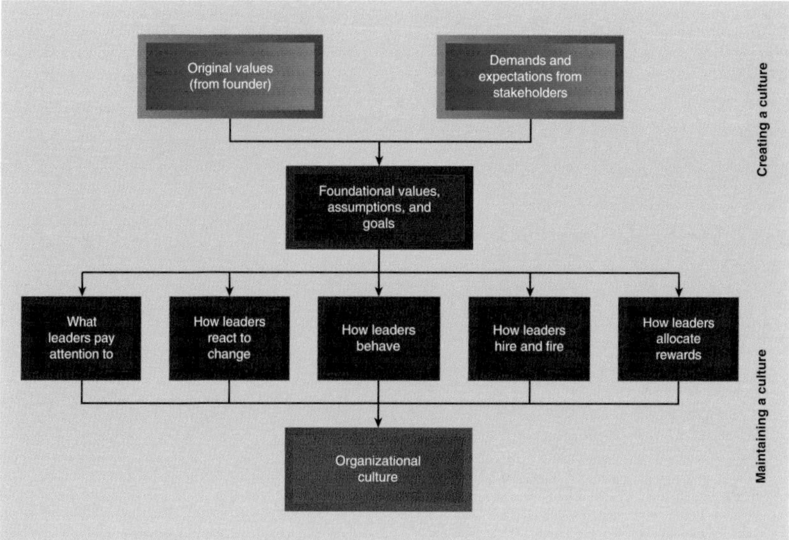

13-6

Describe how culture relates to organizational performance. There are two theories about how culture relates to organizational performance; the first is that strong cultures that are consistent throughout the organization and recognizable to outsiders can help lead the organization to increased performance. The other is that adaptive cultures that encourage risk taking, have leadership that produces change, and focus on the changing needs of customers are better able to ensure success.

CHAPTER REVIEW 14

Learning and Performance Management

KEY CONCEPTS

14-1

Describe classical conditioning and reinforcement theory's approach to learning. Classical conditioning involves modifying by pairing a conditioned stimulus with an unconditioned stimulus to elicit an unconditioned response. Reinforcement theory applies operant conditioning principles to learning. Knowing people change their behaviour in order to gain positive consequences and avoid negative consequences, an organization can deliberately manipulate consequences in order to motivate learning. Basic strategies include positive reinforcement, negative reinforcement, punishment, and extinction.

14-2

Describe Bandura's social learning theory. Bandura argues that people learn through watching others' behaviour and its consequences and then modelling that behaviour. His theory focuses on the importance of task-specific self-efficacy, an individual's beliefs and expectancies about their ability to perform a specific task effectively.

14-3

Describe evidence showing that thinking about learning seems to influence the learning process. Evidence comes from three areas of research: self-regulation prompts in online training, error management training, and after-event reviews. Interspersing prompts in online training that trigger the learner to reflect on the learning leads to better learning and lower dropout. Learners encouraged to make mistakes in a safe training environment transfer the learning better to novel situations and learn to take failure in stride. After-event reviews that ask the learner to reflect on how their specific actions and decisions contributed to the event's success and failure show enhanced learning.

14-4

Explain the aspects of performance management. Performance management is the process of defining, measuring, appraising, and providing feedback, and responding to performance. By taking actions that clarify organizational expectations, indicate results and impact, and support and reward effective performance, the organization can guide the performer's actions to better align with the organization's wishes.

KEY TERMS

learning A change in behaviour acquired through experience.

classical conditioning Modifying behaviour by pairing a conditioned stimulus with an unconditioned stimulus to elicit an unconditioned response.

operant conditioning Modifying behaviour through the use of positive or negative consequences following specific behaviours.

positive reinforcement Attempting to strengthen desirable behaviour by bestowing positive consequences.

negative reinforcement Attempting to strengthen desirable behaviour by withholding negative consequences.

punishment Attempting to eliminate or weaken undesirable behaviour by bestowing negative consequences or withholding positive consequences.

extinction Attempting to eliminate or weaken undesirable behaviour by attaching no consequences to it.

task-specific self-efficacy An individual's beliefs and expectancies about their ability to perform a specific task effectively.

self-regulation prompting Questions that encourage learners to reflect on what and how they are learning.

error management training Immersion in a safe training environment where learners are encouraged to deliberately make mistakes and see what happens.

after-events review Procedure where, following an experience, learners systematically analyze how their actions and decisions contributed to the success and failure of the performance.

CHAPTER REVIEW 14

performance management A process of defining, measuring, appraising, providing feedback on, and responding to performance.

management by objectives (MBO) A goal-setting program based on interaction and negotiation between employees and managers.

360-degree feedback A process of self-evaluation and evaluations by a manager, peers, direct reports, and possibly customers.

mentoring A work relationship that encourages development and career enhancement for people moving through the career cycle.

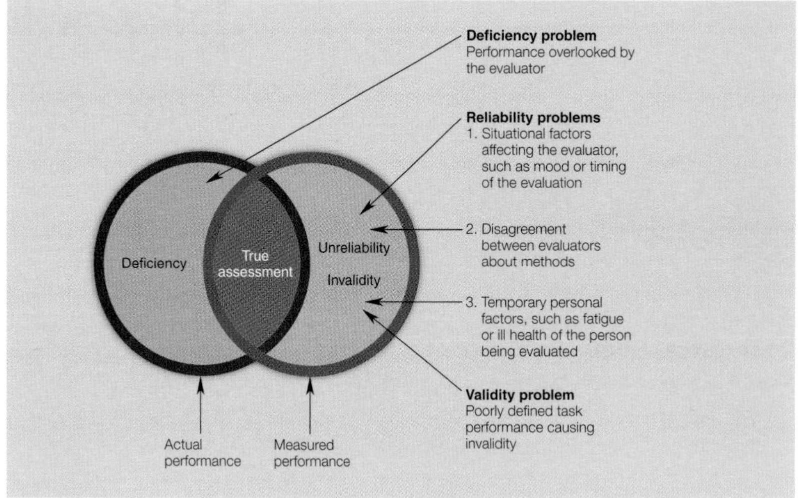

14-5

Explain the importance of performance feedback and how it can be delivered effectively. Feedback can have a powerful influence on behaviour. Good performance appraisal systems develop people, enhance careers, and boost individual and team achievements in an organization. Effective performance appraisal systems have five key characteristics: validity, reliability, responsiveness, flexibility, and equitability. The supervisor must establish mutual trust, be vulnerable and open to challenge, and be a skilled, empathic listener who encourages employees to discuss their aspirations.

14-6

Identify ways managers can reward performance. Individual reward systems (such as commission and merit pay) foster higher effort and are particularly appealing to workers with a high need for achievement and high self-efficacy, but they can also undermine cooperation. Team reward systems (such as gainsharing and profit sharing) encourage cooperation and the sharing of information and expertise but are less motivating for individual contributions. Hybrid plans combine both individual and group reward systems.

14-7

Describe how to correct poor performance. Supervisors need first to identify the cause of the poor performance and then develop a plan for addressing the cause. In determining the cause, the supervisor must be careful to avoid the fundamental attribution error, which may lead to blaming the worker inappropriately. Performance problems are often not self-motivated and may be due to the circumstances. For example, the supervisor may need to address training practices, equipment issues, role ambiguity, or role conflicts.

NOTES

CHAPTER REVIEW 15
Jobs and the Design of Work

KEY CONCEPTS

15-1

Differentiate between *job* and *work*. A *job* is an employee's specific work and task activities in an organization. *Work* is effortful, productive activity resulting in a product or a service. A job is composed of a set of specific tasks, each of which is an assigned piece of work to be done in a specific time period. Work is an especially important human endeavour because it has a powerful effect in binding a person to reality.

15-2

Explain how job enlargement and job enrichment counter Taylor's scientific management concepts. Scientific management focuses on work simplification. The other approaches move away from work simplification. Job enlargement adds tasks to a job in order to overcome the limitations of specialized work, such as boredom. Job enrichment incorporates motivating factors into job design, such as responsibility and opportunities to achieve.

15-3

Explain the job characteristics model, and how it has been expanded by subsequent research. The JCM suggests that five core job characteristics (skill variety, task identity, task significance, autonomy, feedback from the job) create the critical psychological states of experienced meaningfulness of work, experienced responsibility for work, and knowledge of outcomes. These motivate the employee to work hard and enjoy the job. Further research refined the core characteristics (e.g., types of autonomy) and added many broad categories: social, knowledge, and work context.

15-4

Describe the concepts of social information processing (SIP), ergonomics, and job crafting. SIP indicates that employees are more influenced by their subjective perception of the job than the objective facts of job design, and the perception is heavily influenced by social cues about the tasks from those around them. Ergonomics is the science of adapting work and working conditions to the employee or worker. Job crafting suggests people are active architects in shaping their own jobs.

15-5

Identify and describe contemporary issues facing organizations in the design of work. Contemporary job design issues include telecommuting, alternative work patterns, technology at work, and skill development. Work is relationally designed to provide opportunities and increase flexibility for employees. Organizations use these and other approaches to the design of work as ways to manage a growing business while contributing to a better balance of work and family life for employees.

KEY TERMS

work Mental or physical activity that has productive results.

job A set of specified work and task activities that engage an individual in an organization.

work simplification Standardization and the narrow, explicit specification of task activities for workers.

job enlargement A method of job design that increases the number of activities in a job to overcome the boredom of overspecialized work.

job rotation A variation of job enlargement in which workers are exposed to a variety of specialized jobs over time.

cross-training A variation of job enlargement in which workers are trained in different specialized tasks or activities.

job enrichment Designing or redesigning jobs by incorporating motivational factors into them.

job characteristics model (JCM) A framework for understanding person–job fit through the interaction of core job dimensions with critical psychological states within a person.

Job Diagnostic Survey (JDS) The survey instrument designed to measure the elements in the Job Characteristics Model.

social information-processing (SIP) model A model that suggests that the important job factors depend in part on what others tell a person about the job.

ergonomics The science of adapting work and working conditions to the employee or worker.

job crafting Employees take the initiative to redefine their jobs.

CHAPTER REVIEW 15

i-deals Customized employment terms negotiated between employees and their supervisors.

technocentric Placing technology and engineering at the centre of job design decisions.

anthropocentric Placing human considerations at the centre of job design decisions.

telecommuting Employees work away from the company (typically at home) through the use of technology.

job sharing A permanent work arrangement where two or more employees voluntarily share or split one full-time position.

compressed work week Employees work longer shifts in exchange for a reduction in the number of working days.

flextime An alternative work pattern that enables employees to set their own daily work schedules outside core operational hours.

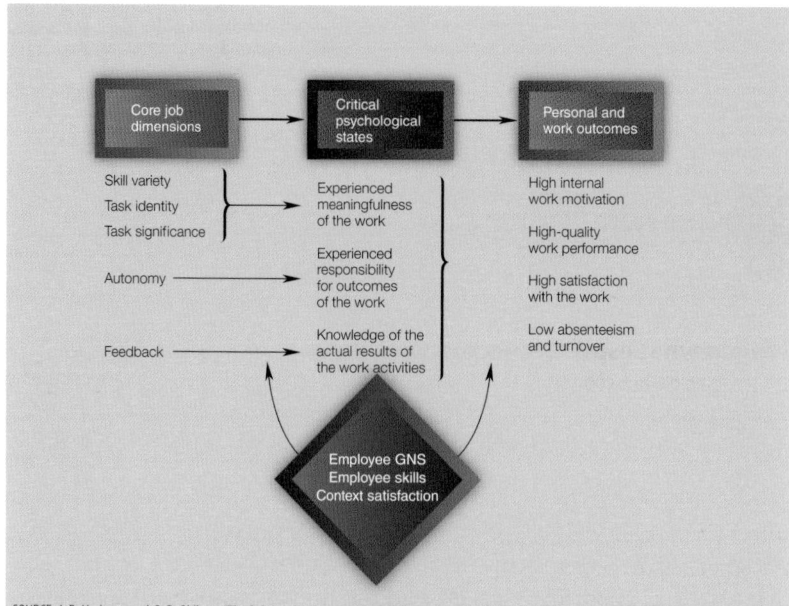

SOURCE: J. R. Hackman and G. R. Oldham, "The Relationship Among Core Job Dimensions, the Critical Psychological States, and On-the-Job Outcomes," *The Job Diagnostic Survey: An Instrument for the Diagnosis of Jobs and the Evaluation of Job Redesign Projects*, 1974. Reprinted by permission of Greg R. Oldham.

virtual office A mobile platform of computer, telecommunication, and information technology and services.

technostress The stress caused by new and advancing technologies in the workplace.

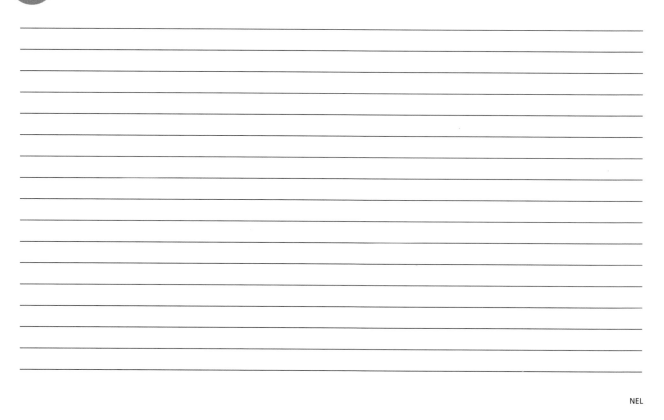

NOTES

CHAPTER REVIEW 16

Organizational Design and Structure

KEY CONCEPTS

16-1

Explain what aspects of organizational structure are represented on an organizational chart. An organizational chart shows the formal lines of authority and responsibility, the basis on which people are grouped for reporting purposes, and the formal systems of communication and coordination.

16-2

Discuss the basic design dimensions managers must consider in structuring an organization. Basic design dimensions combine to yield various structural configurations. Structural dimensions include the following: formalization, centralization, specialization, standardization, complexity, and hierarchy of authority. Henry Mintzberg's alternative approach is to describe what is and is not important to the success of the organization and design structures that fit each organization's unique set of circumstances.

Basic Design Dimensions	Small Organizations	Large Organizations
Formalization	Less	More
Centralization	High	Low
Specialization	Low	High
Standardization	Low	High
Complexity	Low	High
Hierarchy of Authority	Flat	Tall

16-3

Describe the basic organizational structures: simple, functional, divisional, matrix. Simple structures are a centralized form of organization typical of a small company, emphasizing direct supervision and low formalization. Functional structures group people according to functional role (e.g., finance, marketing, production) whereas divisional structures group employees according to product, service, client, or geography. The matrix structure combines functional and divisional forms, typically through the use of project teams whose members report both to the project manager and their functional supervisors.

16-4

Describe four contextual variables that influence organizational structure. Four variables influence the success of an organization's design: size, technology, environment, and strategy and goals. These variables provide a manager with key considerations for the right organizational design. The relationship to size is evident in the table in answer 2 above. The less routine an organization's technology is, the greater the need for an organic structure, whereas companies with routine activities are best supported by a mechanistic structure. The more complex and dynamic the environment, the more an organic structure offers the needed flexibility and responsiveness. Strategy also links to structural fit, e.g., an organization that strategically focuses on cost leadership will likely use a mechanistic structure.

KEY TERMS

organizational design The process of constructing and adjusting an organization's structure to achieve its goals.

organizational structure The linking of departments and jobs within an organization.

differentiation The process of deciding how to divide the work in an organization.

integration The process of coordinating the different parts of an organization.

formalization The degree to which the organization has official rules, regulations, and procedures.

centralization The degree to which decisions are made at the top of the organization.

specialization The degree to which jobs are narrowly defined and depend on unique expertise.

standardization The degree to which work activities are accomplished in a routine fashion.

complexity The degree to which many different types of activities occur in the organization.

hierarchy of authority The degree of vertical differentiation across levels of management.

span of control The number of employees reporting to a supervisor.

simple structure A centralized form of organization that emphasizes direct supervision and low formalization.

functional structure A form of organization that groups people according to the function they perform.

CHAPTER REVIEW 16

divisional structure A form of organization that groups employees according to product, service, client, or geography.

matrix structure A dual-authority form of structure that combines functional and divisional structures, typically through project teams.

mechanistic structure An organizational design that emphasizes structured activities, specialized tasks, and centralized decision making.

organic structure An organizational design that emphasizes teamwork, open communication, and decentralized decision making.

contextual variables A set of characteristics that influences the organization's design processes.

technological interdependence The degree of interrelatedness of the organization's various technological elements.

environment Anything outside the boundaries of an organization.

environmental uncertainty The number of different elements and the rate of change in the organization's environment.

organizational life cycles The differing stages of an organization's life from birth to death.

16-5

Explain the forces reshaping organizations. Several forces reshaping organizations are causing managers to go beyond the traditional frameworks and to examine ways to make organizations more responsive to customer needs. Some of these forces include shorter organizational life cycles, globalization, and rapid changes in information technology. These forces together increase the demands on process capabilities within the organization and emerging organizational structures. To successfully retain their health and vitality, organizations must function as open systems that are responsive to their task environment.

16-6

Identify and describe emerging organizational structures. Network organizations are weblike structures that contract some or all of their operating functions to other organizations and then coordinate their activities through managers and other employees at their headquarters. Virtual organizations are temporary network organizations consisting of independent enterprises.

16-7

Identify the consequences of an inappropriate structure. If organizational structure is out of alignment with its contextual variables, one or more of the following symptoms appear: delayed decision making, low-quality decision making, non-response to changing environment, and interdepartmental conflict.

NOTES

CHAPTER REVIEW 17
Managing Change

KEY CONCEPTS

17-1
Identify the major external and internal forces for change in organizations. *External* forces that demand change are globalization, workforce diversity, technological change, and expectations for ethical behaviour. *Internal* pressures for change are generally recognizable: declining effectiveness, crisis, changes in employee expectations, and work climate. Adaptiveness, flexibility, and responsiveness are characteristics of the organizations that will succeed in meeting the challenges of change.

17-2
Describe how different types of change vary in scope. Change can be of a relatively small scope, such as a modification in a work procedure (an *incremental change*) or of a larger scale, such as the restructuring of an organization (a *strategic change*). The most massive scope of change is *transformational change,* in which the organization moves to a radically different, and sometimes unknown, future state. One of the toughest decisions faced by leaders is the "pace" of change. Researchers agree that pace is important; however, they can't agree on which pace of change is most beneficial.

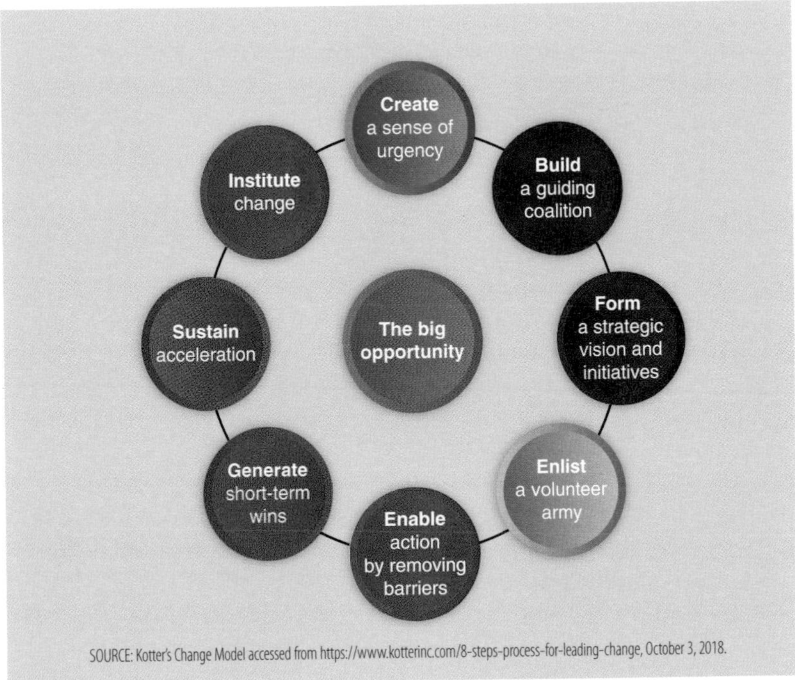

SOURCE: Kotter's Change Model accessed from https://www.kotterinc.com/8-steps-process-for-leading-change, October 3, 2018.

17-3
Discuss methods organizations can use to manage resistance to change. The contemporary view holds that resistance is simply a form of feedback and that this feedback can be used very productively to manage the change process. Three key strategies for managing resistance to change are communication, participation, and empathy and support.

KEY TERMS

planned change Change resulting from a deliberate decision to alter the organization.

unplanned change Change that is imposed on the organization and is often unforeseen.

incremental change Change of a relatively small scope, such as making small improvements.

strategic change Change of a larger scale, such as organizational restructuring.

transformational change Change in which the organization moves to a radically different, and sometimes unknown, future state.

change agent The individual or group that undertakes the task of introducing and managing a change in an organization.

unfreezing The first step in Lewin's change model, in which individuals are encouraged to discard old behaviours by shaking up the equilibrium state that maintains the status quo.

moving The second step in Lewin's change model, in which new attitudes, values, and behaviours are substituted for old ones.

refreezing The final step in Lewin's change model, in which new attitudes, values, and behaviours are established as the new status quo.

organization development (OD) A systematic approach to organizational improvement that applies behavioural science theory and research in order to increase individual and organizational well-being and effectiveness.

survey feedback A widely used method of intervention whereby employee attitudes are solicited using a questionnaire.

management by objectives (MBO) An organization-wide intervention technique that involves joint goal setting between employees and managers.

quality program A program that embeds product and service quality excellence in the organizational culture.

team building An intervention designed to improve the effectiveness of a work group.

process consultation An OD method that helps managers and employees improve the processes that are used in organizations.

skills training Increasing the job knowledge, skills, and abilities that are necessary to do a job effectively.

leadership training and development A variety of techniques that are designed to enhance individuals' leadership skills.

executive coaching A technique in which managers or executives are paired with a coach in a partnership to help the executive perform more efficiently.

job redesign An OD intervention method that alters jobs to improve the fit between individual skills and the demands of the job.

17-4

Explain Lewin's and Kotter's organizational change models.
Lewin's model, the idea of force field analysis, contends that a person's behaviour is the product of two opposing forces; one force pushes toward preserving the status quo and the other force pushes for change. Lewin's change model is a three-step process: *unfreezing*—encouraging individuals to discard old behaviours, *moving*—new attitudes, values, and behaviours are substituted for old ones, and *refreezing*—new attitudes, values, and behaviours are established as the new status quo.

Kotter's model has eight stages: (1) creating a sense of urgency, (2) forming a guiding coalition, (3) developing a strategic vision, (4) enlisting supporters, (5) removing obstacles, (6) generating short-term wins, (7) sustaining acceleration, and (8) locking the change in the organization's culture. He argues that change must proceed sequentially through *all* the stages. His model is derived from research that identified factors which explained why some changes were successful while others were not. Kotter's model is popular among change agents.

17-5

Explain how companies determine the need to conduct an organizational development intervention. *Organization development (OD)* is a systematic approach to organizational improvement. The first step, the diagnosis, should pinpoint specific problems and areas in need of improvement. Six areas to examine carefully are the organization's purpose, structure, reward system, support systems, relationships, and leadership. A needs analysis then determines the skills and competencies that employees must have to achieve the goals of the change.

17-6

Discuss the major group-focused techniques for organization development intervention. Some OD intervention methods emphasize changing the organization itself or changing the work groups within the organization. Intervention methods in this category include survey feedback, management by objectives, product and service quality programs, team building, and process consultation. These OD methods focus on changing the organization or the work group.

17-7

Discuss the major individual-focused techniques for organization development intervention. Managers have a host of organization development techniques to facilitate individual change. Development efforts include skills training, leadership training and development, executive coaching, job redesign, health promotion programs, and career planning. Success depends on techniques used, competence of the change agent, the organization's readiness for change, and top management commitment.

NOTES

CHAPTER REVIEW 18
Career Management

KEY CONCEPTS

18-1

Explain occupational and organizational choice decisions. Today a majority of workers no longer work in one organization for the length of their working life. The new career model is characterized by discrete exchange, occupational excellence, organizational empowerment, and project allegiance. When building a career, individuals first select an occupation that meets their needs, values, abilities, and preferences.

18-2

Identify foundations for a successful career. Two foundations for a successful career are becoming your own career coach and developing your emotional intelligence. To become your own career coach, you must acquire multiple skills, develop self-reliance, and cultivate a flexible, team-oriented attitude. Emotional competencies are of equal or greater importance than technical skills.

18-3

Explain the career-stage model. The career-stage model shows that individuals pass through four stages in their careers: establishment, advancement, maintenance, and withdrawal. Timing of career transitions varies greatly among individuals.

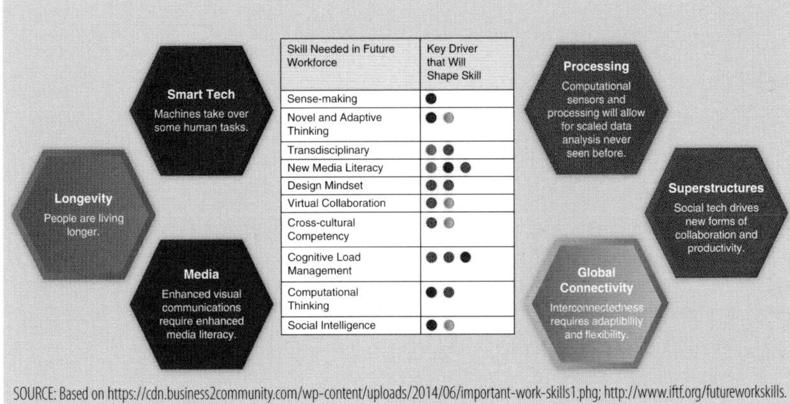

Smart Tech
Machines take over some human tasks.
Longevity
People are living longer.
Media
Enhanced visual communications require enhanced media literacy.
Skill Needed in Future Workforce
Key Driver that Will Shape Skill
Sense-making
Novel and Adaptive Thinking
Transdisciplinary
New Media Literacy
Design Mindset
Virtual Collaboration
Cross-cultural Competency
Cognitive Load Management
Computational Thinking
Social Intelligence
Processing
Computational sensors and processing will allow for scaled data analysis never seen before.
Superstructures
Social tech drives new forms of collaboration and productivity.
Global Connectivity
Interconnectedness requires adaptibility and flexibility.

SOURCE: Based on https://cdn.business2community.com/wp-content/uploads/2014/06/important-work-skills1.phg; http://www.iftf.org/futureworkskills.

18-4

Explain the major tasks facing individuals in the establishment stage of the career model. *Establishment* is the first stage of a person's career. The activities that occur in this stage centre around learning the job and fitting into the organization and occupation. Individuals in this stage begin to work out their psychological contract with the organization and form attachment relationships with coworkers.

KEY TERMS

career The pattern of work-related experiences that span the course of a person's life.

career management A lifelong process of learning about self, jobs, and organizations; setting personal career goals; developing strategies for achieving the goals; and revising the goals based on work and life experiences.

realistic job preview (RJP) Both positive and negative information given to potential employees about the job they are applying for, thereby giving them a realistic picture of the job.

establishment The first stage of a person's career in which the person learns the job and begins to fit into the organization and occupation.

advancement The second, high achievement–oriented career stage in which people focus on increasing their competence.

maintenance The third stage in an individual's career in which the individual tries to maintain productivity while evaluating progress toward career goals.

withdrawal The final stage in an individual's career in which the individual contemplates retirement or possible career changes.

psychological contract An implicit agreement between an individual and an organization that specifies what each is expected to give and receive in the relationship.

career path A sequence of job experiences that an employee moves along during their career.

career ladder A structured series of job positions through which an individual progresses in an organization.

CHAPTER REVIEW 18

mentor An individual who provides guidance, coaching, counselling, and friendship to a protégé.

dual-career partnership A relationship in which both people have important career roles.

flexible work schedule A work schedule that allows employees discretion in order to accommodate personal concerns.

eldercare Assistance in caring for elderly parents and/or other elderly relatives.

career plateau A point in an individual's career in which the probability of moving further up the hierarchy is low.

phased retirement An arrangement that allows employees to reduce their hours and/or responsibilities in order to ease into retirement.

bridge employment Employment that takes place after a person retires from a full-time position but before the person's permanent withdrawal from the workforce.

career anchors A network of self-perceived talents, motives, and values that guide an individual's career decisions.

18-5

Identify the issues confronting individuals in the advancement stage of the career model. *Advancement* is a high achievement–oriented stage in which people focus on increasing their competence. A hallmark of this stage is the exploration of career paths or sequences of job experiences along which employees move during their careers. Some companies use career lattices that move employees laterally through the organization in an attempt to build diverse skills. A mentor provides numerous sponsorship, facilitating, and psychosocial functions for the protégé. Dual-career partnerships are common now and can lead to work–home conflicts.

18-6

Describe how individuals can navigate the challenges of the maintenance stage of the career model. The *maintenance* stage finds the individual trying to maintain productivity while evaluating progress toward career goals. Individuals sustain their performance and continue to grow, although at a slower rate. Individuals in this stage may also become mentors.

18-7

Explain how individuals withdraw from the workforce. The *withdrawal* stage involves contemplation of retirement or possible career change. Increasingly, individuals in this stage are opting for phased retirement, which is a gradual cessation of work. To help workers at this stage of their careers, organizations should provide opportunities for continued involvement with the organization, such as mentoring other employees making career transitions.

18-8

Explain how career anchors help form a career identity. Career anchors are self-perceived talents, motives, and values that guide an individual's career decisions. Five main anchors are technical/functional competence, managerial competence, autonomy and independence, creativity, and security/stability.

18-9

Become familiar with some current tools and practices that will help you develop your own career. The material in Part 2 of the book provides the theory behind understanding who you are, your skills, and your weaknesses. The chapters on teams and decision making provide guidance about the nature of teams and how to make effective decisions in teams. The material on organizational culture is particularly important so you know how to read organizations. Chapter 18 highlights the tools that you can use to shape your career journey.

NOTES